One of the great achievements of the Venerable Bede was the shaping of tools to teach the Latin language—the tongue of Augustine and Hilary and Ambrose and the Vulgate Bible itself—using Christian resources. In this volume Bede's enterprise lives again! Derek Cooper draws us into the condensed, expressive beauty of Latin grammar and vocabulary through passages drawn from the Christian Latin tradition. His exposition is always clear, direct, and accurate. This wonderful volume is an excellent resource, and I recommend it to anyone seeking to learn the Latin language and to discover something of how central it has been in Christian life down the centuries.

LEWIS AYRES, professor of Catholic and historical theology, Durham University

As advertised, this book will give you the basics of the Latin language, tailored specifically to those who wish to read Christian texts, from the Latin Bible to early modernity. While not intended to make you a *Ciceronianus* of the kind Jerome was accused of being *in somniis*, *Basics of Latin* provides a good foundation on which students of ecclesiastical and theological Latin can build.

ERIC HUTCHINSON, associate professor of classics, Hillsdale College

Derek Cooper's *Basics of Latin* fills a void that the usual Latin grammars wholly ignore, for it aims at the vast bulk of the surviving corpus of Latin writings, namely, the patristic, medieval, Renaissance, and Reformation authors. Covering the wealth and variety of the texts of these writers (Augustine is not Bede is not Thomas Kempis is not Lorenzo Valla is not Calvin), Dr. Cooper treats the items that are most regular in this panoply of authors, while touching as well on some of the idiosyncrasies. It meets a great need that in my own education had to have a graduate course to fill. It looks not to supplant the study of the classics but to dive into the vast world of Latin literature that runs up into the seventeenth century and even beyond. Growing up in a time when there is no God but Cicero, and Wheelock is his prophet, this text gives to students the rest of the Latin world.

GARY W. JENKINS, Van Gorden Professor in History and director,
St. Basil Center for Orthodox Thought and Culture, Eastern University

Kudos to Dr. Cooper for accomplishing something never done before: an introduction to Latin grounded in the writings of the Western Fathers, Roman Catholics, and Protestants alike. Derek Cooper has created a beautifully written and conceived textbook that teaches the language in articulate, innovative, and relatable ways to those interested in its Christian expression. He takes nothing for granted, instead teaching from the ground up while avoiding intimidating technicalities. Students will find this book a pleasure to work through. In addition to the lucid grammatical explanations, numerous historical tidbits, anecdotes, and etymologies adorn the book and will sweep the students along a journey of the first sixteen hundred years of church history. This textbook will undoubtedly find its way into many Christian high schools, and rightfully so, but it is also suitable for college students and self-learners.

KIRK SUMMERS, professor of classics, University of Alabama

BASICS of
LATIN

ALSO BY DEREK COOPER

1–2 Samuel, 1–2 Kings, 1–2 Chronicles,
Reformation Commentary on Scripture

Introduction to World Christian History

Thomas Manton:
A Guided Tour of the Life and Thought of a Puritan Pastor

Exploring Church History

Twenty Questions That Shaped World Christian History

Christianity and World Religions:
An Introduction to the World's Major Faiths

Sinners and Saints:
The Real Story of Early Christianity

Translator, Philip Melanchthon's
Commentary on Proverbs

BASICS *of* LATIN

A GRAMMAR WITH READINGS AND EXERCISES FROM THE *CHRISTIAN TRADITION*

DEREK COOPER

ZONDERVAN ACADEMIC

Basics of Latin
Copyright © 2020 by Derek Cooper

Requests for information should be addressed to:
Zondervan, *3900 Sparks Dr. SE, Grand Rapids, Michigan 49546*

ISBN 978-0-310-53899-8 (softcover)

ISBN 978-0-310-53900-1 (ebook)

All Scripture quotations, unless otherwise indicated, are taken from The Holy Bible, New International Version®, NIV®. Copyright © 1973, 1978, 1984, 2011 by Biblica, Inc.® Used by permission of Zondervan. All rights reserved worldwide. www.Zondervan.com. The "NIV" and "New International Version" are trademarks registered in the United States Patent and Trademark Office by Biblica, Inc.®

Any internet addresses (websites, blogs, etc.) and telephone numbers in this book are offered as a resource. They are not intended in any way to be or imply an endorsement by Zondervan, nor does Zondervan vouch for the content of these sites and numbers for the life of this book.

All rights reserved. No part of this publication may be reproduced, stored in a retrieval system, or transmitted in any form or by any means—electronic, mechanical, photocopy, recording, or any other—except for brief quotations in printed reviews, without the prior permission of the publisher.

Cover design: LUCAS Art & Design
Interior design: Kait Lamphere

Printed in the United States of America

*This book is warmly dedicated to my friend
Dr. Cliff Gehret, gatekeeper of reason,
preserver of faith, master of proverbs.*

ACKNOWLEDGMENTS

I would like to thank several people who have played a part in my research, teaching, and writing of Latin, particularly with reference to this book. First off, I am indebted to Chris Beetham for believing in this project from our very first interaction. He has lent a helping hand to the entire project *ab ovō usque ad māla*, "from beginning to end." Thanks also go to all the wonderful staff at Zondervan, including Josh Kessler, Madison Trammel, and Liz England. It has been a pleasure working with you on this book and the accompanying teaching series.

Second, I would like to thank all of the Latin students I have taught over the years. I am particularly grateful to the Latin students who used this present manuscript as their course grammar. You helped me clarify concepts, locate errors, and stay encouraged during the lengthy process of writing a grammar. In a related way, a hearty thanks goes to Carol Ramsey, who reviewed my translations and exercise examples.

Third, I greatly appreciate the comments I received from an anonymous reviewer. You alerted me to several areas that needed to be improved, and the final product is much better thanks to your detailed feedback.

Fourth, my family has been incredibly supportive as I have poured countless hours into this project. My son even pledged to read it if I give him a free copy. You alone know how exhilarating and exhausting it has been. I love you with all my heart!

Finally, I have dedicated this book to Dr. Cliff Gehret. Cliff has been an extraordinary literary partner. Not only did he provide great feedback to each of my chapters, but he diligently checked the accuracy of the practice exercises, corrected inconsistencies, helped with vocabulary words and etymologies, and generally offered support, motivation, and good cheer at just the right moments.

CONTENTS

Abbreviations xvi
Diacritics xvi
Welcome to Latin! xvii
A Guide to the Latin Language: Alphabet, Pronunciation, and More xxi
Overview xxix

PRĪMA PARS: *Nouns and Adjectives*

    Capítula, "Chapters"
    Dictum Latínum, "Latin Saying"
    Opúsculum Theológicum, "Small Theological Excerpt"
    Ōrắtiō Populắris, "Prayer Offered by the People"

1. Nouns and Prepositions 3
    Dictum Latínum: Gospel of Matthew 3
    Opúsculum Theológicum: Sīgnum Crucis 3
    Ōrắtiō Populắris: Sīgnum Crucis 11

2. First-Declension Nouns; Sum, Esse, Fuī, Futū́rus; and Et, -Que, and Ac 12
    Dictum Latínum: Gospel of John 12
    Opúsculum Theológicum: Ego Sum in the Gospel of John 12
    Ōrắtiō Populắris: Glṓria Patrī 20

3. Second-Declension Nouns 22
    Dictum Latínum: Tertullian 22
    Opúsculum Theológicum: Dóminus et Deus 22
    Ōrắtiō Populắris: Sānctus 29

4. Third-Declension Nouns 30
    Dictum Latínum: Cyprian of Carthage 30
    Opúsculum Theológicum: God as Pater and Church as Māter in Cyprian of Carthage 30
    Ōrắtiō Populắris: Pater Noster (Pars Minor I) 37

5. First-, Second-, and Third-Declension Adjectives 38
    Dictum Latínum: Thomas Aquinas 38
    Opúsculum Theológicum: The Five Sṓlae 38
    Ōrắtiō Populắris: Pater Noster (Pars Minor II) 47

6. Fourth-Declension Nouns, Positive, Comparative, and Superlative Adjectives, and Ablatives . . 48
   Dictum Latīnum: Martin Luther 48
   Opúsculum Theológicum: Martin Luther's Dictắta in Psaltḗrium 48
   Ōrắtiō Populắris: Agnus Deī 59

7. Fifth-Declension Nouns, Indeclinable Nouns, and Numbers. 60
   Dictum Latīnum: Cōdex Justīniắnus 60
   Opúsculum Theológicum: Constantine and the Diēs Sōlis 60
   Ōrắtiō Populắris: Ōrắtiō Fắtimae 68

SECÚNDA PARS: *Indicative Mood Verbs: First and Second Principal Parts*

8. Verbs and Four Principal Parts. 71
   Dictum Latīnum: Sýmbolum Apostolṓrum 71
   Opúsculum Theológicum: Crēdō and Creeds 71
   Ōrắtiō Populắris: Sýmbolum Apostolṓrum (Pars Minor I) 77

9. Present Actives and Present Passives. 78
   Dictum Latīnum: Pericle Felici 78
   Opúsculum Theológicum: Habḗmus Pāpam 78
   Ōrắtiō Populắris: Sýmbolum Apostolṓrum (Pars Minor II) 88

10. Imperfect Actives, Imperfect Passives, and Adverbs. 89
    Dictum Latīnum: Vincent of Lérins 89
    Opúsculum Theológicum: Vincent of Lérins and the Vincentian Canon 89
    Ōrắtiō Populắris: Sýmbolum Apostolṓrum (Pars Minor III) 101

11. Future Actives and Future Passives 102
    Dictum Latīnum: Exodus 102
    Opúsculum Theológicum: Decem Verba 102
    Ōrắtiō Populắris: Sýmbolum Apostolṓrum (Pars Minor IV) 111

TÉRTIA PARS: *Nonconforming Verbs*

12. Irregular Verbs. 115
    Dictum Latīnum: Augustine of Hippo 115
    Opúsculum Theológicum: Augustine's Posse, Nōn Posse Theology 115
    Ōrắtiō Populắris: Tē Deum (Pars Minor I) 125

13. Deponents and Semideponents 126
    Dictum Latīnum: Tertullian 126
    Opúsculum Theológicum: Tertullian's Apologḗticus 126
    Ōrắtiō Populắris: Tē Deum (Pars Minor II) 133

QUĀRTA PARS: *Pronouns and Adjectives*

14. Personal Pronouns and Demonstratives... 137
    Dictum Latīnum: Synoptic Gospels 137
    Opúsculum Theológicum: Tū et Hic in the Vulgate 137
    Ōrắtiō Populắris: Ánima Christī (Pars Minor I) 147

15. Reflexives, Possessives, and Intensives 148
    Dictum Latīnum: John Calvin 148
    Opúsculum Theológicum: John Calvin's Use of Brévitās 148
    Ōrắtiō Populắris: Ánima Christī (Pars Minor II) 155

16. Relatives, Interrogatives, and Indefinites... 156
    Dictum Latīnum: Saint Patrick 156
    Opúsculum Theológicum: Saint Patrick's Prayer 156
    Ōrắtiō Populắris: Ánima Christī (Pars Minor III) 166

QUĪNTA PARS: *Indicative Mood Verbs: Third Principal Part*

17. Perfect Actives 169
    Dictum Latīnum: Gospel of Luke 169
    Opúsculum Theológicum: Magníficat 169
    Ōrắtiō Populắris: Magníficat (Pars Minor I) 175

18. Pluperfect Actives and Future Perfect Actives................................. 176
    Dictum Latīnum: John Owen 176
    Opúsculum Theológicum: Epigrams 176
    Ōrắtiō Populắris: Magníficat (Pars Minor II) 184

SEXTA PARS: *Subjunctive Mood Verbs: All Tenses*

19. Present Active and Present Passive Subjunctives............................. 187
    Dictum Latīnum: Ignatius of Loyola 187
    Opúsculum Theológicum: Ignatius of Loyola's Exercítia Spirituália ... 187
    Ōrắtiō Populắris: Dē Profúndīs (Pars Minor I) 198

20. Imperfect Active and Imperfect Passive Subjunctives....................... 200
    Dictum Latīnum: Martin Luther 200
    Opúsculum Theológicum: Martin Luther's Plea to the Emperor 200
    Ōrắtiō Populắris: Dē Profúndīs (Pars Minor II) 207

21. Perfect and Pluperfect Subjunctives and Cum Clauses 209
    Dictum Latīnum: Thomas Aquinas 209
    Opúsculum Theológicum: Thomas Aquinas's Use of Utrum 209
    Ōrắtiō Populắris: Deus Inténde 220

SĒPTIMA PARS: *Participles, Perfect Passives, and Infinitives:*
Second and Fourth Principal Parts

22. Present Active Participles, Future Passive Participles (Gerundives), and Gerunds. 223
   Dictum Latī́num: Peter Ramus. 223
   Opúsculum Theológicum: What is Theology?. 223
   Ōrā́tiō Populā́ris: Psalmus CL. 237

23. Perfect Passive Participles, Future Active Participles, and Periphrastic Constructions 238
   Dictum Latī́num: Acts of Peter. 238
   Opúsculum Theológicum: Ā́cta Petrī́. 238
   Ōrā́tiō Populā́ris: Ā́ctus Contrītiṓnis. 248

24. Perfect, Pluperfect, and Future Perfect Passives; Fíerī; Ablative Absolutes 250
   Dictum Latī́num: Ā́ngelus. 250
   Opúsculum Theológicum: Ā́ngelus. 250
   Ōrā́tiō Populā́ris: Ā́ngelus. 260

25. Present Active and Passive Infinitives; Indirect Speech; Impersonal Verbs. 261
   Dictum Latī́num: Isaac Newton. 261
   Opúsculum Theológicum: Isaac Newton and the Lḗgēs Mṓtūs. 261
   Ōrā́tiō Populā́ris: Ā́ctus Cāritā́tis. 269

26. Perfect and Future Infinitives and More about Indirect Speech 271
   Dictum Latī́num: Damasus I. 271
   Opúsculum Theológicum: Epitaphs. 271
   Ōrā́tiō Populā́ris: Catēchísmus Mā́ior. 279

OCTĀ́VA PARS: *Giving Commands*

27. Imperatives, Prohibitions, and Vocatives. 283
   Dictum Latī́num: Sidonius Apollinaris 283
   Opúsculum Theológicum: Hildegard of Bingen's Epístolae 283
   Ōrā́tiō Populā́ris: Nunc Dīmíttis 293

Conclusion: Ciceronians, Christians, and Fī́nis Librī́ 295

Appendices
   1. *Exercitia* 299
      Exercitium I. 299
      Exercitium II 302
      Exercitium III 304
      Exercitium IV 307
      Exercitium V 309
      Exercitium VI 312
      Exercitium VII. 314
      Exercitium VIII 316

  Exercitium IX 318
  Exercitium X 320
  Exercitium XI 323
  Exercitium XII 325
  Exercitium XIII 327
  Exercitium XIV 329
  Exercitium XV 331
  Exercitium XVI 333
  Exercitium XVII 336
  Exercitium XVIII 338
  Exercitium XIX 340
  Exercitium XX 343
  Exercitium XXI 346
  Exercitium XXII 349
  Exercitium XXIII 352
  Exercitium XXIV 354
  Exercitium XXV 356
  Exercitium XXVI 359
  Exercitium XXVII 361
2. *Answer Key to Exercitia* 365
3. *Latin-English Vocabulary* 383
4. *Bibliography* 399

Index 401

ABBREVIATIONS

A&G	*Allen and Greenough's New Latin Grammar.* Edited by J. B. Greenough et al. Boston: Ginn & Company, 1903
CR	*Corpus Reformatorum.* 101 vols. Edited by K. G. Bretschneider et al. Halle: 1834
PG	*Patrologia Graeca.* 162 vols. Edited by J. P. Migne. Paris: 1857–1866
PL	*Patrologia Latina.* 221 vols. Edited by J. P. Migne. Paris: 1844–1864
WA	*D. Martin Luthers Werke: Kritische Gesamtausgabe, Schriften.* 73 vols. Weimar: H. Böhlau Nachfolger, 1883–2009
WA BR	*D. Martin Luthers Werke: Kritische Gesamtausgabe, Briefwechsel.* 18 vols. Weimar: H. Böhlau Nachfolger, 1930–1985

DIACRITICS

The following diacritics (otherwise known as diacritical marks, coding, or symbols) are used in this text.

- ´ Acute accent (for instance, á), indicating increased emphasis when pronouncing syllable
- ˘ Breve or short vowel (for instance, ă), indicating less time spent pronouncing the syllable
- ¯ Macron or long vowel (for instance, ā), indicating longer time spent pronouncing the syllable
- → Rightward arrow (for instance, sunt → erant), indicating that something changes into something else
- * Asterisk, indicating that the word immediately following it (for instance, *gooder*) is not an actual word

WELCOME TO LATIN!

Arma virúmque canō.[1]
—VIRGIL

WHO IS CATILINE?

For many who learn Latin, it's all about Cicero's speeches, Caesar's memoirs, and Virgil's poems. Which is to say, it's about:

Quō ūsque tandem abūtére, Catilína, patiéntiā nostrā?[2]	For exactly how long, Catiline, will you try our patience?
Gállia est omnis dīvī́sa in pártēs trēs.[3]	All Gaul is divided into three parts.
Arma virúmque canō.[4]	I sing of arms and the man.

These are the three most famous lines in all of Latin literature. Although many of us automatically associate Latin with Romans like Cicero, Caesar, and Virgil, they wrote only a small percentage of the works that exist in Latin. According to historian of Latin Jürgen Leonhardt, Roman writings "constitute at most 0.01 percent of the total output [of the Latin language]."[5] Stated differently, a combined total of the Latin language taught in textbooks, boarding schools, and classrooms from Manchester to Melbourne represents less than 1% of Latin in existence. In contrast to the Latin of Cicero, Caesar, Virgil, and other classical authors, "approximately 80 percent"[6] of Latin comes from Christian authors, few of whom receive as much attention in the traditional Latin curriculum.[7]

I'm no mathematician, but these percentages invite the question: Why would we spend so much more time reading authors who only constitute a small percentage of the Latin *corpus*? To be sure, classical Roman authors like Cicero, Caesar, and Virgil were skilled orators, consummate propagandists, and masterful poets. As the Romans used to say, "they were worth their salt." Like Shakespeare and the King James Bible for the English-speaking world, they have influenced the Latin language in countless

---

1. "I sing of arms and the man."
2. Cicero, *In Catilínam* I.1.
3. Caesar, *Commentáriī dē Bellō Gállicō* I.1.
4. Virgil, *Aenéis* I.1.
5. Jürgen Leonhardt, *Latin: Story of a World Language* (Cambridge, MA: Harvard University Press, 2013), 2.
6. Leonhardt, *Latin*, 2.
7. The other percentage comes from non-Christian Latin writings after the Middle Ages.

ways. More to the point, I like these authors. Their command of the language is inspiring. Their cadence is breathtaking. And they are a true joy to read. There's a reason, after all, the classics are the Classics.

But let's be honest, the same holds true for many Christian authors. Not only did they leave us the overwhelming majority of all Latin writings, they actually managed to say some pretty amazing things in the process. And when it comes to sheer numbers, their output speaks volumes. Think about it: For every Cicero, Caesar, and Virgil, there are a thousand Jeromes, a thousand Thomases, and a thousand Luthers. What's more, these last three Christians uniquely influenced the Western world—particularly when we consider their theological and spiritual influence. Either way, no one would ever describe them as amateurs.

Truth be told, few today could pick Marcus Tullius Cicero out of a historical lineup, but many could probably identify Martin Luther. And he, in fact, is just the start. When it comes to Christian authors of Latin, there is a never-ending smorgasbord of theologians, hymnists, poets, teachers, lawyers, jurists, pastors, and just plain cantankerous polymaths waiting to be consumed by the general public. Here are just three tantalizing dishes served by some of my favorite Christian authors of Latin:

Carō salū́tis est cardō.[8]	Flesh is the hinge on which salvation turns.
Inquiḗtum est cor nostrum dōnec requiḗscat in tē.[9]	Our heart is restless until it rests in you.
Crēdō ut intélligam.[10]	I believe so I may understand.

These are not just inspiring Latin sentences; they are deeply moving ones, spoken out of Christian conviction, lived out of deep experience, and born out of a desire for others to grow in the faith. Here we glimpse the profound theology of Tertullian, the spiritual curiosity of Augustine, and the trusting faith of Anselm.

CLASSICAL AND ECCLESIASTICAL LATIN

With all due respect to Cicero, Caesar, and Virgil, this book takes as its focus only Christian authors of Latin. Caesar, his *amī́cī*, "friends," and, more interestingly, his *inimī́cī*, "enemies," will make rare guest appearances. Christian authors of Latin provide enough interest of their own. (If you don't believe me, just read one of my books on church history and you will see what I mean.) There is no shortage of Latin grammars teaching the classical Latin of Caesar and his contemporaries. These grammars are excellent guides for classical Latin. But this raises the question: Is "Christian" Latin different from "classical" Latin? In terms of the language itself, not at all. Latin is Latin—end of story. There is no such thing as "Christian" Latin any more than there is "Christian" English, a "Christian" pair of socks, or a "Christian" microwave oven. There are only Christians who wrote in Latin.

When people mention "classical" Latin, they are *generally* referring to the literary form of the language that reached its apex around the time of Christ. Of course, there were also classical or Roman Christian and non-Christian authors writing after Christ, but these are not typically given the same attention as the authors listed immediately below. Cicero is probably the quintessential representative of classical Latin, but other noteworthy authors include Caesar, Catullus, Horace, Livy, Ovid, Virgil, and many others. Many educated Christians were exposed to the niceties of the Latin language by reading

---

8. Tertullian, *Dē Resurrēctiōne Carnis* VIII (PL 2.806).
9. Augustine of Hippo, *Cōnfessiōnēs* I (PL 32.661).
10. Anselm of Canterbury, *Proslógion* I (PL 158.227).

these eminent authors, so they became very familiar with what they said and, especially, how they said it (even when they regularly disagreed with the content). However, because the focus of this book is the Latin recorded in the Bible, in theological treatises, in sermons, and in church prayers—which we are categorizing under "ecclesiastical" Latin—these otherwise laudatory authors will not appear.

Instead of Classical authors, all the references, examples, and excerpts in this book come directly from Latin authors in the Christian tradition. Who exactly is a Christian? Here I will give authors the benefit of the doubt. If they consider themselves Christians and speak about Christian topics—and if they do so in Latin—they may be included in this book. I will not assess the theological accuracy of any of the authors or sentences included. You, of course, are welcome to do so, but I encourage you instead to simply drink in their Latin and learn a thing or two from them.

In terms of sheer numbers, most Latin authors belonged to the Roman Catholic faith, but there are countless other varieties of Protestant, humanist, and non-conformist Christians who also wrote in this timeless language. They will not be overlooked. Part of the goal of this book is to expose you to *all* the various kinds of Christians who wrote in Latin as well as to their numerous works with biblical or Christian content.

So you will encounter Bede's biblical commentaries on one page and Sir Isaac Newton's scientific treatises on another; Arminius here and Calvin there; a little bit of Zwingli and a lot of Augustine; a hymn from the Roman Catholic faith and a creed from the Reformed Protestant tradition. There will also be many verses from the Bible and several prayers. To be fair, I should note that some of these authors would not appreciate being placed next to someone they probably regarded as a heretic—or a low-grade Latinist. But the best way to learn Latin is by exposure to multiple styles, and even heretics can write impeccable Latin.

This feature represents one of the most unique elements of this book. Whereas some Latin books offer trite, made-up sentences for students to translate, this book only contains real-life, bona fide sentences from Latin-writing Christians. Here is my pledge to you: I will not make up any Latin sentences in this book. With so many hundreds of thousands of Latin sentences out there waiting to be read, why form new ones from scratch? I cannot think of one good reason. As such, every Latin sentence that you encounter in this book will have been uttered by someone smarter and deader than me.[11] What's more, they will be representative of the Christian tradition—no Caesars allowed. (Even though he wrote fantastic Latin, he has conquered enough.)

By reading this book, you will join a linguistic and ecclesiastical tradition with roots in the Bible but which has also blossomed into hymns, prayers, and creeds. By learning how to read such Latin, you will, with continued effort, breathe in the full fragrance of the Latin Christian tradition—from Perpetua to Jerome to Hildegard of Bingen to Thomas Aquinas to William Ames and beyond.

---

11. Don't worry, I do know that "deader" is not a real word.

A GUIDE TO THE LATIN LANGUAGE: ALPHABET, PRONUNCIATION, AND MORE

Parvus error in prīncípiō magnus est in fīne.[1]
—THOMAS AQUINAS

GETTING OFF TO A GOOD START

I am so glad that you have decided to join me in the study of Latin. I can already tell that you are a smart, sophisticated, and savvy student. Great things are in store for both of us. But before we start, I have a confession to make. We better proceed to the confessional booth so that no other language teachers hear me. They might get upset. Here is *cōnféssiō mea*, "my confession": although I have taught several languages, I think Latin is the most exquisite of all, and it is definitely my favorite. I believe that its precision, beauty, and content surpass that of any rival. It is quite simply the best. There—I feel much better getting that off my chest.

In order to prepare ourselves for our first *capítulum*, "chapter," we need to make sure that we avoid committing—as the ever-astute Thomas Aquinas warns us—*parvus error in prīncípiō*, "a small mistake in the beginning." That is why I will here provide a general overview of the Latin used in this book as well as a summary of the basic features of the Latin language such as the alphabet, pronunciation, and accentuation. Getting these things right in the beginning goes a long way *in fīne*, "in the end." Although I know you are eager to dive into the endless pool of Latin awaiting us, we must first wade in with the basics.

Because this guide prepares us for our first *capítulum*, it will have a slightly different format than the others. Our agenda here is to determine which pronunciation system to adopt so that we can maintain consistency throughout the book. When you have sufficiently learned the basics found in this guide, you are ready to proceed to the next order of business: the genius of the Latin language itself.

---

1. "A small mistake in the beginning is a big one in the end."

BASICS OF LATIN

LATIN ALPHABET

According to Isidore of Seville, a seventh-century Spanish bishop, there are three things associated with each letter of the alphabet: *nōmen, figūra,* and *potéstās*.[2] Isidore explained that a letter's *nōmen,* "name," refers to how it is called; a letter's *figūra,* "shape," to how it is formed; and a letter's *potéstās,* "meaning," to how it is signified. Take the first letter of the Latin alphabet, for example. Its *nōmen* is "a," its *figūra* is its particular shape, and its *potéstās* indicates its meaning.

Because English uses the Latin or Roman alphabet, you are already familiar with the *nōmen, figūra,* and *potéstās* of each letter in the alphabet. Congratulations on achieving your first Latin milestone! With a few exceptions, Latin is identical to English when it comes to the alphabet. There are vowels and consonants; all the letters are written from left to right; and there are also combinations of letters called syllables that produce distinct sounds. Although the pronunciation of Latin differs from English, there are many parallels. Here is the Latin alphabet in upper and lower case.

Aa, Bb, Cc, Dd, Ee, Ff, Gg, Hh, Ii, Jj, Kk, Ll, Mm, Nn, Oo, Pp, Qq, Rr, Ss, Tt, Uu, Vv, Xx, Yy, Zz

Do you see anything missing? As you may have noticed, Latin does not possess the letter *w*, and the letters *k*, *y*, and *z* only appear in words borrowed from Greek.[3] Also, Latin contains two letters called "glides" (or "semiconsonants" when preceding a vowel and "semivowels" when following one), which sometimes appear as vowels and sometimes as consonants. The two glides are *i* and *u*. When the Latin letter *i* is a consonant, it can be represented as *j* or *i*. Similarly, when the Latin letter *u* is a consonant, it can be represented as *v* or *u*. I readily admit that this can be confusing at first, but you will soon get used to it. The variation in spelling does not affect the meaning of the word. So, whether you see the word translated into English as "slave" spelled as *servus* or *seruus,* it means the same thing.

PRONUNCIATION OF THE LATIN LANGUAGE

There is no universal way to pronounce Latin. Instead, pronunciation varies according to time period, geographic region, content focus, and personal preference. The most common systems of pronunciation are what I will call (1) "classical," (2) "ecclesiastical," and (3) "national."

"Classical" pronunciation takes as its model educated Roman authors who lived roughly from the first century BC to the second century AD. Because such authors have been dead for millennia, advocates of this pronunciation use ancient writings to reconstruct how Latin was spoken by these educated classes of Romans. This reconstructed model is the closest that we can get to the actual pronunciation of such classical Roman figures.[4]

"Ecclesiastical" pronunciation, by contrast, does not seek to emulate the way Latin was spoken during the height of the Roman Empire. As the type of pronunciation used by the Roman Catholic Church, located in the Vatican, it is heavily influenced by Italian pronunciation. To many, ecclesiastical pronunciation sounds like Latin with an Italian accent.[5]

"National" pronunciation generally follows the pronunciation of the reader's mother tongue (whether English, Italian, French, etc.). In the words of Renato Oniga, "The most successful national pronunciation

---

2. Isidore of Seville, *Etymologiārum Librī XX* I.4.16 (PL 82.81).
3. The letter *k* only appears at the beginning of two words, and the other two letters are used in words of Greek origin, such as the *z* in *baptīzāre,* "to baptize."
4. If you want a thorough guide to classical pronunciation, see W. Sidney Allen, *Vox Latina: The Pronunciation of Classical Latin,* 2nd ed. (Cambridge: Cambridge University Press, 1978).
5. For more on this style of pronunciation, see William D. Hall, *Latin Pronunciation according to Roman Usage* (Anaheim, CA: National Music, 1971).

of Latin was the Italian one."[6] This makes complete sense. The Roman Catholic Church naturally adopted the style of pronunciation where it was headquartered, and the use of Latin by the church (Latin was the official liturgical language of the Roman Catholic Church until the twentieth century) meant that Latin went where the church went. In many ways, a national pronunciation is the easiest way to pronounce Latin—you simply pronounce letters like you would in your native language (which is greatly facilitated if your native language uses the Roman alphabet).

Which system of pronunciation should you adopt? Traditionally, the classical form has been standard for those studying Classical Latin, while the ecclesiastical form has been customary for those studying church Latin. In other words, the classical pronunciation predominates in secular institutions, boarding schools, and universities, whereas the ecclesiastical pronunciation prevails in Catholic schools, churches, monasteries, and seminaries. National pronunciation, by contrast, is not centralized like the other two and varies from region to region. Despite conventions, there are Christian teachers who employ classical pronunciation and secular teachers who adopt ecclesiastical pronunciation (as well as both who might use a kind of national pronunciation). Personally, I believe any pronunciation is acceptable as long as there is consistency. That stated, I am partial to classical and ecclesiastical pronunciation since these are fairly standardized. And I have used both at different times in my teaching. For instance, although I was originally taught ecclesiastical pronunciation, years later I switched to the classical pronunciation.

Classical and ecclesiastical are mutually intelligible and contain far more similarities than differences. The variances between classical and ecclesiastical parallel those between speakers of the same language from different regions, such as American speakers of English versus British ones. I will include a guide to both classical and ecclesiastical below with no preference for which system you adopt; it is up to you, your instructor, or your institution. Of most importance is that you choose one of these two forms and *consistently* pronounce Latin according to the guidelines offered.[7]

VOWELS

Latin maintains the same number of vowels as English,[8] but Latin distinguishes between short and long vowels. Traditionally, long vowels take about twice as long to enunciate as short ones. Though not essential to understanding Latin and not always easy to remember, it is a good practice to hold long vowels slightly longer than short vowels (even when speaking silently in your head) in order to remind yourself that Latin differentiates the two.

How do you know if a vowel is long or short? In the parentheses after the long and short vowels in the chart below, I provide the mark for long vowels—called "macra," which are represented by ¯ (for example, ā)—and short vowels—called "breves," which are signified by ˘ (for instance, ă). These diacritical marks only appear in Latin grammars or readers, and even in these textbooks you will almost always encounter only macra. When diacritics appear in written works, they have been added by the publisher to help the reader recognize vowel quantity. The grammar you are reading offers the best of both worlds. How so? I will include both macra and acute accent marks in each *capítulum* to encourage consistent pronunciation; however, these diacritics will not be added to the *exercítia* in the appendix (which correspond to the *capítula*) so that you gain exposure to how Latin appears when reading it on your own—whether in the Latin Vulgate, in Augustine, or in Calvin.

---

6. Renato Oniga, *Latin: A Linguistic Introduction* (Oxford: Oxford University Press, 2014), 21.
7. Consult the bibliography for advanced grammars on pronunciation. If you want to learn more, see Oniga, *Latin*, 21–23.
8. Because of Greek influence (specifically the Greek letter *upsilon*), the letter *y* will sometimes appear in Latin; when it does so, it is acting like a vowel. The exact sound is hard to approximate in English. A long *u* sounds like u in French, while a short *u* sounds like *ü* in German.

Keep in mind that the chart below can only approximate Latin vowels (and Latin sounds in general), and that pronunciation of English (let alone Latin) can vary widely from region to region and instructor to instructor. For the sake of simplicity, I am organizing the sound of classical and ecclesiastical vowels into similar sounds, but I highly recommend searching for online recordings of these two pronunciations and listening to how they are pronounced. There are slight variations that are difficult to capture in written form alone.

Classical and Ecclesiastical <u>Long</u> Vowels	English Equivalent	Classical and Ecclesiastical <u>Short</u> Vowels	English Equivalent
a (ā)	father	a (ă)[a]	idea
e (ē)	obey	e (ĕ)	ever
i (ī)	ravine	i (ĭ)	if
o (ō)	over	o (ŏ)	on
u (ū)	tune	u (ŭ)	under
y (ȳ)	move[b]	y (y̆)	über

[a] In this grammar, I will only rarely use breves. There is no need since the absence of macra indicates that the vowel is short. When I do use breves, as in this paradigm, I am pointing out something specific.

[b] This sound is harder to render in English and our example is a mere approximation; try to pronounce the word *move* with a French accent.

Assuming the absence of macra and breves, how do you know if a vowel is long or short? Unfortunately, this can get tricky. Here is the simplest guideline: A syllable is considered long if it (a) contains a diphthong (discussed immediately below), (b) has a vowel followed by two or more consonants (or *x* or *z*),[9] or (c) is long by nature (which is what a macron indicates; if a vowel has no macron, then the vowel is short). But let us make it even simpler. Because vowels that are long by nature are difficult to predict for beginning students, I will provide an acute accent mark (for instance, á) over the syllable that should be accentuated in each word, even when also providing macra (for instance, ā́).

DIPHTHONGS

I will now introduce you to a word that sounds like utensils used on a spaceship. Every time I hear this word, I imagine a conversation taking place in space: "Hey Neil, can you pass me the diphthongs? I need to fix the control system." In actuality, the word derives from ancient Greek, not Latin. What exactly is a diphthong? Whenever two vowels unite to form one sound or syllable, a "diphthong" is born. They are two-vowel yet single-syllable letter combinations. You begin pronouncing a diphthong by articulating the first vowel and then making a slight change (while still holding the original syllable) as you articulate the second vowel. This sounds more difficult than it actually is, so just do your best when practicing the guidelines below. Altogether, there are six diphthongs in Latin, each of which is listed below according to the classical and ecclesiastical pronunciations.[10]

---

9. A vowel that is long because it is followed by two consonants is still pronounced as a short vowel, but the syllable itself is long.
10. Though not a diphthong, in ecclesiastical Latin (but not classical), the *ti* combination sounds like *tsi* in English.

Classical Latin	English Equivalent	Ecclesiastical Latin	English Equivalent
ae[a]	s**ky**	ae	s**ay**
au	n**ow**	au	n**ow**
ei	**eigh**t	ei	**eigh**t
eu	-[b]	eu	-[c]
oe[d]	s**oi**l	oe	s**ay**
ui	**wee**	ui	**wee**

[a] The ligature æ (with *a* and *e* touching) indicates that the two vowels are diphthongs, while the *ae* (not touching) conventionally indicates that the two vowels are separate. However, this is not a universal rule, and this textbook will NOT utilize the ligatures of two conjoined vowels.

[b] Because there is not an exact equivalent in English, a better approach to this diphthong is voicing the *e* and *u* together as one sound.

[c] As with classical pronunciation, this diphthong is pronounced with the *e* and *u* together as one sound.

[d] Like æ and *ae*, the ligature œ may also appear instead of *oe*; when it does, it indicates a diphthong.

Most of the time, diphthongs are easy to recognize. When you see two adjoining vowels, it is common to expect one. When there is confusion as to whether two adjoining vowels are forming one sound (such as a diphthong) or forming distinct sounds (such as two vowels working independently), it may be marked with a "diaresis" (a Greek word that means "division"), which looks like the German umlaut (¨). The diaresis tells you to make two sounds instead of one. The word *Israel*, for example, is sometimes printed as *Israël* to indicate that the adjoining vowels (in this case, *a* and *e*) should be pronounced separately.[11] When the accent mark of a word falls on the diphthong (as it often does since all diphthongs are long), only the second of the two vowels actually receives the accent mark. This will take some getting used to, but the inclusion of both macra and accent marks—in addition to the rules you are learning in this introductory guide—will equip you to pronounce Latin confidently and consistently.

CONSONANTS

The majority of consonants in Latin are pronounced as they are in English.[12] The exceptions to this rule appear below.

Classical Latin	English Equivalent	Ecclesiastical Latin	English Equivalent
c	always hard, as in **c**arol	c	before i, e, ae, oe **ch**ant; otherwise as in **c**arol
ch	always like k in English, as in **Ch**ristmas (same pronunciation as c)	ch	like k in English, as in **Ch**ristmas
g	always hard, as in **g**o	g	before i, e, y, as in **j**ump; otherwise as in **g**o

(cont.)

---

11. We can also see this word marked differently, e.g., *Isrā́ēl* with macra. The word used above, though, is not using macra.
12. Naturally, with an international language as widespread as English, there is a great regional variety. Native English speakers hail from all parts of the world: Asia, the Americas, Oceania, Europe, etc.

Classical Latin	English Equivalent	Ecclesiastical Latin	English Equivalent
h	like h in **hi**	h	Like h in **hi**
-	-	j[a]	like y in **y**es
v[b]	like w in English, as in **w**eep	v	like v in English, as in **v**eto
gn	pronounced as **ng** in English followed by **n**, like ha**ngn**ail	gn	pronounced as one sound, as in can**y**on
ph	like the ph in u**ph**eld	ph	like ph in **ph**ilosophy
r	slightly trilled, as in Italian **R**ōma	r	slightly trilled, as in Italian **R**ōma
sc	Like sk in **sk**ill	sc	before i, e, as in **sh**ip; otherwise as in **sk**ip
th	like th in **th**yme; or th in ho**tth**ouse	th[c]	like th in **th**yme

[a] Remember that *j* is a consonantal *i*. Sometimes you will see *i*, sometimes *j*. Other than when quoting texts, I will generally spell the consonantal *i* as *i* rather than *j* in the vocabulary sections.

[b] Remember that the *u* and *v* are actually the same letter. Before a consonant, the *u* will sound more like an English *u*, and before a vowel, as in this chart, it will sound like the English letter *w*. Thus, the Latin word *servus* ("slave") contains *u* as a consonant (and so is pronounced like English *w*), followed by *u* as a vowel (and so pronounced like English *u*).

[c] As you may have noticed, *ch*, *ph*, and *th* are all Greek imports, just as *k*, *y*, and *z* are.

SYLLABLES

Here we encounter another strange-sounding term that ultimately derives from Greek. Is it a part of the human anatomy or a sickness to be avoided? Neither of the above. Syllables are simply units of pronunciation. They are the building blocks to proper Latin pronunciation. It is important from the beginning to pronounce Latin in a consistent and uniform way so that you can recall words, communicate with others, and maintain some sense of verbal sanity. This is why learning the basic rules of syllabification prove helpful. Each word has as many syllables as it has vowels and diphthongs. To know how many syllables there are in a word, simply count the number of vowels and diphthongs. The number you count is the number of syllables. Then, when pronouncing a word, pause briefly between each syllable.

Here are a few guidelines for syllabification:

1. When there are two adjoining vowels or combinations of a vowel and diphthong, separate them. For instance, *āit*, "he/she/it says," is divided as follows: a-it.
2. When there is a single consonant between two vowels, the consonant goes with the second vowel. For instance, the words *pater* "father," and *māter*, "mother," are divided as follows: pa-ter and ma-ter.
3. When there are two or more consonants between two vowels, the last consonant usually goes with the second vowel. For instance, *prīnceps*, "chief" or "leader," is divided as follows: prin-ceps.

ACCENTS

The concept of accent is often categorized according to (1) pitch or (2) stress. While a pitch accent is increased by articulating a syllable at a higher note, a stress accent is increased by using greater force.

It is easy to confuse these two kinds of accents, but they are quite different. English, for example, is mostly a language of stress while ancient Greek was one of pitch.

As you might imagine, much ink has been spilt on the topic of Latin accentuation. In the past, the so-called French school has argued that classical Latin used a pitch accent, while the German school contended that classical Latin always employed a stress accent.[13] My approach in this book is to offer as much pronunciation guidance as possible, which is why I will include diacritical marks in each chapter.

Having learned the ways to determine the number of syllables per word, the icing on the cake is deciding where to put the stress. That is to say, it is one thing to recognize that *puélla*, "girl," contains three syllables divided as pu-el-la, but it is another thing to understand whether the stress falls on the *u*, *e*, or *a*, or a combination thereof. What is a *puélla* to do?

The good news is that a Latin word will only receive stress on one syllable. In fact, the even better news is that I will always provide the stressed accent mark for you (as seen in the word *puélla* above). However, if you want to learn how to stress a word without my help, you can easily do so. Here are some basic guidelines:

1. In a word with only one syllable (monosyllabic) or two syllables (disyllabic), the stress is ALWAYS on the first syllable (e.g., *hic*, *hīc*, *pater*, and *māter*). In this grammar, I will not include accent marks in words with two or fewer syllables since the stress will always be predictably known.
2. In a word with three or more syllables (polysyllabic), the stress is on the second-to-last (penultimate) syllable if that vowel is long (e.g., *cogitā́re*); or on the third-to-last (antepenultimate) syllable if the second-to-last vowel is short (e.g., *íterum*). This is because Latin generally prefers the accent to be as far back as possible in a word.
3. In any word, the accent will never be further back than the antepenultimate. Romans had standards, after all.
4. In a word that receives the addition of an appendage such as -*ne*, -*ue*, and -*que*, the stress falls on the last syllable of the word (e.g., *fīliō* → *fīliṓque*).

And if you want to identify the Latin words lurking behind the technical terms, here they are:

- The word *última* means "last" (hence "ultima" in English, referring to the last syllable).
- The words *paene última* mean "almost last" (hence "penult" in English, referring to the second-to-last syllable).
- The words *ante paene última* mean "before almost last" (hence "antepenult" in English, referring to the third-to-last syllable).

In summary, I will place an acute accent mark (´) on words with three or more syllables to indicate where the stress is located, and I will also include macra (¯) to designate the length of vowels. The macron helps you know how long to hold a syllable and the accent helps you know which syllable to stress. Although there may be more than one word in Latin with a long vowel, there will only be one accent mark per word. For example, in the word *infīnítum*, the second and third *i*'s are long, but only the *i* in the penult receives the accent mark. Similarly, in the word *spīrítuī* there are three *i*'s: the first and last are long (hence the macra), while the middle one is short (hence no macron). In this instance, it is the short *i* that receives the stress.

---

13. If you want to thoroughly familiarize yourself with this debate, see Philomen Probert, *Latin Grammarians on the Latin Accent: The Transformation of Greek Grammatical Thought* (Oxford: Oxford University Press, 2019), 17–47.

PUNCTUATION

The same punctuation that you encounter in English is generally the same that you will encounter in written Latin.

BUILDING ON THE ABCS

Upon reading this guide—what we may label the ABCs of the Latin language—you are ready to begin the first *capítulum*. The ensuing ABCs of Latin—Augustine, Bede, and Calvin—are anxiously awaiting you. However, if you find yourself later requiring a refresher on how to pronounce Latin correctly, feel free to return to this guide. Augustine and Bede can wait—and Calvin can, too. *Bonam fortúnam*, "Good luck!"

OVERVIEW

This book is organized into eight *partēs*, "parts." Each *pars* will equip you with the skills needed to master a particular grammatical concept. The *Index Rērum*, "Contents," delineates all of the *capítula*, "chapters."

The order of each *capítulum*, "chapter," is always the same. Following the name of the *capítulum*, which summarizes the main contents, these components will always be included and related to the chapter's topic:

- *Dictum Latínum*, "Latin Saying," emerges from one of the authors or writings presented.
- *Opúsculum Theológicum*, "Small Theological Excerpt," features a theme-related introduction.
- *Prōspéctus*, "Overview," encapsulates the major concepts discussed in each *capítulum*.
- *Grammática*, "Grammar," presents all of the relevant grammatical concepts. There will usually be several subsections.
- *Summárium*, "Summary," summarizes the major concepts learned in each *capítulum*.
- *Vocābulṓrum Index*, "List of Vocabulary," lists all twenty-five words to be memorized for each *capítulum*. The vocabulary words are carefully chosen to represent the most common words used in ecclesiastical Latin, culled from the Latin Vulgate and Christian authors. The lists offer glosses of words. (It should be noted here that these lists do not provide every possible meaning of each word.)
- *Ōrắtiō Populắris*, "Prayer Offered by the People," offers a Christian prayer to memorize.

Supplemental material will appear in the appendix under the designation *Exercítia*, "exercises." There is direct correspondence between the *capítulum* and its respective *exercítium*. Just as there are XXVII (27) *capítula*, there are likewise XXVII *exercítia*. Each *exercítium* contains real-life Latin examples that will enhance and assess your mastery of the material. A translation exercise concludes each *exercítium*.

As you can see, each *capítulum* and corresponding *exercítium* in this book will surround you with Latin from all sides and all vantage points with the purpose of setting you up for great success. What is more, each *capítulum* combines history, culture, theology, spirituality, and tradition so that you may delight in the beauty of the Latin language while also learning all of the most important grammatical and linguistic concepts.

PRĪMA PARS

NOUNS *and* ADJECTIVES

> Prīma Pars covers nouns and adjectives. You will learn the five different declensions of nouns as well as the three declensions of adjectives. In addition, your understanding of the noun system will receive reinforcement by means of specific sayings, exercises, prayers, translations, and supplemental materials.

Capítulum

I

NOUNS AND PREPOSITIONS

In nómine Patris et Fílii et Spíritūs Sānctī.[1]
—GOSPEL OF MATTHEW

OPÚSCULUM THEOLÓGICUM: *Sīgnum Crucis*[2]

One of the most ancient yet enduring prayers in Latin is constructed out of the most basic building blocks of any language: nouns. The prayer is called the *sīgnum crucis*, "sign of the cross." Composed of four nouns, it is based *verbấtim*, "word for word," on the Latin version of Matthew XXVIII.19,[3] where Jesus commands his apostles to make disciples of all the nations and to baptize them as follows:

In nómine Patris et Fílii et Spíritūs Sānctī.	In the name of the Father, and of the Son, and of the Holy Spirit.

For centuries, Christian priests have uttered this prayer at the beginning of the *Missa*, "the Mass," while simultaneously offering a gesture of blessing. The practice of combining this simple prayer with the making of the cross upon one's body was widespread in early Christianity and continues to this day. This specific use of the prayer is mentioned by church fathers Tertullian, Hippolytus, Basil, and Jerome. In one of his writings abbreviated *Dē Corṓnā*, "On the Crown," Tertullian describes the specific times at which Christians daily motioned the *sīgnum crucis*:

Ad omnem prōgréssum atque prōmṓtum, ad omnem áditum et éxitum, ad calciátum, ad lavácra, ad mēnsās, ad lū́mina, ad cubī́lia, ad sedília, quāecúmquē nōs conversātiō exércet <u>frontem crucis signáculō térimus</u>.[4]	When moving forward and moving around, when coming in and going out, when putting on shoes, washing, eating, turning on the lights, lying down, sitting down, in whatever situation we find ourselves, <u>we mark our head with the sign of the cross.</u>

---

    1. In this book, the *Dictum Latī́num* will immediately follow the title of each *capítulum* (but it will never be labeled *Dictum Latī́num*). The footnote will always offer a translation. Here, the translation is: "In the name of the Father, and of the Son, and of the Holy Spirit."
    2. In English translation: "Small Theological Excerpt: Sign of the Cross."
    3. In order to help you become more familiar with Roman numerals, I will slightly modify convention when citing Scripture and other ancient sources. Rather than using Arabic numerals, I will use Roman numerals. Granted, this will take some time getting used to, but a later *capítulum* will discuss numerals (ch. 7). They, of course, occur frequently in Latin texts.
    4. Tertullian, *Dē Corŏ́nā Mī́litis* III (PL 2.80).

Following in the footsteps of Tertullian yet making more compact steps, Jerome, the leading translator of the Vulgate Bible, wrote to a friend about the *sīgnum crucis* in a sentence that was as simple as it was sublime:

Ad omnem āctum, ad omnem incéssum manus <u>pingat crucem</u>.[5]	At every moment and every step our hand should <u>draw the cross</u>.

The *sīgnum crucis* provides a delightful introduction to Latin. Not only does it showcase the terseness of the Latin language in comparison to its English counterpart—indeed, the Latin prayer uses roughly half of the words that English requires—but it also suggests the splendor of Latin as a spoken medium. Most noteworthy, however, is the prayer's origin in the Bible and its explicit Christian content. Upon translation into Latin in the second century, the Latin Bible offered a form in which Latin-speaking Christians could write, speak, sing, debate, and pray for more than a millenium. Thus it is no wonder that Tertullian would coin the word *Trī́nitās*, or "Trinity," after reading about the *Pater et Fī́lius et Spī́ritus Sā́nctus* mentioned explicitly in biblical passages such as Matthew XXVIII.19.

Like these skilled Latin writers of ages past, we must begin where they began their study of the Latin language: *in prīncípiō*, "in the beginning." And in the beginning was the *verbum*, "the word"—not surprisingly a noun, the backbone of which provides not only the foundation of the *sīgnum crucis* but also of the Latin language itself.

Prospéctus[6]

In this *capítulum* you will learn that:
- A noun is a person, place, or thing.
- Prepositions introduce phrases describing actions or states.
- The Latin noun system includes case, number, and gender.

GRAMMÁTICA: *English Nouns*

1.1 **Nouns.** As you may remember from Mrs. Watson in elementary school (at least that was the name of my teacher), a noun is commonly defined as a person, place, or thing. This is basic stuff. And it is wonderful to see how this definition has not changed over time. In sentences, nouns tend to be the main event. Stated differently, nouns are those grammatical parts of speech that name things, e.g., "Paul," "Jerusalem," "churches," "salvation." In English, or Latin for that matter, you cannot have a proper sentence without at least one noun (or pronoun, which takes the place of a noun) understood. This is why nouns are the building blocks of a language.

1.2 **Inflection.** English speakers intuitively know the differences between "he," "him," and "his." Though subtle, these all mean different things. The technical term for these differences is "inflection." English words sometimes "inflect," or change their forms, in order to indicate their specific function in a sentence. Thus "he" is used when referring to a male that is functioning as the subject of a sentence, "him" when functioning as the direct object, and "his" when pointing

---

5. Jerome, *Epistula* XXII.37 (PL 22.421).
6. "Overview."

to something he owns. What is going on here? The different forms of his name, though referring to the same person, indicate a different grammatical function.

1.3 **Word Order.** Compared to Latin, English is not even a moderately inflected language. It is as bland as unseasoned oatmeal. For the most part, English nouns no longer make any attempt to change their forms (or endings) to accommodate their different grammatical functions as commonly as nouns in Latin do (German and Greek also do this). Instead, English mostly relies on word order. The rules are quite fixed here (unless you are dealing with poetry, which is not bound by grammatical rules to the same extent). English nouns typically acquire their function-specific meanings from the order in which they appear in a sentence. In other words, we can easily identify the subject of a sentence in English because it usually stands as the first word. For those who like variety, this formation is very dull, but it does get the job done.

1.4 **Case System.** Generally speaking, the English case system contains three grammatical components, which all sound as official as a bureaucratic office: (1) the subjective, (2) the objective, and (3) the possessive.[7] Defined briefly, an English noun may be described as the subject of a clause (subjective), as an object (objective), or as something owned or possessed (possessive). Depending on the noun's function in a particular sentence, it may or may not be required to alter its form, that is, "inflect." If we diagram the English word "name" into its three inflectional categories, or "cases," we get the following chart.

ENGLISH CASE SYSTEM

Case	Singular Form	Plural Form
subjective	name	names
objective	name	names
possessive	name's / of the name	names' / of the names

There is relatively little change in this English noun as its grammatical function changes from one case to another. Latin nouns, however, are quite different. This is exciting, and I hope you will learn to love this aspect of Latin. English, on the other hand, mostly shed its use of cases centuries ago, making it very difficult sometimes to know what role a noun or adjective is playing in a sentence.

GRAMMÁTICA: *Latin Case System*

1.5 **Translation.** Translating from one language to another is as much art as science. When comparing English translations of the Bible, for instance, we see that (1) translation philosophy, (2) ideological commitment, (3) time period, (4) geographic region, and (5) personal preference may play a role when moving from the original language to the target language. This, of course, does not mean that anything goes, but it is helpful as we embark on learning how to read and translate Latin to remember that translations need not be identical to be accurate.

When translating from Latin into our target language—for example, English—there will sometimes be a one-to-one correspondence in the words, but more often there will not be.

---

7. Some grammarians also include a fourth case: the indirect object, which indirectly receives the action of the verb.

Nor should we expect this. As a simple example, Latin does not contain the articles "a," "an," and "the," even though these are staples in the English language. Almost every time we seek to translate a Latin noun into English, therefore, we will have to decide whether we think an English article is required to render the Latin thought accurately. In a similar way, as we begin to discuss cases and prepositions below, we will come to understand that English will often (though not always) require more words to be used than Latin does. Latin is a very terse language, after all. Oftentimes, specific Latin cases will warrant the use of certain English prepositions (or even a cluster of possible prepositions). Ideally, we should first attempt to understand the Latin words and sentence before seeking to render them accurately into English. Instead of immediately attempting a translation, stick with the Latin on its own terms until you understand it; then you can translate it into English.

1.6 **Latin Cases.** A Latin noun (related to *nōmen*, "name") indicates its grammatical function more precisely than an English noun does. This grammatical advantage allows for Latin nouns to convey more exact functional meanings than their English counterparts. It means that Latin students will need to become familiar with many new forms called "cases."[8] In Latin, there are commonly understood to be seven "cases," or ways that nouns function in a sentence. Virtually every sentence in Latin will be comprised of words using one, or a combination, of these cases.

The descriptions below are designed to get you started with Latin, although each case deserves more attention than allocated here. Let's get started!

1.7 **Nominative Case.** This case serves as the subject or predicate nominative[9] of a clause or sentence. Examples: "Ruth," "life," "the apostles," "salvation," "a boat," "Rome."

    Sōlus Petrus respóndet. (John Calvin)[10]   Only Peter replies.

1.8 **Genitive Case.** This case indicates ownership, possession, relationship, or association, or it otherwise qualifies the meaning of another word. When translating the genitive case, it may often be represented by the use of the preposition "of" (more about prepositions below) or by the combination of "apostrophe + s." Examples: "Priscilla's," "of lives," "the church's."

    Ex Jerúsalēm enim éxiēns verbum   For the word of the Lord goes out from
    Dóminī. (Hilary of Poitiers)[11]   Jerusalem.

1.9 **Dative Case.** This case indicates reference or to whom something is given. It is often expressed by the prepositions "for" and "to." Examples: "for the temple," "to Timothy."

    Illustríssimo Príncipī ac Dóminō.   To the most renowned Prince and Lord.
    (Philip Melanchthon)[12]

1.10 **Accusative Case.** This case serves as the direct object of a verb or that which directly receives the action. It can also indicate motion toward something and several other ideas. Sometimes this

---

8. For those interested, the English word "case" is derived from the Latin verb *cadō, cádere, cécidī, cāsus*, "fall." According to the theory of Plato, "cases" were words falling from the heavens indicating an earthly representation. Thus, all words on earth represented real qualities or characteristics in the heavens.
9. A predicative nominative is a noun in the nominative case that completes a (stative) verb such as "to be."
10. John Calvin, *Īnstitūtiō Chrīstiánae Religiónis* VI.6.4 (CR 30.815).
11. Hilary of Poitiers, "Psalm CXXI," in *Tractátus in CXXI Psalmum* (PL 9.663).
12. Philip Melanchthon, *Epístolae* (CR 7.705).

case is expressed in English by the prepositions "to" or "toward." Examples: "toward life," "the churches," "John," "a scroll."

Manichaéus est quī ábnegat vēritátem, quī carnem Christī negat. (Ambrose of Milan)[13]	A Manichaean is he who denies the truth and rejects the flesh of Christ.[14]

1.11 **Ablative Case.** This case may express manner, means, separation, agency, instrumentality, time, place, etc. It also often indicates motion away from something, which is the opposite of the accusative case (indicating direction toward something). When translating the ablative case into English, we will often use one of the following prepositions: "about," "by," "from," "in," "on," or "with." Which do we choose? It depends on context. And, in all truth, you will sometimes have more than one option available—or none at all. But that is why you are studying Latin—it will always keep you on your toes. Examples: "about the letter," "by the path," "from the apostle," "in the city," and "with the women."

Dē Christō ígitur haec ūnivérsa dīcúntur. (Peter the Venerable)[15]	All these things, therefore, are spoken about Christ.

1.12 **Vocative Case.** This is the case of direct address. When translating the vocative case, older English translations often inserted the word "o" in front of it. Example: "O earth." However, since we live in the twenty-first century rather than the seventeenth, the time has come to abandon the drama of the "o." We can simply translate the word itself. Example: "earth."

Please note that we will not include the vocative case in paradigm charts because the vocative is identical to the nominative case (except in the second declension). When used, it is fairly obvious since it is the case of direct address.

Sed glória tibi, Dómine, quī sōlus ómnia potes, ūnā cum benedíctō Deō nostrō et Patre, atque cum Spíritū Sānctō. (Anastasius Bibliothecarius)[16]	But glory to you, Lord, who alone is able to do all things together with our blessed God and Father, and with the Holy Spirit.

1.13 **Locative Case.** This case deals with location. For instance, *domī* means "at home," and *Rōmae* signifies "in Rome." Along with the vocative case, it is fairly obvious when the locative is being used, and it is not uncommon for the ablative case to be used when the locative could have been used instead. As with the vocative case, the locative will not appear in paradigms.

Ecclésiae Deī quae est Corínthī. (I Cor. I.2)	To the church of God that is in Corinth.

Our primary goal in the first several *capítula* is to learn the Latin case system. The order seen above is the order of all our noun paradigms.[17] Finally, please observe the case abbreviations, which will be used interchangeably with the full names of the cases.

---

13. Ambrose of Milan, "Epístola XLII.13" in *Epistolárum Classis* I (PL 16.1128).
14. Manicheans were a group of early gnostics whose founder, Mani, was a prophet in the third century AD. They were active during the time of the early church.
15. Peter the Venerable, *Trāctátus contrā Jūdaéōs* (PL 189.548).
16. Anastasius Bibliothecarius, *Interpretátiō Sýnodī VII Generális* (PL 129.286).
17. Other textbooks order the cases differently. For instance, the British often place the accusative after the nominative. Regardless of order, however, the meaning does not change.

LATIN CASE SYSTEM

Case (Abbreviation)	Roles
Nominative (Nom)	subject, predicate nominative, main thing
Genitive (Gen)	ownership, possession, relationship, association
Dative (Dat)	reference, benefit, indirect object
Accusative (Acc)	direct object, direction toward something
Ablative (Abl)	manner, instrumentality, motion away, accompaniment, separation, location
Vocative (Voc)[a]	direct address
Locative (Loc)	location

[a] Remember that the vocative and locative will not normally appear in charts.

PREPOSITIONS

1.14 **Latin Prepositions.** Many of the cases that we just learned may pair with certain Latin prepositions (the vocabulary list of words that we will learn in this *capítulum* is mostly Latin prepositions). These Latin prepositions help us determine the best possible way to render the Latin phrase into English. But even if the Latin noun does not have a corresponding Latin preposition we will often rely on English prepositions when making our translations.

1.15 **English Prepositions.** As seen above, our translation of Latin cases will often pair with specific words in English. Traditionally, such words are called "prepositions." We may describe prepositions as those words introducing phrases that describe actions or states. By expressing how words are related to each other, they are some of the most frequently used words in the English language. Common prepositions include "at," "by," "for," "in," "into," "of," "to," and "with." The word introducing the phrase that describes action is called the "object of the preposition," and the preposition with its objects constitute a "prepositional phrase." In Latin prose, prepositions appear before nouns.

1.16 **Prepositions Govern the Accusative and Ablative Cases.** Over time, Latin came to rely more heavily on prepositions, which explains, in part, why Romance languages such as Spanish and Portuguese do not use cases as readily as Latin did. Still, prepositions in Latin are often absent, forcing us to rely primarily on a word's ending to determine (1) whether an English preposition should be used in our translation and (2) which English preposition is best.

When Latin prepositions do appear, they only do so in relation to two cases: the accusative and ablative. In other words, when you see a Latin preposition, you should expect one of those two cases to follow. In fact, most Latin prepositions pattern either with the accusative or the ablative, not often with both. The Latin preposition *ad*, for example, only occurs with an accusative noun. Meanwhile, the preposition *coram* only appears in relation to the ablative case. For example:

Testíficor <u>coram</u> <u>Deō</u> et <u>ángelīs</u> suīs. (Saint Patrick)[18]	I bear witness <u>before</u> both <u>God</u> and his <u>angels</u>.

---

18. Saint Patrick, *S. Pātrícii ad Corotícum Epístola* X (PL 53.818).

NOUNS AND PREPOSITIONS

Latin	English (Gloss)	(Etymology)
ā, ab (+ abl)[a]	by, from	(abnormal)
ad (+ acc)	to, toward, near to	(adjunct)
ante (+ acc)	before, in front of	(anterior)
circum (+ acc)	around, about, nearby	(circumference)
contrā (+ acc)	against	(contrary)
cōram	(+ abl)	before, in the presence of
dē (+ abl)	about, concerning, on	(departure)
cum (+ abl)	with	
ē, ex (+ abl)[b]	from, out of	(eloquent)
extrā (+ acc)	outside (of), beyond	(extraterrestrial)
in (+ acc; abl)	into, onto, against (acc); in, on (abl)	(inside)
inter (+ acc)	between	(intervene)
intrā (+ acc)	within, inside	(intramural)
nōn	no, not	(nonbinding)
ob (+ acc)	on account of, according to, towards	(obstruct)
per (+ acc)	through	(persevere)
post (+ acc)	after, behind	(postscript)
praeter (+ acc)	beyond, except, besides	
prō (+ abl)	for, in behalf of, before, instead of	(protect)
propter (+ acc)	on account of, because	
sine (+ abl)	without	
sub (+ acc)	under, before (acc); under, beneath (abl)	(submerge)
super (+ acc; abl)	above, beyond (acc); concerning (abl)	(superlative)
suprā (+ acc)	above, over, beyond	(supralapsarian)

[a] When defined, prepositions will always include the cases they govern. In this case, the parentheses indicate that the preposition *ā, ab* always takes the ablative case. Remember that a preposition may only take the ablative (abl) or accusative (acc) case.

[b] Whereas *ē* only appears before consonants, the form *ex* may appear before consonants or vowels.

Because the preposition *coram*, "before," "in the presence of," only and always takes the ablative case, this means that the two nouns that it governs in this sentence, *Deō* and *ángelīs*, must be in the ablative case.

1.17 *Exémplī Grátiā.* Although most prepositions appear before nouns, there is a class of "post-position" prepositions, such as *causā* and *grátiā*, which developed from nouns and appeared

9

before the noun they described. These prepositions govern the genitive case. One of the most common examples of this is the expression *exémplī grátiā*, "for the sake of an example," which is usually abbreviated into English as e.g. and translated simply as "for example." Here *grátiā* is the preposition and *exémplī* is the noun in the genitive case. (When you see this abbreviation in English sentences from now on, you will know exactly how it works and what it means.)

1.18 No Inflection. Prepositions, unlike nouns, do not generally inflect or change their endings. Although some are slightly variable,[19] prepositions use the same form regardless of their location in a sentence. In short, remember this rule: nouns inflect, but prepositions do not. On the contrary, it is prepositions that govern a noun's case.

NUMBER AND GENDER OF LATIN NOUNS

1.19 Number and Gender. As in English, Latin nouns also contain two more features that we need to discuss: number and gender. The concept of number is easy enough to understand. Every noun in Latin must either refer to one thing (and is thus singular) or more than one thing (and is thus plural). There are no other options.[20] Hence when referring to one "book," *liber*, the word is singular; but when mentioning more than one (whether two books or 2,000), an "s" must be added in English to indicate that it is plural: "books," *librī*.

1.20 Natural and Grammatical Gender. In contrast to number, the concept of gender is slightly more involved. Here we must distinguish between natural and grammatical gender. Other than simple examples such as "boy," "mother," or "uncle," most English words are not assigned to any particular natural gender. Hence, for instance, neither the word "scroll" nor "altar" carries any overtones of maleness or femaleness. And when looking up an English noun in the dictionary, its "gender" will not typically be identified since it is not essential to sentence formations.

The genders of Latin nouns, by contrast, are always listed alongside their dictionary meanings. In fact, a Latin noun's gender is just as important as its definition; without knowing a word's gender, we would not know if any other word in a given sentence is modifying the noun(s), among other things. In other words, gender is a big deal in Latin.

Because of the precision of the Latin language, a noun's gender is seldom in doubt. It will always fall into one of three "genders": masculine, feminine, or neuter (from *neúter*, "neither"). Although it may be tempting to think of "gender" and "biological sex" as interchangeable concepts, they are not. The Latin word for "gender," *genus, géneris*, which is itself neuter, can be translated as "grouping," "category," or "class." In other words, it is best to think of every Latin word as falling into one of three "classes" or "groupings," not into one of three "sexes" or "biological genders." More often than not, a Latin noun's gender has little to do with its biological sex. Again, we must keep natural and grammatical gender separate. Thus:

- *liber, librī*, "book," is masculine
- *vīta, vītae*, "life," is feminine
- *nōmen, nōminis*, "name," is neuter

---

19. One common exception is the preposition *ā, ab*, meaning "by" or "from." Put simply, we use the form *ā* before consonants and *ab* before vowels. Thus, *ab ecclésia*, "from the church" (Acts XII.5) and *ā Dóminō*, "from the Lord" (Ezek. XI.15). This change, however, is not technically inflection.

20. There is something called a "collective" noun, which encompasses both the singular and plural concepts. But we need not cover that in this grammar.

The gender of every Latin noun must be individually memorized—though certain important patterns will be discussed in later *capítula*.

Summárium[21]

In this *capítulum* you learned that:
- Latin nouns inflect, or alter their forms, depending on their function in a sentence.
- There are seven Latin cases: nominative, genitive, accusative, dative, ablative, vocative, and locative (though we will only list the first five in our paradigms).
- Latin nouns may or may not appear with a corresponding preposition.
- Latin nouns are either singular or plural.
- Latin nouns fall into one of three "groupings": masculine, feminine, or neuter.

VOCĀBULŌRUM INDEX[22]

Each vocabulary section in this book contains exactly twenty-five words. Vocabulary words include an etymology as a mnemonic device. Remember that words containing two or less syllables will not be marked with accent marks in this book since the stress is ALWAYS on the first syllable.[23] Words with three syllables or more will contain accent marks over the syllable to be stressed.

One final note: A "gloss" is a simple definition of a word. Please note, therefore, that the glosses below are not exhaustive. The preposition *dē*, for instance, could accurately be translated in a number of ways—many more than are listed below. Because the purpose of this book is to introduce you to the "Basics of Latin," it does not provide exhaustive translations for vocabulary words or comprehensive explanations of all the grammatical components of this wonderful language.

ŌRĀTIŌ POPULĀRIS

Sīgnum Crucis. Each *capítulum* of this book concludes with an *Ōrātiō Populāris*, "a prayer offered by the people." These are time-honored prayers that have been uttered and spoken for centuries by the faithful. In this first *capítulum*, we will memorize the prayer introduced in the *Opúsculum Theológicum*, which is not what we will typically do. An English translation will always immediately follow the prayer in Latin.

In nómine Patris et Fílii et Spíritūs Sānctī.	In the name of the Father, and of the Son, and of the Holy Spirit.

EXERCÍTIA

Be sure to complete the *exercítium* in the appendix corresponding to this *capítulum*.

---

21. "Summary."
22. "List of Vocabulary."
23. Occasionally, an accent will be added on a two-syllable (disyllabic) word for the sake of clarity.

Capítulum

II

FIRST-DECLENSION NOUNS; SUM, ESSE, FUI, FUTÚRUS; AND ET, -QUE, AND AC

Ego sum lūx mundī.[1]
—GOSPEL OF JOHN

OPÚSCULUM THEOLÓGICUM: *Ego Sum in the Gospel of John*

"I am the light of the world." "I am the good shepherd." "I am the way and the truth and the life." The "I am" statements in the Gospel of John—*ego sum* in the Latin Vulgate—are some of the most famous declarations in the entire Bible. According to the Gospel, Jesus spoke these words to many people on many occasions. For our purposes, we may divide Jesus's "I am" statements into two categories (existential and copulative, to use more fancy terms), roughly corresponding to how the Latin verb "to be" (*sum, esse, fuī, futū́rus*) is translated into English.

The first category of "I am" statements are markers of identification (e.g., VI.20; XVIII.5). Serving as responses to questions or reactions, we could translate them as "It is I," or "I am [he]." One of the most famous examples is Jesus's response about his existence even before Abraham was born (e.g., VIII.58). It may be best to translate this statement as "I exist," since the verb *sum, esse, fuī, futū́rus* conveys this existential notion. The expression echoes Exodus III, where God informed Moses that God's name was *ego sum quī sum* (III.14), "I am the one who is" or "I am the one who exists." In this way, Jesus's use of *ego sum* suggests that Jesus is not only a human being (*homō*), but very God (*ipse Deus*).

The second category of "I am" statements serve as linking verbs or copulatives. It is here where Jesus says "I am . . . x" or "I am . . . y" in order to link himself to something else, whether something tangible such as bread (*pānis*) or intangible such as truth (*vḗritās*). There are seven such statements in the Gospel of John:

Ego sum pānis vītae. (VI.35, 48)	I am the bread of life.
Ego sum lūx mundī. (VIII.12; IX.5)	I am the light of the world.
Ego sum ṓstium óvium. (X.7)	I am the gate of the sheep.

---

1. "I am the light of the world."

FIRST-DECLENSION NOUNS

<u>Ego sum</u> pāstor bonus. (X.11, 14)	<u>I am</u> the good shepherd.
<u>Ego sum</u> resurréctiō et vīta. (X.25)	<u>I am</u> the resurrection and the life.
<u>Ego sum</u> via et vĕritās et vīta. (XIV.6)	<u>I am</u> the way and the truth and the life.
<u>Ego sum</u> vītis vēra. (XV.1)	<u>I am</u> the true vine.

In one of the most well-known of these "I am" statements, Jesus compares himself to three nouns in Latin—all of which conveniently begin with the letter *v*: *via*, *vĕritās*, and *vīta*.[2] Interestingly, one of Julius Caesar's most famous utterances also features three Latin words that begin with the letter *v*: *vēnī, vīdī, vīcī*.[3] Speaking in reference to Rome, these words are all verbs that may be translated as follows: "I came, I saw, I conquered." While Julius Caesar's use of *vēnī, vīdī, vīcī* expresses military conquest, Jesus's use of *via, vĕritās,* and *vīta* with the linking verb *sum, esse, fuī, futúrus* connects God and humankind through the bridge of Jesus Christ.

Prospéctus

In this *capítulum* you will learn that:
- There are five noun declensions in Latin.
- The most common Latin verb is *sum, esse, fuī, futúrus*, often translated as "to be," "to exist."
- There are several ways to express the concept of "and" in Latin.

GRAMMÁTICA

2.1 **Nouns.** We will recall from the first *capítulum* that a noun is a person, place, or thing. As such, it is not surprising that nouns appear everywhere in both English and Latin. After all, it is very hard to utter a sentence without mentioning some person, some place, or some thing. (Go ahead; I will wait while you try.)

2.2 **Parts of Latin Nouns.** While nouns in English convey number—that is, something is either one (singular) or more than one (plural)—nouns in Latin reveal several things simultaneously: declension, case, number, and gender. Latin nouns communicate much more than their English counterparts.

2.3 **Five Declensions.** In Latin, there are five categories of nouns or family systems called "declensions." Every noun in Latin falls into one of these five declensions,[4] meaning that every noun inflects or changes its ending in order to disclose its function and meaning in a sentence. The traditional way to categorize these nouns presents us with a lackluster description. They are labeled first, second, third, fourth, and fifth. Despite these rather banal names, the five declensions correspond nicely with the five vowels of Latin: *a, o, i, u,* and *e*. These vowels are traditionally understood to be the thematic vowel, or most dominant vowel, for each respective declensional family. Another way to say this is that each particular declension has that vowel

---

2. The nouns *via* and *vīta* happen to be first-declension nouns, but *vĕritās* is third declension.
3. Suetonius, *Dē Vītā Caésarum* XXXVII.
4. For our purposes, this is a true statement even though many biblical names (coming from Hebrew, for instance) are indeclinable, meaning that they do not change their endings.

as its stem. Thus, for instance, first declensions have a stem of -a, second declensions -o, third-declensions -i (or a consonant), fourth declensions -u, and fifth declensions have a stem of -e.

FIVE DECLENSIONS AND CORRESPONDING THEMATIC VOWELS

Name of Declension	Thematic Vowel or Stem
First declension	-a
Second declension	-o
Third declension	-i (or consonant)
Fourth declension	-u
Fifth declension	-e

[a] The third declension shows the most exceptions to this general pattern.

The chart below is not foolproof—and you should *not* expect that every noun in a particular declension will exclusively or even necessarily contain one of these vowels—but it is a guideline that may prove helpful to you as you begin to learn the different Latin declensions.[5]

2.4 **Word Endings.** We can think of a "regular" Latin sentence as generally following an order of subject, object, and verb (with various modifiers appearing in the mix). As you encounter more Latin sentences, you will observe this common pattern, particularly the pattern of a verb appearing last. At the same time, Latin features far more variety than English since meaning in Latin is conveyed primarily through word endings. This is part of what makes Latin so fun to learn. It is like your very own linguistic puzzle. I recognize that you do not yet know the meaning of the words below, but let's look at an example by focusing our eyes *only* on the endings of the words.

Nōs quoque clārā vōce praedīcámus, servánda esse mandáta sī in opéribus vīta quaéritur. (John Calvin)[6]

There are a lot of different endings here. We see that roughly half of the words end in vowels and the other half consonants. Because we are learning nouns first, here is a list of all the nouns used in the sentence: *vōce*, *mandáta*, *opéribus*, and *vīta*.[7] Latin nouns come in much more variety than this, and the two words ending in -a do not have much in common (the first is plural and the second singular). If we were to translate this sentence according to strict word order, we might get something like this:

> *We also in a clear voice preach to be preserved the commandments if in works life is sought.

This translation is far from satisfactory. I suppose that we might be able to discern the general flow of thought, but it is less than ideal. What we will need to do in Latin is to allow word endings to shape how we render the sentence into English and then to combine what we know about word endings with the Latin word order (for instance, that verbs frequently—but by no means exclusively—appear at the end of a clause, as in this example: *praedīcámus* and *quaéritur*).

---

5. Nouns with a stem ending in a consonant typically fall within the third declension.
6. John Calvin, *Īnstitūtiō Chrīstiānae Religiōnis* III.18.9 (CR 30.611).
7. *Nōs* is a pronoun, which means that it is a word standing in place of a noun.

FIRST-DECLENSION NOUNS

By assessing a Latin sentence's word endings and word order, our English translation could appear as follows:

We also preach in a clear voice that if life is sought in works, the commandments must be kept.

This sounds better and makes more sense. Below we will learn one class of noun used in this sentence: *vīta*, here translated as "life."

2.5 **First-Declension Nouns.** Fortunately for us, all nouns inflect or change their endings in a predetermined fashion. And every noun with a genitive singular in -ae is a first-declension noun. It's that simple. As mentioned above, -a is the thematic, or predominate, vowel for this declension, which you will see amply distributed across it. Below is the pattern, or paradigm, that all first-declension nouns follow. Regardless of the base of the noun, which is where the actual meaning of the noun resides, all first-declension nouns adopt these predetermined endings.

CASE ENDINGS FOR FIRST-DECLENSION NOUNS

Case	Singular	Plural
Nominative	-a	-ae
Genitive	-ae	-árum
Dative	-ae	-īs
Accusative	-am	-ās
Ablative	-ā	-īs

Steps to Form First-Declension Nouns
1. Select a first-declension noun (e.g., *vīta*, *vītae*, "life").[8]
2. Determine its "base" by removing the -ae from the genitive singular form (e.g., *vītae* → **vīt*).[9]
3. Add first-declension endings to the base as needed: -a, -ae, -ae, -am, -ā; -ae, -árum, -īs, -ās, -īs (e.g., *vīta*, *vītae*, *vītae*, *vītam*, *vītā*, etc.).

Although the thematic vowel *a* appears frequently in this declension, we cannot automatically expect all nouns with an *a* to be first declension. It is not that simple. However, we can expect to see the length of vowels disclosed in the paradigm.

2.6 **Feminine Example.** The overwhelming majority of first-declension nouns are feminine, so we will begin with a feminine example before listing a masculine one. It will be my custom in this grammar to isolate distinct letters by putting them **in bold**. In this case, the bold letters indicate those case endings that distinguish the first declension from other declensions.

---

[8]. Every dictionary identifies the declension of a noun (by including the genitive singular after the nominative singular), so there is never any doubt into which declension a noun falls. What's more, a noun's declension is firmly fixed and not able to be changed. So, *terra, terrae* will always be a first-declension noun and cannot be declined according to the endings of a second-, third-, fourth-, or fifth-declension noun.

[9]. Although it seems like we could just as easily determine the base by removing the ending of the nominative singular (in this case, -a), this will not work with all the declensions so it is best to remember from the beginning that the genitive singular is the best source for a noun's base.

TERRA, TERRAE (F), "LAND," "GROUND," "EARTH" (BASE: TERR-)[a]

Case	Singular	Plural
Nominative	terra	terrae
Genitive	terrae	terrárum
Dative	terrae	terrīs
Accusative	terram	terrās
Ablative	terrā	terrīs

[a] I prefer using the language of "base" to refer to what is left of a noun after the genitive singular ending is removed. Another way to say this is that the "base" contains the core meaning of a noun, the various possible endings of which indicate how its core meaning is functioning in any given context. As mentioned above, the "stem" can refer to the thematic vowel. In this framework, for instance, the noun *vītae, vītae* has a "base" of *vīt-but a stem of *a*. Different grammars may use the language of "base" and "stem" somewhat differently.

To begin with, you will need to be thoroughly familiar with each paradigm. Additionally, when you learn any noun, you should prioritize memorizing its nominative *and* genitive singular case endings (thus *terra, terrae*—not just *terra*). This may seem like busywork at first, but you will come to recognize that it will save you a lot of time in the end. How so? The nominative form will enable you to find the word in a dictionary and the genitive form will reveal which declension it is and also how to determine its base. Both are essential parts.

Next, remember that cases identify a noun's particular function in a sentence. So, when translating a noun into English, prepositions (such as "of," "for," "in," "to," "with" etc.) will frequently be part of our translations. For instance, *terrárum* is not accurately translated as "lands" because, as a genitive, it indicates ownership or possession. So it is more accurately rendered in English as "of the lands" or "the lands'." Additionally, we may require the use of an article (such as "a[n]" and "the") to render a noun into English more faithfully.

Furthermore, I encourage you to pay especial attention to the length of vowels. Remember that a macron indicates a long vowel. Therefore, while *terrā* could be translated as, e.g., "with the earth" or "from the earth" depending on context, *terra* could not be accurately translated this way since the previous form is ablative and the latter is nominative.

Finally, you probably noticed that some of the case endings in our paradigm noun are identical. *Terrae*, for example, could be a genitive singular ("of the land"), a dative singular ("to/for the land"), or a nominative plural ("lands"). This can be confusing, especially as we learn additional declensions. How exactly do we translate a noun when it shares an ending with another case? I would be lying if I said that it is always easily apparent. Translating a Latin sentence into English is like assembling a jigsaw puzzle. Just like color and shape help us link pieces together when in doubt, so context and trial by error clarify the function of a word when it has a shared ending. And just as some jigsaw pieces are immediately identifiable while others appear identical, so some Latin words require little effort while others require rigorous concentration. Here is a rather simple example:

Nec erat pānis pópuló terrae. (II Kgs. XXV.3)

In this sentence, *terrae*, in and of itself and if we had no context, could be one of three cases, so we will need to determine which one. We start with the genitive singular: "Neither was there bread for the people of the land." How does that sound? Although a sad verse, it is grammatically logical. What about the dative singular? "Neither was there bread for the people to the land." That does not make as much sense. Now we may plug in the nominative plural: "Neither was there bread for the people lands." That definitely does not work. So, what is the case of *terrae* in this sentence? Everything is pointing us in the direction of the genitive case. Case closed.

2.7 **Masculine Example.** Let's now turn to a masculine noun of the first declension.

SCRĪBA, SCRĪBAE (M), "SCRIBE," "SECRETARY," "WRITER" (BASE: SCRĪB-)

Case	Singular	Plural
Nominative	scrība	scrībae
Genitive	scrībae	scrībárum
Dative	scrībae	scrībīs
Accusative	scrībam	scrībās
Ablative	scrībā	scrībīs

The great news about first-declension nouns is that they employ the same endings regardless of gender. So, there are no new forms to learn here; they are identical to the feminine forms. As it turns out, most first-declension nouns are feminine, but even those that happen to be masculine will have the same case endings as feminine ones. Here is an example from the noun above:

Et accéssit ūnus dē Scrībīs, lēgis doctor, tentāns eum. (Werner of St. Blaise)[10]

And one of the scribes, a teacher of the law, approached to test him.

SOME COMMON FIRST-DECLENSION BIBLICAL NAMES AND TITLES

Names and titles from the Bible appear regularly in the kind of Latin emphasizing the Christian tradition. Here are some common first-declension names and titles, all of which derive from Hebrew.

- *Ādām, Ādae* (m), "Adam"[11]
- *Ábrahām, Ábrahae* (m), "Abraham"
- *María, Maríae* (f), "Mary" or "Miriam"
- *Messíās, Messíae* (m), "Messiah," "Christ"
- *Sátanās, Sátanae* (m), "Satan," "Devil"[12]

Let's look at an example from Abraham's name:

Ábrahae sēmen estis. (Gal. III.29)

You all are Abraham's seed.

Many occupations appear as first-declension nouns (such as *scrība, scrībae*). Common "occupations" (people of the past did not categorize jobs the same way we do today) include the following:

---

10. Werner of St. Blaise, *Defloratiónēs* (PL 157.1117).
11. You will also more commonly see *Ādămus, Ādămī* (m), "Adam," as a second-declension noun (which nouns we will discuss in the next *capítulum*).
12. You will also see this as *Satan, Satan* (indeclinable), but we will talk about such nouns in Capítulum VII.

agrícola, agrícolae (m), "farmer"
ancílla, ancíllae (f), "maid"
dómina, dóminae (f), "lady" or "mistress [of a household]"
nauta, nautae (m), "sailor"
poéta, poétae (m), "poet"

SUM, ESSE, FUĪ, FUTŪRUS, "TO BE," "TO EXIST"

2.8 **The "To Be" Verb.** Although we will reserve our discussion of verbs for *Secúnda Pars*, it is important to briefly introduce the verb *sum, esse, fuī, futúrus*, "to be" or "to exist." As in English, this is the most common verb used in Latin, and you will see it constantly. We will examine the form below before explaining how it works.

PRESENT ACTIVE INDICATIVE[a] OF *SUM, ESSE, FUĪ, FUTÚRUS,* "TO BE," "TO EXIST"

	Singular	Plural
First Person	sum	sumus
Second Person	es	estis
Third Person	est	sunt

[a] There is no need to worry about these terms as well as some of other features of verbs included here. We will discuss verbs in *Secúnda Pars*.

Just as an equal sign (=) indicates equality in mathematics, so, too, does *sum, esse, fuī, futúrus* in grammar. It is sometimes called a "linking" verb because it often connects two words in the nominative case.[13] In the sentence below, both nouns are in the nominative case, but the second one (*ūnus*) is called the "predicate nominative," which is the one that renames the first nominative (*Christus*).

Christus enim ūnus est.   For Christ is one.
(Huldrych Zwingli)[14]

In this sentence, the word *est* links two nominatives, that is, subjects: "Christ" and "one." Although this is not the only use of the verb *sum, esse, fuī, futúrus*, it is the only one we will discuss in this *capítulum* (but keep in mind the two main uses we saw of it in the *Opúsculum Theológicum*: the copulative, discussed here, and the existential, which may warrant the translation of the verb as "to exist" rather than "to be").

ET, -QUE, AND *AC*

2.9 ***Et, -Que,* and *Ac*.** Latin does not have a direct correlation to the word "and," but it does connect one thing to another in sentences. Below are some same Latin examples, with accompanying explanations, that may be rendered as "and" in English:

---

13. Some other ways used to describe this verb are "intransitive" (since it does not take a direct object) or a "state of being" (since it does not express action). Note that this verb can also take an accusative case, not always just the nominative case.
14. Huldrych Zwingli, *Dē Canóne Missae Epichíresis* (CR 89.582).

FIRST-DECLENSION NOUNS

1. *Et* expresses a general connection between concepts. When you encounter *et* used as a pair—meaning that the two occurrences of *et* will be separated by at least a couple of words and function as a unit—it is usually translated "both . . . and."
2. *-Que* is added at the end of a word in a series of two or more parallel terms.
3. *Ac* indicates a closer connection between items and is used before words beginning with consonants. *Atque* is an alternative form of *ac* and is used before vowels. Though perhaps an extreme example, observe below all Latin uses from a celebrated passage describing the character of God.

Dominátor Dómine Deus miséricors <u>et</u> clēmēns pátiēns <u>et</u> multae miserātiónis <u>ac</u> vērus quī cūstódis misericórdiam in mília quī aufers inīquitátem <u>et</u> scélera <u>atque</u> peccáta nūllús<u>que</u> apud tē per sē ínnocēns est quī reddis inīquitátem patrum in fíliīs <u>ac</u> nepótibus in tértiam <u>et</u> quārtam prōgéniem. (Exod. XXXIV.6–7)	The Master, the Lord God, merciful <u>and</u> [*et*] gentle, patient, <u>and</u> [*et*] rich in mercy <u>and</u> [*ac*] true, you who maintains mercy unto thousands, who takes away iniquity <u>and</u> [*et*] wickedness <u>and</u> [*atque*] sins <u>and</u> [*-que*] no one, of himself, is innocent in your presence, who assigns the iniquity of the fathers to the children <u>and</u> [*ac*] grandchildren unto the third <u>and</u> [*et*] fourth generation.

2.10 ***Et* and *Étiam*.** Having just encountered the connecting word *et*, often translated as "and," it is important to mention a word that is often abbreviated as *et* but is actually a different word altogether. I am referring to the adverb *étiam*, which is commonly translated as "also," "even," "indeed," "furthermore," or "besides." *Étiam* is abbreviated quite often to *et*, meaning that when you encounter *et*, you will have to ask whether it is functioning as a conjunction (and so "and" is an appropriate translation since it is linking one item to another) or as an adverb describing a verb or adjective (and so it is really *étiam*).

Summárium

In this *capítulum* you learned that:
- Latin nouns fall into one of five categories of case endings called "declensions." You will need to memorize paradigm nouns for each declension so you can identify how a noun functions in any given sentence. Pay especial attention to the nominative and genitive singular forms; they are like the keys that unlock the door to the noun.
- All first-declension nouns, regardless of gender, have the exact same case endings.
- The verb *sum, esse, fuī, futúrus* is the most common verb in Latin. It often links the subject to something else; it is usually translated "to be," but can also be translated as "to exist" and in other ways.
- *Et, -que,* and *ac* are used in Latin to connect one thing to another. They may be translated into English as "and." The adverb *étiam*, which means something distinct, is sometimes abbreviated as *et*.

VOCĀBULŌRUM INDEX

As we encounter our first nouns in this *capítulum*, I recommend the following procedure when it comes to memorizing them. In addition to memorizing the nominative and genitive singular endings, you will want to also take note of the noun's declension and gender. Although it is very tempting to overlook these features, they are essential to understanding and translating Latin sentences properly, especially as we learn more grammatical concepts. I will mostly group vocabulary words into the same declensions (and then eventually verb conjugations), particularly in the early *capítula*.

And one more thing: As you will remember from the first *capítulum*, Latin does not possess articles such as "a," "an," and "the." Depending on context, the noun *scrība* could be translated as "a scribe," "scribe," or "the scribe."

Latin	English (Gloss)	(Etymology)
āit, āiunt[a]	he/she/it says, they say	
agrícola, agrícolae (m)	farmer	(agriculture)
ánima, ánimae (f)	soul, life, spirit	(animate)
aqua, aquae (f)	water	(aquatic)
doctrína, doctrínae (f)	teaching, learning, doctrine	(doctrine)
ecclésia, ecclésiae (f)	church, assembly, gathering	(ecclesiology)
família, famíliae (f)	family	(familiar)
fília, fíliae (f)	daughter	
glória, glóriae (f)	glory, fame	(glory)
grátia, grátiae (f)	favor, grace	(grace)
īra, īrae (f)	anger, wrath	(irate)
iūstítia, iūstítiae (f)[b]	righteousness, justice	(justice)
língua, línguae (f)	tongue, language	(linguistics)
porta, portae (f)	gate, entrance, door	(portal)
prophéta, prophétae (m)	prophet	(prophecy)
puélla, puéllae (f)	girl	
quia, quod, quóniam[c]	that, because, since	
sapiéntia, sapiéntiae (f)	wisdom	(homosapien)
sciéntia, sciéntiae (f)	knowledge	(science)
scrīptúra, scrīptúrae (f)	writing, scripture	(scripture)
sed	but	
sī	if	
terra, terrae (f)	land, ground, earth	(terrain)

| via, viae (f) | way, path, road | (viable) |
| vīta, vītae (f) | life | (vital) |

[a] This is an irregular verb that is best learned as a separate vocabulary word.

[b] You may also see this form as *jūstítia, jūstítiae*, which has the same meaning. In ecclesiastical Latin, consonantal -i is often spelled with -j.

[c] These are not different forms of the same word, but three words that look alike and mean similar (though not exactly identical) things.

ŌRÁTIŌ POPULÁRIS

Glória Patrī. This prayer, "Glory to the Father," is one of the most significant prayers in the Christian tradition. Based on Matthew XXVIII.19, it has been memorized and put into song and praise for centuries.

> Glória Patrī, et Fíliō, et Spīrítuī Sānctō.
> Sīcut erat in prīncípiō, et nunc, et semper,
> et in saécula saeculórum. Āmēn.

> Glory be to the Father, and to the Son, and to the Holy Spirit.
> As it was in the beginning, and now, and ever shall be, forever and ever. Amen.

EXERCÍTIA

Be sure to complete the *exercítium* in the appendix corresponding to this *capítulum*.

Capítulum

III

SECOND-DECLENSION NOUNS

Dóminus enim meus ūnus est.[1]

—TERTULLIAN

OPÚSCULUM THEOLÓGICUM: *Dóminus et Deus*

With the divine Creator as its principal theme and primary character, it comes as no surprise that two of the most common words in the Latin Bible are *Deus* and *Dóminus*. The first of these, *Deus, Deī*, was the standard Latin word meaning "god." Its corresponding feminine form was *dea, deae*, "goddess." The *deī*,[2] "gods," and *deae*, "goddesses," of the Roman pantheon included the likes of *Iúppiter*, "Jupiter," *Iūnō*, "Juno," *Mercúrius*, "Mercury," and *Venus*, "Venus." It is in the context of this Greco-Roman mindset that the apostle Paul spoke of *magnae deae Diánae templum*, "the temple of the great goddess Diana" in Acts XIX.27.

The term *Dóminus, Dóminī*, an equally common and recurring word in the Christian tradition, is often translated as "lord" or "master." It generally referred to a man of high stature or to a god, later serving as a title for the Roman emperor. When addressing a person in the New Testament, it was typically reserved for the *pater famíliās*, or "head of the household," who naturally enough in the Greco-Roman world was a powerful man who owned *servī* or "slaves" (as in Eph. VI.5, Col. III.22, Titus II.9, and I Pet. II.18). The only instance of the corresponding noun *dómina, dóminae*, "mistress" or "lady," in the New Testament appears in II John, where the *dómina* refers to a known wealthy lady or mystically to an *ecclésia*, "church."

When it comes to the Christian tradition, *Deus* and *Dóminus* usually referred to the God of the Bible. In the Old Testament, *Deus* was a common translation of the Hebrew word "Elohim," just as *Dóminus* was for "Adonai" and "Yahweh." The title of *Dóminus* was applied to Jesus in the New Testament, serving as a noticeable contrast to its use for Roman emperors. Ruling a mere generation after the time of Jesus, for example, the Emperor Domitian ordered others to call him *dóminus et deus noster*,[3] "our lord and god," leading one to wonder if John's Gospel, written around that same time period, understood Thomas's reply to Jesus as *Dóminus meus et Deus meus*, "my Lord and my God," to serve as a social or political rebuttal (XX.28).

---

1. "For my Lord is one."
2. In the nominative plural, *deus* may also appear as *dī* or even *diī*.
3. Suetonius, "Vīta Domitiánī" XIII.2 in *Dē Vītīs Caésarum*.

SECOND-DECLENSION NOUNS

Whatever the case, early Christians seem to prefer the title *Dóminus* to be applied to Jesus. In his work *Apologéticus*, for instance, Tertullian wrote:

Dóminus enim meus ūnus est, Deus omnípotēns et aetérnus, īdem quī et ipsíus.[4]	For my Lord is one, the almighty and everlasting God, the same who is also his.[5]

Later on, early Christians composed the hymn *Sānctus*, "Holy," in celebration of the Holy Trinity's glory and majesty. Eventually incorporated into a Eucharistic prayer in the Western tradition, the opening lines proclaim:

Sānctus, Sānctus, Sānctus	Holy, holy, holy
Dóminus Deus Sábaoth[6]	The Lord God of Hosts
Plēnī sunt caelī et terra glóriā tuā.	Heaven and earth are full of your glory.

Collectively, the two dominating words *Dóminus* and *Deus* refer to the God of the Bible, and they also introduce us to two of the most important second-declension nouns in Latin, which is the topic of the following *capítulum*.

Prospéctus

In this *capítulum* you will learn that:
- Second-declension nouns end in -ī in the genitive singular.
- Most second-declension nouns are masculine or neuter.
- Parsing nouns includes identifying their case, number, gender, dictionary form, and meaning.

GRAMMÁTICA

3.1 **Case Endings.** In the previous *capítulum*, we discussed how Latin nouns inflect or change their endings based on their functions in a sentence. This occurs because meaning in Latin primarily depends on word endings. When seeking to determine the meaning of a Latin noun, in other words, one of our foremost concerns is identifying to which of the noun families or "declensions" it belongs. And because a noun's declension does not vary, a noun's declension is not in doubt. This is a fabulous feature of the Latin language.

3.2 **Second-Declension Nouns.** We will now turn to the second category of Latin nouns. Just as we learned previously that first-declension nouns are nouns that end in -ae in the genitive singular, second-declension nouns end in -ī in the genitive singular.[7] According to the thematic vowel and noun declension chart we discussed previously, the second declension possesses -o as its thematic vowel. However, over time the -o came to be displaced in some cases, meaning that

---

4. Tertullian, *Apologéticus* XXXIV.1 (PL 1.451).
5. Here, the word "his" is referring to the emperor's God.
6. As regularly the case with foreign words like this, the spelling and length of vowels can vary. I will adopt this spelling in this book, but do not be surprised if you encounter this word—and other Hebrew and Greek words from the Bible—spelled in a slightly different way.
7. Remember that the dictionary forms of all nouns will have the nominative singular and the genitive singular. This is why we are memorizing all nouns in two cases rather than one since the case is established only by the genitive singular form.

the presence of the vowel -o should not automatically lead you to believe you are looking at a second-declension noun. Maybe you are, but maybe you are not. It is the genitive singular ending that makes it crystal clear.

Here are the predetermined case endings for second-declension nouns.[8]

CASE ENDINGS FOR SECOND-DECLENSION NOUNS

Case	Singular	Plural
Nominative	-er, -ir, -us; -um (n)[a]	-ī (m); -a (n)
Genitive	-ī	-órum
Dative	-ō	-īs
Accusative	-um	-ōs (m); -a (n)
Ablative	-ō	-īs

[a] The nominative singular forms do not have identical endings, as they do in the first declension. These endings listed are the most common endings. The -um ending occurs exclusively with neuter nouns.

Steps to Form Second-Declension Nouns
1. Select a second-declension noun (e.g., *templum, templī*, "temple").
2. Determine its "base" by removing the -ī from the genitive singular form (e.g., *templī* → **templ*).[9]
3. Add second-declension endings to the base as needed (remembering that the masculine/feminine and neuter are different in the nominative and accusative plurals): -er/-ir/-us/-um, -ī, -ō, -um, -ō; -ī/-a, -ōrum, -īs, -ōs/-a, -īs (e.g., *templum, templī, templō, templum, templō*, etc.).

After locating a noun's base, we then add the appropriate case endings depending on the noun's function. For example, is the noun acting as the indirect object, that is, is it indirectly receiving the action of the verb? Then it must be in the dative case, meaning that it will end in -ō if it is singular or -īs if it is plural. There are no other options.

I want to make note of three additional items. First, as mentioned above, the thematic vowel for the second-declension is -o. Although it is not always apparent in every form, the appearance of that vowel toward the end of a noun is a clue that it *may* be a second-declension noun.

Second, the case ending for the nominative singular varies. This is a helpful reminder that we always determine a noun's base from its genitive singular form and not its nominative form.

Finally, you probably noticed that the nominative and accusative plurals have two possible case endings. The (m) indicates masculine nouns while the (n) represents neuter ones. In short, masculine second-declension nouns end in -ī in the nominative plural and -ōs in the accusative plural. By contrast, neuter second-declension nouns end in -a in both the nominative and accusative plurals. This underscores the importance of learning a noun's gender in addition to its case.

---

8. If you want to learn more about the variations of the o-stem, second-declension nouns, see A&G §§45–51.
9. Although it seems like we could just as easily determine the base by removing the ending of the nominative singular (in this case, -a), this will not work with all the declensions so it is best to remember from the beginning that the genitive singular is the best source for a noun's base.

3.3 **Masculine Example.** Because second-declension nouns are usually masculine or neuter (very rarely feminine[10]), we will include paradigm nouns only for these two genders.

DÓMINUS, DÓMINĪ (M), "LORD," "MASTER," "SIR" (BASE: DOMIN-)

Case	Singular	Plural
Nominative	dóminus	dóminī
Genitive	dóminī	dominórum
Dative	dóminō	dóminīs
Accusative	dóminum	dóminōs
Ablative	dóminō	dóminīs

If you like playing Dominoes or eating Domino's Pizza (or doing both at the same time), this is the paradigm for you. As with first-declension nouns, there are several second-declension nouns with shared endings. It is like a smorgasbord of domino tiles, with one dot (or letter) changing the numeric value (or meaning). This will oftentimes require extra detective work to determine which case is being used, but this is the *gaúdium*, "joy," of learning Latin. Let's pull out our magnifying glasses.

Dāvīd nōn aedíficat Dóminō domum. (Adam of Dryburgh)[11]

Most of these words should be easy enough to detect, but the third and last ones are new to us. The verb *aedíficat* translates as "he/she/it builds," while the noun *domum* signifies "house." Let's now focus on the word *Dóminō*. Because it ends in -ō, we know that it has to be in the dative or ablative case. But which one? First, we search for nearby prepositions since they govern which case may be used. However, there are no prepositions in this sentence. As the Romans would say, *ēheu*, "oh shucks." So, we start plugging in different English prepositions that we have paired with the dative and ablative cases when translating, particularly "to" and "for" for the dative case and "about," "by," and "from" and "with" for the ablative.

As it turns out, our second preposition, "for," sounds the best (never underestimate your ear when translating), and the niceties of grammar indicate that the noun is working as a so-called dative of advantage. In short, *Dóminō* is in the dative case, and here is how we can translate it:

David does not build a house for the Lord.

3.4 **Proper Nouns.** In addition to indicating common nouns, second-declension masculine nouns also provide us with proper nouns such as names. Here are some frequent biblical examples:

- *Ādā́mus, Ādā́mī*, "Adam"[12]
- *Christus, Christī*, "Christ"

---

10. Feminine nouns of the second declension are very uncommon, but they do occur. When they do so, they follow the forms of masculine nouns, not neuter ones. Therefore, the nominative plural of *mālus, mālī* (f), "apple tree," is *mālī*, not **mala*.

11. Adam of Dryburgh, *Dē Tripartítō Tabernáculō* XV (PL198.619).

12. We saw in the previous *capitulum* that this name also appears as *Ādām, Ādae* (m) in the first declension.

- *Iācóbus, Iācóbī*, "James"
- *Paulus, Paulī*, "Paul"
- *Petrus, Petrī*, "Peter"

3.5 **Neuter Example.** We may now turn to an example of a neuter second-declension noun.

VERBUM, VERBĪ (N), "WORD" (BASE: VERB-)

Case	Singular	Plural
Nominative	verbum	verba
Genitive	verbī	verbórum
Dative	verbō	verbīs
Accusative	verbum	verba
Ablative	verbō	verbīs

As mentioned above, neuter nouns differ most noticeably from masculine ones in two instances: the nominative and accusative forms. This phenomenon introduces us to two important and fixed grammatical rules in Latin that should be thoroughly memorized. What we learn here can be applied universally across all nouns. This is good news! Universal rules are friends, indeed.

Two Latin Grammatical Rules for Neuter Nouns
1. Neuter accusative nouns ALWAYS duplicate the nominative, whether singular or plural.
2. Neuter nouns ALWAYS end in -a in the nominative and accusative plurals.

As just mentioned, these *régulae*, "rules," will apply to all noun declensions, so keep them in your memory bank and be prepared to make regular withdrawals from this bank in the *capítula* to come. But note that these rules only apply to neuter nouns, not masculine or feminine ones. As we learned in the first *capítulum*, *neúter* means "neither" in Latin, so it's fitting that these "neither" nouns follow their own paths. They are true trailblazers.

Let's examine one of the most distinct features of neuter nouns: the nominative and accusative plurals.

Haec autem sunt verba novíssima. (I Sam. XXIII.1)[13]

Because we just learned first-declension nouns, we are tempted to immediately classify the word *verba* as a nominative or ablative singular noun of the first declension since it ends in -a. There is no harm in trying to translate it this way, but keep your options open before committing. What occurs in one declension does not necessarily occur in another. So, what happens when we translate it like a first declension?

*Now this word are very last (nominative singular).
*Now this are by/from/with the very last word (ablative singular).

---

13. It may be helpful to know that, here, *haec* means "these," *autem* "now," and *novíssima*, "last."

I don't know about you, but something does not sound right here. Hopefully your ear will help you out when you say it out loud. These translations remind us always to take sufficient time to identify accurately the noun's declension and gender *before* translating. Once we realize that *verbum, verbī* is a neuter noun, we understand that *verba* is either nominative plural or accusative plural. It cannot be anything else. But before we decide its case, let's examine the sentence one last time and hunt for any additional clues. Do you see what I see?

Haec autem sunt verba novíssima. (I Sam. XXIII.1)

Right, we know that the word *sunt*, "are," is a linking verb that often connects a nominative with another nominative (a predicate nominative). Equipped with this information, we are ready to venture a translation. Doesn't this sound better?

Now these are the very last words [of David].

Latin invites us into a conversation. When you encounter a word that can be translated more than one way, you will need to ask different questions in order to ascertain the best possible way to understand it and then render it into English.

PARSING NOUNS

3.6 **Parsing.** Now that we are familiar with a couple of noun cases, it is important to learn how to identify their respective forms succinctly and accurately. Although some poor Latin students have been traumatized by fastidious teachers relishing in the rote recitation of noun paradigms, there is a great benefit to mastering case endings—trauma aside. If you are ever asked to "parse"[14] a noun, do not think that you are being asked to do anything illegal. Parsing a noun means classifying its form in whatever instance it is being used. Typically, parsing a noun entails identifying five features: (1) case, (2) number, (3) gender, (4) dictionary form, and (5) meaning in context. Here is an example.

Interrogábat ergō Dóminus servum. (Augustine of Hippo)[15]

Therefore, the Lord was questioning the slave.

Isolating the noun *servum*, it is "parsed" as follows: (1) accusative, (2) singular, (3) masculine, (4) from *servus, servī*, (5) meaning in context "slave" or "servant." If you are in a classroom setting, the teacher may have a different preference for parsing, but all Latin students are encouraged to learn how to quickly identify how a noun functions in any given context.

Five Parts to Parsing
1. **Case:** Nominative, genitive, dative, accusative, or ablative (or locative or vocative)
2. **Number:** Singular or plural
3. **Gender:** Feminine, masculine, or neuter
4. **Dictionary Form:** Nominative and genitive singular form
5. **Meaning in Context:** Simple "gloss" or translation[16]

---

14. Naturally enough, this word ultimately derives from the Latin noun *pars, partis*, meaning "part."
15. Augustine of Hippo, *Sermō* XII (PL 46.851).
16. Although supplying the meaning in context is not necessarily what is traditionally called "parsing," it is a natural outflow of parsing.

> **Summárium**
>
> In this *capítulum* you learned that:
> - Second-declension nouns are those nouns that end in -ī in the genitive singular.
> - Most second-declension nouns are masculine, though they can appear in any gender.
> - Neuter nouns in the nominative and accusative cases are identical and always end in -a in the plural.
> - Reading Latin is like playing a game of Dominoes. Many dominoes (or for us, words) may look alike at first appearance, but closer inspection will distinguish one from another.

VOCĀBULŌRUM INDEX

Latin	English (Gloss)	(Etymology)
amícus, amícī (m)	friend	(amicable)
ángelus, ángelī (m)	angel, messenger	(angel)
apóstolus, apóstolī (m)	apostle	(apostle)
caelum, caelī (n)[a]	heaven, sky	(celestial)
Christus, Christī (m)	Christ, Messiah, Anointed One	(Christ)
deus, deī (m)	God, god	(deify)
discípulus, discípulī (m)[b]	learner, disciple, student	(disciple)
dóminus, dóminī (m)[c]	Lord, lord, master, sir	(dominion)
fílius, fíliī[d] (m)	son	(filial)
gládius, gládiī (m)	sword	(gladiator)
liber, librī (m)	book	(library)
lignum, lignī (n)	tree, wood	(lignify)
númerus, númerī (m)	number	(numerous)
óculus, óculī (m)	eye	(binocular)
óstium, óstiī (n)	door, entrance	
peccátum, peccátī (n)	sin	(peccant)
pópulus, pópulī (m)	people	(population)
rēgnum, rēgnī (n)	kingdom	(reign)
servus, servī (m)	slave, servant	(servant)
sīgnum, sīgnī (n)	sign, mark, miracle	(sign)
tabernáculum, tabernáculī (n)	tent, tabernacle	(tabernacle)
templum, templī (n)	temple, church	(temple)
verbum, verbī (n)	word	(verb)

| vīnum, vīnī (n) | wine | (vineyard) |
| vir, virī (m) | man, husband | (virile) |

^a This word also appears with the spelling *coelum, coeli* with no difference in meaning. For both sets of spellings, the *ae* and *oe* combinations are diphthongs and thus pronounced as one syllable.

^b This word also appears in the feminine gender as *discípula, discípulae* (f), which is a first-declension noun; however, the translation is the same as the second-declension masculine form.

^c The word *dómina, dóminae* (f), a first-declension noun, corresponds to the masculine form. The feminine form, however, may be translated as "mistress" or "lady."

^d The nouns *fílius, fíliī* and *gládius, gládiī* may appear strange with the two ii's in the genitive singular. But as we have learned, second-declension nouns always end in -ī in the genitive singular, so it does not matter whether an additional -i appears before it. (In fact, the word *fílius, fíliī* often occurs with only one i in the genitive case.) On another note, *fília, fíliae* (f) is a corresponding first-declension noun to *fílius, fíliī*. It translates as "daughter," as we learned previously.

ŌRĀ́TIŌ POPULĀ́RIS

Sānctus. The "Holy" is a prayer that has been included in the Mass since the early medieval period. It is based on Old Testament and New Testament passages, chiefly Isaiah VI.3 and Matthew XXI.9.

Sānctus Sānctus, Sānctus, Dóminus Deus Sábaoth.
Plēnī sunt caelī et terra glṓriā tuā.
Hosánna in excélsīs.
Benedíctus quī venit in nṓmine Dóminī.
Hosánna in excélsīs.

Holy, Holy, Holy [is] the Lord God of Hosts.
Heaven and earth are full of your glory.
Hosanna in the highest.
Blessed is the one who comes in the name of the Lord.
Hosanna in the highest.

EXERCÍTIA

Be sure to complete the *exercítium* in the appendix corresponding to this *capítulum*.

Capítulum

IV

THIRD-DECLENSION NOUNS

Habére jam nōn potest Deum <u>patrem</u> quī Ecclésiam nōn habet <u>mātrem</u>.[1]
—CYPRIAN OF CARTHAGE

OPÚSCULUM THEOLÓGICUM: *God as Pater and Church as Māter in Cyprian of Carthage*

If God is our Father, is the church our Mother? Though by no means the foregone conclusion of many believers, this is a concept with seed form in the New Testament[2] and with deep roots in the early tradition of Christianity. It is attested by early, medieval, and even Protestant reformers. Not only does our earliest theological author in Latin, Tertullian, refer to the church as *dómina māter ecclésia*, "the Lady, our Mother Church,"[3] but writers such as John Calvin do as well. Commenting on Galatians IV.26, the latter explains:

Eccésia vocétur fidélium māter. Et sānē quī recúsat esse ecclésiae fílius, Deum frūstrā patrem habére éxpetit.[4]	The church should be called the mother of the faithful. Indeed, the one who refuses to be a son of the church seeks in vain to have God as father.

In this passage, Calvin pays homage to one of the most memorable oneliners in the history of Latin Christianity. This oneliner springs from a book titled *Dē Ūnitáte Cathólicae Ecclésiae*, "On the Unity of the Catholic Church," written by Cyprian of Carthage several years before his martyrdom in 258. The church in Cyprian's day was rife with division, some of which was directly caused by prosecution and persecution of Christians in the Roman Empire. As *epíscopus*, "bishop," of the Christians in the important Roman city of Carthage, Cyprian was compelled to address the status of those who separated themselves from the historic body of believers.

For Cyprian, the church was one and undivided based on the unity of the bishops (based ultimately on the unity of the Godhead and the authority of Christ). The church was also a mother out of whose

---

1. "He who does not have church as <u>mother</u> cannot now have God as <u>Father</u>."
2. As II John I states in the Vulgate, *sénior eléctae dóminae*, "the elder to the chosen woman." This "woman" likely refers to the church.
3. Tertullian, *Ad Mártyrēs* I.1 (PL 1.619).
4. John Calvin, *Commentárius in Epístolam Paulī ad Gálatās* IV (CR 78.239).

womb the faithful were born and from whose sustenance the faithful were nourished. As Cyprian famously declared:

Habére jam nōn potest Deum <u>patrem</u> quī Ecclésiam nōn habet <u>mātrem</u>.[5]	He who does not have church as <u>mother</u> cannot now have God as <u>Father</u>.

Whether or not we follow Cyprian's line of reasoning regarding the maternal role of the church, we have to admire the *pū́ritās*, "purity," of his prose and the *grávitās*, "heaviness," of his argument. For our purposes, Cyprian's declaration centered on two third-declension nouns: *pater*, "father," and *māter*, "mother." These are two of the most basic of words in any language—Latin included—and they also serve as a wonderful introduction to the largest family of nouns in Latin: the third declension.

> **Prospéctus**
> In this *capítulum* you will learn that:
> - Third-declension nouns end in -is in the genitive singular. They are the most common nouns in Latin, and they occur in all three genders.
> - There are two major sets of third-declension nouns: (1) consonant-stems and (2) i-stems. The first ends in -um in the genitive plural, and the latter ends in -ium in the genitive plural.

GRAMMÁTICA

4.1 **Third Class of Nouns.** Third-declension nouns are the most common category of nouns in Latin. They are like seagulls by the beach; they appear *ubī́que*, "everywhere." Unlike the first- and second-declension nouns, they are rather evenly spread across all three genders: feminine, masculine, and neuter. The characteristic genitive singular form, which distinguishes this grouping of nouns from all others, is the -is ending. In short, any noun that ends in -is in the genitive singular is a third-declension noun regardless of its gender. The thematic vowel for this class of nouns is -i, but stems ending in consonants also appear readily. In this way, there are traditionally understood to be two classes of third-declension nouns. Put most simply, (1) consonant-stem nouns have a genitive plural ending of -um, while (2) i-stems have a genitive plural ending of -ium.[6]

We will begin our discussion with consonant-stem third-declension nouns, but it should be noted again that all third-declension nouns—regardless of their name—are *generally* formed the same way and *all* end in -is in the genitive singular.

There are three steps to form a third-declension noun.

Steps to Form Third-Declension (Consonant-Stem) Nouns
1. Select a third-declension noun (e.g., *cā́ritās*, *cāritā́tis*, "love").
2. Determine its base by removing the -is from the genitive singular form (e.g., *cāritā́t̶i̶s̶* → **cāritāt*).

---

[5]. Cyprian of Carthage, *Dē Ūnitā́te Ecclésiae* VI (PL 4.503).
[6]. Naturally, there are many more ways to classify these kinds of third-declension nouns. Allen and Greenough categorize these nouns into two major classifications in addition to minor ones: (1) consonant-stems with mute, liquid, or nasal stems; and (2) i-stems with pure and mixed i-stems (A&G §54). According to Allen and Greenough, in fact, "The i-declension was confused even to the Romans themselves" (A&G §73). This should not make us despair, but it should make us aware that third-declension nouns, particularly i-stems, are more involved than the other declensions. I recommend consulting A&G for advanced information about this fascinating class of nouns.

NOUNS AND ADJECTIVES

3. Add third-declension endings to the base as needed: -, -is, -ī, -em, -e; -ēs/-a, -um, -ibus, -ēs/-a, -ibus (e.g., cáritās, cāritátis, cāritátī, cāritátem, cāritáte).

CASE ENDINGS FOR THIRD-DECLENSION <u>CONSONANT-STEM</u> NOUNS

Case	Singular	Plural
Nominative	-[a]	-ēs (m, f); -a (n)
Genitive	-is	-um
Dative	-ī	-ibus
Accusative	-em; -[b]	-ēs (m, f); -a (n)
Ablative	-e	-ibus

[a] There is great variety when it comes to the possible endings of third-declension nouns in the nominative singular. As a result, it is best not to expect one particular one. According to Allen and Greenough, nouns of the third declension may end in the vowels *a, e, i, o,* and *y,* and the consonants *c, l, n, r, s, t,* and *x* (A&G §53).

[b] Here, the dash indicates that some accusative singular forms will be identical to their nominative singular forms..

We are now rather accustomed to the notion that nominative singular endings cannot always be predicted. This is not a problem, however, since genitive singular endings are as predictable as the rising sun. In this instance, for example, we always know that a third-declension noun ends in -is in the genitive singular. If we encounter an unfamiliar nominative singular ending, we simply look to the genitive singular to confirm the noun's declension. Despite appearances, in other words, the genitive singular ending always determines a noun's declension—no exceptions.

We are also familiar with neuter (n) nouns utilizing endings that may differ from masculine (m) and/or feminine (f) nouns of the same declension. As we discussed in the previous *capítulum,* neuter nouns employ their own set of endings in the nominative and accusative cases, particularly in the plural where they always end in -a.

4.2 **Masculine Example.** Because third-declension nouns appear in all three genders, we will isolate a commonly used noun from each gender to highlight as our model.

***SERMŌ, SERMÓNIS* (M), "SPEECH," "WORD,"[a] "CONVERSATION" (BASE: SERMŌN-)**

Case	Singular	Plural
Nominative	sermō[b]	sermónēs
Genitive	sermónis	sermónum
Dative	sermónī	sermónibus
Accusative	sermónem	sermónēs
Ablative	sermóne	sermónibus

[a] You may have noticed that *verbum, verbī* and *sermō, sermónis* can sometimes be translated the same way. This is true (and not an uncommon phenomenon in Latin), though the two words have different semantic ranges. Because of their similarities, in the famous opening of the Gospel of John—"In the beginning was the word" (I.1)—the word "word" (λόγος in Greek) has been translated as both *verbum* and *sermō* in ancient manuscripts. Which one is best? You tell me.

[b] Once again, the nominative singular is unpredictable.

Once we become familiar with the specific case endings for consonant-stem third-declension nouns, they should present no challenges.[7] As with other declensions, context is our best ally when it comes to distinguishing cases with shared endings. And it is also important for us not to confuse the genitive plural -um ending of third-declension nouns with the accusative singular ending of second-declension nouns, which is also -um.[8] Nor should we confuse the dative singular ending of this declension (-ī) with the genitive singular and nominative plural of second-declension nouns—also -ī. That stated, let's look at a masculine third-declension noun:

Vōx prophétae sermō est Deī.   The voice of the prophet is God's word.
(Haimo of Halberstadt)[9]

This sentence features two third-declension nouns. The reason why the endings in *x* and *o*, respectively, may appear strange is because they are both in the nominative singular, which, as mentioned, is generally unpredictable in the third declension. Nonetheless, by learning their genitive singular forms—*vōcis* and *sermōnis*, respectively—we can immediately classify them as third-declension nouns since they both end in -*is*.

4.3   **Feminine Example.** Our next model for third-declension nouns is the feminine form.

PĀX, PĀCIS (F), "PEACE" (BASE: PĀC-)

Case	Singular	Plural
Nominative	pāx[a]	pācēs
Genitive	pācis	pācum
Dative	pācī	pácibus
Accusative	pācem	pācēs
Ablative	pāce	pácibus

[a] Keep in mind that there are no key endings with this word since we should not expect most third-declension nouns to end with the letter -x (though some, of course, will). As mentioned above, the nominative singular of the third declension is unpredictable.

As in previous instances, masculine and feminine nouns of the third declension have identical endings. Feel free to thank me now or hold your applause until the end of the *capítulum*. Here is a sentence with two feminine nouns of the third declension.

Tunc Paulus cīvitátis Rōmánae   Then Paul obtains the birthright of
cōnséquitur nātīvitátem. (Tertullian)[10]   Roman citizenship.

The first is in the genitive case, and the second in the accusative; both are singular.

---

7. There is an exception to this when it comes to so-called i-stem third-declension nouns, which will be explained below.
8. And because we remember that the accusative always duplicates the nominative in neuter nouns, this -um ending also applies to second-declension neuter nouns.
9. Haimo of Halberstadt, "*Ēnārrātiō in Hōséae Prophétam* X," in *Ēnārrātiō in Duódecim Prophétās Minórēs* (PL 117.74). Although attributed to this Haimo, it's likely that Haimo of Auxerre was the actual author. You tell me how many friends you have with the name Haimo and you will understand how this happened.
10. Tertullian, *Advérsus Gnósticōs Scorpiácus* XV (PL 2.151).

4.4 **Neuter Example.** The neuter nouns of this declension are very similar to their masculine and feminine counterparts with a few exceptions. Let's see if you can identify those exceptions in the paradigm below. What do you observe?

NŌMEN, NŌMINIS (N), "NAME" (BASE: NŌMIN-)

Case	Singular	Plural
Nominative	nōmen[a]	nōmina
Genitive	nōmin**is**	nōmin**um**
Dative	nōmin**ī**	nōmín**ibus**
Accusative	nōmen	nōmina
Ablative	nōmin**e**	nōmín**ibus**

[a] As mentioned above, the nominative singular of the third declension is unpredictable.

That's right—as we have learned, all neuter nouns (1) have identical nominative and accusative endings and (2) the plural of the nominative and accusative always ends in -a. This will always be the case regardless of a noun's declension. With the application of these standard rules, we will learn to recognize neuter nouns very readily. As in the example below, you will see that, apart from these two differences, neuter nouns appear otherwise just like masculine and feminine forms.

> Mutātiō nōminis benedíctiō fuit.   The change of name was a blessing.
> (Remigius)[11]

I-STEM THIRD-DECLENSION NOUNS

4.5 **I-Stems.** Before there were iPhones and iPads, there were i-stems. Because consonant-stem nouns are customarily regarded as the more common variety, or default, for third-declension nouns, i-stems appear to march to the beat of a different drummer. Whether or not that is an apt description, i-stems do follow a slightly distinct pattern. In contrast to consonant-stem third-declension nouns, i-stems make use of -i in certain forms. However, not all i-stems act alike. Masculine and feminine i-stem nouns decline one way, neuter nouns another.

We will not concern ourselves with exactly how the sub-class of i-stem nouns developed.[12] What is most important is that we recognize that i-stems, regardless of their gender, end in -ium in the genitive plural. What's more, some also make use of an -ī in other forms, but we will define i-stem nouns as those third-declension nouns ending in -ium in the genitive plural. Below are the possible endings for i-stems.

As you can see in the following chart, many of the endings are the same as the consonantal class. The only real exception is the possible presence of an -ī in the ablative case. For the sake of an example, we will isolate one i-stem noun below. The ways in which it slightly differs from regular third-declension nouns are in bold.

---

11. Remigius, *Commentārius in Génesim* XXXII (PL 131.110).
12. If you would like to study this more, see Philip Baldi, *The Foundations of Latin* (Berlin: de Gruyter, 2002), 326–29.

THIRD-DECLENSION NOUNS

CASE ENDINGS FOR THIRD-DECLENSION I-STEM NOUNS

Case	Singular	Plural
Nominative	-	-ēs (m, f); -ia (n)
Genitive	-is	-ium
Dative	-ī	-ibus
Accusative	-em; -	-ēs; -īs (m, f); -ia (n)
Ablative	-e; -ī	-ibus

MARE, MARIS (N), "SEA" (BASE: MAR-)

Case	Singular	Plural
Nominative	mare[a]	mária
Genitive	maris	márium
Dative	marī	máribus
Accusative	mare	mária
Ablative	marī	máribus

[a] As we know by now, we will not expect one particular ending in the nominative case.

Despite the minor problems they present, there is a silver lining with i-stems. First and most important, the i-stem only affects a small portion of the forms. In the case of *mare, maris, márium*, the only form that might cause real confusion is the ablative singular,[13] for here the i-stem causes the word to end in -ī rather than -e. When it comes to the nominative, genitive, and accusative plurals, the presence of the -i might make us scratch our heads and wonder if we really understand Latin, but it does not alter the endings we are expecting to find: -a for neuter nouns in the nominative and accusative plural and -um for the genitive plural.

Second, what all i-stems have in common is their characteristic -ium ending in the genitive plural. This is a fixed rule that applies to all three genders: masculine, feminine, and neuter. In short, if a noun ends in -ium in the genitive plural, it is an i-stem. Of course, a couple of the endings will be marginally different in other cases depending on their genders, but we have covered these distinctives above.

4.6 **Listing Third-Declensions.** Despite what appears intimidating at first, there are *rēgulae* you can learn in order to detect whether a third-declension noun—of whatever gender—is an i-stem. I encouraged you above to consult an advanced Latin grammar for this information, or borrow your teacher's notes. Or you could follow a much simpler solution. Rather than have you memorize several rules like many grammars do, I will instead indicate i-stem nouns by simply including their genitive plural forms in our vocabulary lists.[14] In other words, instead of only

---

[13] And if we were not paying attention to the fact that this is a neuter noun, we may wonder why the accusative singular case has an ending that we would expect of the ablative.

[14] If you want to memorize the rules for identifying i-stem nouns, here is a start. For masculine and feminine nouns: (1) The nominative singular form ends in -is or -es AND has the same number of syllables for the nominative and genitive singular forms; and (2) the nominative singular form ends in -s or -x AND the noun's base ends in least two consonants. For neuter nouns: the nominative singular form ends in -al, -ar, or -e.

offering the nominative and genitive singular forms, we will also offer the genitive plural for i-stem third-declension nouns.

Let's look at an example:

- pānis, pānis, pā́nium (m), "bread"

Whereas the genitive singular form (the second *pānis*) indicates that this noun is a third-declension noun, the genitive plural form (*pā́nium*) indicates that this is an i-stem. Although it may initially seem burdensome to memorize one extra form, you will quickly become accustomed to doing so. In fact, in the *capítula* that follow, we will develop the habit of memorizing three forms for adjectives and four for verbs. (We will not rest on our laurels in this book.) What's more, this phenomenon of using three forms for nouns will only occur with third-declension nouns with i-stems—not consonant-stems or any other nouns. This will make i-stem nouns very easy to notice.

Summárium

In this *capítulum* you learned that:
- Third-declension nouns are those nouns that end in -is in the genitive singular.
- Third-declension nouns may appear in any gender.
- Third-declension nouns are customarily classified into (1) consonant-stems and (2) i-stems. Consonant-stems end in -um in the genitive plural and i-stems end in -ium in the genitive plural.

VOCĀBULŌRUM INDEX

Latin	English (Gloss)	Etymology
caput, cápitis (n)	head	(capital)
cī́vitās, cīvitā́tis (f)	city, citizenship, state	(civilian)
cor, cordis, córdium[a] (n)	heart	(cordial)
corpus, córporis (n)	body	(corporation)
frāter, frātris (m)	brother	(fraternity)
gēns, gentis, géntium (f)	nation, tribe, people	(gentile)
habitā́tor, habitātṓris (m)	inhabitant, resident, dweller	(habitat)
homō, hóminis (m)	person, humankind, man	(hominoid)
lēx, lēgis (f)	law	(legal)
mare, maris, márium (n)	sea	(marine)
māter, mātris (f)	mother	(maternal)
mēnsis, mēnsis, mḗnsium (m)	month	(month)
múlier, mulíeris (f)	woman	(muliebrity)

nōmen, nóminis (n)	name	(name)
nox, noctis, nóctium (f)	night	(nocturnal)
pānis, pānis, pánium (m)	bread, loaf	(pannettone)
pater, patris (m)	father	(paternal)
prīnceps, príncipis (m)	chief, leader, ruler, prince	(prince)
rēx, rēgis (m)	king	(regal)
sacérdōs, sacerdótis (m)	priest	(sacred)
sēmen, séminis (n)	seed	(seminary)
sermō, sermónis (m)	speech, word, conversation	(sermon)
tempus, témporis (n)	time, period, age	(temporal)
Trínitās, Trīnitátis (f)	Trinity	(Trinity)
vōx, vōcis (f)	voice	(vocal)

[a] As mentioned above, nouns with a third component offered (in this case, *córdium*) indicate that the third-declension noun is an i-stem noun.

ŌRĀ́TIŌ POPULÁRIS

Pater Noster (Pars Minor I). The "Our Father" is Jesus's most famous prayer. Contained in Matthew VI.9–13, it is the prayer that Jesus taught his disciples when asked how to pray. We will divide the Lord's Prayer into two parts: verses 9–10 in this *capítulum* and verses 11–13 in the next.

Pater noster	Our father
quī es in caelīs	You who are in heaven.
sānctificétur nōmen tuum	May your name be sanctified.
Advéniat rēgnum tuum	May your kingdom come.
Fīat volúntās tua	May your will be done,
sīcut in caelō et in terrā.	On earth just as in heaven.

EXERCÍTIA

Be sure to complete the *exercítium* in the appendix corresponding to this *capítulum*.

Capítulum
V

FIRST-, SECOND-, AND THIRD-DECLENSION ADJECTIVES

Sōla canónica Scrīptū́rā est régula fídeī.[1]
—THOMAS AQUINAS

OPÚSCULUM THEOLÓGICUM: *The Five Sōlae*

Although we tend to associate the phrase *sōlā Scrīptū́rā*, "by Scripture alone," with the Protestant Reformation, this concept existed centuries before the birth of Protestantism. Among others, the renowned medieval theologian Thomas Aquinas made use of the expression in his commentary on the Gospel of John. He explained:

Sōla canónica Scrīptū́ra est régula fídeī.[2]   Only canonical Scripture is the rule of faith.

Commenting on the end of John's Gospel where the apostle reported that there were many other things that Jesus did not record for posterity, Thomas felt compelled to write that *sōla [canónica] Scrīptū́ra* contained those things which must be believed. Everything else, he advised, must be measured against canonical Scripture.

When it comes to first-generation Protestant Reformers, they actually used the phrase *sōlā Scrīptū́rā* sparingly. Martin Luther, for instance, only wrote the phrase twenty times in his lifetime. And when he did so, he did not mean what people often believe he meant. In his tract *To the Christian Nobility*, for instance, he penned: "Scripture alone is our vineyard in which we must all labor and toil. Above all, the foremost reading for everybody . . ."[3] As Reformation scholars such as Timothy Wengert have noted,[4] what Luther really advocated was *prīma Scrīptū́ra*, "Scripture first," not technically *sōla Scrīptū́ra*,

---

1. "Only canonical Scripture is the rule of faith."
2. Thomas Aquinas, *Sānctī Thómae dē Aquínō Super Ēvangélium S. Iōánnis Lēctū́ra* XXI.6.
3. *To the Christian Nobility of the German Nation 1520*, ed. Timothy J. Wengert and James Estes, The Annotated Luther Study Edition (Minneapolis: Fortress, 2015), 453. Note: Because Luther wanted this book to be immediately read by the people he addressed, he wrote it in German and not in Latin.
4. See, for instance, Timothy J. Wengert, *Reading the Bible with Martin Luther: An Introductory Guide* (Grand Rapids: Baker, 2013), 16–19. Wengert notes that Luther used the Latin phrase *sōlā scrīptū́rā* a mere twenty times. In summary, he explains: "Indeed, we would be better off replacing *sola Scriptura* with the phrase *solus Christus* (Christ alone) and, what amounts to the same thing, *solo Verbo*, by the word alone—where 'the Word' was for Luther not simply the Bible but its proclamation" (18–19).

"Scripture alone." Luther believed that the Bible was the primary authority of the Christian life, not the sole authority.

We are standing on much better ground when we speak of the Protestant Reformers' use of the related phrases *sōlā fidē*, "by faith alone," and *sōlā grātiā*, "by grace alone." Returning again to Luther, the celebrated Wittenberg professor made use of these phrases with much more frequency than that of *sōlā Scrīptūrā*—publishing the Latin slogan *sōlā fidē* on 1,200 separate occasions.[5]

Since at least the twentieth century, two other Latin slogans have gained popularity alongside the renowned three above: *sōlō Chrīstō*, "by Christ alone," and *sōlī Deō glōria*, "glory to God alone." It is believed by some that, collectively, these "five solas" summarize the distinctives of Protestant theology:

Sōlā Scrīptūrā: By Scripture alone
Sōlā fidē: By faith alone
Sōlā grā́tiā: By grace alone
Sōlō Christō: By Christ alone
Sōlī Deō glṓria: Glory to God alone

Besides offering theological food for thought, these rich slogans introduce us to a very important part of speech: words that describe nouns—called "adjectives." What holds these slogans together is their convenient and repeated use of the adjective *sōlus, sōla, sōlum*, meaning "alone," "only," or "sole." In the examples above, the first four *sōlae* are in the ablative case—hence the use of the word "by" in our translation and the letter ā rather than ă for the feminine—whereas the last one is dative.

In the last phrase, *sōlī Deō glōria*, some might incorrectly translate it as "glory alone to God," but this is not possible due to the surgical precision of the Latin language.[6] Because *Deus* and *glōria* are nouns from different genders and different cases—*Deō* is masculine and dative, while *glōria* is nominative and feminine—the masculine and dative form of *sōlus, sōla, sōlum* (*sōlī*) tells us without a shadow of a doubt that it can only be modifying *Deō*, not *glōria*. Otherwise, it would read *Sōla Deō glōria*. Instead, however, the phrase remains *Sōlī Deō glōria*—"To God alone [be the] glory!"

Prospéctus
In this *capítulum* you will learn that:
- Adjectives modify nouns.
- There are two classes of adjectives, those using first- and second-declension noun endings and those using third-declension ones.

GRAMMÁTICA

5.1 Noun Modifiers. Adjectives are noun descriptors. They quantify the number of disciples Jesus called (*duódecim*, "twelve")[7] and describe the temperament of Thomas Aquinas (*mūtum*, "quiet").[8]

---

5. Wengert, *Reading the Bible with Martin Luther*, 16. In comparison, Wengert notes that Luther used the expression *sōlā grātia* two hundred times.

6. As you may have guessed, note that "precision" ultimately comes from the Latin noun *praecísio, praecisiónis* (f), meaning "the act of cutting."

7. Matt. X.1 et al.

8. Claire Le Brun-Gouanvic, ed., *Ystoria Sancti Thome de Aquino de Guillaume de Tocco (1323)*, Studies and Texts 127 (Toronto: Pontifical Institute of Medieval Studies, 1996), 13.117.

Coming from the Latin word *adjéctum*, "added,"[9] adjectives represent words that are often added alongside nouns in order to limit, qualify, modify, or otherwise characterize nouns in some specific way: in color, shape, size, nature, or number. They provide delightful ways to garnish our words. They are like gravy to potatoes, parmesan to pasta, and salt to eggs. For those who love novels, they are the difference between Charles Dickens (who bathed his nouns in adjectives) and Ernest Hemingway (who kept his nouns bone-dry of them).

5.2 **Adjective Placement.** In English, adjectives are rather statically positioned in sentences. They always precede the noun(s) they modify. Latin adjectives, by contrast, enjoy a much greater range of flexibility. Depending on the type used, looking for adjectives in Latin can sometimes feel like going on a scavenger hunt.

On the one hand, a good deal of Latin adjectives follow the nouns they describe, though they may be separated from their nouns by one or many words. If you find it helpful, you could think of that as the default location of adjectives: noun first and then adjective following close afterward. On the other hand, certain adjectives, such as those describing size, quantity, or personal possession prefer to appear before the nouns they modify. When it comes to poetry, however, all bets are off: adjectives may appear in very different places in a sentence.

5.3 **Declension Patterns of Adjectives.** There are two declension patterns that adjectives follow in Latin: (1) those using the first- and second-declension endings (which I will refer to as 2-1-2 adjectives); and (2) those employing the third-declension endings (which I will list as 3-3-3 adjectives).[10] (Keep in mind that third-declension adjectives have subcategories that I will discuss below.) As a perpetual blessing to beginner students, Latin adjectives only utilize case endings from the first three declensions—never the fourth or fifth declensions (which we will discuss in subsequent *capítula*). This makes adjectives relatively easy to recognize since we have already learned their case endings. It also explains why we are examining adjectives at this stage before fourth and fifth declensions nouns. Adjectives simply do not use these last two declensions; they only have eyes for the first, second, and third declensions.

5.4 **Agreement but Not Duplication.** Adjectives always agree with the nouns they modify in case, number, and gender, but they need not agree in declension. This is an important distinction. Stated differently, while adjectives will always share the same case, number, and gender of the noun(s) they modify, they may or may not follow the same declension patterns—in fact, many times they will not. This means adjectives need not share the same endings as the noun(s) they modify. What we are searching for is grammatical agreement, not visual correspondence.

Let's look at an example from the twelfth-century chronicler Orderic Vitalis:

Theódorus pāpa multum pius et bonus fuit. (Orderic Vitalis)[11]	Pope Theodore [I] was a very devout and good pope.

There are two important features to note here. First, the adjectives Orderic used to describe the noun *pāpa*, "pope"—which are *pius* and *bonus*—agree with the noun they are modifying in

---

9. This is related to the Latin verb *adjício* (or: *adício*), *adjícere*, *adjécī*, *adjéctus*, meaning "to throw" and "to add," among many other glosses.
10. Traditional grammars call these "first/second declensions" and "third declensions," respectively. These are acceptable terms but the terminology I am suggesting is more exact. That stated, the language most often used is still "first/second declensions" and "third declensions."
11. Orderic Vitalis, *História Ecclēsiástica* I.2.28 (PL 188.217).

case, number, and gender despite the fact that they make use of different endings. Did you notice that? We may suppose that the two adjectives should be *pia* and *bona* in order to match the ending of the noun *pāpa*, but they are not because *pāpa* is masculine rather than feminine. It is best to get in the mindset *ab prīncípiō*, "from the beginning," of not expecting adjectives to mirror the noun endings they modify. Sometimes they do, but just as often they do not.

Second, and in a related way, Latin adjectives are capable of modifying nouns from all noun declensions. Correct: Adjectives can modify nouns of first, second, third, fourth, and fifth declensions (even though they can never adopt fourth- or fifth-declension endings). In other words, adjective declensions are not exclusively bound to nouns of the same declensions. In the case above, *pius* and *bonus* employ second-declension endings because they happen to be modifying a masculine noun; if they were modifying a feminine noun, however, they would have to use first-declension endings (and so *pia* and *bona* would be the correct forms). But *pāpa, pāpae* is a first-declension masculine noun, and this can never be changed. It is permanent.

This kind of mixing and matching among nouns and adjectives of different declensional families is as common as it is correct. Similar to how nouns are only allowed to be one declension (never more than one), so adjectives can only appear as 2-1-2 adjectives or as 3-3-3 adjectives. So, if an adjective is a 2-1-2 adjective and it is modifying a third-declension noun, the adjective can never change its declension pattern to match the noun's declension; it can only alter its case, number, and gender. That is all. To whatever declension family an adjective belongs, it remains forever; so, too, with nouns. As a result, *Sāncta Maria*, "Holy Mary," *Fēlīx Maria*, "Blessed [or Fortunate] Mary," and *Fidélis Maria*, "Faithful Mary" are all grammatically correct even though each adjective ends in a different letter. Again, we are not looking for visual correspondence, only grammatical agreement.

THREE FUNCTIONS OF LATIN ADJECTIVES

5.5 **Adjectival Functions.** Adjectives occur regularly in Latin sentences. For our purposes in this *capítulum*, we will isolate three ways that adjectives function: (1) as attributive adjectives; (2) as predicate adjectives; and (3) as substantival adjectives. Depending on its role in any given sentence, an adjective in Latin may function in any one of these three ways. For instance, an adjective may be attributive in one instance but substantival in another.

(1) Attributive Adjectives. Attributive adjectives attribute a certain quality or characteristic to a noun. These adjectives usually appear near—whether before or after—the noun they modify, though in English we will translate them right before the noun in accordance with English style, which is quite boring in relation to Latin.

Quasi bonus et vērus doctor.   Like a good and true teacher.
(Cyprian of Carthage)[12]

Here the adjectives *bonus* and *vērus* are attributing a quality to the noun *doctor*.

(2) Predicate Adjectives. Predicate adjectives assert or "predicate" something about a noun, that is, the subject of the sentence.

---
12. Cyprian of Carthage, *Epístola* LIIVIII.2 (PL 4.421).

| Vērum prōmíssiō nova poeniténtiae et dōnátiō clávium novae lēgis <u>própria</u> est. (Martin Luther)[13] | But the new promise of repentance and the gift of the keys are <u>particular</u> to the new law. |

In this sentence, both uses of the adjective *novus, nova, novum*, "new," are attributive,[14] so we are focusing on the last adjective listed: *própria*. Because *própria* is predicating something about the noun, we designate it a predicate adjective.

(3) Substantival Adjectives. Substantival adjectives stand in place of the noun(s) they modify. In this way, they are acting "substantively" or as a "substantive,"[15] namely, as a noun. For what it's worth, a substantival adjective will always agree with the absent noun it is modifying in gender and number, even though the noun is not present. The adjective's case, however, will depend upon its function in the sentence.

| Beátī <u>paúperēs</u> spíritū. (Matt. V.3) | Blessed are <u>the poor</u> in spirit. |

In this first of Jesus's beatitudes (from *beātitū́dō*, "blessedness"), the lack of a noun indicates that at least one adjective is acting as a substantive, thus the adjective assumes its gender and number from an antecedent (whether stated or implied). In this case, *paúperēs* is the substantive and *beátī* is the predicate.

THE GOSPEL OF ADJECTIVES

1. Adjectives modify nouns and agree with them in case, number, and gender.
2. Though agreeing with nouns in case, number, and gender, the endings of adjectives need not look identical to the nouns they modify. Sometimes they do; oftentimes they do not.
3. Adjectives, which only use the case endings of first, second, or third declension nouns, modify nouns of any declension.
4. Adjectives may function as attributives, predicates, or substantives.

TWO DECLENSION PATTERNS OF ADJECTIVES

5.6 **First- and Second-Declension Adjectives.** We will begin with the first set of adjectives—those making use of the first- and second-declension case endings. I will refer to these as 2-1-2 adjectives since they acquire their masculine endings from the second declension, their feminine endings from the first declension, and their neuter endings from the second declension.

Though intimidating at first glance, there are no new endings here. We have already learned each of the case endings for this pattern of adjective: first- and second-declension ones. In other words, we are accustomed to the cases and their endings as well as to the lack of a constant nominative singular masculine ending: Sometimes it ends in -us, sometimes it does not.

Let us look at an example of a 2-1-2 adjective in the following chart. As is true of nouns, we generate adjective case endings from the word's base, which is discovered upon removing the ending of the genitive masculine singular (-ī).

---

13. Martin Luther, *Dē Cāptivitā́te Babylónicā Ecclḗsiā* (WA 6.552).
14. Notice also that the adjective *novus, nova, novum* does not mirror the endings of the noun in either occurrence in this sentence.
15. The term comes from *substantī́vus*, "self-existent."

FIRST-, SECOND-, AND THIRD-DECLENSION ADJECTIVES

2-1-2 ADJECTIVES (ADJECTIVES USING THE SECOND-, FIRST-, SECOND-DECLENSION ENDING PATTERNS)

Case	Masculine	Feminine	Neuter
Nominative Sg	-us; -	-a	-um
Genitive Sg	-ī	-ae	-ī
Dative Sg	-ō	-ae	-ō
Accusative Sg	-um	-am	-um
Ablative Sg	-ō	-ā	-ō
Nominative Pl	-ī	-ae	-a
Genitive Pl	-órum	-árum	-órum
Dative Pl	-īs	-īs	-īs
Accusative Pl	-ōs	-ās	-a
Ablative Pl	-īs	-īs	-īs

SĀNCTUS, SĀNCTA, SĀNCTUM (2-1-2), "HOLY," "GODLY" (BASE: SĀNCT-)

Case	Masculine	Feminine	Neuter
Nominative Sg	sānctus	sāncta	sānctum
Genitive Sg	sānctī	sānctae	sānctī
Dative Sg	sānctō	sānctae	sānctō
Accusative Sg	sānctum	sānctam	sānctum
Ablative Sg	sānctō	sānctā	sānctō
Nominative Pl	sānctī	sānctae	sāncta
Genitive Pl	sānctórum	sānctárum	sānctórum
Dative Pl	sānctīs	sānctīs	sānctīs
Accusative Pl	sānctōs	sānctās	sāncta
Ablative Pl	sānctīs	sānctīs	sānctīs

Dictionaries typically list 2-1-2 adjectives as follows: *sānctus, -a, -um*. This specifies the adjective pattern[16] by listing the full form of the nominative masculine singular followed by abbreviations for the feminine and neuter nominatives, respectively. In short, all adjectives that have as their dictionary forms -us,[17] -a, -um are 2-1-2 adjectives and will follow the predetermined

---

16. Dictionaries always label them first and second declensions.
17. The most common exception to this rule is 2-1-2 adjectives that do not use -us in the nominative masculine singular, e.g., *sacer, sacra, sacrum*, an adjective also meaning "holy." Its dictionary form is slightly different from *sānctus, -a, -um* due to the lack of the -us in the masculine nominative singular. And because we already know that bases are generated from the genitive singular form (rather than the nominative), we are not surprised that the feminine and neuter forms are slightly different. Either way, it is still a 2-1-2 adjective and will use the same case endings as all other 2-1-2 adjectives.

pattern that we have seen above (and have learned in previous *capítula* for first- and second-declension nouns).

5.7 **Ūnus Nauta, "One Sailor": Nine Irregular 2-1-2 Adjectives.** As we might expect, there are a group of unruly and bad little adjectives that defy the heaven-ordained rules of first- and second-declension case endings in a couple of forms. In total, there are nine such adjectives, conveniently assembled into an acronym meaning "one sailor," *ūnus nauta* in Latin.

The characteristic difference of these adjectives is -ius and -i case endings in the genitive and dative singular. Otherwise, these adjectives follow normal declensional patterns. I do not recommend memorizing the divergent endings of each of these adjectives. After all, this is only a handful of words. Instead, I suggest memorizing only the acronym and remembering that all such "*ūnus nauta*" adjectives follow their own patterns in a couple of forms.

Here is the list of such adjectives in the order of the acronym.

- *Ūnus, ūna, ūnum*, "one"
- *Neúter, neútra, neútrum*, "neither"
- *Uter, utra, utrum*, "either"
- *Sōlus, sōla, sōlum*, "alone," "sole"
- *Nūllus, nūlla, nūllum*, "none"
- *Alter, áltera, álterum*, "other," "another"
- *Ūllus, ūlla, ūllum*, "any"
- *Tōtus, tōta, tōtum*, "total," "entire"
- *Álius, ália, áliud*, "other," "another"

5.8 **Third-Declension Adjectives.** Besides first- and second-declension patterns, the other pattern of adjectives is third-declension adjectives. I will refer to these as 3-3-3 adjectives since they acquire their masculine, feminine, and neuter forms from third-declension endings.

Note that 3-3-3 adjectives follow the pattern of the i-stem third-declension nouns that we learned in the previous *capítulum*. In case you forgot, here are the i-stem essentials:

- All three genders in the ablative singular end in -ī.
- Nominative and accusative neuter plurals end in -ia.
- All genders in the genitive plural end in -ium.
- In every other way, 3-3-3 adjectives mostly mirror consonant-stem third-declension noun endings.

3-3-3 ADJECTIVES (ADJECTIVES USING THE THIRD-DECLENSION I-STEM ENDING PATTERNS)

Case	Masculine	Feminine	Neuter
Nominative Sg	-	-	-
Genitive Sg	-is	-is	-is
Dative Sg	-ī	-ī	-ī
Accusative Sg	-em	-em	-
Ablative Sg	-ī	-ī	-ī
Nominative Pl	-ēs	-ēs	-ia
Genitive Pl	-ium	-ium	-ium

Dative Pl	-ibus	-ibus	-ibus
Accusative Pl	-ēs	-ēs	-ia
Ablative Pl	-ibus	-ibus	-ibus

5.9 **Three Possible Nominative Singular Forms.** Besides following the pattern of third-declension i-stems, 3-3-3 adjectives may be further divided into three groupings based on how many different forms there are in the nominative singular, or "dictionary" forms: (1) one-form nominative singulars; (2) two-form nominative singulars; and (3) three-form nominative singulars. These groupings are purely for classification purposes and have no intrinsic meaning. In other words, this is my own language that I have used in teaching, but it is not used in other grammars. On the flip side, attending cocktail parties will never get old when you can dish out terms like these: one-form nominative singular adjectives with i-stem third-declension endings. Let's take a closer look at them.

(1) One-Form Nominative Singulars. These contain the same form for all nominative singulars, regardless of gender. For example, *ínnocēns, ínnocēns, ínnocēns,* "blameless," "pure," is the same in the masculine, feminine, and neuter singular forms.

(2) Two-Form Nominative Singulars. These share the same masculine and feminine forms in the singular yet diverge in the neuter. (Remember that neuters are the bachelors of the grammatical gender world—happy to do things on their own.) Observe, therefore, that it is always true that the masculine and feminine are the same and the neuter is different. For example, *fidélis, fidélis, fidéle,* "faithful," appears as *fidélis* in the masculine and feminine nominative singular but as *fidéle* in the neuter nominative singular. This is the most common form of 3-3-3 adjective.

(3) Three-Form Nominative Singulars. These utilize different forms for each gender in the nominative singular. For example, *celer, céleris, célere,* "fast" or "swift," makes use of three different forms. In short, the three-form nominative singular adjectives are individualists. They all do their own thing.

5.10 *Cáveat Léctor,* **"Reader Beware."** There is one *cáveat* that I must offer. Other than the differences appearing in the nominative singular forms, 3-3-3 adjectives follow the standard i-stem third-declension patterns in all other forms. The three forms mentioned above have nothing to do, therefore, with the adjective's meaning. They exist to keep grammarians employed and students sane.

CELER, CÉLERIS, CÉLERE (3-3-3), "FAST," "SWIFT" (BASE: CELER-)

Case	Masculine	Feminine	Neuter
Nominative Sg	celer	céler**is**	céler**e**
Genitive Sg	céler**is**	céler**is**	céler**is**
Dative Sg	céler**ī**	céler**ī**	céler**ī**
Accusative Sg	céler**em**	céler**em**	céler**e**
Ablative Sg	céler**ī**	céler**ī**	céler**ī**
Nominative Pl	céler**ēs**	céler**ēs**	celér**ia**
Genitive Pl	celér**ium**	celér**ium**	celér**ium**

(cont.)

Case	Masculine	Feminine	Neuter
Dative Pl	celéribus	celéribus	celéribus
Accusative Pl	célerēs	célerēs	celéria
Ablative Pl	celéribus	celéribus	celéribus

5.11 Third-Declension Example. Let us look at an example of a 3-3-3 adjective. As with 2-1-2 adjectives, we generate these adjective case endings from the word's base, which is discovered upon removing the ending of the genitive masculine singular (-is).

Here is an example from one of the oldest Western liturgies:

Dómine Deus omnípotēns sempitérne,　　　　Almighty and Eternal Lord and God, you
quī peccātórum indulgéntiam　　　　　　　　who have ordained remission of sins in
in cōnfessiōne <u>célerī</u> posuístī.　　　　　　　a <u>swift</u> confession.
(*Sacrāmentárium Gelasiánum*)[18]

The adjective *célerī* is modifying the singular feminine noun *cōnfessiōne*, which occurs in the ablative case.

Note also that the rule of neuter nouns is completely in effect, which explains the same forms in the nominative and accusative neuter as well as the standard neuter ending in -ia in the plural.

Summárium

In this *capítulum* you learned that:
- Adjectives are words that modify nouns.
- Adjectives consist of two patterns, those using first- and second-declension endings and those using third-declension ones.
- Adjectives of whatever declension may modify nouns of any declension; adjectives of all types may modify nouns of all types.

VOCĀBULÓRUM INDEX

Latin	English (Gloss)	(Etymology)
aliénus, aliéna, aliénum	strange, foreign, belonging to another	(alien)
altus, alta, altum	high, deep, tall	(altitude)
benedíctus, benedícta, benedíctum	blessed	(benediction)
bonus, bona, bonum	good	(bonus)
brevis, brevis, breve	short, brief, small, little	(brevity)
celer, céleris, célere	fast, swift	(accelerate)

---

18. *Sacrāmentárium Gelasiánum* III.106 (PL 74.1244).

FIRST-, SECOND-, AND THIRD-DECLENSION ADJECTIVES

cūnctus, cūncta, cūnctum	all, whole	
dignus, digna, dignum[a]	worthy, fitting, appropriate	(dignity)
fidélis, fidélis, fidéle	faithful, loyal, trustworthy	(confidential)
fortis, fortis, forte	strong, brave	(fortitude)
īrátus, īráta, īrátum	angry	(irate)
iūstus, iūsta, iūstum[b]	righteous, just	(justice)
līber, líbera, líberum	free	(liberty)
magnus, magna, magnum	great, large, big	(magnificent)
malus, mala, malum	bad, evil	(malicious)
multus, multa, multum	many, much	(multitudinous)
omnípotēns, omnípotēns, omnípotēns	all-powerful, omnipotent, almighty	(omnipotent)
prīmum	first, at first	(primary)
sānctus, sāncta, sānctum	holy, godly	(sanctify)
sápiēns, sápiēns, sápiēns	wise	(sapiental)
símilis, símilis, símile	similar	(similar)
tōtus, tōta, tōtum	whole, complete, entire, total	(total)
ūnivérsus, ūnivérsa, ūnivérsum	whole, entire	(universe)
vērus, vēra, vērum	true, real	(verify)
vetus, vetus, vetus	old, ancient, aged, former	(veteran)

[a] Note that this adjective (and its antonym: *indígnus, indígna, indígnum*) pattern with the ablative case.
[b] This adjective will often also appear as *jūstus, jūsta, jūstum*.

ŌRÁTIŌ POPULÁRIS

Pater Noster (Pars Minor II). The second and final section of the *Pater Noster*, coming from Matthew VI.11–13, completes the rest of the prayer.

Pānem nostrum quotīdiánum	Give us today
dā nōbīs hódiē	Our daily bread
et dīmítte nōbīs débita nostra	And forgive us our debts
sīcut et nōs dīmíttimus dēbitóribus nostrīs	As we also forgive those indebted to us
Et nē nōs indúcās in tentātiónem	And lead us not into temptation
sed líberā nōs ā malō. Āmēn.	But deliver us from evil. Amen.

EXERCÍTIA

Be sure to complete the *exercítium* in the appendix corresponding to this *capítulum*.

Capítulum
VI

FOURTH-DECLENSION NOUNS, POSITIVE, COMPARATIVE, AND SUPERLATIVE ADJECTIVES, AND ABLATIVES

Spíritū psállere est spīrituálī dēvōtióne et afféctū psállere.
—MARTIN LUTHER[1]

OPÚSCULUM THEOLÓGICUM: *Martin Luther's Dictắta in Psaltḗrium*

As a newly minted *Dóctor Theológiae*, "Doctor of Theology," from the University of Wittenberg, the young German monk Martin Luther offered his first lectures to students on the book of Psalms. It's not at all surprising that Luther inaugurated his teaching career with this book. As countless monks before him, Luther had memorized the psalms in Latin while an Augustinian monk at Erfurt and had sung through the Psalter in Latin on a regular basis. Why not teach what you know?

The title of Luther's lectures, delivered from 1513 to 1515, was *Dictắta in Psaltḗrium*, "Lectures on the Psalter." While students worked from a printed copy of the Latin Psalter,[2] Luther dictated his notes on the biblical text, called *glōssae*, "glosses." Due to the recently invented printing press (in Germany, of all places), professors like Martin Luther "were able to commission local printers to print the biblical text with space between the lines and wide margins,"[3] enabling eager students to record interlinear and marginal notes in the printed text. All of this naturally took place in Latin, the language of the academy. In short, Luther made use of a Latin biblical text, lectured in Latin, and his students took notes in Latin. It was a Latinist's dream come true.

Luther's opening lines from his lectures on the Psalter indicate both his admiration of the psalms as well as his deep love of singing.

---

1. "To sing psalms with the Spirit means to sing psalms with both spiritual devotion and with affection."
2. Luther used a Latin version of the psalms printed in Leipzig. There were many Latin versions of the Psalter by this time.
3. Robert Kolb, *Martin Luther and the Enduring Word of God: The Wittenberg School and Its Scripture-Centered Proclamation* (Grand Rapids: Baker Academic, 2016), 132.

Psallam spíritū, psallam et mente. Spíritū psállere est spīrituálī dēvōtióne et afféctū psállere, quod dícitur contrā eōs, quī carne tantum psallunt.[4]	"I will sing psalms both with my spirit and with my mind" [I Cor. XIV.15]. To sing psalms with the Spirit means to sing psalms with both spiritual devotion and with affection, which is spoken against those who sing psalms only in the flesh.

After quoting Paul, Luther declares that a true recitation of the psalms necessitates doing so "with the Spirit" and "with affection." As we know by now, Latin is quite concise. It achieves in two words what English clumsily does in six. The two key words from Luther's opening remarks are *spíritus* and *afféctus*, terms with a longstanding theological history. They are both used here in the ablative case, meaning that we will probably have to use one of a number of possible prepositions ("by," "through," "with," etc.) when translating into English. For our purposes, these two key words introduce us to a new set of case endings: those of fourth-declension nouns.

Prospéctus

In this *capítulum* you will learn that:
- Fourth-declension nouns end in -ūs in the genitive singular.
- Comparative and superlative adjectives are used to compare two or more items.
- The ablative case is often used when comparing one thing to another.

GRAMMÁTICA

6.1 Fourth Class of Nouns. In comparison to third-declension nouns, fourth-declension nouns are simpler to master and fewer to manage. This is good news, to be sure. You will be delighted to note that, unlike those fiendish third-declension nouns, there are no subcategories associated with them (such as i-stems). In fact, nouns of the fourth declension are few and far between (at least compared to third declensions); there are only a handful that occur with regularity in the biblical or theological *corpus*. The majority of fourth-declension nouns are masculine, though they can also occur in the feminine and neuter genders.

6.2 Characteristic Vowel. The thematic vowel for this class of nouns is -u. As such, when you encounter a noun with this letter appearing toward the end of a word, there is a *possibility* that it is a fourth-declension noun.[5] However, as always, you can only truly know the identity of a noun's declension by its form in the genitive singular. For fourth-declension nouns, that ending is -ūs. Forming fourth-declension nouns is not difficult. It follows the basic rules learned before.

Steps to Form Fourth-Declension Nouns
1. Select a fourth-declension noun (e.g., *cultus, cultūs*, "worship").
2. Determine its base by removing the -ūs from the genitive singular form (e.g., *cultūs* → **cult*).

---

4. Martin Luther, "Glossa: Praefátio," in *Dictáta in Psaltérium* (WA 3.11).
5. The word just mentioned above, for instance, is *corpus, córporis* (n). Despite the *u* toward the end of the word in the nominative singular, it is third declension because the genitive singular has an ending of -is.

NOUNS AND ADJECTIVES

3. Add fourth-declension endings to the base as needed: -us/-ū, -ūs, -uī/-ū, -um/-ū, -ū; -ūs/-ua, -uum, -ibus, -ūs/-ua, -ibus (e.g, *cultus, cultūs, cúltuī, cultum, cultū*, etc.).

CASE ENDINGS FOR FOURTH-DECLENSION NOUNS

Case	Singular	Plural
Nominative	-us (m, f); -ū (n)	-ūs (m, f); -ua (n)
Genitive	-ūs	-uum
Dative	-uī (m, f); -ū (n)	-ibus
Accusative	-um (m, f); -ū (n)	-ūs (m, f); -ua (n)
Ablative	-ū	-ibus

While masculine and feminine fourth-declension nouns share the same set of endings, the neuter gender endings are largely distinct. In fact, only the genitive of the singular is declined.

You will have noticed that the case ending of every singular neuter form except one (the genitive) is the same: -ū. What is going on here? This is confusing and takes time to get used to, but the good news is that the use of prepositions and adjectives will reduce the uncertainty of the case. What is more, some fourth-declension nouns, such as *spíritus, spíritūs*, occur so frequently and with so much theological context that you will have little difficulty discerning their case.

Looking at other forms in the paradigm above, you will notice that the -us and -um endings in the nominative and accusative (masculine and feminine) cases look familiar; however, be careful not to confuse them with second-declension nouns. Similarly, the -ibus ending of the dative and ablative plurals is identical to third-declension nouns. Why is it -ibus instead of -ubus? The characteristic -u vowel weakens before the -bus, resulting in the form we are familiar with in the third declension: -ibus.

Finally, I hope you remember the two grammatical rules we have already learned: (1) Neuter accusative nouns always duplicate the nominative, and (2) neuter nouns always end in -a in the nominative and accusative plurals. This explains the identical forms in the nominative and accusative and also the -ua endings in the plural.

6.3 **Masculine Example.** Most fourth-declension nouns are masculine. The very small number of feminine fourth-declension nouns[6] follow the same case endings as the masculine, so there is no need to supply an additional paradigm just for them.

***SPÍRITUS, SPÍRITŪS* (M), "SPIRIT," "BREATH," "WIND," "BLOWING" (BASE: SPĪRIT-)**

Case	Singular	Plural
Nominative	spíritus	spíritūs
Genitive	spíritūs	spírit**uum**
Dative	spīrítuī	spīrít**ibus**
Accusative	spíritum	spíritūs
Ablative	spíritū	spīrít**ibus**

---

6. The most common feminine forms are found in the vocabulary list at the end of the *capítulum*.

As mentioned above, the fourth declension contains many forms with identical endings: particularly -us (where the *u* may be long [ū] or short [ŭ]). There are four places where this occurs: nominative and genitive singular (depending on the macron), and nominative and accusative plural. We also often encounter this ending with second-declension masculine singular endings (though there it will be -us and not -ūs). Though initially ambiguous, context will almost always clarify the case of the noun. I write "almost always," since Latin does sometimes leave ambiguity. As we have already discussed, prepositions and adjectives are our allies when it comes to cracking the code of a noun's case. And as we encounter verbal forms in the *capítula* to come, we will learn how they also help distinguish the different cases.

As for other forms, note that -uum is a dead giveaway of a fourth-declension noun, and that -ibus always indicates dative and ablative plural forms.

Let's look at an example from the word *spíritus, spíritūs*.

Adjuvánte Dóminō nostrō Jēsū Christō, quī cum Patre et Spíritū Sānctō vīvit et rēgnat Deus per īnfīníta saécula saeculórum. Āmēn. (Caesarius of Arles)[7]

It is very clear that *Spíritū* here is ablative, especially since it is patterning with the preposition *cum*, which only and always patterns with the ablative case. This means that we will translate the word as something like "with the Spirit." And what about its gender? In short, we know its gender only because we will have memorized *spíritus, spíritūs* as a masculine noun (though the use of the adjective *Sānctō* limits the gender to either masculine or neuter). That stated, here is our translation:

With the help of our Lord Jesus Christ, who with the Father and with the Holy Spirit lives and reigns as God for ever and ever. Amen.

IĒSUS, IĒSŪ ("JESUS")

The most important Latin name in the Christian tradition comes directly from the Greek word Ἰησοῦς, which derives from the Hebrew word יֵשׁוּעַ. Not unusual for a term of foreign origin, *Iēsus, Iēsū* (m) follows an irregular pattern. Although it is a fourth-declension masculine noun, its case endings are unpredictable and so must be memorized. There are no plural forms—unless you are *haeréticus*, a "heretic."

Nominative: Iēsus
Genitive: Iēsū
Dative: Iēsū
Accusative: Iēsum
Ablative: Iēsū
Vocative: Iēsū

Keep in mind that the letter *I* is a consonant rather than a vowel, which is why you will commonly see this name spelled *Jēsus, Jēsū*. There is no difference in meaning; the first letter

---

7. Caesarius of Arles, *Homílía* X (PL 67.1069).

is a consonant, meaning that there are only two syllables in this word. And because there are only two syllables, the stress must be put on the first syllable—in this case over the long vowel ē.

6.4 **Neuter Example.** There are only a handful of neuter fourth-declension nouns that you will typically encounter when reading Latin, but we will include an example in the paradigm below since their case endings differ, especially in the singular, from the masculine or feminine forms in several instances.

GENŪ, GENŪS (N), "KNEE" (BASE: GEN-)

Case	Singular	Plural
Nominative	genū	génua
Genitive	genūs	génuum
Dative	genū	génibus
Accusative	genū	génua
Ablative	genū	génibus

The most distinctive feature of neuter nouns of this declension are the repeated uses of the -ū ending. Whereas this ending only occurs in the ablative singular of masculine fourth-declension nouns, it occurs in four places in neuter nouns: nominative, dative, accusative, and ablative singulars. These identical endings must be memorized and distinguished from one another according the context of each given sentence.

All other endings of this gender follow standard patterns we have already encountered. Here is an example:

In advéntū Dóminī Salvātóris, quandō   At the coming of our Lord the Savior,
in nómine ejus omne genū flectétur.   when in his name every knee will bow.
(Rufinus of Aquileia)[8]

BENDING THE KNEE

The English term "genuflection" derives from the fourth-declension neuter noun *genū, genūs*, "knee," and the verb *flectō, fléctere, flexī, flexus*, "to bend." In the Middle Ages, this coalesced into the verb *genūfléctō, genūfléctere, genūflexī, genūfléxus*, "to bend the knee." Genuflection is done in Roman Catholic Churches by bending the right knee to the ground toward the "host" (*hóstia* or consecrated bread, though originally the word meant "sacrificial victim" in Latin and "offering"), which is stored within a locked box before and after a service in the church tabernacle near the altar.

---

8. Rufinus of Aquileia, *Apológiae Liber Prīmus* XXXI (PL 20.571).

FOURTH-DECLENSION NOUNS; POS., COMP. AND SUPERL. ADJS.; ABLATIVES

6.5 **Adjective Comparisons and "Degrees."** As in other languages, Latin often compares one thing to another in order to determine the relationship between someone or something. Thus, the comparison of a living dog to a dead lion in Ecclesiastes IX.4: *Mélior est canis vīvēns leōne mórtuō*, "better a living dog than a dead lion." In English, we typically make comparisons by using adjectives, that is, by adding -er to the adjective itself (e.g., tall*er*) or inserting the word "more" or "most" before the adjective (e.g., *more* tall or the *most* tall). Latin follows a very similar procedure for making comparisons, but one that is different in a few respects.

Scholars of both English and Latin classify adjectives of comparison into three forms or "degrees": (1) positive, (2) comparative, and (3) superlative. Note the example below for the adjective "holy," *sānctus*, in Latin.[9]

MASCULINE SINGULAR EXAMPLE OF ENGLISH AND LATIN ADJECTIVE "DEGREES"

Language	Positive	Comparative	Superlative
English	Holy	Hol*ier*	Hol*iest*
Latin	Sānct*us*	Sānct*ior*	Sānct*íssimus*

While English often adds -y, -[i]er, and -[i]est to the different degrees of adjectives, Latin normally adds -us, -ior, and -issimus true or -imus to its.[10]

(1) Positives. Positive adjectives are adjectives that stand alone, that is, they are not compared to someone or something else. I like to describe them as adjectives in plain or regular form. They are like manila envelopes. In the sentence following, the (proper) noun "Peter" is being modified by the adjective "holy," but the adjective is not being compared to anything in particular—neither to Paul, nor to another apostle, nor to anyone else. It is simply describing Peter.

<u>Sānctus</u> Petrus aetérnō anathémate damnávit. (Alcuin of York)[11]

<u>Holy</u> Peter has condemned him with an everlasting anathema.

Adjectives that are not compared to anything are considered to be in the "positive degree." Although we have refrained from introducing this phrase until now, we learned about positive adjectives in the previous *capítulum*. How so? Everything we previously learned about adjectives was actually about "positive" adjectives, but I simply did not use the term because it was not necessary then. But now that we are making comparisons, it is necessary. In this way, we are familiar with all their forms since all regular or stand-alone adjectives are "positive" adjectives, that is, adjectives of the "positive degree."

There is nothing additional to mention about positive adjectives other than repeating the rules of ("positive") adjective formation from the last *capítulum*. In short, 2-1-2 adjectives acquire their masculine endings from the second declension, their feminine endings from the first declension, and their neuter endings from the second declension. Meanwhile, 3-3-3 adjectives obtain all of their case endings from third-declension forms. After identifying the base of the adjective, we simply remove the genitive singular ending and add the corresponding endings for 2-1-2 or 3-3-3 adjectives, respectively.

---

9. The chart only contains the nominative masculine singular forms. A complete chart appears later in this chapter.
10. Once again, we must recognize that this is for a masculine singular adjective, and also for a 2-1-2 adjective rather than a 3-3-3 adjective, which will be different in the "positive" degree.
11. Alcuin of York, *Epístula* LIV (PL 100.220).

(2) Comparatives. Comparative adjectives are adjectives that compare one noun to another. Whereas such adjectives are formed in English by adding -[i]er to the adjective or placing the word "more" in front of it—thus, "holi*er*" or "*more* holy," respectively—in Latin we add -ior to masculine and feminine bases and -ius to neuter ones. Thus: *sānctus → sā́nctior → sā́nctius*.

We may translate Latin comparatives into English by adding -[i]er to the end, or suffix, of the adjective or by inserting the word "more" or "rather" in front of it.

Nēmō sā́nctior vīxit in lēge. (Bruno of Cologne)[12]	No one has lived holier according to the law. No one has lived more holy according to the law.

When it comes to their precise forms, comparative adjectives follow the third-declension endings, even if an adjective is a 2-1-2 adjective in the "positive degree" (as is the case with *sānctus, sāncta, sānctum*). As we learned from the previous *capítulum*, this means (1) two-form nominative singulars use two nominative forms—one for the masculine and feminine, which is identical, but another for the neuter—and (2) 3-3-3 adjectives are those that adopt third-declension endings. This explains why the nominative comparative forms mentioned above are *sā́nctior, sā́nctior, sā́nctius*. The first two forms, which are the same, are the masculine and feminine forms; while the last one is the neuter form.

At the same time, keep in mind what we discussed in the previous *capítulum*: Adjectives—whatever their declension family—may, and do, modify nouns from *any* declension family. This always throws beginner students for a loop. The new "degrees" that we are learning now do not alter that rule. In brief, comparative adjectives modify nouns of all five declensions but employ third-declension endings (again, even if they use second-declension forms in the "positive degree").

As we know well, we generate (noun and adjective) case endings by removing the genitive singular ending, inserting the comparative infix, and adding each particular case ending. What is the genitive singular ending for comparatives? It is -ió́ris. Therefore, in order to generate or recognize a comparative adjective, we simply remove this genitive singular ending, insert the suffix -iōr-, and then add our case endings for the third declension.

Steps to Form Comparative Adjectives
1. Select an adjective (e.g., *fēlīx, fēlīx, fēlīx*, "happy").
2. Determine its base by removing the -is from the genitive masculine singular of the (positive) adjective (e.g., *fēlīciṓris → *fēlīc*).
3. Insert the suffix -iōr- (e.g., *fēlī́cior, fēlī́cior, fēlī́cius*, etc.).[13]
4. Add the 3-3-3 endings as needed (e.g., *fēlī́cior*,[14] *fēlīcióris, fēlīcióri*, etc.), highlighted in bold in the following chart.

We have discussed these case endings in depth in previous *capítula*, so there is nothing new to learn here. Naturally, there are always exceptions to general rules, but the case endings you see here are representative of the basic formation of the comparative adjective.

---
12. Bruno of Cologne, *Expositiō in Omnēs Epístolās Paulī*, "Ad Rōmǎnōs" III (PL 153.37).
13. As we will see frequently, long vowels shorten before words ending in -r, which is why the nominative has a short -o.
14. Remember that the nominative singular is somewhat unpredictable. In this instance, nothing is added.

Notice that, unlike positive adjectives of the third declension, comparative adjectives do not use i-stem endings.

SĀNCTIOR, SĀNCTIOR, SĀNCTIUS (3-3-3), "HOLIER/MORE HOLY" (BASE: SĀNCT-)

Case	Masculine	Feminine	Neuter
Nominative Sg	sā́nctior	sā́nctior	sā́nctius[a]
Genitive Sg	sānctió̄ris	sānctió̄ris	sānctió̄ris
Dative Sg	sānctió̄ri	sānctió̄ri	sānctió̄ri
Accusative Sg	sānctió̄rem	sānctió̄rem	sā́nctius
Ablative Sg	sānctió̄re	sānctió̄re	sānctió̄re
Nominative Pl	sānctió̄rēs	sānctió̄rēs	sānctió̄ra
Genitive Pl	sānctió̄rum	sānctió̄rum	sānctió̄rum
Dative Pl	sānctió̄ribus	sānctió̄ribus	sānctió̄ribus
Accusative Pl	sānctió̄rēs	sānctió̄rēs	sānctió̄ra
Ablative Pl	sānctió̄ribus	sānctió̄ribus	sānctió̄ribus

[a] You can expect the -ius ending for the neuter in the singular form (both nominative and accusative) and, of course, the -a ending in the nominative and accusative plural forms. Even super-duper adjectives like the comparatives and superlatives have to bend the knee to neuter rules.

(3) Superlatives. Superlative adjectives are adjectives that compare three or more nouns, or simply wish to attribute a very high quality. They are the granddaddy of adjectives. When making such comparisons, the superlative takes the adjective to the highest degree, thus describing the noun as the "most" of something: "the most faithful," *fīdíssimus*, "the holiest," *sānctíssimus*, and "the happiest," *fēlīcíssimus*. When translating Latin superlative adjectives into English, we typically insert the word "most" in front of the adjective, though there are some words that allow the letters -iest to be added to the endings: "holiest," "happiest," but "most faithful" rather than "*faithfuliest," since the latter is not an English word (at least according to my elementary teacher).

Just as comparative adjectives use only 3-3-3 case endings, so superlative adjectives use only 2-1-2 adjectives. So even if an adjective in the positive degree employs 3-3-3 case endings, it will switch to 2-1-2 endings when used as a superlative. Wait, what did I just write? Yes, we have to change from 3-3-3 case endings for comparatives to 2-1-2 case endings for superlatives—regardless of what case endings an adjective follows in the "positive" degree.

To make a superlative adjective, we simply remove the genitive (masculine) singular form and add the requisite infix and case endings.

Steps to Form Superlative Adjectives
1. Select an adjective (e.g., *fēlīx, fēlīx, fēlīx*, "happy").
2. Determine its base by removing the -is from the genitive masculine singular of the (positive) adjective (e.g., *fēlīcíssimī* → *fēlic*).
3. Insert the suffix -issim- (e.g., *fēlīcissim, *fēlīcissim, *fēlīcissim*, etc.).
4. Add the 2-1-2 endings as needed (e.g., *fēlīcíssim**us**, fēlīcíssim**ī**, fēlīcíssim**ō***, etc.), highlighted in bold below.

SANCTÍSSIMUS, SANCTÍSSIMA, SANCTÍSSIMUM (2-1-2), "HOLIEST/MOST HOLY" (BASE: SĀNCT-)

Case	Masculine	Feminine	Neuter
Nominative Sg	sānctíssimus	sānctíssima	sānctíssimum
Genitive Sg	sānctíssimī	sānctíssimae	sānctíssimī
Dative Sg	sānctíssimō	sānctíssimae	sānctíssimō
Accusative Sg	sānctíssimum	sānctíssimam	sānctíssimum
Ablative Sg	sānctíssimō	sānctíssimā	sānctíssimō
Nominative Pl	sānctíssimī	sānctíssimae	sānctíssima
Genitive Pl	sānctissimórum	sānctissimárum	sanctissimórum
Dative Pl	sānctíssimīs	sānctíssimīs	sānctíssimīs
Accusative Pl	sānctíssimōs	sānctíssimās	sānctíssima
Ablative Pl	sānctíssimīs	sānctíssimīs	sānctíssimīs

Here is an example:

In tálibus sepúlcrīs nóluit mórtuum suum sepelíre sānctíssimus Patriárcha (Bernard of Clairvaux).[15]

The <u>holiest</u> patriarch did not want to bury his dead in such graves.
The <u>most holy</u> patriarch did not want to bury his dead in such graves.

Although technically a new form, the use of the 2-1-2 case endings for the superlative adjective makes it rather straightforward to identify and nothing new to master. Even better, the characteristic suffix of -imus is easily recognizable and even easier to generate all remaining case endings.

IRREGULAR ADJECTIVE COMPARISONS

Perhaps the most common adjective in English is "good, better, best"—an adjective, we clearly see, that is irregular. While we might expect the forms "good, *gooder, *goodest," we encounter two completely different forms in the comparative and superlative degrees.

This same type of irregular pattern also occurs in Latin. The adjective "good, better, best" in Latin is *bonus, mélior, óptimus*—not *bonus,* **bónior,* *boníssimus. Rather than looking for a rule to learn, it's best simply to recognize that many of the most common adjectives have irregular forms in Latin.[16] Here are the most common irregular adjectives in their nominative masculine singular forms. Though irregular, they follow the same declension forms as regular adjectives.

---

15. Bernard of Clairvaux, *Meditátiō in Passiónem et Resurrēctiónem Dóminī* IX (PL 184.755).
16. Moreover, there are several "defective" adjectives of comparison in Latin, which may lack a "positive," "comparative," or "superlative" degree, and/or make use of irregular forms when filling in those *lacúnae*, "absences." Rather than listing all such adjectives, it is best simply to be aware that defective adjectives do occur in Latin (as in English). For instance, the adjective *novus, -, novíssimus* does not have a comparative form—which we would surmise to be *nóvior. To say "newer" in Latin, we say *recéntior* (from the "positive" adjective *recēns*) rather than *nóvior.

- *bonus, mélior, óptimus*, "good, better, best"
- *malus, peior, péssimus*, "bad, worse, worst"
- *magnus, maior, máximus*, "great, greater, greatest"
- *multus, plūs, plúrimus*, "much/many, more, most/very many"
- *parvus, minor, mínimus*, "small, smaller, smallest"

THE GOSPEL OF COMPARATIVE ADJECTIVES

1. Positives are un-compared adjectives, which use both 2-1-2 and 3-3-3 case endings.
2. Comparatives are adjectives comparing two nouns, which use only 3-3-3 case endings.
3. Superlatives are adjectives that compare three or more nouns or simply attribute a high degree to an adjective, which use only 2-1-2 case endings.

6.6 **Comparatives, Superlatives, and Quam.** When comparing adjectives in Latin, the word *quam* is sometimes used. Although this Latin word can be translated in several ways, it should be translated as "than" when used in a comparative manner—whether in the comparative or superlative degree. In this regard, it is very similar to the way English uses "than" when comparing one thing to another. Thus, we see below the use of the comparative adjective *mélius*, "better," used in conjunction with the word *quam*, "than."

Sánguinis sparsiónem mélius loquéntem quam Abel. (Heb. XII.24)

The sprinkling of [Jesus's] blood speaks better than [the blood] of Abel.[17]

6.7 **Ablative of Comparison.** When Latin compares one thing to another, it may use the ablative case to do so. This use of the ablative is called the "ablative of comparison," and its usage informs us that the case forms we learned in the first *capítulum* possess a greater range of meaning than initially indicated.

We learned in the Capítulum I, for example, that most of the cases require the use of a preposition when translating Latin into English. For the ablative case, I recommended inserting the word "about," "by," "from," "in," "on," or "with" before the noun. This is still true, but all cases—including the ablative—may also be translated into English in other ways based on the word's function in any given context.

One of these additional ways to translate the ablative case, as mentioned above, is called the "ablative of comparison." As its name implies, Latin places the second of two nouns in the ablative case when the initial noun or adjective is used in either the nominative or accusative case. For example:

Quid enim mélius Deō?
(Rufinus of Aquileia)[18]

For what is better than God?

---

17. Do not worry if you say that I have translated the accusative as if it were a nominative. We are abbreviating this sentence for the sake of the example. Focus on the use of *quam*.
18. Rufinus of Aquileia, "Psalmus" XXXIV.9, in *Psalmos LXXV Commentárius* (PL 21.769).

Consider another example:

Multis passéribus meliōrēs estis vōs. (Matt. X.31)	You all are more valuable than many sparrows.

While the pronoun *vōs*, "you all," is in the nominative case, the noun and adjective modifying it, *passer*, "sparrow," and *multus*, "many," are in the ablative case (*passéribus* and *multis*).

Does it feel like this *capítulum* will continue *ad naúseam*? Not to worry—we have arrived at the end. Good job with working through so much material!

Summárium

In this *capítulum* you have learned that:
- Fourth-declension nouns are those nouns that end in -ūs in the genitive singular.
- Most fourth-declension nouns are masculine, some are feminine, and a very few are neuter.
- The different "degrees" of adjectives are positive, comparative, and superlative. The positives use both 2-1-2 and 3-3-3 case endings; comparatives use only 3-3-3 endings; and superlatives use only 2-1-2 endings.
- The word *quam* may appear in Latin when comparing things.

VOCĀBULŌRUM INDEX

Latin	English (Gloss)	(Etymology)
advéntus, advéntūs (m)[a]	coming, arrival, approach	(advent)
afféctus, afféctūs (m)	devotion, love, affection	(affection)
aspéctus, aspéctūs (m)	appearance, sight	(aspect)
concéptus, concéptūs (m)	conception, embryo	(concept)
cōnspéctus, cōnspéctūs (m)	sight, presence, view	(conspicuous)
cornū, cornūs (n)	horn	(cornucopia)
cultus, cultūs (m)	worship, church service	(cult)
domus, domūs (f)[b]	home, house, household	(domicile)
exércitus, exércitūs (m)	army, host	(exercise)
frūctus, frūctūs (m)	fruit, crop, outcome, produce	(fruit)
genū, genūs (n)[c]	knee	(genuflect)
gradus, gradūs (m)	step, degree, rank, position	(grade)
hábitus, hábitūs (m)	habit, appearance, garment	(habit)
intelléctus, intelléctūs (m)	reason, understanding, intellect	(intellect)
manus, manūs (f)	hand	(manual)

FOURTH-DECLENSION NOUNS; POS., COMP. AND SUPERL. ADJS.; ABLATIVES

metus, metūs (m)	fear, dread	(meticulous)
nātus, nātūs (m)[d]	child, son, offspring	(neonatal)
pōtus, pōtūs (m)	drink	(potable)
rītus, rītūs (m)	ceremony, rite	(ritual)
sēnsus, sēnsūs (m)	feeling, sentiment, sense	(sense)
spíritus, spíritūs (m)	spirit, breath, wind	(spirit)
tractátus, tractátūs (m)	treatment, treatise, tract	(tract)
tribus, tribūs (f)	tribe	(tribe)
ūsus, ūsūs (m)	practice, skill, use	(use)
vultus, vultūs (m)	countenance, face, expression	

[a] As mentioned earlier, the -ū in all fourth-declension genitive singulars is long. Therefore, when memorizing vocabulary, you could hold the characteristic genitive singular vowel slightly longer than the nominative form, making it easier to distinguish the two forms. In other words, a native Latin speaker would immediately hear a difference between the two forms due to the nominative masculine and feminine being short and all the genitive forms being long.

[b] This noun also appears as a second declension noun as *domus, domī* (f), with no difference in meaning.

[c] Be careful not to confuse this with the third-declension noun *genus, géneris* (n), "nation," "race," "people."

[d] The feminine form is *nāta, nātae* (f), a first-declension noun that is translated as "daughter."

ŌRÁTIŌ POPULÁRIS

Agnus Deī. The "Lamb of God" prayer is brief and beloved in the Latin tradition. Adapted from John 1.29, it is traditionally prayed during the liturgy.

Agnus Deī, quī tollis peccáta mundī, miserére nōbīs.
Agnus Deī, quī tollis peccáta mundī, miserére nōbīs.
Agnus Deī, quī tollis peccáta mundī, dōnā nōbīs pācem.

Lamb of God, you who take away the sins of the world, have mercy on us.
Lamb of God, you who take away the sins of the world, have mercy on us.
Lamb of God, you who take away the sins of the world, grant us peace.

EXERCÍTIA

Be sure to complete the *exercítium* in the appendix corresponding to this *capítulum*.

Capítulum
VII

FIFTH-DECLENSION NOUNS, INDECLINABLE NOUNS, AND NUMBERS

Omnēs iúdicēs urbānaéque plēbēs et ártium offícia
cunctárum venerábilī <u>diē sōlis</u> quiéscant.[1]
—CŌDEX JUSTĪNIÁNUS

OPÚSCULUM THEOLÓGICUM: *Constantine and the Diēs Sōlis*

Although scholars continue to debate the *vērácitās*, "veracity," of Emperor Constantine I's faith before his deathbed baptism to Christianity in the year 337, there is no doubt that he was a longtime *patrṓnus*, "patron," of the Christian religion before his official conversion. Among many other ways he showed his patronage of Christianity, Constantine declared Sunday a day of rest in March of 321. The decree subsequently appeared in *Cōdex Justīniánus*, "Justinian's Code," part of the much larger book of Roman civil law published in the sixth century:

Omnēs iúdicēs urbānaéque plēbēs et ártium offícia cunctárum venerábilī <u>diē sōlis</u> quiéscant.	All judges, those who dwell in cities, and all workshops must rest <u>on the</u> venerable <u>day of Sunday</u>.[2]

For three hundred years, the *diēs sōlis* (literally "day of the Sun") marked the day on which Christians assembled for worship. Due to the church's growth across the Roman Empire in the fourth century, it only took a generation before this day came to be called the *diēs domínica* (as in Rev. I.10), which established this day of the week as more revered than every other day.

Like English, the word for "day" in Latin, *diēs, diḗī*, is used in conjunction with many other words. Here we will briefly examine three combined usages: (1) days of the week; (2) times of the day; and (3) biblical and Christian phrases.

To begin with, there are the seven days of the week:

Diēs sōlis—Day of the Sun (Sunday)
Diēs lūnae—Day of the Moon (Monday)

---

[1] "All judges, those who dwell in cities, and all workshops must rest <u>on the</u> venerable <u>day of Sunday</u>."
[2] *Cōdex Justīniánus* III.12.2.

FIFTH-DECLENSION NOUNS, INDECLINABLE NOUNS, AND NUMBERS

Diēs Mártis—Day of Mars (Tuesday)
Diēs Mercúriī—Day of Mercury (Wednesday)
Diēs Ióvis—Day of Jupiter (Thursday)
Diēs Véneris—Day of Venus (Friday)
Diēs Satúrnī—Day of Saturn (Saturday)

Next, there are different times of the day:

Hódiē—today
Prídiē—yesterday
Postrídiē—on the next day
Merídiēs—midday
Ante merídiem—before noon ("a.m." in English)
Post merídiem—after noon ("p.m." in English)

Finally, there are a host of biblical and Christian phrases associated with the word:

Diēs īrae—day of judgment/day of wrath
Diēs novíssimus—the last day
Diēs hebdómadis[3]—day of the week/the seventh day

For our purposes, the Latin word *diēs, diéī* and its related terms introduce the final and smallest class of Latin nouns: the fifth declension.

Prospéctus
In this *capítulum* you will learn that:
- Fifth-declension nouns are the smallest group of Latin nouns.
- Latin has nouns that do not decline, called "indeclinables."
- Numbers are divided into (1) cardinal, (2) ordinal, and (3) Roman numerals.

GRAMMÁTICA

7.1 **Fifth Class of Nouns.** We have arrived at the last family of nouns in Latin. Congratulations! All of your hard work so far has paid off. You can expect your noun diploma to arrive in the mail in the next six to eight weeks. By now, you know exactly how nouns are formed: A genitive singular case ending reveals a noun's declension, and there are always a couple of shared case endings that we have to watch out for in order to establish an accurate translation. While masculine and feminine nouns of the same declension typically utilize the same case endings, neuter nouns follow a path of their own for a few forms.

7.2 **Singular Form.** I have great news about fifth-declension nouns. Not only are there just a handful of them that appear with any regularity, but they often occur only in their singular forms,

---

3. The word *hébdomas, hebdómadis* (f) comes from a Greek word meaning "seventh," which came to represent a week since a week equals seven days.

meaning that there is much less to memorize. What's more, except for the very common word *diēs, diéī,* "day," and its related forms, all fifth-declension nouns are feminine.[4]

7.3 **Distinctives.** All genitive singular nouns that end in -eī (or -ēī) are fifth-declension nouns. This class of noun also ends in -ēs in the nominative singular.[5] The thematic vowel of -e distinguishes fifth declensions from other declensions and makes them fairly easy to recognize. To generate or identify a fifth-declension noun, all we have to do is remove the -eī (or -ēī) suffix from the genitive singular and add our particular endings to the base.

Steps to Form Fifth-Declension Nouns
1. Select a fifth-declension noun (e.g., *fidēs, fídeī,* "faith," "faithfulness").
2. Determine its base by removing the -eī ending from the genitive singular form (e.g., *fídeī* → **fid*).
3. Add fifth-declension endings to the base as needed: -ēs, -eī, -eī, -em, -ē; -ēs, -ērum, -ēbus, -ēs, -ēbus (e.g., *fidēs, fídeī, fídeī, fidem, fidē,* etc.).

CASE ENDINGS FOR FIFTH-DECLENSION NOUNS

Case	Singular	Plural
Nominative	-ēs	-ēs
Genitive	-eī; ēī	-ērum
Dative	-eī; ēī	-ēbus
Accusative	-em	-ēs
Ablative	-ē	-ēbus

As we have grown to appreciate and expect, there are various shared endings among cases, which can sometimes cause confusion. For instance, (a) the nominative singular, nominative plural, and accusative plural all end in -ēs; (b) the genitive and dative singulars both end in -eī or ēī; and (c) the dative and ablative plurals end in -ēbus.

7.4 **Feminine Example.** Because fifth-declension nouns are feminine,[6] we will only use one form in our paradigm below.

FÁCIĒS, FACIÉĪ (F), "FACE," "FORM," "APPEARANCE" (BASE: FACI-)

Case	Singular	Plural
Nominative	fácies	faciés
Genitive	faciéī	faciérum
Dative	faciéī	faciébus
Accusative	fáciem	fáciēs
Ablative	fáciē	faciébus

---

4. As we will see below, *diēs, diéī* can be either masculine or feminine depending on the exact circumstances.
5. Of course, a nominative singular ending of -ēs is not enough to determine that a noun is in the fifth declension; we need to confirm such a suspicion with the genitive singular ending.
6. Once again, the one common exception to this rule is the noun *diēs, diéī,* which is masculine; however, when combined with specific

Note, particularly, the thematic vowel of -e. This is the best (though not error-free) clue when identifying this class of nouns. Any cause for confusion of case endings is mentioned above. The distinctive endings are in bold.

Let us look at an example, which contains two instances of the noun *fáciēs, faciḗī*:

Neque enim fidélēs olim ália dē causā **fáciem** Deī in sānctuáriō quárere iussī sunt, idque tótiēs repétitur in lēge, nisi quia lēgis doctrína et prophéticae exhortātiónēs erant illīs vīva Deī imágō, sícutī Paulus in suā praedicatióne lūcére ásserit glóriam Deī in **fáciē** Christī (John Calvin).[7]	For no other reason were the faithful in former times commanded to seek the face of God in the sanctuary— a command so often repeated in the law—than because the teaching of the law and the prophetic exhortations were to them the living image of God, just as Paul in his preaching asserts that God's glory shone in the face of Christ.

INDECLINABLE NOUNS

7.5 **Unclassified Nouns.** We learned in the first *capítulum* that all nouns in Latin fall into one of five boringly named classes or declensions: first, second, third, fourth, and fifth. Though accurate, there is a group of nouns that do not follow this rule. These nouns are called "indeclinable nouns," which means that they do not decline (or, at least, not in the way we expect). Despite the intimidating description, indeclinable nouns only utilize one form for all cases—that's right, you only have to memorize one form instead of the usual ten (or fourteen forms if we take into consideration the vocative and locative cases).

As we might expect, indeclinable nouns do not follow the standard rules for the simple reason that many are foreign words that entered Latin at some point in the past. Due to the Hebraic influence upon Christianity, many of the indeclinable words that we encounter in ecclesiastical Latin derive from Hebrew, the language of the Old Testament.[8] For reasons that do not concern us here, some names in Hebrew were incorporated into Latin noun declensions while others were not. Consider the following examples:

1. *María, Maríae* (f) became a first-declension noun.
2. *Petrus, Petrī* (m) became a second-declension noun.
3. *Iōánnēs, Iōánnis* (m) became a third-declension noun.
4. *Iēsus, Iēsū* (m) became a fourth-declension noun.
5. *Dāvīd, Dāvīd* (m) became an indeclinable noun.
6. *Moÿsēs, Moÿsēs* [*Moÿsis*] (m) became an irregular declension.[9]

---

days and dates, the gender usually changes to feminine, as in *diēs domínica*. Regardless, however, *diēs, diḗī* shares the same case endings with masculine forms.

7. John Calvin, *Instítūtiō Chrīstiánae Religiónis* IV.1.5 (CR 30.750–51).

8. The same is true for other foreign words as well, such as Greek words, though many Greek words were distributed across the first three declensions in Latin.

9. The bracket indicates that you will see more than one form. Proper nouns like this from other languages can appear in great variety, so we have to take them with a grain of salt. This name, in particular, has alternative spellings, so do not be surprised if you see it spelled differently.

7.6 **Not Standardized.** Perhaps a source of confusion, while some Latin authors may decline a certain Hebrew proper noun, others may not. This is true even within the same text. In the Vulgate, for instance, Tobit VI.22 reads: *in sémine Ábrahae,* "in the seed of Abraham," while VII.15 reads *Deus Ábrahām,* "the God of Abraham." What kind of linguistic sorcery is taking place here? Despite the fact that both instances concerning Abraham are genitives (hence "of Abraham"), the first was declined and the second was not. These kinds of inconsistencies are very common in ancient writings before professional editors were introduced into the publishing enterprise and saved the world from literary malfeasance. In my opinion, when it comes to foreign names, just take them and their declension patterns *cum grānō salis,* "with a grain of salt."

7.7 **Different Spelling and Different Gender.** There are also slight differences in foreign words when it comes to spelling. The word *Hierúsalēm* "Jerusalem," for example, may be declined as a first- or second-declension noun, and there are any number of potential spellings employed (I will typically use the spelling *Jerúsalēm,* but do not be surprised if you see something different in primary texts).[10] What's more, indeclinable nouns may occur in any gender. Thus, *Beélzebub,* "Beelzebub," is masculine; *Capharnáum,* "Capernaum," is feminine; and *Hierúsalēm,* is neuter.

7.8 **Suggested Practice.** There are too many Hebrew-based indeclinable Latin words to mention in one list, but they are especially common as place names and proper names: *Abiáthār, Béthlehem, Ephráim, Iehóva[h], Hierúsalēm,* etc. Here is what I recommend: When you encounter a Hebrew name in Latin,[11] remind yourself that there is a good possibility that it is not declinable—or at least not as consistently as you might expect. Although you should attempt to identify its case, do not be surprised if it does not appear to make sense (in which instance it is probably indeclinable). Although this sounds intimidating, you will get used to it, and you will come to anticipate such words that do not follow a predictable pattern. Here is an example:

Sīcut suprā jam díximus, per Dāvīd fidélis ánima accipítur. (Gregory I)[12]	As I already stated above, a faithful spirit is received through David.

Even though you may not understand all of the words in this sentence, you know enough to identify how *Dāvīd* is used. How so? Since we can surmise that *Dāvīd* is originally a Hebrew term,[13] we should already anticipate that it will be indeclinable. So, the word itself will help us by context, not form. There are two clues in this sentence: first, context (which only becomes clearer as we learn more words); and, second, an accompanying preposition. In the present example, the preposition *per* indicates that the name *Dāvīd* is used here to show agency since this preposition carries that meaning with the name of persons. As you see, context will always unlock the meaning.

LETTERS IN LATIN

Letters in Latin, of whatever language, are not declined. This means, for example, that *a* (in Latin) or *alpha* (in Greek) will not be declined when used in a sentence.

---

10. Truth is, this word can sometimes appear in the singular, sometimes the plural; and sometimes feminine, sometimes neuter. But this is not the norm for indeclinable words, and it's a very recognizable word regardless of its form.
11. In general, we should assume that names from the Old Testament have Hebrew origins.
12. Gregory I, "In Secúndum Psalmum Poeniteniálem," in *Expositiō in Septem Psalmōs Poenitentiálēs* (PL 79.558).
13. We surmise this not only because it is in the Bible, but specifically because it is in the Hebrew Bible.

FIFTH-DECLENSION NOUNS, INDECLINABLE NOUNS, AND NUMBERS

NUMERALS / NUMBERS

7.9 **Numerals / Numbers.** Despite initial appearances, indeclinable nouns are actually our *amīcī*, "friends," since they do not require us to learn another set of case endings. The same holds true for the first class of Latin numerals or numbers, which are called "cardinals" (from *cardō, cárdinis*, "hinge"). With a few exceptions, cardinal numbers are indeclinable adjectives. Another class of numerals, called "ordinals" (from *ōrdō, ŏrdinis*, "order" or "rank"), follow first- and second-declension endings. Finally, so-called "Roman" numerals represent the numbers ancient Romans used when writing numbers. We will organize our discussion of numbers into three parts: (1) cardinal, (2), ordinal, and (3) Roman numerals.

(1) Cardinal Numerals. Cardinal numerals are the ones we use when counting: "one," "two," "three," etc. Apart from the numbers "one," "two," and "three," most cardinal numbers in Latin from one to 100 (as well as 1,000) are indeclinable adjectives.[14] This means that most cardinal numerals are not modified according to case, number, or gender. What you see in one form is essentially what you get in all of them.

> Ūnus diēs apud Dóminum sīcut mīlle
> anni et mīlle anni sīcut diēs ūnus.
> (II Pet. III.8)

> One day with the Lord is like 1,000
> years, and 1,000 years are like one day.

Note that *ūnus* is declined in accordance with the case, number, and gender of the noun *diēs* while *mīlle* is indeclinable.[15]

(2) Ordinal Numerals. Ordinal numerals are numerals ranked in order: "first," "second," "third." Naturally, there are as many ordinal numbers as there are cardinal ones. Unlike cardinal numbers, however, ordinals are declined as 2-1-2 adjectives. They therefore follow the word endings that we have already encountered: -us, -a, -um.

> Prīmus ex géntibus Hierosólymae
> Mārcus epíscopus cōnstitúitur.
> (Ado of Vienne)[16]

> Marcus was established as the first
> bishop in Jerusalem from among
> the Gentiles.

Here the cardinal for "first" ends in -us because the noun it modifies (*epíscopus*) is a masculine singular noun of the second declension.

(3) Roman Numerals. Roman numerals are the numbers Romans used when writing. While the first four numerals (I, II, III, IV) represent a single *dígitus* "finger," on the hand, the numeral for five (V) and ten (X) signify one hand and two hands, respectively. Larger numbers such as 100 (*centum*) and 1,000 (*mīlle*) were represented by the first letters of the word—hence "C" for 100 and "M" for 1,000.

When reading Latin, we will perhaps come across Roman numerals most often in the front matter and table of contents in books. However, for the sake of getting used to Roman numerals, I have slightly altered citation conventions in this book to always include the first book, section, or chapter in Roman numerals. The example from the index of the book below,

---

14. The numerals "one," "two," and "three" naturally represent incomplete forms, as "one" is always singular and "two" and "three" are always plural (although "two" used to possess a dual number that fell into disuse). While "one" is declined as a 2-1-2 adjective with -ius in the genitive (*ūnus, ūna, ūnum*), "two" (*duo, duae, duo*) and "three" (*trēs, trēs, tria*) follow irregular patterns. "Two" in Latin makes use of a characteristic -o in its forms while "three" resembles a two-form nominative third-declension noun.

15. When in the singular form (as in the example), *mīlle* is not declined; in the plural, however, it is. It is a semi-indeclinable numeral. Sorry, I don't make the rules. I only enforce them.

16. Ado of Vienne, *Chrónicon* VI (PL 124.82).

for instance—William Perkins's *Cathólicus Refōrmắtus*—indicates that it was printed in the year MDCIII, that is, 1603. And here is a sample of the table of contents from one of William Perkins's books.[17]

Index Cápitum Religiṓnis Contrōversiắrum quae in hoc librō tractắntur
    I. Dē līberō arbítriō
   II. Dē peccắtō orīginắlī
  III. Dē certitǘdine salǘtis
  IV. Dē iūstificātiṓne
   V. Dē mérītīs
  VI. Dē satisfactiṓnibus prō peccắtīs
 VII. Dē trāditiṓnibus
VIII. Dē vōtīs
  IX. Dē imāgínibus
   X. Dē reắlī praeséntiā

Index of Disputed Topics of Religion Handled in This Book
1. Free Will
2. Original Sin
3. The Certainty of Salvation
4. Justification
5. Merits
6. Satisfactions for Sins
7. Traditions
8. Vows
9. Images
10. The Real Presence

You are bound to come across Latin numerals quite regularly in writings (the nature of the topic at hand will naturally determine how often they are used), and it is good practice to begin converting numbers and dates into Roman numerals.

TÁBULA NÚMERĪ, "TABLE OF NUMBERS"

Roman Numerals (Arabic Numerals)	Cardinal Numerals (Largely Indeclinable)	Ordinal Numbers (2-1-2 Endings)
I (1)	ūnus, ūna, ūnum	prīmus, prīma, prīmum
II (2)	duo, duae, duo	secúndus, secúnda, secúndum
III (3)	trēs, trēs, tria	tértius, tértia, tértium
IV (4)	quáttuor	quārtus, quārtua quārtum
V (5)	quīnque	quīntus, quīnta, quīntum
VI (6)	sex	sextus, sexta, sextum
VII (7)	septem	séptimus, séptima, séptimum

---
17. William Perkins, *Cathólicus Refōrmắtus* (Hanau, Germany: William Antonius, 1603), index.

FIFTH-DECLENSION NOUNS, INDECLINABLE NOUNS, AND NUMBERS

VIII (8)	octō	octávus, octáva, octávum
IX (9)	novem	nōnus, nōna, nōnum
X (10)	decem	décimus, décima, décimum
XX (20)	vīgíntī	vīcésimus, vīcésima, vīcésimum
L (50)	quīnquāgíntā	quīnquāgésimus, quīnquāgésima, quīnquāgésimum
C (100)	centum	centésimus, centésima, centésimum
D (500)	quīngéntī	quīngentésimus, quīngentésima, quīngentésimum
M (1000)	mīlle	mīllésimus, mīllésima, mīllésimum

Summárium

In this *capítulum* you learned that:
- Fifth-declension nouns are those nouns that end in -eī (or -ēī) in the genitive singular.
- All fifth-declension nouns except for one are feminine.
- Latin has nouns that do not decline, called "indeclinables."
- There are various numerals in Latin, some of which are cardinals, ordinals, and Roman numerals.

VOCĀBULŌRUM INDEX

Latin	English (Gloss)	(Etymology)
áciēs, aciéī (f)	sharpness, edge, line of sight or battle	(acidic)
adhūc	still, yet, now, as, thus far	
bis	twice, two times	(bicycle)
centum	one hundred	(century)
dēprecátiō, dēprecātiónis (f)	prayer, deprecation	(deprecating)
diēs, diéī (m)	day	(day)
duo, duae, duo	two	(duet)
effígiēs, effigéī (f)	image, figure, likeness	(effigy)
fidēs, fídeī (f)	faith, faithfulness	(fideism)
hódiē	today	
mīlle	one thousand	(millennium)
ōrátiō, ōrātiónis (f)	prayer, speech, sentence	(oration)

(cont.)

Latin	English (Gloss)	(Etymology)
parvus, parva, parvum	small, little, cheap	
prex, precis (f)[a]	prayer, request, entreaty	(imprecatory)
prídiē	day before	
prōgéniēs, prōgeniéī (f)	race, progeny, offspring	(progeny)
prīmus, prīma, prīmum	first	(primal)
quam	than, as	
rēs, reī (f)	thing	(reify)
secúndus, secúnda, secúndum	second	(second)
spéciēs, speciéī (f)	species, form, appearance	(species)
spēs, speī (f)	hope	
trēs, trēs, tria	three	(tricycle)
ūnus, ūna, ūnum	one	(unicycle)
vīsus, vīsūs (m)	sight, vision	(vision)

[a] If you have been counting, you will have noticed the introduction of three (feminine) third-declension nouns all meaning "prayer." As indicated in the translations, they each mean something slightly different, but each can also be translated as "prayer" in English. However, ōrātio is probably the most generic of the three, which is why it will be used as a section in each *capítulum* for "prayer."

ŌRÁTIŌ POPULÁRIS

Ōrátiō Fátimae. The "Fátima Prayers" are a series of prayers that emerged out of the Marian apparitions occuring within the Catholic Church in Fátima, Portugal in 1917. Here is one of the prayers.

Ō mī Iēsū,	My Jesus,
Dīmítte nōbīs peccáta nostra.	Forgive us our sins.
Cōnsérvā nōs ab īgne īnférnī.	Protect us from the fire of hell.
Condūc in caelum omnēs ánimās,	Lead all souls into heaven,
Praesértim illās quae misericórdiae tuae máximē índigent.	Especially those who most need your mercy.

EXERCÍTIA

Be sure to complete the *exercítium* in the appendix corresponding to this *capítulum*.

SECÚNDA PARS

INDICATIVE MOOD VERBS: FIRST *and* SECOND PRINCIPAL PARTS

Secúnda Pars introduces us to the engines of all sentences: verbs. Although we will focus here only on the indicative mood—the mood of factuality and reality—we will begin by learning the four principal parts before then turning to the present, imperfect, and future tenses. Because they modify verbs, we will also devote time to adverbs.

It is important always to learn each of the four principal parts of every verb. These specific parts will later be used to form additional tenses and moods. As for the three verb tenses that we will learn in Secúnda Pars, the present tense refers to an ongoing action taking place in the present, the imperfect is the past continuous tense, while the future tense indicates an ongoing future event. Each of these tenses occurs in both active and passive voices, meaning the subject is either performing an action (active voice) or receiving it (passive voice).

The three tenses you will learn here—present, imperfect, and future—are formed from the first principal part. They are all part of the so-called present system.

Capítulum
VIII

VERBS AND FOUR PRINCIPAL PARTS

Crēdō in Deum Patrem . . . et [credō] in Iēsum Christum . . .
et [credō] in Spíritum Sānctum.¹
—SÝMBOLUM APOSTÓLORUM

OPÚSCULUM THEOLÓGICUM: *Crēdō and Creeds*

Christianity has always been about beliefs. The apostle Paul, perhaps quoting an existing statement of faith or hymn, wrote in his letter to the Romans:

*Sī cōnfiteáris in ōre tuō Dóminum Iēsum et in corde tuō crēdíderis quod Deus illum excitávit ex mórtuīs salvus eris.*²	If you confess with your mouth that Jesus is Lord and believe in your heart that God raised him from the dead, you will be saved.

Decades earlier, when a despairing man presented his deaf child to Jesus after the disciples were unable to offer relief, the boy's father confessed faith in Jesus's power to heal with one word: *crēdō*, "I believe."³

As Christianity developed, it never lost its emphasis on belief. The countless statements of faith that emerged out of the biblical text highlight how important a role belief has played in the Christian life. In fact, due to the initial verb appearing in the opening lines of these faith statements, many of us call these documents "creeds" rather than "statements of faith." Since the word *creed* derives from the Latin verb *crēdō, crēdere, crēdidī, crēditus*, "to believe," theologian Alistair McGrath defines it as an "attempt to summarize the main points of what Christians believe."⁴ Creeds, in other words, are where belief and confession intersect. Whether in the Apostles' Creed, the Nicene Creed, or declarations emerging from countless churches and councils, creeds convey the Christian faith in both confessional and public language.

In the Western Christian tradition, the Apostles' Creed is probably the most well-known creed used today. Originally believed to have its origins in the faith of the twelve apostles—hence the name *Sýmbolum Apostólorum*, "symbol [or creed] of the apostles"—the Apostles' Creed confesses faith in the

---

1. "I believe in God the Father . . . and I believe in Jesus Christ . . . and I believe in the Holy Spirit."
2. Rom. X.9–10.
3. Mark IX.24.
4. Alistair McGrath, *Apostles' Creed* (Downers Grove, IL: InterVarsity Press, 2016), 5.

INDICATIVE MOOD VERBS: FIRST AND SECOND PRINCIPAL PARTS

Holy Trinity by use of the Latin verb *crēdō*, "I believe." Although the Latin verb only appears explicitly in the first sentence about God the Father, it is implied for the other members of the Trinity as well: *Jēsus Chrīstus* and the *Spīritus Sānctus*. In the original Latin, those lines are:

Crēdō in Deum Patrem omnipoténtem...	I believe in God the Father Almighty.
Et [crēdō] in Jēsum Chrīstum...	And [I believe] in Jesus Christ...
Et [crēdō] in Spíritum Sānctum.[5]	And [I believe] in the Holy Spirit.

The Apostles' Creed was affirmed by countless Christian fathers, including bishops such as Cyprian, Augustine, Ambrose, and Gregory. Regardless of the regional differences in faith and practice, belief in God the Father, God the Son, and God the Holy Spirit has characterized the body of believers all across the globe.

In this *capítulum*, we will witness the power of verbs such as *crēdō* in the Latin language. Illustrating action and activity, verbs bring everything else in a sentence together.

> **Prospéctus**
> In this *capitulum* you will learn that:
> - A verb is the engine of a language. It expresses action.
> - There are four regular classes (or "conjugations") of Latin verbs: first, second, third, and fourth. (The fifth class, which is irregular, will be discused in a subsequent *capítulum*.)
> - Each verb should be memorized according to its four principal parts.

GRAMMÁTICA

8.1 Overview of Verbs. This *capítulum* introduces verbs, one of the most essential grammatical features of any language. Because verbs are so important, so pervasive, and so varied, we will dedicate many *capítula* to them. As such, there is no need to memorize all of the material presented now. For the time being, simply breathe in the essence of the *capítulum* as if you were inhaling a fresh ocean breeze. In fact, feel free to read it on the beach before turning to subsequent *capítula*. Observe patterns and make note of anything that you will want to review in subsequent lessons.

8.2 Action Words. Who doesn't love verbs? They convey action. They get things done. They indicate existence. Deriving from the Latin word *verbum*, "word," verbs are like engines in a car, brains in a body, and batteries in a flashlight. Without them, there is no movement, no action, and no life. Without verbs, there is no real sentence. There is nothing more than a puddle of stagnating words.

With verbs come life. For instance, when Jesus stated in John VII.38, *quī crēdit in mē sīcut dīxit scrīptūra flūmina dē ventre eius fluent aquae vīvae*, "the one who believes in me, as Scripture has said, 'from his stomach will flow rivers of living water,'" all of the action words —"believe" (*crēdit*), "said," (*dīxit*), and "flow" (*fluent*)—are verbs. They keep the flow of thought moving along like a rapid river. Without these verbs, the sentence is a motionless pool.

---

5. Philip Schaff, *The Greek and Latin Creeds*, vol. 2 of *The Creeds of Christendom* (New York: Harper, 1905), 47. In the Nicene Creed, the verb changes from first-person singular (*crēdō*, "I believe") to first-person plural (*crédimus*, "we believe").

8.3 **Five Characteristics of Verbs.** Because of their *grávitās*, verbs carry a lot of "weight" in sentences. For our purposes, verbs indicate five features about themselves every time they are used: person, number, tense, mood, and voice (abbreviated in this book as P, N, T, M, V). The information below may appear daunting at first but remember that this *capítulum* serves as a general overview of verbs, which subsequent *capítula* will unpack in more detail. Keep in mind, also, that verbs follow an existing pattern that we have witnessed with nouns and adjectives: The numerous endings of Latin words are more varied than English ones but there is sense and order to Latin sentences.

1. **Person (*Persŏna*).** This refers to the "person" doing the action in a sentence. The grammatical phenomenon of *person* answers the question, "who is doing the action?" There are three kinds of performers.
    i. *First person*: the person(s) speaking or doing ("I," "we").
    ii. *Second person*: the person(s) being spoken to ("you," "you all").
    iii. *Third person*: the person(s) being spoken about ("he," "she," "it," "they").
2. **Number (*Númerus*).** This refers to the "number" of people acting. It answers the question, "how many people are involved in the action?" There are two possibilities.
    i. *Singular*: one.
    ii. *Plural*: more than one.
3. **Tense (*Tempus*).**[6] This refers to the "time" the action happened. It answers the question, "when did this action occur?" There are six tenses, or time sequences, of Latin verbs. We will learn all of them soon enough.
    i. *Present*: action occurring in the present ("walks").
    ii. *Future*: action occurring in the future ("will walk").
    iii. *Imperfect*: action occurring in the past but with attempt (conative), habituation (customary), starting (inceptive), or repetition (continuous) ("was walking").
    iv. *Perfect*: action completed in the past but having ongoing significance ("has walked").
    v. *Future Perfect*: action that will be completed in the future ("will have walked").
    vi. *Pluperfect*: action fully completed in the past which had ongoing significance but no longer does ("had walked").
4. **Mood (*Modus*).** This refers to the "manner" of the action that occurred. It answers the question, In what way did the action occur? There are three moods in Latin.
    i. *Indicative*: represents reality.
    ii. *Subjunctive*: represents possibility, probability, or uncertainty.
    iii. *Imperative*: represents commands or orders.
5. **Voice (*Vōx*).** This refers to the "voice" of the action that occurred. This last grammatical feature answers the question, How are the subject and verb related? There are two ways verbs are related in Latin.
    i. *Active*: the subject performs the action.
    ii. *Passive*: the subject receives the action.

Every time we encounter a verb in Latin, we will need to identify its PNTMV, that is, person, number, tense, mood, and voice. (Even if we do not always use the same exact order, it still has the same meaning.)

---

6. The concept of *aspect* is intimately connected to tense, but we will reserve discussion of aspect in relation to specific tenses (beginning with the next *capítulum*).

INDICATIVE MOOD VERBS: FIRST AND SECOND PRINCIPAL PARTS

8.4 **Conjugation.** We learned in the previous *capítula* how to identify the case, number, and gender of nouns and adjectives. When seeking to uncover these features with nouns and adjectives, grammarians use the term "declension." *Mūtā́tīs mūtándīs*, "the necessary changes having been made," this term changes from "declension" to "conjugation"[7] when applied to verbs. In short, whereas *declining* a noun or adjective entails identifying its case, number, and gender, *conjugating* a verb entails identifying its person, number, tense, mood, and voice. It's the same concept, just a different name.

As discussed in Capítulum I, the umbrella term for both of these grammatical features is "inflection." Because Latin relies so heavily on word endings rather than merely word order, inflection is a big deal. After all, we will never know the totality of a sentence's meaning or function in Latin without knowing the ending of individual words: nouns, adjectives, verbs, and so on.

8.5 **Regular Verbs.** Just as "regular" Latin nouns fall into one of five declensions, so too do "regular" Latin verbs fall into one of four conjugations. We have already learned that there are always exceptions to the rules, but the rules are important, nonetheless. And here are the rules for verbs: Verbs in Latin end in one of four predetermined ways. As was the case with noun endings, scholars have labeled these verbal endings as follows: first conjugation, second conjugation, third conjugation, and fourth conjugation (see specific forms below).

In this book, the four paradigm verbs used are *amā́re*, "to love," *monḗre*, "to warn," *osténdere*, "to show," and *audī́re*, "to hear." Every time a new form of a verb is presented, it will use these four verbs to serve as illustrations.

PARADIGM FORMS FOR CONJUGATIONS

Conjugation Name	Infinitive Form (Ending)	Alternative Name	Sample Verb Principal Parts
First	-āre	(Long) ARE Verbs	amṓ, amā́re, amā́vī, amā́tus
Second	-ēre	Long ERE Verbs	móneō, monḗre, mónuī, mónitus
Third	-ĕre	Short ERE Verbs	osténdō, osténdere, osténdī, osténtus
Fourth	-īre	(Long) IRE Verbs	aúdiō, audī́re, audī́vī, audī́tus

There are several items to note about this paradigm. To begin with, the most common designation for verbs appears in the column all the way to the left: first, second, third, fourth. These conjugations correspond to the endings -āre, -ēre, -ĕre, -īre, which are called "infinitive forms." Briefly stated, the infinitive form is traditionally the dictionary form of a word; it is usually translated as "to . . ." Thus, the infinitive form of *amā́re* is "to love." The "alternative name" for these verbs provides more detail about their endings (particularly since second and third conjugations appear the same in the absence of diacritical marks such as macra or acute accents), but it is not a universal way to label them.

---

7. This comes from the Latin verb *coniugā́re*, "to bring together."

I put the word "Long" in parentheses for the first and fourth conjugations but kept them out of parentheses for the second and third conjugations. Why? Regarding second- and third-conjugation verbs, note that the second-to-last (or "penultimate") -e in second-conjugation verbs is long (thus ē), whereas the penultimate -e in third-conjugation verbs is short (thus ĕ). This slight difference will be important to remember when conjugating these verbs, as second-conjugation verbs preserve a characteristic -e throughout while third-conjugation ones weaken to a characteristic -i due to the length and shortness of their -e vowels, respectively.

The short -e in third-conjugation verbs also explains why the accent falls on the last vowel before the penultimate -e in the infinitive form (*osténdere* rather than *ostendére). According to Latin rules of accentuation, words with three or more syllables have an accent on the penultimate vowel *if it is long*. Because the penultimate vowel in third-conjugation verbs is always short (it really is a weak link), the accent appears one vowel to the left. When memorizing vocabulary, it will be necessary to distinguish the accent marks of second- and third-conjugation verbs in the infinitive forms.

8.6 **Principal Parts.** You probably noticed that each of the sample verbs from our paradigm contains four separate forms. What are these forms and why are they listed? Of the six different tenses in which a Latin verb may appear, scholars have determined that four parts are especially important to memorize since they provide the basis of all the other forms. These four forms are called "principal parts."

In this book, we will list each of the principal parts for verbs. Although the temptation will be to remember only the first or second forms, I strongly encourage, nay, implore you to memorize all four principal parts *ab prīncípiō*. By doing so, you will be much better prepared for subsequent *capítula*. I assure you that the extra work upfront will pay off in the end.

Although we will encounter them in due time, the four principal parts consist of:

1. First-person singular present active: -ō (e.g., "I verb").
2. Present active infinitive: -āre, -ēre, -ere, -īre (e.g., "to verb").
3. First-person singular perfect active: -ī (e.g., "I have verbed").
4. Masculine nominative singular perfect passive participle: -us (e.g., "having been verbed").[8]

Do not concern yourself about what each of these forms mean at the present time; most important right now is simply to memorize these forms.

8.7 **Verbs Last.** We have learned in this grammar that Latin enjoys more variety of word order than English. This is true, but we must also recognize that Latin is very precise and orderly. When it comes to word order in sentences, verbs have conventionally been put last. (If you have studied a language like German, you know German does this as well.) I love this feature of Latin. It is an elegant component to the language. As you continue to read more Latin on your own, pay attention to where the verbs appear and what percentage of sentences delay the main verb until the end. You will also find quite a bit of variety, so it is best to allow the Latin sentence to do as it pleases and instead keep your eyes on the endings of words.

---

8. For the fourth principal part, you will sometimes see an ending in -um rather than -us. This is due to the use of the neuter singular form (-um) instead of the masculine singular (-us). It is called the supine. We will not concern ourselves with the supine in this book.

INDICATIVE MOOD VERBS: FIRST AND SECOND PRINCIPAL PARTS

> **Summārium**
>
> In this *capítulum* you learned that:
> - Verbs convey action or express a state of being.
> - Verbs are conjugated by identifying their five constituent components (PNTMV).
> - Regular verbs follow one of four predetermined set of endings, called "conjugations" (first, second, third, fourth).
> - Principal parts refer to four specific forms of verbs, which we will memorize when learning new verbs.
> - The main verb often appears last in a Latin sentence or clause, but be prepared for it to appear anywhere by focusing on the endings of words (and not just where you expect them to appear).

VOCĀBULŌRUM INDEX

Notā Bene, "Note Well": The specific conjugation of each verb will be provided in parentheses (1, 2, 3, 4). When it comes to second- and third-conjugation verbs, remember that the macra or long marks (in the second principal part) make all the difference; a long -e (that is, -ē) indicates the second conjugation, while a short -e (that is, -ĕ) reveals the third.

Also, some verbs do not always have each of their four principal parts. When a verb lacks one of them, a dash (-) will appear in its place.

Latin	English (Gloss)	(Etymology)
ábeō, abíre, ábiī (abívī), ábitus (2)	to go away, to depart	
aedíficō, aedificáre, aedificávī, aedificátus (1)	to build, to erect	(edify)
ascéndō, ascéndere, ascéndī, ascénsus (3)	to go up, to climb (up), to ascend	(ascend)
aúdiō, audíre, audívī, audítus (4)	to hear, to listen (to)	(audio)
débeō, dēbére, débuī, débitus (2)	to owe, ought, to keep from	(debt)
dīcō, dícere, dīxī, dictus (3)	to say, to speak, to talk	(contradict)
dō, dare, dedī, datus (1)	to give, to offer, to yield	(datum)
dúbitō, dubitáre, dubitávī, dubitátus (1)	to doubt, to waver, to hesitate	(dubious)
fáciō, fácere, fēcī, factus (3)	to do, to make, to construct	(manufacture)
gignō, gígnere, génuī, génitus (3)	to give birth to, to produce, to beget	(genetic)
hábeō, habére, hábuī, hábitus (2)	to have, to hold, to consider	(prohibit)
mittō, míttere, mīsī, missus (3)	to send, to let go, to discharge	(mission)
percútiō, percútere, percússī, percússus (3)	to beat, to strike, to pierce	(percussion)

plangō, plángere, plānxī, plānctus (3)	to mourn, to bewail, to lament	(plangent)
portō, portáre, portávī, portátus (1)	to carry, to bear, to sustain	(porter)
praecípiō, praecípere, praecépī, praecéptus (3)	to command, to order, to enjoin	(precept)
recédō, recédere, recéssī, recéssus (3)	to fall back, to retreat, to withdraw	(recede)
reddō, réddere, réddidī, rédditus (3)	to give back, to return, to restore	
respóndeō, respondére, respóndī, respónsus (2)	to reply, to respond, to answer	(respond)
surgō, súrgere, surréxī, surréctus (3)	to rise, to arise, to get up	(surge)
vādō, vádere, vāsī, - (3)	to go, to hasten	(invade)
véniō, veníre, vēnī, ventus (4)	to come, to approach	(convenient)
vídeō, vidére, vīdī, vīsus (2)	to see, to look at, to understand	(video)
vīvō, vívere, vīxī, vīctus (3)	to live, to be alive	(revive)
vocō, vocáre, vocávī, vocátus (1)	to call, to name, to designate	(vocation)

ŌRÁTIŌ POPULÁRIS

Sýmbolum Apostolórum (Pars Minor I). The "Apostles' Creed" is traditionally ascribed to the disciples of Christ, one line per disciple. In truth, the exact origins are not known; it is possible that Christians were reciting this confession of faith as early as the second century. Due to the length of the *Sýmbolum*, we will divide it into several sections, beginning with the opening statement.

Crēdō in Deum Patrem omnipoténtem, Creātórem caelī et terrae, et in Iēsum Christum, Fílium eius únicum, Dóminum nostrum.	I believe in God the Father, Almighty, the Creator of heaven and earth, and in Jesus Christ, his only Son, our Lord.

EXERCÍTIA

Be sure to complete the *exercítium* in the appendix corresponding to this *capítulum*.

Capítulum

IX

PRESENT ACTIVES AND PRESENT PASSIVES

Adnúntiō vōbīs gaúdium magnum: Habḗmus Pāpam![1]
—PERICLE FELICI

OPÚSCULUM THEOLÓGICUM: *Habḗmus Pāpam*

In the fall of 1978, the recently elected pope—John Paul I—died only a month after taking office as Roman Pontiff (from *póntifex, pontíficis*, "high priest") of the Roman Catholic Church. His tenure, though only thirty-three days in length, introduced two innovations. First, desiring to pay homage to his recent predecessors, he choose two separate names—John and Paul. By doing so, he became the first pope to adopt more than one name. Second, this pope not only called himself John Paul, but John Paul I. This sobriquet paved the way for successors to adopt his name upon his death.

As fortune would have it, that is exactly what happened just weeks after his own election to the papacy. Following the untimely death of Pope John Paul I, his successor, the first Polish man to be so elected, adopted the name John Paul II out of respect for his immediate predecessor.

Pericle Felici, the Senior Cardinal at this time, received the honor of introducing the pope to the world. Speaking in Latin, and pausing between triumphal shouts and cheers from the crowds, Cardinal Felici proclaimed:

Adnúntiō vōbīs gaúdium magnum: Habḗmus Pāpam! Ēminentíssimum ac reverendíssimum dóminum, Dóminum Cárolum Sānctae Rōmánae Ecclḗsiae Cardinálem Wojtyła, quī sibi nōmen impósuit Jōánnis Paulī.	I announce to you all a great joy: We have a pope! The most eminent and most reverend lord, Lord Karol Wojtyła, Cardinal of the Holy Roman Church, who has taken for himself the name of John Paul.

Over the centuries, the rituals associated with the election of the highest office in the Catholic Church have become as fixed as they are famous. After the cardinals elect the pope, they usher him to the Sistine Chapel, where he is dressed in white, adored with praise, and asked what pontifical name he would like to assume. Eventually, the new pope is presented to an eager crowd waiting in St. Peter's

---

1. "I announce to you all a great joy: We have a pope!"

Square in front of the Vatican. After the Senior Cardinal pronounces the formulaic words, particularly the famous sentence *Habḗmus Pāpam*, the Roman Pontiff utters his first words to the audience.

The notion of the *pāpa*, "the pope," as the leading authority in the Western Church developed in the fourth and fifth centuries, although its roots may stretch back earlier. The formulaic announcement of the pope's election, however, emerged only a thousand years later, during the Late Middle Ages. As attentive biblical readers will no doubt notice, the language of the declaration is based on Luke's accouncement of Jesus's birth to the shepherds assembled in Bethlehem:

Ecce enim ēvangelī́zō [or adnū́ntiō] vōbīs gaúdium magnum quod erit omnī pópulō quia nātus est vōbīs hódiē salvā́tor quī est Christus Dóminus in cīvitā́te Dāvī́d. (Luke II.10–11)	Behold, I announce to you all a great joy that will be for all the people because today a Savior has been born for you all in the city of David, who is Christ the Lord.

Whereas some former Latin translations of the Bible used the verb *adnū́ntiō*, the Vulgate opted for a transliteration (or lexical transcription) of the Greek term, thus the creation of the verb *ēvangelī́zō*. Both words, however, share a semantic range.

For our purposes, the importance of the Latin formula introducing the newly elected pope lies in its use of two verbs, both occuring in the present tense: *adnū́ntiō*, "I announce," and *habḗmus*, "we have." As we will learn in this *capítulum*, the present tense generally indicates action occuring at the time of the speaker.

Prospéctus

In this *capítulum* you will learn that:
- Present indicative active verbs express an action normally occurring in the present, in which the subject performs the action.
- Present indicative passive verbs communicate an action normally occurring in the present, in which the subject is acted upon.

GRAMMÁTICA

9.1 **Conjugating Verbs.** We learned in the previous *capítulum* that the classification of a verb according to its person, number, tense, mood, and voice (summarized as PNTMV) is called "conjugation." Despite its strange name, it is an important concept for us to master. After all, unless we conjugate a verb, we will never know who is acting (P), how many people are acting (N), when the action occurs (T), in what manner it does so (M), or how the subject and verb are related (V).

9.2 **English and Additional Words.** In English, we rely on the addition of one or two extra words to identify the PNTMV of any given verb. For example, the verb "love," in and of itself, tells us very little about what we need to know in order truly to understand what is going on in a sentence. Do you "love" puppy dogs? Does Billy "love" hot dogs? Does Paula "love" corn dogs? More information is needed. If we want to recognize who is loving (P), therefore, we need to add a pronoun such as "I love" or "they love." Alternatively, if we want to learn when an action occurs (T), we usually need to add an auxiliary word of some kind, for instance, "I will love" or "they have loved."

INDICATIVE MOOD VERBS: FIRST AND SECOND PRINCIPAL PARTS

Or, if we want to determine whether the subject is doing or receiving the action (V), we need to either include or not include the verb "to be," for example, "I love" versus "I am loved."

9.3 **Latin Precision.** The genius of the Latin language is that it can indicate PNTMV in just one word. That's right—no additional words are typically required. (It is almost like Latin was invented by geniuses.) And, as we now know well, Latin indicates these grammatical features through word endings rather than word order. This is quite different, of course, from English, which relies so heavily on word order and the addition of accompanying words. This makes Latin appear much more sleek than English. And it is why English translations of Latin sentences can easily contain twice as many words as the Latin original. If you agree with the expression that "less is more," then you are well on your way to loving Latin.

PRESENT TENSE (INDICATIVE)

9.4 **Tenses.** Due to Latin's precision and ability to accomplish so much with so little, there are a limited number of ways that Latin verbs can end. In order to pace ourselves and not learn too many forms too quickly, however, we will distribute the tenses of Latin verbs over the course of the next several *capítula*.

In this *capítulum*, we will encounter the most basic of Latin verbs: the present tense.[2] In general, the present tense describes an action that occurs in the present. Nothing difficult there. The action of the verb, therefore, is said to be contemporaneous with the speaker.

9.5 **Aspect.** In addition to tense, verbs also indicate what is called "aspect." Derived from the Latin word *aspéctus*, "sight" or "appearance,"[3] aspect refers to the way an action appears or is represented. The aspect of present tense verbs may be brought out in three distinct ways when translating:

- as a simple or undefined action (e.g., "I love," "I am loved")
- as a continuous or progressive action (e.g., "I am loving," "I am being loved")
- as an emphatic or deliberative action (e.g., "I do love")[4]

Depending on context and custom, translators bring out aspect in different ways. In British English, for instance, it is more commonplace to say something like "I do love," whereas in American English this use of the helping (or auxiliary) verb "do" more often indicates emphasis. All things the same, I recommend translating present tense verbs with the simple or undefined aspect ("I love," "I am loved") unless context offers a compelling reason to do otherwise. Of course, as you become more familiar with Latin, you will begin to discern subtly contextual clues that will require more variety when translating verbs.

PRESENT ACTIVE (INDICATIVE)

9.6 **Present Active Personal Endings.** We will now turn our attention to the shared and predetermined endings of the present active tense. We need only list the person and number since,

---

2. We will only look at the present tense in the indicative mood for this *capítulum*. Discussion of other "moods" come much later in this book.
3. This word comes from the verb *aspício, aspícere, aspéxī, aspéctus*, "to look at," "to observe."
4. It's much harder to bring out the emphatic aspect in passive constructions.

PRESENT ACTIVE PERSONAL ENDINGS ("PRESENT-SYSTEM" ACTIVE ENDINGS)

	Singular	Plural
First Person	-ō, -m[a]	-mus
Second Person	-s	-tis
Third Person	-t	-nt

[a] Many verbal forms end in -m rather than -ō. However, we will see more of these in future *capítula*.

as already stated, we are only considering the present tense in this *capítulum* as well as the indicative mood in the next subsequent *capítula*. Moreover, because the passive voice uses different personal endings, we will discuss them in the next section.

All present active verbs use these same personal endings, regardless of their distinct conjugation patterns (discussed below). Though quite different from English, it may be helpful to think of Latin's present active personal endings as implying the following English equivalents:

-ō, m, "I"	-mus, "we"
-s, "you"	-tis, "you all"
-t, "he, she, it"	-nt, "they"

The only possible confusion is that Latin does actually possess personal pronouns that mean "I" and "they" (that is, all of the words in quotation marks immediately above). The difference between English and Latin, however, is that English *always* requires the use of personal pronouns with verbs (or at least an explicit subject). For instance, as mentioned above, the word "speaks" means nothing by itself in English; it requires a personal pronoun such as "he" or "she," or a proper name such as "Priscilla," to clarify and complete its meaning. Latin, however, does not need such words since the identity of the speaker is always implied by the verb's ending. Because Latin verbs do not require personal pronouns, they will never be included in verbal paradigms. Therefore, we will reserve discussion of pronouns for subsequent *capítula*.

9.7 **Present Tense Conjugations: Stem Vowels.** We have just observed how all regular present active verbs share the same personal endings. Now we turn to the ways in which present active verbs differ. You will recall from the previous *capítulum* that there are four verbal conjugations, that is, four different predetermined patterns of endings for all regular verbs. These different forms are illustrated in the paradigm below. Observe the different vowels as well as their quantity (length or shortness): -ā, -ē, -e, and -ī. The quantity and distinctness of these vowels indicate how they will differ from one form to another before the same personal endings (discussed above) are added.

In order to conjugate a present active verb, we remove the -re from the end of the infinitive form (which is the second principal part) and add the personal endings listed above. Other than the characteristic vowel differences from the different conjugations, present active verbs will appear very similar. Pay attention to the patterns of the four conjugations that will appear consecutively below, noting both their similarities and differences. For the purpose of clarity, I have put the distinctive endings in bold. This is only to make the forms as distinct as possible; obviously, the actual forms will not be in bold in primary writings.

INDICATIVE MOOD VERBS: FIRST AND SECOND PRINCIPAL PARTS

PARADIGM FORMS FOR CONJUGATIONS

Conjugation Name	Infinitive Form (Ending)[a]	Alternative Name[b]	Sample Verb
First	-āre	(Long) ARE Verbs[c]	amō, amāʹre, amāʹvī, amāʹtus
Second	-ēre	Long ERE Verbs	móneō, monére, mónuī, mónitus
Third	-ere	Short ERE Verbs	osténdō, osténdere, osténdī, osténtus
Fourth	-īre	(Long) IRE Verbs	aúdiō, audīʹre, audīʹvī, audīʹtus

[a] Keep in mind two things when it comes to the length of vowels here. First, because I will use both macra and accent marks, the long vowels here will often have an accent mark added on top of them (for instance, āʹ) in a real word since their length often (though not always) makes them receive the stress in any given word. Second, although they are included here, you will never see them in primary works.

[b] The conjugation of verbs is universally called "first, second, third, and fourth." This alternative name is what I will sometimes use, but it is not universal.

[c] Remember that we usually put the word "long" in parenthesis when it comes to -āre and -īre verbs; for -ēre and -ere verbs, however, we will keep the term more prominent since the difference in these verbs is significant.

9.8 **Present Active Indicative: First Conjugation (Long ARE).** Not surprisingly, -ā is the characteristic stem vowel for ARE verbs. It is a long vowel (thus -ā), but the stress or accent of the -ā only appears in the first and second-person plurals (amā́mus, amā́tis) since most of the forms only have two syllables.

You will observe that the length of the characteristic vowel (-ā) is not completely distributed across each form. Why not? Long vowels tend to be shortened when occuring immediately before certain letters or letter combinations. Three examples of this phenomenon will suffice. They occur when long vowels appear (a) before other vowels, (b) before the letters -nd or -nt, and (c) before the consonants -m, -r, and -t when occuring at the end of the word. This explains, for instance, why it is *amat*—not **amāt*. The vowel was shortened.

Another related feature occurs when vowels drop out altogether before certain letters. You probably noticed, for example, that there is no -ā in the first-person singular form. You were likely anticipating something like **amā́ō*, but the -ā dropped out when it contracted with the -ō, resulting in *amō*. This is a fairly common phenomenon, occurring in the third conjugation as well. To make a long story short: Do not be concerned if you notice that the vowels are not perfectly preserved in every form. This is quite standard. Simply memorize the forms as they appear in the paradigm. For the most part, we will leave discussion of the exact reasons for this to the experts.

When it comes to translation, keep in mind our discussion above about aspect. Depending on context, we may translate *amat* as "he/she/it loves," "he/she/it is loving," or "he/she/it does love." (Obviously, context will clarify whether we use "he," "she," or "it"—we will not use them simultaneously.) If it is simpler, feel free to translate present verbs with a simple aspect ("he/she/it loves") unless context suggests otherwise.

Our example comes from Augustine of Hippo:

Beā́tus quī <u>amat</u> tē.   Blessed is the one who <u>loves</u> you.
(Augustine of Hippo)[5]

---

5. Augustine of Hippo, *Cōnfessiṓnēs* IV.9 (PL 32.699).

PRESENT ACTIVES AND PRESENT PASSIVES

AMŌ, AMÁRE, AMÁVĪ, AMÁTUS, "TO LOVE" (STEM: AMĀ-)

	Singular	Plural
First Person	amō	amámus
Second Person	amās	amátis
Third Person	amat	amant

Similarly, look at the example below, which contains both a positive and a negative translation of the forms. In particular, notice that the use of the negating word *nōn* will often require that our translation uses the word "does" or "do":

Sī enim <u>laudās</u> Deum, ut det tibi áliquid, <u>jam</u> <u>nōn</u> grātīs <u>amās</u> Deum. (Peter Abelard)[6]

For if <u>you praise</u> God so that he gives you something, <u>you do not love</u> God freely any longer.

9.9 **Present Active Indicative: Second Conjugation (Long ERE).** The next conjugation is Long ERE verbs. Other than when shortened (before -t and -nt, for instance), they retain their characteristic -ē throughout their distinct forms. We simply add the shared present-system personal endings to the stem. There is one form, however, that does the opposite of what the -āre verbs do: You might have expected that the -ē would drop out before -ō, resulting in something like **monō*. But no such thing happens. Although the -ē did not drop out in this instance, its length was shortened (in accordance with the rule we learned above that long vowels are sometimes shortened before other vowels). Thus, the correct form is: *móneō*.

MÓNEŌ, MONÉRE, MÓNUĪ, MÓNITUS, "TO WARN," "TO ADVISE" (STEM: MONĒ-)

	Singular	Plural
First Person	móneō	monémus
Second Person	monēs	monétis
Third Person	monet	monent

9.10 **Present Active Indicative: Third Conjugation (Short ERE).** When it comes to the four conjugations, the third conjugation is the outlier. Unlike the other three conjugations, it is the only one with a short stem vowel. The shortness of this characteristic -e vowel causes it to weaken when the personal endings are added, and this also explains why we do not see the -i stressed or accented. Despite this imperfection, the verbal show must go on. Because this class of verbs occurs constantly in Latin, it is essential that we become familiar with them and learn to appreciate their idiosyncrasies.

Also, note that both the first-person singular and third-personal plural have no -i at all (*osténdō* and *osténdunt*). We have already encountered this phenomenon with first-person singular forms; in the case of the third-person plural, the -i becomes -u. Be sure to make a mental note of this when memorizing its forms.

---

6. Peter Abelard, *Sīc et Nōn* III.138 (PL 178.1575).

INDICATIVE MOOD VERBS: FIRST AND SECOND PRINCIPAL PARTS

OSTÉNDŌ, OSTÉNDERE, OSTÉNDĪ, OSTÉNTUS, "TO SHOW" (STEM: OSTENDE-)

	Singular	Plural
First Person	osténdō[a]	osténdimus
Second Person	osténdis	osténditis
Third Person	osténdit	osténdunt

[a] Some third-conjugation verbs end in -iō in the first person.

Let us look at an example:

Osténdunt opus lēgis scrīptum in córdibus suīs. (Rom. II.15)

They show that the work of the law has been written on their hearts.

9.11 **Present Active Indicative: Fourth Conjugation (Long IRE).** The Long IRE verbs look very similar to Short ERE verbs, so be *valdē*, "exceedingly," careful when comparing them.

Also, as with the third conjugation, -u appears immediately before the personal endings are added to the third-person plural. (Vowels like this are sometimes added for the sake of pronunciation.) What is the difference? Here the long -i (thus ī) remains in the fourth conjugation, while only the -u appears in the third. This is a reminder of how important the length of vowels is. Latin is such a great language that we have to always pay attention to the most minute of variations. Something as innocuous as the length of a vowel can make a big difference.

AÚDIŌ, AUDÍRE, AUDÍVĪ, AUDÍTUS, "TO HEAR" (STEM: AUDĪ-)

	Singular	Plural
First Person	aúdiō	audímus
Second Person	audīs	audítis
Third Person	audit	aúdiunt[a]

[a] Note that "u" is added before the endings here; this is to ease pronunciation.

There should be no surprises here. We have discussed all of the forms that might be slightly different than expected.

PRESENT PASSIVE (INDICATIVE)

9.12 **Present Passive Personal Endings.** Now that we have learned the present active, the present passive will be a piece of *lībum*, "cake." The active patterns we encountered above apply to passives except that now, of course, we will add passive personal endings to the four conjugations rather than active endings. Substituting passive personal endings for active ones also means that we have now shifted from the verb performing the action to receiving the action. In terms of translation, this indicates that we move, for instance, from "we love" or "we are loving" (in the active voice) to "we are loved" or "we are being loved" (in the passive). Someone else is now performing the action.

Once again, Latin proves itself a much more concise language than English. Whereas we are forced to include the "to be" verb in English passive forms, we simply change our word ending

PRESENT ACTIVES AND PRESENT PASSIVES

in Latin. In Latin, as we have discovered, the addition of just a couple of letters makes a great deal of difference.

PRESENT-SYSTEM PASSIVE PERSONAL ENDINGS

	Singular	Plural
First Person	-r, -or	-mur
Second Person	-ris, -re	-minī
Third Person	-tur	-ntur

We know the drill by now. In order to conjugate a verb, we add the present-system personal endings to the stem of any of the four conjugation verbs: (Long) ARE, Long ERE, Short ERE, and (Long) IRE. In our specific case, we remove the -re ending of the present infinitive (or second principal part) and add the passive personal endings to what remains (which is the stem of the verb).

For the first- and second-person singular forms, you will see two possible endings. They carry the same meaning. Note that the second of the second-person singular form looks identical to the infinitive. This can potentially cause confusion.

If it is helpful, you could think of the passive personal endings as essentially meaning the following in English. (Note that the inclusion of the "to be" verb indicates that it is passive rather than active.)

-r, -or, "I am -ed"	-mur, "we are -ed"
-ris, -re, "you are -ed"	-minī, "you all are -ed"
-tur, "he, she, it is -ed"	-ntur, "they are -ed"

9.13 **Reminder about Aspect.** Whereas the present active may indicate three different aspects, the passive form is able to be brought out in two ways depending on context:

- as a simple or undefined action (e.g., "I am advised")
- as a continuous or progressive action (e.g., "I am being advised")

Using the simple aspect is the easiest and most basic way to translate this tense and voice, but you can opt for whatever your instructor prefers and what makes the most sense in context.

9.14 **Present Passive Indicative: First Conjugation (Long ARE).** Just like with the active forms, the long -a (-ā) is retained in all passive forms other than the first-person singular.

AMŌ, AMÁRE, AMÁVĪ, AMÁTUS, "TO LOVE" (STEM: AMĀ-)

	Singular	Plural
First Person	amor	amámur
Second Person	amáris, amáre	amáminī
Third Person	amátur	amántur

INDICATIVE MOOD VERBS: FIRST AND SECOND PRINCIPAL PARTS

9.15 **Present Passive Indicative: Second Conjugation (Long ERE).** The long ERE verbs retain their characteristic -ē throughout their distinct forms (as we would expect with a strong vowel), so these forms are easy to generate and identify.

MÓNEŌ, MONÉRE, MÓNUĪ, MÓNITUS, "TO WARN," "TO ADVISE" (STEM: MONĒ-)

	Singular	Plural
First Person	móneor	monémur
Second Person	monéris, monére	monéminī
Third Person	monétur	monéntur

The German Lutheran theologian Andreas Osiander provides us with an example:

Monéntur spectrīs diábolī et praestígiīs. (Andreas Osiander)[7]	They are (being) warned through the appearances of the devil and delusions.

9.16 **Present Passive Indicative: Third Conjugation (Short ERE).** As we know, the third conjugation acts differently from the other conjugations. It is the only one with a short stem vowel. The shortness of this characteristic -e vowel causes it to undergo change when the personal endings are added.

OSTÉNDŌ, OSTÉNDERE, OSTÉNDĪ, OSTÉNTUS, "TO SHOW" (STEM: OSTENDE-)

	Singular	Plural
First Person	osténdor	osténdimur
Second Person	osténderis, osténdere	ostendíminī
Third Person	osténditur	ostendúntur

Let us look at an example:

Nam in hoc osténditur Deus omnípotēns esse iūstus. (Haimo of Halberstadt)[8]	For in this the Almighty God is shown to be righteous.

9.17 **Present Passive Indicative: Fourth Conjugation (Long IRE).** As with the active, IRE verbs look very similar to Short ERE verbs in the passive, so be careful when comparing them. Here is the key difference: Because the -ī in the fourth conjugation is long, we put accentuation on the -ī in several forms, while the third-conjugation does not typically receive stress on the -i.

AÚDIŌ, AUDÍRE, AUDÍVĪ, AUDÍTUS, "TO HEAR" (STEM: AUDĪ-)

	Singular	Plural
First Person	aúdior	audímur
Second Person	audíris, audíre	audíminī
Third Person	audítur	audiúntur

---

7. Andreas Osiander, *In Ēvangélium Secúndum Lucam* XVII (Geneva: Robert Stephanus, 1553), 291.
8. Haimo of Halberstadt, "Ad Rōmānōs VIII," in *In Dīvī Paulī Epístolās . . . Expositiō* (Munich: 1528), n.p.

PRESENT ACTIVES AND PRESENT PASSIVES

Here is an example:

Aequitáte tamen suādénte semper audítur. (Cassiodorus)⁹

Nevertheless, one is always heard when justice is one's advocate.

Summārium

In this *capítulum* you learned that:
- The present tense refers to an action occurring at the time of the speaker and it may bring out two or three different aspects when being translated.
- A verb's voice is active or passive; active verbs perform the action of a sentence and employ one set of predetermined endings, while passive verbs receive the action of a sentence and use a different set of predetermined endings.
- All four principal parts of a verb need to be learned.

VOCĀBULŎRUM INDEX

Latin	English (Gloss)	(Etymology)
accípiō, accípere, accḗpī, accéptus (3)	to take, to receive	(accept)
adnū́ntiō, adnūntiáre, adnūntiávī, adnūntiátus (1)	to announce, to proclaim, to report	(announce)
agō, ágere, ēgī, āctus (3)	to do, to act, to make	(act)
appáreō, appārḗre, appáruī, appáritus (2)	to appear, to be visible	(appear)
aspíciō, aspícere, aspéxī, aspéctus (3)	to look at, to observe, to regard	(aspect)
benedī́cō, benedī́cere, benedī́xī, benedíctus (3)	to bless, to praise, to speak well of	(benediction)
cápiō, cápere, cēpī, captus (3)	to take, to capture, to seize	(capture)
cognóscō, cognóscere, cognṓvī, cógnitus (3)	to learn, to recognize, to be acquainted with	(cognizant)
dēmíttō, dēmíttere, dēmī́sī, dēmíssus (3)	to send down, to bring down, to forgive	(demit)
dērelínquō, dērelínquere, dērelī́quī, dērelíctus (3)	to abandon, to forsake, to desert, to leave	(derelict)
dēspíciō, dēspícere, dēspéxī, dēspéctus (3)	to look down upon, to despise, to disdain	(despise)
dī́ligō, dīlígere, dīléxī, dīléctus (3)	to love, to esteem, to cherish	(diligent)
dūcō, dū́cere, dūxī, ductus (3)	to lead, to guide	(duct)
éligō, ēlígere, ēlḗgī, ēléctus (3)	to choose, to elect	(elect)

(cont.)

---

9. Cassiodorus, *Epístola* VIII (PL 69.774).

INDICATIVE MOOD VERBS: FIRST AND SECOND PRINCIPAL PARTS

Latin	English (Gloss)	(Etymology)
ēvangelízō, ēvangelīzáre, ēvangelīzávī, ēvangelīzátus (1)	to evangelize, to preach the gospel	(evangelize)
impónō, impónere, impósuī, impósitus (3)	to place upon, to set upon, to lay upon	(impose)
legō, légere, lēgī, lēctus (3)	to read, to select, to choose	(lectern)
máneō, manére, mānsī, mānsus (2)	to stay, to remain	(remain)
mānō, mānáre, mānávī, mānátus (1)	to flow, to run, to drop	(immanent)
nōscō, nóscere, nōvī, nōtus (3)	to know, to recognize	(notice)
praédicō, praedicáre, praedicávī, praedicátus (1)	to preach, to announce, to declare	(predicate)
scrībō, scríbere, scrīpsī, scrīptus (3)	to write	(scribe)
stō, stāre, stetī, status (1)	to stand, to stay	(status)
téneō, tenére, ténuī, tentus (2)	to have, to hold, to grasp	(tenant)
tímeō, timére, tímuī, - (2)	to fear, to be afraid	(timid)

ŌRÁTIŌ POPULÁRIS

Sýmbolum Apostolórum (Pars Minor II). Below is the second part of the *Sýmbolum Apostolórum*, which centers on the person of Jesus Christ.

Quī concéptus est dē Spíritū Sānctō, nātus ex Maríā Vírgine, passus sub Póntiō Pilátō, crucifíxus, mórtuus, et sepúltus, dēscéndit ad ínferōs, tértiā diē resurréxit ā mórtuīs, ascéndit ad caelōs, sedet ad déxteram Deī Patris omnipoténtis, inde ventúrus est iūdicáre vīvōs et mórtuōs.	Who was conceived by the Holy Spirit, born from the Virgin Mary, suffered under Pontius Pilate, crucified, dead, and buried. He descended into Hell. On the third day he rose again from the dead, ascended into Heaven, and sat at the right hand of God the Father, the Almighty. From there he will come to judge the living and the dead.

EXERCÍTIA

Be sure to complete the *exercítium* in the appendix corresponding to this *capítulum*.

Capítulum
X

IMPERFECT ACTIVES, IMPERFECT PASSIVES, AND ADVERBS

Ut id teneámus quod <u>ubíque</u>, quod <u>semper</u>, quod ab ómnibus créditum est.[1]
—VINCENT OF LÉRINS

OPÚSCULUM THEOLÓGICUM: *Vincent of Lérins and the Vincentian Canon*

Vincent of Lérins was a fifth-century monk who lived on a tiny island close to the modern-day city of Cannes in France. Here, surrounded by a few monks and lots of water, in the year 434 he wrote an anonymous book titled *Commonitórium Peregrínī advérsus Haeréticōs*, "A Pilgrim's Reminder against Heretics."[2] One of the constant thorns in the side of figures like Vincent was deciding how to distinguish between authentic and inauthentic Christianity. Vincent, of course, was a Catholic Christian who adhered firmly to the traditions of the ancient church, but there was always, it seemed, a new individual and group claiming to be Christians but offering novel interpretations of the Bible.

One would think that the truth of one's faith could be measured easily enough by comparing it to the standard of the *verbum Deī*. But even in the 400s, there were rival interpretations about how to interpret the word of God. As Vincent so elegantly put it in his book:

Quot hóminēs sunt, tot illinc senténtiae.[3]	There are as many interpretations [of Scripture] as there are people.

Because anyone could—and did—interpret the Bible in any way he or she saw fit, Vincent believed it was necessary to establish a rule or canon apart from the Bible that determined correct belief. Vincent's solution has been called "the Vincentian canon." In short, Vincent contended that true Christianity consisted of that kind of faith which has been believed *ubíque*, "everywhere," *semper*, "always," and *ab ómnibus*, "by all."

The full sentence reads as follows:

---

1. "That we may hold what has been believed <u>everywhere</u>, <u>always</u>, and by everyone."
2. For the likely title and likely year of composition, see Thomas Guarino, *Vincent of Lérins and the Development of the Christian Tradition* (Grand Rapids: Baker, 2013), xvi.
3. Vincent of Lérins, *Commonitŏrium* II.2, *The Commonitorium of Vincent of Lerins*, ed. Reginald Stewart Moxon (Cambridge: Cambridge University Press, 1915), 8.

INDICATIVE MOOD VERBS: FIRST AND SECOND PRINCIPAL PARTS

In ipsā item cathólicā ecclésiā magnópere cūrándum est, ut id teneámus quod <u>ubī́que</u>, quod <u>semper</u>, quod ab ómnibus créditum est.[4]	Likewise, in the universal church itself, we must take great care to hold that which has been believed <u>everywhere</u>, <u>always</u>, and by all.

There are two major items to note from this beautiful Latin sentence. The first is the reference to *cathólica ecclésia*. The earliest known reference to this phrase, particularly the adjective *cathólica*, arose from Ignatius of Antioch, a bishop in Asia Minor who was a former disciple of the apostle John. Making use of two Greek terms meaning "according to the whole," Ignatius instructed Christians in the city of Smyrna that "wherever Jesus Christ is, there is the universal church."[5] Ignatius himself was writing in the first decade of the second century to Christians scattered across the Roman Empire, encouraging them to submit to the bishops from each respective diocese. I translated both Ignatius's phrase from Greek and Vincent's from Latin as "universal church" rather than "Catholic Church," but both are equally sound translation options.

The second item to note from Vincent's sentence are the three phrases mentioned briefly above: *ubī́que*, *semper*, and *ab ómnibus*. As he stated in this same paragraph, these standards are preserved:

Sequámur ūnīversitátem, antīquitátem, cōnsēnsiónem.[6]	If we follow universality, antiquity, consent.

As succinctly as ever, Vincent intends for *ubī́que* to correspond to *ūnīvérsitās*; *semper* to *antī́quitās*; and *ab ómnibus* to *cōnsḗnsiō*. Regardless of these explanatory nouns that Vincent provided, the Vincentian canon has become forever synonymous with *ubī́que*, *semper*, and *ab ómnibus*. For our purposes, not only are they the core of one of the most famous slogans in all of Christianity, but they also introduce us to the linguistic power of words that modify verbs—"adverbs." In this slogan, the adverbs *ubī́que* and *semper* offer a deeper understanding of the verb *crédere*, "to believe."[7] True Christianity, for Vincent, is not merely believing but holding to that which has been believed everywhere, always, and by all.

> **Prospéctus**
>
> In this *capítulum* you will learn that:
> - Adverbs modify verbs, adjectives, and other words like adverbs.
> - Imperfect indicative verbs indicate past continuous or incomplete time. They are formed by inserting an infix (-bā-) and then adding the present-system personal endings.
> - Like present-tense verbs, imperfects can be either active or passive in voice.

GRAMMÁTICA: *Adverbs*

10.1 Introducing Adverbs. We have already learned that adjectives are words that modify nouns. This means that they describe, characterize, or provide greater detail about nouns in some particular way. Adverbs are quite similar. In fact, despite the fact that "adverb" sounds a lot like "verb," adverbs do not just modify verbs; they are also quite content to modify adjectives and even other

---

4. Vincent of Lérins, *Commonitórium* II.3.
5. Ignatius of Antioch, *Epístola ad Smyrnaéōs* VIII.2 (PG 5.713–14). The Latin translation of the Greek original in PG is: "... ubi fúerit Christus Jēsus, ibi cathólica est Ecclésia."
6. Vincent of Lérins, *Commonitórium* II.3.
7. *ab ómnibus* is a prepositional phrase.

adverbs. Deriving from the Latin word *advérbium*, "next to the verb," adverbs typically appear next to the word they are describing (though not always, of course, since Latin likes to keep you guessing and never reveals all its secrets). If you like to think of it this way, adverbs ask the question of "how" a certain action is taking place, e.g., "quickly," "more enjoyably," "easily," "most refreshingly," etc. But more than just -ly words, adverbs are also capable of describing many other features of how something occurs in relation to verbs, adjectives, or other adverbs, for instance: *rārē*, "seldom"; *semper*, "always"; *ferē*, "almost"; or *nusquam*, "nowhere."

10.2 **Adverbs: A New Species of Modifiers.** Though this does not apply to all adverbs, you could characterize many of them as ambitious adjectives that aspired to more in life. Not content to modify nouns, they outgrew their trivial adjective selves and searched for a way to also modify verbs—the real powerhouse of the Latin language. For 2-1-2 adjectives that wanted more, they simply added a customary -ē[8] to the "positive" adjective base (hence *rēctus*, "correct" → **rēct* → *rēctē*, "correctly"). Meanwhile, for 3-3-3 adjectives that desired more, they added -er or -iter to the "positive" adjective base (hence *fēlīx*, "happy" → **fēlic* → *fēlíciter*, "happily").

With the customary -ē and -iter/-er endings, these evolved adjectives become their own species: adverbs. Standing atop the modifying taxonomic ranks, they began modifying, describing, and limiting as much as they could.

Here is an example:

Presbýterī uxóribus <u>líberē</u> cōpuléntur.   Priests should be united <u>freely</u> with
(Philip of Harveng)[9]   their wives.

As this adverb illustrates, adverbs exercise dominion in some way—in this case expanding how priests are to be united with their wives.

10.3 **Comparing Adverbs.** This new species of adverb wanted to do everything that an adjective could do—including making comparisons. Just like adjectives are divided into three "degrees"—positive, comparative, and superlative—so, too, adverbs decided that they would also make such comparisons. In truth, adverbs are not that original in how they are formed and in how they are compared. They mostly just followed the pattern set by adjectives, including using *quam*, "than," when making comparisons. For this reason, we will not go into as much detail as we did with adjectives. That stated, below is the way that many adverbs moved from the following: positive adjective to positive adverb to comparative adverb to superlative adverb. It is quite a linguistic evolutionary journey that they have taken.

The Basics of Adverbs
- "Positive" adverbs often end in the following ways: -ē, -iter, -er. In English, we usually translate them with -ly at the end (e.g., "happi<u>ly</u>").
- "Comparative" adverbs often end in -ius. In English, we usually translate them as "more -ly" (e.g., "<u>more</u> happi<u>ly</u>").
- "Superlative" adverbs often end in -ē, which can frequently appear in Latin words as -errime, -issime, or -illime. In English, we usually translate them as "most -ly" (e.g., "<u>most</u> happi<u>ly</u>").
- Adverbs often use *quam* when comparing more than one thing (e.g., "more happily <u>than</u> . . .").

---
8. Do not be surprised, of course, if you encounter an "irregular" adverb that has a short -e, for instance, *male*, "badly."
9. Philip of Harveng, *Dē Continéntiā Clericórum* LXVII (PL 203.754).

INDICATIVE MOOD VERBS: FIRST AND SECOND PRINCIPAL PARTS

Latin Ending	English Ending
-ē, -iter, -er	-ly
-ius	more -ly
-errime, -issime, -illime	most -ly

10.4 Common Endings for Adverbs. As noted above, not all adverbs are formed from adjectives (or at least not in the way we might expect). In fact, there are many ways that adverbs developed—whether from a distinct adjective form, a noun, or another way altogether. Below are some common ways that adverbs may end:

- Ending in -am: e.g., pal*am*, "openly"; cl*am*, "secretly"
- Ending in -im: e.g., part*im*, "partly"; stat*im*, "immediately"
- Ending in -ō: e.g., cit*ō*, "quickly"; fals*ō*, "falsely"
- Ending in -um: e.g., íter*um*, "again"; paul*um*, "a little"
- No particular ending: e.g., cūr, "why," "for what reason"; crās, "tomorrow"

10.5 Degrees of Adverbs. Below is a list of some common adverbs in their different degrees of comparison. The list below is by no means exhaustive; it simply provides several examples of adverbs so that you will gain familiarity with how they look.

SAMPLE ADVERBS AND THEIR DEGREES

Latin (English)	("Positive") Adjective	Positive Adverb	Comparative Adverb	Superlative Adverb
Latin (English)	ācer, ācris, ācre (bitter)	acriter (bitterly)	ácrius (more bitterly)	ācérrimē (most bitterly)
Latin (English)	amícus, amíca, amícum (friend)	amícē (friendly)	amícius (more friendly)	amīcíssimē (most friendly)
Latin (English)	celer, céleris, célere (quick)	celériter (quickly)	celérius (more quickly)	celérrimē (most quickly)
Latin (English)	fácilis, fácilis, fácile (easy)	fácile[a] (easily)	facílius (more easily)	facíllimē (most easily)
Latin (English)	fidélis, fidélis, fidéle (faithful)	fidéliter (faithfully)	fidélius (more faithfully)	fidēlíssimē (most faithfully)
Latin (English)	līber, líbera, líberum (free)	líberē (more freely)	líberius (more freely)	líbérrimē (most freely)
Latin (English)	malus, mala, malum (bad)	male (badly)	peíus (worse)	péssimē (worst)
Latin (English)	sápiēns, sápiēns, sápiēns (wise)	sapiénter (wisely)	sapiéntius (more wisely)	sapientíssimē (most wisely)

[a] This and many other "irregular" adverbs do not perfectly follow the rules. As we know by now, we should always expect some forms that do not perfectly follow the rules.

Here is an example:

Sapiénter psallunt. (Rupert of Deutz)[10] They sing psalms wisely.

GRAMMÁTICA: *Imperfect Verbs*

10.6 **The Imperfect.** And now we turn to the objects that adverbs were so intent on modifying—verbs. Specifically, this next section of the *capítulum* is focused on verbs of the imperfect (indicative) tense. In Latin, there are different ways to describe past actions, and each way corresponds to a specific verb tense (and mood). The most basic way to designate past actions is by employing the so-called imperfect tense. Related to the Latin adjective *imperféctum*, "unfinished" or "incomplete," the imperfect tense describes an action in the past that was not finished or completed (or at least it is not *explicitly* stated to have been finished or completed). Despite the meaning of the English word "imperfect," the Latin imperfect tense is far from flawed. In fact, it may soon become one of your favorite Latin tenses. It definitely gets a lot of bang for its buck.

10.7 **Verbal Aspect.** If you recall our discussion of verbal aspect from the previous *capítulum*, you might remember that there are three different aspects common to the present tense:

- simple or undefined action ("I love," "I am loved")
- continuous or progressive action ("I am loving," "I am being loved")
- emphatic or deliberative action ("I do love")

In the imperfect tense, we may use similar concepts but add some more (the exact terminology of which may vary from grammar to grammar). Naturally, there is some overlap among the different uses of the imperfect tense, but I am only drawing your attention to some of the most common ones:

- simple action ("I loved")
- continuous action ("I was loving," "I kept loving")
- customary action ("I used to love")
- inceptive action ("I began loving")
- conative action ("I tried to love," "I attempted to love")

Within this framework of understanding, the imperfect tense in Latin indicates the habitual, ongoing, incomplete, or repetitive nature of a past action. It may be helpful to think of the imperfect as the continuous-aspect past tense.

10.8 **Incomplete Actions of Some Kind.** When it is either not known or not explicitly stated whether an event being described in the past was ever completed, the "unfinished" or "not finished" (again, *imperféctum*) nature of the imperfect tense is utilized in Latin. It does not matter whether the speaker or hearer actually knows whether the past action was brought to completion or even when it began; it only matters that the speaker chose to describe the action by highlighting its continuous or progressive aspect. (If the speaker were to refer to an explicitly finished or

---

10. Rupert of Deutz, *Commentária in Apocalýpsim* X.19 (PL 169.1157).

completed past action in Latin, he or she would use the "perfect" tense, which will be discussed in a future *capítulum*.)

IMPERFECT ACTIVE (INDICATIVE) TENSE

10.9 Present-System Personal Endings. We are learning the imperfect tense immediately after the present tense for the simple reason that the imperfect uses the same endings as the present stem. Together, the present, imperfect, and future tenses use what is called the "present-system" endings. (This also explains the occasional use of the equal sign to indicate that present, imperfect, and future tenses share personal endings.) Hopefully by now the chart below is as familiar to you as your phone number. There is nothing new to note, other than that I have made explicit what I previously placed in a footnote for the first-person singular ending. While the present active tense applies the -ō ending to the first person-singular, the imperfect active utilizes the -m ending. Other than that, there is no difference between the endings.

PRESENT-SYSTEM ACTIVE PERSONAL ENDINGS

	Singular	Plural
First Person	-ō; -m	-mus
Second Person	-s	-tis
Third Person	-t	-nt

10.10 Recognizing the Imperfective Active Verb: -bā- Infix. The imperfect tense is very easy to recognize due to the "infix" (or insert) -bā-.[11] In short, when you come across the combination -ba- in the middle of a Latin word, begin using those inferential skills that are so crucial to Latin: Deduce that the word is very possibly in the imperfect tense.[12]

If you find this helpful, you could think of the imperfect actives as the English equivalents of the following:

-bam, "I was -ing"	-bámus, "we were -ing"
-bās, "you were -ing"	-bátis, "you all were -ing"
-bat, "he, she, it was -ing"	-bant, "they were -ing"

When it comes to the active tense, you can think of -bā- as the equivalent of "was/were + ing" in English. It may initially strike you as scandalous to see -bā- in all four conjugation forms of the imperfect, under the (noble but erroneous) assumption that the -bā- form has betrayed its ARE heritage and begun fraternizing with the other three conjugations. But fret not: The -ā- in -bā- is not exclusive to ARE verbs; on the contrary, it will be used in all four conjugations: (Long) ARE, Long ERE, Short ERE, and (Long) IRE. In fact, it will be used in both the active and passive tenses. That stated, as we learned previously, long vowels can be shortened before certain letters and letter combinations, so it will not be long in every form.

---

11. Both dashes enclosing -bā- are important to note. In the imperfect tense, the verbal stem always immediately precedes -bā- and at least one personal ending always immediately follows it.

12. That stated, -bā- does not guarantee that a Latin word will be an imperfect tense, for it could be a noun or something else. Nonetheless, it is still recommended to get in the habit of associating the infix -bā- with the imperfect tense.

IMPERFECT ACTIVES, IMPERFECT PASSIVES, AND ADVERBS

Steps to Form Imperfect Active (Indicatives)
1. Locate the second principal part of a verb (e.g., *laudā́re*).
2. Remove the -re ending (e.g., *laudā́-*).
3. Attach the infix -bā- (e.g., **laudābā-*).
4. Add the present-system personal active endings: -m, -s, -t; -mus, -tis, -nt
   (e.g., *laudā́bam, laudā́bās, laudā́bat, laudābā́mus, laudābā́tis, laudā́bant*).

In this way, the imperfect tense contains three parts: the verb's stem, the infix -bā-, and the present-system personal endings. I like to compare the imperfect tense to atoms in chemistry. Just as atoms are composed of tiny particles containing protons, neutrons, and electrons, so imperfect Latin verbs are composed of the present stem, the infix -bā-, and the present-system personal ending. It is that simple.

One final note: Although the -ā is long in the infix -bā-, its length will shorten in several forms in accordance with the rules that we learned in the previous *capítulum*.

10.11 Translating the Imperfect. As mentioned above, there are many ways to translate the imperfect tense into English accurately. When you encounter this tense, you can plug in the different concepts mentioned above about action to see which one you think best applies to the context. Probably the two most common ways to translate the imperfect tense into English are as follows:

1. "was/were + -ing" (e.g., "she was listening," "they were listening")
2. "used to" (e.g., "she used to listen," "they used to listen")

I am intentionally steering us away from the simple or undefined aspect for the imperfect, e.g., "I loved," "they advised," etc. Why? We will soon encounter another past tense called the "perfect" tense, which is sometimes translated with a simple aspect. It is best to avoid confusion for the time being. Of the two options I listed above, I recommend using the first as your default translation but be sure to keep the second one visible in your detective's notebook—and also feel free to experiment with the different options listed above in relation to aspect.

In brief, if you are not exactly sure how an author was describing an event (other than the fact that he or she was using the imperfect tense), then choose the default "was/were + -ing" translation. If, however, the context of the passage leads you to believe that the author was emphasizing one of the actions described under aspect, then pat yourself on the back for your Latin prowess and translate the word with one of those constructions. As in most circumstances, context is king.

IMPERFECT ACTIVE CONJUGATION PARADIGMS

10.12 Imperfect Active First Conjugation (Long ARE). As we know by now, -ā is the characteristic vowel for (Long) ARE verbs. Notice that the acute accent falls on the -ā preceding the -bā- in all forms except in the first-person plural and second-person plural (*amābā́mus, amābā́tis*). This, by the way, is similar to what occurs in the present tense, and so we are familiar with the reasons why this occurs. What's more, we will observe this same pattern throughout all the imperfect active forms: The singular and third-person plural forms place the stress on the vowel before the -b, while the first-person and second-person plural place the stress on the vowel (always -ā) after it.

AMŌ, AMÁRE, AMÁVĪ, AMÁTUS, "TO LOVE" (STEM: AMĀ-)

	Singular	Plural
First Person	amā́bam	amābā́mus
Second Person	amā́bās	amābā́tis
Third Person	amā́bat	amā́bant

Quid hīc volēbās, quid amābās? Mandūcáre et bíbere? Ipse tibi erit cibus, ipse tibi erit pōtus. (Augustine of Hippo)[13]

What were you wanting here, what were you loving? To eat and to drink? He himself will be your food and he himself will be your drink.

10.13 Imperfect Active Second Conjugation (Long ERE). The second-conjugation forms are exactly what we should expect in all ways.

MÓNEŌ, MONḖRE, MÓNUĪ, MÓNITUS, "TO WARN," "TO ADVISE" (STEM: MONĒ-)

	Singular	Plural
First Person	monḗbam	monēbā́mus
Second Person	monḗbās	monēbā́tis
Third Person	monḗbat	monḗbant

10.14 Imperfect Active Third Conjugation (Short ERE). We know by now that the third-conjugation forms are the ones that present the most trouble for us. However, the characteristic short -e (ĕ) is not displaced in the imperfect tense (as it is in the present), so you will see it throughout as -ē. In fact, it will contain the stress of the word in all forms except the first- and second-person plurals.

OSTÉNDŌ, OSTÉNDERE, OSTÉNDĪ, OSTÉNTUS, "TO SHOW" (STEM: OSTENDE-)

	Singular	Plural
First Person	ostendḗbam	ostendēbā́mus
Second Person	ostendḗbās	ostendēbā́tis
Third Person	ostendḗbat	ostendḗbant

This example also comes from Augustine of Hippo:

In interióribus meīs latḗbam, nōn ostendḗbam quis essem. (Augustine of Hippo)[14]

In my interior parts I was concealing; I was not showing who I was.

---

13. Augustine of Hippo, *Sermō* CLVIII.9 (PL 38.867).
14. Augustine of Hippo, *Ēnārrātiō in Psalmum* LXXXVII.8 (PL 37.1114).

10.15 Imperfect Active Fourth Conjugation (Long IRE). As is common, the long -i (-ī) shortens before the long -e (-ē), meaning that the forms of the fourth conjugation will match the third conjugation in the imperfect tense. Be sure to make note of this.

AÚDIŌ, AUDÍRE, AUDÍVĪ, AUDÍTUS, "TO HEAR" (STEM: AUDĪ-)

	Singular	Plural
First Person	audiḗbam	audiēbā́mus
Second Person	audiḗbās	audiēbā́tis
Third Person	audiḗbat	audiḗbant

Let us look at an example:

| Christus... víderit... flēre Marī́am quae atténtē <u>audiḗbat</u> verbum Deī. (Ambrose of Milan)[15] | Christ... will have seen... Mary crying as she <u>used to listen</u> attentively to the word of God. |

Here I translated the imperfect with a habitual aspect, suggesting that Mary, sister of Martha, was in the habit of listening to the word of God.

10.16 Imperfect Passive Forms and Aspect. Moving from imperfect actives to imperfect passives is very straightforward. We simply substitute passive personal endings for active ones. It's that simple. As we do so, of course, we have shifted from the verb performing the action to receiving the action. Thus, we should often expect the use of -ed in English to reflect that change. We will follow the same general pattern with the imperfect active when translating:

1. "was/were + being -ed" (e.g., "I was being loved," "they were being loved").
2. "used to be -ed" (e.g., "I used to be loved," "they used to be loved").

As always, we notice how concise Latin is compared to English. Latin can accomplish in one word what English must do in many words. The ending of -r, for instance, effectively means "I am verbed" or "I am being verbed." As we know, Latin can be a spectacularly compressed language.

PRESENT-SYSTEM PASSIVE PERSONAL ENDINGS

	Singular	Plural
First Person	-r	-mur
Second Person	-ris, -re	-minī
Third Person	-tur	-ntur

In order to conjugate an imperfect verb, we insert the infix -bā- between the present (= imperfect) tense stem and the present (= imperfect) personal endings. Remember that the present system—which includes the present, imperfect, and future—uses the same endings.

---

15. Ambrose of Milan, *Dē Poeniténtiā* II.VII.54 (PL 16.510).

INDICATIVE MOOD VERBS: FIRST AND SECOND PRINCIPAL PARTS

If you find this helpful, you could think of the imperfect passives as the equivalent of the following:

-bar, "I was being -ed"	-bámur, "we were being -ed)"
-báris, "you were being -ed"	-bámini, "you all were being -ed)"
-bátur, "he, she, it was being -ed)"	-bantur, "they were being -ed)"

Steps to Form Imperfect Passive (Indicatives)
1. Locate the second principal part of a verb (e.g., *laudáre*).
2. Remove the -re ending (e.g., *laudá-*).
3. Attach the infix -ba- (e.g., **laudābā-*).
4. Add the present-system personal passive endings: -r, -ris/-re, -tur; -tur, -mur, -minī, -ntur (e.g., *laudábar, laudābáris/-re, laudābátur, laudābámur, laudābámini, laudābántur*).

10.17 Imperfect Passive First Conjugation (Long ARE). These forms are as right as rain.

AMŌ, AMÁRE, AMÁVĪ, AMÁTUS, "TO LOVE" (STEM: AMĀ-)

	Singular	Plural
First Person	amábar	amābámur
Second Person	amābáris, amābáre	amābámini
Third Person	amābátur	amābántur

Here is an example of a first-conjugation imperfect passive:

Vīdī ímpiōs sepúltōs, quī étiam cum adhuc víverent in locō sānctō erant, et laudābántur in cīvitáte quasi jūstórum óperum. (Ecc. VIII.10)

I saw the wicked buried, who also when they were still living were in the holy place, and they were being praised in the city as those of righteous works.

10.18 Imperfect Passive Second Conjugation (Long ERE). Here is an example of a second-conjugation verb.

MÓNEŌ, MONĒRE, MÓNUĪ, MÓNITUS, "TO WARN," "TO ADVISE" (STEM: MONĒ-)

	Singular	Plural
First Person	monḗbar	monēbámur
Second Person	monēbáris, monēbáre	monēbámini
Third Person	monēbátur	monēbántur

10.19 Imperfect Passive Third Conjugation (Short ERE). In these forms, a long -e (-ē) appears throughout, just like the Long ERE verbs. So, be careful when distinguising them from the second conjugation. This underscores the importance of noting a verb's conjugation family when memorizing vocabulary.

IMPERFECT ACTIVES, IMPERFECT PASSIVES, AND ADVERBS

OSTÉNDŌ, OSTÉNDERE, OSTÉNDĪ, OSTÉNTUS, "TO SHOW" (STEM: OSTENDE-)

	Singular	Plural
First Person	ostendḗbar	ostendēbā́mur
Second Person	ostendēbā́ris, ostendēbā́re	ostendēbā́minī
Third Person	ostendēbā́tur	ostendēbā́ntur

10.20 Imperfect Passive Fourth Conjugation (Long IRE). Our final example comes from of a fourth-conjugation verb. It, too, is exactly as expected. There are no surprises.

AÚDIŌ, AUDÍRE, AUDÍVĪ, AUDÍTUS, "TO HEAR" (STEM: AUDĪ-)

	Singular	Plural
First Person	audiḗbar	audiēbā́mur
Second Person	audiēbā́ris, audiēbā́re	audiēbā́minī
Third Person	audiēbā́tur	audiēbā́ntur

Our example comes from I Samuel:

Porrō Anna loquēbā́tur[16] in corde suō, tantúmque lábia illíus movēbántur, et vōx pénitus nōn audiēbā́tur. Aestimā́vit ergō eam Heli temuléntam. (I Sam. I.13)	Then Anna was speaking in her heart, and only her lips were moving but her voice was not being heard thoroughly. Therefore, Eli suspected that she was drunk.

This verse offers a nice contrast between the imperfect tense (all the -bā- verbs), which highlights ongoing or habitual action, and the perfect tense (seen in the word *aestimā́vit*), which emphasizes completed action. (And, as a side note, *pénitus* is the adverb; it is modifying the activity of not being heard, not the noun *vōx*.)

Summā́rium

In this *capítulum* you learned that:
- Adverbs modify verbs, adjectives, and other words.
- The imperfect tense refers to an action occurring at the time of the speaker and it may bring out three or four different aspects when being translated.
- The imperfect tense uses the -bā- infix and the present-system endings: active endings for the imperfect active and passive endings for the imperfect passive.

---

[16]. This verb has a passive form but an active meaning. It's called a "deponent" verb, which we will soon discuss.

VOCĀBULŎRUM INDEX

Latin	English (Gloss)	(Etymology)
abscóndō, abscóndere, abscóndī, abscónditus (3)	to conceal, to hide, to cover	(abscond)
adṓrō, adōrā́re, adōrā́vī, adōrā́tus (1)	to worship, to adore, to revere	(adore)
addū́cō, addū́cere, addū́xī, addū́ctus (3)	to bring in, to lead in, to draw in	(adduction)
cómedō, comédere, comḗdī, comḗsus (3)	to eat, to eat up, to chew up, to consume	(comestible)
cóngregō, congregā́re, congregā́vī, congregā́tus (1)	to gather, to assemble, to congregate	(congregate)
clāmō, clāmā́re, clāmā́vī, clāmā́tus (1)	to proclaim, to cry out, to shout	(clamor)
effū́ndō, effū́ndere, effū́dī, effū́sus (3)	to pour (forth), to shed, to cast out	(effusive)
fugō, fugā́re, fugā́vī, fugā́tus (1)	to put to flight, to chase, to drive into exile	(fugitive)
iam (jam)	already, now, anymore	
inde	from there, thence, thereafter, since	
invéniō, invenī́re, invḗnī, invéntus (4)	to find, to discover, to come upon, to obtain	(invent)
mandō, mandā́re, mandā́vī, mandā́tus (1)	to order, to command, to give charge to	(mandate)
partim	in part, partly	(partly)
passim	everywhere	
porrō	furthermore, further, onwards	
quidem	indeed, in fact	
quasi	as it were, nearly, almost	(quasi)
resístō, resístere, réstitī, - (3)	to resist, to withstand, to oppose	(resist)
scī́licet	naturally, certainly, namely	
semper	always	(sempiternal)
simul	at the same time, simultaneously	(simultaneously)
sū́bitō	quickly, at once, immediately	
statim	immediately, at once, then	(stat)
vidḗlicet	namely, that is, that is to say	
ubī́que[a]	everywhere	(ubiquitous)

[a] This word is a synonym with *passim*.

ŌRĀTIŌ POPULĀRIS

Sýmbolum Apostolṓrum (Pars Minor III). Below is the final part of the *Sýmbolum Apostolṓrum*, which centers on the Holy Spirit and the church.

Et in Spíritum Sānctum, sānctam Ecclḗsiam cathólicam, sānctṓrum commūniṓnem, remissiṓnem peccātṓrum, carnis resurrēctiṓnem, vītam aetérnam. Āmēn.

And [I believe] in the Holy Spirit, the holy Catholic Church, the communion of the saints, the remission of sins, the resurrection of the flesh, and eternal life. Amen.

EXERCÍTIA

Be sure to complete the *exercítium* in the appendix corresponding to this *capítulum*.

Capítulum
XI

FUTURE ACTIVES AND FUTURE PASSIVES

Nōn habḗbis deōs aliḗnōs.[1]
—EXODUS

OPÚSCULUM THEOLÓGICUM: *Decem Verba*

The Ten Commandments are the most famous laws in history. Since the day Moses chiseled them into stone on Mount Sinai, they have been recorded in law, engraved on plaques, dramatized in movies, and inscribed on buildings. Though popularly known as the "ten commandments," many scholars refer to this set of laws as the "Decalogue," a term deriving from the Greek Old Testament—what scholars refer to as the Septuagint.[2] In the Septuagint, the Hebrew phrase "the ten words" [עֲשֶׂרֶת הַדְּבָרִים] was translated directly into Greek as τὰ δέκα ῥήματα, "the ten words" (Deut. IV.13), hence the English term *Decalogue*.[3] The Vulgate follows the practice of the Septuagint by translating this phrase as "ten words," *decem verba* in Latin.

So, what are the *decem verba*? In abbreviated form, here are the *decem verba* from the Vulgate:[4]

1. Nōn habḗbis deōs aliḗnōs.

   You shall not have foreign gods.

2. Nōn fáciēs scúlptile neque omnem similitúdinem.

   You shall not make a graven image nor any likeness.

3. Nōn adsū́mēs nōmen Dóminī Deī tuī in vanum.

   You shall not take God's name in vain.

4. Meméntō ut diem sábbatī sānctíficēs.

   Remember to keep as holy the Sabbath day.

5. Honṓrā patrem tuum et mātrem tuam.

   Honor your father and your mother.

---

1. "You shall not have foreign gods" (Exod. XX.3).
2. The term *Septuagint* comes from the Latin word meaning "seventy," *septuāgíntā*. Unlike the Latin term, the English word *Septuagint* has its stress over the *u*, so it is pronounced Sep-tú-a-gint, with a soft *g*.
3. This phrase also appears in Exod. XXXIV.28 and Deut. X.4.
4. These commands come from Exod. XX.3–17.

6. Nōn <u>occídēs</u>.	<u>You shall</u> not murder.
7. Nōn <u>moechā́beris</u>.	<u>You shall</u> not commit adultery.
8. Nōn fūrtum <u>fáciēs</u>.	<u>You shall</u> not steal.
9. Nōn <u>loquéris</u> contrā próximum tuum falsum testimṓnium.	<u>You shall</u> not speak false testimony against your neighbor.
10. Nōn <u>concupī́scēs</u> domum próximī tuī.	<u>You shall</u> not covet your neighbor's house.

Other than the fourth and fifth positive commandments, each of the negative commandments begins with *nōn* and is followed by a verb. Most importantly for our purposes, each of these negative commandments in the *decem verba* are in the future tense. In addition to indicating something that will happen in the future, the future tense in Latin can also indicate something that *should* happen in the future. Here both the English and Latin languages are similar.

Prospéctus

In this *capítulum* you will learn that:
- Future indicative verbs indicate something that will happen in the future. They are formed with an infix (-bi- or -ē-) and the present-system personal endings.
- Future active verbs indicate future events in which the subject performs the action; future passive verbs express events in which the subject receives action.

GRAMMÁTICA

11.1 Welcome to the Future. The future tense in Latin refers to an action occurring in the future. As mentioned above, the future tense can also be used to convey future obligation, which is why it works well when giving commands.[5] When acting as a command, it should be translated either as "shall . . ." (if positive) or "shall not . . ." (if negative, as in the case of the *decem verba*). Either way, we should think of the future tense as a verb indicating a future action or activity.

When translating the future tense (both active and passive forms), there are three major translation options. I label them as follows: "simple," "colloquial," or overly dramatic—I mean "formal." Please note that these are my own labels, not the consensus of scholarship. Take them or leave them as you like.

1. **Simple.** "Will," "will be" (e.g., "I will love," "I will be loved").
2. **Colloquial.** "Going to," "going to be" (e.g., "I am going to love," "I am going to be loved").
3. **Formal.** "Shall," "shall be" (e.g., "I shall love," "I shall be loved").

In general, I recommend allowing context to determine which translation you think is best. And it is also important to keep in mind your target audience.

---

[5]. We will discuss commands and prohibitions in Capítulum XXVII.

INDICATIVE MOOD VERBS: FIRST AND SECOND PRINCIPAL PARTS

11.2 **Forming the Future.** In the previous *capítulum*, we learned one of the simplest tenses in Latin: the imperfect. You will remember that the imperfect tense is easily formed by inserting the infix -bā- between a verb's stem (the second principal part after removing the -re) and then adding its present-system personal endings. This is true for both active and passive verbs.

The future tense follows the same method for the first and second conjugations, but it throws off the shackles of conformity in the third and fourth conjugations by deciding to adopt a different *modus vīvéndī*, "mode of living" or "lifestyle." For this reason, we will divide our discussion of the future tense into first and second conjugations and, subsequently, third and fourth conjugations.

FIRST- AND SECOND-CONJUGATIONS (ACTIVE AND PASSIVE) FOR THE FUTURE TENSE

11.3 **Future Tense: First and Second Conjugations (-bi- Forms).** We are learning the future tense immediately after learning the imperfect tense because the two possess almost identical forms and follow the same patterns (at least in the first and second conjugations). Just as the imperfect contains the infix -bā- between a verb's stem and its present-system personal endings, in a similar way, the first- and second-conjugation future contains the infix -bi- between a verb's stem and its present-system personal endings.

As you may have noted, there is only one letter that distinguishes the imperfect (-bā-) from the future (-bi-).[6] This is initially confusing, but here is a way to remember this distinction: The -ā reminds us of "wa̲s" in English (thus the imperfect tense), and the -i reminds us of "wi̲ll" in English (thus the future tense). Because both the imperfect and the future tenses use present-system personal endings, there is not much else to learn. You are already thoroughly familiar with all of these endings for both the active and passive forms.

In summary, to conjugate a first- or second-conjugation future, we simply remove the -re of a verb's second principal part (the present active infinitive), append the infix -bi-, and then attach the present personal endings. This holds true for both the active and passive voices. Also, note that the short *i* in -bi- will mean that the accent or stress for words will precede the infix.

Steps to Form Future Tenses for First and Second Conjugations
1. Locate the second principal part (e.g., *laudā́re*).
2. Remove the -re (e.g., **laudā́-*).
3. Append the infix -bi- (e.g., **laudā́bi*).
4. Add the present-system personal endings: the active for active forms and passive for passive forms. (You are already very familiar with these endings, so I will not include them here.)

11.4 **First- and Second-Conjugation Active Forms.** We will begin with the active forms. If you find this helpful, you could think of the first and second conjugations as the equivalent of the following for future active tenses:[7]

All active future verbs of the first and second conjugations will end this way.

---

6. You probably also observed that the *a* in the imperfect is long (thus, ā), while the *i* in the future tense is short. The length of the vowels affects the stress in individual words.
7. Again, this is only for the first and second conjugations.

FUTURE ACTIVES AND FUTURE PASSIVES

-bō, "I will"	-bimus, "we will"
-bis, "you will"	-bitis, "you all will"
-bit, "he, she, it will"	-bunt, "they will"[a]

[a] Naturally, you could substitute one of the other two translation options as needed.

11.5 **First-Conjugation (Long ARE) Future Active.** The forms of this conjugation are delightfully simple. The characteristic -bi- is present throughout all forms except the first-person singular (*amábō*) and third-person plural (*amábunt*). Why is this? As mentioned above, it is because the *i* is short in all forms and so has been absorbed in *amábō* and modified in *amábunt*. This also explains why the *i* is never stressed or accentuated.

Finally, due to the presence of *u* in the third-personal plural, you may occasionally confuse this form for a third- or fourth-conjugation present tense. Under such circumstances, the -b- is a clue (though not a conclusive one) that the verb may be future tense rather than present tense.

AMŌ, AMÁRE, AMÁVĪ, AMÁTUS, "TO LOVE" (STEM: AMĀ-)

	Singular	Plural
First Person	amábō	amábimus
Second Person	amábis	amábitis
Third Person	amábit	amábunt

Here is an example:

Beátī mundō corde, quóniam ipsī Deum vidébunt (Matt. v, 8): *vidéntēs amábunt, amántēs laudábunt.* (Theobald of Étampes)[8]

"Blessed are the pure in heart, for they will see God" (Matt. V.8): in seeing, they will love; in loving, they will praise.

11.6 **Second-Conjugation (Long ERE) Future Active.** Here is an example of a second-conjugation verb. Upon substituting the -ē for the -ā (we do this because this is a Long ERE verb while the one above is a Long ARE verb), everything is identical. Note, too, the same phenomenon for the first-person singular and third-personal plural. While the former ends with -ō, the latter is modified to -u.

MÓNEŌ, MONÉRE, MÓNUĪ, MÓNITUS, "TO WARN," "TO ADVISE" (STEM: MONĒ-)

	Singular	Plural
First Person	monébō	monébimus
Second Person	monébis	monébitis
Third Person	monébit	monébunt

---

8. Theobald of Étampes, *Epístola* I (PL 163.762). Hopefully you noticed that *vidébunt* is also in the future tense; it's a second-conjugation verb, so we will examine it next.

Peter of Celle provides a delightful example:

Docébō tē? Sed hoc esset deméntia: laudábō tē? Sed hoc esset stultítia: monébō tē? Sed hoc esset audácia. (Peter of Celle)[9]	Shall I teach you? But that would be madness. Shall I praise you? But that would be foolishness. Shall I instruct you? But that would be brazenness.

11.7 **First- and Second-Conjugation Passive Forms.** We will now turn to the passive forms of the first and second conjugations. The -bi- infix still applies. The only difference is that passive present-system endings are added to -bi- rather than active ones.

If you find this helpful, you could think of the first and second conjugations as the equivalent of the following for future passive tenses:

-bor, "I will be -ed"[a]	-bimur, "we will be -ed"
-beris, "you will be -ed"	-bíminī, "you all will be -ed"[b]
-bitur, "he, she, it will be -ed"	-buntur, "they will be -ed"[c]

[a] The (-ed) indicates that the verb in English will be past tense, e.g., "I will be loved."

[b] Note the placement of the accent over the first *i*. The reason is because the *i* in -bi- is short, so we have to go back one further for the accented vowel, in accordance with the rules of Latin accentuation. At the same time, even though the final *i* is long, but we cannot put stress on it.

[c] Naturally, you could substitute one of the other two translation options as needed.

11.8 **First-Conjugation (Long ARE) Future Passive.** As with the active forms, the imperfect passive and future passive forms are virtually identical in every way other than the use of -a in the imperfect (evident in all imperfect passive forms, whether long or short) and the use of -o, -e, -i, or -u in this conjugation of the future.

AMŌ, AMÁRE, AMÁVĪ, AMÁTUS, "TO LOVE" (STEM: AMĀ-)

	Singular	Plural
First Person	amā́bor	amā́bimur
Second Person	amā́beris, amā́bere	amābíminī
Third Person	amā́bitur	amābúntur

Here is an example:

Nec tantum dīlígere áliquid potérimus in terrā, quantum beáta amā́bitur réquiēs in coelō. (Alcuin of York)[10]	And we will not be able to cherish anything on earth as much as the blessed rest of heaven will be loved.

11.9 **Second-Conjugation (Long ERE) Future Passive.** Here is an example of a second-conjugation verb. There is nothing surprising here. The forms are identical to those in the first conjugation except the presence throughout of the stem vowel -ē rather than -ā.

---

9. Peter of Celle, *Epístola LXIII* (PL 202.492). Remember this saying if ever attempting to offer me instruction or criticism.
10. Alcuin of York, *Epístola XLIII* (PL 100.208).

FUTURE ACTIVES AND FUTURE PASSIVES

MÓNEŌ, MONÉRE, MÓNUĪ, MÓNITUS, "TO WARN," "TO ADVISE" (STEM: MONĒ-)

	Singular	Plural
First Person	monḗbor	monḗbimur
Second Person	monḗberis monḗbere	monēbímini
Third Person	monḗbitur	monēbúntur

THIRD- AND FOURTH-CONJUGATIONS (ACTIVE AND PASSIVE) FOR THE FUTURE TENSE

11.10 Future Tense: Third and Fourth Conjugations. Unfortunately, the third and fourth conjugations are an unruly bunch in the future tense; they are nonconformists, electing to turn their backs on the -bi- infix that we have grown to love.[11] Instead of the infix -bi-, they opt for -ē.

As you may perceive, this infix could cause confusion when it comes to distinguishing clearly between second-conjugation present tenses and third-conjugation future ones. For example, consider the following:

Dóminus . . . docet. (Ps. CVIII.1)   Dūcet Dóminus. (Deut. XXVIII.36)

Despite the exact same -et endings, one of these is in the present tense and the other is in the future tense. How do you know which is which? Unless you have been diligently memorizing all the principal parts of verbs and notating their exact family of conjugations, there is no real way to intuit the tense of these two verbs. Memorization is our only *amícus*, "friend." As it turns out, here is the translation:

The Lord . . . teaches (present tense).   The Lord will lead (future tense).

When push comes to shove, we only know this because we memorized *docet* as a second-conjugation verb and *dūcet* as a third-conjugation one. However, since I trust you have been *discípulī bonī*, "good students," studiously taking precise notes on verbs, we can end the lecture and resume learning this category of future tenses.[12]

Fortunately, there is some grace. As mentioned above, both third- and fourth-conjugation future verbs make use of a long -e (thus, -ē). However, in accordance with a lesson we have already learned—namely, that long vowels can shorten before certain letter endings and letter combinations—the long -e in *docet* shortened before the -t.

The formula for creating third- and fourth-conjugation future verbs (both active and passive) is the same.

Steps to Form the Third- and Fourth-Conjugation Future Tenses
1. Locate the second principal part (e.g., *audī́re*).
2. Remove the -re (e.g., *audī́-*).

---

[11]. Why so unruly? I mentioned previously that the short -e in third-conjugation verbs makes them subject to the most variation of any class of conjugations. As for the fourth conjugation, even though its characteristic vowel is long, the -i causes it to undergo change as well.

[12]. If you have not been memorizing all four principal parts and noting each verb's conjugation, the Roman author Livy provides the best retort: *pótius sērō quam numquam*, "better late than never" (Livy, *Ab Urbe Condítā* 4.2).

3. Append the infix -ē- (e.g., *audiē)
4. Add the present-system personal endings: active ones for actives and passive ones for passives.

If you like, you can think of this class of future active verbs as equivalent to the following:

-am,[a] "I will"	-émus, "we will"
-ēs, "you will"	-étis, "you all will"[b]
-et, "he, she, it will"	-ent, "they will"[c]

[a] The first-singular person form is the outlier here. It is most distinct from the other forms.
[b] Note the placement of the accent over the first -i. The reason is because all the i's in -bi- are short, so we have to go back one further for the accented vowel.
[c] Naturally, you could substitute one of the other two translation options as needed.

Once again, note how the long -e shortens before -t and -nt.

11.11 Third-Conjugation (Short ERE) Future Active. Third-conjugation verbs are upgraded in the future tense. How so? Instead of their characteristic short -e (that is, -ĕ), they are given new life with a long -e (-ē). This -ē changes where the stress would otherwise be in a couple of forms. Here is an example of a third-conjugation verb.

OSTÉNDŌ, OSTÉNDERE, OSTÉNDĪ, OSTÉNTUS, "TO SHOW" (STEM: OSTENDE-)

	Singular	Plural
First Person	osténdam	ostendémus
Second Person	osténdēs	ostendétis
Third Person	osténdet	osténdent

The apostle James, who was big on evidence, shows us how the verb *osténdō* can be used:

Osténdam tibi ex opéribus fidem meam.   I will show you my faith from works.
(Jas. II.18)

11.12 Fourth-Conjugation (Long IRE) Future Active. Because the -i in a fourth-conjugation verb is long (thus, -ī), it stays; consequently, we simply add the long -e (-ē) infix after it. Once it is added, however, -ī shortens before it, which is why -i is not accentuated. Note that the combination of -iē does not conclusively corroborate the future tense. The combination of these two letters can also appear in the third-conjugation present tense.[13] Finally, even though the -i precedes the infix -ē-, do not fail to forget that the -i is still fully present in each form (though it is now short rather than long).

---

13. This combination is particularly prominent among so-called third-conjugation -iŏ types.

FUTURE ACTIVES AND FUTURE PASSIVES

AÚDIŌ, AUDÍRE, AUDÍVĪ, AUDÍTUS, "TO HEAR" (STEM: AUDĪ-)

	Singular	Plural
First Person	aúdiam	audiḗmus
Second Person	aúdiēs	audiḗtis
Third Person	aúdiet	aúdient

11.13 Third- and Fourth-Conjugation Passive Forms. We will now turn to the passive forms of the third and fourth conjugations. The -ē- infix still applies. The only difference is that passive present endings are added to -ē- rather than active ones.

Once again, if you find this helpful, you could think of the third and fourth conjugation passives as the equivalent of the following in the future tense:

-ar, "I will be -ed"[a]	-ḗmur, "we will be -ed"
-ḗris, "you will be -ed"	-ḗminī, "you all will be -ed"
-ḗtur, "he, she, it will be -ed"	-entur, "they will be -ed"[b]

[a] The (-ed) indicates that the verb in English will be past tense, e.g., "I will be warn<u>ed</u>," or "I will be shown." Also, as with future actives, you could substitute one of the other two translation options as needed for future passives.

[b] If you are wondering why there is no accent over this -e, it's for reasons that we already know. Long vowels shorten before words ending in -t or -nt. The accent may or may not fall on the -e in -entur depending on which vowels appear before it. (If so, the stress would be on the -e in -entur not because it is long by nature, but because it would be long by position—due to it being followed by two consonants.)

Other than the -ar for the first-personal singular, there is nothing surprising here to note.

11.14 Third-Conjugation (Short ERE) Future Passive. All the forms below should be anticipated. There is an -a in the first-personal singular instead of the -e as in the other forms, and we know (from the two previous *capítula*) that the personal passive endings end in -r.

OSTÉNDŌ, OSTÉNDERE, OSTÉNDĪ, OSTÉNTUS, "TO SHOW" (STEM: OSTENDE-)

	Singular	Plural
First Person	osténdar	ostendḗmur
Second Person	ostendḗris	ostendḗminī
Third Person	ostendḗtur	ostendḗntur

Here is an example:

Áliquot exémplīs <u>ostendḗtur</u>.   <u>It will be shown</u> through several
(Hilary of Poitiers)[14]   examples.

---

14. Hilary of Poitiers, *Praefătiō Generâlis* CCV (PL 9.118).

11.15 Fourth-Conjugation (IRE) Future Passive. As noted above, the long -i remains in all forms of the future passive but shortens when preceding the infix -e, which is long.

AÚDIŌ, AUDÍRE, AUDÍVĪ, AUDÍTUS, "TO HEAR" (STEM: AUDĪ-)

	Singular	Plural
First Person	aúdiar	audiémur
Second Person	audiéris	audiéminī
Third Person	audiétur	audiéntur

Here is an example:

Et lūx lucérnae nōn lucébit in tē ámplius: et vōx sponsī et sponsae nōn audiétur adhuc in tē. (Rev. XVIII.24)	And the light of the lamp will shine no more in you; and the voice of the bride and groom <u>will be heard</u> no longer in you.

Despite the ominous words, this verse illustrates well two kinds of future tense formations; the first instance employs the infix -bi- and is in the active voice (*lucébit*); the second uses the -ē- infix and is in the passive voice (*audiḗtur*).

Summārium

In this *capítulum* you learned that:
- The future tense refers to an action occurring in the future; it can also sometimes be used to convey future obligation.
- While the first and second conjugations make use of the -bi- infix, the second and third conjugations use the infix -ē-; both use the present-system personal endings. Regardless of whether a future-tense verb is a first, second, third, or fourth conjugation, it is still translated the same way.

VOCĀBULŎRUM INDEX

Latin	English (Gloss)	(Etymology)
accéndō, accéndere, accéndī, accénsus (3)	to kindle, to light (a fire), to inflame	(incensed)
altáre, altáris (n)	altar, place for burnt offerings	(altar)
apériō, aperíre, apéruī, apértus (4)	to open, to uncover	(aperture)
donec	while, until, as long as	
dórmiō, dormíre, dormívī, dormítus (4)	to sleep, to lie down	(dormant)
eō, īre, iī (īvī), ītus (4)[a]	to go, to proceed, to advance	(iterate)

éxeō, exíre, éxiī (exívī), éxitus (4)	to go out (from), to exit, to depart	(exit)
exhíbeō, exhibére, exhíbuī, exhíbitus (2)	to reveal, to show, to exhibit	(exhibit)
ígitur	therefore, consequently, thus	
inquiétus, inquiéta, inquiétum	restless	(quiet)
intrō, intráre, intrávī, intrátus (1)	to enter, to go in	(intravenous)
intróeō, introíre, intróiī, intróitus (4)	to enter, to go in[b]	(introvert)
mandúcō, mandūcáre, mandūcávī, mandūcátus (1)	to eat, to chew, to devour, to goble up	(mandable)
nam	for, because, thus	
num(quid)	if, whether, surely not?[c]	
óbeō, obíre, óbiī (obívī), óbitus (4)	to go towards, to die	(obituary)
ōs, ōris (n)	mouth, face, appearance	(orifice)
os, ossis (n)[d]	bone, soul	(ossuary)
peccō, peccáre, peccávī, peccátus (1)	to sin, to transgress	(peccadillo)
récitō, recitáre, recitávī, recitátus (3)	to recite	(recite)
rēgína, rēgínae (f)	queen	
rēgnō, rēgnáre, rēgnávī, rēgnátus (1)	to rule, to govern, to reign[e]	(reign)
regō, régere, rēxī, rēctus (3)	to rule, to govern	(regent)
régulō, rēguláre, rēgulávī, rēgulátus (1)	to rule, to govern, to regulate	(regulate)
soror, soróris (f)	sister	(sorority)

[a] This is an irregular fourth-conjugation verb. Not only is it used often, but it has attracted many prepositions that slightly modify the meaning of the word, e.g., *introéō*, "to go in."

[b] You are not seeing double! I have put these verbs adjacent to each other because they look alike and also mean similar things. Be sure to note this in your vocabulary cards.

[c] This word can occur as *num* or *numquid*. It is used when a negative answer is expected.

[d] Again, you are not seeing things—this word has the same nominative form as the one above it (other than the length of vowel), even though they are different words.

[e] This verb, and the two immediately afterward, all look very similar and have the same range of meanings. Be sure to keep this in mind when notating them.

ŌRĀTIŌ POPULĀRIS

Sýmbolum Apostolórum (Pars Minor IV). Below is the entirety of the *Sýmbolum Apostolórum*. You should be able to translate it completely on your own by now. As such, no translation will be offered.

Crēdō in Deum Patrem omnipoténtem, Creatórem caelī et terrae, et in Iēsum Christum, Fílium Eius únicum, Dóminum nostrum, quī concéptus est dē Spíritū Sānctō, nātus ex María Vírgine, passus sub Póntiō Pilátō, crucifíxus, mórtuus, et sepúltus, dēscéndit ad ínferōs, tértiā diē resurréxit ā mórtuīs, ascéndit ad caelōs, sedet ad déxteram Deī Patris omnipoténtis, inde ventúrus est iūdicáre vīvōs et mórtuōs.

Et in Spíritum Sānctum, sānctam Ecclésiam cathólicam, sānctórum commūniónem, remissiónem peccātórum, carnis resurrēctiónem, vītam aetérnam. Āmēn.

EXERCÍTIA

Be sure to complete the *exercítium* in the appendix corresponding to this *capítulum*.

TÉRTIA PARS

NONCONFORMING VERBS

> While the previous part discussed all the present-system verbs (present, imperfect, and future) that play by the rules, Tértia Pars introduces us to the nonconforming verbs of Latin. Capítulum XII includes the most common verbs in all of Latin such as *esse, posse*, and *ferre*. You will see these verbs constantly. Despite the irregular formations they adopt, you will come to recognize them very quickly.
>
> Capítulum XIII presents what are called "deponent" and "semideponent" verbs. For the most part, these verbs use passive forms but have active meanings. As a result, particularly with respect to deponents (and not to the same extent with semideponents), they do not have active forms; nor do they have passive meanings. You will initially want to translate them as verbs in the passive voice, but you will need to give them an active translation in English instead. Deponent verbs have three principal parts rather than four. The principal part they do not contain is the perfect active. Semideponent verbs are "active" in the present system, but act like deponents in the perfect system.
>
> Finally, you will recall from Secúnda Pars that verbs display PNTMV, the last of which abbreviations stand for "voice." Verbs in Latin are either active in voice (in which case the subject performs the action) or passive in voice (in which case the subject is acted upon). Since you are already familiar with this concept, Capítulum XIII will not be as challenging as initial appearances suggest.

Capítulum
XII

IRREGULAR VERBS

Pótuit enim nōn peccáre prīmus homō,
pótuit nōn morī, pótuit bonum nōn dēsérere.[1]
—AUGUSTINE OF HIPPO

OPÚSCULUM THEOLÓGICUM: *Augustine's Posse, Nōn Posse Theology*

One of the earliest discussions about the freedom of the will in Christianity involved one of Roman Catholicism's four official "teachers of the church" (*doctórēs ecclḗsiae*), Augustine of Hippo. In the early 400s, Augustine refuted the arguments of Manicheans and Pelagians by employing one of the most common verbs in Latin: *possum, posse, pótui*, translated as "to be able" or "can." Unlike other Latin verbs we have learned thus far, this one is irregular, meaning that it doesn't follow the regular patterns of conjugation as seen in verbs such as *amō, amā́re, amā́vī, amā́tus*.

Despite its morphological irregularity, Augustine used *possum, posse, pótuī* with *potéstās*—a related noun meaning "power"—to cleverly communicate the state of humankind before and after the fall. According to Augustine, Adam and Eve originally possessed freedom of choice to either sin (*posse peccā́re*, "to be able to sin") or refrain from sinning (*posse nōn peccā́re*, "to be able not to sin"). After the fall, however, human beings lost the freedom to be able not to sin (*nōn posse nōn peccā́re*, "not to be able not to sin"). But not all hope was lost. In the future life of blessedness, sin will be a faded memory. In Heaven, a human being will not be able to sin (*nōn posse peccā́re*, "not be able to sin").

I acknowledge that this precise language can be difficult to keep straight, but Augustine was nothing if not a careful theologian who chose his words strategically.

We get an example of Augustine's *posse-nōn posse* theology in his work *Dē Corruptiṓne et Grā́tiā*:

> Therefore, it is necessary for us to carefully and cautiously consider in what way these pairs differ from each other: to be able not to sin [*posse nōn peccā́re*], and not to be able to sin [*et nōn posse peccā́re*], to be able not to die [*posse nōn morī*], and not to be able to die [*et nōn posse morī*], to be able not to forsake good [*bonum posse nōn dēsérere*], not to be able to forsake good [*et bonum nōn posse dēsérere*]. For the first person was able not to sin, was able not to die, and was able not to forsake good [*Pótuit enim nōn peccā́re prīmus homō, pótuit nōn morī, pótuit bonum nōn dēsérere*].[2]

---

1. "For the first person was able not to sin, was able not to die, and was able not to forsake good."
2. Augustine of Hippo, *Dē Corruptiṓne et Grā́tiā* XXXIII (PL 44.936).

Interestingly, I John, an epistle that Augustine preached on three decades before writing *Dē Corruptiōne et Grātiā*, offers a caveat to his *posse-nōn posse* theology. First John III.9 reads as follows:

Omnis quī nātus est ex Deō peccátum nōn facit, quóniam sēmen ipsíus in eō manet; et nōn potest peccáre quóniam ex Deō nātus est.	No one who has been born from God commits sin, because God's seed remains in him; and he is not able to sin because he is born from God.

For our purposes, the last clause is the most interesting: *nōn potest peccáre*, "he is not able to sin." Is John stating that God's children are unable to sin? If so, does that make Augustine's teachings null and void?

To his credit, Augustine felt the the full weight of this passage on his theology, but he neither dismissed nor ignored it. On the contrary, he simply juxtaposed it with another passage from I John. Translated from the Vulgate, I John I.8 states: "If we say, 'we do not possess sin [*peccátum nōn habēmus*],' we deceive ourselves, and the truth is not in us.'" Like all interpreters, Augustine used one biblical passage to interpret another; in this case, he interpeted I John III.9 in light of I.8.[3] As he did so, he made ample use of one of the most irregular, but still most common, verbs in the Latin language: *possum, posse, pótuī*.

Prospéctus

In this *capítulum* you will learn that:
- Irregular verbs are those that do not follow one of the four conjugations.
- Some of the most common verbs in Latin follow irregular conjugation patterns.

GRAMMÁTICA

12.1 **"Regular" Verbs.** Thus far we have discussed "regular" verbs, that is, those verbs that follow a standard pattern of conjugation. They are every teacher's pet verbs: stable, predictable, yawningly consistent. Theoretically, every "regular" verb can be generated quite simply by applying predetermined infixes and endings to a verb's stem. The four paradigm verbs used to illustrate regular verbs in this book are listed as follows:

- *amō, amáre, amávī, amátus* (Long ARE, or first-conjugation, verbs)
- *móneō, monére, mónuī, mónitus* (Long ERE, or second-conjugation, verbs)
- *osténdō, osténdere, osténdī, osténtus* (Short ERE, or third-conjugation, verbs)
- *aúdiō, audíre, audívī, audítus* (Long IRE, or fourth-conjugation, verbs)

12.2 **"Irregular" Verbs.** As in other languages, some verbs in Latin do not play by the *régulae*, "rules." For the sake of simplicity, grammarians, perhaps a bit insensitively, call this class of verbs "irregular," even though they are otherwise perfectly capable and common verbs. In fact,

---

3. For more on Augustine's interpretation of these passages, see Augustine, *Homilies on the First Epistle of John*, trans. Boniface Ramsey, The Works of Saint Augustine: A Translation for the 21st Century 3/14 (New York: New City, 2008), 75–77.

as we will see below, they are some of the most important verbs we will learn in Latin. One of the quickest ways to identify an "irregular" verb is to glance at the verb's second principal part, which is the present active infinitive. If it does not end in *-āre*, *-ēre*, *-ĕre*, or *-īre*, it is considered irregular.[4]

SUM, ESSE, FUĪ, FUTŬRUS, "TO BE," "TO EXIST"

12.3 **Esse.** We have actually learned one irregular verb already, assuredly the most important verb in all of Latin: *sum, esse, fuī, futŭrus*, "to be" or "to exist." Because this verb does not fit precisely into one of the four conjugations, it is deemed irregular. In a similar way, all of the verbs below are considered irregular because they fall outside of the standard fourfold pattern of Latin verbs.

We will generate their forms for the present, imperfect, and future active indicatives, beginning with the most common one. Because we are presenting a horizontal comparison of three forms for each verb, we will change the standard paradigm to account for these "irregular" verbs. After all, if they have worked so hard at trying to stand out from the crowd, we might as well play along.

	Present Active	**Imperfect Active**	**Future Active**
	"be"	"was"	"will be"
	"exist"	"existed"	"will exist"
1 sg	sum	eram	erō
2 sg	es	erās	eris
3 sg	est	erat	erit
1 pl	sumus	erámus	érimus
2 pl	estis	erátis	éritis
3 pl	sunt	erant	erunt

Here is an example:

Sī autem [volúntās] rēcta est, nōn sōlum inculpábilēs, vērum étiam laudábilēs <u>erunt</u>. (Eugippius)[5]

But if the will is righteous, <u>they will be</u> not only blameless but even praiseworthy.

---

4. This is because verbs are assigned to one of the four conjugations according to the second principal part; thus, a verb with a second principle part that does not follow the normal rules is considered irregular. This practice makes good sense in some ways, but it also adds unnecessary complications since many "irregular" verbs are quite "regular" once understood in more depth. For our purposes, however, we will follow the traditional terminology.

5. Eugippius, *Thēsaúrus* III (PL 62.573).

NONCONFORMING VERBS

POSSUM, POSSE,[6] *PÓTUĪ,* "TO BE ABLE," "CAN"

12.4 **Building on *Esse*.** Though appearing new to us, we have seen *possum, posse, potuī* many times before and should be able to conjugate it without the aid of notes. Why am I so confident of this? That's because it follows the same conjugation pattern of the Latin verb detailed above meaning "to be," "to exist." In other words, all we have to do is remove the letters *pot-* from this Latin verb,[7] and the familiar forms of *sum, esse, fuī, futūrus* magically appear.

POT- + SUM = POSSUM

12.5 ***Pot- + Sum*.** In truth, there is an even simpler way to understand the connection between these two verbs. Once we recognize that the root *pot-*[8] means "able" (think "potent" or "potential" in English) and *sum* is the first-person singular of "to be," all we do is combine these into one, dare I say, potent form and, *voilà*, we have a new verbal creation that means "to be able." In mathematical terms, *pot- + sum = possum*. Here are their forms in the present, imperfect, and future active indicatives. Note that the imperfect and future tenses appear "regular."

	Present Active "be able" "can"	**Imperfect Active** "was able" "could"	**Future Active** "will be able" -
1 sg	**pos**sum	**pó**teram	**pó**terō
2 sg	**pot**es	**pó**terās	**pó**teris
3 sg	**pot**est	**pó**terat	**pó**terit
1 pl	**pós**sumus	**pot**erámus	**pot**érimus
2 pl	**pot**éstis	**pot**erátis	**pot**éritis
3 pl	**pos**sunt	**pó**terant	**pó**terunt

Below is an example from this verb:

Nam quómodo est vēra resurréctiō, sē vēra esse nōn póterit carō? (Gregory I)[9]

For how is the resurrection true if true flesh <u>will</u> not <u>be able</u> to exist?

12.6 **Complementary Infinitive.** As in English, *possum, posse, pótuī* is a verb that ordinarily requires another verb to complete or "complement" its meaning. This is what grammarians call a "complementary infinitive." Hence, when we see *possum, posse, pótuī*, we should always be on the lookout for a verb nearby in its infinitive form—or second principal part—that works in tandem with it.

---

6. It may be helpful to think of *posse*, which is irregular, as originally being *potésse.
7. This rule works for every form except three in the present tense. But what happens here is simple enough to understand. The grammatical term is "assimilation." Assimilation occurs when a consonant will transform into the consonant next to it. In the case of the three exceptions to our *pot-* rule, the *t* has assimilated into an *s* resulting in: *possum, póssumus,* and *possunt* rather than **potsum,* **pótsumus,* and *potsunt. If you think about it, is it easier to pronounce these words with "ss" than "ts"? Latin speakers thought so, too.
8. Technically, *potis, potis, pote*.
9. Gregory I, *Mōrálium Librī* LV.71 (PL 75.1077).

IRREGULAR VERBS

TRANSLATING *POSSUM, POSSE, PÓTUĪ*

12.7 **Are You Able or Can You?** When translating *possum, posse, pótuī* into English, we will typically have to choose whether to render it as "to be able" or "can." Because these two translations may convey different senses of ability,[10] here is a general guideline (not ironclad rule) to follow: First translate *possum, posse, pótuī* as "to be able"; then do so as "can." Afterward, decide which translation fits the context. Here is an example from the present tense:

Quis <u>potest</u> fácere mundum? (Job XIV.4)

We first translate it as follows: "Who <u>is able</u> to make clean?" Now we substitute "can" for "is able": "Who <u>can</u> make clean?" Which translation is best? Arguably, the former better conveys the sense that no one except God, or those God so empowers, is capable of making someone clean, while the latter is more informal and direct. Our next example is from the imperfect tense. The book Job is proving to offer an interesting illustration, so we will continue with it:

<u>Póteram</u> et ego simília vestrī loquī. (Job XVI.4)

Our first translation is: "<u>I was</u> also <u>able</u> to speak similar things as you all." After making our substitution, it is: "<u>I could</u> also speak similar things as you all." Arguably the latter translation is better since it is more idiomatic, and we could even make it sound more colloquial by translating it as follows: "I could also speak like you." Our final example comes from the future tense.

Dīxítque Dóminus num cēláre <u>pótero</u> Ábrahām quae gestúrus sum. (Gen. XVIII.17)

As it turns out, the use of the word *num* indicates in Latin that a negative answer is expected. But we can still run through our translation options. First we have: "And the Lord said, '<u>Will I be able</u> to hide from Abraham what I am about to do?'" When translating with "can," we will notice an immediate problem: The verb "can" does not have a future tense in English. (Go ahead and try to "can" something in the future; I will wait for you.) This means that we must either adopt the first translation or we must get creative and think of other ways of expressing the idea of "can-ness."

This might eventually lead us to translate it as one of the following: "And the Lord said, '<u>Can / Could I</u> hide from Abraham what I am about to do?'" Arguably neither of these best fits the context; in such a case, we might opt for one of the following: "And the Lord said, '<u>Shall / Should I</u> hide from Abraham what I am about to do?'" Context will ultimately decide which translation is best—and, again, the use of *num* indicates the answer God is expecting—but arguably this last rendition sounds better in English than the others. However, in my humble opinion, the helping verb "shall" is best saved for legal documents and Shakespearean plays.

FERŌ, FERRE, TULĪ, LĀTUS, "TO BRING," "TO BEAR," "TO CARRY"

12.8 **Defective Verb.** *Ferō, ferre, tulī, lātus* is probably the most unusual verb we have seen thus far. You may be wondering if you need to schedule an *óculus* exam. Although it initially looks

---

10. In English, "can" is a modal auxiliary verb, while "to be able" is not. Although their meanings can overlap, "to be able" sometimes sounds more formal.

like it follows some of the rules for the third conjugation in the present form, it is missing some letters that we would expect.[11] More troubling, however, is the marked differences among its principal parts. In short, *tulī* and *lātus* do not look anything like *ferō*, let alone much like each other. It looks like the verb is falling off the train tracks. What is going on here?

But let's not get concerned just yet. Despite its irregularity, there is something beautifully logical taking place. The first two parts of the verb *ferō, ferre* changed verbal forms when moving from the present system to the perfect one. Trouble is, the cognate verb that it acquired happens to look nothing like it.[12] (Apparently the Roman in charge of choosing a substitute verb had drunk too much *vīnum* that day.) Oh well, the two forms stuck together and found a way to work out their differences.

12.9 **Compound Verbs.** Despite its peculiar form, *ferō, ferre, tulī, lātus* is a very common and important verb. We will see it frequently in Latin and so must become comfortable with it from the beginning. At its core, it means something like "to bring," "to bear," or "to carry," but there are actually any number of acceptable ways to render it into English. In fact, one of its most frequent uses is as a "compound verb," that is, as a verb that has been compounded, or combined, with a preposition, particle, or prefix. For instance:

- auférre, "to bring [take] away" (combined with the preposition *ab*)
- cōnférre, "to bring together" (combined with the preposition *cum*)
- dēférre, "to bring down" (combined with the preposition *dē*)
- efférre, "to bring out" (combined with the preposition *ex*)
- prōférre, "to bring forth" (combined with the preposition *prō*)
- reférre, "to bring back (combined with the prefix *re*)

We will not memorize all of these verbs, but I highly recommend getting in the habit of observing prefixes and prepositions. Although you may not know the translation of a certain verb, your ability to combine a Latin prefix or preposition with the root of the verb can oftentimes uncover its general meaning. For instance, after learning that verbs with a second-principal part of *ferre* mean something like "to bring," its combination with the preposition *cum* (which, not surprisingly, undergoes a slight alteration when combined: thus cōnférre) logically carries the meaning of "to bring together."

12.10 *Ferre.* At this point, we are reserving our discussion of the perfect tense for another *capitulum*. This is good news for you. That's because the present, imperfect, and future forms of *ferre* are based only on the first two principal parts, meaning that we do not have to tackle the forms of *tulī* and *lātus* at this time. What's more, other than the phenomenon of the present active tense lacking the connecting vowel -i in three forms and the present passive tense in two, *ferre* follows the third conjugation pattern of verbs quite regularly. Turns out, in other words, that *ferō, ferre, tulī, lātus* is not as intimidating as it first appeared. Here are the active

---

11. The grammatical term for this is "syncope," or the dropping of a sound from a word. The letter *r* is particularly susceptible to syncope. Thus, in the present active form, *fers, fert,* and *fertis* are each missing an *i*; and *ferre* should have an *e* between the two *r*'s: **férere*.

12. The grammatical term for this phenomenon is "suppletion." An example in English is "I go" (for the present tense) and "I went" (for the past tense). The reason why these two words look different is because they are based on different verbal forms. As regards *ferō, ferre*, it made the verb *tollō, tóllere* its perfect form, which is how it became *tulī, lātus*. (And for those really interested, the form *lātus* was initially **tlātus*, but dropped or syncopated the *t*. Because *tollō, tóllere* lost its perfect forms, it had to take new perfect forms, which it did in the verb *súfferō, suférre*—resulting in *sústulī, sublātus*.)

and passive forms of the verb based on the first two principal parts. The words footnoted indicate slight irregularities.

	Present Active "bring"	**Imperfect Active** "was bringing" "brought"	**Future Active** "will bring"
1 sg	ferō	ferḗbam	feram
2 sg	fers[a]	ferēbās	ferēs
3 sg	fert[b]	ferḗbat	feret
1 pl	férimus	ferēbā́mus	ferḗmus
2 pl	fertis[c]	ferēbā́tis	ferḗtis
3 pl	ferunt	ferḗbant	ferent

	Passive "be brought"	**Imperfect Passive** "was being brought"	**Future Passive** "will be brought"
1 sg	feror	ferḗbar	ferar
2 sg	ferris[d] (ferre)	ferēbā́ris (ferēbā́re)	ferḗris (ferḗre)
3 sg	fertur[e]	ferēbā́tur	ferḗtur
1 pl	férimur	ferēbā́mur	ferḗmur
2 pl	feríminī	ferēbā́minī	ferḗminī
3 pl	ferúntur	ferēbā́ntur	ferḗntur

[a] Note that the verb is regular if we imagine an "i" between "r" and "s": *feris.
[b] Note that the verb is regular if we imagine an "i" between "r" and "t": *ferit.
[c] Note that the verb is regular if we imagine an "i" between "r" and "t": *féritis.
[d] Note that the verb is regular if we imagine an "e" between "r" and "r": *fereris.
[e] Note that the verb is regular if we imagine an "i" between "r" and "s": *féritur.

Here is an example:

Nōn agunt poeniténtiam ibi, nec ferunt laudēs omnipoténtī Deō. (Haymo of Halberstadt)[13]

They neither do penance there nor bring praise to the almighty God.

VELLE, NELLE, AND *MĀLLE*

12.11 Irregular Verbs. The last irregular verbs we will discuss in this *capítulum* are words following the same irregular pattern. We can think of these verbs as generally falling within the third conjugation, though some of their forms are more easily memorized than understood.

---

13. Haymo Halberstadt, *Commentária in Isaíam* II.XXXVIII (PL 116.905).

VOLŌ, VELLE, VÓLUĪ, "TO WANT," "TO WISH," "TO WILL"

12.12 Velle. The first of our verbs is *volō, velle, vóluī*. It is a verb that is used often in Latin, and it encompasses the semantic range of "to want," "to wish," or "to will."

	Present Active[a]	**Imperfect Active**	**Future Active**
	"want" "wanting"	"was wanting"	"will want"
1 sg	volō	volébam	volam
2 sg	vīs	volébās	volēs
3 sg	vult (volt)	volébat	volet
1 pl	vólumus	volēbámus	volémus
2 pl	vultis (voltis)	volēbátis	volétis
3 pl	volunt	volébant	volent

[a] Note that this verb does not occur in the passive voice; it is always active in meaning.

Here is an example of this verb:

| Quid ámplius vólumus? Commentítiōs omnēs cultūs Deus réspuit, dámnat, excēcrátur. (John Calvin)[14] | What else do we want? God rejects, condemns, and detests all false worship. |

12.13 To Want, To Wish, To Will. Probably the most challenging feature of *volō, velle, vóluī* is deciding exactly how to render it into English. As mentioned above, the most generic translation options are "to want," "to will," "to wish." The semantic ranges of these words overlap in English as they do in Latin (and Greek), but the Latin word could also be translated as "to desire" or even "to intend" or "to mean." When encountering this verb in Latin, I recommend plugging in our three basic translation options and then deciding which sounds best according to context; in other words, trust your ear. If these do not sound good, then you could consider the other three translation options just listed (or dig deeper into the context and find another translation option).

DEUS VULT

The word *volō, velle, vóluī* has been used in various ways in the history of Christianity. One well-known phrase is *Deus vult*. It translates as "God wills it," and it was the rallying cry for the First Crusade. According to one account of the speech that Pope Urban II gave at the Council of Clermont in France in the year 1095 (the speech that effectively launched the Crusades), those present unanimously shouted *Deus vult* in response to Urban II's passionate plea for the Frankish Christians to liberate the Christians under Muslim occupation in the East.[15]

---

14. John Calvin, *Dē Necessitáte* (CR 6.464).
15. See *Robert the Monk's History of the First Crusade: Historia Iherosolimitana*, trans. Carol Sweetenham, Crusade Texts in Translation 11 (Ashgate: Aldershot, 2006), 43.

IRREGULAR VERBS

NŌLŌ, NŌLLE, NŌLUĪ, "TO NOT WANT," "TO NOT WISH," "TO NOT WILL"

12.14 Nōlle. One additional irregular verb, following on the heels of the one above, is very easy to master. For not only does *nōlō, nōlle, nōluī* follow the same pattern as *volō, velle, vóluī*, it actually is the same word in several forms in the present tense—it is simply preceded by the word *nōn*, "not." Here are their active forms (as there are no passive ones).

	Present Active	Imperfect Active	Future Active
	"do not want"	"was not wanting"	"will not want"
	"did not want"		
1 sg	nōlō	nōlébam	nōlam
2 sg	nōn vīs	nōlébās	nōlēs
3 sg	nōn vult	nōlébat	nōlet
1 pl	nólumus	nōlēbámus	nōlḗmus
2 pl	nōn vultis	nōlēbátis	nōlḗtis
3 pl	nōlunt	nōlébant	nōlent

Paul exemplifies the battle between *velle* and *nōlle* in the following *versículus*, "verse."

Nōn enim quod <u>volō</u> bonum hoc
fáciō sed quod <u>nōlō</u> malum hoc agō.
(Rom. VII.19)

For I do not do the good that <u>I want</u> to do but I do the bad that <u>I do not want</u> to do.

MĀLŌ, MĀLLE, MĀLUĪ, "TO PREFER," "TO WANT MORE"

12.15 Mālle. There is one more irregular verb that complements *nōlle* and *velle*. Translated as "to prefer" or "to want more," *mālō, mālle, máluī* forms very similarly to the two above. This is because it is actually a compound of the adverb *magis* and *velle*, "to want more." Depending on the exact form, this verb mirrors *velle* and *nōlle*. As such, we will not include full paradigms for its forms since you should be able to identify it quite easily.

Summárium

In this *capítulum* you learned that:
- Irregular verbs are those verbs that do not follow the standard fourfold conjugation discussed in previous *capítula*. However, many of these still follow somewhat predictable patterns.
- Several of these irregular verbs can be translated in many ways, so we must be patient and pay close attention to context.
- Irregular verbs are some of the most commonly used verbs in Latin. We will see them frequently.

VOCĀBULŌRUM INDEX

Latin	English (Gloss)	(Etymology)
aúreus, aúrea, aúreum	golden, of gold	(aureole)
ferō, ferre, tulī, lātus (3)	to bring, to bear, to carry	(fertile)
grex, gregis (m)	flock, herd, crowd	(gregarious)
hábitō, habitáre, habitávī, habitátus (1)	to dwell, to live, to inhabit, to abide	(habitat)
méminī, meminísse, -, - (3)[a]	to remember, to be mindful of	(reminisce)
mercēs, mercédis (f)	pay, wages, reward, salary, ransom	(mercenary)
nōlō, nōlle, nóluī	to not wish, to not want, to not will	
ovis, ovis (f)	sheep	(ovine)
paúper, paúper, paúper	poor	(pauper)
possum, posse, pótuī, -	to be able, can	(potential)
poténtia, poténtiae (f)	power, might	(potent)
potéstās, potestátis (f)[b]	power, ability, authority	
pulvis, púlveris (m)	dust, powder, ashes	(pulverize)
réliquus, réliqua, réliquum	remaining, surviving	(relic)
sciō, scīre, scīvī (sciī), scītus (4)	to know, to understand	
sōl, sōlis (m)	sun	(solar)
tollō, tóllere, sústulī, sublātus (3)	to take away, to take up, to lift up	(sublate)
tunc	then, at that time	
vítulus, vítulī (m)	bull, calf	(vituline)
volō, velle, vóluī, -	to wish, to want, to will	(volition)
urbs, urbis (f)	city	(urban)
uxor, uxóris (f)	wife	(uxorious)
valdē	greatly, exceedingly, very	
venter, ventris (m)	womb, stomach, belly, bowels	(ventricle)
vincō, víncere, vīcī, victus (3)	to conquer, to win, to defeat	(victory)

[a] As you can see, this is considered a "defective" verb. (It's actually in a tense we have not learned yet: the "perfect," though it is translated as if it were in the "present.") For the time being, simply memorize its forms.

[b] What is the difference between *poténtia* and *potéstās*? The first emphasizes capacity, while the latter emphasizes authority. Our translations, however, will not always be able to bring out these subtleties.

ŌRĀTIŌ POPULĀRIS

Tē Deum (Pars Minor I). This is one of the classic prayers in the Catholic Church. Due to its length, we will only memorize the first two parts.

Tē Deum laudámus: tē Dóminum cōnfitémur.	We praise you, God: We confess you as Lord.
Tē aetérnum Patrem omnis terra venerátur.	All the earth worships you, the everlasting Father.
Tibi omnēs Ángelī; tibi caelī et univérsae potestátēs.	All the Angels cry out to you; the heavens and all powers cry out to you.
Tibi Chérubīm et Séraphīm incessábilī vōce prōclámant:	In an unceasing voice the Cherubim and Seraphim cry out to you:
Sānctus, Sānctus, Sānctus, Dóminus Deus Sábaoth.	Holy, Holy, Holy, the Lord God of Hosts.
Plēnī sunt caelī et terra majestátis glóriae tuae.	The heavens and the earth are full of the majesty of your glory.

EXERCÍTIA

Be sure to complete the *exercítium* in the appendix corresponding to this *capítulum*.

Capítulum
XIII

DEPONENTS AND SEMIDEPONENTS

Cūr querimini, quod vōs īnsequámur?[1]
—TERTULLIAN

OPÚSCULUM THEOLÓGICUM: *Tertullian's Apologéticus*

Tertullian was one of the earliest Christian authors of the Latin language. Born in the middle of the second century in the Roman province of Africa, his full Latin name was more elegant than his English one: Quīntus Septímius Flōrēns Tertulliánus. Although we do not know all of his background or how he made a living, he was clearly very educated and well trained in both oratory and theology. Personally, I think he is one of the most interesting and entertaining Christian Latin writers of all time.

In total, about thirty of his writings have come down to us. Not only do these writings display an author who is as spirited as he is spiritual, but they also contain some the earliest uses of some of the most well-known phrases in Christian theology such as *Trínitās*, "Trinity"; *trēs persónae, ūna substántia*, "three persons and one substance"; *Novum Testāméntum*, "New Testament"; and *Vetus Testāméntum*, "Old Testament."

Among his highly distinguished writings, one of his most famous ones is called *Apologéticus prō Chrīstiánīs*, "Defense in Behalf of Christians"—but most known simply as "Apology." Probably written at the end of the second century, it is Tertullian's attempt to correct misunderstandings about Christianity. The most memorable line uttered in the book, which has reverberated across the centuries, is surprisingly brief:

Sēmen est sanguis Chrīstiānórum.[2]   The blood of Christians is seed.

Perhaps you are more familiar with the classic way this Latin sentence has been translated: "The blood of the martyrs is the seed of the church." I have always loved this translation. It has a great ring to it. Although it is not a mistranslation, it only makes sense to translate the short sentence in this way in order to provide necessary context for the reader who otherwise encounters it without having read Tertullian's actual work, which, of course, takes as its subject the whole notion of Christian persecution.

---

1. "Why do you all complain when we persecute you?"
2. Tertullian, *Apologéticus prō Chrīstiánīs* L (PL 1.535).

Whatever the case, the section in which this famous Latin appears is in the context of the final chapter of Tertullian's treatise: the fiftieth. Tertullian sets up his argument for *sēmen est sanguis Chrīstiānōrum* in the earliest lines of this *capítulum*. He writes:

Cūr queríminī, quod vōs īnsequámur, sī patī vultis, cum dīlígere dēbeátis per quōs patíminī quod vultis? . . . tamen et proeliátur ómnibus víribus et vincēns in proéliō gaúdet quī dē proéliō querēbátur, quia et glóriam cōnséquitur et praedam.³	Why do you all complain when we persecute you? Instead, you ought to love those through whom you suffer what you want [to suffer] . . . Nevertheless, the one who was complaining about the battle fights with all his strength and, when victorious, he rejoices in battle because he obtains both glory and spoil.

There are six verbs of note that Tertullian presents here: *queror, īnsequor, pátior, proélior, gaúdeō,* and *cōnsequor*. Respectively, they can be succinctly translated as "to complain," "to persecute," "to suffer," "to fight," "to rejoice," and "to obtain."⁴ You may have noticed that some of these verbs possess forms that look somewhat familiar, but not necessarily in the place we expect them. This is a new class of verbs that we will encounter in this *capítulum*: "deponent" and "semideponent" verbs.

Prospéctus

In this *capítulum* you will learn that:
- Deponent verbs have passive forms but active meanings; they only have three principal parts.
- Semideponent verbs have active forms in the first two principal parts but are deponent in the third principal part. They do not have a fourth principal part either.
- Neither deponent nor semideponent verbs conjugate in all their parts. However, there is logic behind their formations, and they are easy enough to recognize.

GRAMMÁTICA

13.1 Regular Verbs. By now, we are *bona fide* experts when it comes to understanding and identifying "regular" verbs. These, as we have come to recognize, are the goody-goody verbs that always obey the teacher's rules and never get detention for unruly behavior. They follow one of four predetermined patterns of conjugation, generically labeled first, second, third, and fourth. Before we condemn them to the underworld, however, we must recognize that they allow our brains to go on autopilot when coming across them. Like clockwork, they can be depended on to be formed in a consistent way. They are definitely worth keeping.

13.2 Deponents and Semideponents. In the last couple of *capítula*, we have seen a pattern. In addition to the regular verbs that conform to the rules, there are many other verbs that do not. If the "regular" verbs are the ones sitting on the side of conformity, the verbs we encountered in

---

3. Tertullian, *Apologḗticus prō Chrīstiā́nīs* L (PL 1.530).
4. Naturally, these verbs have much greater ranges of meaning, but I am here only providing one basic translation.

the last *capítulum*—"irregular" and even "defective" ones—are on the other side. Like people, when examined closer, these "irregular" and "defective" verbs are not as bad as their reputations suggest. They are actually quite normal once properly understood. But they do take their beats from a different drummer.

If we imagine a spectrum of Latin verbs—with "regular" ones on the far right and "irregular" and "defective" ones on the far left—deponents and semideponents sit snugly in the middle. Here is why: On the one hand, they look and are conjugated just like "regular" active verbs (and they therefore fall into the four classes of verbs we know by heart: first, second, third, and fourth). On the other *manus*, these verbs mostly use the passive voice forms even though they must be translated in the active voice.

What does this mean for you? Two things. First, and most important, there are not any new paradigms to learn for deponent and semideponent forms. Since they follow regular patterns, you already know the predetermined ways they will end. This is the good news. Second, and here it is less than ideal, the only guaranteed way to spot a deponent or semideponent verb out of a crowd is to memorize it as such. Otherwise, you will translate it in the passive voice, in which case it will not make sense. Let us look at an example:

Angústiās pátior. (Gerhoh of Reichersberg)[5]

When we come across any sentence in Latin, I encourage you to first locate the nominative (subject) and then find the accusative (direct object). In the example provided, the subject is contained in the verb, which means we can now immediately hunt for the direct object. Although we have not learned the word *angústiās*, you see the -ās ending, which is a clue (though not a definitive one) that the word could be in the accusative plural.[6] And because the other word is the verb, this is what it has to be.

Good enough, but how exactly do we translate it? If we did not recognize the verb as a deponent, we would initially translate it (and incorrectly so) in the passive voice: "*I am suffered." Fortunately, our common sense should eventually kick in and remind us that we do not use the verb "to suffer" in this way in English (at least I don't), leading us to change our course of action and also change our translation to the active voice: "I suffer." This sounds much better (only grammatically speaking, that is) and, by checking in the dictionary, we discover that our common sense was correct. Here is how we translate the sentence, *Angústiās pátior*:

I suffer trials.

This is a short example, but it prepares us for the discussion below.

13.3 **Deponent or Semideponent?** We know by now that deponent and semideponent verbs differ from other verbs, but we do not yet know the difference between them. Let us crack the case. While deponent verbs have passive forms but active meanings across both the present and perfect systems, semideponent verbs act normally in the present system but deponent in the perfect system. In other words, deponent verbs are always active even though they appear passive; semideponent verbs are sometimes active and sometimes passive depending on their tense. Let us dig a little deeper.

---

5. Gerhoh of Reichersberg, *Commentárium in Psalmōs* X.CXVIII.82 (PL 194.783).
6. What else could it be? Right—it could be a second-person singular active verb of the first conjugation, such as *amās*, "you love."

DEPONENTS AND SEMIDEPONENTS

13.4 **Deponents.** As stated above, deponent verbs have passive forms but active meanings. They look passive, but they will be translated as active. In fact, deponent verbs have no active forms and no passive meanings. They are easy to recognize in the dictionary because their principal parts use the passive forms. For example, the principal parts of the verb "to suffer" are as follows: *pátior, patī, passus sum*. These three forms are all passive, but we will, nonetheless, translate them as active. This is initially perplexing, so below is a deponent guide that you may find helpful.

DEPONENT CONJUGATIONS

Conjugation Name	Active Infinitive Form (Ending)	Alternative Name	Deponent (or Passive) Infinitive Form (Ending)
First	-áre	(Long) ARE Verbs	-árī
Second	-ére	Long ERE Verbs	-érī
Third	-ĕre	Short ERE Verbs	-ī[a]
Fourth	-íre	(Long) IRE Verbs	-írī

[a] As always, the short -e (ĕ) in the third conjugation keeps it from hardly ever following the rules. Even if the third-conjugation verb is a so-called -iō verb, it still uses the -ī ending here.

As this chart indicates, we classify deponent verbs just like normal verbs: first, second, third, and fourth. It's only that they look different than what we have learned because they are now in the passive (= deponent) form rather than an active form.

Let us return to the principal parts. We will begin with the first one. *Pátior* is simply the passive form of a verb we would otherwise anticipate to be *pátio. Not only is *pátio not Roman outdoor furniture, it's not even a Latin word. The reason should be dawning on you: Deponent verbs do not have active forms. Therefore, the (first-person) present *passive* form is the first principal part.

As for the second principal part, *patī*, this is simply the present *passive* infinitive. As seen in the chart, -ī is the normal ending for a third-conjugation passive infinitive. We will learn infinitives in due course; for now, remember that infinitives are the dictionary forms of verbs. They are the "to . . ." verbal form, for instance, "to suffer." The second principal part of deponent verbs end in -árī, -érī, -ī, or -írī in correspondence with the first, second, third, and fourth conjugations, respectively.

Finally, there is the third principal part. This is the one that is most distinct from what we have previously learned. In short, the third principal part in deponent verbs is the perfect passive—the "to have been -ed" tense—which we will discuss in much greater detail in a subsequent *capítulum*. Because the perfect passive is a compound verb—meaning that it uses two words to form it rather than one—we memorize it alongside the verb *sum*.

What about the fourth principal part? Deponent verbs do not have them. Instead of four, they simply have three. In summary, deponent verbs use only the first three principal parts; in every instance, they appear passive in form, even though they are to be translated as active in meaning. Let us look at a paradigm verb in full. This comes from a third-conjugation verb, but the same concept applies to all four conjugations.

As you see, there are no new forms here. Celebrate accordingly. In an ideal universe, you should be able to reproduce this chart from memory. The forms look identical to the present passive, imperfect passive, and future passive; the only difference is that they are to be translated in the active voice.

PÁTIOR, PATĪ, PASSUS SUM, "TO SUFFER"

	Present	Imperfect	Future
	"suffer"	"was suffering"	"will suffer"
1 sg	pátior	patiébar	pátiar
2 sg	páteris (pátere)	patiēbáris (patiēbáre)	patiéris (patiére)
3 sg	pátitur	patiēbátur	patiétur
1 pl	pátimur	patiēbámur	patiémur
2 pl	patíminī	patiēbáminī	patiéminī
3 pl	patiúntur	patiēbántur	patiéntur

But enough of suffering; let us now discuss the deponent verb's cousin: the semideponent verb. Hopefully we can find a more uplifting paradigm verb for it.

13.5 **Semideponents.** Semideponent, or what we could designate as half-deponent, verbs are identical to deponent verbs except in one very important way: Semideponent verbs have active (and passive) forms throughout the entire present stem, but passive forms in the perfect system. Because this is so, the first two principal parts in semideponents will look entirely regular; it is only the third principal part that will give us a run for our money.

Additionally, because the present system in semideponents has both active and passive forms, you will translate them as active or passive depending upon their specific form: Translate it as active if in the active voice and passive if in the passive voice. It is only in the third principal part—which is part of the perfect system—where we will translate the passive form actively. Stated differently, semideponent verbs are deponent verbs only in the third principal part.

Let us look at a paradigm verb. This is another third-conjugation verb, but the rule applies across the board to all semideponents.

CŌNFÍDO, CŌNFÍDERE, CŌNFÍSUS SUM, "TO TRUST," "TO CONFIDE IN," "TO BE CONFIDENT OF"

	Present	Imperfect	Future
	"trust"	"was trusting"	"will trust"
1 sg	cōnfídō	cōnfīdébam	cōnfídam
2 sg	cōnfídis	cōnfīdébās	cōnfídes
3 sg	cōnfídit	cōnfīdébat	cōnfídet
1 pl	cōnfídimus	cōnfīdēbámus	cōnfīdémus
2 pl	cōnfíditis	cōnfīdēbátis	cōnfīdétis
3 pl	cōnfídunt	cōnfīdébant	cōnfídent

As you see, there is nothing new here to learn (other than the change in the presentation of the principal parts). Despite the beads of sweat forming on your face, you know all of these forms. In terms of contract law, we might state it as follows: Whereas the present stem includes the present, imperfect, and future tenses; and whereas semideponents only use passive/deponent forms in the perfect system; now, therefore, semideponents will not substantially impact us until we learn the perfect system.

If you did not attend law school, here is the summary: We do not need to be overly concerned with semideponent verbs. Why? The first two principal parts of semideponents are delightfully normal; and the only remaining principal part—the third—will not concern us until we learn the perfect system.

This raises a question: Why are we talking about it, then? We only include a brief discussion of semideponent verbs here for two reasons. First, they are connected to deponent verbs, which will impact our translations immediately; and, second, we need to be familiar with their principal parts since we will start learning them in vocabulary starting now. In fact, compared to deponent verbs, there are only a handful of semideponent verbs. They are fairly easy to distinguish from deponent verbs since their first two forms are active while only the last one is passive.

> **Summārium**
>
> In this *capítulum* you learned that:
> - Deponent verbs possess passive forms but active meanings, while semideponent verbs have passive forms only in the perfect system; in every other way, however, they look and translate like active verbs.
> - There are a good number of such verbs in Latin, and the only way to recognize them is to memorize them as such in the dictionary or vocabulary section. Deponents and semideponents only have three principal parts (rather than four). As such, when you learn a vocabulary word that only has three principal parts, you should assume that it is a deponent or semideponent verb.

VOCĀBULŌRUM INDEX

Be sure to annotate deponent and semideponent verbs carefully. The fact that they only possess three principal parts should make this rather easy. Remember that deponent verbs maintain passive forms in all three principal parts, while semideponent verbs only have passive forms in the third principal part. Finally, do not be intimidated by the fact that several of these words share very similar—if not identical—meanings. In fact, many of these words mean essentially the same thing, whether we add or substitute an English preposition in front of them or not. Once again, take careful notes.

Latin	English (Gloss)	(Etymology)
aúdeō, audḗre, ausus sum (2)[a]	to dare, to risk, to venture	(audacious)
cōnfídō, cōnfídere, cōnfísus sum (3) (+ dat)[b]	to trust (in), to confide (in), to confess	(confide)
cōnfíteor, cōnfitḗrī, cōnféssus sum (2)	to confess, to acknowledge, to praise	(confess)

(cont.)

NONCONFORMING VERBS

Latin	English (Gloss)	(Etymology)
cōnor, cōnā́rī, cōnā́tus sum (3) (+ inf)c	to strive, to try, to attempt	(conation)
cónsequor, cónsequī, cōnsecū́tus sum (3)	to follow, to pursue, to obtain	(consequence)
cōnsólor, cōnsōlā́rī, cōnsōlā́tus sum (1)	to console, to soothe, to alleviate	(console)
diffī́dō, diffī́dere, diffī́sus sum (3) (+ dat)	to distrust (in), to despair (of)	(diffidence)
fáteor, fatḗrī, fassus sum (2) (+ acc; dat)d	to confess, to admit, to praise	
fīdō, fī́dere, fī́sus sum (3)	to trust, to rely (on), to put confidence (in)	(fiduciary)
gaúdeō, gaudḗre, gāvī́sus sum (2)	to rejoice, to be glad	(gaudy)
glṓrior, glōriā́rī, glōriā́tus sum (1)	to boast, to brag, to glory	(glory)
hortor, hortā́rī, hortā́tus sum (1)	to urge, to exhort, to encourage	(exhort)
lóquor, loquī, locū́tus sum (3)	to speak, to say, to tell, to talk	(loquacious)
méditor, meditā́rī, meditā́tus sum (1)	to meditate (on), to contemplate	(meditate)
míseror, miserā́rī, miserā́tus sum (1)	to have pity on, to lament, to feel sorry for	(commiserate)
mīror, mīrā́rī, mīrā́tus sum (1)	to be amazed (at), to wonder (at)	(admire)
mórior, morī, mórtuus sum (3)	to die	(morgue)
óperor, operā́rī, operā́tus sum (1)	to work, to labor	(operator)
ṓrdior, ōrdī́rī, ōrsus sum (4)	to begin, to commence	(order)
órior, orī́rī, ortus sum (4)	to arise, appear, to rise, to get up	(orient)
pátior, patī, passus sum (3)	to suffer, to endure, to allow	(passion)
recórdor, recordā́rī, recordā́tus sum (1)	to remember, to call to mind, to recollect	(record)
téstor, testā́rī, testā́tus sum (1)	to witness, to testify, to attest	(testify)
ūtor, ūtī, ūsus sum (3) (+ abl)	to use, to employ, to enjoy, to experience	(use)
véreor, verḗrī, véritus sum (2)	to revere, to worship, to fear	(revere)

a Do not confuse this verb with aúdiō, which means "to hear."

b This verb is part of a number of verbs that take the dative as their object (instead of the accusative). Verbs that take a case other than the accusative for the object will subsequently be indicated as such in parenthesis.

c This means that the verb necessitates an infinitive after it, that is, a "to . . ." verb.

d When taking the accusative, it is best translated as "to confess" or "to acknowledge"; with the dative, it is "to praise."

ŌRĀTIŌ POPULĀRIS

Tē Deum (Pars Minor II). Below is the second part of the *Tē Deum* prayer. Although the prayer contains more words than here provided, we will only memorize the first and second parts.

Tē glōriósus Apostolórum chorus;	The glorious chorus of the Apostles praise you.
Tē Prophētárum laudábilis númerus;	The praiseworthy fellowship of the Prophets praise you.
Tē Mártyrum candidátus laudat exércitus.	The shining[7] army of Martyrs praise you.
Tē per orbem terrárum sāncta cōnfitétur Ecclésia:	The Holy Church through all the world confesses you:
Patrem imménsae mājestátis;	Father of infinite Majesty;
Venerándum tuum vērum et únicum Fílium;	Your true and only Son who is to be worshiped.
Sānctum quoque Parāclítum Spíritum.	And also the Holy Spirit, the Comforter.
Tū Rēx glóriae, Christe.	You are the King of Glory, Christ.
Tū Patris sempitérnus es Fílius.	You are the everlasting Son of the Father.

EXERCÍTIA

Be sure to complete the *exercítium* in the appendix corresponding to this *capítulum*.

---

7. The adjective *candidátus* could also be translated as "dressed in white," among other ways.

QUĀRTA PARS

PRONOUNS *and* ADJECTIVES

> Having gained sufficient exposure to verbs in Secúnda Pars and Tértia Pars, we are ready to return to pronouns and adjectives.
>
> Everything we learned in Prīma Pars about nouns and adjectives will come in handy for Quārta Pars. Pronouns, after all, are simply words used in place of nouns, and adjectives often act like nouns. Collectively, there are eight kinds of pronouns used in Latin. In Quārta Pars, each kind will be carefully explained. The good news is that the forms are very similar (in most instances, almost identical) to all the forms we discussed in Prīma Pars. So, despite all the new paradigms that will come your way, you should be able to recognize almost all of the endings.

Capítulum
XIV

PERSONAL PRONOUNS AND DEMONSTRATIVES

Hic est fílius meus dīléctus.[1]
—SYNOPTIC GOSPELS

OPÚSCULUM THEOLÓGICUM: *Tū et Hic in the Vulgate*

Three of the canonical Gospels narrate the baptism of Jesus in the Jordan River, and each of these Synoptic Gospels (Matthew, Mark, and Luke) narrates God's proclamation as Jesus rises out of the baptismal waters. The scene, as famous as any portrayed in the Bible, has inspired countless artists over the centuries, just as it has fascinated scholars and captivated believers. Although the Synoptic writers describe the same story, they record slightly different versions of God's pronouncement to Jesus and those assembled:

Hic est fílius meus dīléctus in quō mihi conplácuī. (Matt. III.17)	This is my beloved son in whom I am well pleased.
Tū es fílius meus dīléctus in tē conplácuī. (Mark I.11)	You are my beloved son; I am pleased with you.
Tū es fílius meus dīléctus in tē conplácuit mihi. (Luke III.22)	You are my beloved son; I am pleased with you.

In Matthew's version, the primary receiver of God's declaration is John the Baptist, or possibly those near the river. In Mark and Luke's, by contrast, Jesus is the subject, and it is unclear whether anyone else hears the Father's proclamation.

A similar scene unfolds in the story of the transfiguration.[2] Here, in the Latin Vulgate, the Synoptic Gospels share identical wording except the last term. As seen below, the Vulgate translates as follows: "beloved" (Matt. XVII.5), "dearest" (Mark IX.7), and "chosen" (Luke IX.35).

---

1. "This is my beloved son."
2. The term "transfiguration," *trānsfigūrātiō*, means "change in form" in Latin and derives from Matthew and Mark's versions: *trānsfigūrātus est* ("[Jesus] was changed") in Matt. XVII.2 and Mark IX.2.

Hic est fílius meus dīléctus. (Matt. XVII.5)
Hic est fílius meus cāríssimus. (Mark IX.7)
Hic est fílius meus ēléctus. (Luke IX.35)

As endlessly interesting as these theological features are for us to explore, I want us to focus on the first word appearing in all six verses: *tū* or *hic*. Although they are classified somewhat differently, both are pronouns, which are words that replace nouns. In the examples provided, the noun to which they are referring is Jesus (*Iēsus* in Latin), but grammarians categorize the pronouns into different subclasses.

We learned in the introductory *capítulum* on verbs that personal pronouns such as *tū*, "you," are already implied in the verb. I love this feature of Latin. Because the personal pronoun is implied, its inclusion in a sentence is one of emphasis: It draws added attention to the person being addressed.

In two of the verses being discussed, the biblical writers are emphasizing that it is not just anyone who is God's beloved son; it's "you" (*tū*)—Jesus. As for *hic*, here translated as "this one," it is what grammarians call a "demonstrative pronoun," namely, a word pointing out someone or something in particular. Though not addressed to Jesus himself (as with *tū*), the use of *hic* still designates a specific person. Once again, it's not just anyone who is God's beloved son; it's "this one" (*hic*)—Jesus. Through the use of pronouns, the gospel writers convey an important theological message: It is through Jesus, and not anyone else, that God's promises to the world are to be fulfilled.

> **Prospéctus**
> In this *capítulum* you will learn that:
> - There are eight kinds of pronouns.
> - Pronouns can be used in place of nouns or adjectives (though personal and reflexive pronouns can only be used to replace nouns).
> - Personal pronouns are used in the first, second, and third person.
> - Demonstrative pronouns and adjectives point out people and things.

GRAMMÁTICA

14.1 **Noun Replacers.** Pronouns are words that replace nouns. Related to the Latin *prōnōmen*, meaning "instead of a noun," writers make frequent use of pronouns instead of constantly referring back to the same noun. In short, pronouns are placeholders that facilitate reading. We owe them a debt of gratitude, as there is nothing worse than words that get in the way of good writing. The authors of the Gospels, among many other classical writers, understood this principle and regularly referred to Jesus as "he" or "him" after establishing "Jesus" as the primary character in a narrative section. Otherwise, reading would become quite cumbersome.

14.2 **Case, Number, and Gender in Pronouns.** Pronouns function exactly as nouns do since pronouns simply replace them. In this way, all pronouns include case, number, and gender. Like nouns, pronouns function as nominatives (subjects), datives (indirect objects), accusatives (direct objects), vocatives (forms of direct address), and more.

14.3 **Eight Kinds of Pronouns.** Due to the frequency of nouns in Latin as well as the need to substitute pronouns for them rather than mention nouns *ad naúseam*, pronouns appear repeatedly in the

PERSONAL PRONOUNS AND DEMONSTRATIVES

Latin *corpus* of writings. You will see them in virtually every Latin sentence. For our purposes, we will organize pronouns into eight subclasses and dedicate the next three *capítula* to them.

1. **Personal pronouns** refer to a person or thing (e.g., "I," "you").
2. **Demonstrative pronouns** designate someone or something (e.g., "this one," "those").
3. **Reflexive pronouns** indicate the same subject and object (e.g., "myself," "itself").
4. **Intensive pronouns** add emphasis to a person or thing (e.g., "myself," "itself").
5. **Possessive pronouns** show ownership (e.g., "mine," "theirs").
6. **Relative pronouns** connect a clause (e.g., "who," "whomever").
7. **Interrogative pronouns** ask something (e.g., "which," "what").
8. **Indefinite pronouns** refer to someone or something (e.g., "some," "none").

Note that many of these categories of pronouns equally apply to adjectives (in fact, all of them—except personal and reflexive pronouns—can be used in place of nouns or adjectives). In this way, just as there are demonstrative pronouns that designate people or things by replacing nouns, so there are demonstrative adjectives that designate people or things by modifying nouns. Pronouns and adjectives function in a similar way; the key difference is that pronouns replace nouns while adjectives modify them and thus appear near them. You can think of it this way: pronouns "placehold,"[3] while adjectives amplify. If we want to use the theater as a simile, pronouns are like understudies who replace the main actor when needed, while adjectives are like backdrops that enhance the scene.

14.4 **Personal Pronouns.** As in English, Latin personal pronouns include first person, second person, and third person. Logically enough, a first-person personal pronoun indicates the speaker who is speaking (such as "I" or "us"); a second-person pronoun specifies the person(s) being directly addressed (such as "you" or "your"); and a third-person pronoun designates the person, place, or thing being discussed (such as "she" or "they").

14.5 **First-Person Personal Pronoun Forms.** Here are the Latin forms for the first-person personal pronouns.

FIRST-PERSON PERSONAL PRONOUNS: *EGO, NŌS* ("I," "WE")

Case	Singular	Plural
Nominative	ego[a]	nōs
Genitive	meī	nostrum; nostrī
Dative	mihi[b]	nōbīs
Accusative	mē	nōs
Ablative	mē	nōbīs

[a] You may also see this word with the long vowel at the end as *egō*. In this book, however, I will not use a macron.

[b] You may also see this with the last *i* having a long vowel: *mihī* or *mī*. In this book, however, I will not use a macron.

---

3. I do recognize that "placehold" is not technically a verb; however, what's the fun of learning a new language if you can't invent new words every once in a while? That's how languages started, anyway. Besides, I think most of you get the drift of the meaning.

PRONOUNS AND ADJECTIVES

The various forms of the personal pronoun occur with such frequency in Latin that you will have little difficulty learning them. In the meantime, focus on their commonalities. What's more, remember that the accent will always be located on the first syllable (since none of these words contains more than two syllables). Also, be sure to remember that translating into English may require the use of more than one word. For example, *mihi* may mean "to me" or "for me," or just "me."

As we are accustomed to experiencing in Latin, a few of the forms are identical to one another, such as *mē* in the accusative and ablative singular; *nōs* in the nominative and accusative plural; and *nōbīs* in the dative and ablative plural. However, prepositions do occasionally appear before these forms, which will more easily alert us to their cases. Finally, in the genitive plural, both *nostrum* and *nostrī* are used. *Nostrum* is what is called a "partitive genitive," denoting something that can be divided, such as *pars nostrum*, "part of us." Meanwhile, *nostrī* refers to what is called an "objective genitive," indicating that they act like the object of a noun, such as *liber nostrī*, "the book [comprised] of us" (rather than *liber noster*, which means "our book"[4]). In fact, *meī* and *nostrī*, in addition to *tuī* and *vestrī* (below), maintain this concept of being an objective genitive. Though a subtle distinction, it will be important when understanding and translating accurately.

Let us look at an example of a first-person personal pronoun:

Christus prō nōbīs immolátus est.   Christ was sacrificed for us.
(Ordinary Gloss)[5]

Whereas the pronoun *nōbīs* could be construed as either dative or ablative plural, the use of the preposition *prō*, which does not take the dative, establishes the fact—by process of elmination—that *nōbīs* must be in the ablative case. As we have learned, prepositions tend to clarify a noun's case when in doubt.

14.6 Second-Person Personal Pronoun Forms. Below are the second-person personal pronouns.

SECOND-PERSON PERSONAL PRONOUN: *TŪ, VŌS* ("YOU," "YOU ALL")

Case	Singular	Plural
Nominative	tū	vōs
Genitive	tuī	vestrum; vestrī
Dative	tibi	vōbīs
Accusative	tē	vōs
Ablative	tē	vōbīs

We see the same pattern with first-person personals as with second-person ones. That is to say, there are identical forms in the accusative and ablative singular (*tē*); nominative and accusative plural (*vōs*); and dative and ablative plural (*vōbīs*). Also as before, the distinction holds true of *vestrum* as a partitive genitive and *tuī* and *vestrī* as objective genitives.

Let us look at an example of a second-person personal pronoun:

---

4. The next *capítulum* will discuss how the possessive adjective is used in Latin to indicate possession.
5. Glossa Ordinária, *Liber Lēvíticus* XVI (PL 113.341).

Quia <u>tibi</u> lēx, <u>tibi</u> prophētía, <u>tibi</u> templum, <u>tibi</u> sacerdótium, <u>tibi</u> sacrifícia, <u>tibi</u> rēgnum, <u>tibi</u> múnera. (Peter Chrysologus)[6]

Because [it is] the law <u>for you</u>, prophecy <u>for you</u>, the temple <u>for you</u>, the priesthood <u>for you</u>, the offerings <u>for you</u>, the kingdom <u>for you</u>, [and] the gifts <u>for you</u>.

This sentence is chock-full of second-person personal pronouns.

CUM + PREPOSITION

When appearing with certain pronouns, the preposition *cum*[7]—often translated as "with" and taking the ablative—is appended to the end of the pronoun. As such, Jesus says *Pater <u>mēcum</u> est* (John XVI.32), "The Father is <u>with me</u>," rather than **Pater cum mē est*. Similarly, Exodus XVIII.19 states: *Erit Deus <u>tēcum</u>*, "God will be <u>with you</u>," instead of **Erit Deus cum tē*.

14.7 **Third-Person Personal Pronoun Forms.** Finally, here are the third-person personal pronouns.[8] They are a bit more involved than the forms above, but they are much less intimidating than expected.

THIRD-PERSON PERSONAL PRONOUN: *IS, EA, ID* ("HE," "SHE," "IT"; "THIS," "THAT")

Number	Case	Masculine	Feminine	Neuter
Singular	Nominative	is	ea	id
	Genitive	eius[a]	eius	eius
	Dative	eī	eī	eī
	Accusative	eum	eam	id
	Ablative	eō	eā	eō
Plural	Nominative	eī; iī	eae	ea
	Genitive	eórum	eárum	eórum
	Dative	eīs	eīs	eīs
	Accusative	eōs	eās	ea
	Ablative	eīs	eīs	eīs

[a] Note that this form will also appear as *ejus* for masculine, feminine, and neuter.

Fortunately, there is very little for us to learn here. Despite their initial appearance, the forms of *is, ea, id* follow the pattern of the 2-1-2 adjectives in the plural that we have already mastered, such as: *sānctus, sāncta, sānctum*. Whereas first- and second-person personal pronouns only encompass people, third-personal personal pronouns include people and things. *Ergō*, "hence," the neuter case has joined the pronoun party and is found in the last column.

---

6. Peter Chrysologus, *Sermō* V (PL 52.201).
7. Sometimes *cum* is understood to be an adverb.
8. Some grammar books classify the third-personal pronouns as "demonstratives" rather than "personal" pronouns, arguing that personal pronouns only occur in the first and second person. In fact, most pronouns are demonstrative adjectives that are then used without a noun, that is, as substantives As such, I have decided to discuss them in the context of both kinds of pronouns.

Several of these forms are identical, so you will want to pay close attention to context when translating them. Note also that the rules of neuter nouns are fully in force, meaning that the accusative duplicates the nominative (in both the singular and plural) and that the nominative and accusative plurals both end in -a.

Finally, our discussion in the chart about demonstrative pronouns and demonstrative adjectives also applies to *is, ea, id*. Depending on context, we may translate *is, ea, id* as "he," "she," "it"; or as "this," "that."

ĪDEM, EÁDEM, IDEM

It is common for the Latin suffix -dem, which translates as "same," to be appended to each of the forms of the demonstrative *is, ea, id*. This is the main way Latin speakers communicated the notion of sameness. Other than the nominatives, which we are accustomed to encountering as slightly irregular,[9] the -dem suffix is simply added to the end of the demonstrative: thus *idem, eídem, eísdem, eósdem*, and so on. Though the case, number, and gender differ, the English translation is literally the same for all of them: "the same." Let us look at an example:

Loquéndum est enim semper eísdem verbīs. (Johannes Murmellius and Rodolphus Agricola)[10]

For it is always necessary to speak by means of the same words.

14.8 **Demonstratives.** The second class of pronouns we will learn in this *capítulum* are demonstrative pronouns and adjectives. Deriving from the Latin verb *dēmónstrō, dēmōnstrāre, dēmōnstrāvī, dēmōnstrātus*, "to point out," these are what I refer to in my classes as pointing-out pronouns. As pronouns, they "placehold," or replace nouns; as demonstratives, they point out or call attention to specific ones. When demonstratives appear alongside nouns, they are acting as adjectives and so are regarded as demonstrative adjectives; when no noun is present, they are demonstrative pronouns. The distinction between a demonstrative-pronoun use and a demonstrative-adjective use appears in the two verses below from the Gospel of John, both of which contain the demonstrative *hic*.

Hic as Demonstrative Pronoun	*Hic* as Demonstrative Adjective
Hic vēnit ad eum nocte. (III.2)	Nōn est hic homō ā Deō. (IX.16)
This one [or "he"] came to him by night.	This man is not from God.

In nuce, "in short," pronouns appear *in place of* nouns (meaning they "placehold"), while adjectives appear *in proximity to* them (meaning they "amplify"). When no noun is present, the translation of the pronoun must consider the word it is replacing (in this case a nominative masculine singular person). A textbook translation of the first example is "this one," but a more idiomatic translation is "he" (as discussed below).

When the noun is present, as in the second example, we simply translate the noun (in this case, *homō*) alongside the adjective amplifying it. Either way, whether a pronoun or an adjective,

---

9. For instance, *is* turns into *idem*; and *eī* and *iī* to *idem*.
10. Johannes Murmellius and Rodolphus Agricola, *In Librōs dē Cōnsōlātiōne Philosóphiā Commentāria* (PL 63.925).

PERSONAL PRONOUNS AND DEMONSTRATIVES

because both examples feature demonstratives, they are pointing out or designating a specific person. It is not just any person; it is "this one," "this man."

14.9 **Nearness and Farness.** The three forms of demonstratives below can be classified according to nearness and farness. In general, a speaker uses *hic, haec, hoc* in reference to people or objects nearest to the speaker; *ille, illa, illud* for people or objects nearest to the hearer; and *iste, ista, istud* for people nearest to the third party (or, if there is none, then out of earshot of the speaker and hearer). The Spanish language, ultimately descended from Latin, has preserved the essence of these demonstratives (minus the neuter forms). Consider the chart below.

DEMONSTRATIVES IN LATIN, SPANISH, AND ENGLISH

Latin	Spanish	English
hic, haec, hoc	este, esta	this (one)
ille, illa, illud	ese, esa	that (one)
iste, ista, istud	aquel, aquella	that (one) over there

Other Romance languages behave similarly. If you have studied a Romance language before—whether Spanish, Portuguese, French, Italian, and so on—consider their use of demonstratives and how they relate back to Latin.

14.10 **Hic, Haec, Hoc.** Like a sergeant's commands in the military, the various forms of this word have been drilled into the minds of beginning Latin students for centuries. You are joining an esteemed cohort of Latin veterans by memorizing them. Be sure to recite the forms with both class and cadence.

In the classroom, I call these the "H-demonstratives" as a handy mnemonic device to reinforce that each form begins with the letter *h*.

DEMONSTRATIVE NEAREST TO SPEAKER: *HIC, HAEC, HOC* ("THIS," "THIS ONE")

Number	Case	Masculine	Feminine	Neuter
Singular	Nominative	hic	haec	hoc
	Genitive	huius[a]	huius	huius
	Dative	huic[b]	huic	huic
	Accusative	hunc	hanc	hoc
	Ablative	hōc	hāc	hōc
Plural	Nominative	hī	hae	haec
	Genitive	hōrum	hārum	hōrum
	Dative	hīs	hīs	hīs
	Accusative	hōs	hās	haec
	Ablative	hīs	hīs	hīs

[a] *Huius* only contains two syllables (hui-us), in which *ui* is a diphthong; so, the accent falls on the first part and sounds like hui-yus.

[b] *Huic* has one syllables, with *ui* forming a diphthong.

As with *is, ea, id*, the H-demonstratives will be easily learned since you will see them constantly.

Et haec natúrae divínae descríptio primum omnis Religiónis fundaméntum est. (Jacob Arminius)[11]	And this description of divine nature is the main basis of all religion.[12]

14.11 ***Hic* vs. *Hīc*.** One letter can make all the difference in Latin. The same may be said of vowel length. A clear example of this appears in two words that look alike but one has a short vowel and the other a long one. While *hic* means "this (one)," *hīc* means "here." Both are extremely common in Latin.

When encountering these words "in the field," that is, when there are no macra used, here is what I recommend: First translate the word as a demonstrative ("this" or "this one"—*hic*); if it does not sound right in context, then it is probably the adverb *hīc* ("here"). Latin speakers could more easily distinguish these two words since *hic*, pronounced with a short -i (*hĭc*), was the demonstrative; while, *hic*, with a long -i (*hīc*), was the adverb. No such distinctions exist in most written Latin, however. We are privileged to decipher the meaning in a more interesting way—by trial and error.

14.12 ***Ille, Illa, Illud*.** And now we present the cousins of *hic, haec, hoc*. The first is *ille, illa, illud*. These are what I like to refer to as ILL-demonstratives, since each form begins with those three letters. As with all demonstratives, this word points out someone or something, and it can also be used as a pronoun or as an adjective.

DEMONSTRATIVE NEAREST TO HEARER: *ILLE, ILLA, ILLUD* ("THAT [ONE]")

Number	Case	Masculine	Feminine	Neuter
Singular	Nominative	ille	illa	illud
	Genitive	illíus	illíus	illíus
	Dative	illī	illī	illī
	Accusative	illum	illam	illud
	Ablative	illō	illā	illō
Plural	Nominative	illī	illae	illa
	Genitive	illórum	illárum	illórum
	Dative	illīs	illīs	illīs
	Accusative	illōs	illās	illa
	Ablative	illīs	illīs	illīs

Sed tū, miséricors Pater, ad fontem illum misericórdiae convértere. (Anselm of Canterbury)[13]	But you, merciful Father, return to that source of mercy.

---

11. Jacob Arminius, "Index Disputatiónum Privátárum" XXIII.8, in *Disputatiónēs Públicae et Prīvátae* (Leiden: G. Basson, 1614), 47.
12. Or, if *primum* is functioning as an adverb rather than an adjective: "And this description of divine nature is, first of all, the basis of all religion."
13. Anselm of Canterbury, *Meditātiōnēs* VII (PL 158.745).

14.13 Iste, Ista, Istud. The other cousin of *hic, haec, hoc* is *iste, ista, istud*. It works like all other demonstratives but begins with ist- in all forms. This word can sometimes be used in a pejorative sense, particularly with the form *iste*; but be sure to infer such a sense only in context.

DEMONSTRATIVE NEAREST TO THIRD PARTY: *ISTE, ISTA, ISTUD* ("THAT [OF YOURS]," "THOSE [OF YOURS]," "THAT [ONE] OVER THERE")

Number	Case	Masculine	Feminine	Neuter
Singular	Nominative	iste	ista	istud
	Genitive	istíus	istíus	istíus
	Dative	istī	istī	istī
	Accusative	istum	istam	istud
	Ablative	istō	istā	istō
Plural	Nominative	istī	istae	ista
	Genitive	istórum	istárum	istórum
	Dative	istīs	istīs	istīs
	Accusative	istōs	istās	ista
	Ablative	istīs	istīs	istīs

Let us look at an example:

In istō saeculō in quō tōta vīta hóminis tentátiō est, unicuíque tribúitur quod merétur. (Eligius)[14]	In this age in which all of human life is a temptation, each of us is given what is deserved.

14.14 Biblical Use of *Hic, Ille,* and *Iste*. Despite the precise definitions provided above, biblical Latin frequently employs *hic, ille,* and *iste* (and even *ipse*)[15] as a third-person personal pronoun (a common feature of Romance languages). In the Vulgate, all three forms of demonstrative pronouns can oftentimes be translated as "he," "she," or "it," rather than "this one," "that one over there," and "that of yours," respectively. Observe each of the following instances from the Gospel of Mark where the demonstratives are just as easily translated as "he" as some other way.

Hic fílius Deī erat. (XV.39)	He was God's son.
Nōnne iste est faber? (VI.3)	Is he not the carpenter?
Ille autem dīxit. (V.34)	And he said.
Et ipse vōbīs dēmōnstrábit. (XIV.15)	And he will show you all.

---

14. Eligius, *Homíliae* VIII (PL 87.622).
15. We will learn this word in the next *capítulum*.

Naturally, you could provide the stock translations used above; they would work, but we want to increasingly become more nuanced in our translations as we advance in the study of Latin.

> **Summārium**
>
> In this *capítulum* you learned that:
> - There are eight different kinds of pronouns.
> - The personal pronouns do not have to appear with verbs (as in English); however, they do occur frequently.
> - Demonstrative pronouns and adjectives point things out. There are three subclasses of demonstrative pronouns and adjectives in Latin, universally abbreviated in paradigms as: (1) *hic, haec, hoc*; (2) *ille, illa, illud*; and (3) *iste, ista, istud*.

VOCĀBULŌRUM INDEX

Latin	English (Gloss)	(Etymology)
ámbulō, ambulắre, ambulắvī, ambulắtus (1)	to walk, to travel	(ambulance)
apprehéndō, apprehéndere, apprehéndī, apprehénsus (3)	to lay hold of, to understand, to seize	(apprehend)
cōnfúndō, cōnfúndere, cōnfúdī, cōnfúsus (3)	to confound, to confuse, to shame, to unite	(confuse)
convéniō, convenīre, convḗnī, convéntus (4)	to come together, to agree, to be suited	(convenient)
convértō, convértere, convértī, convérsus (3)	to turn (back), to convert, to change	(convert)
creō, creāre, creāvī, creātus (1)	to create, to produce, to make, to cause	(create)
custṓdiō, custōdīre, custōdīvī, custōdītus (4)	to guard, to protect, to watch	(custody)
ēnárrō, ēnārrāre, ēnārrāvī, ēnārrātus (1)	to explain, to expound, to show, to relate	(narrate)
exténdō, exténdere, exténdī, exténtus (3)	to extend, to stretch, to prolong, to enlarge	(extend)
índicō, indicắre, indicắvī, indicắtus (1)	to indicate, to point out, to show, to declare	(indicate)
iū́dicō, iūdicắre, iūdicắvī, iūdicắtus (1)	to judge, to determine, to decide	(judge)
occī́dō, occī́dere, occī́dī, occī́sus (3)	to kill, to murder, to slay, to beat	(homicide)
occúrrō, occúrrere, occúrrī, occúrsus (3)	to meet, to go to meet, to come to, to charge	(occur)
ódium, ódiī (n)	hatred, ill will, bitterness	(odious)

PERSONAL PRONOUNS AND DEMONSTRATIVES

ōrō, ōráre, ōrávī, ōrátus (1)	to pray, to plead, to deliver a speech	(oration)
núntiō, nūntiáre, nūntiávī, nūntiátus (1)	to announce, to declare, to proclaim, to tell	(announce)
péreō, períre, périī [perívī], péritus (4)[a]	to perish, to pass away, to die, to disappear	(perish)
persólvō, persólvere, persólvī, persolátus (3)	to explain, to recite, to perform (a duty)	
pervéniō, pervenīre, pervénī, pervéntus (4)	to come, to arrive, to attain, to reach	
rédeō, redíre, rédiī (redívī), réditus (4)[b]	to turn back, to return, to go/come back	
sōlémnitās, sōlemnitátis (f)[c]	solemnity, feast day, festival	(solemnity)
sōlémne, sōlémnis (n)[d]	feast (day), ceremony, festival	(solemn)
stēlla, stēllae (f)	star	(interstellar)
súscitō, suscitáre, suscitávī, suscitátus (1)	to encourage, to stir up, to awaken	(resuscitate)
vínciō, vincíre, vinxī, vinctus (4)	to bind, to tie up, to fasten, to fetter	(vinculum)

[a] This is a slightly irregular verb. Either form of the third principal part could appear. It is to be distinguished from another verb that looks like it, which we have already encountered: *reddō, réddere, réddidī, rédditus* (3) "to give back," "to return," "to restore."

[b] Both forms may appear.

[c] Sometimes this word has a double "ll" instead of a single "l."

[d] This word, too, sometimes has a double "ll" and sometimes a single "l." Also, take note of the similarity with the word above.

ŌRÁTIŌ POPULÁRIS

Ánima Christī (Pars Minor I). This is an anonymous Roman Catholic prayer dating to the Middle Ages. It is often prayed after Mass. We will divide this beautiful prayer into three parts to memorize. Observe the exquisite grammatical pattern of the Latin: vocative, genitive, imperative (also called command), and, last but not least, the accusative case of the personal pronoun: *mē*.

Ánima Christī, sānctíficā mē.	Spirit of Christ, sanctify me.
Corpus Christī, salvā mē.	Body of Christ, save me.
Sánguis Christī, inébriā mē.	Blood of Christ, fill me.
Aqua láteris Christī, lavā mē.	Water from the side of Christ, wash me.
Pássiō Christī, cōnfórtā mē.	Suffering of Christ, strengthen me.

EXERCÍTIA

Be sure to complete the *exercítium* in the appendix corresponding to this *capítulum*.

Capítulum
XV

REFLEXIVES, POSSESSIVES, AND INTENSIVES

Deī cognitiṓne et nostrī.[1]
—JOHN CALVIN

OPÚSCULUM THEOLÓGICUM: *John Calvin's Use of Brévitās*

John Calvin's opening lines of the *Īnstitū́tiō Chrīstiā́nae Religiṓnis*, "Institutes of the Christian Religion," remain some of the most famous in the Protestant tradition. He begins his treaty as follows:

Tōta ferē sapiéntiae nostrae summa... duábus pártibus cōnstat, Deī cognitiṓne et nostrī.[2]	Nearly the total sum of our wisdom consists of two parts: knowledge of God and knowledge of ourselves.

There are several items to note here from the prowess and pen of Calvin, a writer of great skill and style. First, Calvin shows finesse in both his word choice and word order. By delaying the subject of the sentence (*summa*) until the fifth word, he creates suspense in the mind of the reader. In between the nominative adjective (*tōta*) and the noun it modifies (*summa*), Calvin inserts an adverb (*ferē*), the object (*sapiéntiae*), and its corresponding adjective (*nostrae*). Also, by placing *Deī* in front of *cognitiṓne* and *nostrī* at the very end of the sentence, Calvin enshrines his theology in his actual word structure: God first, humans afterward.

Second, in stately Latin fashion, Calvin reserves the verb (*cōnstat*) for the end of the clause. This was the common way that Cicero and other great stylists penned their sentences. Although it is proper to vary one's sentence structure, the Latin verb itches to be the last word in the sentences (or clauses) of celebrated writers.

Third, Calvin does not weigh down the sentence with unnecessary verbiage. As becomes clearer as the opening paragraph continues, Calvin does not tend to utilize prepositions, and he does not include redundancies. He is single-minded and word-sensitive. As a writer, he pursued *brévitās*: "conciseness," "terseness," "brevity."

Finally, for our purposes, we may isolate the pronoun Calvin uses in this sentence: *nostrī*. Here, it is acting as an objective genitive, which I have rendered as "knowledge of ourselves," refering to

---

1. "Concerning the knowledge of God and of ourselves."
2. John Calvin, *Īnstitū́tiō Chrīstiā́nae Religiṓnis* I.1 (CR 30.31).

REFLEXIVES, POSSESSIVES, AND INTENSIVES

the knowledge of whom we are. By isolating this example of a pronoun, we will now turn to our next discussion of Latin pronouns.

> **Prospéctus**
> In this *capítulum* you will learn that:
> - Reflexives pronouns turn back to the subject (and only replace pronouns).
> - Intensive pronouns and adjectives offer emphasis.
> - Possessive pronouns and adjectives indicate non-reflexive possession.

GRAMMÁTICA

15.1 **Pronoun Review.** As you will recall from the previous *capítulum*, pronouns "placehold" previously stated people and objects rather than mentioning them *ad naúseam*. As much as we like Peter, for instance, we still do not want to read a sentence that says: "Peter breathes. Peter eats. Peter walks." Once we establish Peter as the subject, it is natural to move onto less distracting ways of referring back to him.

15.2 **Reflexives.** Reflexive pronouns have little to do with athletic ability, but they do contribute to our game plan of understanding the different kinds of pronouns in Latin. Related to the Latin verb *refléctō, refléctere, refléxī, refléxus*, "to turn back," reflexive pronouns turn back to the subject. Stated differently, reflexive pronouns "reflect" the subject of the sentence or clause. (If they do not "turn back" to the subject, they are not reflexives but some other kind of pronoun.)

Reflexives find their home in the predicate, which is that part of a sentence pointing back to the subject. As a result, reflexives do not contain nominative forms; nor do they serve as subjects of verbs. When learning reflexives, therefore, we have one less form to memorize: the nominative case. To be sure, this does not lighten the paradigm load too much, but we will have to take any help we can get.

When translating the reflexive into English, we will use the suffix "-self" or "-selves." It does not matter whether key words appear immediately before "-self" or "-selves" (such as "<u>by</u> myself" or "<u>from</u> themselves"; or whether "-self" or "-selves" is preceded by an adjoining word ("<u>him</u>self" or "<u>them</u>selves"). However they appear, they are all "turning-back-to" pronouns.

15.3 **Forms of Reflexives.** Below are all the different forms of reflexives.

REFLEXIVE: *MEÍ, TUÍ, SUÍ*ᵃ ("OF MYSELF," "OF YOURSELF," "OF HIMSELF/HERSELF/ITSELF")

Case	1st Person	2nd Person	3rd Person
Nominative Sg	-	-	-
Genitive Sg	meī	tuī	suī
Dative Sg	mihi	tibi	sibi
Accusative Sg	mē	tē	sē
Ablative Sg	mē	tē	sē

(cont.)

PRONOUNS AND ADJECTIVES

Case	1st Person	2nd Person	3rd Person
Nominative Pl	-	-	-
Genitive Pl	nostrī	vestrī	suī
Dative Pl	nōbīs	vōbīs	sibi
Accusative Pl	nōs	vōs	sē (sēsē)
Ablative Pl	nōbīs	vōbīs	sē (sēsē)

[a] Because there are no nominative forms, I am using the genitive forms here. Sometimes it is referred to by the third-person forms: *suī, sibi, sē, sē*.

Let us unpack these forms. First, I trust that most of them look familiar. The first- and second-person are identical to the personal pronouns learned in the previous *capítulum*. This is a curse and a blessing. On the one hand, they do not require additional memorization; on the other, they do require additional differentiation.

As for the third-person forms, these are new. Take note of the way each of these words begins with the letter "s"; also recognize how *sē* is used for both singular and plural accusatives and ablatives. (In the accusative and ablative, *sēsē* may also be used.) It is recommended to immediately begin associating *suī, sibi,* and *sē* with the suffix "-self" and "-selves" in English. When I was a wee lad memorizing these forms, for instance, I repeated the phrase "*suī, sibi, sē,* -self" in one part of my brain; in another, "*suī, sibi, sē, sē*"; and in another, I linked *sē* and *sē* with *sēsē*. (Although this made sense to me, you may want to experiment with your own mnemonic jingle.)

Second, as alluded to above, do not forget to incorporate the use of prepositions—such as "by," "for," "from," "of," "to," and "with"—into your translations when appropriate. Sometimes they are required to complete an accurate English translation, and sometimes they are not. When they are required, we should never think of them as additional words to add; rather, they are ideas implicit in the Latin and simply must be made explicit in English.

Finally, because reflexives do not specify gender (and the third person is both singular and plural), they could be translated in various ways. This is most apparent in the third person since, as just mentioned, this form does not designate gender or number; it only indicates case—and that poorly. For instance, *se* could be translated as: "himself," "herself," "itself" or "themselves." This is embarassingly ambiguous. How do you know which gender and number to supply in English translation? Correct, the subject is our fearless guide. Because reflexives "turn back" to the subject (always a noun, not an adjective), we will always need to identify the subject *before* translating the reflexive that refers back to the subject. Otherwise we would not know the correct translation.

Let us look at a couple of examples of reflexives.

Iēsus exinānívit sē. (Phil. II.7)   Jesus emptied himself.

Tū tē in humilitáte deprímerēs.   You were humbling yourself
(Peter Damian)[3]   in lowliness.[4]

I hope you saw how both reflexives referred back to the subject: *Iēsus* and *tū*, respectively.

---

3. Peter Damian, *Liber Gomorrhiánus* XVIII (PL 145.179).
4. And you are doing the same thing by learning the language of the greatest masters.

15.4 **Possessives.** Possessive pronouns are sometimes called "reflexive possessives." This nomenclature reveals why they are introduced immediately after we learn reflexives. They are also referred to as "possessive adjectives" and "possessive pronouns." In short, there are four possible names for just one type of pronoun, but, in fact, traditional grammars were more correct when they classified them as adjectives rather than pronouns. Related to the Latin verb *possídeō, possidére, possédī, posséssus*, "to own" or "to possess," possessives have to do with possessing or owning something, for instance, "*my* church," "*her* Bible," "*their* prayers." As adjectives, you also know that possessives must agree with the noun(s) they modify in case, number, and gender.[5]

15.5 **Forms of Possessive Adjectives.** Here are the possessive adjectives in all their *glŏria*—in their nominative glorious forms, at least.

First and Second Person (Singular and Plural)
- *meus, mea, meum*, "my," "my own" (first-person singular)
- *tuus, tua, tuum*, "your," "your own" (second-person plural)
- *noster, nostra, nostrum*, "our," "our own" (first-person plural)
- *vester, vestra, vestrum*, "your," "your own" (second-person plural)

Third Person (Singular and Plural)
- *suus, sua, suum*, "his," "his own"; "her," "her own"; "its," "its own" (singular and plural)

As you surely noticed, possessives follow the pattern of 2-1-2 adjectives. Thus, their endings are never in doubt: -us, -a, -um, etc. They are just like clockwork: precise, orderly, comforting. Because you have already memorized the 2-1-2 paradigm, it is not necessary to list each of the forms in their entirety. Therefore, the paradigm below only contains the 2-1-2 endings of the different forms mentioned elsewhere. If you need to review these, consult Capítulum V.

2-1-2 ADJECTIVE ENDINGS (ADJECTIVES USING THE SECOND-, FIRST-, SECOND-DECLENSION ENDING PATTERNS)

Case	Masculine	Feminine	Neuter
Nominative Sg	-us; -	-a	-um
Genitive Sg	-ī	-ae	-ī
Dative Sg	-ō	-ae	-ō
Accusative Sg	-um	-am	-um
Ablative Sg	-ō	-ā	-ō
Nominative Pl	-ī	-ae	-a
Genitive Pl	-órum	-árum	-órum
Dative Pl	-īs	-īs	-īs
Accusative Pl	-ōs	-ās	-a
Ablative Pl	-īs	-īs	-īs

---

5. In the third person, however, the possessive is not an adjective but a pronoun.

15.6 **Potential Confusion with *Suus, Sua, Suum*.** There are two potentially confusing attributes of third-person possessives. One is a problem intrinsic to Latin, and the other to English. First, we will address the problem inherent in the Latin language. In a word, *suus, sua, suum* may refer to either a singular or a plural noun. How will you be able to know which one? You guessed it—context is your best ally.

The second potentially confusing aspect of *suus, sua, suum* has little to do with Latin. The fault lies with English, unfortunately. In English, we translate the demonstrative *is, ea, id* as "his," "her," or "their" in the genitive singular and plural (the Latin is *eius, eórum, eárum*). This is problematic because it is also how we translate *suus, sua, suum* into English. In reality, the two forms have quite different meanings in Latin (*is, ea, id*, for instance, only shows non-reflexive possession); but you would not know that based on English translations.

In short, we can clarify the ambiguity between this demonstrative pronoun and a reflexive pronoun by recognizing *eius, eórum, eárum* as referring to something owned by someone <u>other than</u> the subject; and *suus, sua, suum* as referring to something owned <u>by</u> the subject. Because reflexives, as we learned above, "refer back" to the subject, so, too, do possessives. Like a boomerang, a reflexive pronoun returns to the subject, not anything else. To continue the analogy, if the boomerang does not return to the subject (the one who throws it), it is not reflexive and, instead, is likely a possessive.

Let us look at an example from the Vulgate.

Páriet autem fílium: et vocábis nōmen <u>ejus</u> Iēsum: ipse enim salvum fáciet pópulum <u>suum</u> ā peccátīs <u>eórum</u>. (Matt. 1.21)	She will give birth to a son, and you will call <u>his</u> name Jesus: For he himself will save <u>his</u> people from <u>their</u> sins.

This beautiful sentence features pronouns as the star of the show, eclipsing the future tense by frequency in this sentence[6] with four pronoun guest appearances. I have underlined the featured pronouns: *ejus, suum, eórum* (*ipse* will make its debut below).

Even though our English translation correctly renders both *ejus* and *suum* as "his," these words express different concepts in Latin. The first use of "his" (*ejus*) is possessive because the subject ("you") is different from the object ("his"). We cannot employ *suum* here unless we want to suggest that the "you" mentioned is Jesus, which, of course, it is not (it is Joseph). Meanwhile, the second use of "his" (*suum*) is possessive and reflexive because the predicate ("his") refers back to the subject ("he"). To use *ejus* in this instance would indicate that "he" is different from Jesus, which makes neither grammatical nor theological sense. The moral of the story: Matthew (technically, Jerome) knew his Latin, and he correctly distinguished the reflexive from the possessive. You must, too. (In case you are curious, the use of *eórum* confirms that Jesus is not implicated in the sin of the world; otherwise *suum* would have been used.)

15.7 **Intensives.** Intensives became a common way for Romans to emphasize a noun or pronoun. They share affinities with both demonstratives (pointing-out words) and reflexives (reflecting-back words), but also differ in noteworthy ways. Unlike a demonstrative, *ipse, ipsa, ipsum* intensifies a noun or pronoun rather than merely identifying it; and unlike a reflexive, it refers to any part of the sentence rather than simply the subject.

---

6. I trust you observed that every verb in the sentence (there are three in total) is in the future tense: *páriet, vocábis,* and *fáciet.*

15.8 Forms of Intensives.
Below are the forms of intensives.

INTENSIVE: *IPSE, IPSA, IPSUM* ("HIMSELF," "HERSELF," "ITSELF"; "HE," "SHE," "IT")

Number	Case	Masculine	Feminine	Neuter
Singular	Nominative	ipse	ipsa	ipsum
	Genitive	ipsíus	ipsíus	ipsíus
	Dative	ipsī	ipsī	ipsī
	Accusative	ipsum	ipsam	ipsum
	Ablative	ipsō	ipsā	ipsō
Plural	Nominative	ipsī	ipsae	ipsa
	Genitive	ipsórum	ipsárum	ipsórum
	Dative	ipsīs	ipsīs	ipsīs
	Accusative	ipsōs	ipsās	ipsa
	Ablative	ipsīs	ipsīs	ipsīs

Other than the declensional pattern it shares with demonstratives in the genitive and dative singular, *ipse, ipsa, ipsum* does have several overlaps with 2-1-2 adjectives, though not perfectly.

As its name suggests, *ipse, ipsa, ipsum* brings emphasis to a noun or pronoun, which, in English, often requires the translation of "-self" and "-selves" once again. This is problematic for English-speakers because it sounds like a reflexive. Sometimes this is alleviated by using the word "very" (as in "by that very reason"), but it is not always the case.

Though traditionally indicating emphasis, *ipse, ipsa, ipsum* also eventually came to play the part of a run-of-the-mill personal pronoun, which we can simply translate as "he," "she," or "it." This use of the intensive is common among Christian authors of Latin. You will see it often in the Vulgate.

In summary, there are several acceptable ways to translate *ipse, ipsa, ipsum* into English in accordance with context: "he himself," "she herself," "itself"; "very," "actual[ly]," "real[ly]"; and "he," "she," "it." Note, however, that *ipse, ipsa, ipsum* does not mean "[the] same." Latin uses other words to convey that notion, as discussed in the previous *capítulum*, for instance.

Let us look at some examples of this intensive from the Gospels—this time from the Gospel of Luke. Observe how many ways *ipse, ipsa, ipsum* may be translated.

Et <u>ipse</u> Jēsus erat incípiēns quasi annórum trīgíntā. (III.23)	And Jesus <u>himself</u> was coming into his thirtieth year [of birth].
<u>Ipse</u> autem sēcēdébat in dēsértum, et ōrábat. (V.16)	<u>He</u>, however, was retiring to the desert and began to pray.
Vidéte manūs meās, et pedēs, quī ego <u>ipse</u> sum. (XXIV.39)	Look at my hands and my feet, for it is <u>really</u> me.

15.9 Trifecta: Three Uses of -Self in English (But Not in Latin). One of the most confusing parts of this *capítulum* has little to do with Latin but a lot to do with that other language we know: English. So, let us clear the English air.

There are effectively three ways that English uses the suffix "-self" or "-selves." Examples below appear from the book of Acts.

1. **Reflexive**—using the reflexive pronouns and adjectives
   Jūdās . . . āvértit pópulum post sē, "Judas . . . draws the people toward himself." (VII.15)

2. **Intensive**—using the intensive pronouns and adjectives
   Simōn et ipse crédidit, "Simon himself also believed." (VIII.13)

3. **Alone**—using the adjective *sōlus, sōla, sōlum*
   Jūdās autem sōlus ábiit, "Judas departed by himself." (XV.34)

As you observed, Latin makes use of a different word each time the English word is translated as "-self" in these examples. This highlights the distinction that we must make between English and Latin with reference to translations of certain terms.

Summārium

In this *capítulum* you learned that:
- Reflexives occur in the predicate and turn back to the subject; they never occur in the subject (that is, nominative form).
- Intensives emphasize someone or something.
- Possessives indicate non-reflexive possession of someone or something.

VOCĀBULŌRUM INDEX

Latin	English (Gloss)	(Etymology)
aliquándō	sometimes, formerly, at one time	
árbitror, arbitrārī, arbitrātus sum (1)	to judge, to witness, to observe, to consider	(arbitration)
cessō, cessāre, cessāvī, cessātus (1)	to stop, to cease, to delay	(cessation)
cōncípiō, concípere, concēpī, concéptus (3)	to conceive, to comprehend, to contain	(concept)
díves, díves, dívitis	rich, wealthy	
dóceō, docēre, dócuī, dóctus (2)	to teach, to instruct, to show, to inform	(indoctrinate)
ímpleō, implēre, implēvī, implētus (2)	to fill (up), to satisfy, to cover, to complete	(implement)
ingrédior, ingrédī, ingréssus sum (3)	to go into, to enter, to walk	(ingredient)
ínsequor, ínsequī, īnsecūtus sum (3)	to follow, to pursue	
interfíceō, interfícere, interfēcī, interféctus (3)	to kill, to destroy, to murder	

laetor, laetắrī, laetắtus sum (1)[a]	to rejoice, to be glad	
levō, levắre, levắvī, levắtus (1)	to raise, to lift up, to elevate, to lighten	(levitate)
nímius, nímia, nímium	too much, too great, excessive	
pótior, potī́rī, potī́tus sum (4)	to be more able, to be more capable	(potent)
proélior, proeliắrī, proeliắtus sum (1)	to fight, to battle, to contest	
profī́teor, profitḗrī, proféssus sum (2)	to profess, to declare, to acknowledge	(profess)
prōícīō, prōícere, prōiḗcī, prōiḗctus (3)	to throw, to thrust, to cast away	(projectile)
quéror, querī, questus sum (3)	to complain, to lament, to be indignant	(querulous)
respíciō, respícere, respéxī, respéctus (3)	to look at, to respect, to have regard for	(respect)
revértor, revértī, revérsus sum (3)	to return, to turn back	(revert)
séquor, sequī, secū́tus sum (3)	to follow, to pursue	(sequence)
sóleō, solḗre, sólitus sum (2)	to be accustomed to, to be used to	(insolent)
suscípiō, suspícere, suspéxī, suspéctus (3)	to look up to, to regard, to suspect	(suspicious)
trādō, trā́dere, trā́didī, trā́ditus (3)	to hand over, to deliver, to betray	(trade)
túeor, tuḗrī, túitus sum (3)	to protect, to look at, to guard, to preserve	(tuition)

[a] This word can be understood as a "regular" verb: *laetō, laetāre, laetāvī, laetātus* (1), which means almost the same thing: "to cause to rejoice."

ŌRĀ́TIŌ POPULĀ́RIS

Ánima Christī (Pars Minor II). Below is the second part of the *Ánima Christī* prayer that we will memorize.

Ō bone Iēsū, exaúdī mē.
Intrā tua vúlnera, abscónde mē.
Nē permíttās mē sēparắrī ā tē.
Ab hoste malígnō, defénde mē.
In hora mortis meae, vōcā mē.

O good Jesus, hear me.
Within your wounds, hide me.
Let me never be separated from you.
From my evil enemy, defend me.
In the hour of my death, summon me.

EXERCÍTIA

Be sure to complete the *exercítium* in the appendix corresponding to this *capítulum*.

Capítulum
XVI

RELATIVES, INTERROGATIVES, AND INDEFINITES

Christus in corde omnis hóminis <u>quem</u> álloquar.[1]
—SAINT PATRICK

OPÚSCULUM THEOLÓGICUM: *Saint Patrick's Prayer*

Saint Patrick is one of the most celebrated saints in the Christian tradition. *Patrícius* in Latin, he is the *sānctus patrōnus*, or "patron saint," of Ireland. The patronage system in the Roman empire was widespread and pervasive. Under this system, a *patrōnus* was the protector, benefactor, and sponsor (all English nouns derived from Latin ones) of a *cliēns* or "client." As such, Sānctus Patrícius is regarded as the special guardian over Ireland, with his feast day celebrated on March 17.

The events, stories, and miracles involving Patrick are steeped in legend. There is not a consensus regarding the exact dates of his life or even in what region he was born (though Roman Britain is the most common guess). Although there are several works attributed to Patrick, two of them have survived that continue to be regarded as authentic: *Letter to Coroticus* and *Confession*, both written in Latin.[2]

What can be loosely gathered about Patrick's life comes to us partly through the book *Confession*, or *Cōnféssiō* in Latin. This *liber*, written in a colloquial style, contains episodes in Patrick's life such as his enslavement by Irish pirates at the age of sixteen, his eventual escape from slavery, his growing relationship with Christ, his ministry, and the many confrontations he encountered. However, this book also ignores many details about Patrick's life that have been filled by other sources. Much of what is attributed to Patrick, for instance, comes from these other sources, which were written centuries after Patrick lived. One such source records one of my favorite prayers attributed to *Patrícius*.

Christus mēcum. Christus ante mē. Christus mē pōne. Christus in mē. Christus īnfrā mē. Christus suprā mē. Christus ad dextram meam. Christus ad laevam meam. Christus hinc. Christus íllinc. Christus ā tergō.[3]	Christ with me. Christ before me. Christ behind me. Christ in me. Christ below me. Christ above me. Christ on my right. Christ on my left. Christ here. Christ there. Christ from the back.

---

1. "Christ in the heart of every person <u>who</u> speaks."
2. For a contemporary translation of these, see *The Confession of Saint Patrick and Letter to Coroticus*, trans. John Skinner (New York: Image, 1998).
3. Ulick Bourke, *The College Irish Grammar* (Dublin: John O'Daly, 1856), 189.

According to legend, Patrick composed this hymn on Easter Sunday in the year 433 on his way to the royal palace in Tara (also called Temoria). He, along with his clerical companions, uttered the prayer to shield themselves from the magical powers of the Druids and from the violent hands of the warriors stationed to intercept and slay the mighty bishop. Patrick had been invited to the palace under the guise that the pagan lord would make a public confession of the Christian faith. The lord's real plan, however, was to kill Patrick. After arriving safely to the palace, Patrick recorded the hymn in the vernacular (titled *Feth-fiada*) and also in Latin (*Lōrīca*). In English it has been passed down with the title *St. Patrick's Breastplate* (in Latin, *Lōrīca Patrīciī*), though other names are also used, including "The Deer's Cry." Here is an excerpt, with several key words underlined:

Christus in corde omnis hóminis <u>quem</u> álloquar. Christus in ōre cūjúsvīs <u>quī</u> mē alloquátur. Christus in omnī óculō <u>quī</u> mē vídeat. Christus in omnī aure <u>quae</u> mē aúdiat.[4]

Christ in the heart of every person to <u>whom</u> I speak. Christ in the mouth of anyone <u>who</u> speaks to me. Christ in every eye <u>that</u> sees me. Christ in every ear <u>that</u> hears me.

Whatever it is called, and whoever exactly composed it, these words are a beautiful prayer as well as a grand introduction to a new kind of pronoun in Latin: the relative pronoun. In a word, relative pronouns are the "who," "what," "which," and "that" pronouns (see underlined). Appearing frequently in Latin, they complete our study of the different kinds of Latin pronouns.

Prospéctus

In this *capítulum* you will learn that:
- Relative pronouns relate one thing to another.
- Interrogative pronouns ask questions.
- Indefinite pronouns do not explicitly designate people or things.

GRAMMÁTICA

16.1 The Last of the Pronouns. In many ways the *ossa* of the Latin language, nouns have served as the backbone of this book from the first *capítulum* onward. We dedicated the first seven *capítula* to them and returned to them yet again in these last three. As the latter uttered in the play *Romeo and Juliet*, "parting is such sweet sorrow," but we will have to pull ourselves together as we bid adieu to nouns (and to all their extended family: adjectives, pronouns, and so on) in this section. Having learned of the hidden beauty of personal pronouns, demonstratives, reflexives, intensives, and possessives, we now turn to the last of the pronouns: relatives, interrogatives, and indefinites, which all begin with the letters qu- or cu-. When you think of relatives, interrogatives, and indefinites, think of the letters qu- as well.

16.2 Relatives. We know by now that a pronoun replaces a noun rather than a noun undergoing repetition *ad īnfīnītum*. However, Latin goes several steps further by furnishing a variety of pronoun options to replace that noun—whether offering a demonstrative, intensive, reflexive, possessive, *et cétera*. We will begin this *capítulum* by examining one of the most common pronouns of all: the relative pronoun.

---

4. Ulick Bourke, *The College Irish Grammar* (Dublin: John O'Daly, 1856), 189.

I describe relative pronouns as "relating-back-to" pronouns. (Be sure not to confuse these with "turning-back-to" or reflexive pronouns, discussed in the previous *capítulum*.) Related to the Latin verb *réferō, reférre, réttulī, relātus*, "to relate back," relative pronouns relate back to the subject and, in this way, relate one thing to another like a bridge joining separate clauses into one show-stopping sentence. (A clause is any complete idea.)[5]

Instead of using conjunctions like "and" or "or," relative pronouns directly join two clauses, thereby building more intricate sentences. When they do so, the clause containing the relative pronoun is called the "relative clause," which, by design, is a clause subordinate to the main clause standing on its own merit. Observe the example below wherein the relative pronoun *quī* effectively follows three rules: (1) it builds a more complicated sentence, (2) it cannot stand on its own and be regarded as a "complete" sentence, and (3) it serves as the beginning of the relative clause.

Joánnes Baptísta, quī replétus Spíritū Sānctō ex úterō mātris suae sīcut dē ipsō ángelus patrī prōmíserat, in eádem Spíritus Sānctī grátiā iúgiter perseverāvit et prōfécit. (Gunther of Paris)[6]	John the Baptist, who was filled with the Holy Spirit out of his mother's womb just as the angel had promised concerning him to his father, likewise continually persisted and progressed in the same grace of the Holy Spirit.

As you see, *quī* builds clauses into one more complex sentence. Here, as elsewhere, the relative pronoun (again, *quī*) essentially acts like an adjective to the noun it modifies (*Joánnes Baptísta*), furnishing more detail than we otherwise have about the subject. The relative pronoun sets in motion a relative clause, which, when linked with the subject and main verb, extends and amplifies the sentence.

16.3 Relatives and Long Sentences. Unlike contemporary American culture, which increasingly avoids using relatives in speech and in writing, the Romans loved their relative pronouns. Classical figures like Cicero sometimes constructed colossal sentences out of them, stacking them layer by layer like scaffolding, garnished with subordinate clauses. When surveying that kind of architectural sentence, you will patiently need to translate the relative clauses one at a time, as if brick by brick. Rather than assembling an example from Cicero, however, let us turn to the weighty sentence of another *cīvis Rōmānus*, "Roman citizen": Paul, or *Paul(l)us* in Latin.[7]

Benedíctus Deus et Pater Dóminī nostrī Jēsū Christī, quī benedíxit nōs in omnī benedictióne spīrituálī in caeléstibus in Christō, sīcut ēlégit nōs in ipsō ante mundī cōnstitutiónem, ut essémus sānctī et immaculātī in cōnspéctū ejus in cāritáte, quī praedestināvit nōs in adoptiónem filiórum per Jēsum Christum in ipsum: secúndum prōpósitum voluntātis suae, in laudem glóriae grátiae suae, in quā grātificāvit nōs in dīléctō Fíliō suō; in quō habémus redēmptiónem per sánguinem ejus, remissiónem peccātórum secúndum dīvítiās grátiae ejus, quae superabundāvit in nōbīs in omnī sapiéntiā et prudéntiā: ut nōtum fáceret nōbīs sacrāméntum voluntātis suae, secúndum beneplácitum ejus, quod prōpósuit in eō, in dispēnsātióne plēnitúdinis témporum, īnstaurāre ómnia in Christō, quae in caelīs et quae in terrā sunt, in ipsō; in quō étiam et nōs sorte vocátī sumus praedestinátī secúndum

---

5. A "simple" sentence is usually defined as containing a single subject and single predicate; a "multiple" one
6. Gunther of Paris, *Dē Ōrātióne, Jejúniō, et Eleēmósyna* XII (PL 212.187).
7. I recognize that Paul wrote this letter originally in Greek rather than in Latin, but the example still stands. Besides, we all have our faults, even apostles. Paul did not want to be the lone ranger writing in Latin in the Greek New Testament.

prōpósitum ejus <u>quī</u> operátur ómnia secúndum cōnsílium voluntátis suae: ut sīmus in laudem glóriae ejus nōs, <u>quī</u> ante spērávimus in Christō; in <u>quō</u> et vōs, cum audīssétis verbum vēritátis, ēvangélium salútis vestrae, in <u>quō</u> et crēdéntēs sīgnátī estis Spíritū prōmissiónis Sānctō, <u>quī</u> est pignus haerēditátis nostrae, in redēmptiónem acquisītiónis, in laudem glóriae ipsíus. (Eph. I.3–14)

Wow, what a mouthful. Congratulations for making it through. Instead of translating this magnificent yet lengthy sentence into English (feel free to give it a whirl—you should be able to understand most of it by the end of the *capítulum*), I have merely underlined the relative pronouns. These reveal the importance of relatives in connecting clauses and building upon similar ideas. You will not necessarily often encounter such long sentences; but, when you do so, you will translate them the same way as shorter ones: clause by clause, recognizing that the clause, like an adjective, is adding more detail to the noun that it is modifying.

16.4 **Translating Relatives.** In many Latin sentences, it is relatively easy to determine the appropriate English translation of the relative pronoun. In other circumstances, however, it requires more effort. The most common translations are:

- who
- whom
- whose
- which
- what
- that

How will you know which is best? You, of course, know the *respōnsum*, "the answer": context decides. By way of example, just as we do not typically call inanimate objects "who" or "whom," nor people "which," so, too, depending on the context supplied, we will need to translate the relative pronoun the best possible way in accordance with how it is functioning in its respective clause (and in agreement with the niceties of English, which, all too recently in spoken English, omit the relative clause altogether).[8]

That stated, it will not usually be possible to convey completely the elegance and precision of the Latin relative pronoun since it—like every pronoun—possesses case, number, and gender (which is less evident in English), and because Latin style prefers relatives to stand first in clauses (which may or may not happen in English). As bridge-builders, relatives look back to the antecedent they are connecting to another clause; in this role, relatives ape their antecedent's number and gender, but elect their case according to the role they are playing (as a subject, object, and so on).

16.5 **Unidentified Relative Pronouns.** I hasten to add one more *cáveat léctor*, unfortunately. There are many occasions in which Latin sentences do not supply the antecedent. Naturally, this represents no sweat off of the writer's back—the writer knew exactly to what he or she was referring—but it does cause us to perspire as we look frantically and in vain for an antecedent. If you are translating a sentence and experiencing difficulty finding the antecedent, do not sweat it. Stay calm and translate on.

Consider the following example:

---

8. How many relative clauses did I use in this sentence?

| Quī Deum nōn timent, necésse est ut īnférnum dēscéndant, et ab eō nōn éxeant. (Hélinand of Froidmont)[9] | The ones who do not fear God must descend into Hell [upon death], and from there do not exit. |

Latin loves to start clauses with unidentified relative pronouns like this. You will come to delight in this feature of the language as well. In the meantime, just know that there will be many instances in which a relative pronoun appears—sometimes first in the sentence or clause—with little clue as to the antecedent's true identity. This is especially common in the Bible. Many verses in Proverbs, for instance, begin with "The one who . . ." or "That which . . ." Latin conveys this notion in only one word, for instance, *quī* or *quod*. When translating into English, analyze all the words in the clause and make a translational deduction. This habit will become instinct over time and you will immediately intuit how best to render the pronoun into English.

16.6 Forms of Relatives. Below are the forms of relatives.

RELATIVES: *QUĪ, QUAE, QUOD* ("WHO," "WHOM," "WHICH," "WHAT," "WHOSE," "THAT")

Case	Masculine	Feminine	Neuter
Nominative Sg	quī	quae	quod
Genitive Sg	cuius	cuius	cuius
Dative Sg	cui	cui	cui
Accusative Sg	quem	quam	quod
Ablative Sg	quō	quā	quō
Nominative Pl	quī	quae	quae
Genitive Pl	quórum	quárum	quórum
Dative Pl	quibus	quibus	quibus
Accusative Pl	quōs	quās	quae
Ablative Pl	quibus	quibus	quibus

Did I mention that the Romans also loved their qu- sounds? Despite the differences in spelling between qu- and -cu, the pronunciation of the first syllable is the same for all relatives—and, in fact, there are many more qu-sounding Latin words than in English—several of which will appear below.

As you see in the paradigm, the endings of the relative pronoun are both intrestingly foreign and vaguely familiar. Other than the peculiarity of the cu- and qu- sound, the actual endings of the relative pronoun are rather straightforward and require no great effort to recognize since they mostly follow the endings that we learned for demonstratives like *is, ea, id; ille, illa, illud;* and *iste, ista, istud*. The most unanticipated form is the neuter plural: *quae*. As a rule, the neuter nominative and accusative are the same, but *quae* is not expected, so be careful when you encounter it, especially since it is the form used both for the nominative feminine singular and plural forms.

---

9. Hélinand of Froidmont, *Sermō* XVI (PL 212.617).

Here is an example from our friend Saint Patrick in his *Letter to Coroticus*:

Quāprópter sciat omnis homō timēns Deum quod ā mē aliḗnī sunt et ā Christō Dóminō meō pro <u>quō</u> lēgātiṓne fungor. (Saint Patrick)[10]	For this reason, let every person who fears God know that he is separate from me and from Christ my Lord, for <u>whom</u> I serve as an ambassador.

16.7 **Interrogatives.** The interrogative shares many similarities with the relative pronoun. Not only are most of its forms identical in Latin, but they also seek to identify a person or thing. Related to the Latin verb *intérrogō, interrogāre, interrogāvī, interrogātus*, "to ask," "to inquire," interrogatives ask, inquire, question, and examine. As a result, many of them in modern texts are followed by a question mark. Let us look at their forms before discussing them in more depth.

16.8 **Forms of Interrogatives.** Below are the forms for one extremely frequent interrogative, which are almost identical for pronouns and adjectives.

INTERROGATIVES: *QUIS, QUIS, QUID* ("WHO," "WHAT")

Case	Masculine	Feminine	Neuter
Nominative Sg	quis[a]	quis	quid
Genitive Sg	cuius	cuius	cuius
Dative Sg	cui	cui	cui
Accusative Sg	quem	quem	quid
Ablative Sg	quō	quō	quō
Nominative Pl	quī	quae	quae
Genitive Pl	quṓrum	quārum	quṓrum
Dative Pl	quibus	quibus	quibus
Accusative Pl	quōs	quās	quae
Ablative Pl	quibus	quibus	quibus

[a] Note that the nominative singular is different depending on whether referring to an adjective or pronoun. The examples provided in the chart are for pronouns. The nominative masculine singular adjective is qui, the feminine quae, and the neuter quod.

You should be thinking to yourself: *These forms look oddly familiar.* Yes, they do. In the singular, their forms are identical to the relative pronoun except for the nominative forms. And when it comes to the plural, each of their forms is exactly identical to the relative pronoun, including their nominative forms. In this way, you will not be able to detect any real difference between interrogatives and relatives at first glance. An exception, as mentioned previously, occurs in the nominative singular forms, including the following neuter example:

<u>Quid</u> ígitur? (Johannes Oecolampadius)[11]	<u>What</u> therefore?

---

10. Saint Patrick, *S. Pātriciī ad Corotícum Epístola* III (PL 53.815). He is referring to murderers in context.
11. Johannes Oecolampadius, *Apologḗtica* (Zurich: Froschauer, 1526), no page.

16.9 **Distinguishing Relatives from Interrogatives.** Because it will not be readily evident whether a qu-sounding word is a relative or interrogative pronoun (or, indeed, something entirely different), distinguishing the two requires practice. The following list is neither exhaustive nor infallible, but it offers some guidelines. Take them *cum grānō salis*, "with a grain of salt."

- If you see a question mark at the end of the sentence, the qu-sounding word is possibly an interrogative; if you do not see a question mark, it is possibly a relative.
- If the qu-sounding word is preceded by a comma, it is possibly a relative; if it is not preceded by a comma, it is possibly an interrogative. (However, keep in mind that commas are completely at the discretion of the author.)
- If the qu-sounding word has an antecedent, it is a relative; if it clearly does not have an antecedent, it is an interrogative.
- If the qu-sounding word is (eventually) followed by a corresponding noun of the same case, number, and gender, it is possibly an interrogative; if it is not, it is possibly a relative.

Again, these guidelines will not always equip you to clearly distinguish the two pronouns from each other. However, on the plus side, the translations of the two in English are often the same, so do not be overly concerned if you find yourself unable to decide which pronoun is being used.

Consider the following example:

Quae ūtílitās cibī istíus spīrituális? (Johannes Oecolampadius)	What [kind of usefulness] is the usefulness of that spiritual food?

Here the qu- word presents itself as a possible candidate for being a relative or an interrogative, but which one? As it turns out, the qu- word is an interrogative adjective. It is nominative feminine singular, modifying the noun *ūtílitās*. No worries if you do not recognize that. For all practical purposes, it does not affect our translation. We know that qu-sounding words are usually translated as "who," "whom," "which," "what," or "that." In this example, "what" makes the most sense. How do I know? After plugging in each of the possible words, what other word would you suggest sounds better?

16.10 **Indefinites.** If demonstrative pronouns are those that explicitly point out someone or something, indefinite pronouns and adjectives are those that shrug their shoulders when asked to identify actors and actions. We may wonder exactly who did something or what occurred, but an indefinite is not going to explicitly tell us. Instead, it will casually indicate that "someone" said or did something or that "something" occurred, leaving us to piece together the who's and the what's for ourselves. This is why I often refer to them as "unspecified" pronouns. The use of the indefinite Latin pronoun *quīdam*, for instance, was so common that it was carried over into English in the sixteenth century as a noun meaning "an unknown individual," "somebody," and even a "nobody."

16.11 **Forms of Indefinites.** There are many varieties of indefinites. Other than the fact that they display apathy when it comes to labeling an actor or action precisely, they prefer to have the sound qu- somewhere in the word. After including one of the most common indefinites (*quīdam, quaedam, quiddam*), I will additionally list a variety of other unspecified pronouns and adjectives. For the word below, you can think of the suffix -dam as being roughly equivalent to "some . . ." or "a certain . . . ," in which case the qui- or cui- form (in front of it) indicates "one" or "thing."

INDEFINITES: *QUĪDAM, QUAEDAM, QUIDDAM* ("SOMEONE," "SOMETHING," "A CERTAIN ONE," "A CERTAIN THING")

Case	Masculine	Feminine	Neuter
Nominative Sg	quīdam	quaedam	quiddam[a]
Genitive Sg	cuiúsdam	cuiúsdam	cuiúsdam
Dative Sg	cuidam	cuidam	cuidam
Accusative Sg	quendam	quandam	quiddam
Ablative Sg	quōdam	quādam	quōdam
Nominative Pl	quīdam	quaedam	quaedam
Genitive Pl	quōrúndam	quārúndam	quōrúndam
Dative Pl	quibúsdam	quibúsdam	quibúsdam
Accusative Pl	quōsdam	quāsdam	quaedam
Ablative Pl	quibúsdam	quibúsdam	quibúsdam

[a] This is the pronoun form; the adjective form will be *quoddam*. The same holds for the neuter accusative singular as per the rules that neuters are identical in the nominative and accusative. Also, take note of the double "d" in the neuter in contrast to the single "d" in the masculine.

If you remove the suffix -dam, you should anticipate these forms or, at least, recognize them when encountered. They are simply compounds of the interrogative pronoun *quis, quis, quid* or the adjective *quī, quae, quod*. As *sacerdṓtēs bonī*, "good priests," we will have to forgive the Romans for inventing so many words that sound alike and contain similar meanings. They were too busy conquering the world. Perhaps losing sight of all the people they conquered, they simply referred to them in indistinct ways.

Whatever the case, do not confuse these forms with the word *quidem*, which is an adverb meaning "indeed" or "in fact." In fact, now would be a good time to open a Latin dictionary to the letters "qu-" and familiarize yourself with all the many words that begin with these two letters. You may be surprised at how many there are.

Let us look at an example of an indefinite:

Quṓmodo dīvīnṓrum Librṓrum cōnsīderā́tur auctṓritās? Quia quīdam perfēctae auctōritā́tis sunt, quīdam médiae, quīdam nūllī́us. (Junilius Africanus)[12]

How must the authority of the divine Scriptures be considered? For <u>some</u> are of a complete authority, <u>some</u> of partial authority, and <u>others</u> of no authority.

16.12 Additional Unspecified Pronouns. Below is a list of different indefinite pronouns and adjectives that you may encounter when translating Latin. This list is not exhaustive. Each one contains only the nominative singular forms and thus needs to be declined like all pronouns. Remember that if the word does not contain an accent, the stress falls on the first syllable.

---

12. Junilius Africanus, *Dē Pártibus Dīvī́nae Lḗgis* I.7 (PL 68.20).

- *quīcúmque, quaecúmque, quodcúmque*, "who[so]ever," "what[so]ever"[13]
- *quílibet, quaélibet, quódlibet*, "anyone [at all]," "anything [at all]"
- *quíspiam, quídpiam, quídpiam*, "anybody," "anything," "somebody," "something"
- *quisquam, quaequam, quidquam* (*quicquam*), "anyone," "anything"
- *quisque, quaeque, quidque* (*quodque*), "each [one]," "each [thing]," "whoever," "whatever"
- *quīvīs, quaevīs, quidvīs* (*quodvīs*), "anyone," "anything, "whoever you will," "whatever you will"

Be sure not to practice reciting these words in public, for someone may fear you are preparing for a role as a duck. I admit that these words can come across as a bit strange to the ears of English speakers, but they seemed to work for the Romans.

16.13 Ali Who? To add even more adventure to all the qu-sounding Latin words, I would like to point out one additional suffix that appears frequently with indefinites. It is the suffix ali-. Allow me to ask a question: How do you turn an interrogative into an indefinite? Answer: You simply add ali-. For example, the interrogative *quis, quis, quid*, "who" or "what," can change from a question-asking pronoun into an unspecified one in a Roman minute through the addition of ali-: thus *áliquis, áliquis, áliquid*, "someone," "something," "anyone," "anything."

In fact, ali- is such an exciting word that it comes with its own rule: if a clause or sentence begins with the words *sī, nisi, num*, or *nē*, the prefix ali- is dropped. How will you ever remember this? Just mentally download this clever rhyme: "After *sī, nisi, num*, and *nē*, all the alis go away."

Below is a list of several interrogatives that, like butterflies, have undergone a metamorphosis from interrogatives into indefinites with the addition of the suffix ali-.

Interrogative Form and Meaning	Indefinite Form and Meaning
quis, quis, quid, "who," "what," etc.	*áliquis, áliquis, áliquid*, "someone," "something," "anyone," "anything"
quandō, "when"	*aliquándō*, "sometime"
quantum, "how much"	*aliquántum*, "some amount"
quántulus, quántula, quántulum, "how little"	*aliquántulum*, "a little"
quot, "how many"	*áliquot*, "some"

The list of such words could continue, but these are provided only as examples.

Summārium

In this *capítulum* you learned that:
- Relatives are relating-back-to pronouns and adjectives.
- Interrogatives are question pronouns and adjectives.
- Indefinites are unspecified pronouns and adjectives.

---

13. This word is also used in a negative sense, as in *nec quīcúmque*, "and not," as the Romans did not like to say things like *et nēmō*, "and no one."

VOCĀBULŌRUM INDEX

Latin	English (Gloss)	(Etymology)
acceptábilis, acceptábilis, acceptábile	acceptable	(acceptable)
addō, áddere, áddidī, ádditus (3)	to add	(addition)
advérsus (+ acc)	against	(adverse)
aurum, aurī (n)	gold	
bibō, bíbere, bibī, bíbitus (3)	to drink	(imbibe)
bráchium, bráchiī (n)	arm	(brachial artery)
canō, cánere, cécinī, cantus (3)	to predict, to prophesy, to foretell, to sing	(chant)
cantō, cantáre, cantávī, cantátus (1)	to sing, to chant	
cánticus, cánticī (n)	song, chant	(canticle)
carō, carnis (f)	flesh, meat	(carnal)
dōnō, dōnáre, dōnávī, dōnátus (1)	to give, to grant; to forgive, to pardon	(donate)
ēgrédior, ēgrédī, ēgréssus sum (3)	to go out, to go forth, to land, to disembark	(egress)
exáltō, exaltáre, exaltávī, exaltátus (1)	to exalt, to praise, to elevate	(exalt)
fleō, flēre, flēvī, flētus (2)	to cry, to weep, to lament, to grieve (for)	
lac, lactis (n)[a]	milk	(lactose)
pertíneō, pertinére, pertínuī, -(2)	to stretch out, to reach, to belong to	(pertinent)
possídeō, possidére, possédī, posséssus (2)	to possess, to inherit, to own	(possess)
praeváricor, praevāricárī, praevāricátus sum (1)	to sin against, to transgress	(prevaricate)
pugnō, pugnáre, pugnávī, pugnátus (1)	to fight, to battle, to combat, to struggle	(pugnacious)
quoque	also, even, indeed, likewise	
sagínō, sagīnáre, sagīnávī, sagīnátus (1)	to fatten, to feed, to nourish	
sédeō, sedére, sēdī, séssus (2)	to sit, to be seated, to be established	(sedentary)

(cont.)

Latin	English (Gloss)	(Etymology)
sustíneō, sustinére, sustínuī, susténtus (2)	to uphold, to support, to sustain, to restrain	(sustain)
vítium, vítiī (n)	crime, fault, sin, vice	(vice)
virtūs, virtū́tis (f)	power, virtue, character, strength	(virtue)

[a] This word only occurs in the singular.

ŌRĀ́TIŌ POPULĀ́RIS

Ánima Christī (Pars Minor III). The following contains the last part of the *Ánima Christī* prayer.

Et iubē mē venī́re ad tē,	Order me to come to you,
Ut cum Sānctīs tuīs laudem tē	That I may praise you in the company
in saécula saeculórum. Āmēn.	Of your holy ones for all eternity. Amen.

EXERCÍTIA

Be sure to complete the *exercítium* in the appendix corresponding to this *capítulum*.

QUĪNTA PARS

INDICATIVE MOOD VERBS: THIRD PRINCIPAL PART

> Thus far, we are familiar only with present-system verbs. This system includes three tenses: present, imperfect, and future. These three are learned together because they are formed from the first and second principal parts and because they use the same personal endings: one set for the active voice and another for the passive voice.
>
> Quīnta Pars introduces us to the other system of verbs: perfect-system ones. This includes three tenses: perfect, pluperfect, and future perfect. The active voice of these verbs is formed from the third principal part and mostly share the same sets of endings. These tenses may be new to you, but the concepts are very easy to understand. In general, we can translate the perfect active with "has -ed," the pluperfect active with "had -ed," and the future perfect active with "will have -ed." This is very straightforward. When dealing with the passive voice, we simply add one more component: "has <u>been</u> -ed" for the perfect passive, "had <u>been</u> -ed" for the pluperfect, and "will have <u>been</u> -ed" for the future perfect. All three tenses indicate completed aspect.

Capítulum
XVII

PERFECT ACTIVES

Dēpósuit poténtēs dē sēde: et exaltávit húmilēs.[1]
—GOSPEL OF LUKE

OPÚSCULUM THEOLÓGICUM: *Magníficat*

The Magníficat is one of the most beloved prayers of the church. Taken directly from the Vulgate version of Luke I.46–55, in which Mary composes a hymn to God after her cousin Elizabeth greets her, it has been prayed daily by countless Christians for centuries.

Magníficat ánima mea Dóminum.
Et exultávit spíritus meus: in Deō salūtárī meō.
Quia respéxit humilitátem ancíllae suae:
Ecce enim ex hoc beátam mē dīcent omnēs generātiónēs.
Quia fēcit mihi mágna quī potēns est: et sānctum nōmen eius.
Et misericórdia eius in prōgéniēs et prōgéniēs timéntibus eum.
Fécit poténtiam in bráchiō suō: dispérsit supérbōs mente cordis suī.
Dēpósuit poténtēs dē sēde: et exaltávit húmilēs.
Ēsuriéntēs implévit bonīs: et dívitēs dīmísit inánēs.
Suscépit Isrāél púerum suum: recordátus misericórdiae suae.
Sīcut locútus est ad patrēs nostrōs: Ábrahām, et sémini eius in saécula.

Reminiscent of Hannah's prayer to God after she dedicated her firstborn Samuel to the Lord's work in Shiloh in I Samuel II.1–10, the Magníficat is a beautiful prayer about thanksgiving and the reversal of fortunes.

Although the first word of the prayer—which is the prayer's official name—is in the present tense, most of the successive verbs are in a different tense: the perfect. The shift in verbal tense is essential to the meaning of the hymn. Mary's soul "praises" (in the present tense) the Lord on account of all the many things that the Lord "has done" (in the perfect tense). In other words, it is due to God's past and completed faithfulness to Mary that she can now presently praise the Lord. It is a wonderful reminder of how God has worked in the lives of the faithful.

---

[1]. "God has displaced the powerful from their seat, and he has exalted the lowly" (Luke I.52).

INDICATIVE MOOD VERBS: THIRD PRINCIPAL PART

In this *capítulum* and the next, we will memorize the *Magníficat* in full. In the meantime, observe below all the underlined words from our English translation. These underlined words are all in the perfect tense, which is the verbal tense of completed action. As we will learn in this *capítulum*, the perfect tense is the second most common tense in Latin after the present. In fact, in just eleven lines, the Magníficat uses the perfect tense twelve times.

My soul magnifies the Lord.
And my spirit has rejoiced in God my Savior.
Because he has regarded the lowliness of his servant.
For, see, from henceforward all generations will call me blessed.
Because the one who is powerful has done great things for me, and holy is his name.
And his mercy follows those who fear him, generation after generation.
He has demonstrated power with his arm, and he has scattered the proud in the imagination of their hearts.
He has displaced the powerful from their seat, and he has exalted the lowly.
He has filled the hungry with good things, and he has sent away empty the rich.
He has acknowledged Israel as his son, and he has remembered his mercy.
Just as he has spoken to our forefathers: Abraham and his seed forever.

Prospéctus

In this *capitulum* you will learn that:
- The perfect (active) tense is the present completed tense. It indicates an action completed in the past that can have ongoing significance. It is translated as "to have -ed."
- The perfect system includes the perfect, pluperfect, and future perfect tenses. These tenses can occur in the active or passive voice.

GRAMMÁTICA

17.1 The "Completed" Tense: The Perfect. At long last, we come to my favorite tense in Latin. With a name like "perfect," it had better be good—and it is. Related to the verb *perfício, perfícere, perféci, perféctus*, "to finish" or "to complete," the perfect tense is a high-achieving verb. Unlike the "imperfect" tense, which merely describes an ongoing event in the past, the "perfect" tense represents a verb that actually finished the job. It is a highly motivating tense.

What's more, you are in luck if you are tired of learning four separate conjugations for each verb. High-achievers that the perfect verbs are, they make no distinctions among conjugations. Each of them is perfectly high-achieving. Practically speaking, this means that we can use verbal endings that are virtually the same across all four conjugation families.

17.2 Forms of the "Completed" Tense. For those who still feel uncomfortable calling a tense "perfect," let me suggest another name: completed aspect verbs. What do I mean? Because the perfect tense indicates completed aspect, we could just as easily focus on the finished nature of the tense. Whatever we decide to call this tense, the perfect active is the first of three perfect system tenses that use the third principal part as its base, which may be called the perfect stem.

PERFECT ACTIVE PERSONAL ENDINGS

	Singular	Plural
First Person	-ī	-imus
Second Person	-ístī	-ístis
Third Person	-it	-érunt[a]

[a] You may see -ére as well, though it is most common in poetry.

Steps to Form Perfect Active (Indicatives)
1. Locate a verb's third principal part (e.g., *laudā́vī*).
2. Remove the -ī at the end of the third principal part (e.g., *laudā́vī*), thus isolating the perfect tense's stem (*laudāv*).
3. Add the distinct personal endings for the perfect active (e.g., *laudā́vī*, *laudāvístī*, *laudā́vit*, *laudā́vimus*, *laudāvístis*, *laudāvérunt*).

There are a couple of items to note. First, the third principal part can differ from verb to verb. The perfect stem cannot necessarily be predicted, thus underscoring the importance of memorizing all four principal parts of verbs. Regardless of conjugation, however, the same procedure is followed: drop the -ī and add the perfect active personal endings. So, as long as you are still memorizing all four principal parts, you are in great shape.

Second, the stress will always fall on the first -i in -ístī and -ístis, as per the rules that a vowel followed by two consonants is long by position (though not long by nature). In a similar way, the -ē in -ērunt is long by nature so the stress will be put on it (as indicated in the paradigm box, hence -érunt). For all the other forms, the stress will be placed on the vowel appearing before the -i or -ī. (The only exception lies with fourth-conjugation verbs, which contain an -ī and therefore receive the stress.)

Finally, the perfect tense is often syncopated, or "shortened." In such instances, it is the -vi or -v that is dropped. You will see the syncopated form of the perfect so often that you may wonder what the "regular" form is. For instance, the "regular" form of *amō* in the second personal singular is *amāvístī*, but you will often encounter the form as *amā́stī*. The meaning is the same. They both can be translated as "you have loved" or "you loved."

Similarly, the "regular" form of *aúdiō* in the first-person singular is *audī́vī*, but you are also likely to see *aúdiī*. When you encounter such shortened forms, once again, there is no difference in meaning. I will not list the syncopated forms in the paradigms, but do not be surprised when they appear in Latin texts.[2]

17.3 **Comparison of Verbs in the Perfect Active.** Below is a comparison of our four paradigm verbs distributed by conjugation. The main thing for you to memorize are the personal endings: -ī, -ístī, -it, -imus, -ístis, and -érunt (-ére). That is all.

Below is an example of how a perfect active indicates a completed action in the past. In this instance, Augustine of Hippo cites what Cyprian of Carthage "has demonstrated" with regard to a common church practice.

---

2. One of the starkest examples of this phenomenon occurs with the common verb *īre*, "to go." You are probably more likely to see the syncopated forms in each instance (meaning that it will very frequently drop the -v). Here are the syncopated forms: *iī*, *īstī*, *iit*, *ī́mus*, *īstis*, *iérunt*. The form *iī* throws off beginning students; however, not only is it a perfectly correct Latin word, but it is also a complete sentence! You can translate it as "I have gone."

COMPARISON OF FOUR CONJUGATIONS OF PERFECT ACTIVE

Verb (Conjugation)	Amō, Amā́re, Amā́vī, Amā́tus (1)	Mṓneō, Monḗre, Mónuī, Mónitus (2)	Osténdō, Osténdere, Osténdī, Osténtus (3)	Aúdiō, Audī́re, Audī́vī, Audī́tus (4)
First Personal Singular	amā́vī	mónuī	osténdī	audī́vī
Second Person Singular	amāvístī	monuístī	ostendístī	audīvístī
Third Person Singular	amā́vit	mónuit	osténdit	audī́vit
First Personal Plural	amā́vimus	monúimus	osténdimus	audī́vimus
Second Person Plural	amāvístis	monuístis	ostendístis	audīvístis
Third Person Plural	amāvḗrunt	monuḗrunt	ostendḗrunt	audīvḗrunt

Vērúmtamen quae solḗret esse Ecclḗsiae cōnsuētū́dō, satis idem Cypriā́nus <u>osténdit</u>, quī āit, in praetéritum dē haéresī ad Ecclḗsiam veniéntēs sine Baptísmō admíssōs. (Augustine of Hippo)[3]

Nevertheless, that same Cyprian <u>has demonstrated</u> sufficiently what the custom of the Church was when he said that in the past that those coming to the Church from heresy were admitted without baptism.

17.4 **The "To Be" Verb in the Perfect.** There really is no need to include the perfect active forms of the "to be" verb in Latin since they are able to be precisely predicted according to the three rules about the formation of the perfect above. However, I am including the verb due to its great frequency in Latin texts. You will see these forms constantly. Usually, you can just translate these forms with the simple past tense (discussed more below), such as "I was" and "they were."

SUM, ESSE, FUĪ, FUTŪ́RUS, "TO BE," "TO EXIST" (STEM: FU-)

	Singular	Plural
First Person	fuī	fúimus
Second Person	fuístī	fuístis
Third Person	fuit	fuḗrunt

17.5 **Translation of Perfect Active: "Has -ed" or "Have -ed."** While the imperfect tense describes an ongoing or habitual action in the past, the genius of the perfect tense is its ability to describe a completed action that has ongoing effects or results. Put in a different way, the perfect indicates a "past" time significance and a "completed" aspect significance.

---

3. Augustine of Hippo, *Dē Baptísmō contrā Dōnātístās* III.5.7 (PL 43.143). Technically, the verb *osténdit* could be a present active or perfect active. The similarity between third-person singulars in the present active and perfect active is common, but the length of the vowel will often distinguish them, for instance, *venit*, "he comes," as opposed to *vēnit*, "he came." In our example, however, the -nd- keeps any long vowel from forming, so context is our only clue.

PERFECT ACTIVES

There are two common ways to translate the perfect active into English:

- Present Completed: "has -ed" and "have -ed"[4] (e.g., "she has loved," "they have loved")
- Simple Past: "-ed" (e.g., "I loved")

I recommend that you emphasize the completed aspect of the perfect tense, thus "has -ed" or "have -ed." (An exception can be made, however, for the "to be" verb, for reasons that should be obvious when translating into English.) This practice of using "has -ed" and "have -ed" will help you distinguish the perfect from the imperfect. As you advance in your knowledge of Latin, though, you will understand how context determines the best way to render the perfect.

Let us look at an example from the famous thirteenth-century poem titled *Diēs Īrae*, "the Day of Wrath." The following section contains three back-to-back perfect actives.

Quī Maríam absolvístī,	You who have forgiven Mary,
Et latrónem exaudístī,	And have heard the thief,
Mihi quoque spem dedístī.[5]	You have also given me hope.

Although we must certainly recognize that the genre of poetry allows for greater flexibility than prose, the fact that these lines are punctuated with perfect indicatives (rather than imperfect ones) indicates the complete and decisive nature of the events. Mary's guilt is completely forgiven, the thief's prayer is completely heard, and the author's hope has been restored.

17.6 **Perfect Passive?** Perhaps you noticed the two anomalies in the perfect tense from the Magníficat. If you did not, review the Magníficat in Latin again and choose the two underlined words that contain endings different from the regular active endings used for the perfect tense.

You should have chosen *locūtus est* and *recordātus [est]*. Make no mistake—these verbs must be translated into English as actives. But they are compound verbs, meaning that they require another word (namely the "to be" verb) to make sense. The reason why they look different is because they are deponents. Yes, those darn deponents strike again! In short, because they are deponents, they use the perfect passive form (which we will learn soon enough), but they must be translated in the active voice, as per the rules for deponents that we have already learned. Because they look so different, we are only focusing in this *capítulum* on perfect actives.

Summārium

In this *capítulum* you learned that:
- The perfect active indicates a completed action. It is sometimes referred to as the "completed present."
- The perfect system includes the perfect active tense along with the pluperfect and future perfect (discussed in the next *capítulum*).
- The present system—which includes the present, imperfect, and future tenses—makes use of different personal endings. They are not used in the perfect system.
- The perfect passive indicative, which we will study in another *capítulum*, is a compound tense using a form of the perfect (participle) together with the "to be" verb.

---

4. Although I am using -ed as an example, there are many instances in English where -en is used instead, e.g., "I have eaten." Thus, -en is also included in the acceptable ways to translate the perfect tense.
5. *Diēs Īrae*, ed. Abraham Coles, 2nd ed. (New York: D. Appleton, 1861), 3.

VOCĀBULŌRUM INDEX

Latin	English (Gloss)	(Etymology)
ádiuvō, adiuváre, adiúvī, adiútus (1)	to help, to assist	(adjunct)
aéstimō, aestimáre, aestimávī, aestimátus (1)	to think, to judge, to reckon, to value	(estimate)
appéllō, appelláre, appellávī, appellátus (1)	to call by name	(appellate)
arbor, árboris (f)	tree	(arboretum)
assúmō, assúmere, assúmpsī, assúmptus (3)	to take up, to accept, to assume	(assume)
āvértō, āvértere, āvértī, āvérsus (3)	to turn away, to avoid, to avert	(avert)
citō	quickly	
clārēscō, clārēscere, clāruī, -(3)	to flourish, to brighten, to become clear	(clarify)
cōnsúmō, cōnsúmere, cōnsúmpsī, cōnsúmptus (3)	to consume, to devour, to eat	(consume)
dēfíciō, dēfícere, dēfécī, dēféctus (3)	to waste, to forsake, to abandon	(defecate)
dívidō, dīvídere, dīvísī, dīvísus (3)	to divide, to separate	(divide)
errō, erráre, errávī, errátus (1)	to go astray, to wander, to err, to be wrong	(err)
expónō, expónere, expósuī, expósitus (3)	to set forth, to explain, to expound	(exposition)
extínguō, extínguere, extínxī, extínctus (3)	to extinguish, to quench	(extinguish)
fundō, fúndere, fūdī, fūsus (3)	to pour (out), to shed	(effusive)
pósteā	afterward, then, next	(post)
prōdúcō, prōdúcere, prōdúxī, prōdúctus (3)	to produce, to bring forth, to beget	(produce)
refórmō, refōrmáre, refōrmávī, refōrmátus (1)	to renew, to reform, to transform, to remake	(reform)
regénerō, regeneráre, regenerávī, regenerátus (1)	to regenerate, to reproduce, to bring back	(regenerate)
restítuō, restitúere, restítuī, restitútus (3)	to restore, to replace, to revive	(restitution)
salvátor, salvātóris (m)	Savior	(Savior)

salvō, salvā́re, salvā́vī, salvā́tus (1)	to save	(salvific)
suffíciō, suffícere, sufféci, sufféctus (3)	to be sufficient, to be enough	(suffice)
ségregō, sēgregā́re, sēgregā́vī, sēgregā́tus (1)	to separate, to segregate, to remove	(segregate)
volúntās, voluntā́tis (f)	will	(voluntary)

ŌRĀ́TIŌ POPULĀ́RIS

Magníficat (Pars Minor I). The following prayer is one of the most beloved in the Christian tradition, uttered by the Virgin Mary to the Lord. Before memorizing this prayer, be sure to reread the introduction to this *capítulum* for needed context. In the *capítulum próximum*, "next chapter," we will memorize the second half of the prayer.

Magníficat ánima mea Dóminum.	My soul magnifies the Lord.
Et exultā́vit spíritus meus: in Deō salūtā́rī meō.	And my spirit has rejoiced in God my Savior.
Quia respéxit humilitā́tem ancíllae suae:	Because he has regarded the lowliness of his maidservant.
Ecce enim ex hōc beā́tam mē dī́cent omnēs generātiónēs.	For, see, from henceforward all generations will call me blessed.
Quia fēcit mihi mágna quī́ potēns est: et sānctum nōmen eius.	Because the one who is powerful has done great things for me, and holy is his name.
Et misericórdia eius in prōgéniēs et prōgéniēs timéntibus eum.	And his mercy follows those who fear him, generation after generation.

EXERCÍTIA

Be sure to complete the *exercítium* in the appendix corresponding to this *capítulum*.

Capítulum
XVIII

PLUPERFECT ACTIVES AND FUTURE PERFECT ACTIVES

Christus utī clausīs <u>penētráverat</u> óstia portīs . . .[1]
—JOHN OWEN

OPÚSCULUM THEOLÓGICUM: *Epigrams*

In the ancient world, epigrams were the currency of gossip, humor, and social critique. Coming directly from the Greek word meaning "inscription" (ἐπίγραμμα, hence the Latin *epigrámma*), an epigram was a pithy or witty saying used to publicly lambaste, scandalize, satirize, or entertain. In the Roman world, Martial was the consummate epigrammist. Like Cicero for Latin prose or Virgil for Latin poetry, Martial set the bar for Latin epigrams. His epigrams were characterized by brevity, meter (often elegiac couplet), universal concepts, and a pithy punch line. Here is a classic:

Chīrū́rgus <u>fúerat</u>, nunc est vispíllō Diaúlus.	Diaulus <u>had been</u> a surgeon, but now he's an undertaker.
Coepit quō póterat clī́nicus esse modō.[2]	He started to be a doctor the only way he knew how.

Or consider a variation of the same epigram by Martial:

Nūper erat médicus, nunc est vispíllō Diaúlus;	Recently a doctor, Dialus is now an undertaker.
Quod vispíllō facit, <u>fécerat</u> et médicus.[3]	What he does as an undertaker he <u>had already done</u> as a doctor.

Although the lyrical quality (and certainly the elegiac couplet) is lost in translation, the punch line remains: Because Diaulus lost so many patients on the operating table as a surgeon, he changed his profession to an undertaker. Now he actually performs well at his job.

---

1. "As Christ <u>had entered</u> even though the doors were locked . . ."
2. Martial, *Epigrams*, ed. Shackleton Bailey, Loeb Classical Library 94 (Cambridge, MA: Harvard University Press, 1993), 60.
3. Martial, *Epigrams*, ed. Shackleton Bailey, Loeb Classical Library 94 (Cambridge, MA: Harvard University Press, 1993), 72.

During the time of the Renaissance and Reformation, it was customary for British intellectuals to compose their own epigrams in the style of Martial. All schoolboys, after all, had been exposed to epigrams during their classical education, and some of them gained notoriety for their ability to master this kind of poetry. Perhaps the most renowned was the Welshman John Owen (not to be confused with the Welsh theologian John Owen). Owen published his first installment of epigrams in the year 1606. They were instant hits. Since he only published in Latin, and since so many schoolboys looked back fondly to epigrams learned in school, he was able to successfully penetrate the entire European market. Even before his death in 1622, modern translations of his Latin epigrams were underway across Europe.

Owen wrote on funny and sometimes scandalous topics, just as Martial had. However, he also composed epigrams touching on Christians themes. One of my favorites appears as a prayer in elegiac meter:

Christus utī clausīs <u>penētráverat</u> óstia portīs Sīc caelī penétrant ínvia claustra precēs.[4]	As Christ <u>had entered</u> the doors though the passageways were closed, In the same way, our prayers enter heaven's locked gates.

As we have already learned, verbs are the real engines of the Latin language. In these three epigrams, the importance of the tense of the underlined verbs cannot be ignored; they are each in the pluperfect tense, which is the tense of finished actions with only past ramification (often translated as "had -ed"). Whereas Martial had used the pluperfect to convey that Diaulus had been a doctor—but was no longer—Owen used the pluperfect to communicate how Jesus had entered the *óstia* though the doors were locked after his resurrection.

In this *capítulum*, we will come to appreciate the precision of the pluperfect tense (along with its companion: the future perfect).

Prospéctus

In this *capitulum* you will learn that:
- The pluperfect tense communicates completed past action without present ramification.
- The future perfect tense conveys future completed action.
- Both of these tenses, along with the perfect tense, comprise the perfect system of verbs.

GRAMMÁTICA

18.1 Perfecting the Perfect System. This *capítulum* concludes the "completed" (or perfect) active system. Having learned the perfect tense in the previous *capítulum*, we now turn to the pluperfect and future perfect tenses. These are the final two tenses that we will learn out of a combined six in the Latin language (at least in the indicative mood). This includes three in the "present system": present, imperfect, and future; and three in the "perfect system": perfect, pluperfect, and future perfect.

---

4. John Owen, *Epigrammátum Joánnis Owēnī*, ed. Albert Ines, *Epigrámma* III.52 (Amsterdam: Lodewijk Elzevir, 1679), no page.

INDICATIVE MOOD VERBS: THIRD PRINCIPAL PART

While the present system forms its verbs from the first principal part, the perfect system does so from the third and fourth. We are learning all three perfect actives together since they are derived from the third principal part; in a subsequent *capítulum*, we will then turn to the perfect, pluperfect, and future perfect <u>passives</u>, which are formed from the fourth principal part—the past perfect (participle).

A word on nomenclature: You will encounter slight variations of the names of these different tenses (as seen in the diagram below). The most logical way to refer to these perfect system verbs is as follows: (1) completed present, (2) completed past, and (3) completed future. More often than not, however, the perfect system is referred to as (1) perfect, (2) pluperfect, and (3) future perfect.

PERFECT SYSTEM

Name	Emphasis (Aspect)	How to Translate
(Present) Perfect	Completed action (completed present)	"has -ed" or "have -ed"
(Past Perfect) or Pluperfect	Action fully completed before next action (completed past)	"had -ed"
Future Perfect	Action will be completed in the future (completed future)	"will have -ed"

18.2 Escalating Verbs: Basement, Ground, Second. When teaching the perfect system, I like to compare its verbs to a book in a building. Imagine a Latin grammar that was left all alone on an escalator at a department store. By the time the *liber* makes its way to you on the ground (that is, "first") floor, the book "had passed" (past perfect) through the basement; by the time it is on the ground floor with you, it "has passed" (present perfect) to the ground floor; and by the time it reaches the next floor in the building, it "will have passed" (future perfect) the ground floor. With this analogy in view, we will now turn our attention to the book when it is in the basement and when it will be on the second floor.

18.3 Pluperfect Active. The term "pluperfect" ultimately comes from the Latin words *plūs quam perféctum*, "more than complete."[5] It communicates completed past action without present ramifications.

18.4 Forming the Past Perfect (Pluperfect) Active Tense: Perfect Stem + *Eram*. The formation of the past perfect is easy as *crustum*, or "pie." It is simply the combination of the perfect stem with the past tense (imperfect) of the verb "to be"—all in one form. Nothing more, nothing less.

To make things even easier, we already learned the imperfect tense of *sum, esse, fuī, futū́rus* back in Capítulum XII, so there is not really anything to memorize here. It is unfortunate that the pluperfect tense uses different personal endings than the perfect, but that grievance is alleviated by the ease of the personal endings used: the past tense of "to be." Note, though, that the past tense of "to be" in Latin is directly appended to the perfect stem, meaning that the pluperfect active is one word.[6]

---

5. In Latin, the pluperfect tense is called the *tempus praetéritum plūsquamperféctum*, or "more than completed time past tense." That's quite a mouthful.

6. An exception is deponent verbs, which use passive forms (though they have active meanings).

Pluperfect Active Personal Endings

	Singular	Plural
First Person	-eram	-erámus
Second Person	-erās	-erátis
Third Person	-erat	-erant

Steps to Form Pluperfect Active (Indicatives)
1. Locate a verb's third principal part (e.g., *laudāvī*).
2. Remove the -ī at the end of the third principal part (e.g., *laudā́vī*), thus isolating the perfect tense's base (*laudāv*).
3. Add the distinct personal endings (e.g., *laudā́veram, laudā́verās, laudā́verat, laudāverā́mus, laudāverā́tis, laudā́verant*).

As is the case in other tenses, there is more than one way to form this tense. For instance, you could simply insert -erā after the third principal part upon removing -ī, and then add the active personal endings for the present system. Here are those steps:

1. Locate a verb's third principal part (e.g., *laudāvī*).
2. Remove the -ī at the end of the third principal part (e.g., *laudā́vī*), thus isolating the perfect tense's base (*laudāv*).
3. Insert the prefix -erā (*laudāverā*).
4. Add the present-system personal active endings: -m, -s, -t, -mus, -tis, -nt (e.g., *laudā́veram, laudā́verās, laudā́verat, laudāverā́mus, laudāverā́tis, laudā́verant*).

Both methods work just fine. However, I prefer first approach because it more clearly distinguishes the perfect system from the present system.

Regardless of the approach you adopt, it is useful to note that the second-person singular (-erās), first-person plural (-erāmus), and second-person plural (-erātis) each retain the long -a (thus, -ā). In the last two forms, it will also receive stress (as illustrated); otherwise, however, the stress will go two vowels before the -a (that is, one vowel before the -e, which is always short). What is going on? The -a suffix is technically -ā (thus -erā), but, for reasons that we have already learned, the long vowel tends to shorten before certain letters and letter combinations, which is why the long vowel only appears in three of the six forms.

18.5 Comparison of Verbs in the Pluperfect Active. As mentioned in the previous *capítulum*, the perfect system does not alternate its personal endings based on conjugation type. This makes the perfect system much easier to learn. Still, for the point of illustration, I am including our paradigm verb for each of the four conjugations of the pluperfect active.

There is nothing here to note other than to draw your attention to where the accent mark is located on each of these forms.

Let us look at an example from Bede's commentary on the book of James:

Monúerat suprā verbum Deī nōn sōlum audíre, sed et fácere. (Bede)[7]	James <u>had warned</u> previously not just to hear the word of God but also to do it.

---

7. Bede, "In D. Iācŏ́bī Epístola I," in *Expósítiō super Epístolās Cathólicās* (PL 93.17).

COMPARISON OF FOUR CONJUGATIONS OF PLUPERFECT ACTIVE

Verb (Conjugation)	Amō, Amā́re, Amā́vī, Amā́tus (1)	Mṓneō, Monḗre, Mónuī, Mónitus (2)	Osténdō, Osténdere, Osténdī, Osténtus (3)	Aúdiō, Audī́re, Audī́vī, Audī́tus (4)
First Personal Singular	amā́veram	monúeram	osténderam	audī́veram
Second Person Singular	amā́verās	monúerās	osténderās	audī́verās
Third Person Singular	amā́verat	monúerat	osténderat	audī́verat
First Personal Plural	amāverā́mus	monuerā́mus	ostenderā́mus	audīverā́mus
Second Person Plural	amāverā́tis	monuerā́tis	ostenderā́tis	audīverā́tis
Third Person Plural	amā́verant	monúerant	osténderant	audī́verant

18.6 **The "To Be" Verb in the Pluperfect.** You should be able to generate fully the pluperfect of *sum, esse, fuī, futū́rus*, but I will, nonetheless, include the full paradigm. Usually, you can just translate these forms with the simple past tense (discussed more below), such as "I had been" and "they had been."

SUM, ESSE, FUĪ, FUTŪ́RUS, "TO BE," "TO EXIST" (STEM: FU-)

	Singular	Plural
First Person	fúeram	fuerā́mus
Second Person	fúerās	fuerā́tis
Third Person	fúerat	fúerant

Here is an example from the fabulous pen of Tertullian. Think long and hard before you answer his question:

Quī ergō nihil fúerās priúsquam essēs, īdem nihil factus cum esse dēsíeris, cūr nōn possīs esse rūrsus dē níhilō, ejúsdem ipsíus auctóris voluntā́te, quī tē vóluit esse dē níhilō? (Tertullian)[8]	You, therefore, who had been nothing before you existed, and the same reduced to nothing when you will cease to be, why are you not able to exist again from nothing, at the will of the same creative source that willed you to exist from nothing?

Other than the deep philosophical thinking required to navigate this sentence, the grammatical use of the pluperfect is straightforward.

---

8. Tertullian, *Apologéticus* XLVIII (PL 1.523–24).

18.7 Translating the Pluperfect. The simplest way to translate the pluperfect active is to use the helping verb "had" along with the simple past tense ending "-ed" or "-en": hence "had loved" for *amáverat*.

GRAMMÁTICA: *Future Perfect*

18.8 Future Perfect: Completed Future. The future perfect describes an action or event that will be complete in the future. It is extremely rare in the Latin *corpus*. After all, most verbs describe something that happened, is happening, or will happen, but not too many describe something that will have happened at some point in the future. We will still learn its forms, however, and you are more likely to encounter it in wills or similar documents, but do not expect to see it very frequently. When it does appear, naturally enough, it usually does so alongside other future-oriented verbs.[9]

FUTURE PERFECT ACTIVE PERSONAL ENDINGS

	Singular	Plural
First Person	-erō	-erimus
Second Person	-eris	-eritis
Third Person	-erit	-erint[a]

[a] The future of "to be" in Latin is *erunt*, but the third person plural ending substitutes the *u* for an *i*, thus -erint.

18.9 Forming the Future Perfect Tense: Perfect Stem + *Erō*. The formation of the future perfect is identical to the past perfect (pluperfect), except that the future tense of the verb "to be" is used instead of the past. Otherwise, it is the same procedure. We simply append the endings directly to the perfect stem. Quite literally, the future perfect is the combination of the future tense of *sum, esse, fuī, futūrus* with the perfect stem.

Steps to Form Future Perfect Active (Indicatives)
1. Locate a verb's third principal part (e.g., *laudā́vī*).
2. Remove the -ī at the end of the third principal part (e.g., *laudā́vī*), thus isolating the perfect tense's base (*laudā́v*).
3. Add the distinct personal endings (e.g., *laudā́verō, laudā́veris, laudā́verit, laudāvérimus, laudāvéritis, laudā́verint*).

As mentioned with the formation of the pluperfect active, however, you may also form this tense differently, substituting -eri- for the future perfect instead of -erā- in the pluperfect. Thus, it would be the third principal part (minus the -ī) + -eri- + present-system active personal endings. Here are the steps:

1. Locate a verb's third principal part (e.g., *laudā́vī*).
2. Remove the -ī at the end of the third principal part (e.g., *laudā́vī*), thus isolating the perfect tense's base (*laudā́v*).
3. Insert the infix -eri- (*laudā́veri*).

---

[9] We will discuss this in its proper place, but the future perfect in many forms is identical to the perfect subjunctive. Contextual clues can help you distinguish the two.

4. Add the present-system personal active endings: -ō, -s, -t, -mus, -tis, -nt
   (e.g., laudā́ve**rō**, laudā́ve**ris**, laudā́ve**rit**, laudāvé**rimus**, laudāvé**ritis**, laudā́ve**rint**).

I prefer the first method because I like to keep the present-system personal endings separate from the perfect-system ones. However, your or your instructor may prefer the second approach. Note that, unlike the long vowel (-ā) in the pluperfect, the future perfect has a short vowel (-i). This affects where the stress goes.

18.10 Comparison of Verbs in the Future Perfect Active. The same for the pluperfect goes for the future perfect. The personal endings for the future perfect are the same for all conjugation families.

COMPARISON OF FOUR CONJUGATIONS OF FUTURE PERFECT ACTIVE

Verb (Conjugation)	Amō, Amā́re, Amā́vī, Amā́tus (1)	Mónēō, Monḗre, Mónuī, Mónitus (2)	Osténdō, Osténdere, Osténdī, Osténtus (3)	Aúdiō, Audī́re, Audī́vī, Audī́tus (4)
First Personal Singular	amā́verō	monúerō	osténderō	audī́verō
Second Person Singular	amā́veris	monúeris	osténderis	audī́veris
Third Person Singular	amā́verit	monúerit	osténderit	audī́verit
First Personal Plural	amāvérimus	monuérimus	ostendérimus	audīvérimus
Second Person Plural	amāvéritis	monuéritis	ostendéritis	audīvéritis
Third Person Plural	amā́verint	monúerint	osténderint	audī́verint

Below is an example of a future perfect active:

Deus . . . per eum tot mīrācula <u>osténderit</u>. (Sigebert of Gembloux)[10]   God <u>will have demonstrated</u> so many miracles through him.

18.11 The "To Be" Verb in the Future Perfect. You can translate the future perfect as "will have -ed," thus "I will have been" and "they will have been." As you will observe, the actual forms of the future perfect are very similar to the pluperfect. Be sure to distinguish them.

SUM, ESSE, FUĪ, FUTŪ́RUS, "TO BE," "TO EXIST" (STEM: FU-)

	Singular	Plural
First Person	fúerō	fuérimus
Second Person	fúeris	fuéritis
Third Person	fúerit	fúerint

---
10. Sigebert of Gembloux, *Vīta S. Theodárdī* XVIII (PL 160.757).

Here is an example from Minicius Felix:

Quod discípulī Jōánnis Baptístae nōn fúerint in statū grátiae. (Minicius Felix)[11]

Since the disciples of John the Baptist will not have been in a state of grace.

18.12 Translating the Future Perfect. To translate the future perfect, we simply aim to capture both the futurity or future-ness of a verb (hence "will") and the perfectness or completeness of it (hence "have"). The "will have -ed" nature of the translation conveys that an action will be complete at some point in the future. Note, however, that English often uses the present tense where Latin prefers the future perfect. In such instances, initially translate the Latin form as "will have -ed." As you become more comfortable in Latin, however, feel free to select a more contextually appropriate translation (even if that means translating it into English with the present tense).

Summárium

In this *capítulum* you learned that:
- The pluperfect and future perfect are the last two tenses in the perfect active indicative system.
- While the pluperfect describes a fully completed past action, the future perfect indicates an action that will be complete in the future.

VOCĀBULŎRUM INDEX

Latin	English (Gloss)	(Etymology)
adóleō, adolére, -, - (2)	to smell	(redolent)
ambō, ambōnis (m)	lectern, pulpit	(ambo)
ars, artis, ártium (f)	skill, art, craft, knowledge	(art)
auris, auris, aúrium (f)	ear	(aurist)
cadō, cádere, cécidī, cāsus (3)	to fall (down)	(cadence)
cālígō, cālíginis (f)	mist, fog, gloom, darkness	(caliginous)
clam	secretly	
conclúdō, conclúdere, conclúsī, conclúsus (3)	to enclose, to shut in, to conclude	(conclude)
concupíscō, concupíscere, concupívī, concupítus (3)	to covet, to desire, to be desirous of	(concupiscence)
currō, cúrrere, cucúrrī, cursus (3)	to run, to hasten	(current)
festínō, festīnáre, festīnávī, festīnátus (1)	to hurry, to hasten	(festinate)

(cont.)

---

11. Minicius Felix, *Dē Firmiliánī ad Cypriánum Epístola* L.1.1 (PL 3.1389). Minicius Felix is referring to what he believes to be the erroneous teachings of Pseudo-Cyprian.

INDICATIVE MOOD VERBS: THIRD PRINCIPAL PART

Latin	English (Gloss)	(Etymology)
iáciō, iácere, iēcī, iáctus (3)	to throw, to cast, to hurl	(eject)
ignṓrō, ignōráre, ignōrávī, ignōrátus (1)	to not know, to ignore	(ignore)
lītúrgia, lītúrgiae (f)	liturgy, service	(liturgy)
missa, missae (f)	Mass	(Mass)
pācíficō, pācificáre, pācificávī, pācificátus (1)	to make peace, to negotiate peace, to pacify	(pacify)
perdō, pérdere, pérdidī, pérditus (3)	to destroy, to ruin	(perdition)
praecéptum, praecéptī (n)	lesson, command, precept	(precept)
prohíbeō, prohibḗre, prohíbuī, prohíbitus (2)	to forbid, to prohibit, to hinder, to restrain	(prohibition)
putō, putáre, putávī, putátus (1)	to think, to consider, to reckon	(putative)
quiéscō, quiéscere, quiévī, quiétus (3)	to cease, to rest, to be still, to be at peace	(acquiesce)
servō, serváre, servávī, servátus (1)	to keep, to preserve	(preserve)
tendō, téndere, teténdī, tentus (3)	to stretch, to extend, to bend	(tension)
vídeor, vidḗrī, vīsus sum (2)[b]	to seem	(videography)
vōtum, vōtī (n)	vow, prayer	(votive)

[a] It is possible that this word is not directly related to the verb, but the concepts are overlapping so it is a good mnemonic.

[b] This construction is used in tandem with the infinitive of another verb.

ŌRÁTIŌ POPULÁRIS

Magníficat (Pars Minor II). The following is the continuation of Mary's prayer to the Lord.

Fēcit poténtiam in bráchiō suō: dispérsit supérbōs mente cordis suī.
Dēpósuit poténtēs dē sēde: et exaltávit húmilēs.
Ēsuriéntēs implévit bonīs: et dívitēs dīmísit inánēs.
Suscépit Isrāél púerum suum: recordátus misericórdiae suae.
Sīcut locútus est ad patrēs nostrōs: Ábrahām, et sḗminī eius in saécula.

He has demonstrated power with his arm, and he has scattered the proud in the imagination of their hearts.
He has displaced the powerful from their seat, and he has exalted the lowly.
He has filled the hungry with good things, and he has sent the rich away empty.
He has acknowledged Israel as his son, and he has remembered his mercy.
Just as he spoke to our forefathers: Abraham and his seed forever.

EXERCÍTIA

Be sure to complete the *exercítium* in the appendix corresponding to this *capítulum*.

SEXTA PARS

SUBJUNCTIVE MOOD VERBS: ALL TENSES

> We come now to the subjunctive mood, one of the most significant moods in all of Latin. Although some are intimidated by the subjunctive mood, there really is no reason to fear. The subjunctive mood expresses contingency and possibility, but we are quite familiar with this concept in English. Perhaps part of the challenge comes from the many ways that the subjunctive mood can be translated into English. In Latin, however, the subjunctive mood is crystal-clear. Each of the tense forms and meanings is concise and straightforward. It will not take long before you begin to observe all the clues for the subjunctive as well as the subtle differences between it and the indicative mood.

Capítulum
XIX

PRESENT ACTIVE AND PRESENT PASSIVE SUBJUNCTIVES

Creátus est homō . . . ut Dóminum Deum suum laudet.[1]
—IGNATIUS OF LOYOLA

OPÚSCULUM THEOLÓGICUM: *Ignatius of Loyola's Exercítia Spīrituália*

Born in 1491, Íñigo López de Loyola, better known as Ignatius of Loyola, was a Spaniard reared on the noble stories of El Cid and the life of the knight-errant. It was his dream to be a valiant soldier. However, after his military career was cut short by a war injury sustained in 1521, he turned inward and began meditating. Before he knew it, his life had changed from fighting physical battles to spiritual ones. While recovering from surgery and enduring physical therapy, he composed one of the most famous spiritual retreat handbooks of all time. Although he would later become famous for founding the Society of Jesus, *Socíetās Iēsū*—whose members were called *Iēsuítae*, "Jesuits" or "followers of Jesus"—most people know Ignatius as the author of the *Exercítia Spīrituália*, "Spiritual Exercises."

From the years 1522 to 1524—while contemporaries like Martin Luther were developing new theological and ecclesiastical models for the fledging Protestant community—Ignatius of Loyola was seeking to create a series of spiritual reflections in submission to the *Magistérium*, or "Teaching Office," of the Roman Catholic Church.

The *Exercítia Spīrituália* consist of meditations on Scripture, prayers, confessions, and imaginative mental exercises. They are designed to offer sustained spiritual reflection over the course of a month-long retreat. These opening lines of Loyola's masterpiece express the magnitude of the book:

Creátus est homō ad hunc fīnem, ut Dóminum Deum suum laudet, ac revereátur, eíque sérviēns tandem salvus fīat. Réliqua vērō suprā terram sita, creáta sunt hóminis ipsíus causā, ut eum ad fīnem ceatiónis suae prosequéndum iuvent: unde séquitur uténdum illīs, vel abstinéndum eátenus esse, quátenus ad prosecutiónem fīnis vel cónserunt, vel obsunt. Quaprópter debémus absque differéntia nōs habére circā rēs creátas omnēs (prout lībertátī arbítriī nostrī subiéctae sunt, et nōn prohíbitae). Ita, ut (quod in nōbīs est) nōn quaerámus sanitátem magis, quam aegritúdinem: neque

---

[1] "Humankind was created . . . that it would praise its Lord God."

dīvítiās paupertátī, honórem contémptuī, vītam longam brevī <u>praeferámus</u>. Sed cōnsentáneum est, ex ómnibus ea dēmum, quae ad fīnem dūcunt, ēlígere ac desideráre.[2]

Wow, this is a lot of text. But it is so good that I thought it best to include a full translation below.

Humankind was created toward this end: that it <u>would praise</u> and <u>would worship</u> its Lord God, serving him, and ultimately that it <u>would be saved</u>. All the other things set forth on the earth are created for the sake of humankind: that they <u>would aid</u> him in the pursuit of that for which he was created. Hence it follows that humanity is to make use of them or is to abstain from them inasmuch as they strengthen or harm him in the performance of this end. For this reason, we must make distinction among all created things (as they are subject to the choice of our free will and not prohibited). In this way, inasmuch as it is within us, <u>we should</u> not <u>prefer</u> health to sickness, riches to poverty, honor to contempt, and <u>we should</u> not <u>anticipate</u> a long life over a short one. Instead, it is proper for us, out of all the things that exist, to choose and to desire only those things that lead toward the end.

There are many points that we could make from this text, but we will stick solely with the grammar. You may have noticed that our friend Ignatius could convey in one word what always took at least two to express in English. You may have also noticed that every verb underlined in English was preceded by the helping verb "should" or "would." The presence of this helping verb is not insignificant; it signals, in the most literal of ways, a change in perspective. That is, it conveys that we have moved out of the realm of reality into one of contingency. Grammarians call this realm of contingency the "subjunctive mood," which is distinct from the realm with which we are most familiar: the "indicative mood." In this *capítulum*, we will begin a three-part discussion of the subjunctive.

Prospéctus

In this *capítulum* you will learn that:
- The subjunctive is the "mood" of contingency, possibility, indirect question, uncertainty, and sometimes command.
- There are four tenses in the subjunctive: present, imperfect, perfect, and pluperfect.
- In Latin, subjunctives are characterized by vowels that differ from the indicative stem vowels. This is -e for the first conjugation and -a for the second, third, and fourth.
- We often translate the subjunctive into English with a helping verb like "may," "might," "should," or "would."

GRAMMÁTICA

19.1 **The Subjunctive: It's about Time.** *Dóminae domini̅que*, "ladies and gentlemen," I introduce you to the *capítulum* that you have all been waiting for: welcome to the subjunctive mood! When I was a student learning Latin and other Romance languages, the subjunctive mood was a linguistic train wreck waiting to happen. Throughout the semester, the teacher would make a comment about how hard the subjunctive would be once we began studying it later in the term.

---

2. Ignatius of Loyola, *Exercítia Spīrituália* I (Rome: Roman College, 1615), 20–21.

PRESENT ACTIVE AND PRESENT PASSIVE SUBJUNCTIVES

Not surprisingly, by the time we approached that fated day, we were scared out of our *mentēs*, "minds." For what reason, I do not know. Despite the stories you may have heard, the subjunctive mood is not scary or even difficult to grasp. Admittedly, it does take time to get used to, but you will soon become comfortable with it. We cannot place any blame on Latin here; the difficulty of learning it has to do with English, which fumbles about with the subjunctive mood like an opening-day juniors' football match.

19.2 **What Is the Subjunctive? All about What "Could" Be.** We begin with the basics. You will remember from our earliest discussions about verbs that they contain PNTMV, that is, person, number, tense, mood, and voice. Of these five verbal components, mood refers to the "manner" of the action that occurred. It answers the question, "in what way did the action occur?" There are three moods in Latin: (1) indicative, (2) subjunctive, and (3) imperative. To generalize, the indicative mood indicates facts, the subjunctive expresses hypotheticals, and the imperative issues commands.

19.3 **Indicative and Subjunctive Moods.** Whereas the indicative mood operates from within a world of reality, objectivity, and facts, the subjunctive mood deals with contingency, possibility, and hypotheticals. We can get a sense of the different takes on reality based on the Latin roots of our English grammatical terms for "indicative" and "subjunctive." Related to the verb *indicăre*, "to point out," the indicative "points out" real actions and events—whether such events happened in the incomplete past (imperfect), the completed present (perfect), the completed past (pluperfect), right now (present), or whether the events will very likely occur in the future (future) or in the completed future (future perfect).

By contrast, the subjunctive involves what "may" happen or what "might have" happened. The adjective *subjūnctīvus* is related to the verb *subiúngere*, "to subjoin" or "to subordinate." The subjunctive often (but certainly not always) "subordinates" to the indicative, meaning that it is dependent on it. And if it is dependent on it, this suggests that the subjunctive cannot stand on its own. This is often (but, again, not always) the case. Most sentences with a verb in the subjunctive also contain an indicative verb that subordinates to it. The subjunctive describes something that may have happened (imperfect, perfect, and pluperfect) or may be happening now (present). Because of the hypothetical nature of the mood, it does not make any sense for it to have a future tense. If an event is likely to take place, the indicative will be used; if it is unlikely or uncertain, the subjunctive will be used (but not in the future tense).

19.4 **Moving from Latin to English.** Unfortunately, our mother tongue, English, offers little help for us when it comes to the subjunctive. When English speakers want to express possibility or hypothetical actions, we turn to helping verbs like "may," "might," "ought," "should," or "would." Latin is much more precise—and, it goes without saying, concise. Indeed, it can change as little as one small vowel to switch from the indicative to the subjunctive mood.

I, personally, love the subjunctive mood. I appreciate how Latin can so concisely convey contingency. There is no fuss and no drama. The subjunctive mood is just as efficient and direct as the indicative. English, in this regard, is sorely wanting; it takes too many words and conflates too many competing helping verbs to express contingency. In English, for instance, I have to wonder: What is the difference between "I could," "I may," "I might," "I ought," "I should," "I were," "I would"? Enough already—Latin uses one simple word to cut through all this ambiguity: *possim*. Thanks a lot, English, for making things so complicated! But enough complaining about English—let's talk about the subjunctive in Latin.

SUBJUNCTIVE MOOD VERBS: ALL TENSES

19.5 **Only Four Subjunctive Tenses.** The advantages of the subjunctive in Latin are many. As alluded to above, rather than six tenses in the indicative mood—present, imperfect, future, perfect, pluperfect, and future perfect—we only encounter four tenses in the subjunctive mood: present, imperfect, perfect, and pluperfect. This means no future and no future perfect. This should lift your mood, indeed.

19.6 **Functions of the Subjunctive Mood.** Another fantastic feature of the subjunctive mood in Latin are the clues that come with it. For example, whereas the indicative mood uses *nōn* to negate, the subjunctive employs *nē*. When you see this word, therefore, you know that you have left the mood of reality. Also, particles like *ut* often trigger the subjunctive, indicating purpose, intention, result, indirect command, or fear. There are many other such words, as well. These context clues take us to another important point of discussion: These clues signal something specific occurring at a grammatical level. What is that exactly?

With such an arsenal of helping verbs at its disposal, you can probably tell that the subjunctive mood is capable of communicating several kinds of tentative or hypothetical situations. Below are some of the most common; however, keep in mind that these are general guidelines and not ironclad rules. There are many more words that prompt and describe the subjunctive. Also, my list of possible Latin clue words is not at all complete. It merely provides a sampling.

COMMON FUNCTIONS OF THE SUBJUNCTIVE

Function	Possible Translations	Possible Latin Clue Words
Signal adverbial purpose	"so that," "so as to," "in order to"	ut, nē
Display relative purpose[a]	"that," "in order that"	relative pronouns
Show result	"with the result that," "that"	ut, ut . . . nōn, ut . . . nūllus, ita, sīc, tālis, tam, tantus, tot
Express desire	"want," "would like"	
Give command	"let," "may"	nē
Show possibility	"could," "may," "were"	
Communicate fear	"lest," "that"	ut, nē, nē nōn
Ask indirect question	"should," "was," "would"	cūr, utrum
Make concession	"lest," "if . . . then"	cum, sī, quamvīs, quantúmvīs
Reveal uncertainty	"should," "were"	
Illustrate characteristic	"who/which is the kind"	
Utter unattainable wish	"would that," "I wish that"	útinam
Indicate what will not happen or is contrary to fact	"if . . . then"	sī

[a] If this is helpful, you can think of the "adverbial" purpose clause as seeking to answer the question "why?" while a "relative" purpose clause seeks to answer the question "who[m]?"

In each of these instances, the verb triggered by these clauses will be in the subjunctive mood (but the word triggering it will not). The exact person, number, tense, and voice of the subjunctive will depend upon the subject. For example, the present subjunctive is used when the main (= indicative) verb is present, future, or future perfect. By contrast, the imperfect subjunctive is used when the main verb is imperfect, perfect, or future perfect. There are very specific instances that more comprehensive grammar books provide, but it is beyond the scope of our study here.[3]

19.7 **Translating Subjunctives.** As you see in the chart listed above, there are a variety of ways to translate these different kinds of clauses into English. Most of the time, we will allow a helping verb to assist the main verb. Depending on the exact context, we may translate a subjunctive with one of the following helping verbs (or none at all, which is represented by the dash):

- may
- might
- let
- ought
- should
- were
- would
- -

Naturally, these are just guides. As always, each Latin sentence and its unique context determines how we are to understand and translate it into English.

19.8 **One Long Question Should Do the Trick.** Unfortunately, with such a long list, you may have anticipated what is coming next: there is no stock translation for the subjunctive. Instead, we are required to examine the Latin text in more depth and ask ourselves one long question. Which question is that? Here it is:

- Does this subjunctive indicate purpose, result, desire, a command, possibility, fear, a question, a concession, a characteristic, just plain uncertainty, or something else?

This question is not perfect, but it is intended to get you to think deeply about why the subjunctive is being used. Depending on how you answer that question, you may mix and match any of the helping verbs above with the particular kind of subjunctive clause (or use no helping verbs at all). Our translations will become easier as we become more familiar with the various causes of the subjunctive.

19.9 *Exémplī Grātiā.* Before we look at the present subjunctive forms, let us turn to an example. We will revisit the first sentence of Ignatius's *Exercítia Spīrituália*.

Creátus est homō ad hunc fīnem,	Humankind was created toward this
ut Dóminum Deum suum <u>laudet</u>,	end: that it <u>would praise</u> and <u>would</u>
ac <u>revereátur</u>, eíque sérviēns tandem	<u>worship</u> its Lord God, serving him,
salvus <u>fīat</u>.[4]	and ultimately that it <u>would be saved</u>.

---

3. I am referring to so-called "conditional" clauses, which contains several subcategories. If you would like to study these conditional clauses, I recommend A&G §§511–25.
4. Ignatius of Loyola, *Exercítia Spīrituália* I (Rome: Roman College, 1615), 20.

What a magnificently constructed Latin sentence. You will notice that Ignatius deferred to the standard practice of deploying his verbs last in their clauses, and he also nicely bookended the sentence with *creātus* and *fīō*, which combination of words features heavily in the creation story of Genesis. More to the point, observe how Ignatius conveyed in three words what English could only clumsily convey in seven. This is the genius of the Latin language. It is so precise and orderly.

But enough of our fawning over this language—let us take a closer look at the individual words used in each of the Latin verbs underlined. Everything should appear normal (that is, "normal" from the perspective of the indicative mood) except for one tiny letter. Can you detect which letter per word?[5] In *laudet*, it should be the -e that throws you; in *revereātur*, the -ā; and in *fīat* also the -ā. Why so? It is because the subjunctive replaces the stem vowel with a different vowel. This sleight of hand is all it takes to move from the realm of reality into the realm of possibility. What you just witnessed was a move from the indicative to the subjunctive.

PRESENT SUBJUNCTIVE

19.10 Divide and Conquer. We will divide our discussion of the present subjunctive into four parts, the first two of which cover first-conjugation verbs and the second two of which focus on second-, third-, and fourth-conjugation ones. (Whereas the third conjugation is the outlier in the present indicative, it is the first person in the present subjunctive.) We can remember the characterstic vowels for the present active subjunctive with the following acronym: "Peter fears a paterfamilias." This can be illustrated as such:

P<u>e</u>ter
F<u>ea</u>rs
<u>a</u>
Paterfamili<u>as</u>

Here, the -e indicates the characteristic vowel for the first conjugation; -ea for the second; -a for the third; and -ia for the fourth. If this makes you scratch your *caput*, more clarity will be provided below.

19.11 Present Active Subjunctive: (Long) ARE Verbs. For both first-conjugation active and passive subjunctives of the present tense, the stem vowel is long -e (that is, -ē). You will recall that this differs in only one way from present tense verbs in the indicative mood, which always use the stem vowel -ā. In theory, this switch to -ē makes it look similar to a "regular" second-conjugation verb of the present tense and indicative mood. However, in practice, you will not fall for this trick since you have been memorizing the principal parts *ab prīncípiō*.

After replacing the stem vowel with -ē, we then add the present tense endings: -m, -s, -t, -mus, -tis, and -nt, respectively.[6] You know these by heart, as you already memorized them in our discussions of the present, imperfect, and future indicative tenses. In case you do not

---

5. Of course, if you have not been learning your principal parts, you may not know what I am talking about. However, knowing what a great student you are, I am fully confident that you have memorized the principal parts of all the verbs learned thus far in the book.

6. You may be confused by the -m ending rather than -ō. In the indicative, you will often see -ō, but it will be -m in the subjunctive. This is not a new concept. We have encountered this phenomenon before.

remember, these are the present-system personal endings. And in case you are wondering, yes, the same personal endings are used for the present-system indicative mood as the present-system subjunctive mood.

> **Steps to Form Present Active Subjunctives of the First Conjugation**
> 1. Locate the second principal part (e.g., *laudắre*).
> 2. Remove the -re ending (e.g., *laudắre* → *laudā*).
> 3. Change the stem vowel of -ā to -ē (e.g., *laudā* → **laudē*).
> 4. Add the present-system personal active endings: -m, -s, -t, -mus, -tis, -nt (e.g., *laude**m***, *laudē**s***, *laude**t***, *laudḗ**mus***, *laudḗ**tis***, *laude**nt***).

PRESENT ACTIVE SUBJUNCTIVE FORMS: *(Long) ARE Verbs*

AMŌ, AMÁRE, AMÁVĪ, AMÁTUS, "TO LOVE" (STEM: AMĀ-)

	Singular	Plural
First Person	amem	amḗmus
Second Person	amēs	amḗtis
Third Person	amet	ament

19.12 Contrasting Moods. The change from -ā to -ē provides a clear contrast between the indicative and the subjunctive. Here is an easy way to remember the difference: Because the indicative indicates the mood of reality, it only makes sense that it retains the stem vowel. However, the subjunctive, as the mood of possibility, replaces the stem vowel with a different one—in this instance -ē. As you move from the indicative to the subjunctive, you move from -ā to -ē.

Let us look at an example:

Sē quisque in áltero <u>cógitet</u> et <u>amet</u>. (Gregory I)[7]	<u>May</u> everyone <u>know</u> and <u>love</u> himself in the other.

As subjunctives, these -āre verbs switch to -ē.[8] No big deal. And because they are subjunctives, we signal the grammatical shift by adding the helping verb "may." We could substitute any number of helping verbs:

- <u>Let</u> everyone know and love himself in the other.
- Everyone <u>should</u> know and love himself in the other.
- Everyone <u>must</u> know and love himself in the other.
- Everyone <u>may</u> know and love himself in the other.

As always, allow context to determine what you think is the best translation. First attempt to understand the Latin sentence, and then determine how to render it best into English.

---

7. Gregory I, *Mōrálium in Iōb* IV.34.53 (PL 75.757).
8. Of course, as we know, long vowels shorten before certain words, such as those ending in -t.

QUADRIGA: THE MEDIEVAL GUIDE TO HERMENEUTICS

The *quadríga*, etymologically related to *quáttuor*, "four," and *iugum*, "yoke," refers to the four-horse carriage that carried drivers. In ancient times, it simply meant "carriage." In the Christian tradition, however, the term came to refer to the mainstream view that there is a "fourfold" sense of interpreting the Bible. Over time, a medieval poem came to signify this fourfold reading of the Bible.

Líttera gesta docet	The letter teaches what happened.
Quid <u>crēdās</u> allēgória	Allegory teaches that which <u>you should believe</u>.
Mōrália quid <u>agās</u>	
Quō <u>tendās</u> anagógia.	Morality teaches what <u>you should do</u>.
	Anagogy teaches where <u>you are headed</u>.

According to this method, each word (excluding the literal/historical) corresponds to an accompanying attribute of the Christian life: **allegory** to what <u>we should believe</u>; **morality** to how <u>we should live</u>; and **anagogy** to what <u>we should hope for</u>. In this way, the entire method encompassed not only the historical sense (which anyone—regardless of religion or maturity—could understand) but, more importantly, the spiritual senses of the Bible. This method of interpretation was famous in the Middle Ages. And what held together this pithy saying was a string of present active subjunctives.

19.13 **Present Passive Subjunctive.** Everything we learned about present subjunctives in the first conjugation above applies here to the passive voice. The only difference is that active subjunctives adopt present-system active endings while passive ones employ passive endings. Once again, both sets of endings are the same ones that we learned in the present system (which includes the present, imperfect, and future), so you are already completely familiar with them. All that is left to do is substitute -ē to the vowel stem of first-conjugation verbs.

Steps to Form Present Passive Subjunctives of the First Conjugation
1. Locate the second principal part (e.g., *laudā́re*).
2. Remove the -re ending (e.g., *laudā́re* → *laudā*).
3. Change the stem vowel of -ā to -ē (e.g., *laudā* → *laudḗ*).
4. Add the present-system personal passive endings: -r, -ris, -tur, -mur, -minī, -ntur (e.g., *lauder, laudḗris, laudḗtur, laudḗmur, laudḗminī, laudḗntur*).

19.14 **Present Passive Subjunctive: (Long) ARE Verbs.** The first conjugation is formed by adding -ē to the stem vowel before then inserting the personal passive endings: -m, -ris, -tur, -mur, -minī, and -ntur, respectively. Similar to the active forms, the length of the -ē is retained in all passive forms other than the first-person singular.

PRESENT PASSIVE SUBJUNCTIVE FORMS: *(Long) ARE Verbs*

The example below contains no less than three passive subjunctives of the first conjugation:

PRESENT ACTIVE AND PRESENT PASSIVE SUBJUNCTIVES

Vīta ánimae quaerátur, salūs <u>cōgitétur</u>,
Deus <u>amétur</u>, memória patriae
<u>celebrétur</u>. (Peter Cellensis)[9]

The life of the soul should be sought, salvation <u>should be pondered</u>, God <u>should be loved</u>, and remembrance of our homeland <u>should be celebrated</u>.

AMŌ, AMÁRE, AMÁVĪ, AMÁTUS, "TO LOVE" (STEM: AMĀ-)

	Singular	Plural
First Person	amer	amémur
Second Person	améris[a]	amémini
Third Person	amétur	améntur

[a] You may also see the form *amére*.

Using the passive endings and the characteristic -ē for the subjunctive of this conjugation type, each of the verbs is transformed into a beautiful first-conjugation present passive subjunctive.

What about *quaerắtur*, the verb I did not underline? As you may have guessed, it too perfectly illustrates the present passive subjunctive, but with one difference—it is not a first-conjugation verb. But this question takes us directly to our next discussion: present subjunctives of the second, third, and fourth conjugations.

PRESENT SUBJUNCTIVE OF *SUM, ESSE, FUĪ, FUTÚRUS*

Forming the present subjunctive of the "to be" verb is easy. Because it has no passive, there is only one form to learn:

1 sg	sim	1 pl	sīmus
2 sg	sīs	2 pl	sītis
3 sg	sit	3 pl	sint

Exémplum. Ita fīet, ut omnis, quī invocáverit nōmen Dóminī, salvus <u>sit</u>. (Martin Luther)[10]

Thus, it will come to pass that everyone who calls upon the name of the Lord <u>shall be</u> saved.

19.15 Present Active Subjunctive: Long ERE, Short ERE, and (Long) IRE Verbs. Now that we understand how present subjunctives form in the first conjugation, we can proceed effortlessly through the second, third, and fourth conjugations. Whereas (Long) ARE verbs replace the characteristic -ā with -ē in the subjunctive, Long ERE, Short ERE, and (Long) IRE verbs add or replace the characteristic -ē, -ĕ, and -ī with -ā. It is that simple. To be precise, -ā is added to the stem vowels -ē and -ī for the second and fourth conjugations, respectively (with the result that -e and -i are shortened); meanwhile, -ā replaces -ĕ in the third conjugation.

Or, if you remember the acronym I displayed above, you can just chant: "Peter f<u>ea</u>rs <u>a</u> paterfamili<u>as</u>." While the -ē is for the first conjugation ("P<u>e</u>ter"), -eā, -ā, and -iā is for the second,

---

9. Peter Cellensis, *Mosaícī Tabernắculī Mýstica et Morắlis Expositiō* I (PL 202.1057).
10. Martin Luther, *Sermō Praescríptus in Litzka 1512* (WA 1.16).

third, and fourth ("f<u>ea</u>rs," "<u>a</u>," and "paterfamil<u>ia</u>s"). If you think about why this is the case, it should make sense. The second and fourth conjugation already have long vowels in the vowel stem: -ē and -ī. However, because the third conjugation has a short vowel (ĕ), it is overpowered and displaced by a long vowel that can get the job done: -ā.

Steps to Form Present Active Subjunctives of the Second, Third, and Fourth Conjugations
1. Locate the second principal part (e.g., *dícere*).
2. Remove the -re ending (e.g., *dícere* → **díce*).
3. Change the stem vowel to -ā (e.g., *díce* → **dícā*). Note that, for second and fourth conjugations, you simply add the -ā to the existing stem vowel (e.g., **hábeā*).
4. Add the present-system personal active endings: -m, -s, -t, -mus, -tis, -nt (e.g., *dícam, dícās, dícat, dicámus, dicátis, dícant*).

PRESENT ACTIVE SUBJUNCTIVE FORMS: LONG ERE, SHORT ERE, AND (LONG) IRE VERBS

Verb (Conjugation)	Móneō, Monére, Mónuī, Mónitus (2)	Osténdō, Osténdere, Osténdī, Osténtus (3)	Aúdiō, Audíre, Audívī, Audítus (4)
First Personal Singular	móneam	osténdam	aúdiam
Second Person Singular	móneās	osténdās	aúdiās
Third Person Singular	móneat	osténdat	aúdiat
First Personal Plural	moneámus	ostendámus	audiámus
Second Person Plural	moneátis	ostendátis	audiátis
Third Person Plural	móneant	osténdant	aúdiant

19.16 Present Passive Subjunctive: Long ERE, Short ERE, and (Long) IRE Verbs. We need no prefatory comments for the passive subjunctive of the remaining conjugations. They proceed in the same way as the active forms. To form them, we remember our acronym: ~~Peter~~ f<u>ea</u>rs <u>a</u> paterfamil<u>ia</u>s. I put a line through Peter since he represents first-conjugation verbs. However, the other vowels follow in perfect form: -eā (second conjugation), -ā (third conjugation), and -iā (fourth conjugation). Stated differently, we add -ā to second- and fourth-conjugation verbs, while we replace the vowel stem with -ā for the third-conjugation ones. Then we add our passive personal endings. That is all there is to it.

Steps to Form Present Passive Subjunctives of the Second, Third, and Fourth Conjugations
1. Locate the second principal part (e.g., *dícere*).
2. Remove the -re ending (e.g., *dícere* → **díce*).
3. Change the stem vowel to -a (e.g., *díce* → **dícā*). Note that, for second and fourth conjugations, you simply add the -ā to the existing stem vowel (e.g., **hábeā*).
4. Add the present-system personal passive endings: -r, -ris, -tur, -mur, -minī, -ntur (e.g., *dicar, dicáris, dicátur, dicámur, dicáminī, dicántur*).

As we know by now, long vowels shorten before certain letters and letter combinations appearing at the end of words. In this instance, the -ā shortens before -r and -ntur. In all other forms, however, expect to see the -ā distributed throughout.

PRESENT PASSIVE SUBJUNCTIVE FORMS: LONG ERE, SHORT ERE, AND (LONG) IRE VERBS

Verb (Conjugation)	Móneō, Monére, Mónuī, Mónitus (2)	Osténdō, Osténdere, Osténdī, Osténtus (3)	Aúdiō, Audíre, Audívī, Audítus (4)
First Personal Singular	mónear	osténdar	aúdiar
Second Person Singular	moneáris[a]	ostendáris[b]	audiáris[c]
Third Person Singular	moneátur	ostendátur	audiátur
First Personal Plural	moneámur	ostendámur	audiámur
Second Person Plural	moneáminī	ostendáminī	audiáminī
Third Person Plural	moneántur	ostendántur	audiántur

[a] You may also see the form moneáre.
[b] You may also see the form ostendáre.
[c] You may also see the form audiáre.

There is nothing out of the ordinary here. Let us look at an example:

Audiátur clāmor dē dómibus eórum. (Jer. 18:22)   Let a cry be heard out of their houses.

> **Summárium**
>
> In this *capítulum* you learned that:
> - The subjunctive mood is the mood of contingency, possibility, and (sometimes) command.
> - There are four tenses in the subjunctive, with no future and no future perfect.
> - The characteristic vowel for the present subjunctive is -ē (in the first conjugation) and -ā (in the last three).
> - The personal endings for the present subjunctive (both active and passive voice) are the same ones from the present-system personal endings used in the indicative mood.

VOCĀBULŐRUM INDEX

Latin	English (Gloss)	(Etymology)
abscónditus, abscóndita, abscónditum	hidden, concealed, secret	(abscond)
blasphémō, blasphemáre, blasphemávī, blasphemátus (1)	to blaspheme	(blaspheme)
caecus, caecus, caecum	blind (blind person)	(caecilian)
caécitās, caecitátis (f)	blindness, darkness	

(cont.)

SUBJUNCTIVE MOOD VERBS: ALL TENSES

Latin	English (Gloss)	(Etymology)
copiósus, copiósa, copiósum	abundant, full, copious	(copious)
custódia, custódiae (f)	guard, custody; prison, cell	(custody)
dēféndō, dēféndere, dēféndī, dēfénsus (3)	to defend, to guard, to protect	(defend)
dēlíctum, dēlíctī (n)	crime, fault, offense, sin	(delict)
exaúdiō, exaudíre, exaudívī, exaudítus (4)	to hear (favorably), to hearken	(audio)
misericórdia, misericórdiae (f)	mercy	(misericord)
haéresis, haéresis (f)	heresy	(heresy)
imperítus, imperíta, imperítum	inexperienced, unskilled	
iníquitās, iníquitátis (f)	iniquity, unfairness, injustice	(iniquity)
magistérium, magistériī (n)	office of authority, teaching office	(magisterium)
nisi	unless, if not, except	
puer, púerī (m)	boy, child, servant	(puerile)
quaérō, quaérere, quasívī, quasítus (3)	to seek, to inquire, to ask, to require	(question)
quátenus	so, so that, insofar as	
quidquid	whatever	
redémptiō, redēmptiónis (f)	redemption, ransoming	(redemption)
redímō, redímere, redémī, redémptus (3)	to redeem, to ransom	(redeem)
restaúrō, restauráre, restaurávī, restaurátus (1)	to restore, to renew	(restore)
ut	as, when; that, so that[a]	
útinam	would that	
vel	or[b]	

[a] When used with the indicative mood, this word means "as" or "when." When used with the subjunctive mood, however, it means something like "that," "so that," or many other things.

[b] This word means "either . . . or" when two uses of *vel* appear in relation to each other: "*vel . . . vel.*"

ŌRĀ́TIŌ POPULĀ́RIS

Dē Profúndīs (Pars Minor I). This prayer originates from Psalm CXXIX in the Vulgate (Psalm 130 in English versions). The words *Dē Profúndīs* derive from the opening lines, "From the Depths." In the Christian tradition, this psalm represents one of the "penitential" psalms, a series of psalms (traditionally seven in number) characterized by sorrow for one's sin. We will divide our memorization of the prayer into two parts.

PRESENT ACTIVE AND PRESENT PASSIVE SUBJUNCTIVES

Dē profúndīs clāmávī ad tē, Dómine:	I have cried out to you, Lord, from the depths.
Dómine, exaúdī vōcem meam:	Lord, hear my voice.
Fīant aurēs tuae intendéntēs,	May your ears be attentive
in vōcem dēprecātiónis meae.	To the voice of my prayer.
Sī inīquitátēs observáveris, Dómine:	If you would regard iniquities, Lord,
Dómine, quis sustinébit?	Who, Lord, could stand firm?
Quia apud tē propitiátiō est:	For with you there is forgiveness.
et propter lēgem tuam sustínuī tē, Dómine.	And on account of your law I am sustained, Lord.
Sustínuit ánima mea in verbō eius:	My soul has stayed in his word.
spērávit ánima mea in Dóminō.	My soul has hoped in the Lord.

EXERCÍTIA

Be sure to complete the *exercítium* in the appendix corresponding to this *capítulum*.

Capítulum
XX

IMPERFECT ACTIVE AND IMPERFECT PASSIVE SUBJUNCTIVES

Verbum Deī nōn negárem.[1]
—MARTIN LUTHER

OPÚSCULUM THEOLÓGICUM: *Martin Luther's Plea to the Emperor*

Martin Luther's summons before the Diet of Worms in 1521 represents a watershed moment in Western history. Departing on April 3, the Wednesday after Easter, Luther rode at the front of a long procession embarking on a three-hundred-mile journey from Wittenberg to Worms.

Luther and his entourage arrived in Worms on the morning of April 16. The proceedings were formal, direct, and conducted in Latin and German. The tribunal only had two questions for Luther—whether he wrote the dozens of booklets assembled on the table and whether he wanted to recant any of them. Luther—conscientious, surprised, and not good with "yes" or "no" questions—asked for an extension, which he was astonishingly granted. When asked the same two questions the following day, Luther uttered one of the most famous speeches in all of Western history, not just once but twice—first in German and then again in Latin.

Upon leaving Worms, Luther immediately wrote a letter to Emperor Charles V, who had presided over the meeting in Worms and who was still in that city. In little more than 1,200 Latin words, Luther managed to write a concise, insistent, yet respectful letter to this most powerful of men. The force of the letter becomes apparent in Luther's high cluster of imperfect subjunctives, for example:

Verbum Deī nōn negárem.	I would not deny the Word of God.
Nōn libéllōs meōs revocárem.	I would not recant my booklets.
Libéllōs meōs īgnī tráderem.	I would hand over my booklets to the fire.
Pédibus conculcárem.	I would trample [them] under my feet.

---

1. "I would not deny the Word of God."

IMPERFECT ACTIVE AND IMPERFECT PASSIVE SUBJUNCTIVES

Simplíciter et plānē respondérem.	I would reply simply and plainly.
Jūdíciō submítterem.	I would submit to judgement.
Ēvidéntī ratióne docérer.	Unless I were instructed by plain reason.
Áliquot excérptōs artículōs concéderem et concréderem.	I would concede and surrender certain excerpted portions.
Ratióne submítterem.	I would submit with an explanation.
Concíliī dēterminātiónī concréderem.	I would commit to the decision of the council.[2]

After a long stretch of such verbs in sentences that lingered like Cicero's, Luther punctuated his words with an unforgettably concise phrase: *Hic fuit contrōvérsiae tōtíus cardō*, "This was the heart of the whole controversy."

Despite the rhetorical flare of Luther's letter, the emperor promulgated the so-called Edict of Worms approximately four weeks afterward, calling for the German reformer's immediate arrest. Regardless of the results, Luther's letter to the emperor stands as a monument to this most historic of occasions. Not only does it enshrine the theology of one of the most influential people of all time, but it also preserves a letter written in his own hand.

For our purposes, Luther's letter offers an impressive introduction to our next form of the subjunctive mood: the imperfect. As you saw, Luther's use of the imperfect subjunctive adeptly captured the disconnect between what the emperor had wanted when it came to an event that occurred in the past but was nonetheless still ongoing and not yet complete. For such an occasion, the imperfect subjunctive was the perfect match. To be sure, my simple translations of the imperfect subjunctive verbs as "I would . . ." do not do full justice to Luther's Latin, but I have chosen to translate them this way here to underscore their shared tenses and moods.

Prospéctus

In this *capítulum* you will learn that:
- The imperfect subjunctive indicates contingency or possibility in the past.
- The imperfect subjunctive—in both the active and passive voice—is formed by adding present-system personal endings to the second principal part.
- Imperfect subjunctives are delightfully regular in their formation.

GRAMMÁTICA

20.1 Subjunctive Mood (Take Two). We come now to our second lesson for the subjunctive. Everything that we learned in the previous *capítulum* will aid us. As you remember, the subjunctive deals

---

2. The entire Latin letter is found in WA BR 2.307–10. For the sake of example, I have preserved the exact word order, but removed some of the words in between the object and verb.

SUBJUNCTIVE MOOD VERBS: ALL TENSES

with contingency, possibility, chance, suggestion, and hypotheticals, which in English translates into a lot of helping verbs like "may," "might," "ought," "should," and "would." Unfortunately, it will not always be easy to determine the exact way to render the subjunctive. The fault here lies with English, not Latin. Still, as speakers of English, we are left to figure out how to move out of Latin and into our target language. But do not worry at all. With practice, you will find accurate ways to convey the subjunctive in English.

20.2 **Good News with the Imperfect Subjunctive.** The imperfect subjunctive embraces us with good news from the start. All four conjugations are formed the exact same way. And what way is that? We simply add present-system personal endings to the second principal part (active voice endings for actives and passive voice endings for passives). In fact, even deponents behave in the imperfect subjunctive. Deponent verbs use the active forms of the imperfect subjunctive (as we will see in the illustrated sentence below). If you are looking for a grammatical breather, this *capítulum* is for you.

20.3 **Imperfect Active Imperfect Subjunctive: All Conjugations.** Now back to business. As alluded to above, forming the imperfect active subjunctive is fabulously simple and predicatably dependable. All you do is add the personal active endings to the second principal part (being sure to lengthen the final -e). That is it. And because all four conjugations follow the same procedure, there is no need to divide our discussion into different conjugations like we did in the previous *capítulum*. There is one method to bind them all.

Steps to Form Imperfect Active Subjunctives
1. Locate the second principal part (e.g, *laudáre*).
2. Lengthen the final letter from -e to -ē (e.g., *laudā́rē*).[3]
3. Add the present-system personal active endings: -m, -s, -t, -mus, -tis, -nt
 (e.g., *laudā́rem, laudā́rēs, laudā́ret, laudārḗmus, laudārḗtis, laudā́rent*).

20.4 **Out of the Crowd.** This formation makes the imperfect active very easy to spot in a crowd of verbiage. This mood and tense is virtually spilling over with letters. Once you see a verb not only housing the entire second principal part but also possessing additional endings, you know that you have an imperfect active subjunctive on your hands.

IMPERFECT ACTIVE SUBJUNCTIVE FORMS: ALL FOUR CONJUGATIONS

Verb (Conjugation)	Amō, Amā́re, Amā́vī, Amā́tus (1)	Móneō, Monḗre, Mónuī, Mónitus (2)	Osténdō, Osténdere, Osténdī, Osténtus (3)	Aúdiō, Audī́re, Audī́vī, Audī́tus (4)
First Personal Singular	amā́rem	monḗrem	osténderem	audī́rem
Second Person Singular	amā́rēs	monḗrēs	osténderēs	audī́rēs
Third Person Singular	amā́ret	monḗret	osténderet	audī́ret

---

3. Of course, the -ē will only appear in half of the forms. Why? For reasons we know by heart—long vowels like to shorten before words ending in -m, -t, and -nt.

First Personal Plural	amārḗmus	monērḗmus	ostenderḗmus	audīrḗmus
Second Person Plural	amārḗtis	monērḗtis	ostenderḗtis	audīrḗtis
Third Person Plural	amā́rent	monḗrent	osténderent	audī́rent

There are no surprises here. We are ready to look at an example:

Sī vērō duo vel trēs vel multō plūrēs idípsum habérent, tantúmdem prō síngulīs, quantum prō teipsō gaudérēs; sī síngulōs, sīcut teipsum, amárēs. (Anselm of Canterbury)⁴	But if two, three, or many more <u>were to have</u> the same [joy], <u>you would rejoice</u> as much for each one as for yourself, if you <u>loved</u> each as yourself.

The sentence above contains three imperfect active subjunctives: *habérent*, *gaudérēs*, and *amárēs*. However, as you can see, I chose to translate each one a slightly different way: "were to have," "you would rejoice," and "loved," respectively. What is going on here? This sentence perfectly captures both the opportunities and challenges involved in translating the subjunctive into English. In Latin, the subjunctive is a piece of cake. One word communicates everything we need to know.

In English, however, it is a different story. In our maternal language, we signal contingency, possibility, and uncertainty in many different ways. Do not be concerned if you translated these verbs differently than I did. Here is what is really important: First, you recognize the imperfect tense is being used in Latin and, second, you attempt to convey the subjunctive mood into English as best as you can.⁵

20.5 Translating the Imperfect Active Subjunctive: I "Might" Help You. I hate to continue throwing English under the wagon, but the ubiquity of options available to us to communicate uncertainty in this language makes it difficult for us to systematically choose one stock translation over another. In English, we like our options and are used to saying things in lots of different ways. This is foreign to Latin. But since we are translating from Latin into English, we need to think more about translation options.

We know by now that the subjunctive is all about possibility, potential, hypotheticals, and non-factual actions and events, but we have added a new layer of complexity with the introduction of the imperfect tense. Put simply, how do you convey uncertainty about a past event? There are many ways, to be sure. As with the previous *capítulum*, you have to determine why the subjunctive is being used in the first place. By way of a reminder, here are some of the most common uses of the subjunctive:

- To signal purpose (e.g., "so that," "so as to," "in order to")
- To show result (e.g., "with the result that," "that")
- To express desire (e.g., "want," "would like")

---

4. Anselm of Canterbury, *Proslógion* XXXV (PL 158.241).
5. As mentioned in the previous *capítulum*, I recommend reviewing A&G §§511–25, which discusses so-called conditionals and counterfactuals. The subjunctive is often used with these constructions, and there are specific situations in which they are used.

- To give a command (e.g., "let," "may")
- To show possibility (e.g., "could," "may," "were")
- To communicate fear (e.g., "lest," "that")
- To ask an indirect question (e.g., "should," "was," "would")
- To make a concession (e.g., "lest," "if . . . then")
- To reveal uncertainty (e.g., "should," "were")
- To illustrate characteristic ("who/which is the kind")
- To utter an unattainable wish ("would that," "I wish that")
- To indicate what is not going to happen or is contrary to fact ("if . . . then")

As always, I strongly urge you to take time to understand the Latin and determine from context how best to render it into English—regardless of the illustrative phrases included above.

20.6 **Things Specific to the Imperfect.** Once you determine how the subjunctive is functioning, you can then decide how to convey it in the past. The imperfect conveys aspect that is contemporaneous with that of the main verb. What is more, there are also certain uses of the subjunctive that are confined to a tense other than the present. For instance, the Latin particle *útinam*, "would that, or "I wish that," is usually combined with the imperfect (or pluperfect) tense.

IMPERFECT SUBJUNCTIVE OF *SUM, ESSE, FUĪ, FUTÚRUS*

Forming the imperfect subjunctive is even easier than forming the present subjunctive. We simply add the personal active endings to the present infinitive:

1 sg	essem	1 pl	essémus
2 sg	essēs	2 pl	essétis
3 sg	esset	3 pl	essent

Exémplum. Ego sī salútem nōn quaérerem audiéndam, ante tribúnal tuum nōn <u>essem</u>. (Anastasius Bibliothecarius)[6]

If I were not seeking to hear a greeting, <u>I would</u> not <u>be</u> before your greatness.

IMPERFECT PASSIVE SUBJUNCTIVES

20.7 **Imperfect Passive Subjunctive: All Conjugations.** We are now ready to turn to imperfect passives. These are formed in the exact same way as actives. The only difference, of course, is that we add passive personal endings (rather than active ones) to the second principal part. It is that simple. You know that I do not like using a stock translation for the subjunctive mood, but opt for "might be -ed" if you find yourself unable to translate the verb accurately. But, as always, let context be your ultimate guide.

---

6. Anastasius Bibliothecarius, *Ācta Sānctae Crispínae* (PL 129.728). In Latin, this is a good example of a conditional clause. Because both main verbs are in the imperfect subjunctive, and thus a "present contrary-to-fact condition," we translate it in a fairly standardized way.

IMPERFECT ACTIVE AND IMPERFECT PASSIVE SUBJUNCTIVES

Steps to Form Imperfect Passive Subjunctive
1. Locate the second principal part (e.g, *laudā́re*).
2. Lengthen the final letter from -e to -ē (e.g., **laudā́rē*).
3. Add the present-system personal passive endings: -r, -ris, -tur, -mur, -minī, -ntur (e.g., *laudā́rer, laudārḗris, laudārḗtur, laudārḗmur, laudārḗminī, laudārḗntur*).

IMPERFECT ACTIVE SUBJUNCTIVE FORMS: ALL FOUR CONJUGATIONS

Verb (Conjugation)	Amṓ, Amā́re, Amā́vī, Amā́tus (1)	Mṓneō, Monḗre, Mṓnuī, Mṓnitus (2)	Osténdō, Osténdere, Osténdī, Osténtus (3)	Aúdiō, Audī́re, Audī́vī, Audī́tus (4)
First Personal Singular	amā́rem	monḗrem	osténderem	audī́rem
Second Person Singular	amā́rēs	monḗrēs	osténderēs	audī́rēs
Third Person Singular	amā́ret	monḗret	osténderet	audī́ret
First Personal Plural	amārḗmus	monērḗmus	ostenderḗmus	audīrḗmus
Second Person Plural	amārḗtis	monērḗtis	ostenderḗtis	audīrḗtis
Third Person Plural	amā́rent	monḗrent	osténderent	audī́rent

Let us look at an example:

| Nam proptéreā homō vīsíbilis factus sum, ut ā tē vīsus <u>amā́rer</u>. (Bernard of Clairvaux)[7] | Therefore, I, a man, was made visible with the result that <u>I, having been seen by you, would be loved</u>. |

20.8 All Good Things Must Come to an End: Deponents. Before we ride off into the sunset, we need to revisit a comment that I made at the very beginning of this *capítulum*. I said that all verbs, even the cranky ones, follow the rules in the imperfect subjunctive. This is the case for practically all verbs—except one unruly lot at which we have grown accustomed to furrowing our brows: deponents.

However, before getting too upset, I hasten to add that deponents mostly follow the rules here. Yet, as we would expect with such a rogue brand of verbiage, they like to veer away from the pack when an opportunity presents itself. Here is how they do it. Rather than adding the present-system personal endings to their second principal, they look like what an active second principal part would look like and then add the present-system personal endings to that. In a strange way, this actually makes sense. Turns out, deponents are not as unique as they think they are. But, still, it could cause confusion, so let us pay attention. Here are the specific steps to make a deponent into an active verb.

---

7. Bernard of Clairvaux, *Vītis Mýstica* XLIV.152 (PL 184.726).

Steps to Form Deponent Imperfect Subjunctives
1. Locate the second principal part of a deponent (e.g., *loquī*).
2. Re-create what an active second principal part would look like (e.g., *loquī* → *lóquere*).
3. Add the present-system passive endings:[8] -r, -ris, -tur, -mur, -minī, -ntur
   (e.g., *lóquerer, loquerḗris, loquerḗtur, loquerḗmur, loquerḗminī, loqueréntur*).

These look just like imperfect passive subjunctives. The only difference, of course, is that they retain the active meanings. Here is an example:

Quómodo enim, frātrēs meī, putā́tis quod beā́ta Catharī́na, simplex utī́que puélla, contrā tyránnum, et contrā quīnquiāgíntā exquīsī́tōs sapiéntēs, tam argū́tē disputā́ret, et eōs convínceret, nisi Spī́ritus Sānctus in eam et per eam loquerḗtur? (Raoul Ardens)[9]	For, my brothers, how do you reckon that the blessed Catherine, certainly a simple girl, was so shrewdly debating against fifty sought-after wise men and defeating them, unless the Holy Spirit was speaking in her and through her?

Because we have already learned the principal parts of deponents, they present no challenge to us once we recognize what they are doing. They will look just like your garden-variety imperfect passive subjunctives, even though we know that they will translate into the active voice in English. After all is said and done, in other words, the imperfect subjunctive is one of the easiest forms of verbs to master in Latin.

Summā́rium

In this *capítulum* you learned that:
- The imperfect subjunctive describes past contingency. It is formed by adding present-system personal endings (for both the active and passive voices) to the second principal part.
- Stock translations are hard to come by in the subjunctive. It is best to try to understand first why the subjunctive is being used and then to decide how to convey this into English.
- One always has to be aware of deponent verbs, which appear passive but are translated as active.

VOCĀBULŎRUM INDEX

Latin	English (Gloss)	(Etymology)
annus, annī (m)	year	(annual)
arma, armṓrum (n)[a]	weapons, arms	(armor)
causa, causae (f)	purpose, reason, motive, cause	(cause)

---

8. Naturally, we would not add active endings to a deponent. Their forms are passive (though, of course, they have active meanings).
9. Raoul Ardens, *Homī́lia* VI (PL 155.1512).

coépiō, coépere, coepī, coeptus (3)	to begin	incipient
compléctor, compléctī, compléxus sum (3)	to embrace, to surround, to hug	(complexion)
coróna, corónae (f)	crown, wreath, tonsure	(coronation)
corónō, corōnáre, corōnávī, corōnátus (1)	to crown	(coronate)
dēmóror, dēmorárī, dēmorátus sum (1)	to delay, to abide, to linger, to dwell	
diábolus, diábolī (m)	devil, Satan	(diabolic)
dísputō, disputáre, disputávī, disputátus (1)	to dispute, to argue, to debate, to discuss	(dispute)
obsum, obésse, óbfuī, obfutúrus (+ dat)	to be against, to do harm to	
optō, optáre, optávī, optátus (1)	to wish, to desire, to hope for	(optative)
indígeō, indigére, indíguī, - (2)	to need, to want, to lack	(indigence)
índigēns, indegéntis (m, f, n)[b]	needy (person), in want	(indigent)
probō, probáre, probávī, probátus (1)	to test, to prove, to try, to examine	(probe)
relígiō, religiónis (f)	religion, devotion, reverence	(religion)
rēvérā	actually, in fact, in truth, truthfully	
senténtia, senténtiae (f)	thought, sentiment, sentence	(sentence)
sumō, súmere, sumpsī, sumptus (3)	to take (up), to seize, to obtain, to acquire	(sumptuous)
summópere	exceedingly, very much	
tam[c]	so, so much, to such a degree	
trādítiō, trāditiónis (f)	tradition, teaching, instruction	(tradition)
utérque, utráque, utrúmque	each of two	
velut	like, as	
vērō	but, indeed, in truth	

[a] This noun is always plural.
[b] This is a participle from the verb above, but you see it often acting like a noun.
[c] This adverb can pair with the adverb quam to mean something like "so . . . as."

ŌRÁTIŌ POPULÁRIS

Dē Profúndīs (Pars Minor II). We will conclude our memorization of the *Dē Profúndīs* from the previous *capítulum* with the remaining section.

SUBJUNCTIVE MOOD VERBS: ALL TENSES

Ā custódiā mātūtī́nā ūsque ad noctem:	From the morning watch until night
spēret Isrāél in Dóminō.	Let Israel hope in the Lord.
Quia apud Dóminum misericórdia:	Because with the Lord there is mercy
et cōpiṓsa apud eum redémptiō.	And with him unceasing redemption.
Et ipse rédimet Isrāél,	And he will himself redeem Israel
ex ómnibus inīquitā́tibus eius.	From all its iniquities.
Glória Patrī, et Fíliō,	Glory to the Father and to the Son
et Spīrítuī Sānctō.	And to the Holy Spirit.
Sīcut erat in prīncípiō, et nunc, et semper,	As it was in the beginning, is now,
et in saécula saeculórum. Āmēn.	and is always
	World without end. Amen.

EXERCÍTIA

Be sure to complete the *exercítium* in the appendix corresponding to this *capítulum*.

PERFECT AND PLUPERFECT SUBJUNCTIVES AND CUM CLAUSES

Utrum Christus in trī́duō mortis fúerit homō.[1]
—THOMAS AQUINAS

OPÚSCULUM THEOLÓGICUM: *Thomas Aquinas's Use of Utrum*

Born in the year 1225, Thomas Aquinas was an Italian theologian, Catholic priest, Dominican friar, university professor, and eminent philosopher. He has deeply influenced Western theology, particularly the Roman Catholic tradition, where his thought is referred to as Thomism. According to philosopher Peter Kreeft, "More doctoral dissertations have been written on St. Thomas than on any other philosopher or theologian who ever lived."[2] Whether cosmology, metaphysics, law, ethics, or theology proper, it seems that Thomas was always thinking and always writing.

Of all his theological works, two stand out: *Summa Contrā Gentī́lēs*, "Summary against the Nations," and *Summa Theológiae*, "Summary of Theology." Even though he died before completing it, the *Summa Theológiae* (also known as *Summa Theológica*) is perhaps the most influential theological textbook ever written. Thomas began composing the *Summa* in 1266 and continued until December of 1273, a few months before his death. Centuries later, the book is still in print.

What deep idea would you like to explore: life, death, sin, nature, Scripture, science, divinity? The *Summa*, no doubt, discusses it. Well before Wikipedia became an informational catchall for satisfying any factual curiosity, the *Summa*—totaling more than a dozen volumes in most English translations—was a veritable encyclopedia of theological knowledge.

Like the Talmud in the Jewish tradition and the Sunnah in the Muslim tradition, the *Summa* contains a unique style of its own. The book is structured around three *Partēs* or "Parts," which are further divided into more than six hundred *Quaestiṓnēs*, "Questions." The *Quaestiṓnēs* are distributed across more than three thousand *Artículī*, "Articles." The *Summa* discusses God in *Prīma Pars*, humanity and ethics in *Secúnda Pars*, and Christ in *Tértia Pars*. Thomas uses the same method throughout.

---

1. "Whether Christ was a human being during the three days of his death."
2. Peter Kreeft, *A Summa of the Summa* (San Francisco: Ignatius, 1990), 19.

SUBJUNCTIVE MOOD VERBS: ALL TENSES

After introducing a question, he provides objections, cites important theologians, philosophers, and biblical verses, responds to the objections, and then offers his answer.

Let us look at an example from *Tértia Pars, Quaéstiō L, Dē Morte Christī*, "Part Three, Question Fifty, about the Death of Christ." Thomas introduces the section as follows: *Deinde cōnsīderándum est dē morte Christī, et circā hōc quaeréntur sex*, "Then we must consider the death of Christ, about which six points shall be treated." Here are the six points:

1. Utrum <u>fúerit</u> convéniēns Christum morī.
2. Utrum per mortem Christī <u>fúerit</u> separáta dīvínitās ā carne.
3. Utrum <u>fúerit</u> sēparáta dīvínitās ab ánimā.
4. Utrum Christus in trīduō mortis <u>fúerit</u> homō.
5. Utrum <u>fúerit</u> ídem númerō corpus Christī vīvum et mórtuum.
6. Utrum mors Christī sit áliquid operáta ad nostram salútem.[3]

1. Whether it <u>was</u> fitting that Christ should die.
2. Whether Christ's divinity <u>was</u> separated from his flesh by his death.
3. Whether his divinity <u>was</u> separated from his soul.
4. Whether Christ <u>was</u> a human being during the three days of his death.
5. Whether the body of Christ <u>was</u> the same alive and dead.
6. Whether the death of Christ has anything to do with our salvation.

To be sure, there are many fascinating topics to be considered in these questions, but we will only focus on the grammar. You surely noticed that each statement began with an unfamiliar word—*utrum*—and that every sentence but one contained an identical underlined word—*fúerit*.

The first word, *utrum*, comes from *uter, utra, utrum*. Here it is best translated as "whether." The indeterminate nature of this word signals the subjunctive, the mood of uncertainty and possibility. This is exactly why every verb was in the subjunctive mood rather than the indicative; the answers were up for discussion. The verb used every time was the "to be" verb, specifically the pluperfect subjunctive form of it: *fúerit*.[4] In this *capítulum*, we will continue our discussion of how Latin conveys uncertainty and contingency in the past by focusing on the perfect and pluperfect subjunctive.

Prospéctus

In this *capítulum* you will learn that:
- The subjunctive mood is used in all past tenses in Latin: imperfect, perfect, and pluperfect. Each tense is represented by different forms.
- The perfect and pluperfect subjunctives indicate prior action in future situations; yet unlike imperfect subjunctives, they are formed from different principal parts.
- So-called *cum* clauses are constructions that involve the Latin word *cum*. Some are in the indicative mood and others are in the subjunctive. When in the subjunctive mood, three common uses indicate cause, concession, and circumstance.

---

3. Thomas Aquinas, *Summa Theológiae* III.50.1.
4. The one exception was the imperfect subjunctive: *sit*.

PERFECT AND PLUPERFECT SUBJUNCTIVES AND CUM CLAUSES

GRAMMÁTICA

21.1 **Subjunctive Mood (Revisited).** Despite the scary name—who would not become uneasy when hearing the term "pluperfect subjunctive"?—there is nothing either novel or frightening presented in this *capítulum*. After all, you are thoroughly familiar with both the subjunctive mood and the perfect and pluperfect tenses. As we know, the subjunctive mood signals contingency while the perfect and pluperfect tenses indicate completed aspect. All we have to do in this *capítulum* is combine these two worlds. Perfect-system actives use the third principal part, while perfect-system passives employ the fourth principal part.

21.2 **The *Dōnum*, "Gift," of the Perfect System.** Fortunately for us, all four conjugations conjugate the same way in the perfect active subjunctive. This is definitely reason to celebrate. In order to draw out similarities among "voices," we will first discuss the perfect and pluperfect active voices before then discussing the perfect and pluperfect passive voices.

PERFECT ACTIVE SUBJUNCTIVE

21.3 **Perfect Active Subjunctive: "May Have -ed."** The perfect active subjunctive expresses contingency or doubt about a past completed action. Although I am reluctant to offer a stock translation for the subjunctive mood, a possible example here could be "may have -ed." Naturally, however, depending on the exact function of the subjunctive, you may translate the verb in any number of ways.

21.4 **Forming the Perfect Subjunctive.** The formation of this verb can be achieved in more than one way. The most common way is to insert the suffix -erī- in between the perfect base and the present-system active personal endings

Steps to Form Perfect Active Subjunctives
1. Locate the third principal part (e.g., *laudāvī*).
2. Remove the -ī at the end, thus isolating the perfect active base (e.g., **laudāv-*).
3. Insert the suffix -erī (e.g., **laudāverī*).
4. Add the present-system personal active endings: -m, -s, -t, -mus, -tis, -nt
   (e.g., *laudáverim, laudáverīs, laudáverit, laudāverímus, laudāverítis, laudáverint*).

COMPARISON OF VERBS IN THE PERFECT ACTIVE SUBJUNCTIVE: ALL FOUR CONJUGATIONS

Verb (Conjugation)	Amō, Amáre, Amávī, Amátus (1)	Móneō, Monére, Mónuī, Mónitus (2)	Osténdō, Osténdere, Osténdī, Osténtus (3)	Aúdiō, Audíre, Audívī, Audítus (4)
First Personal Singular	amáverim	monúerim	osténderim	audíverim
Second Person Singular	amáverīs	monúerīs	osténderīs	audíverīs
Third Person Singular	amáverit	monúerit	osténderit	audíverit

(cont.)

SUBJUNCTIVE MOOD VERBS: ALL TENSES

Verb (Conjugation)	Amō, Amā́re, Amā́vī, Amā́tus (1)	Mōneō, Monḗre, Mónuī, Mónitus (2)	Osténdō, Osténdere, Osténdī, Osténtus (3)	Aúdiō, Audī́re, Audī́vī, Audī́tus (4)
First Personal Plural	amāverī́mus	monuerī́mus	ostenderī́mus	audīverī́mus
Second Person Plural	amāverī́tis	monuerī́tis	ostenderī́tis	audīverī́tis
Third Person Plural	amā́verint	monúerint	osténderint	audī́verint

Here is an example from our *amī́cus* Thomas Aquinas:

Utrum occī́sorēs ejus eum <u>cognṓverint</u>. (Thomas Aquinas)[5]

Whether his [Christ's] murderers <u>recognized</u> him.

21.5 **Seeing Double?** I trust these forms look quite familiar. In fact, if you look close enough, you will see that they are virtually identical to the future perfect indicative. The only exception is the first person singular and the length of the -i vowel in certain forms (here it is -erī rather than -erĭ in the future perfect indicative). So, how will you know the difference between the two? As you know, context is *rēx*. If you see subjunctive triggers, such as *ut* or *an* or *utrum*, then the verb is likely subjunctive. There are also many interrogative adjectives and pronouns used as indirect questions, thereby prompting the subjunctive. But if you notice an indicative future verb in the sentence, this is a good clue that you are working with a future perfect.

In nuce, "in short," the verb is future perfect if you are in the indicative mood and perfect subjunctive if your surrounding verbs are also in the subjunctive mood. We know from the example above, for instance, that *cognṓverint* has to be perfect subjunctive because of the word that triggered the subjunctive: *utrum*. This is one of our clue words for the subjunctive.

However, for the sake of argument, let us say that you are still unsure and cannot determine whether the verb is a perfect subjunctive or a future perfect indicative. Worst case scenario, you can hedge your bets by translating the verb in question, first, as a future perfect indicative and, then, as a perfect subjunctive. Then, you can make the best decision possible based on context clues and everything else you know about Latin.

PLUPERFECT ACTIVE SUBJUNCTIVES

21.6 **Pluperfect Active Subjunctive.** The intimidating name notwithstanding, this verb is easy enough to understand. In fact, we have met each of the individual components in previous *capítula*. While the perfect tense indicates the completion of an action prior to another one, the pluperfect indicates the completion of an action prior to another action in the past.

21.7 **Translating the Pluperfect Active Subjunctive: "Might Have -ed."** How exactly do you translate contingency in the past completed tense? If you discover the answer, please let me know. In all seriousness, it is simply not possible to offer a universal way to translate the pluperfect active subjunctive. However, for the sake of a base-line translation I reluctantly suggest "might have

---

5. Thomas Aquinas, *Summa Theológiae* III.47.1.

-ed." For most of us, this does not sound too different from the perfect active subjunctive. This is true. In the end, any translation that accurately conveys both the uncertainty of an event as well as the past completed nature of it will suffice, though this cannot always be accomplished in a tidy and consistent way. As is the case with all subjunctives, we need to first identify *why* a verb is in the subjunctive mood to begin with; after we determine that, it will be easier to determine *how* to translate it.

21.8 **Forming the Pluperfect Active Subjunctive: Perfect Stem + *-issē*.** The formation of the pluperfect active subjunctive is uncomplicated. We simply combine the perfect stem (minus the -ī) with the—surprise, surprise—pluperfect subjunctive of the "to be" verb (minus the fu-). This method, though my preference, is not the standard way to form it. Below we will list two ways to form the pluperfect active subjunctive: my preferred way and the more standard way.

Steps to Form Pluperfect Active Subjunctives
1. Locate the third principal part (e.g., *laudávī*).
2. Remove the -ī at the end, thus isolating the perfect active base (e.g., **laudāv-*).
3. Add the pluperfect subjunctive of the "to be" verb minus the fu-: ~~fu~~íssem, ~~fu~~íssēs, ~~fu~~ísset, ~~fu~~issēmus, ~~fu~~issētis, ~~fu~~íssent (e.g., *laudāvíssem, laudāvíssēs, laudāvísset, laudāvissēmus, laudāvissētis, laudāvíssent*).

The standard way to form this verb will now be offered. You could simply insert the suffix -issē between the perfect base and the present-system personal active endings. Here are the steps:

1. Locate the third principal part (e.g., *laudávī*).
2. Remove the -ī at the end, thus isolating the perfect active base (e.g., **laudāv-*).
3. Insert the suffix -issē (e.g., **laudāvissē*).
4. Add the present-system personal active endings: -m, -s, -t, -mus, -tis, -nt (e.g., *laudāvíssem, laudāvíssēs, laudāvísset, laudāvissēmus, laudāvissētis, laudāvíssent*).

COMPARISON OF VERBS IN THE PLUPERFECT ACTIVE SUBJUNCTIVE: ALL FOUR CONJUGATIONS

Verb (Conjugation)	*Amō, Amáre, Amávī, Amátus* (1)	*Móneō, Monére, Mónuī, Mónitus* (2)	*Osténdō, Osténdere, Osténdī, Osténtus* (3)	*Aúdiō, Audíre, Audívī, Audítus* (4)
First Personal Singular	amāvíssem	monuíssem	ostendíssem	audīvíssem
Second Person Singular	amāvíssēs	monuíssēs	ostendíssēs	audīvíssēs
Third Person Singular	amāvísset	monuísset	ostendísset	audīvísset
First Personal Plural	amāvissḗmus	monuissḗmus	ostendissḗmus	audīvissḗmus
Second Person Plural	amāvissḗtis	monuissḗtis	ostendissḗtis	audīvissḗtis
Third Person Plural	amāvíssent	monuíssent	ostendíssent	audīvíssent

Once again, I prefer the first method, but you are welcome to adopt the second one instead—or, if you are interested, put on your thinking cap and feel free to discover another way to form the tense.

Here is an example of a pluperfect active subjunctive:

Eṓdem témpore Jovī quoque Pistṓrī āra pósita est, quod eōs quiétē <u>monuísset</u>, ut ex omnī frūméntō, quod habḗbant, pānem fácerent, et in hóstium castra jactárent. (Lactantius)[6]	At the same time, an altar was also erected to Jupiter Pistor[7] because <u>he had warned</u> them in a dream to make all the grain which they had into bread and to throw it into the camp of their enemies.

PERFECT AND PLUPERFECT SUBJUNCTIVE OF *SUM, ESSE, FUĪ, FUTŪRUS*

Perfect Subjunctive				Pluperfect Subjunctive			
"may be"				"might be"			
1 sg	fúerim	1 pl	fuerímus	1 sg	fuíssem	1 pl	fuissḗmus
2 sg	fúerīs	2 pl	fuerítis	2 sg	fuíssēs	2 pl	fuissḗtis
3 sg	fúerit	3 pl	fúerint	3 sg	fuísset	3 pl	fuíssent

There is no passive of the "to be" verb, so that only leaves two forms for this *capítulum*, the perfect and pluperfect subjunctives:

Exémplum. Quia etiámsī nōn collápsa <u>fuísset</u>[8] Adae intégritās, símilis <u>fuísset</u> Deō cum ángelīs; neque tamen proptéreā necésse <u>fuísset</u> fīlium Deī fíerī vel hóminem vel ángelum. (John Calvin)[9]	Because, even if the blamelessness of Adam had not been lost, he, <u>would have been</u> like God with the angels. Yet, nevertheless, <u>it would</u> not for this reason <u>have been</u> necessary for the Son of God to become either a human or an angel.

PERFECT PASSIVE FORMS: *Indicative and Subjunctive*

21.9 Perfect Passive Forms: Indicative and Subjunctive. Forming the passive forms of the perfect system are so easy even an *īnfāns* could do it. All we do is combine the fourth principal part with a particular tense and mood of the "to be" verb. For the sake of comparison, below is an abbreviated chart of the perfect passive system in both the indicative and subjunctive forms.

---

6. Lactantius, *Dīvīnārum Īnstitūtiṓnum Librī* I.20 (PL 6.226).
7. The word *pistor, pistṓris* (m) means "baker" or "miller."
8. Because this first use of *fuísset* is a compound tense working with *collápsa*, we will not illustrate here.
9. John Calvin, *Īnstitūtiṓ Chrīstiánae Religiṓnis* II.12.7 (CR 30.345).

COMPARISON OF INDICATIVE AND SUBJUNCTIVE FORMS OF THE PERFECT PASSIVE

The perfect uses the present tense of "to be," the pluperfect uses the imperfect of "to be," and the future perfect uses the future of "to be." Meanwhile, the fourth principal part remains the same.

INDICATIVE

Perfect	Pluperfect	Future Perfect
audítus sum	audítus eram	audítus erō
audítus es	audítus erās	audítus eris
audítus est	audítus erat	audítus erit
audítī sumus	audítī erámus	audítī érimus
audítī estis	audítī erátis	audítī éritis
audítī sunt	audítī erant	audítī erunt

SUBJUNCTIVE

Perfect	Pluperfect	Future Perfect
audítus sim	audítus essem	-
audítus sīs	audítus essēs	-
audítus sit	audítus esset	-
audítī sīmus	audítī essémus	-
audítī sītis	audítī essétis	-
audítī sint	audítī essent	-

Exémplum. Nec vērō spéculum esset inaestimábilis Deī grátiae homō Christus, nisi in eum <u>colláta esset</u> haec dígnitās ut sit ac vocétur ūnigénitus Deī fílius. (John Calvin)[10]

Nor could Christ as a man be a mirror of God's immeasurable grace, unless this dignity <u>had been conferred</u> on him with the result that he would exist and would be called God's only begotten Son.

PERFECT PASSIVE SUBJUNCTIVES

21.10 Perfect Passive Subjunctive: "May Have Been -ed." This form indicates the completed tense of the event (thus the "have" part), the passive voice (the "been" part), and the subjunctive mood (the "may" part). Altogether, this leads us to a possible translation of something like "may have been -ed." Nonetheless, as we have come to expect with the subjunctive, it is important to first determine the function of the subjunctive before translating.

---

10. John Calvin, *Īnstitútiō Chrīstiánae Religiónis* II.14.5 (CR 30.357).

21.11 Forming the Perfect Passive Subjunctive. Because this is a compound tense—meaning that it requires more than one word—we will require two components. The first is the perfect passive participle (the fourth principal part) and the second is the present subjunctive of the "to be" verb. In other words, this works exactly like the perfect passive indicative (which we will soon learn); the only difference is that we use the subjunctive rather than the indicative. Otherwise, their forms are identical.

Steps to Form Perfect Passive Subjunctives
1. Locate the fourth principal part (e.g., *laudátus/láudatī*).
2. Combine the fourth principal part with the present subjunctive forms (e.g., *sim, sīs, sit, sīmus, sītis, sint + laudátus*).
3. Align the case, number, and gender of the fourth principal part (which use 2-1-2 endings) with the person and number of the present subjunctive.

PERFECT PASSIVE SUBJUNCTIVES: REPRESENTATIVE EXAMPLE

Masculine	Feminine	Neuter	Translation
mónitus sim	mónita sim	mónitum sim	I may have been warned
mónitus sīs	mónita sīs	mónitum sīs	You may have been warned
mónitus sit	mónita sit	mónitum sit	He / she / may have been warned
mónitī sīmus	mónitae sīmus	mónita sīmus	We may have been warned
mónitī sītis	mónitae sītis	mónita sītis	You all may have been warned
mónitī sint	mónitae sint	mónita sint	They may have been warned

Let us look at an example:

. . . licet plērīque Hebraeórum arbitréntur quod tunc prīmum in nómine Dóminī et in similitúdine ejus <u>fabricáta sint</u> ídóla. (Angelomus of Luxeuil)[11]	. . . even if most of the Hebrews think that idols then <u>were</u> first <u>made</u> in the name of the Lord and in his likeness.

In this sentence, the subjunctive has ultimately been triggered by the deponent verb *árbitror*, though technically, at this stage in Latin, the word *quod* introduced indirect statement.

PLUPERFECT PASSIVE SUBJUNCTIVES

21.12 Pluperfect Passive Subjunctive: "Might Have Been -ed." The last of our passive subjunctives follows the same trail taken by the perfect subjunctive. The only difference is the use of the

---

[11]. Angelomus of Luxeuil, *Commentárius in Génesim* IV.26 (PL 115.153).

imperfect subjunctive of the "to be" verb rather than the present tense. Otherwise, the forms are identical. We form the pluperfect passive subjunctive from the fourth principal part and then combine it with the imperfect subjunctive of *sum, esse, fuī, futūrus*. One possible translation is "might have been -ed," but you will also encounter various ways to convey the sense of the Latin into English depending on why the subjunctive is being used in the first place. Also, as expected, the exact word order of this compound tense varies. Do not be surprised if you see the "to be" verb first, the fourth principal part first, or several words separating the two. It is still a compound tense, and the two are still working together to convey one concept.

Steps to Form Pluperfect Passive Subjunctives
1. Locate the fourth principal part (e.g., *laudātus*).
2. Combine the fourth principal part with the imperfect subjunctive forms
    (e.g., *essem, essēs, esset, essēmus, essētis, essent + laudātus*).
3. Align the case, number, and gender of the fourth principal part (which use 2-1-2 endings) with the person and number of the present subjunctive.

PLUPERFECT PASSIVE SUBJUNCTIVE: REPRESENTATIVE EXAMPLE

Masculine	Feminine	Neuter	Translation
mónitus essem	mónita essem	mónitum essem	I might have been warned
mónitus essēs	mónita essēs	mónitum essēs	You might had been warned
mónitus esset	mónita esset	mónitum esset	He / she / might had been warned
mónitī essémus	mónitae essémus	mónita essémus	We might had been warned
mónitī essétis	mónitae essétis	mónita essétis	You all might had been warned
mónitī essent	mónitae essent	mónita essent	They might had been warned

Here is an example of a pluperfect passive subjunctive:

Quia nisi Spíritūs Sānctī grátiā <u>essent illūminátī</u>, neque daemónia ējícerent, neque virtūtēs fácerent, neque illum verum Deum esse créderent. (Haimo of Halberstadt)[12]

Because unless they <u>had been enlightened</u> by the grace of the Holy Spirit, they would not cast out demons, perform miracles, or believe that he was the true God.

CUM CLAUSES

21.13 ***Cum* Clauses in the Subjunctive Mood.** As we bring our discussion of the subjunctive mood to a close, let us take a look at one final construction. These are often called "*cum* clauses" due to

---
12. Haimo of Halberstadt, *Homílīa* LXXXI (PL 118.492).

the use of the Latin word *cum*. Before we tackle *cum* clauses, it is important to distinguish two identical words. We have already learned the meaning of *cum* when functioning as a preposition with the ablative; it means "with." However, there is another word, spelled the same way, that means something different. This use of *cum* occurs as a conjunction, and it is this use of *cum* that concerns us here since it often prompts the subjunctive mood. Below are three ways the *cum* clause may function in Latin when triggering the subjunctive mood.

1. **Causal.** Explaining the cause of something. Often translated as "because," "inasmuch," "seeing that," "since," and "whereas."
2. **Concessive.** Making a concession. Often translated as "although," "even though," "granted that," and "though."
3. **Circumstantial.** Describing the circumstances around an action. Could be translated as "under the circumstances."

21.14 *Cum in the Indicative Mood—Plus Dum, Donec, and Quoad.* When *cum* is followed by the present, future, or future perfect, often the indicative follows. In such a construction, you will translate *cum* as "when" or "while"—or even more specifically, "after" and "before." This is sometimes called the "temporal" use of the *cum* clause. When functioning temporally, you will sometimes not see *cum*, but instead will encounter similar types of conjunctions, such as *dum*, *donec*, and *quoad*. These words will contain similar translations as *cum*, but they are also able to branch out semantically into meanings such "as long as," "until," etc.

21.15 *Cum, Quum, or Quom?* After I learned Latin and began translating for myself, I came across so many words that I had never learned—or so I thought. One of these was *quum*. For the life of me, I could not figure out how this word was different from *cum*, even though I would encounter authors who used both forms. To make a long story short, there are different spellings for this word. Although *cum* is the textbook spelling, you might also encounter *quum* or *quom*. The exact spelling and usage depend on the era, style, and region of the author. Nonetheless, translate it according to the guidelines above, as this word carries many meanings.

Summārium

In this *capítulum* you learned that:
- The perfect system is a very understandable system regardless of whether it is in the indicative or subjunctive mood.
- The perfect and pluperfect tenses occur in the subjunctive mood (the future perfect subjunctive does not exist). The perfect and pluperfect subjunctive indicate past contingency.
- There are many acceptable ways to translate the perfect and pluperfect subjunctives into English. One possibility is "may have -ed" and "may have been -ed" for the perfect active and passive, respectively; and "might have -ed" and "might have been -ed" for the pluperfect active and passive, respectively.
- The perfect and pluperfect passive subjunctives are formed in a way very similar to perfect and pluperfect passive indicatives (which we will soon learn).
- The word *cum* means many different things. When it is not a preposition meaning "with," it may introduce a clause with a variety of possible meanings.

VOCĀBULŌRUM INDEX

Latin	English (Gloss)	(Etymology)
alō, álere, áluī, altus (3)	to nourish, to foster, to feed	(alimony)
ancílla, ancíllae (f)	female servant, maid	(ancillary)
ángulus, ángulī (m)	corner, angle	(angle)
amplus, ampla, amplum	large, abundant, ample, splendid	(ample)
aula, aulae (f)	class, hall, church, court, palace	
aut	or[a]	
castus, casta, castum	chaste	(chaste)
cēra, cērae (f)	wax	(cerated)
céreus, céreī (m)[b]	candle	(cerements)
clāvis, clāvis, clávium (f)	key	(clavicle)
cōgō, cógere, coḗgī, coáctus (3)	to collect, to compel, to assemble, to force	(coagulate)
mūtō, mūtā́re, mūtā́vī, mūtā́tus (1)	to change, to move, to modify, to transform	(mutate)
pāstor, pāstóris (m)	shepherd	(pastor)
porténdō, porténdere, porténdī, porténtus (3)	to foretell, to predict, to portend	(portend)
praefigū́rō, praefigūrā́re, praefigūrā́vī, praefigūrā́tus (1)	to prefigure	(prefigure)
tangō, tángere, tétigī, tāctus (3)	to touch	(tactile)
saepe	often	
sīve	or[c]	
supérnus, supérna, supérnum	heavenly, celestial	(supernal)
spīrō, spīrā́re, spīrā́vī, spīrā́tus (1)	to breathe	(perspire)
umbra, umbrae (f)	shadow	(umbrela)
ventus, ventī (m)	wind	
vénia, véniae (f)	indulgence, kindness, forgiveness	(venial)
vērā́citer	in truth, truthfully, really	
vínculum, vinculī (n)	bond, chain	

[a] Like *vel*, this word means "either . . . or" when two uses of *aut* appear in relation to each other: "*aut . . . aut.*"
[b] There is an adjectival form that looks very similar: *céreus, cérea, céreum,* meaning "waxen" or "of wax."
[c] Like *aut* and *vel*, this word means "either . . . or" when two uses of *sive* appear in relation to each other: "*sive . . . sive.*"

SUBJUNCTIVE MOOD VERBS: ALL TENSES

ŌRĀTIŌ POPULĀRIS

Deus Inténde. Below is Psalmus LXIX, which is numbered as Psalm 70 in English versions. This is a daily prayer in the Breviary, a collection of liturgical texts and prayers in the Roman Catholic Church. You are certainly welcome to memorize all of the prayer, but I have underlined only the second, fifth, and sixth verses of the psalm to memorize.

In fīnem, Psalmus Dāvīd, in remorātiónem, quod salvum fécerit eum Dóminus.	At the end, a psalm of David, in memory that the Lord had saved him.
<u>Deus, in adiūtórium meum inténde.</u>	<u>God, come to my help.</u>
<u>Dómine, ad adiuvándum meum festínā.</u>	<u>Lord, hasten to help me.</u>
Cōnfundántur et revereántur quī quaérunt ánimam meam.	Let those who seek my life be confounded and afraid.
Āvertántur retrórsum et ērubéscant quī volunt mihi mala.	Let those who wish to do me evil be turned backward and be embarrassed.
Āvertántur statim ērubēscéntēs quī dīcunt mihi: euge, euge!	Let those who say to me—hurrah, hurrah—be turned away and be embarrassed.
<u>Exsúltent et laeténtur in tē omnēs quī quaérunt tē</u>	<u>Let all who seek you rejoice and be joyful in you.</u>
<u>et dīcant semper: magnificétur Deus quī díligunt salūtáre tuum.</u>	<u>And let those who love your salvation always say: "May God be praised!"</u>
<u>Ego vērō egénus et pauper sum.</u>	<u>But I am desperate and poor.</u>
<u>Deus, ádiuvā mē.</u>	<u>God, help me!</u>
<u>Adiútor meus et līberátor meus es tū.</u>	<u>You are my helper and my liberator.</u>
<u>Dómine, nē moriēris.</u>	<u>Lord, do not delay!</u>

EXERCÍTIA

Be sure to complete the *exercítium* in the appendix corresponding to this *capítulum*.

SÉPTIMA PARS

PARTICIPLES, PERFECT PASSIVES, *and* INFINITIVES: SECOND *and* FOURTH PRINCIPAL PARTS

There are many concepts presented in Séptima Pars. For the most part, this section introduces us to participles and infinitives.

Participles are verbal adjectives and infinitives are verbal nouns. As such, both of them can do many of the things that verbs can do. But they can also do much more. This dexterity allows for participles and infinitives to be used for a variety of purposes. You will see them everywhere, performing a whole host of duties along the way.

Here is the great news: By the time you complete Séptima Pars, you will be well on your way toward mastering the Latin language, since familiarity with the participle and infinitive unlock the language in countless ways. While learning about the participle and infinitive, do not forget to make connections with the different verbal tenses you have already learned as well as the specific endings and usages of nouns and adjectives. You know more than you think you do.

Capítulum
XXII

PRESENT ACTIVE PARTICIPLES, FUTURE PASSIVE PARTICIPLES (GERUNDIVES), AND GERUNDS

Theológia est doctrína bene vīvéndī.[1]
—PETER RAMUS

OPÚSCULUM THEOLÓGICUM: *What Is Theology?*

What is theology? There have been many attempts to succintly define this term in the history of Christianity. Anselm, the archbishop of Canterbury, offered a classic definition. In his most celebrated work *Proslógion*, "Discourse," written in 1077–1078, he suggested that theology is:

Fidēs quaerēns intelléctum.[2]　　　　　　　　　Faith seeking understanding.

In the late sixteenth century, a French Protestant logician named Peter Ramus moved in a different direction. In his book *Commentāriṓrum dē Religiṓne Chrīstiā́nā Librī Quattuor*, "Four Books of Comments on the Christian Religion," published posthumously in 1576, he wrote:

Theológia est doctrína bene vīvéndī.[3]　　　　　Theology is the doctrine of living well.

The framework that Peter Ramus developed, called Ramism, influenced countless thinkers in the generations to come. Among many others, two English theologians thoroughly adopted Ramist principles: William Perkins and William Ames.

---

1. "Theology is the doctrine of living well."
2. Anselm of Canterbury, *Proslógion*, Prooémium (PL 158.223).
3. Peter Ramus, *Commentāriṓrum dē Religiṓne Chrīstiā́nā Librī Quattuor* I.1 (Frankfurt: Andreas Wechel, 1576), 6.

In his book *Armílla Aúrea*, "Golden Chain," originally published in 1590, Perkins only slightly modified Ramus's definition of theology:

Theológia est sciéntia beátē <u>vīvéndī</u> in aetérnum.[4]	Theology is the science <u>of living</u> happily in eternity.

Perhaps Perkins's most prized pupil at Cambridge was William Ames, who spent his career in the Netherlands. In his *magnum opus*, titled *Medúlla Theológica*, "Theological Marrow," Ames defined theology in a very similar way:

Theológia est doctrína Deō <u>vīvéndī</u>.[5]	Theology is the doctrine <u>of living</u> for God.

Ames's contemporary, a Polish theologian named Johannes Maccovius (in Polish, Jan Makowski), expanded the base of this definition. He described theology as follows:

Theológia est disciplína, partim Theōrética, partim práctica <u>docēns</u> modum bene beatéque <u>vīvéndī</u> in aetérnum.[6]	Theology is a discipline, partly theoretical and partly practical, <u>teaching</u> a way <u>of living</u> both well and happily forever.

This is a beautifully concise definition, encompassing both the intellectual and experiential dimensions of the theological enterprise. But was it missing something?

Dutchman Peter Van Mastricht, living a generation after Ames and Maccovius, but still very much part of the Reformed tradition, put theology under a microscope. In his life's labor, *Theōrético-práctica Theológia*, "Theoretical-Practical Theology," published in the later part of the seventeenth century, he examined theology from a different perspective:

Theológia ista Chrīstiána, theōrético-práctica, nōn est nisi doctrína Deō <u>vīvéndī</u> per Christum; seu doctrína, quae est secúndum pietátem.[7]	That Christian theology is not theoretical-practical if it is not the doctrine <u>of living</u> for God through Christ; or if it is not the doctrine that exists according to piety.

So, what can we learn about these different definitions of theology? Many things, to be sure. We observe both the great variety and unity in how theologians from many traditions and time periods have defined this term. For our purposes, though, we must take note of two new grammatical concepts: participles and gerunds, which are verbal adjectives and verbal nouns, respectively. Curiously, in every definition provided, the author defined theology using either a participle or a gerund (which I have underlined to illustrate). Given the importance of defining theology well, they must play significant roles in Latin.

---

4. William Perkins, *Armílla Aúrea* I (Basel: Conrad Waldkirch, 1596), 5.
5. William Ames, *Medúlla Theológica* I.1 (Amsterdam: Ioannes Ianbonius, 1556), 1.
6. Johannes Maccovius, *Locī Commúnēs* I (Franeker: Nicholas Arnold, 1650), 1.
7. Peter van Mastricht, *Theōrético-práctica Theológia* I.40 (1698), 21. This was a multivolume work, the first four parts of which were published in 1682 and the second four in 1687.

PRESENT ACTIVE PARTICIPLES, FUTURE PASSIVE PARTICIPLES, AND GERUNDS

> **Prospéctus**
>
> In this *capítulum* you will learn that:
> - Participles are verbal adjectives.
> - There are four kinds of participles in Latin.
> - Present active participles are contemporaneous with the main tense of the verb.
> - Future passive participles, also called gerundives, often imply obligation or necessity.
> - Gerunds are neuter, singular, oblique (no nominative!) verbal nouns that sometimes look like gerundives.

GRAMMÁTICA

22.1 Participles: Verbal Adjectives. If participles were analyzed by psychologists, they would be diagnosed as extroverts. Energetic, outgoing, and sociable, they are words that quite literally love to take "part"—from the Latin *pars, partis*—of verbal activities of all kinds. Related to the noun *particípium*, "partaking" or "participation," participles participate in the social life of both adjectives and verbs since they are essentially adjectives assembled from verbs.

In a word, participles do many things that adjectives and verbs do, but still retain their own distinct identity. As adjectives, they describe nouns and agree with them in case, number, and gender.[8] Nothing complicated there. As verbs, participles express action and so convey tense and voice (but not person).[9] Participles maintain three verbal tenses and two different voices.

THE COMPONENTS OF A LATIN PARTICIPLE

As an Adjective	As a Verb
case	~~person~~
number	voice
gender	tense

22.2 *Exémplī Grátiā*, **"For the Sake of an Example."** Let us look at an example of how participles can draw out the verbal and adjectival component of adjacent words.

Et ego Jōánnes vīdī sānctam cīvitátem Jerúsalēm novam <u>dēscendéntem</u> dē caelō ā Deō, <u>parátam</u> sīcut spōnsam <u>ōrnátam</u> virō suō. (Rev. XXI.2)	And I, John, saw the holy and new city Jerusalem, <u>descending</u> out of heaven from God, having been <u>prepared</u> and <u>adorned</u> like a bride for her husband.

As mentioned above, participles are verb-based adjectives that describe nouns. Sometimes your translation will make participles sound exactly like adjectives and sometimes your translation will make them sound like verbs. Technically, both components are at work in the Latin

---

8. Similarly, as adjectives, they can also take the place of adjectives (as substantives).
9. They may also govern a direct object or modify an adverb.

participle. *Dēscendéntem*, for example, is accusative, singular, and feminine to match the noun *cīvitắtem*, but it is also in the active voice and present tense to indicate the performance of action (thus active voice) and the contemporaneous nature of the action to the main verb (thus present tense). Both *parắtam* and *ōrnắtam* share the same adjectival characteristics (accusative, singular, and feminine) for the same reasons mentioned above, but the voice (passive) and tense (perfect) indicate something different about *cīvitắtem*—it is now receiving action (thus passive voice) and indicating action prior to the main verb (thus perfect tense).

As alluded to above, English sometimes requires our translations to sound either more like a verb or an adjective (or even an adverb). This will take some time getting used to since English does not make use of the participle in the same way and with the same frequency as Latin. But enough of our introductory example—let us examine the different kinds of participles.

22.3 **Four Participles.** Like true extroverts, participles keep up their social appearances: They appear frequently in Latin sentences of all kinds. The Romans loved them. Despite their frequency, however, there is not much variety. Latin only contains four kinds of participles: (1) present active, (2) perfect passive, (3) future active, and (4) future passive (gerundive). Below is a paradigm of the four kinds of participles that appear in Latin, which are constructed out of the building blocks of principal parts and which utilize common case endings.[10]

PARTICIPLE FORMS

Tense	Active Voice	Passive Voice
Present	2nd princ. part + -ns, -ntis 3-3-3 adjective endings (English: "-ing")	-
Perfect	-	4th princ. part + -us, -a, -um 2-1-2 adjective endings (English: "having been -ed")
Future	4th princ. part + -úrus, -úra, -úrum 2-1-2 adjective endings (English: "about to-," "going to-")	2nd princ. part + -ndus, -nda, -ndum 2-1-2 adjective endings (English: "to be -ed")

You probably noticed the blank forms in this paradigm. Latin lacks a participle for the present passive ("being -ed") and perfect active ("having -ed"). Such forms do not exist. Latin makes up for these insufficiencies in different ways. For instance, rather than using a present passive participle, Latin could communicate a similar concept by combining adverbs such as *cum* or *dum* with a finite verb; and instead of using a perfect active participle, Latin could sometimes express such a notion by deploying a deponent form of the perfect passive participle, or by combining a perfect passive participle with an ablative absolute (discussed in a subsequent *capítulum*). Whatever the case, as the saying goes, "life finds a way." Latin does, too. The Romans, and later Latin writers, devised different ways to discharge sentences with only four participles in their quiver. So do not feel too much sympathy for them. Latin has managed quite well.

Perhaps the second item you noted from the paradigm was the two sets of principal parts used to form participles: the second and the fourth. I will refer to this phenomenon as the 2-4-4-2

---

10. I have abbreviated principal parts as princ. part.

pattern. Put simply, the present active and future passive participles make use of the second principal part (2 PP), while the perfect passive and future active participles draw from the fourth principal part (4 PP). It is for this reason that I will divide our discussion of participles into two separate *capítula*. First, in this *capítulum*, we will explore second-principal part participles; and then, in the *próximum*, "the next one," we will isolate fourth-principal part participles.

2 PP Participles
- Present Active: Second principal part, 3-3-3 endings
- Future Passive: Second principal part, 2-1-2 endings

4 PP Participles
- Perfect Passive: Fourth principal part, 2-1-2 endings
- Future Active: Fourth principal part, 2-1-2 endings

22.4 *Cáveat Léctor*, **"Reader Beware."** Participles come with a warning. Despite explicit language to the contrary, "present" participles do not necessarily occur in the present; "perfect" participles do not necessarily indicate past action; and "future" participles do not necessarily refer to what is to come. It is a bit more nuanced. Just as adjectives can be used with any noun declension, so, too, participles can essentially be combined with any main verbal tense. The most important rule to remember is that, whatever main verb or participle combination you may encounter, the participle receives its orders from the tense of the main verb—not *vice versā*. In this way, a participle reveals relative time; that is to say, the tense of a participle is relative to the tense of the main verb—whether present, past, or future.

It is traditionally taught that a "present" participle is one that occurs *contemporaneously* with the main—what we call "finite"—verb. For you math majors out there, it represents + or −0 time value. *Mūtátīs mūtándīs*, a "perfect" participle communicates something that was completed *prior to* the main verb (−1 time value); and, you surely guessed it, a "future" participle indicates completion *subsequent to* the main verb (+1 time value).[11] You might ask why we do not go ahead and abandon the traditional language altogether. To be sure, some have.[12] However, there are two immediate problems that present themselves once we do so. First, the language used—present, perfect, and future—is linked to more than participles. Indeed, we are already accustomed to this language, so adding new terminology would introduce confusion when comparing it to different verbal tenses. Second, it is not exactly easy to find suitable, one-word replacements to the traditional terms handed down to us. That stated, we will retain the traditional terminology and just make note that the time-value of the participle used is relative to the rest of the sentence, particularly the main verb.

22.5 Translating Participles. When translating participles into English, I recommend sticking to the basic translation formula provided in our initial paradigm, but then branching out once you get comfortable with them. You will eventually discover that participles can be rendered in many ways in English depending on tense, voice, and context. Let us look at a simple example:

---

11. To be fair, there are always exceptions to these general rules. For example, in the Vulgate, the present active participle is often used to convey the aorist participle in Greek, which is one of the past-tense participles. However, these kinds of things are bound to happen when moving from one language to another.

12. Mostly notably, the eminent Latinist Reginald Foster has abandoned most of the traditional language. See his *Ossa Latīnitātis Sōla ad Mentem Regináldī Ratiōnémque: The Mere Bones of Latin according to the Thought and System of Reginald* (Washington, DC: Catholic University of America Press, 2016), 318–20. But, then again, he fought against most all traditional terminology.

Véniēns domum cónvocat amícōs et vīcínōs. (Luke XV.6)[13]

Coming home, he called together his friends and neighbors.
While coming home, he called together his friends and neighbors.
After coming home, he called together his friends and neighbors.
When he came home, he called together his friends and neighbors.
Although he came home, he called together his friends and neighbors.
Because he came home, he called together his friends and neighbors.

As you see, there are many acceptable ways to translate this sentence (focusing just on the use of the participle). These translation options are not meant to frighten you, but merely to illustrate how a simple participle can be rendered many different ways into English. Because our goal at this stage in translation is learning new forms, I, once again, recommend using a basic, predetermined translation (as found in the paradigm box and in each participle discussion) and then considering more nuanced translations as you progress in Latin. We crawl before we walk.

SECOND-PRINCIPAL PART PARTICIPLES: *Present Active and Future Passive*

22.6 **Deponents and Participles.** As mentioned above, we will divide our discussion of participles into those that draw upon second principal parts and those that make use of fourth principal parts. But, *in prīmīs*, "first and foremost," a word about deponents. As participles, many deponent verbs are translated as passive in English translation rather than just looking passive in form; or, conversely, they retain their passive forms but adopt active meanings and are thereby used by authors to express an "active" participle (rather than a "passive" one). The Roman people were clever and found a way to navigate this class of verbs quite well. You will, too. Removing this deponent obstacle now will allow us to focus on second-principal-part participles.

THE PRESENT PARTICIPLE: *-ing*

22.7 **Present Active Participles.** Since there is no present passive participle in Latin, you can also think of this form as simply the "present participle." The present participle is used very often in Latin, so you will become familiar with it in no time. Present participles denote action in progress. As such, our stock translation will be "-ing." As noted above, the time of the present active participle is contemporaneous with that of the main verb. Rather than indicating something that has been completed, in other words, the present active participle is progressive in nature, signaling that something is ongoing. You can think of it as indicating same-time action, which is why many translators translate it as "as -ing" or "while -ing."

---

13. You may wonder why I do not translate the present active verb *cónvocat* below in the present tense. It is because it is what grammarians call a "historical present," meaning that the author uses the present tense to describe a past event. It is fairly common in the Gospels.

PRESENT ACTIVE PARTICIPLES, FUTURE PASSIVE PARTICIPLES, AND GERUNDS

22.8 Participle Formation. The present active participle is formed by removing the -re ending from the second principal part (the present active infinitive) and adding -ns, -ntis.[14] The use of the term "present" in English is not coincidental. It carries over directly from the Latin present active participle *praésēns, praeséntis*, "present." As you detect from this example, implanted in the (nominative and genitive) Latin forms are the letter combinations -ns (*praesē**ns***) and -nt (*praesé**nt**is*). When you think of the present active participle, always keep these two letter combinations in mind.

Steps to Form Present Active Participles
1. Locate the second principal part and remove -re (e.g., *laudā-*).
2. Insert the ending -ns, -ntis (.e.g, *laudāns, laudántis*), which is the nominative and genitive singular forms, respectively.
3. Remove the -is ending of the genitive singular (*laudánt*is) and add 3-3-3 endings: -, -is, -ī, -em, -e/-ī, etc. (e.g., *laudāns, laudántis, laudántī, laudántem, laudánte/laudántī*, etc.). (See the full endings in the chart below.)

22.9 Present Participle = Third-Declension Adjectival Endings. Hopefully the -ntis ending in the genitive also signaled something else to you: the third declension, which is always -is in the genitive singular. In fact, as a point of Latin trivia, the present participle is the only participle that adopts third-declension endings.[15] It does not matter one iota which declension the noun it modifies happens to be (first, second, third, fourth, fifth—or twenty-seventh).[16] The rules of grammar are fixed here, so you will encounter all five noun declensions paired with present active participles.

PRESENT ACTIVE PARTICIPLES

Conjugation Type	Paradigm Verb	Nominative and Genitive Singular Forms
(Long) ARE Verbs	amō, amáre, amávī, amátus	am**ā**ns, am**á**ntis
Long ERE Verbs	móneō, monére, mónuī, mónitus	mon**ē**ns, mon**é**ntis
Short ERE Verbs	osténdō, osténdere, osténdī, osténtus	osténdēns, ostendéntis
(Long) IRE Verbs	aúdiō, audíre, audívī, audítus	aúdi**ē**ns, audi**é**ntis

This chart lists the present participle as a third-declension adjective, from which you can now generate the predetermined endings that we all memorized when learning nouns and adjectives.

There are several items to observe in this paradigm. First, as I have illustrated in bold, the characteristic -ā, -ē, -e, and -ī from the four conjugations are retained in this form (even though there are some slight differences—discussed next). Second, as usual, the third conjugation is the outlier; for the nominative singular, however, the stem vowel lengthens before -ns (but never before -nt). Third, the accent always falls on the vowel immediately before the genitive singular form (-ntis). Fourth, -iō third-conjugation and regular fourth-conjugation verbs require the insertion of an -ē immediately before the suffix.

---

14. For fourth-conjugation verbs, an extra -ē is added before the -ns or -nt: thus *áudiēns, audiéntis* (from *audíre*) rather than **audins, *audintis*. The same is true for third-conjugation (or Short ERE) -iō verbs.
15. All other participles use 2-1-2 endings.
16. Do not worry—there are only five declensions in Latin.

Finally, as mentioned above, the present participle always follows the third-declension pattern. You already know these forms by heart, but I will also include these endings below for review. Note that the present participle applies the i-stem endings, and that the ablative singular may appear with an -ī or -e ending.[17]

3-3-3 ADJECTIVES (ADJECTIVES USING THE THIRD-DECLENSION I-STEM ENDING PATTERNS)

Case	Masculine	Feminine	Neuter
Nominative Sg	-	-	-
Genitive Sg	-is	-is	-is
Dative Sg	-ī	-ī	-ī
Accusative Sg	-em	-em	-
Ablative Sg	-ī, -e[a]	-ī	-ī
Nominative Pl	-ēs	-ēs	-ia
Genitive Pl	-ium	-ium	-ium
Dative Pl	-ibus	-ibus	-ibus
Accusative Pl	-ēs	-ēs	-ia
Ablative Pl	-ibus	-ibus	-ibus

[a] As noted above, you may encounter either form.

Here are two examples of a present active participle:

Invénta ígitur audítum recēpísse, vēnit glōríficāns Deum, et Deī Fámulō grátiās agēns. (Gaufrid of Clairvaux)[18]	Therefore, when she was found to have recovered hearing, she went glorifying God and giving thanks to the servant of God.

Here, the two present active participles—*glōríficāns* and *agēns*—modify the implicit subject (a woman who had been healed). You will notice that the two participles are present active despite the fact that the main verb (*vēnit*) is perfect active.[19]

22.10 ***Dīcēns.*** We discussed in an earlier *capítulum* the peculiar feature of biblical Latin. Because it is a translation of Hebrew and Greek, the translators sometimes allowed the original biblical idiom to carry over into Latin, creating a form of Latin that was not necessarily spoken on the streets, but which served as a basis for ecclesiastical Latin for centuries to come. One common carryover from Greek (which, in itself, was a carryover from Aramaic) is the use of the present active participle *dīcēns*, "speaking." You will encounter this word dozens and dozens of time in biblical narrative, particularly in the Gospels. However, it is rather redundant in the text. For example:

---

17. For those who want to get technical, the -e ending is used when functioning verbally and the -ī ending when used adjectivally.
18. Gaufrid of Clairvaux, *Ācta S. Bernárdī Bollandiāna* IV.8.49 (PL 185.349).
19. The verb *vēnit* is the same in the present active and perfect active, except that that it has no macron in the present. In actual writings, however, no diacritical marks are used, so context determines the tense. Based on the context of the passage in Latin, I am taking it as a perfect active.

PRESENT ACTIVE PARTICIPLES, FUTURE PASSIVE PARTICIPLES, AND GERUNDS

> Et apériēns ōs suum docébat eōs <u>dīcēns</u>. (Matt. V.2)
>
> And after opening his mouth, he began teaching them, <u>saying</u> . . .

Technically, the participle *dīcēns* is not necessary, but is rather added to preserve the biblical idiom. When you encounter such words, it is up to you to determine whether you want to render the literal meaning or ignore it altogether (if implied from context). Many times, you can effectively regard the participle *dīcēns* as quotation marks, signaling the beginning of a quote (as in the instance above).

FUTURE PASSIVE PARTICIPLES

22.11 Future Passive Participles (Gerundives). While the first three words are certainly a mouthful to say, all of the terms should make complete sense individually. But what on earth does "gerundive" mean? The English word "gerundive" is built on the Latin future passive participle (aka, gerundive) *geründus*, "to be carried on," which is formed from the common verb *gerō, gérere, gessī, gestus*.[20]

To make a long story short, "future passive participles" and "gerundives" are interchangeable terms. This means that you can take your pick of which you would like to use. The phrase "future passive participle" usefully designates the function of the form. However, the term "gerundive"—in addition to being one word rather than three—contains two nifty clues embedded in the word itself: -nd and -ive. While the letters -nd reveal the characteristic infix of the future passive participle, the -ive ending indicates its identity as an adject<u>ive</u>. You are free to disagree, but I suggest embracing the term "gerundive" and dazzling your *amícī* at dinner parties when using such an exotic word.

22.12 Denoting Obligation. With a name like "gerundive," you know this part of speech is going to be pushy. Indeed, a gerundive often indicates passive necessity, obligation, or compulsion. It specifies that something needs to be done (which is why it is future—it has not happened yet) and that it needs to be done to the noun it describes (which is why it is passive—the noun is receiving the action). Some common ways to translate it are "to be -ed," "has to be -ed," or "must be -ed."

22.13 Participle Formation. Forming the future passive participle is rather straightforward. Of the two common ways to generate it,[21] I suggest the method of removing the -re ending from the second principal part (the present active infinitive) before then inserting the suffix -ndus, -nda, -ndum (which follows 2-1-2 adjective endings).[22] As with the present active participle, so, too, with future passive participles: they modify nouns of any declension; so even though they will always use 2-1-2 adjective endings, the nouns they modify may utilize any and every noun declension. They are equal-opportunity modifiers.

Steps to Form Future Passive Participles (Gerundives)
1. Remove the -re ending from the second principal part (*amā́-, monḗ-, osténde-, audī́-*).
2. Add the suffix -ndus, -nda, -ndum (*amándus, monéndus, ostendéndus, audiéndus*, etc.).
3. Decline using 2-1-2 endings.

---

20. You will also see the form *geréndus* appear with no difference in meaning.
21. One other way is to use the present active participle (learned above), removing the -ns ending of the masculine nominative singular form and then adding -ndus, -nda, -ndum.
22. In the third -iō and fourth conjugations, there is an -iē before the ending added.

Be sure to note that the long stem vowels shorten before -nd, which is why none of the stem vowels are long; however, as per the rules of accentuation, the stress remains with that vowel before -nd.

FUTURE PASSIVE PARTICIPLES (GERUNDIVES)

Conjugation Type	Paradigm Verb	Nominative Forms
(Long) ARE Verbs	amō, amáre, amávī, amátus	amándus, amánda, amándum
Long ERE Verbs	móneō, monére, mónuī, mónitus	monéndus, monénda, monéndum
Short ERE Verbs	osténdō, osténdere, osténdī, osténtus	ostendéndus, ostendénda, ostendéndum
(Long) IRE Verbs	aúdiō, audíre, audívī, audítus	audiéndus, audiénda, audiéndum

Once we convert the future passive participle (gerundive) into first- and second-declension adjectives, all we do now is apply the rest of the 2-1-2 endings to generate each and every form.

2-1-2 ADJECTIVES (ADJECTIVES USING THE SECOND-, FIRST-, SECOND-DECLENSION ENDING PATTERNS)

Case	Masculine	Feminine	Neuter
Nominative Sg	-us; -	-a	-um
Genitive Sg	-ī	-ae	-ī
Dative Sg	-ō	-ae	-ō
Accusative Sg	-um	-am	-um
Ablative Sg	-ō	-ā	-ō
Nominative Pl	-ī	-ae	-a
Genitive Pl	-órum	-árum	-órum
Dative Pl	-īs	-īs	-īs
Accusative Pl	-ōs	-ās	-a
Ablative Pl	-īs	-īs	-īs

Let us consider an example:

Coena Dómini secúndum Jōánnem, adjuvánte ipsō, débitīs est explicánda tractátibus, et ut nōbīs posse dōnáverit, explānánda. (Augustine of Hippo)[23]

The Lord's Supper according to John, with the Lord's assistance, has to be explained with the lectures it deserves and, as He shall have granted us ability, it has to be exegeted.

---

23. Augustine of Hippo, *In Jōánnis Ēvangélium* LV.1 (PL 35.1784).

PRESENT ACTIVE PARTICIPLES, FUTURE PASSIVE PARTICIPLES, AND GERUNDS

As an adjective, the gerundive agrees with the noun it modifies in case, number, and gender. In this sentence, both *explicánda* and *explānánda* are nominative, singular, and feminine to match the noun *coena*. Also as illustrated, this gerundive implies obligation.

22.14 Combination with "To Be." There is also one more item to observe from the example above: if the gerundive is used with a verb, it is *sum, esse, fuī, futūrus*. When this construction occurs, it is technically called a "[passive] periphrastic" or "gerundive of obligation," scary terms, to be sure, necessitating an entire *capítulum* unto themselves.[24] For the time being, just recognize that most instances of the gerundive will occur in tandem with the "to be" verb.

GERUNDS

22.15 Gerunds: The Other Verbal -ing. Before there was Coke and Pepsi, Ford and Chevy, Tylenol and Aspirin, there was Gerund and Gerundive. Cut from the same cloth but showcasing a fabric design all their own, these Latin grammatical terms are best threaded together. We learned above that gerundives represent alternative names for future passive participles. And, like a hidden surprise, gerundives conceal the letters -nd (the characteristic suffix of the future passive participle) and -ive (showing that it is an adject<u>ive</u>) in the term itself. What a trick!

22.16 Fancy Word for Nouns. Whereas gerundives are verbal adjectives that only occur in the future passive form, gerunds are verbal nouns that are translated with an active force.[25] In other words, gerunds are part verb and part noun, just as gerundives are part verb and part adjective. As such, gerunds share features of both verbs and nouns.

22.17 Distinguishing Gerunds from Gerundives. Fortunately, gerunds can be distinguished from gerundives—their fiendish doppelgangers. Truth is, the two are highly related, so let us unpack their relationship. Gerunds are specific forms of gerundives. That is to say, gerunds are gerundives that are used only in the neuter gender and singular number. They are effectively nouns formed out of verbs, which are always active in meaning and never in the nominative case.

To take a different approach to gerunds, we could describe what gerunds are NOT: They do <u>not</u> occur in the nominative, they do <u>not</u> occur in the masculine or feminine, they do <u>not</u> occur in the plural, they do <u>not</u> occur in the passive, and they do <u>not</u> have the same case, number, and gender as a nearby noun. In case this makes gerunds sound too negative, let us make things much simpler and precise below.

Six Features of Gerunds
1. They are always in oblique cases.[26]
2. They are always neuter.
3. They are always singular.
4. They are always active in meaning.

---

24. The nominative will always be used under such circumstances, but more about that in a later *capitulum*.
25. Granted, as adjectives, gerundives can also be substantives, in which case they act like nouns as well.
26. The oblique cases are the genitive, accusative, dative, and ablative—NOT the nominative. The term "oblique" stems from the subject of geometry. For instance, *in rēctō* indicates a vertical right angle and *in oblíquō* indicates a horizontal line, revealing a progression. (The vocative is sometimes considered an oblique case as well, but we need not include it in this discussion.) Also, the present infinitive is essentially the nominative of the gerund.

5. They are sometimes preceded by prepositions.
6. They will never share the nearby noun's case, number, and gender.[27]

In nuce, gerunds are oblique, neuter, singular active verbal nouns that sometimes follow prepositions. I readily admit that this is a mouthful to say, which is why it is perhaps easier to isolate their constituent parts in the six features above.

By process of elimination, recognizing these distinct features of gerunds will empower you to distinguish gerunds from gerundives most of the time. It should also be noted that gerunds can indicate purpose and that they can function as the object of prepositions (such as *ad*, *in*, and *inter*). What's more, once we recognize that gerunds (unlike gerund<u>ives</u>) are not adject<u>ives</u>—but are instead nouns—we can appreciate why they will not modify the primary noun(s) in the sentence or clause. This is important to remember: if the gerundive-looking word does not modify a noun, then assume it to be a gerund. Although this is not a foolproof rule, it is a useful guide.

22.18 Forms of Gerunds: Always Oblique, Always Singular, Always Neuter. Below are the forms of gerunds from our four paradigm verbs. Remember that if you ever encounter what *looks* like a gerund but it is nominative or plural or masculine or feminine, it CANNOT be a gerund. (Also, because gerunds are specific forms of gerundives, they are formed the same way.)

GERUND FORMS

Case, Number, Gender	Amō, Amáre, Amávī, Amátus (1)	Móneō, Monére, Mónuī, Mónitus (2)	Osténdō, Osténdere, Osténdī, Osténtus (3)	Aúdiō, Audíre, Audívī, Audítus (4)
Nom Sg Neut	amáre	monére	osténdere	audíre[a]
Gen Sg Neut	amándī	monéndī	ostendéndī	audiéndī
Dat Sg Neut	āmándō	monéndō	ostendéndō	audiéndō
Acc Sg Neut	amándum	mondéndum	ostendéndum	audiéndum
Abl Sg Neut	amándō	monéndō	ostendéndō	audiéndō

[a] The nominative of the gerund is the infinitive—the "to-" form of the verb. I said that the gerund does not have a nominative form. That is correct—sort of. The infinitive, which we have not yet learned, stands for the nominative form. If this is too confusing, forget I ever said anything. Just memorize the gerund as having no nominative form.

22.19 Translating Gerunds = -ing. When ambiguity still remains in the passage, however, your best bet is to translate the unclear term both as a gerundive (that is, as a verbal adjective) and then as a gerund (that is, as a verbal noun). When you translate it as a gerund—as a noun—our stock translation is -ing. If you think your translation shares more in common with an adjective, consider it a gerundive; if it has more in common with a noun, regard it as a gerund.

Still unclear how a gerund works? Several examples of Latin gerunds have found their way into the English language, such as:

- *Ad captándum vulgus*, "[in order] to capture the crowd"
- *Modus operándī*, "way of working"

---

27. This makes sense if you remember that gerunds are nouns. If the gerund does hypothetically share the same case, number, and gender of a nearby noun, the gerund is still not modifying the noun.

- *Modus vīvéndī*, "way of living"
- *Rátiō decidéndī*, "reasoning for the decision"

Each of these translations utilize the -ing option except for the first, which uses "in order to . . ." or "for the purpose of." The "in order to . . ." or "for the purpose of" phrase indicates purpose; it is quite common to translate a gerund in one of these ways. Under such instances, the gerund will serve as the object of the preposition *ad*; or the gerund will be in the genitive case and will follow the word *causā*, *exémplī*, or *grātiā*.

Let us look at an example from a well-known passage in the Vulgate that uses no less than four gerunds:

Omnis scrīptū́ra dīvī́nitus īnspīrā́ta, ū́tilis est ad <u>docéndum</u>, ad <u>arguéndum</u>, ad <u>corripiéndum</u>, ad <u>ērudiéndum</u> in iūstítiā. (II Tim. III.16)	All Scripture inspired by God is useful for <u>teaching</u>, for <u>rebuking</u>, for <u>correcting</u>, and for <u>instructing</u> in righteousness.[28]

These underlined words sure look like gerundives, don't they? Yes, absolutely. However, after filtering them through the six distinct features of gerunds, we begin to observe that they are, indeed, gerunds. How so? The four underlined Latin words are oblique (which means that they are not nominative), neuter, singular, active in meaning, preceded by a preposition (*ad*), and not sharing the same case, number, or gender as the noun (*scrīptū́ra*). Therefore, the verdict is in; they must be gerunds. Goodbye, gerundive imposters!

I translated the gerunds with -ing in English. However, a case could be made that these gerunds indicate purpose, especially with the preposition *ad* appearing before each gerund. This, therefore, would invite one of two translations:

All Scripture inspired by God is useful for the purpose of teaching, for the purpose of rebuking, for the purpose of correcting, and for the purpose of instructing in righteousness.	All Scripture inspired by God is useful in order to teach, in order to rebuke, in order to correct, and in order to instruct in righteousness.

As always, context is king. So let the king decide how best to render the gerunds into English.

Want one more example of a gerund? How about one from the first line of Martin Luther's *Ninety-Five Theses*?

Dóminus et magíster noster Iēsūs Christus <u>dīcéndō</u> 'Poeniténtiam ágite &c.' omnem vītam fidélium poeniténtiam esse vóluit. (Martin Luther)[29]	Our Lord and Master Jesus Christ, <u>by saying</u> "Repent, etc.," meant for the entire life of believers to be repentance.

There are a number of ways to translate this sentence, but the underlined word has to be a gerund rather than a gerundive. Can you explain why? We use our stock translation of -ing and also accommodate for its use in the ablative case.

---

28. You may have noticed the absence of the "to be" verb. This was omitted in Latin in order to mirror the original Greek sentence, which lacks the "to be" verb. This omission allows for two different translation options: (1) "All Scripture is inspired by God and . . ." or (2) "All Scripture that is inspired by God is . . ."

29. Martin Luther, *Disputā́tiō prō Dēclārātiṓne Virtū́tis Indulgentiā́rum* (WA 1.233).

PARTICIPLES, PERFECT PASSIVES, INFINITIVES: SECOND, FOURTH PRIN. PARTS

> **Summárium**
>
> In this *capítulum* you learned that:
> - Present active participles use 3-3-3 adjective endings.
> - Future passive participles, also called gerundives, adopt 2-1-2 adjective endings.
> - No matter which particular adjectival ending a participle may take, it can modify a noun of any of the five declensional noun patterns.
> - Gerunds are oblique, neuter, singular active verbal nouns.

VOCĀBULÓRUM INDEX

Latin	English (Gloss)	(Etymology)
accéndō, accéndere, accéndī, accénsus (3)	to kindle, to light (a fire), to inflame	(incensed)
altáre, altáris (n)	altar, place for burnt offerings	(altar)
apériō, aperíre, apéruī, apértus (4)	to open, to uncover	(aperture)
donec	while, until, as long as	
dórmiō, dormíre, dormívī, dormítus (4)	to sleep, to lie down	(dormant)
eō, īre, iī (īvī), ītus (4)[a]	to go, to proceed, to advance	(iterate)
éxeō, exíre, éxiī (exívī), éxitus (4)	to go out (from), to exit, to depart	(exit)
exhíbeō, exhibére, exhíbuī, exhíbitus (2)	to reveal, to show, to exhibit	(exhibit)
ígitur	therefore, consequently, thus	
inquiétus, inquiéta, inquiétum	restless	(quiet)
intrō, intráre, intrávī, intrátus (1)	to enter, to go in	(intravenous)
intróeō, introíre, intróiī, intróitus (4)	to enter, to go in[b]	(introvert)
mandúcō, mandūcáre, mandūcávī, mandūcátus (1)	to eat, to chew, to devour, to goble up	(mandable)
nam	for, because, thus	
num(quid)	if, whether, surely not?[c]	
óbeō, obíre, óbiī (obívī), óbitus (4)	to go towards, to die	(obituary)
ōs, ōris (n)	mouth, face, appearance	(orifice)
os, ossis (n)[d]	bone, soul	(ossuary)
peccō, peccáre, peccávī, peccátus (1)	to sin, to transgress	(peccadillo)
récitō, recitáre, recitávī, recitátus (3)	to recite	(recite)
regína, regínae (f)	queen	

rēgnō, rēgnā́re, rēgnā́vī, rēgnā́tus (1)	to rule, to govern, to reign[e]	(reign)
regō, régere, rēxī, rēctus (3)	to rule, to govern	(regent)
rḗgulō, rēgulā́re, rēgulā́vī, rēgulā́tus (1)	to rule, to govern, to regulate	(regulate)
soror, sorṓris (f)	sister	(sorority)

[a] This is an irregular fourth-conjugation verb. Not only is it used often, but it has attracted many prepositions that slightly modify the meaning of the word, e.g., *intróeō*, "to go in."

[b] You are not seeing double! I have put these verbs adjacent to each other because they look alike and also mean similar things. Be sure to note this in your vocabulary cards.

[c] This word can occur as *num* or *numquid*. It is used when a negative answer is expected.

[d] Again, you are not seeing things—this word has the same nominative form as the one above it (other than the length of vowel), even though they are different words.

[e] This verb, and the two immediately afterward, all look very similar and have the same range of meanings. Be sure to keep this in mind when notating them.

ŌRĀ́TIŌ POPULĀ́RIS

Psalmus CL. This is the final psalm in the Psalter, which concludes the so-called Laudā́te psalms, "Praise psalms." As a *psalmus* centered on praising the Lord, it provides a fitting conclusion to the Psalter as a whole. Every verse begins with an imperative—a verbal mood that we will soon encounter—and the last verse is a "hortatory" subjunctive. Not surprisingly given its content, this psalm was incorporated into the divine office in the Christian tradition.

Allelū́ja.[30] Laudā́te Dóminum in sānctīs ejus; laudā́te eum in firmāmḗntō virtū́tis ejus.	Hallelujah. Praise the Lord in his holy places; praise him in the firmament of his power.
Laudā́te eum in virtū́tibus ejus; laudā́te eum secúndum multitū́dinem magnitū́dinis ejus.	Praise him in his power; praise him according to the multitude of his greatness.
Laudā́te eum in sonō tubae; laudā́te eum in psaltḗriō et cítharā.	Praise him in the sound of the trumpet; praise him in the harp and lyre.
Laudā́te eum in týmpanō et chorō; laudā́te eum in chordīs et orgánō.	Praise him in timbrel and in chorus; praise him in chords and with instrument.
Laudā́te eum in cýmbalīs benesonā́ntibus; laudā́te eum in cýmbalīs jūbilātiṓnis.	Praise him in fair-sounding cymbals; praise him in cymbals of joy.
Omnis spíritus laudet Dóminum! Allelū́ja.	Let everything with breath praise the Lord. Hallelujah.

EXERCÍTIA

Be sure to complete the *exercítium* in the appendix corresponding to this *capítulum*.

---

30. You will see this Semitic word spelled in a variety of ways in Latin; however, the meaning should never really be in doubt.

Capítulum XXIII

PERFECT PASSIVE PARTICIPLES, FUTURE ACTIVE PARTICIPLES, AND PERIPHRASTIC CONSTRUCTIONS

In eō Dóminus esset passúrus.[1]
—ACTS OF PETER

OPÚSCULUM THEOLÓGICUM: *Ācta Petrī*

The *Ācta Petrī*, "Acts of Peter," is one of the most intriguing Christian books in the early church. It is not to be confused with I or II Peter in the New Testament or the apocryphal Gospel of Peter, although both the Gospel of Peter and Acts of Peter are non-canonical books likely written in the second century.

Narrating the stories, teachings, and miracles of Jesus's closest disciple, the *Ācta Petrī* depicts the rivalry between Simon Peter and Simon Magus. As you might surmise, Simon Peter is the protagonist and Simon Magus the antagonist. The story takes place in Rome. Toward the end of the book, Simon Peter defeats Simon Magus, but a plot was hatched by the leading authorities in Rome to kill Peter for his scandalous preaching about abstinence.

Perhaps the most famous section of the book appears in Capítulum XXXV. In this *capítulum*, a prominent Roman noblewoman—who had recently embraced Peter's teachings—informs Peter of the plot to kill him. Peter's associates understand Peter's importance for the wellbeing of the fledgling church and so encourage him to flee Rome immediately and live to see another *diem*. Peter agrees but encounters Christ on the way outside of the city. It is best to quote the relevant section in full:

Ut autem portam cīvitátis vóluit égredī, vīsit sibi Christum occúrrere. Et adórāns eum āit; Dómine, quō vādis? Respóndit eī Christus: Rōmam véniō íterum crucifígī. Eī āit ad eum Petrus: Dómine, íterum crucifīgéris?	As he strove to leave the gate of the city, he saw the Lord entering. And worshiping him, he said: "Lord, where are you going?" Christ replied to him: "I go again to Rome to be crucified." And Peter said to him: "Lord, will you be crucified again?"

---

1. "In him the Lord was about to suffer."

PERFECT PASS., FUTURE ACT. PARTICIPLES; PERIPHRASTIC CONSTRUCTIONS

Et dīxit ad eum Dóminus: Étiam, íterum crucifígar. Petrus autem dīxit: Dómine, revértar et séquar tē. Et hīs dictīs Dóminus ascéndit in caelum. Petrus autem prōsecútus est eum multō intúitū atque dulcíssimīs lácrimīs. Et post haec rédiēns in sē ipsum intelléxit dē suā dictum passióne, quod in eō Dóminus <u>esset passúrus</u>.[2]

And the Lord said to him: "Yes, I will be crucified again." But Peter said: "Lord, I will return and follow you." And with these words, the Lord ascended into heaven. And Peter returned with much contemplation and with sweet tears. And coming to himself, he understood that Christ spoke about his suffering, which in him the Lord was <u>about to suffer</u>.

Naturally shocked to see his Lord entering the city of Rome, Peter asks: *Dómine, quō vādis?* That is, "Lord, where are you going?" This exact phrase predates the encounter between Peter and Jesus in Rome. It first appears in the exchange between Peter and Jesus outside of Jerusalem on the night of the latter's arrest. As the Gospel of John states:

Dīcit eī Sīmon Petrus: Dómine <u>quō vādis</u>? Respóndit Iēsus: Quō ego vādō nōn potes mē modo sequī, sequéris autem pósteā. (John XIII.36)[3]

Simon Peter says to him: "Lord, <u>where are you going</u>?" Jesus responded: "Where I go you are not able to follow just now, but you will follow me afterward."

The author of the *Ācta Petrī* knowingly connects the story in Rome to the story in Jerusalem. In the *Ācta Petrī*, Peter interprets Jesus's response to his question to mean that Peter himself is to return to the city and undergo death by crucifixion just as his Lord had. Peter, in other words, is given a second chance to die with Jesus. Although he had fled the scene in Jerusalem, he now agrees to enter into his death in Rome. And, as a subsequent *capítulum* in the *Ācta Petrī* explicitly states, Peter requests to be crucified upside down.

For our purposes, however, I am intrigued by the phrase *in eō Dóminus* <u>*esset passúrus*</u>, "in [Peter] the Lord <u>was about to suffer</u>." As we will learn in this *capítulum*, the combination of these two Latin terms is called an "active periphrastic," and the latter word in Latin is a future active participle indicating imminence. The Latin periphrastic is a useful Latin construction that combines a participle with one of six tenses and three moods of the verb *sum, esse, fuī, futúrus*. Now that you are aware of it, you will see it often in Latin literature.

Prospéctus

In this *capítulum* you will learn that:
- The perfect passive and future active participles are formed from the fourth principal part.
- Perfect passive participles are past-tense verbal adjectives.
- Future active participles are verbal adjectives indicating an impending event.
- Periphrastics are "round-about" ways of saying something. They contain a participle + almost any tense or mood of *sum, esse, fuī, futúrus*.

---

[2]. *Ācta Petrī*, in David Eastman, trans., *The Ancient Martyrdom Accounts of Peter and Paul* (Atlanta: SBL Press, 2015), 42, 44. The most intact manuscript coming from the Acts of Peter is in Latin, though the original story was composed in Greek. This Latin manuscript is preserved in Codex Vercellensis 158. For more about the Acts of Peter, see J. K. Elliot, ed., *The Apocryphal New Testament: A Collection of Apocryphal Christian Literature in an English Translation* (Oxford: Oxford University Press, 1993), 390–426.

[3]. The phrase *Quō vādis* also appears in John XIV.15 and XVI.5.

GRAMMÁTICA

23.1 4 PP Participles. In the previous *capítulum*, we discussed 2 PP participles, that is, those participles—the present active and future passive—that build their houses from the building materials of second principal parts. This *capítulum*, by contrast, showcases 4 PP participles—the perfect passive and future active—which are those participles constructed out of fourth principal parts, sometimes called "participial stems."

PERFECT PASSIVE PARTICIPLES

23.2 Perfect Passive Participles. This is the past-tense participle. In fact, because the perfect passive participle is the only participle in Latin that describes an action prior to that of the main verb, and because there is no perfect active participle, some prefer to simply call it the "past participle." This makes sense, but I still prefer to refer to it by its longer name to remind us of its most essential and distinct features: It indicates an action that was completed (not just happening) in the past, and one that was being acted upon (and so passive) rather than acting upon.

23.3 Translating Perfect Passive Participles: Denoting Past Activity. Before looking at how we form this particular participle, let us offer a stock translation. Our recommended translation for perfect passive participles is "having been -ed." This translation accounts for (1) the completed aspect, (2) the passive voice, and (3) the presence of a participle. At the same time, we must remember that participles sometimes function as nothing other than the adjectives they are. In such instances, it is best to translate the perfect passive participle as such.

Let us consider an example:

Pulchrē hīc prophéta praévidēns <u>pervérsa</u> dógmata, omnem sensum haeréticae perversitátis exclúsit. (John Cassian)[4]

This sentence contains two participles. The first—*praévidēns*—is a present active participle.[5] The second—*pervérsa*—is a perfect passive participle.[6] I recommend translating the first participle with the stock translation of -ing and the second as an adjective:

Here the prophet, beautifully foreseeing <u>false</u> teachings, has prevented all sense of heretical perverseness.

Some dictionaries list *pervérsa* as an adjective coming from *pervérsus, pervérsa, pervérsum*. This is exactly what we should expect: Many adjectives stem directly from the fourth principal part, revealing that a perfect passive participle is sometimes virtually identical to a "regular" 2-1-2 adjective.

23.4 Participle Formation. Forming the perfect passive participle is as easy as apple pie. Assuming you have been memorizing the principal parts all along, it is a one-step process. Ready? Simply locate the fourth principal part. That is because the fourth principal part is the perfect passive participle. You, of course, will want to substitute the endings as needed since the form you

---

4. John Cassian, *Dē Incarnātiōne Christī* IV.9 (PL 50.87).
5. It comes from *praevídeō, praevidére, praevídī, praevísus* (2), "to see before," "to foresee."
6. This participle is formed out of *pervértō, pervértere, pervértī, pervérsus* (3), "to corrupt," "to pervert," "to turn around."

see is masculine singular nominative. However, because the perfect passive participle adopts a conventional 2-1-2 declensional pattern, you will not encounter any problems here. That stated, here is my Public Service Announcement: Because the fourth principal part cannot always be predicted, I heartily encourage you to continue memorizing the principal parts of all verbs. Other than that, you are now on your way to doing more important things—like locating vanilla bean ice cream for your apple pie.

Steps to Form Perfect Passive Participles
1. Locate the fourth principal part (e.g., *laudắtus*).[7]
2. Remove the -us ending (e.g., *laudāt-*).
3. Add the appropriate endings in accordance with 2-1-2 adjective endings: -us, -a, -um, etc. (e.g., *laudắtus*, *laudắta*, *laudắtum*, etc.).

PERFECT PASSIVE PARTICIPLES: ALL CONJUGATIONS

Conjugation Type	Paradigm Verb	Nominative Singular Forms
(Long) ARE Verbs	amō, amắre, amắvī, amắtus	amắtus, amắta, amắtum
Long ERE Verbs	móneō, monḗre, mónuī, mónitus	mónitus, mónita, mónitum
Short ERE Verbs	osténdō, osténdere, osténdī, osténtus	osténtus, osténta, osténtum
(Long) IRE Verbs	aúdiō, audī́re, audī́vī, audī́tus	audī́tus, audī́ta, audī́tum

Here is an example of a perfect passive participle from Hilary of Poitiers:

Cessat ergō per impietắtem blasphēmántium vitiósae intelligéntiae excūsắtiō: cum per Apóstolī auctōritắtem, sub sīgnificātiốne nātīvitắtis, prōpríetās nātūrắlis <u>osténsa sit</u>. (Hilary of Poitiers)[8]

Therefore, the excuse of the defectiveness of understanding holds back the wickedness of blasphemers after the true nature [of Christ] <u>had been revealed</u> through the apostle's authority under the sign of his birth.

Or we could translate it as follows, focusing just on the clause containing the participle:

. . . the true nature [of Christ] <u>having been revealed</u> through the apostle's authority under the sign of his birth.

Of these two translations, the second one helpfully uses our stock translation, but the first sounds better in English. When "in the field," that is, when translating on your own, it will be up to you to decide when and where to choose a more idiomatic translation over against the stock translation ("having been -ed"). When unsure, take comfort in the security of the stock

---

7. What if you have not been memorizing the principal parts? For starters, no apple pie for you. Next, you will need to find the principal part another way. Drop the -re from the second principal part (the present active infinitive), and add -tus, -ta, -tum. For the second conjugation, you will need to reduce the long -ē to short -i. For the third conjugation, make a mental note that the form may not be as predictable. If in doubt, look in a dictionary for the fourth principal part.

8. Hilary of Poitiers, *Dē Trīnitắte* VII.15 (PL 10.211). The use of *osténsa* (with an -s) is the same word as *osténta*; it just uses a different spelling.

translation. However, burst out of the shackles of translational conformity when you are more confident about the context and grammatical concepts presented.

FUTURE ACTIVE PARTICIPLES

23.5 **Future Active Participles.** We discovered in the previous *capítulum* that the future participle is the lone participial verbal tense in Latin to possess both an active and passive voice. However, we only learned its passive forms together with the present active participle since both of them utilize the second principal part in their constructions. Now we turn to the (future) active form, which, like the perfect passive, employs the fourth principal part as its foundation.

23.6 **Denoting Something about to Happen.** The future active participle describes an action that will occur in the future. Specifically, it indicates an action occurring subsequent to the main verb in the clause. We do not have an exact equivalent of this form of speech in English, but the concept is simple enough to understand. In fact, the English word "future" derives from *futúrus, futúra, futúrum*, which is, naturally enough, the future active participle of *sum*.[9] Allow the -ūr- in *futúrus* to loom large in your thinking: for all practical purposes, we can act like this simple letter combination means "about to happen."

This "about to happen" construction also helps us distinguish the "regular" future tense from the future active participle. Although there is overlap, the future active participle classically indicates the imminence of a future activity more so than the future tense, the latter of which simply reveals that something will occur in the future. Also, because the future active participle is an adjective, it will agree with the noun it describes in case, number, and gender.

23.7 **Translating Future Active Participles.** There are several acceptable ways to translate the future active participle into English: "about to-," "has to-," "going to-," "will," "would," or, for those who want to speak Latin with a Texas accent, "fixing to-."

Here is one of the most well-known theological uses of the future active participle, emerging from the *Sýmbolum Apostolórum*, "the Apostles' Creed":

Et íterum <u>ventúrus est</u> cum glóriā iūdicáre vīvōs et mórtuōs. (Sýmbolum Apostolórum)	And he <u>is about to come</u> again with glory to judge the living and the dead.

23.8 **Participle Formation.** It is rather simple to form this participle. Remove the -us ending from the fourth principal part, insert -ūr, and then add the 2-1-2 adjective endings.

Steps to Form Future Active Participles
1. Locate the fourth principal part (e.g., *laudátus*).
2. Remove the -us ending (e.g., *laudāt-).
3. Insert -ūr (*laudātúr).
4. Add the appropriate endings in accordance with 2-1-2 adjective endings: -us, -a, -m, etc. (e.g., *laudatúrus, laudatúra, laudatúrum*, etc.).

---

9. How is this possible? Because *sum, esse, fuī, futúrus* does not have a perfect passive participle, the fourth principal part is supplied by the only participle form of the verb that does exist, which happens to be a future active: *futúrus*. However, normally, you should expect the fourth principal part to be the perfect passive participle. The "to be" verb happens to be special.

Of course, you could skip a step and simply insert -úrus, -úra, -úrum to the fourth principal part (upon removing the -us), keeping in mind that the forms will follow 2-1-2 endings. This is a common method that works just as well.

FUTURE ACTIVE PARTICIPLES

Conjugation Type	Paradigm Verb	Nominative Forms
(Long) ARE Verbs	amō, amáre, amávī, amátus	amātúrus, amātúra, amātúrum
Long ERE Verbs	móneō, monére, mónuī, mónitus	monitúrus, monitúra, monitúrum
Short ERE Verbs	osténdō, osténdere, osténdī, osténtus	ostentúrus, ostentúra, ostentúrum
(Long) IRE Verbs	aúdiō, audíre, audívī, audítus	audītúrus, audītúra, audītúrum

The message from the author of Ecclesiastes applies here, as in many places in our grammar book: *nihil sub sōle novum*, "there is nothing new under the sun" (Eccl. I.10). There are no new concepts here. You are fully aware of the following: how 2-1-2 endings work, how adjectives function, and how participles act. You are ready for translating.

Here is another example of this kind of participle:

Nec mīrum hōc dē amícō et prophétā et lēgíferō Deī, cum omnis pópulus accessúrus ad montem Sina, et Deī audītúrus ēlóquium, tribus diébus sānctificárī jussus sit, et sē ab uxóribus abstinére. (Jerome)[10]

Nor is this surprising about a friend, prophet, and lawgiver of God, when all the people about to approach Mount Sinai and about to hear the voice of God, were commanded to sanctify themselves in three days and to keep themselves from their wives.

As illustrated, the future active participle indicates futurity, that is, something that will happen subsequent to the time of the main verb. There are several ways to render these two participles here, but the "about to-" translation accurately conveys the future nature of the event of approaching and hearing.

PERIPHRASTIC CONJUGATIONS

23.9 **"Round about" Constructions.** We learned in *Capítulum* XXII that gerundives (which is to say, future passive participles) indicate something that is to be done or completed. It is, therefore, traditionally translated as "to be -ed," "has to be-," or "must be -ed." After all, it indicates (passive) necessity. I also explained that the gerundive mostly occurs in tandem with the Latin verb *sum, esse, fuī, futúrus*, otherwise called the "copulative." When the gerundive combines with the copulative, its name changes yet again—we call it a "passive periphrastic,"[11] indicating

---

10. Jerome, *Advérsus Joviniánum* I.20 (PL 23.237).
11. It can also be called a "gerundive of obligation." And it is, in fact, a "compound tense," revealing that two parts are necessary.

that it is the passive form of a periphrastic construction. This is a lot of verbal mumbo jumbo, so let us first look at an example:

Fílius hóminis trādéndus est.　　　　　　The Son of Man is to be betrayed.
(Matt. XVII.21)

In this sentence, both the participle and the "to be" verb collaborate to form a periphrastic construction. However, the "to be" verb is happy to work together with more than the gerundive. Let us return to the same example of a future active participle we encountered previously:

Et íterum ventúrus est cum　　　　　　And he is about to come again with
glóriā iūdicā́re vīvōs et mórtuōs.　　　　glory to judge the living and the dead.
(Sýmbolum Apostolórum)

The use of the periphrastic is very common.

23.10 Participles and Periphrastics: A Marriage Made in *Caelum*. At this point, the greatest takeaway is that a periphrastic construction occurs with more than the gerundive. It comes in all shapes and sizes. Indeed, periphrastics are peppered throughout Latin writings, adding spice to otherwise bland sentences. The term "periphrastic" ultimately comes from a combination of Greek terms that literally means "speaking around." This Greek concept suggests that a person uses more terms than is necessary, offering a roundabout way of saying something rather than being direct and concise in language. This same notion transfers into Latin.

For those who like equations, a periphrastic construction in Latin is a participle + some form of *sum, esse, fuī, futū́rus*. The combination of forms makes it a "compound tense," implying more than one form. Periphrastics appear in the past, present, and future; indicative and subjunctive; and they also may be active or passive. They are very handy grammatical constructions. What is more, the participle form will only appear in the nominative or accusative case, whether singular or plural.

23.11 To Be or Not to Be. And one more thing: the "to be" verb need not always present in order to constitute a periphrastic construction. It is very common, in fact, for Latin writers to omit the "to be" verb, even though it is implied. If it is implied, it is still a periphrastic construction.

23.12 Two General Kinds of Periphrastics. Because periphrastics may occur with any kind of participle, you will see them used often and in different ways.[12] In our discussion, we will divide periphrastics into two general kinds: actives and passives.

(I) (Future) Active Periphrastics (aka, First Periphrastic Conjugations). The active periphrastic entails the use the future active participle in the nominative case + *sum, esse, fuī, futū́rus* in the nominative case. However, the copulative (that is, the "to be" verb) may be in one of various tenses: present, imperfect, future, perfect, pluperfect, or future perfect. And the copulative can be in one of two moods: indicative or subjunctive.

The active periphrastic indicates that an action is going to happen. As such, there are several acceptable ways to translate it: "going to-," "will-," "about to-," "intending to-."

To view the full scope of what an active periphrastic can be, consider the totality of this periphrastic with just the first-person singular forms of our paradigm verb *amō, amā́re, amā́vī, amā́tus*.

---

12. Although they can occasionally occur with the present (active) participle, they are most common with the future active and future passive participles.

PERFECT PASS., FUTURE ACT. PARTICIPLES; PERIPHRASTIC CONSTRUCTIONS

INDICATIVE FORMS

"To Be" Verb Tense	Periphrastic Form	Translation
Present	amātúrus sum	I am about to love
Imperfect	amātúrus eram	I was about to love
Future	amātúrus erō	I will be about to love
Perfect	amātúrus fuī	I have been about to love
Pluperfect	amātúrus fúeram	I had been about to love
Future Perfect	amātúrus fúerō	I will have been about to love

INFINITIVE FORMS

"To Be" Verb Tense	Periphrastic Form	Translation
Present	amātúrus esse	to be about to love
Future	amātúrus fuísse	to have been about to love

SUBJUNCTIVE FORMS

"To Be" Verb Tense	Periphrastic Form	Translation
Present	amātúrus sim	I would be about to love
Imperfect	amātúrus essem	I was about to love
Perfect	amātúrus fúerim	I would have been about to love
Pluperfect	amātúrus fuíssem	I had been about to love

There is much information contained in these paradigms, and it is easy to feel overwhelmed. Please do not be so. These paradigms are only intended to introduce you to the full range of what an active periphrastic can do. It accomplishes a lot in a paucity of words. You will see this construction very often. It is beyond the scope of this book to explore all of the different forms, but you can get a picture here of how useful the construction is.

Because the active periphrastic uses 2-1-2 endings, there is never any doubt as to their identity or conjugation. They all conjugate the same way. But one more note: Despite the word order illustrated in the paradigms, the periphrastic construction may appear in any order and may also appear separated by many words (e.g., *amatúrus sum, sum amatúrus, amatúrus . . . sum,* or *sum . . . amatúrus*). In other words, do not cling to word order in Latin; instead, be on the lookout for the actual combination of terms.

(2) (Future) Passive Periphrastics (aka, Second Periphrastic Conjugation). In contrast to the active, the passive periphrastic uses the future passive participle + *sum, esse, fuī, futúrus*.

INDICATIVE FORMS

"To Be" Verb Tense	Periphrastic Form	Translation
Present	amándus sum	I am to be loved
Imperfect	amándus eram	I was to be loved
Future	amándus erō	I will have to be loved
Perfect	amándus fuī	I had to be loved
Pluperfect	amándus fúeram	I had had to be loved
Future Perfect	amándus fúerō	I will have had to be loved

INFINITIVE FORMS

"To Be" Verb Tense	Periphrastic Form	Translation
Present	amándus esse	to have to be loved
Future	amándus fuísse	to have had to be loved

SUBJUNCTIVE FORMS[a]

"To Be" Verb Tense	Periphrastic Form	Translation
Present	amándus sim	I would to be loved
Imperfect	amándus essem	I was to be loved
Perfect	amándus fúerim	I would have to be loved
Pluperfect	amándus fuíssem	I had had to be loved

[a] Translating subjunctive periphrastics is not easy. It is hard to convey the sense of the Latin into English. I have chosen to have more awkward translations in order to render what is taking place in Latin. In a professional translation, however, it is important to render the Latin into more idiomatic English.

The passive periphrastic is often translated in the same way that a gerundive is translated: "has to be-," "must be-," "should be-."

Once again, please do not be overwhelmed here. This information is simply intended to paint a picture of how this form may be used.

BIBLICAL EXAMPLE

We may use the former verse from Matthew XVII.21 to illustrate how easy it is to move between tenses. Below are some possibilities for the indicative mood.

Present. Fílius hóminis <u>tradéndus est</u>.   The Son of Man <u>is to be betrayed</u>.

Imperfect. Fílius hóminis <u>tradéndus erat</u>.   The Son of Man <u>was to be betrayed</u>.

Future. Fílius hóminis <u>tradéndus erit</u>.   The Son of Man <u>will have to be betrayed</u>.

Perfect. Fílius hóminis <u>tradéndus fuit</u>.   The Son of Man <u>had to be betrayed</u>.

Pluperfect. Fílius hóminis <u>tradéndus fúerat</u>.   The Son of Man <u>had had to be betrayed</u>.

Future Perfect. Fílius hóminis <u>tradéndus fúerit</u>.   The Son of Man <u>will have had to be betrayed</u>.

PERFECT PASS., FUTURE ACT. PARTICIPLES; PERIPHRASTIC CONSTRUCTIONS

A SPECIAL USE OF THE DATIVE CASE

23.13 Dative of Agent. With a name as debonair as "dative of agent," you know that something good is coming. What is it? In a word, it's a particular use of the dative case. It is used with (passive) periphrastics to indicate by whom an action is performed.

23.14 Translating a Dative of Agent. Your inclination (and rightly so) will be to translate the dative with the words "with" or "to," but the dative of agent is best translated actively.

Here is an example:

| Nam remīsī vōs ad illum, et ecce nihil dignum morte āctum est eī. (Luke XXIII.15) | For I sent you all to him and look, nothing worthy of death has been done by him. |

I offered a more literal translation, but a much better way to express the dative of agency is in an active way:

For I sent you to him and look, <u>he</u> has done nothing worthy of death.

Summārium

In this *capítulum* you learned that:
- The fourth principal part serves as the basis for the perfect passive and future active participles.
- Perfect passive participles are verbal adjectives used to describe an activity in the past.
- Future active participles are verbal adjectives indicating imminence.
- Participles are frequently combined with *sum, esse, fuī, futūrus*. This combination is called a periphrastic. Such a combination occurs across tenses, voices, and moods.
- The dative of agency is used to indicate when the dative case is acting as the subject.

VOCĀBULŌRUM INDEX

Latin	English (Gloss)	(Etymology)
accómodō, accomodáre, accomodávī, accomodátus (1)	to suit, to arrange, to accommodate	(accommodate)
alter, áltera, álterum	the other (of two), the second	(alternative)
cēna, cēnae (f)	dinner, supper	
cēnō, cēnáre, cēnávī, cēnátus (1)	to dine, to eat supper	
combúrō, combúrere, combússī, combústus (3)	to burn up, to consume (with fire)	(combustible)
cōnstítuō, cōnstítuere, cōnstítuī, cōnstitútus (3)	to establish, to confirm, to set up	(constitute)

(cont.)

Latin	English (Gloss)	(Etymology)
contíneō, continére, contínuī, conténtus (2)	to hold together, to contain	(continence)
décorō, decoráre, decorávī, decorátus (1)	to adorn, to decorate, to beautify, to honor	(decorate)
gustō, gustáre, gustávī, gustátus (1)	to taste, to sample	(gustation)
ígnis, ígnis, ígnium (m)	fire	(ignite)
ínferus, ínfera, ínferum[a]	of hell, below	(infernal)
multíplicō, multiplicáre, multiplicávī, multiplicátus (1)	to multiply, to increase	(multiply)
mystérium, mystériī (n)	mystery, sacrament	(mystery)
nārrō, nārráre, nārrávī, nārrátus (1)	to narrate, to report, to tell, to recount	(narrate)
páriō, párere, péperī, partus (3)	to bear, to produce, to beget	(postpartum)
Pascha, Paschae (f)	Passover, Easter, Pesach	(paschal)
prōdō, pródere, pródidī, próditus (3)	to bring forth, to produce, to bear	
prōfíciō, prōfícere, prōfécī, prōféctus (3)	to avail, to prevail	(proficient)
sacrāméntum, sacrāméntī (n)	sacrament, mystery, oath	(sacrament)
succéndō, succéndere, succéndī, succénsus (3)	to kindle, to inflame, to set on fire	
ténebrae, tenebrárum (f)[b]	darkness	(tenebrous)
tránseō, trānsíre, tránsiī, tránsitus (4)	to go across, to traverse, to pass away	(transition)
turba, turbae (f)	crowd, multitude	(disturbance)
vestis, vestis, véstium (f)	garment, clothing	(vest)
vīcínus, vīcína, vīcínum[c]	neighboring	(vicinity)

[a] There is a very similar adjective also used in Latin, meaning roughly the same thing: īnférnus, īnférna, īnférnum.

[b] This word only occurs in the plural, which is reflected in the nominative and genitive plural form provided.

[c] The corresponding noun looks very similar: vīcínus, vīcínī (m), "neighbor."

ŌRÁTIŌ POPULÁRIS

Āctus Contrītiṓnis. The "Act of Contrition" is a prayer expressing sorrow for one's sins. It is prayed in many Christian traditions but has historically been part of the Sacrament of Penance in the Roman Catholic Church. Pay attention to all the grammatical features in the prayer that we have learned in the last two *capítula*.

PERFECT PASS., FUTURE ACT. PARTICIPLES; PERIPHRASTIC CONSTRUCTIONS

Deus meus, ex tōtō corde paénitet mē ómnium meórum peccātórum,	My God, I repent of my sins with all my heart, And I detest them,
éaque dētéstor, quia peccándō, nōn sōlum poenās ā tē iūstē statū́tās prōméritus sum,	because in sinning not only do I deserve the penalties that you have justly established, But especially because I have offended you,
sed praesértim quia offéndī tē, summum bonum, ac dignum quī super ómnia dīligā́ris.	The greatest good, worthy to be loved above all things.
Ideō fírmiter prōpṓnō, adjuvánte grā́tiā tuā, dē céterō mē nōn peccātū́rum peccandī́que occāsiṓnēs próximās fugitū́rum. Āmēn.	Therefore, I firmly purpose, By the help of your grace, To sin no more and to flee the closest occasions leading me to sin. Amen.

EXERCÍTIA

Be sure to complete the *exercítium* in the appendix corresponding to this *capítulum*.

Capítulum
XXIV

PERFECT, PLUPERFECT, AND FUTURE PERFECT PASSIVES; FÍERĪ; ABLATIVE ABSOLUTES

Grátiam tuam, quaésumus, Dómine, méntibus nostrīs īnfúnde; ut quī, Ángelō nūntiánte, Christī Fíliī tuī incarnātiónem cognóvimus, per passiónem eius et crucem ad resurrēctiónis glóriam perdūcámur.[1]
—ÁNGELUS

OPÚSCULUM THEOLÓGICUM: *Ángelus*

Originating in the Middle Ages, the Ángelus Prayer celebrates one of the most important theological topics in the Christian life: the incarnation of Jesus. Prayers like this were ubiquitous in the history of the church, and the Ángelus Prayer guides the Christian along the path of belief, confession, prayer, and resolve. In order to assess the full scope of the prayer, I am including its entirety below. You will notice the "V" and "R" for each section. These abbreviations stand for "Versicle" and "Response."

How does it work? After an ecclesial leader reads the versicle, the laypeople offer the response. And, as you surely surmised, both these terms come from Latin. The first term derives from *versículus*, "little verse," while the following originates from *respónsum*, "response." Prayer follows each versicle and response. As you read through the prayer, identify as many words and grammatical features as possible.

V. Ángelus Dóminī nūntiávit Maríae.
R. Et concépit dē Spíritū Sānctō.
Avē María, grátiā plēna; Dóminus tēcum: benedícta tū in muliéribus, et benedíctus frūctus ventris tuī Iēsus. Sāncta María, Māter Deī ōrā prō nōbīs peccātóribus, nunc et in hōrā mortis nostrae. Āmēn.
V. Ecce ancílla Dóminī,
R. Fīat mihi secúndum verbum tuum.
Avē María, grátiā plēna; Dóminus tēcum: benedícta tū in muliéribus, et benedíctus frūctus ventris tuī Iēsus. Sāncta María, Māter Deī, ōrā prō nōbīs peccātóribus, nunc et in hōrā mortis nostrae. Āmēn.

---

1. "Pour forth your grace into our minds, we beseech you, Lord; that we who, <u>with the angel announcing</u>, have known the incarnation of Christ your Son, may be brought to the glory of his resurrection through his suffering and cross."

PERFECT, PLUPERFECT, FUTURE PERFECT PASSIVES; FÍERĪ; ABLATIVE ABSOLUTES

V. Et Verbum carō factum est,
R. Et habitávit in nōbīs.
Avē María, grátiā plēna; Dóminus tēcum: benedícta tū in muliéribus, et benedíctus frūctus ventris tuī Iēsus. Sāncta María, Māter Deī ōrā prō nōbīs peccātóribus, nunc et in hōrā mortis nostrae. Āmēn.
V. Ōrā prō nōbīs, sāncta Deī Génetrīx,
R. Ut dignī efficiámur prōmissiónibus Christī.
Ōrēmus. Grátiam tuam, quaésumus, Dómine, méntibus nostrīs īnfúnde; ut quī, <u>Ángelō nūntiánte</u>, Christī Fílī tuī incārnatiónem cognóvimus, per passiónem eius et crucem ad resurrēctiónis glóriam perdūcámur. Per eúmdem Christum Dóminum nostrum.
R. Āmēn.

Rather than translate the entirety of the prayer, I will only translate the section most pertinent to our discussion, the very last one:

Let us pray. Pour forth your grace into our minds, we beseech you, Lord; that we who, <u>with the angel announcing</u>, have known the incarnation of Christ your Son, may be brought to the glory of his resurrection through his suffering and cross. Through the same Christ, our Lord. Amen.

The underlined section contains a new grammatical feature: the "ablative absolute." This is a peculiar term. Whatever could it mean? As we will learn in this *capítulum*, the ablative absolute is a phrase—grammatically separate from the rest of the sentence—which describes circumstances surrounding the action of the sentence.

Prospéctus

In this *capítulum* you will learn that:
- Compound tenses contain at least two components working together as one grammatical unit.
- The perfect, pluperfect, and future perfect passives are compound tenses, which combine a form of the verb *sum, esse, fuī, futúrus* with a participle.
- The irregular verb *fīō, fíerī, factus sum* means "to be made," "to become," "to come to pass," etc. It is very common in Latin.
- The ablative case is used in many ways. One special usage, the ablative absolute, contains a noun or pronoun in the ablative case in combination with a participle in the ablative case.

GRAMMÁTICA

24.1 Compound Tenses. We have learned about compound tenses in previous *capítula*. In a word, they are tenses formed by more than one part—typically a "helping"[2] verb plus the main verb, for example, "I <u>have</u> loved," "she <u>had</u> warned," "they <u>will have</u> heard." These underlined words are helping verbs, which are used in conjunction with main verbs to help express tense and mood.

---

2. "Helping verbs" also go by the name "auxiliary verbs."

24.2 **The Perfect Passive System Is a Compound Tense.** In Latin, the perfect passive system is a compound tense. As such, it requires two component parts: the helping verb *sum, esse, fuī, futūrus* and a main verb in the fourth principal part (the perfect passive participle). It makes NO difference at all whether the "to be" verbs are placed before, after, or many words from the participle. You will remember that the "perfect system" transcends the "perfect tense": This system encompasses three tenses: the perfect, pluperfect, and future perfect tenses.

24.3 **Periphrastic Constructions, Compound Tenses, and Perfect Passive Systems.** By now, you may be saying to yourself: "Isn't the combination of the 'to be' verb with a participle called a periphrastic construction?" Yes, indeed! Exactly right. The next thing you should be saying to yourself is: "What is the difference between a periphrastic construction and a verb in the perfect passive system?"

Here is the answer: nothing at all. Because Latin verbs in the perfect passive system (a) require the presence of *sum, esse, fuī, futūrus* and (b) make use of a participle (the perfect passive participle, to be exact), they qualify as both compound tenses AND periphrastic constructions. I recognize that this truth invites confusion, and I apologize to you on behalf of all the Latin grammarians who have ever lived. *Nostra culpa*—"Our bad."

Now that we have cleared the air, let us return to the perfect passive system. Exactly how is it formed in all of its tenses, and how does it function?

24.4 **Mastering the Perfect Passive System Is Easy.** Despite the confusion elicited above, it is extremely easy to understand the perfect passive system. There are two reasons for this.

1. **You Already Know It.** Believe it or not, you already know all of the different forms of the system. That is, you know (a) the present, imperfect, and future tenses of *sum, esse, fuī, futūrus*; and (b) the perfect passive participle, which is nothing more than the fourth principal part. As you may recall, I mentioned in previous *capítula* that participles often occur in tandem with *sum, esse, fuī, futūrus*. As such, you have already encountered the perfect passive system.
2. **There Are No Changes in Conjugation.** Just as we discovered in the perfect active system, so, too, here: the perfect passive system does not require different endings according to conjugation type. First-, second-, third-, and fourth-conjugation verbs conjugate the same way in the perfect system (whether active or passive). This is one reason why the perfect system is so, well, "perfect."

24.5 **Perfect Passive Indicative Tense.** As the very name indicates, the perfect passive entails completed action (and so perfect) as well as being acted upon (and so passive). As a verb, the perfect passive indicative uses the present tense of *sum, esse, fuī, futūrus*; and as an adjective, it agrees with its corresponding noun in case, number, and gender. The fourth principal part adopts 2-1-2 endings, which you know like the back of your *manus*. Because the perfect passive indicative is simply the present tense of the "to be" verb + the fourth principal part, we only need to use one type of verb conjugation to illustrate an example.

It is time to look at an example:

Similitúdine comparándum eō, vel quī nōn est purgátus baptísmō, vel nōn mónitus crucis signáculō. (Germain of Paris)[3]	We must compare these as to their similarity, namely, the one who has not been cleansed by baptism and the one who has not been marked by the sign of the cross.

---

3. Germain of Paris, *Expositiō Brevis Antiquae Liturgiae Gallicánae* I (PL 72.92).

PERFECT PASSIVE INDICATIVE FORMS: ONE REPRESENTATIVE CONJUGATION

Masculine	Feminine	Neuter	Translation
mónitus sum	mónita sum	mónitum sum[a]	I have been warned
mónitus es	mónita es	mónitum es	You have been warned
mónitus est	mónita est	mónitum est	He / she / it has been warned
mónitī sumus	mónitae sumus	mónita sumus	We have been warned
mónitī estis	mónitae estis	mónita estis	You all have been warned
mónitī sunt	mónitae sunt	mónita sunt	They have been warned

[a] Granted, it would be rare to encounter the neuter form with first person and second person, but they are included for the sake of understanding the range of combinations.

As we have already learned, it is commonplace for the "to be" verb to be absent. Whether absent or present, however, it is still a perfect passive (and still a compound).

24.6 **Slight Variance: Perfect of "To Be" Rather Than Present.** It is not uncommon for writers to use the perfect active indicative of the "to be" verb rather than the present in the perfect passive indicative. This entails seeing *fuī, fuístī, fuit, fúimus, fuístis, fuḗrunt* instead of *sum, es, est, sumus, estis, sunt*. The use of *fuī* and its related forms can indicate that a state of existence is no longer in force, while the use of *sum* and its related forms can indicate that a state of existence continues. However, your translation in English may sound very similar.

24.7 **Translating the Perfect Passive Indicative.** In our discussion of the perfect active tense, I suggested the stock translation of "have -ed." This translation accurately conveys (a) the completed nature of the tense and (b) the passive nature of the voice. In a similar way, I recommend translating the perfect passive as "have been -ed." This rendering is sometimes referred to as the "completed present," in contrast to the "simple past," which is the equivalent of "-ed." When translating, context may favor one translation over another. Either one is acceptable. However, all things being the same, I suggest allowing "have been -ed" to be your stock translation.

24.8 *Cáveat Discípulus,* **"Learner Beware."** It is tempting for beginning students to see the present tense of the "to be" verb and then immediately assume that the perfect passive should be translated in the present tense. Thus, for example, you might be tempted to translate *mónitus es* as "you <u>are</u> warned" rather than "you <u>have been</u> warned." On the surface, this mistranslation makes sense, but it is important to keep in mind that the perfect passive is a <u>compound tense</u>, meaning that you have to translate it as a unit rather than as two individual parts.[4] Latin prefers to express simple concepts like the present tense without resorting to compound tenses.

---

4. To say "you are warned" in Latin, we use the regular present passive indicative *monḗris*, which is NOT a compound tense.

CERTUM EST QUIA IMPOSSÍBILE

Tertullian famously quipped that Jesus's resurrection from the dead "is certain because it is impossible." The larger context for this phrase contains several perfect passive verbs, two of which are deponents:

Nātus est Deī fīlius; nōn pudet, quia pudéndum est. Et mórtuus est Deī fīlius; prōrsus credíbile est, quia inéptum est. Et sepúltus, resurréxit; certum est, quia impossíbile.[5]	The Son of God was born; it does not cause shame because it is shameful. The Son of God died; it is immediately believable because it is ridiculous. The Son of God was buried, and he rose again; it is certain because it is impossible.

24.9 **Pluperfect Passive Indicative Tense.** The pluperfect passive indicative is identical to the perfect passive in every way other than its use of the imperfect tense of *sum, esse, fuī, futúrus* rather than the present tense. The change in tense emphasizes the past completed aspect of the event. By using the imperfect of "to be," the past completed nature of the event rises to the surfaces.

PLUPERFECT PASSIVE INDICATIVE FORMS: ONE REPRESENTATIVE CONJUGATION

Masculine	Feminine	Neuter	Translation
mónitus eram[a]	mónita eram	mónitum eram	I had been warned
mónitus erās	mónita erās	mónitum erās	You had been warned
mónitus erat	mónita erat	mónitum erat	He / she / it had been warned
mónitī erámus	mónitae erámus	mónita erámus	We had been warned
mónitī erátis	mónitae erátis	mónita erátis	You all had been warned
mónitī erant	mónitae erant	mónita erant	They had been warned

[a] As with the perfect passive, you will sometimes see the pluperfect of "to be" accompanying a fourth principal part to comprise the pluperfect passive indicative: *fúeram, fúerās, fúerat, fuerámus, fuerátis, fúerant*. The translation is the same as a normal pluperfect passive indicative.

24.10 **Translating the Pluperfect Passive Indicative.** The pluperfect passive indicative expresses past completed aspect. And because it is passive, the subject is being acted upon. Our stock translation is exactly what you should expect: "had been -ed." We simply move from "has to be -ed" in the perfect passive to "had to be -ed" in the pluperfect. Nothing surprising here.

Let us illustrate by way of an example:

---

5. Tertullian, *Dē Carne Christī* V (PL 2.761).

Dénique et ab hómine Deī <u>mónitus erat</u>. (Ambrose of Milan)⁶

And finally he <u>had been warned</u> by the man of God.

This is completely straightforward.

24.11 Future Perfect Passive Indicative Tense. There is nothing new to add to our discussion. All the concepts are the same. The only change is the use of the <u>future tense</u> of *sum, esse, fuī, futū́rus* rather than the present or imperfect tense. The future perfect passive indicates an event that will have been completed.

FUTURE PERFECT PASSIVE INDICATIVE FORMS: ONE REPRESENTATIVE CONJUGATION

Masculine	Feminine	Neuter	Translation
mónitus erō	mónita erō	mónitum erō	I will have been warned
mónitus eris	mónita eris	mónitum eris	You will have been warned
mónitus erit	mónita erit	mónitum erit	He / she / it will have been warned
mónitī érimus	mónitae érimus	mónita érimus	We will have been warned
mónitī éritis	mónitae éritis	mónita éritis	You all will have been warned
mónitī erunt	mónitae erunt	mónita erunt	They will have been warned

24.12 Translating the Future Perfect Passive. Our stock translation for the future perfect passive indicative should be anticipated: "will have been -ed." As with the other perfect tenses, some authors prefer to use the future perfect of "to be" (*fúerō, fúeris, fúerit, fuérimus, fuéritis, fúerint*) rather than the future. There is no difference in meaning.

Here is an example of a pluperfect passive indicative:

Quodcúnque ligáveris super terram, <u>erit ligátum</u> et in coelīs. (Isidore of Seville)⁷

Whatever you have bound on earth, it <u>will have been bound</u> also in heaven.

The grammar behind this sentence should be as right as rain. There is nothing out of the ordinary.

FĪŌ, FÍERĪ, FACTUS SUM

24.13 An Irregular Verb: *Fīō, Fíerī, Factus Sum*. You will remember that we discussed some of the most common irregular verbs in a previous *capítulum*. Now is a good time to introduce another noteworthy verb that does not follow the "regular" rules: *fīō, fíerī, factus sum*. This is an exotic

---

6. Ambrose of Milan, *História dē Excídiō Hieros. Urbis* V.16 (PL 15.2151).
7. Isidore of Seville, *Prolegómena* I.45 (PL 81.296). You probably sensed that Isidore is quoting a well-known verse from Matthew XVI.19.

verb that may be translated in many ways depending on context: "to be made," "to become," "to be done," "to be," "to happen," "to occur," and "to come to pass." There are three points to be made about this important verb:

1. **It Is Very Common.** You will see this verb often in Latin. Together with *sum* and *fáciō*, it is one of the most common verbs in Latin. It is especially common in the Vulgate, where narrative writers love to begin sentences with *factum est* . . . , "it came to pass," "it happened," etc. (In this way, it corresponds to the Greek Bible's use of ἐγένετο.)
2. **It Is Used As the Passive of *Fáciō* in the Present Tense.** Rather than using the present passive of *fáciō*, "to do" or "to make," the Romans preferred to use *fīō* as a passive verb (even though it is technically active in voice). This means that whenever you encounter *fīō* in the present tense, it is to be translated in the passive voice.
3. **It Uses *Fáciō* in the Perfect Passive System.** *Fīō* was a bit embarrassed by its perfect passive system, so it decided to use *fáciō* instead. *Fáciō*, in case you are wondering, did not put up too much of a fight and agreed to share. Because *fīō* hijacked the forms of *fáciō* in the perfect passive, both *fīō* and *fáciō* are identical in the perfect passive "system" (thus encompassing the perfect passive, pluperfect passive, and future perfect passive). When you see the perfect passive system (such as *factus est, factus erat*, or *factus erit*), it can be translated as "has become," "had become," and "will have become."

24.14 Forms of *Fīō*. Here are the forms of *fīō* in the "present system" (present, imperfect, and future in the active) and "perfect system" (perfect, pluperfect, and future perfect in the passive) in the indicative mood. As you will observe, *fīō* occurs by itself in the present system, but always as a compound tense in the perfect (passives).

FĪŌ, FÍERI, FACTUS SUM (STEM: FĪ), "TO BE MADE," "TO BECOME," "TO BE DONE," "TO BE," "TO HAPPEN," "TO OCCUR," "TO COME TO PASS"

	Present Active "become"	**Imperfect Active** "was becoming"	**Future Active** "will become"
1 sg	fīō	fiébam	fīam
2 sg	fīs	fiébās	fīēs
3 sg	fit	fiébat	fīet
1 pl	fīmus	fiebámus	fiémus
2 pl	fītis	fiebátis	fiétis
3 pl	fīunt	fiébant	fīent

	Perfect Passive[a] "was made"	**Pluperfect Passive** "had been made"	**Future Passive** "will have been made"
1 sg	factus sum	factus eram	factus erō
2 sg	factus es	factus erās	factus eris
3 sg	factus est	factus erat	factus erit
1 pl	factī sumus	factī erámus	factī érimus
2 pl	factī estis	factī erátis	factī éritis
3 pl	factī sunt	factī erant	factī erunt

[a] Remember that the perfect passive system of *fīō* is identical with that of *fáciō*.

PERFECT, PLUPERFECT, FUTURE PERFECT PASSIVES; FÍERĪ; ABLATIVE ABSOLUTES

The sentence below illustrates the frequent use of the perfect passive of *fīo* in the Vulgate:

Et verbum carō <u>factum est</u>, et habitávit
in nōbīs (John I.14).

And the Word <u>was made</u> flesh and
dwelt among us.

Factum is neuter here to agree with the noun *verbum*. And, as explained earlier, it occurs as a compound tense with the perfect passive.

ABLATIVE CASE REVISITED

24.15 Different Uses of the Ablative. We learned in the first *capítulum* that the ablative case carries the significance of separation or motion away from something, among other usages. It is often translated into English by the preposition "by" or "from." This is still true. However, it is now time to invite you into the circle of trust with respect to the ablative case. It is actually used in numerous ways. In this *capítulum*, we will isolate one of the most common uses of the ablative.

24.16 Ablative Absolute: More Than Soap Detergent. Of all the intimidating terms we have learned in Latin, this takes us to a new level. Is the term "ablative absolute" talking about a soap detergent, a boy band, or a comic book? It is actually a new grammatical concept, directly rolled over from the Latin *ablātívus absolū́tus*, "the ablative having been set free." (Come to think of it, this might make a great rock band name.) If you ever studied Greek, you are familiar with the "genitive absolute," which fulfills a similar role through a different case (the genitive). In effect, the ablative absolute presents circumstances regarding the action of a verb. In other words, it is an adverbial phrase occurring in a subordinate construction. It provides a little more detail than the sentence or verb alone provides, but never stands alone on its own two *pedēs*, "feet."

The "ablative" nature of the grammatical concept signals to us that the ablative has to be used (no other case impostors allowed). What is more, the "absolute" nature of it indicates that the expression is set apart or independent from the rest of the sentence. This may be why Caesar loved to use the ablative absolute in his writing: he loved *lībértās*, his "freedom."

There are two components typically needed to form an ablative absolute: (1) a noun or pronoun in the ablative case, and (2) a modifying participle, also in the ablative case. In addition, the ablative absolute, as the name *absolute* means in Latin—"having been separated from"—indicates a formation that is grammatically separate from the rest of the sentence.

24.17 Latin Ablative Absolutes Common in English. Believe it or not, you are familiar with several Latin ablative absolutes already. Consider the following:

- *Deō volénte*, "with God willing"
- *Mūtā́tīs mūtándīs*, "with the necessary things having been changed"
- *His dictīs*, "with these things having been said"
- *Vice versā*, "with the change having been turned"

So, before we proceed any further, just know that you are familiar with this concept.

24.18 Translating Ablative Absolutes. There are many acceptable ways to translate an ablative absolute:

- **Causal.** Explaining why: "because"
- **Concessive.** Conceding something: "although," "though"
- **Temporal.** Having to do with time: "when," "while"
- **Unclear.** Uncertain how it is functioning: "with -ing"

It takes practice to determine exactly how an ablative absolute is being used. As always, allow context to determine the best translation.

Let us look at an example:

Vidēs ergō quod, dīcénte Apóstolō, mīsit Deus Fílium suum, suum utíque Fílium, ut ipsíus verbīs ūtar Apóstolī, suum Fílium Deus mīsit. (John Cassian)[8]

You no doubt have deduced that *dīcénte Apóstolō* is our ablative absolute. Both the participle and noun are in the ablative case, and they are also helpfully separated from the rest of the sentence. Now the million dollar question is: Is the phrase causal, concessive, temporal, or unclear? When in doubt, plug in all four options and choose which one makes the most sense in context and in translation.

Causal Translation: Therefore, you see that because the apostle said that "God sent his own son," truly his own son, I will make use of the apostle's very words: "God sent his own son."[9]

Concessive Translation: Therefore, you see that although the apostle said that "God sent his own son," truly his own son, I will make use of the apostle's very words: "God sent his own son."

Temporal Translation: Therefore, when the apostle said that "God sent his own son," truly his own son, I will make use of the apostle's very words: "God sent his own son."

Stock Translation: Therefore, with the apostle saying that "God sent his own son," truly his own son, I will make use of the apostle's very words: "God sent his own son."

Which sounds better? I would suggest that the causal translation makes the most sense; however, when you encounter an ablative absolute in Latin, you will sometimes need to plug in different translation options and choose the best one based on context.

24.19 **More Uses of the Ablative.** The ablative case is used frequently in Latin. Sometimes a Latin preposition will occur alongside it, but oftentimes there will be no Latin preposition. Grammarians have classified the different uses into convenient categories. Such classifications include, among others:

- ablative of accompaniment
- ablative of agent
- ablative of description
- ablative of manner
- ablative of means or instrument
- ablative of place
- ablative of separation
- ablative of time

---

8. John Cassian, *Dē Incarnātiōne Christī* IV.2 (PL 50.77).
9. Cassian seems to be basing his biblical reference on Romans VIII.3.

As you can probably surmise, these different usages tend to correspond to certain English phrases or prepositions. For instance, it is not uncommon for the ablative of accompaniment to be translated as "with . . . ," the ablative of agent as "by . . . ," and the ablative of means as "through . . . ," since they are indicating accompaniment, agency, and means, respectively. (Of course, there are many ways to render these usages in English.)

Every time you encounter the ablative case, you will need to be asking yourself to which usage it belongs—regardless of whether there is a Latin preposition alongside it (remember that there are few one-to-one correspondences from Latin to English). Rather than discuss all the various uses of the ablative, I encourage you to consult advanced grammars on this topic.[10]

Summārium

In this *capítulum* you learned that:
- The perfect passive system is a compound tense using the fourth principal part + various tenses of *sum, esse, fuī, futúrus*.
- The frequently used verb *fíō, fíerī, factus sum* follows an irregular pattern.
- The ablative case is used in diverse ways. One such usage, the ablative absolute, is capable of great nuance. It is a construction in the ablative case comprised of a participle and a noun or pronoun.

VOCĀBULŌRUM INDEX

Latin	English (Gloss)	(Etymology)
albus, alba, album	white	(albino)
ántequam	before	
ampléctor, ampléctī, ampléxus sum (3)	to embrace, to esteem, to cherish	(amplect)
baptísma, baptísmatis (n)[a]	baptism	(baptism)
baptízō, baptizáre, baptizávī, baptizátus (1)	to baptize	(baptize)
célebrō, celebráre, celebrávī, celebrátus (1)	to celebrate	(celebrate)
clēmēns, clēmēns, clēmēns	merciful, mild, peaceful, clement	(clemency)
cólligō, collígere, collégī, colléctus (3)	to gather, to assemble, to infer	(collect)
dēclínō, dēclināre, dēclinávī, dēclinátus (1)	to bend, to deflect	(decline)
exclámō, exclāmáre, exclāmávī, exclāmátus (1)	to cry out, to exclaim	(exclaim)
expéctō, expectáre, expectávī, expectátus (1)	to wait for, to expect	(expect)

(cont.)

---

10. See AE §§398–431.

Latin	English (Gloss)	(Etymology)
ōrnō, ōrnáre, ōrnávī, ōrnátus (1)	to equip, to prepare, to adorn	(ornate)
prōmíttō, prōmíttere, prōmísī, prōmíssus (3)	to promise, to send forth	(promise)
répleō, replére, replévī, replétus (2)	to fill again, to replenish, to refill	(replete)
rogō, rogáre, rogávī, rogátus (1)	to pray, to beseech, to ask for	(prerogative)
sémīnō, sēmināre, sēminávī, sēminátus (1)	to sow, to plant	(inseminate)
spectō, spectáre, spectávī, spectátus (1)	to observe, to watch, to look at, to consider	(spectacle)
spōnsus, spōnsī (m)	groom	
táceō, tacére, tácuī, tácitus (2)	to be silent, to say nothing, to be quiet	(taciturn)
tamen	nonetheless, nevertheless	
testis, testis, téstium (m)	witness	(testimony)
trahō, tráhere, trāxī, tractus (3)	to draw, to drag	(traction)
virgō, vírginis (f)	virgin	(virgin)
vīvus, vīva, vīvum	alive, living	(vivacious)
vīvíficō, vīvificáre, vīvificávī, vīvificátus (1)	to bring (back) to life, to vivify	(vivify)

[a] You will also see this form: *baptísmus, baptísmī* (m). However, it means the same thing.

ŌRÁTIŌ POPULÁRIS

Ángelus. Our prayer for this *capítulum* is the last prayer uttered in the *Ángelus*.

Grátiam tuam, quaésumus, Dómine,
  méntibus nostrīs īnfúnde;
ut quī, Ángelō nūntiánte, Christī Fíliī tuī
  incārnatiónem cognóvimus,
per passiónem eius et crucem ad
  resurrēctiónis glóriam perdūcámur.
Per eúmdem Christum Dóminum nostrum.

Pour forth your grace into our minds,
  we beseech you, Lord;
that we who, with the angel announcing,
  have known the incarnation of Christ
  your Son,
may be brought to the glory of his
  resurrection through his suffering
  and cross.
Through the same Christ our Lord.

EXERCÍTIA

Be sure to complete the *exercítium* in the appendix corresponding to this *capítulum*.

Capítulum XXV

PRESENT ACTIVE AND PASSIVE INFINITIVES; INDIRECT SPEECH; IMPERSONAL VERBS

Āctiṓnī contrā́riam semper et aequā́lem <u>esse</u> reāctiṓnem.[1]
—ISAAC NEWTON

OPÚSCULUM THEOLÓGICUM: *Isaac Newton and the Lēgēs Mōtūs*

Isaac Newton is one of the most important figures in the history of science. Born in England in 1642, he was buried at Westminster Abbey upon his death in 1727. Newton made seminal contributions to the fields of science, mathematics, mechanics, optics, and physics. Less known are his achievements and interest in theology. Raised an Anglican, Newton devoted significant time and energy to theological topics such as exegesis, textual criticism, philosophical theology, and church history. He published widely in these fields.

Newton's most famous work, however, was *Philosóphiae Nātūrā́lis Prīncípia Mathēmática*, "Mathematical Principles of Natural Philosophy," first published in 1687. It is often referred to as *Prīncípia*. This treatise was written during the height of the Scientific Revolution, when constant advances were being made in mathematics and science.

Newton's choice to pen this treatise in Latin was not coincidental. Although written in the late seventeenth century, Latin still provided the most immediate and widespread medium to disseminate important ideas internationally.

Some of the most long-lasting principles emerging from Newton's treatise were his *lēgēs mōtūs*, "laws of motion."[2] Newton's three laws of motion appear below in their original form:

| Lēx I. Corpus omne <u>persevērā́re</u> in statū suō quiēscéndī vel movéndī ūnifórmiter in dirḗctum, nisi quátenus ā vī́ribus imprḗssīs cṓgitur statum illum <u>mūtā́re</u>. | Law 1: Every object <u>continues</u> in its own state of rest or of uniform motion in a straight line unless it is compelled <u>to change</u> that state by the forces applied to it. |

---

1. "For every action, there <u>is</u> always an equal reaction."
2. Isaac Newton, *Philosóphiae Nātūrā́lis Prīncípia Mathēmática* (London: Societatis Regiae, 1686), 16. All quotes below come from this page.

This axiomatic law, often called "the law of inertia," states that an object will continue at rest or in motion until something else, whether air or an object, gets in its way.

Lēx II. Mūtātiṓnem mōtūs prōportiōnā́lem esse vī mṓtricī imprḗssae, et fíerī secúndum líneam rēctam quā vīs illa imprímitur.	Law 2: The change of motion is proportional to the motive force applied, and it is made in the direction of the straight line by which that force is applied.

This second law speaks of the force that alters the course of an object. There is constant velocity without the application of force.

Lēx III. Āctiṓnī contrā́riam semper et aequā́lem esse reāctiṓnem: sī́ve corpórum duṓrum āctiṓnēs in sē mū́tuō semper esse aequā́lēs et in partēs contrā́riās dī́rigī.	Law 3: For every action, there is always an equal and opposite reaction; or the mutual actions of two objects upon themselves are always equal and are set in opposite directions.

This final law asserts that whatever presses upon an object must itself also be pressed upon. The force applied is equal to the force received.

Altogether, Newton's *lēgēs mōtūs* have been the subject of continuous study since their debut in 1687, and they have provided a scientific foundation for the field of classical mechanics, which analyzes how objects move. Our purpose in this book, however, is not to shed light on Newton's scientific achievements, but to allow his use of language to help us better understand Latin. Curiously, every one of Newton's laws of motion contained at least one infinitive, which is a type of verbal noun that constitutes the "dictionary" form of a verb. Newton's use of infinitives is intriguing, almost like adding a timeless component to his theories. In this *capítulum*, we will be introduced to these verbal nouns.

> **Prospéctus**
> In this *capítulum* you will learn that:
> - Infinitives are verbal nouns.
> - There are six infinitives: two in the present, two in the past, and two in the future.
> - The present active infinitive normally ends in -re, while the present passive infinitive normally ends in -ī.
> - The infinitive is used in a variety of ways, including as a complementary infinitive and to report indirect speech.
> - Impersonal verbs do not conjugate like "regular" verbs; they assume an impersonal "it" as their subjects.

GRAMMÁTICA

25.1 Infinitives: The Other Verbal Noun. We have previously learned that gerunds are verbal nouns. This is still true. However, there also exists another class of verbal noun in Latin.[3] No offense

---

[3]. However, some grammarians consider infinitives to be the "nominative" form of gerunds, as I mentioned in our discussion of gerunds.

to gerunds, but I think you will like these verbal nouns much better. As verbs, most infinitives contain a subject (whether explicit or implicit), sometimes an object, and always tense and voice. They are also modified by adverbs (rather than adjectives). Infinitives are not conjugated in the same way that regular "finite" verbs are. On the contrary, deriving from the adjective *īnfīnítus*, "unlimited" or "boundless," infinitives are unbounded in that they have no person and no number. They are not yoked to the same conjugation rules as normal finite verbs. As nouns, infinitives may serve as the subject or object of a sentence. The subject of an infinitive is in the accusative case (rather than the nominative case, as we might assume).

Because infinitives do not undergo the same degree of change as finite verbs, grammarians have historically deployed them as the "dictionary" forms of individual verbs. This practice, however, is not universal; many dictionaries prefer to use the first-person singular of the present active indicative of a verb. Whatever the case, you will encounter infinitives often, and you will quickly become accustomed to their distinct -re and -ī endings (for the present active and passive forms, respectively).

25.2 **Time Significance of Infinitives.** Because infinitives are verbs, they possess tense. In traditional terminology, infinitives occur in the past, present, and future tenses. However, as we have discussed elsewhere, particularly with participles, it is oftentimes best to think of the present as indicating action *contemporaneous* with the main verb, perfect as indicating action *prior* to the main verb, and future as indicating action *subsequent* to it.

25.3 **2 Present + 2 Past + 2 Future = 6 Forms.** Altogether, there are six different kinds of infinitives. This entails two in the present, two in the perfect, and two in the future. Each tense contains both an active and passive voice. There is no imperfect, no pluperfect, and no future perfect. We will learn the present infinitives in this *capitulum* and the other two (perfect and future) in the following.

PRESENT ACTIVE INFINITIVES

25.4 **Present Active Infinitive: Contemporaneous Aspect.** This tense and voice indicate action contemporaneous with the main (finite) verb and action that the subject performs. It is customarily translated as "to-": "to love," "to warn," "to show," "to hear," etc.

25.5 **Forming the Present Active Infinitive.** It is easy to form the present active infinitive. Ready? Find the second principal part. Bingo! Task complete. Because the second principal part is the present active infinitive, there is nothing really to learn. You already know these forms.

Step to Form Present Active Infinitives
1. Locate the second principal part (e.g., *laudáre*). This is the present active infinitive.

However, if you would still like the ten-*dēnáriī* tour, here is a more detailed explanation of how you generate the present active infinitive: Add the -re ending to a verb's present stem. When that stem is combined with the thematic vowels of the four conjugations (-ā, -ē, -ĕ, and -ī), you will get -āre, -ēre, -ĕre, and -īre, respectively. And, as we know by now, three of these will receive the stress on the infinitival ending itself, which is why I often add both the accent mark and the macron to make this explicit: -áre, -ére, -íre. (As usual, that wily third-conjugation verb is our outlier: -ere, which has no accent mark and no macron.)

The one major exception to the infinitive endings is the most important verb of all in Latin: *sum, esse, fuī, futūrus*. However, we have encountered it so often that you have already memorized the infinitive as *esse*. This is old news by now. (And, by the way, as you should also know, there is no passive form of "to be." It is always active.)

Below are the "regular" forms of the present active infinitive.

PRESENT ACTIVE INFINITIVE FORMS: ALL FOUR CONJUGATIONS

Verb Conjugation	Infinitive Form	Translation
(Long) ARE (1)	amā́re	to love
Long ERE (2)	monḗre	to warn
Short ERE (3)	osténdere	to show
(Long) IRE (4)	audī́re	to hear

25.6 **How Infinitives Work.** Infinitives are used in a variety of ways. We will not discuss every possible usage. However, I am providing below six common ways that infinitives may be used in Latin. Each example comes from Tertullian.

1. **Subject of Sentence.** This is when the infinitive is simply serving as the subject of a sentence. If there is an accompanying adjective that modifies the subject infinitive, it will have a nominative singular ending. *Bonum est spērā́re in Dóminum quam spērā́re in prī́ncipēs.*[4] "To hope in the Lord is better than to hope in rulers."

2. **Complementary Infinitive.** This is when the infinitive acts as a complement to a particular verb. *Habḗre enim fī́lium dḗbeō ut pater sim.*[5] "For I ought to have a son if I am a father." Here the verb *dḗbeō* requires the help of an infinitive to complete its meaning.

3. **Object Infinitive.** This is when the infinitive explains something. *Nḗmō enim ante voluísset ōrā́re nōsse, quam didicísset quem ōrā́ret.*[6] "For no one would have wanted to learn how to pray before knowing to whom to pray."

4. **Impersonal Verb.** The impersonal verb[7] usually has an accusative and infinitive as its subject. *Ítaque audiéntēs optā́re īntīnctiṓnem, nōn praesū́mere opórtet.*[8] "Therefore, catechumens ought to wish for baptism, but it is not becoming [for them] to presume [baptism]."

5. **Taking an Object.** This is when the infinitive takes on an object of some kind. *Excíderat illī, cum ūnivérsa nāscī jubḗret, purpúreās et coccíneās ovēs mandā́re.*[9] "It had escaped [God], when he was ordering the universes to be born, to command [the creation of] purple and scarlet sheep."

6. **Indirect Statement.** This is when the infinitive takes a subject. When it does so, the subject will be in the accusative case. *Hoc est ergō quod dīcō, ejus Deī fidem esse, cujus est fōrma grātiae fídeī.*[10] "This, therefore, is what I say: that it is that faith in God which prefigured the grace of faith."[11]

---

4. Tertullian, *Advérsus Mārciṓnem* IV.15 (PL 2.394). This quote comes from Psalm CXVIII.9.
5. Tertullian, *Advérsus Práxeam* X (PL 2.165).
6. Tertullian, *Advérsus Mārciṓnem* IV.26 (PL 2.425).
7. We will discuss impersonal verbs below.
8. Tertullian, *Liber dē Poeniténtiā* VII (PL 1.1239–1240).
9. Tertullian, *Dē Cūltū Feminā́rum* II.10 (PL 1.1327).
10. Tertullian, *Advérsus Mārciṓnem* V.3 (PL 475).
11. This is a tricky sentence to translate. I have chosen to translate it in such a way as to highlight how the infinitive is used along with an accusative acting as the subject. Below I will provide another example.

PRESENT PASSIVE INFINITIVES

25.7 Present Passive Infinitive. Everything above applies to passive infinitives. There are only two differences. First, passives are, of course, passive in voice. They are acted upon rather than acting on something. Second, the passive infinitive has a slightly different ending than the active voice. The characteristic ending for passive infinitives is -ī. How do you get this -ī ending? For regular verbs in the first, second, and fourth conjugations, you simply change the -e ending to -ī. That is it. For the third conjugation, however, there is one more step involved: Remove the stem vowel and -re ending of the present active infinitive and then change the -e ending to -ī. For regular verbs other than the third conjugation, you will quickly become accustomed to the -ārī, -ērī, and -īrī endings, which naturally look like this with the accent mark and macron added: -ā́rī, -ḗrī, and -ī́rī. For the third conjugation, be sure not to confuse it with the third-person singular of the perfect active indicative.

Steps to Form Present Passive Infinitives
1. Locate the second principal part (e.g., *laudā́re*).
2. Change the -e ending to -ī (e.g., *laudā́re* → *laudā́rī*) if the verb is in the first, second, or fourth conjugations.
3. If the verb is in the third conjugation (e.g., *dī́cere*), remove both the stem vowel and the -re ending (e.g., *dī́c-*) and then add -ī (e.g., *dī́cī*).

PRESENT PASSIVE INFINITIVE FORMS: ALL FOUR CONJUGATIONS

Verb Conjugation	Infinitive Form	Translation
(Long) ARE (1)	amā́rī	to be loved
Long ERE (2)	monḗrī	to be warned
Short ERE (3)	osténdī	to be shown
(Long) IRE (4)	audī́rī	to be heard

25.8 Possible Confusion with Gerundive. You may have noted that our English translation of the passive infinitive ("to be -ed") is similar to our suggested translation of the gerundive (otherwise known as the future passive participle). This is true. Unfortunately, we sometimes translate both the same way. However, in terms of grammatical function in Latin, they are quite distinct. Although both are verbs—participles are verbal <u>adjectives</u> while infinitives are verbal <u>nouns</u>—they maintain different roles in Latin and are not linguistically transferable in that language.

Let us look at an example of a present passive infinitive:

Nūlla ars <u>docḗrī</u> praesū́mitur, nisi inténta prius meditātiṓne discā́tur. (Gregory I)[12]

No art is presumed <u>to be taught</u> unless it is first learned through serious meditation.

INDIRECT SPEECH

25.9 Indirect Speech vs. Direct Speech. Although we briefly discussed the concept of "indirect speech" above, it is worth revisiting. By now, it is well ingrained in our thinking that the subject

---
12. Gregory I, *Rḗgulae Pāstōrā́lis Liber* I.1 (PL 77.14).

occurs in the nominative case and the verb describing it is finite, that is, conjugated. This is often the case. It is so standard, in fact, that grammarians refer to it as "direct speech" (or "right speech"). The opposite is "indirect speech." That is what we will discuss now.

25.10 Slight Change in the Rules. As you may remember above, indirect speech causes the subject to change to the accusative case and for the finite verb to flex to the infinitive. These changes are as universal as they are common, so it is important to remember this slight change.

Let us look at an example of indirect speech.

Propter eōs quíppe disputátiō illa suscépta est, quī negant, ex líberō voluntátis arbítriō malī oríginem dúcī, et Deum, sī ita est, creātórem ómnium nātūrárum culpándum esse conténdunt. (Augustine of Hippo)[13]	Of course this disputation was taken up because of persons who deny that the source of evil is derived from free choice of the will and who contend that God, if this is true, is culpable as the creator of all natures.

There are four points to make here. First, we see that indirect speech elicits (a) the subject (which we would expect to be in the nominative case) to be put in the accusative case and (b) for the finite verb to be made into an infinitive. Because there are two examples of indirect speech in this sentence, we see this phenomenon twice: *oríginem* (our subject) and *dúcī* (our verb); and then *Deum* (our next subject) and *esse* (our verb). Second, it makes no difference whether the infinitive is active or passive; or present, past, or future. Indirect speech will occur in any of these voices or tenses.[14] Third, indirect speech is sometimes translated in English with a subordinating conjunction and the word "that," or by only using the word "that." Finally, I have also underlined the two words that introduce the indirect speech: *negant* and *conténdunt*. As it turns out, there are a whole host of Latin verbs that elicit indirect speech.

Essentially, any verb related to saying, perceiving, thinking, and knowing can trigger indirect speech. After all, the Latin word *ōrátiō* implies each of these concepts and can be translated in many ways: "speech," "discourse," sentence," "message," "prayer," "address," and "sentiment." The whole notion of indirect speech has to do with relaying some other person's thoughts, feelings, ideas, or perceptions. Grammatically, indirect speech functions as a noun clause.

SAMPLE VERBS PROMPTING INDIRECT SPEECH

Category	Sample Verbs
Saying	āit, árguō, conténdō, dīcō, dóceō, éxplicō, opínor, osténdō, negō, respóndeō, scrībō
Perceiving	aúdiō, gaúdeō, séntiō, spḗrō, vídeō
Thinking	árbitror, cṓgitō, crēdō, hábeō, putō
Knowing	discō, intélligō, nésciō, sciō

So, how exactly do you turn direct speech into indirect speech? It is actually quite straightforward.

---

13. Augustine of Hippo, *Retractiónum* I.9.2 (PL 32.595).
14. And, in fact, there is an exact science on how tenses work with indirect speech. We will not go into that detail in this grammar, but I encourage interested readers to find an advanced Latin grammar that explains these concepts.

Steps to Convert "Direct Speech" into "Indirect Speech"
1. A verb having to do with saying, perceiving, thinking, knowing, etc., introduces a statement, triggering the use of indirect speech afterward.
2. We change the subject (normally in the nominative case) to the accusative case.
3. We change the verb (normally a finite verb) into an infinitive.

IMPERSONAL VERBS

25.11 Impersonal Verbs. In addition to indirect speech, I also briefly mentioned impersonal verbs when speaking about infinitives. Although they can be conjugated like regular verbs, you will usually see them appear in the third person. Often a good way to translate an impersonal verb is with "it" as its implied subject (although context must always shape our translations). As we will see below, impersonal verbs were significant verbs for scholastic theologians, for they allowed precision of thought without clutter or emotion. You encounter them often when reading theological writings.

25.12 Impersonal Verbs and Infinitives. Impersonal verbs are close friends with infinitives, which do not conjugate like finite verbs. When these two verbal forms join forces, the infinitive is used as the subject. Some of the most common impersonal verbs that also occur frequently with infinitives are:

- *áccidit*, "it happens"
- *cōnstat*, "it is agreed," "it costs"
- *decet*, "it is becoming," "it is proper"
- *évenit*, "it results"
- *ínterest*, "it concerns"
- *libet*, "it pleases"
- *licet*, "it is allowed," "it is permitted"
- *necésse est*, "it is necessary"
- *opórtet*, "it is fitting"
- *opus est*, "there is need"
- *placet*, "it pleases"
- *restat*, "it remains"
- *relínquitur*, "it remains"
- *vidḗtur*, "it seems"

Let us observe an example:

Ad castitátis quoque decórum <u>necésse est attíngere</u> per jējūniórum et vigiliárum labórem. (Sicard of Cremona)[15]

<u>It is necessary</u> also <u>to approach</u> the propriety of chastity through the work of fasting and vigils.

25.13 *Vidḗtur* **in Thomas Aquinas.** As we learned in Capítulum XXI, Thomas Aquinas wrote one of the most famous theological treatises in Christianity titled *Summa Theológiae*. This text was organized in a very methodical way. In the first part of any theological question, Thomas

---

15. Sicard of Cremona, *Mitrále* II.8 (PL 213.85).

typically made a theological query by means of objections with the impersonal verb *vidétur*, "it seems," before proceeding to his responses. The constancy of this approach provides a steady rhythm to the book.

Here is an example from the very first question from this massive work, which also features the use of an infinitive.

<u>Vidétur</u> quod nōn sit necessárium, praeter philosóphicās disciplínās, áliam doctrínam habérī. (Thomas Aquinas)[16]	<u>It seems</u> that it is not necessary for any doctrine besides philosophical teachings to be held.

The use of the impersonal verb here, *vidētur*, allows theologians like Thomas to make generic assertions, which he can later qualify when speaking about specific biblical passages and authors. When reading through theological or philosophical writings in Latin, observe how authors make use of impersonal verbs like *vidētur*.

Summárium

In this *capítulum* you learned that:
- Infinitives are verbal nouns.
- There are six infinitives in Latin: two in the present, two in the past, and two in the future.
- The present active infinitive ends in -re; the present passive infinitive ends in -ī.
- The infinitive is used in many different ways, the stock translation of which is "to-" in the active and "to be -ed" in the passive.
- Impersonal verbs are third-person singular verbs with an implied "it" as the subject.

VOCĀBULŌRUM INDEX

Notā Bene: This *capítulum* includes a large list of impersonal verbs. Although many of these verbs can conjugate quite regularly (and thus adopt first-, second-, third-, or fourth-conjugation endings),[17] impersonal verbs appear most frequently in the third-person singular and have an implied "it" as its subject. In the vocabulary list, impersonal verbs will be followed with a parenthesis and an abbreviation of "impersonal" (impers). Some impersonal verbs will have limited principal parts; if they do, it will be the third-person singular present active indicative, the present active infinitive, and the third-person perfect active indicative. Others will have no principal parts.

Latin	English (Gloss)	(Etymology)
áccidit, accídere, accídit (impers)	it happens	
árguō, argúere, árguī, argútus (3)[a]	to assert, to declare, to accuse	(argue)
conténdō, conténdere, conténdī, conténtus (3)	to strive, to assert, to contend	(contend)

---

16. Thomas Aquinas, *Summa Theológiae* I.1.1
17. For example, you could list *évenit* as a regular verb: *ēvéniō, ēvenīre, ēvénī, ēvéntus* (4). Many dictionaries do, but I prefer to classify it as an impersonal verb.

PRESENT ACT. AND PASS. INFINITIVES; INDIRECT SPEECH; IMPERS. VERBS

cōnstat (impers)	it is agreed, it costs	(constant)
decet, decḗre, décuit (impers)	it is becoming, it is proper	(decent)
disséntiō, dissentī́re, dissḗnsī, dissḗnsus (4)	to dissent, to differ	(dissent)
évenit, ēvenī́re, ēvénit (impers)[b]	it results	(event)
ínterest (impers)	it concerns	(interest)
iūstíficō, iūstificā́re, iūstificā́vī, iūstificā́tus (1)	to make righteous, to justify	(justify)
libet, libḗre, líbuit (impers)	it pleases	
licet, licḗre, lícuit (impers)	it is allowed, it is permitted	(leisure)
métior, mētī́rī, mēnsus sum (4)[c]	to measure, to distribute	
necésse est (impers)	it is necessary	(necessary)
númerō, numerā́re, numerā́vī, numerā́tus (1)	to count, to number, to reckon	(numerous)
ófferō, oférre, óbtūlī, oblā́tus (3)	to present, to offer, to sacrifice	(offer)
opī́nor, opinā́rī, opinā́tus sum	to suppose, to deem, to think	(opinion)
opórtet (impers)	it is fitting	
opus est (impers)	there is need	
placet (impers)	it pleases	(placebo)
praesū́mō, praesū́mere, praesū́mpsī, praesū́mptus	to presume, to take for granted	(presume)
ratiócinor, ratiōcinā́rī, ratiōcinā́tus sum (1)	to reckon, to consider, to compute, to argue	
restat (impers)	it remains	
relínquitur (impers)	it remains	(relinquish)
spḗrō, spērā́re, spērā́vī, spērā́tus (1)	to hope, to expect, to await	(desperate)
vidḗtur (impers)[d]	it seems	(video)

[a] You may also see the fourth principal part listed as *argúitus*.

[b] Correct, the present and perfect are identical here except for the accent mark.

[c] You will also see the last principal part as *mētī́tus sum*.

[d] Yes, this is the third-person singular passive of the common verb *vídeō, vidḗre, vī́dī, vī́sus*, "to see." However, because *vidḗtur* appears so often, it is best to include it as an impersonal verb.

ŌRĀ́TIŌ POPULĀ́RIS

Āctus Cāritā́tis. Translated as "Act of Love" or "Act of Charity," this short prayer is a favorite in the Catholic tradition. You will notice its aim to put into practice Christ's instruction to love both God and one's neighbor.

Dómine Deus,	Lord God,
amō tē super ómnia	I love you above all things
et próximum meum propter tē,	And I love my neighbor on account of you
quia tū es summum,	Because you are the highest,
īnfīnítum et perfectíssimum bonum,	Boundless, and most perfect good,
omnī dīlēctiṓne dignum.	Worthy of all love.
In hāc cāritā́te vī́vere et morī státuō.	In this love I intend to live and to die.
Āmēn.	Amen.

EXERCÍTIA

Be sure to complete the *exercítium* in the appendix corresponding to this *capítulum*.

Capítulum
XXVI

PERFECT AND FUTURE INFINITIVES AND MORE ABOUT INDIRECT SPEECH

Hīc habitásse prius sānctōs cognóscere dēbēs
nómina quisque Petrī páriter Paulíque requíris.[1]
—DAMASUS I

OPÚSCULUM THEOLÓGICUM: *Epitaphs*

Thus far in this book, we have focused on Latin originating from literary documents. This makes sense since most of us are seeking to learn Latin in order to read ancients texts—whether hymns, theological treatises, historical narratives, ancient manuals, or devotional writings. But one of the benefits of learning this magnificent language is that we will be empowered to read Latin in any place we may find it—whether inscribed on a church ceiling, carved on an artifact, or engraved on a tombstone.

This last example provides more examples of Latin than you might think. Death, after all, is a universal concept, applying to all people and all places. People in the ancient world were just as preoccupied with it as we are today, particularly since they generally had shorter life expectancies. In fact, Christians were especially prone to think about death since, unlike most other religions, the entire Christian faith is predicated upon the death of its founder Jesus Christ. "Of all religions," writes one historian, "Christianity is the one most concerned with dead bodies."[2]

And with dead bodies come written memories. Epitaphs, coming from the Greek word "relating to a funeral," were commemorations of the deceased in the form of eulogies, inscriptions, poems, and short orations. They were often engraved on or near tombstones. Thousands of epitaphs have survived from the ancient world. Many are located in Italy. Of the thousands in existence, I will include two. The first appears in its original form in all upper case letters before I then list the letters in lower case for ease of understanding:

PRESBYTER HIC SITVS EST CELERINVS NOMINE DIC[TVS] CORPOREOS RVMPENS NEXVS
QVI GAVDET IN ASTRIS

---

1. "Each of you seeking the names of Peter together with Paul must recognize that these saints formerly dwelt here."
2. Robert Bartlett, *Why Can the Dead Do Such Great Things?: Saints and Worshippers from the Martyrs to the Reformation* (Princeton: Princeton University Press, 2013), 3.

Présbyter hīc situs est Celerínus nómine dictus	Here was laid an elder called by the name Celerinus.
Corpóreōs rumpēns nexus quī gaudet in astrīs.³	Who, breaking the bodily bonds, rejoices in the stars.

This epitaph was engraved on a tombstone in Rome in the year 381, the same year of the renowned Council of Constantinople.

The second epitaph, also located in Rome, dates to the same time period. It eulogizes the two mightiest pillars of the early church, Peter and Paul, both of whom died as martyrs in Rome in the 60s AD. Like the first epitaph, the dead in Christ are understood to be in the "stars."

Hīc <u>habitásse</u> prius sānctōs cognóscere dēbēs	Each of you seeking the names of Peter together with Paul
nómina quisque Petrī páriter Paulíque requíris	Must recognize that these saints formerly <u>dwelt</u> here.
discípulōs óriēns misit quod sponte fatémur	That the East sent the disciples we willingly confess.
sánguinīs ob méritum Christúmque per astra secútī	In virtue of their blood seeking to follow Christ through the stars
aethériōs petiére sinūs rēgnáque piórum	They sought the heavenly hearts and kingdoms of the saints.
Rōma suōs pótius méruit defénderre cīvēs	Rome has deserved to preserve them as its citizens.
haec Damásus vestrās réferat nova sídera laudēs.⁴	May Damasus relate these things to your praises, you new stars!

This epitaph contains seven hexameters in Latin, which is why we have had to rearrange the words in English translation. (In meter, what is most important is how many feet per line, not word order.⁵) As mentioned above, what unites these two epitaphs is not only the celebration of the death of Christian leaders, but also their current location in the stars—with even Peter and Paul being referred to as "new stars."

From a grammatical perspective, this second epitaph introduces us to a new form: the perfect infinitive, traditionally translated as "to have -ed," but, in practice, it is an infinitive that is often translated as a finite perfect verb. As we learned in the previous *capítulum*, infinitives occur in one of three tenses: present, perfect, and future. In this *capítulum*, we will learn how infinitives function in the perfect and future tenses.

Prospéctus

In this *capítulum* you will learn that:
- There are two more tenses of Latin infinitives to learn: perfect (active and passive) and future (active and passive). These infinitives will function in a similar way to present (active and passive) infinitives.
- Indirect speech plays an important part in Latin. Indirect speech uses all the infinitive tenses.

---

3. Matthew Hartnett, *By Roman Hands: Inscriptions and Graffiti for Students of Latin*, 2nd ed. (Indianapolis: Focus, 2012), 58.
4. Tyler Lansford, *The Latin Inscriptions of Rome: A Walking Guide* (Baltimore: John Hopkins University Press, 2009), 214.
5. For a primer on Latin metrics, see Renato Oniga, *Latin: A Linguistic Introduction* (Oxford: Oxford University Press, 2014), 32–38.

PERFECT AND FUTURE INFINITIVES AND MORE ABOUT INDIRECT SPEECH

GRAMMÁTICA

26.1 Perfect and Future Infinitives. If you enjoyed learning about infinitives in the previous *capítulum*, you are in luck. This *capítulum* resumes our discussion. You will remember that infinitives appear in six forms: two in the present, two in the past (specifically the perfect), and two in the future, each tense containing both an active and passive voice. Because infinitives involve many other grammatical concepts—such as indirect speech and impersonal verbs—we limited our discussion in the previous *capítulum* to present infinitives. Now we turn to the past and future tenses. Each of these forms, other than the perfect active, are compound forms. This means not only that two words are required to complete the meaning rather than just one, but also that these forms signal double the fun.

26.2 Infinitives Always = Verbal Nouns. There is one more point to make about infinitives. Everything that we learned in the previous *capítulum* applies in our discussion below. For instance, regardless of the particular tense, infinitives are still used in a variety of ways. Nothing changes just because we move from the present tense to the perfect or future. An infinitive is still an infinitive, that is to say, it is still a verbal noun. And as a verbal noun, it exercises both verbal and substantival (or noun-like) characteristics across tense and voice.

26.3 Perfect Active Infinitive = Infinitive's Only Past Tense. The infinitive only has one past tense: the perfect. There is no imperfect or pluperfect. As we know, the perfect tense indicates completed or finished aspect. We translate it into English with the helping verb "to have . . ." When this completed aspect is combined with an infinitive, our stock translation is perfectly predictable: "to have -ed."

We are already thoroughly familiar with how the perfect base is formed. There are only three steps to follow with the perfect active infinitive.

Steps to Form Perfect Active Infinitives
1. Locate a verb's third principal part (e.g., *laudā́vī*).
2. Remove the -ī at the end of the third principal part (e.g., *laudā́vī̵*), thus isolating the perfect tense's stem (**laudā́v*).
3. Add the distinct personal ending of the present active infinitive, which is -ísse (e.g., *laudāvísse*).

26.4 Characteristic Ending of the Perfect Active Infinitive: -Vísse (or -Ísse). The characteristic -[v]ísse ending is a dead giveaway for the present active infinitive. When you see a word ending with this letter combination, you should assume it to be a present active infinitive—unless it has additional endings, in which case it is a pluperfect active subjunctive. There is, however, one caveat: As we learned in Capítulum XVII, the perfect tense is often syncopated, or "shortened." In such instances, it is the -vī or -v that is dropped. This -ísse ending is not as noticeable as -vísse, but it still makes for a distinct verbal ending.

There should be no surprises in the forms listed. Do not be concerned that the endings do not perfectly end in -āvísse, -ēvísse, -ĕvísse, and -īvísse, respectively. As we know, the third principal part can sometimes stray from the pack of regular verbs, especially in the second and third conjugations. However, this presents no problem at all since we always memorize a verb's principal parts.

You may have noticed the accent over the last -i in each example. Because the -i ending is long by position (though not by nature), it receives the accent mark but no macron. Furthermore, as explained above, we should not always expect the -vī or -v to be present in this formation. Sometimes it is, sometimes it is not. Many verbs, in fact, only use the -ísse ending, including some of the most important verbs in Latin:

- *fuísse* (from *sum, esse, fuī, futūrus*), "to have been," "to have existed"
- *potuísse* (from *possum, posse, pótuī*), "to have been able"
- *voluísse* (from *volō, velle, vólui*), "to have wished," "to have willed," "to have wanted"

PERFECT ACTIVE INFINITIVE: ALL FOUR CONJUGATIONS

Verb Conjugation (Present Active Infinitive)	Perfect Active Infinitive	Translation
(Long) ARE (amā́re)	amāvísse	to have loved
Long ERE (monḗre)	monuísse	to have warned
Short ERE (osténdere)	ostendísse	to have shown
(Long) IRE (audī́re)	audīvísse	to have heard

Let us look at an example of a perfect active infinitive:

Péssimum sermṓnem dīcit <u>audīvísse</u> pópulum, hoc est, crūdēlíssimum atque moestíssimum. (Glossa Ordinária)[6]	He says that the people <u>heard</u> a very bad sermon, that is, a very rude and somber one.

I have chosen to illustrate the perfect active infinitive with an example that does not allow for the regular "to have -ed" translation for two reasons. First, despite my recommendation to strive for the "to have -ed" translation, it is not always possible to translate the perfect active infinitive as such. Second, I want us to revisit the noun clause that appears frequently with the infinitive: indirect speech.

As you previously recall, indirect speech is prompted by a trigger word (namely, a verb indicating speech, feeling, perception, or thought). In the example above, that trigger word was *dīcit*. Its triggering of indirect speech prompted the subject to change to the accusative case (*pópulum*) and the finite verb to be put in an infinitive form (*audīvísse*). We need to continue our discussion of it from the previous *capítulum*.

26.5 **Indirect Speech and the Perfect Infinitive: More Explanation.** The perfect infinitive is used to report indirect speech in one of three ways: (1) prior time in the present, (2) prior time in the past, and (3) prior time in the future. In each instance, the infinitive will be in the perfect tense (active or passive), while the main verb will be in one of three tenses: (1) present, (2) past, or (3) future.

In the sentence illustrated above, the perfect infinitive was used to indicate *prior time in the present*, namely, that the time of indirect speech took place *prior* to that of the main verb. This is why *dīcit* was used—the indirect speech happened *beforehand*. Hence our translation was as follows: "He <u>says</u> [present tense] that the people <u>heard</u> [perfect tense] . . ." If you think about it, this construction makes sense.

---

6. Glossa Ordinária, *Éxodus* XXIII.4 (PL 113.288).

PERFECT AND FUTURE INFINITIVES AND MORE ABOUT INDIRECT SPEECH

If the main verb provided is changed to the past tense, this shift in tense indicates *prior time in the past*. Here is an example:

Ex iīs quae <u>dīximus</u> fácile patet píleōs Pontíficīs et Sacerdótum ex līnō <u>fuísse</u>. (Salomon Van Til)[7]	From these things <u>we have said</u> it is quite evident that the hats of both high priests and priests <u>were</u> of linen.

The shift from the present tense (in the example above) to the past (in this sentence) is seamless and exactly as we should expect. If the main verb were in the future tense (*dīcémus*), it would indicate *prior time in the future*, and our translation would change to: "From these things <u>we will say</u> . . . that the hats of both high priests and priests <u>were made</u> [or <u>will have been made</u>] from linen."

26.6 Final Thoughts. I have already stated the main point: Indirect speech alters the rules of sentence formation. Learn how to recognize and identify it when it happens. Because indirect speech occurs so frequently in Latin, you will begin seeing it everywhere. This is a good thing.

COMPOUND TENSES: *Forms with Two Parts*

26.7 Word Order and Word Presence: A Word to the Wise. When it comes to compound tenses, word order is flexible. We have witnessed this before with compound tenses. As we will learn with regard to perfect passive infinitives below, you will see the combination of *esse* + participle in different ways—right next to each other, or separated by several words. What is more, you may not even see *esse* at all! Remember that the "to be" verb in Latin does not like commitments; sometimes it shows up in a sentence, sometimes it does not. Either way, the translation is the exact same. We will have to keep these realities in mind in each of the compound tenses below. I have included the regular word order in the paradigms, but you may encounter the compound tense in a different order (again, without any change in meaning).

26.8 Perfect Passive Infinitive. As luck would have it, you are already familiar with this form. How so? When the perfect passive participle (only in the neuter singular) is combined with the present active infinitive of "to be"—*esse*—a new name magically appears: the perfect passive infinitive. Stated differently, the perfect passive infinitive is the present infinitive of *sum, esse, fuī, futūrus*—which is *esse*—in combination with the fourth principal part (the perfect passive participle). Naturally, this word combination makes the perfect passive infinitive a compound form.

26.9 Translating the Perfect Passive Infinitive. Our stock translation for the perfect passive infinitive is exactly as you should expect: "to have been -ed." This form indicates the completed aspect of the event (thus the "have" part), the passive voice (the "been" part), and the non-finite component (the "to-" part). Despite the simplicity of the forms, it is not always possible to translate perfect passive infinitives as "to have been -ed." As is always the case, context is king. Do your best to convey the perfect passive non-finite nature of the compound tense into English.

---

7. Salomon Van Til, *Commentārius dē Tabernāculō Mōsis* (Amsterdam, 1714), 8.

PERFECT PASSIVE INFINITIVES: ALL FOUR CONJUGATIONS

Verb Conjugation (Present Active Infinitive)	Perfect Passive Infinitive	Translation
(Long) ARE (amā́re)	amā́tus esse	to have been loved
Long ERE (monḗre)	mónitus esse	to have been warned
Short ERE (osténdere)	osténtus esse	to have been shown
(Long) IRE (audī́re)	audī́tus esse	to have been heard

Here is an example:

Sīmon quīdam magus, quī indū́xit novam haéresim, dīcēns sē esse virtū́tem coeléstem, et ūnivérsās quae sunt creātū́rās nōn esse ā Deō factās, sed ā virtū́te quādam supérnā; ideóque sē dēscendísse inquit, ut ovem salvā́ret pérditam, Christum autem apud Jūdaéōs nōn esse passum. (Isidore of Seville)[8]

There was a certain Simon the magician, who introduced a new heresy, saying that he was the heavenly power, and that all creatures which exist were not made by God, but by some celestial power; and therefore he said that he had descended to save the lost sheep, and that Christ had not suffered among the Jews.

There are two examples of the perfect passive infinitive here, both occurring in indirect speech. As we are used to expecting, it is not always possible to make use of our stock translation. Still, the construction is the same: *esse* + the fourth principal part (perfect passive participle). When translating, we have to do our best with respect to context. Also, hopefully you noticed that the second example is a deponent verb, that is, one with a passive form but active meaning.

26.10 The Last Tense: Future Infinitives. We now turn to the last tense of the infinitive: the future. As with each of the other infinitives, the future infinitive appears in the active and passive voices. And, like the perfect infinitives, both forms of the future are compound tenses. Hence, they contain two parts: the "to be" verb (*esse*) and a future participle. The only difference between them is the tense of the "to be" verb and the tense of the participle. Can you guess which voices go with what tenses?

26.11 Future Active Infinitives. The future active infinitive is simply the infinitive *esse* + future participle. Naturally enough, the exact tense and voice of the participle is future active. Stated differently, we form the future active infinitive by combining the future active participle with *esse*. You will remember that the future active participle is formed from the fourth principal part: Simply remove -us from the fourth principal part and add -ū́rus, -ū́ra, -ū́rum in accordance with 2-1-2 adjective endings.

26.12 Translating Future Active Infinitives. This kind of infinitive indicates something about to happen. Our stock translation is: "to be about to-."

---

8. Isidore of Seville, *Prolegómena* III.86.4 (PL 81.637).

FUTURE ACTIVE INFINITIVES: ALL FOUR CONJUGATIONS

Verb Conjugation (Present Active Infinitive)	Future Active	Translation
(Long) ARE (amáre)	amātúrus esse[a]	to be about to love
Long ERE (monére)	monitúrus esse	to be about to warn
Short ERE (osténdere)	ostentúrus esse	to be about to show
(Long) IRE (audíre)	audītúrus esse	to be about to hear

[a] Instead of *esse*, you may encounter the future active infinitive form *fore* instead. For more about *fore*, see the section below.

26.13 Future Passive Infinitives: Rare, Indeed. Let us start off in an unconventional way—first with a translation and then an explanation. Here is how you translate the future passive infinitive: "to be about to be -ed." This is a mouthful, even for a person who likes to talk a lot. Although it only amounts to two words in Latin, the Romans rarely used it. However, we will list the forms below in case you encounter one.

26.14 Translating Future Passive Infinitives. The formation and translation of the future passive infinitive is not complex, even though it is very uncommon. As a future tense, it indicates futurity, that is, something that is going to happen in the future. As a passive verb, it is receiving action rather than performing it. And as an infinitive, it is being used as a non-finite verbal noun. We form this compound tense with the future infinitive of "to be"—which is *fore*—in combination with the fourth principal part. Alternatively, instead of *fore*, you may encounter *īrī*—which is the present passive infinitive of the verb *eō, īre, īvī, ītus*.

26.15 Where Did You Get *Fore*? It is at this point that I have lost most of the room. We face several curve balls with the future passive infinitive, which is why many grammars do not even include it. It is not worth all the fuss. So, let us be terse in explaining what is going on. To begin with, we should expect that the "to be" verb is highly irregular. It does not play by the rules. In fact, in this instance, it has a card up its sleeve. Whereas we might expect *futúrus esse* to be the future active infinitive—and, indeed, it is—there is another form of the future active infinitive. Can you guess what it is? I will give you a clue: It is not *īrī*. Correct—it is *fore*. *Fore* is a different form of the future active infinitive of *sum, esse, fuī, futúrus*. If you think about it, this combination of perfect passive participle + future active infinitive is genius. I only wish I could have gotten credit for inventing such a verbally precise tour de force.

FUTURE PASSIVE INFINITIVES: ALL FOUR CONJUGATIONS

Verb Conjugation (Present Active Infinitive)	Infinitive Form	Translation
(Long) ARE (amáre)	amátus fore	to be about to be loved
Long ERE (monére)	mónitus fore	to be about to be warned
Short ERE (osténdere)	osténtus fore	to be about to be shown
(Long) IRE (audíre)	audítus fore	to be about to be heard

Here is a short example from the revered Archbishop of Canterbury, Thomas Becket:

<u>Salvum fore</u>. (Thomas Becket)[9] He is about to be safe.

Although we translate this sentence as if it is in the passive voice—"be safe"—it is in the active voice in Latin. We have encountered a similar phenomenon before.

Summārium

In this *capítulum* you learned that:
- Infinitives generally function the same way regardless of tense or voice.
- The perfect and future infinitives each contain an active and passive voice.
- Indirect speech occurs frequently in Latin. In it, the subject changes to the accusative case and the finite verb becomes an infinitive.
- Some infinitives are composed of compound tenses, which contain two parts working together.

VOCĀBULŌRUM INDEX

Latin	English (Gloss)	(Etymology)
accédō, accédere, accésī, accéssus (3)	to go to(ward), to approach	(access)
accū́sō, accūsā́re, accūsā́vī, accūsā́tus (1)	to accuse, to blame, to reproach	(accuse)
acquisī́tiō, acquisītiónis (f)	acquisition	(acquisition)
antī́quus, antī́qua, antī́quum	old, ancient; (plural) forefathers	(antique)
antístes, antístis (m)	bishop, overseer	
appropínquō, appropinquā́re, appropinquā́vī, appropinquā́tus (1) (+ dat)	to come near, to approach	(propinquity)
benedíctiō, beneditiónis (f)	blessing, benediction	(benediction)
cathólicus, cathólica, cathólicum	catholic, universal	(Catholic)
clārus, clāra, clārum	clear, famous, bright, renowned	(clarity)
calix, cálicis (m)	cup, chalice	(chalice)
cēdō, cédere, cessī, cessus (3)	to go, to proceed, to happen, to surrender	(accede)
cēnáculum, cēnáculī (n)	dining room, upper room	(cenacle)
cernō, cérnere, crēvī, crētus (3)	to discern, to distinguish, to separate, to see	(discern)
claudō, claúdere, clausī, clausus (3)	to close, to shut	(claustrophobic)
clērus, clērī (m)	clergy	(clergy)

---

9. Thomas Becket, *Epístola* CXXXVIII (PL 190.613).

cógitō, cōgitáre, cōgitávī, cōgitátus (1)	to think, to consider	(cogitate)
ocúrrō, occúrrere, ocúrrī, occúrsus (3)	to (go to) meet, to come to, to occur	(occur)
precor, precárī, precátus sum (1)	to pray, to ask, to beseech	(imprecatory)
prōcédō, prōcédere, prōcéssī, prōcéssus (3)	to advance, to proceed	(proceed)
salútō, salūtáre, salūtávī, salūtátus (1)	to preserve, to keep safe, to salute, to greet	(salutation)
sistō, sístere, stitī, status (3)	to stand, to cause to stand, to set, to place	(state)
vēndō, véndere, véndidī, vénditus (3)	to sell	(vendor)
vestígium, vestígiī (n)	footstep	(vestige)
únitās, ūnitátis (f)	unity, oneness	(unity)
vītis, vītis, vítium (f)	vine	(vise)

ŌRÁTIŌ POPULÁRIS

Catēchísmus Māior. The Westminster Confession of Faith is a historic confession used by Reformed and Presbyterian churches. It was drafted by the Westminster Assembly, which met over the course of several years in London, but which only published the *Cōnféssiō*, "Confession," in 1646. The Larger and Shorter Catechisms, designed together with the Confession, were completed in 1647. Below are the first two *quaestiōnēs*, "questions," (Q) and *respónsa*, "responses," (R) from the *Catēchísmus Māior*, "Larger Catechism."

Q: Quīnam est hóminis fīnis summus ac praecípuus?
R: Fīnis hóminis summus ac praecípuus est Deum glōrificáre, eōdémque perféctē fruī in aetérnum.

Question: What is the chief and highest end of humankind?
Response: The chief and highest end of humankind is to glorify God and enjoy him completely forever.

Q: Unde cōnstat esse Deum?
R: Ipssísimum in hómine nātúrae lūmen, operáque Deī esse Deum lūculénter maniféstant: sōlum antem ipsíus verbum Spīritúsque eum homínibus revélant sufficiénter ac efficáciter ad salútem.

Question: What indicates that there is a God?
Response: The very light of nature in humankind and the works of God plainly reveal that there is a God. But only his word and Spirit sufficiently and efficaciously reveal him to humankind for salvation.

EXERCÍTIA

Be sure to complete the *exercítium* in the appendix corresponding to this *capítulum*.

OCTĀVA PARS

GIVING COMMANDS

> We come now to the final section of the book. Congratulations! Here we will encounter the imperative mood. This is the mood of commands, orders, and directives. Its sole purpose is to order people to do things. Imperatives mostly occur in "positive" commands. To make "negative" commands, any Latin mood may be used: indicative, subjunctive, or imperative.
>
> By the time you finish this last section, you will have been exposed to all the major concepts that Latin has to offer. What is more, the constant reinforcement you will have gotten through prayers, sayings, exercises, supplementary materials, and ancient authors will give you the tools needed to read virtually any author or text in the Latin *corpus*. Great job!

Capítulum
XXVII

IMPERATIVES, PROHIBITIONS, AND VOCATIVES

Valē in Christō.[1]
—SIDONIUS APOLLINARIS

OPÚSCULUM THEOLÓGICUM: *Hildegard of Bingen's Epístolae*

Hildegard of Bingen was one of the most accomplished Christian women in the Middle Ages. Born in Germany in 1098, she was an abbess, visionary, administrator, author, music composer, natural philosopher, and teacher. As was common practice in the Middle Ages, Hildegard's parents offered her as an oblate (literally in Latin, an "offering") to a Benedictine monastery when she was a child with the result that all of her life was spent in service to God.

As early as she could remember, even before being offered as an oblate at a monastery, Hildegard had received *vīsiōnēs*, "visions." Reluctant to share them with the world, she only agreed to record her visions after receiving approval from the Catholic Church while in her forties. The series of books that resulted lay bare the revelations that Hildegard claimed to receive from the Lord over the course of many decades.

In addition to her books that recorded her visions, Hildegard was also a prolific letter writer. In fact, she penned more letters than most of her male contemporaries, exchanging letters with the most influential people in all of Western society: popes, archbishops, abbots, kings, and princes. These letters capture the full range of Hildegard's personality and disposition. Sometimes humble, sometimes bold, and always interesting, Hildegard was both deferential to the powers that were in place as well as eager to interject her opinions. We will look at two examples of her letters.

The first is Hildegard's earliest surviving letter. Written in 1147 to Bernard of Clairvaux, one of the most influential churchmen of the Catholic Church at this time (though he was never appointed pope), Hildegard requested permission to share her visions publicly. She began and ended the *epístola* as follows:

---

1. "Farewell in Christ" or "Be strong in Christ." Sidonious Apollinaris, "Epístula XIV," in *Epístolae et Carmína* (PL 58.585).

GIVING COMMANDS

In spíritū mystēriórum tibi dīcō, ō venerábilis Pater, quī mīrābíliter in magnīs honóribus virtū́tis Deī, valdē metuéndus es . . .	I say to you in the spirit of mysteries, venerable Father, who is wonderfully endowed with great honors in the character of God, you are to be greatly revered . . .
Sed ea in cor tuum pōne, ita ut nōn cessēs, tum tránseās per fōrmam ánimae tuae, ad Deum prō mē aspíciēns, quia ipse tē vult. Valē, valē in ánimā tuā, et estō rōbústus in certámine in Deō.[2]	But put these things in your heart, so that you do not cease to traverse through the form of your spirit, looking to God instead of me, because He himself desires you. Be strong, be strong in your spirit, and be mighty in the battle in God.

Despite the deference demonstrated in her letter to Bernard, Hildegard was not afraid to offer criticism and even stern rebuke. In her *epístola* to Pope Anastasius IV, in the year 1153, she minced no words.

Unde tū, ō homō, quī sedēs in prīncipā́lī cáthedra Dóminī, contémnis quandō malum amplécteris, ita quod illud nōn ábjicis, sed ōsculā́ris, quóniam ipsum sub siléntiō in prāvīs homínibus sústinēs. Et ídeō omnis terra turbā́tur per magnam vicissitū́dinem errórum, quia quod Deus dēstrū́xit, homō amat. Et tū, ō Rōma, velut in extrémīs jacēns, conturbā́beris ita.	So then you, man, who sits in the principal seat of the Lord, you show contempt when you disregard the evil that surrounds you. In fact, you not only ignore it but embrace it, for you support the evil in depraved men through your silence. And, as a result, all of the earth is in a whirlwind through a great alternation of errors, because humanity loves what God has destroyed. And you, Rome, lying on the brink of destruction, you will be thus thrown into confusion.
Tū autem, ō homō, ápparēns cōnstitū́tus pāstor, surge, et curre cítius ad jūstítiam.[3]	But you, man, who appear among us in the role of a shepherd, get up and run quickly toward righteousness.

These are powerful words uttered against one of the most powerful men in the Western world. There are many interesting historical features worthy of comment, but we will keep our eyes firmly fixed on the Latin. In both excerpts from Hildegard, we see at work three important grammatical features (which I have underlined) that often appear together: imperatives, prohibitions, and vocatives. Respectively, they issue commands, make prohibitions, and address persons. And fortunately for us, they will provide the focus of our final *capítulum* together.

Prospéctus

In this *capítulum* you will learn that:
- Imperatives issue commands to people and things. They mostly appear in the present imperative, but they can also be future.
- Prohibitions are effectively negative imperatives. They order people and things not to do something. There are three primary ways to form prohibitions.
- Vocatives are the case of direct address. Usually, they follow the same declension pattern as the nominative case.

---

2. Hildegard of Bingen, *Epístola* XXIX (PL 197.189–90).
3. Hildegard of Bingen, *Epístola* II (PL 197.152–53).

IMPERATIVES, PROHIBITIONS, AND VOCATIVES

GRAMMÁTICA

27.1 *Salvéte*! After spending an entire book together, it is only fitting that we learn how to officially greet one another. It is our last *capítulum*, after all. So, without further ado, *salvéte, sodálēs*, "welcome, comrades!" If you have ever taken Latin before, you are no doubt familiar with the word *salvéte*. In my Latin classes, it is actually the first word that I utter to students each time we come together. If I happen to arrive to class early and there is only one student in the room, all I need to do is adjust the verb from *salvéte* to *salvē*, which means the same thing but is used when only one person is addressed (and the singular vocative of the noun changes to *sodális*).

27.2 Imperatives and Vocatives. Believe it or not, the pleasantries that we just exchanged take us to the heart of our *capítulum últimum*, our "final chapter." The phrase *salvéte, sodálēs* contains two different kinds of words that are often paired together: imperatives and vocatives. I like to call imperatives "commando words," for they are a primary way that languages issue commands and give directives.

Related to the Latin verb *ímperō, imperáre, imperávī, imperátus*, "to command," the imperative is actually a mood unto itself. With a name like "command," you can already perceive that this is a pushy mood that takes no prisoners; it means business. In fact, in Roman society, the word *impérium* meant "right to power" or "absolute command." In short, a person with *impérium* yielded tremendous power to rule and, thus, to issue commands. Not surprisingly, the person with the greatest *impérium* in Rome was the emperor himself—whose Latin title was *imperátor*, the "commander-in-chief," the one with the greatest authority to give orders.

What does this have to do with "vocatives," a term that we learned in the very first *capítulum*? Quite a lot, actually. If you think about it, it is pretty difficult to give a command without addressing someone in particular. Even the *imperátor* was powerless until directly ordering someone to do something. And, as we will hopefully remember, the vocative is all about direct address. When Latin speakers speak directly to someone, they use the vocative case.

We will divide our *capítulum* into three sections: positive commands (imperatives), negative commands (prohibitions), and direct address (vocatives).

IMPERATIVES

27.3 Previous Encounters with Demanding Verbs. We have already encountered two sets of pushy verb formations in previous *capítula*. The first appeared during our discussion of the future active indicative tense. Perhaps you remember our examples from the *Decem Verba*, the "Ten Commandments." Most of the Ten Commandments issue commands by using future indicatives rather than imperative actives. The second example of commands comes from the subjunctive mood. One of the many usages of the subjunctive is to give commands. This feature of the subjunctive is called the "jussive" or "hortatory" subjunctive,[4] both of which words also mean "command" and "urge"—apparently the Romans really liked to order people around.[5] The jussive or hortatory subjunctive is the equivalent of saying "please" before giving a directive, and they are used in the first person and third person: e.g., "let me . . . ," "may she . . . ," or "that

---

4. Some grammarians use the term "jussive" subjunctive exclusively for third-person commands and "hortatory" subjunctive for first-person commands.

5. For those interested, "jussive" derives from the verb *iúbeō, iubére, iussī, iussus* (hence "jussive" in English), "to command." Meanwhile, the word "hortatory" is related to the deponent verb *hortor, hortári, hortátus sum*, "to exhort" or "to urge." We will memorize the first verb in the *vocābulórum index* for this *capítulum*; we have already learned the other verb.

they would . . ." Both of these non-imperative mood command forms will become important to our discussion when learning how to make so-called negative commands. In fact, because the subjunctive does such a great job giving commands in the first and third persons—that is, ordering ourselves and others not directly addressed—we will only discuss second-person (singular and plural) forms of imperatives in this *capítulum*. But here is the moral of the story: The subjunctive mood is used frequently to make positive commands and negative prohibitions—in the first person, second person, or third person.

27.4 *Modus Imperátīvus*: **The Real Deal.** As mentioned above, imperatives comprise their very own mood, making them the third and final mood that we will learn in Latin: (1) indicative, (2) subjunctive, and (3) imperative. The *modus imperátīvus*, "imperative mood," is the real deal when it comes to issuing commands. It is all about ordering people around. Indeed, the entire mood is literally focused on giving commands. In a word, using the imperative mood is the most direct way to make something happen. As such, it is a general's favorite form of speech. With the imperative, there are no if, ands, or buts; there is no ambiguity. When someone orders you to "listen," you listen; when they command you to "speak," you speak; and when they direct you to "leave," you leave.

27.5 **Imperatives: Two Tenses, Two Persons, Two Voices.** For all the reasons just mentioned, the imperative mood is the easiest mood to understand. It works in English the same way it does in Latin. In fact, the imperative is also the easiest mood to form. For our purposes, there are two tenses, two persons, and two voices: present and future, second-person singular and second-person plural, and active and passive.[6] The present imperative indicates immediate commands, while the future imperative is used to issue a command when there is a specific reference to future time. We will focus on the imperative mood used in the second person—the "you" (singular) and "you all" (plural) forms. Finally, as we know, the active voice entails the subject acting upon something; the passive involves the subject being acted upon by someone or something else.

27.6 **Positively Commanding.** There is one more component to the imperative to discuss. It is mostly (though not exclusively) used for "positive commands," that is, commands ordering someone to do something rather than NOT to do something. If you want to issue what grammarians call a "prohibition," there are more common moods available in Latin. For the sake of clarity, we will focus on imperatives—which are always "positive"—before then discussing how to make "negative" commands in Latin. (For "negative" commands, we will discuss three possible ways to form them.)

27.7 **Present Active Imperative.** We will begin with the present active imperative.[7] This is by far the most common kind of imperative that you will encounter. Forming the present active imperative could not be easier. It is simply the second principal part minus the -re. That is all. If you want to issue a command to more than one person, you simply append -te. And because imperatives are formed the same way regardless of conjugation type, there is no need to worry about different kinds of endings. The only real trouble caused by the present active imperative comes from the third conjugation. Because of its short -e (that is, -ĕ) stem vowel, it changes to -i when adding the

---

[6]. I write "for our purposes," because, as mentioned, the imperative can occur outside of the second-person singular and plural, but we will not discuss it in this book. It is rarer than the other forms we will discuss, and it is not usually difficult to recognize it when you see it.

[7]. One school of thought prefers to call the "present" imperative the "first" imperative. If you encounter that language, it still means the same thing.

-te to plural imperatives. Other than in the third conjugation, the accent mark will naturally fall on the long stem vowel directly before the -te, thus -ā́, -ḗ, and -ī́ for the other three conjugations.

Steps to Form Present Active Imperatives
1. Locate the second principal part (e.g., *laudā́re*).
2. Remove the -re (e.g., *laudā́re* → *laudā́*). Bingo, this is the present active imperative.
3. Add -te when wanting to order around more than one person (e.g., *laudā́te*).

PRESENT ACTIVE IMPERATIVE FORMS: ALL CONJUGATIONS

Present Active Infinitive (Verb Type)	Singular	Plural	Translation[a]
amā́re (1)	amā	amā́te	Love![b]
monḗre (2)	monē	monḗte	Warn!
osténdere (3)	osténde	osténdite	Show!
audī́re (4)	audī	audī́te	Listen!

[a] The translation will be the same in the singular and plural forms.

[b] We should not expect that all English translations of Latin imperatives will require an exclamation point. That will be decided by context. They are only inserted here to underscore their directive nature.

Let us look at an example:

Audī et discérne. (Odo of Tournai)[8]   Listen and discern.

Naturally, these are singular imperatives; but, if we wanted to make them plural, we would simply add -te (and change the last -e to -i for third-conjugation verbs). The translation would be the same.

For example:

Audī́te, ō prócerēs. (Ermoldus Nigellus)[9]   Listen, nobles!

FIVE IRREGULAR IMPERATIVES IN THE SINGULAR

The imperative mood is delightfully regular in its formation. However, there are always a few exceptions to the rules. You can guess the offenders—it's a Who's Who of the Third Conjugation. This includes the most common verbs in that irregular-prone conjugation family: *dī́cere*, *dū́cere*, *fácere*, and *ferre*. And, of course, the most irregular verb of all: *esse*. How are these different from "regular" imperatives? They do not contain a stem vowel, so the "irregularity" is quite minimal. What is more, the irregularity only occurs in the singular; in the plural, they are "regular" (though *es* becomes *este* in the plural and *fer* becomes *ferte*).[10]

---

8. Odo of Tournai, *Dē Peccātō Orīginālī* II (PL 160.279).
9. Ermoldus Nigellus, *Dē Rēbus Gestīs Ludovīcī Piī* II (PL 105.587).
10. You may be wondering why irregular verbs like *posse* and *velle* did not make the list. They actually do not occur in the imperative.

Present Active Infinitive	Singular Imperative	English Translation
Esse	es	Be!
Dícere	dīc	Tell!
Dúcere	dūc	Lead!
Fácere	fac	Make!
Ferre	fer	Bring!

Exémplum. Ádjuvā nōs, Dómine, et fac nōbíscum secúndum prōmissiónēs tuās. (Thomas Becket)[11]

Help us, sir, and do to us according to your promises.

27.8 **Present Passive Imperatives (and Deponents).** The passive imperative is just as easy to understand and form as the active. But instead of the active voice, we use the passive voice. This switch in voice provides a stock translation for the passive imperative as: "be -ed." The notable exception, of course, are deponents. Deponents are unchanged in the imperative mood; they are passive in form but should be translated active. Translate them the same way you would a present active imperative.

For instance, when little Samuel seeks to hear from God in I Samuel, he commands God as follows:

Lóquere, Dómine, quia audit servus tuus. (I Sam. III.10)

Speak, Lord, because your servant is listening.

Here, *lóquere* is a deponent verb, so we render its passive form as if it were in the active voice.

27.9 **Forming Present Passive Imperatives.** Forming the present passive imperative only involves one step. For singulars, simply locate the second-person singular present passive indicative (which often is identical to the present active infinitive). That is all. For plurals, locate the second-person plural present passive indicative. And that is it. Naturally, context is everything with these two forms, since they will always look exactly like another form.

Steps to Form Present Passive Imperatives: Singular and Plural
1. For singulars, locate the second-person singular present passive indicative (e.g., *laudāre*).[12] This is the same form as the passive imperative.
2. For plurals, locate the second-person plural present passive indicative (e.g., *laudāminī*). This is the same form as the passive imperative.

It will take some time getting used to these forms since both of them are shared by verbs in other tenses. This illustrates a rare inadequacy in the Latin language; it should be better able to distinguish imperatives from passive indicatives. If it turns out that the verb does not make sense translated one way, then remember that it could also be an imperative or a passive indicative.

---

11. Thomas Becket, *Epístola* X, in *Epístolae ad Alexándrum Pāpam* (PL 190.453).
12. You may remember that the present passive indicative has two forms in the singular: one that ends in -re and one that ends in -ris. For the imperative, we will use the one ending in -re, that is, the one looking like the present active infinitive.

PRESENT PASSIVE IMPERATIVE FORMS: ALL CONJUGATIONS

Present Active Infinitive (Verb Type)	Singular Imperative	Plural Imperative	Translation[a]
amā́re (1)	amā́re	amā́minī	Be loved!
monḗre (2)	monḗre	monḗminī	Be warned!
osténdere (3)	osténdere	ostendíminī	Be shown!
audī́re (4)	audī́re	audī́minī	Be heard!

[a] The translation will be the same in the singular and plural forms.

Below is an example:

Venī́te ergō et <u>congregā́minī</u>, et eā́mus ante sepúlcrum beā́tī virī, et invocḗmus nōmen Dóminī. (Stephen of Muret)[13]

Therefore, come and <u>be gathered</u>, and let us go before the grave of that blessed man and let us invoke the name of the Lord.

Here we have a few points to note. First, you surely saw the present active imperative *venī́te*. It was almost immediately followed by the present passive imperative *congregā́minī*. Although the form is the same as a present passive indicative, "you are gathered," context demands that we understand it is an imperative. In addition, did you notice that the final two verbs—*eā́mus* and *invocḗmus*—were being used as hortatory subjunctives? As mentioned previously, the subjunctive happily issues commands, especially in the first person (as in the examples here). Although *venī́te* and *congregā́minī* happen to be in the imperative mood while *eā́mus* and *invocḗmus* are in the subjunctive mood, they effectively operate on the same grammatical level—they are all issuing commands to do something: "come," "be gathered," "let us go," and "let us invoke." Because ordering people around is so much fun, every mood found a way to do so (though the imperative really came to specialize in it).

27.10 Future Imperatives.[14] Theoretically, the future imperative is designed to issue commands at a future time, which would ideally be paired with a word, for instance, like *crās*, "tomorrow." Practically, though, the difference in meaning between present and future imperatives is an aspect difficult to express in English. In fact, there are only a few verbs that even employ the future imperative form with regularity. As such, we will only include the most commonly used forms below.

27.11 Forming Future Imperatives: Active and Passive Voices. How do you form the future imperative? Effectively, you remove -re from the second principal part and then add -to: hence *laudā́tō* for "Praise!" And to make it plural, simply add -te to that ending: *laudātóte*. Although the future passive imperative exists, it is very rare and so we will not concern ourselves much with it. But if you would like to know how to form it, you simply add -r to the ending of the future singular active imperative. Thus, *laudā́tō* is converted to *laudā́tor*, "Be praised!" This is for the future singular passive imperative form, as you will likely never encounter a future passive plural imperative.

---

13. Stephen of Muret, *Vīta S. Stéphanī Grandimonténsis* III (PL 204.1050).
14. As you may have surmised, for those who like to call the "present" imperative a "first" imperative, they call this class of imperative a "second" imperative.

Steps to Form Future Active Imperatives: Singular and Plural
1. Locate the second principal part (e.g., *laudāre*).
2. Remove the -re (e.g., *laudā-*).
3. Add -tō (e.g., *laudātō*).
4. Add -te when wanting to order around more than one person (e.g., *laudātōte*).

FUTURE (ACTIVE) IMPERATIVE FORMS: MOST COMMON VERBS

Present Active Infinitive	Singular	Plural	Translation[a]
esse	estō	estōte	Be!
habēre	habētō	habētōte	Consider!
fácere	fácito	facitōte	Make! Do!
scīre	scītō	scītōte	Know!
mémini	meméntō	mementōte	Remember!

[a] The meaning will be the same in the singular and plural forms.

Let us look at an example:

Estō benévolus. (Martin Luther)[15]   Be kind.

PROHIBITIONS

27.12 Prohibitions: Issuing Negative Commands. What is the benefit of ordering someone to do something if you cannot also indicate what not to do? The switch from commanding to prohibiting is more involved than perhaps anticipated. You might think we simply preface the command with the word *nōn* (which indicates the indicative mood). Although this is technically possible, it is much more common to make prohibitions using either the imperative mood or the subjunctive mood.

(1) Nōlī / Nōlīte + Infinitive: Imperative Mood Prohibitions. Instead of *nōn* in the indicative mood, we use *nōlī* and *nōlīte* from the imperative mood + an infinitive. This is actually quite brilliant. Why so? Because *nōlī* and *nōlīte* are themselves imperatives. Coming from the verb *nōlō, nōlle, nōluī*, "to be unwilling," "to not want," "to refuse," *nōlī* is the singular imperative form and *nōlīte* is the plural form. To order someone not to do something, you simply use the imperative of *nōlō* and then add the present infinitive of the verb you are negating. The infinitive may appear in the active or passive voice. Observe the example below:

Ō dēliciārum dēlíciās habēre Deum sócium et cómitem, hóspitem et convīvam. Nōlīte eī auférre dēlíciās suās; nē ipse vōbīs aúferat vestrās. (Hélinand of Froidmont)[16]

It is the delights of delights to have God as a companion, partner, host, and guest. Do not take away his delights from him, lest God himself take away yours from you.

---

15. Martin Luther, *Domínica Ante Férīas Iācōbī* (WA 17.337).
16. Hélinand of Froidmont, *Sermō* XXVIII, *Dē Potestāte et Probitāte Ecclēsiae* (PL 212.719).

(2) Nē + Subjunctive:[17] ***Subjunctive Mood Prohibitions.*** Another way to prohibit is to use *nē* + the subjunctive mood. The subjunctive mood's ability to make prohibitions should not be surprising at all, since we know that the subjunctive performs many actions, including making commands and offering suggestions. You might sometimes encounter *nē* + subjunctive preceded by the imperative *vidē* or *vidéte*: "see." This is the trifecta: imperative + negative + subjunctive. It functions the same way English sometimes issues prohibitions: "See that you do not do it." This is exactly what the angel said to John in Revelation XIX.10, *Vidē nē fécerīs*. But let us also look at another example:

Nē putétis vōs posse circumcídī, nisi onus lēgis per ómnia portétis. (Bruno of Cologne)[18]	Do not think that you can be circumcised unless you would bear the burden of the law through all things.

(3) Nōn + Future: Indicative Mood Prohibitions. One final way to prohibit in Latin is to use the negating particle *nōn* + the second-person future indicative. This is the indicative's way to give orders. You will remember seeing examples of this formation in the *Decem Verba*:

Nōn habḗbis deōs aliḗnōs. (Exod. XX.3)	You shall not have foreign gods.

As I mentioned above, ordering people around was so enjoyable that every mood wanted to get in on the action. However, Latin prefers to use the imperative or subjunctive mood for prohibitions, not the indicative mood.

CHART OF PROHIBITIONS

Imperative Mood Formation	Subjunctive Mood Formation	Indicative Mood Formation
nōlī or *nōlī́te* + present infinitive	*nē* + present subjunctive	*nōn* + future indicative

VOCATIVES

27.13 Vocatives: For When You Want to Address People and Things. We learned about vocatives in the very first *capítulum* of this book. We have now come full circle. This is the case of direct address. I encouraged you there and then to kindly abandon Shakespearean English—what with its fondness for dramatizing the vocative with "o"—and to just stick with stating the person, place, or thing addressed: whether a saint, a city, or your favorite farm animal.

27.14 Forming the Vocative. We have not included the vocative case in paradigm charts because the vocative is identical to the nominative case (except in the second declension) and because it is the least common case used in normal speech (although it is common in other speech, such as prayers or commands). To form the vocative in the second declension, you simply add the letter -e at the end of the word if it is singular. Hence *Dóminus, Dóminī* becomes *Dómine*, "Lord," in the vocative case. However, there are a couple of notable exceptions. For example, you use *Deus*

---

17. You may also encounter *cavē* + subjunctive. If so, it means the same thing.
18. Bruno of Cologne, *Expósitiō in Epístolās Paulī, Ad Gálatās* V (PL 153.310).

for "God" and *Jēsū* (= *Iēsū*) for "Jesus." And second-declension nouns that end in -ius drop the -us yet retain the -ī, thus *fílius, fílii* becomes *fīlī* in the vocative, "son."

Apart from these specific rules, the vocative case is always very easy to identify. It should present no challenges.

Let us look at an example:

Nōstis, frātrēs cāríssimī, quóniam Dóminus ac Redémptor noster in véterī lēge pontíficēs fíerī praecépit, ut pópulō suō praeéssent, et Domínicīs praecéptīs pópulum sibi súbditum īnstrúerent. (Munio Alfonso of Mondoñedo)[19]	You know, my beloved brothers, that our Lord and Redeemer commanded in the old law that there be priests, so that they would have charge of his people, and that they would instruct the people thus subdued to them with the Lord's precepts.

There are no surprises here. The vocative cases—a noun and its accompanying adjective—form exactly as we should expect.

Summárium

In this *capítulum* you learned that:

- The imperative mood is the mood of commands, directives, and orders.
- Imperatives are used primarily as "positive commands."
- Although the present imperative is the most common form, the future imperative does exist.
- Prohibitions issue forth "negative commands." You may utter prohibitions in Latin in any of the following moods: indicative (which is very rare), subjunctive, and imperative.
- Vocatives are used to directly address someone or something.

VOCĀBULŌRUM INDEX

Latin	English (Gloss)	(Etymology)
adsum, adésse, ádfuī, adfutúrus (+ dat)	to be present, to arrive	
atténdō, atténdere, atténdī, atténtus (3)	to pay attention, to attend (to)	(attend)
aúferō, auférre, ábstulī, ablátus (3)	to take away, to remove	(ablative)
cáveō, cavére, cāvī, cautus (2)	to beware, to take care	(caution)
comes, cómitis (m, f)	companion, partner; count, earl	
convíva, convívae (m)	guest	(convivial)

---

19. Munio Alfonso of Mondoñedo et al., *História Compostellána* I.89 (PL 170.979).

dēsístō, dēsístere, déstitī, déstitus (3)	to cease, to desist	(destitute)
ferrum, ferrī (n)	iron	(ferric)
hospes, hóspitis (m)	host, guest	(hospitality)
ímperō, imperā́re, imperā́vī, imperā́tus (1) (+ dat)	to command, to give orders to, to rule	(imperative)
íncitō, incitā́re, incitā́vī, incitā́tus (1)	to incite, to quicken, to provoke, to hasten	(incite)
íncrepō, increpā́re, increpā́vī, increpā́tus (1)[a]	to rebuke, to reprove, to blame	(increpation)
intúeor, intuḗrī, intúitus sum (2)	to look at, to consider, to observe, to regard	(intuitive)
ínvocō, invocā́re, invocā́vī, invocā́tus (1)	to invoke, to call by name, to call upon	(invoke)
iúbeo, iubḗre, iussī, iussus (2)	to command, to order	(jussive)
mūtus, mūta, mūtum	silent, mute, quiet	(mute)
negṓtium, negṓtiī (n)	business, employment, labor, matter	(negotiate)
ṓsculor, ōsculā́rī, ōsculā́tus sum (1)	to kiss, to embrace	(osculation)
ṓsculum, ṓsculī (n)	kiss	(oscular)
pū́niō, pūnī́re, pūnī́vī, pūnī́tus (4)	to punish, to avenge	(punitive)
quaesō, quaésere, quaesī́vī, - (3)	to beseech, to ask; please[b]	(question)
sálveō, salvḗre, -, - (2)	to be well, to be healthy	(safe)
scelus, scéleris (n)	crime, sin	
sūrsum	above, upwards	
váleō, valḗre, váluī, válitus (2)	to be well, to be able, to be worth	(value)

[a] You may also see this verb with the second and third principal parts as *incrépuī* and *incrépitus*.

[b] Sometimes it is best to translate this verb simply as "please," especially in the first person.

ŌRĀ́TIŌ POPULĀ́RIS

Nunc Dīmíttis. This prayer, "Now Dismiss," derives from Luke II.29–32. It records the words of Simeon as Christ was presented at the temple in Jerusalem. This prayer is traditionally uttered at Compline, which is the Night Prayer spoken before retiring for the evening. As the opening lines indicate, the *Nunc Dīmíttis* provides a wonderful conclusion to our learning of Latin. As we are sent our own ways in the study of this magnificent language, may we proceed in peace and illumination.

Nunc dīmíttis servum tuum, Dómine,
secúndum verbum tuum in pāce:
Quia vīdérunt óculī meī salūtā́re tuum
Quod parā́stī ante fáciem ómnium
  populṓrum:
Lūmen ad revēlātiṓnem géntium,
et glṓriam plēbis tuae Isrāḗl.
Glṓria Patrī, et Fī́liō, et Spīrítuī Sānctō,
Sīcut erat in prīncípiō, et nunc, et semper,
  et in saécula saeculṓrum. Āmēn.
	Now dismiss your servant, Lord,
	according to your word, in peace.
	Because my eyes have seen your salvation
	Which you prepared before the face of
	  all people:
	A light for the revelation of the gentiles,
	and glory of your people Israel.
	Glory to the Father and to the Son and to
	  the Holy Spirit,
	Just as it was in the beginning, is now, and
	  will always be forever and ever. Amen.

EXERCÍTIA

Be sure to complete the *exercítium* in the appendix corresponding to this *capítulum*.

CONCLUSION

Ciceronians, Christians, and Fīnis Librī

Chrīstiánum mē esse respóndī.[1]
—JEROME

"WHAT DOES ATHENS HAVE TO DO WITH JERUSALEM?"

By the year 374, Jerome was probably the world's greatest biblical scholar. Though he resided in Antioch, he had formerly traveled east to test life as a desert monk. As a monk-in-training, however, he found bitter herbs. Despite his best efforts, he had a habit he just couldn't break—his love of ancient literature. Tormented by a guilty conscience for preferring to read the classical texts of Cicero or Virgil over Mark or Paul, he experienced a vision in which he said that he was "dragged before God's judgment seat." When God asked the ashamed man what he was, he blurted out: *Chrīstiánum mē esse respóndī*, "I answered that I was a Christian." Unsatisfied with his reply, God thundered back: *Mentíris . . . Cicerōniánus es, nōn Chrīstiánus,* "You're lying. You're a Ciceronian, not a Christian!"[2]

The inner turmoil that Jerome experienced as a *Chrīstiánus* and an aficionado of ancient literature—here, a *Cicerōniánus*—was as commonplace as it was conflicting in the ancient world. For early Christians, to read great Latin literature meant turning to the classics. And turning to the classics meant turning away from Christ. In fact, due to the instrinsic link between a classical education and a pagan worldview, some early church decrees forbad Christians from the teaching profession altogether out of fear that it would contaminate their faith. The two were perceived as that incompatible.

It is from this context that the earliest Christian author of Latin, Tertullian, famously asked:

Quid ergō Athénīs et Hierosólymīs? Quid Acadēmíae et Ecclésiae? Quid haeréticīs et Chrīstiánīs?	What does Athens have to do with Jerusalem? The Academy with the Church? Heretics with Christians?[3]

---

1. "I answered that I was a Christian."
2. Jerome, *Epístola* XX.30 (PL 22.416). Here is an excerpt of the Latin most germane to our discussion. "*Interrogátus dē conditióne, Chrīstiánum mē esse respóndī. Et ille quī praesidḗbat: Mentíris, áit, Cicerōniánus es, nōn Chrīstiánus.*" Cicero is the most famous Latin writer of all time, whose Latin set the standard for all subsequent written Latin, even among Christians. He lived during the first century BC, a contemporary of both Caesar and Augustus.
3. Tertullian, *Liber dē Praescriptiónibus* VII.9 (PL 2.20).

Jerome agreed, and he asked a similar set of questions several generations after Tertullian:

Quid facit cum Psaltériō Horátius? Cum Ēvangéliīs Marō? Cum Apóstolō Cícerō?	What does Horace have to do with the Psalter? Virgil with the Gospels? Cicero with the Apostle?[4]

Fortunately, we do not find ourselves in the same situation as Jerome and Tertullian. If they were alive today, they may still regard Christianity and classical literature as incompatible, but they would not do so because excellent Latin Christian writings do not exist. On the contrary, the world is replete with such Latin writing from Christians.

As we learned from the introduction to this book, the writings of classical Latin authors represent less than 1% of the entire Latin *corpus*.[5] The overwhelming majority of Latin in existence was written by Christian authors, not pagan or non-Christian ones. Despite these staggering statistics, classical Latin—the language of Caesar, Cicero, and Virgil—still dominates and overshadows what is variously called "biblical," "church," "ecclesiastical," "theological," or even "Christian" Latin. It is not that non-Christian authors of Latin like Cicero or Virgil are unworthy of reading. These authors were incredible. Nobody could turn a phrase like Virgil, and nobody could construct a sentence as intricate as Cicero. These *virī* could write, and only a *stultus* would say otherwise. Rather, it is that the Latin writings of so many Christian authors sit unread, remain untranslated, and go unappreciated in schools, monasteries, and museums from Canterbury to Christchurch.

ONE LANGUAGE

Although it is tempting to think of "classical" Latin as different from "ecclesiastical" Latin, they are not different languages. Both are Latin. To imagine the Latin of a Christian as fundamentally different from that of Catullus or Ovid is tantamount to saying that a pair of shoes or a toothbrush is "Christian" if used by a member of the church. No such battle lines need to be drawn. The term "classical" refers to the elite and literary form of that language that experienced its golden age from the first century BC to the first AD. Classical Latin is often distinguished from the spoken form of the language, that is, the everyday vernacular that even aristocrats spoke to their *amícī*, *servī*, and even *canēs*, "dogs." It is this spoken form of Latin that eventually gave rise to Romance languages across the European continent.

When all is said and done, "ecclesiastical" Latin has more in common with "classical" Latin than it does with the vernacular spoken by the everyday people. In this way, changes in the Latin language from so-called classical to ecclesiastical are observable but often exaggerated. The categories we impose on the history of this language can sometimes lead us to imagine that a vast chasm separated the different eras of the language. But as medievalist Keith Sidwell wrote, "There was no 'special language' which only Christians used."[6] In other words, we should not conceive of ecclesiastical Latin as being any more or less authentic than classical Latin. In fact, as Latinist Reginald Foster wrote, "[Post-Roman forms of] Latin belong as much to the knowledge and beauty of Latin as anything in the classical period."[7] Although Christians favored particular terms and adopted particular forms, the distinctions between ecclesiastical and classical Latin have more to do with the themes and topics authors discussed,

---

[4]. Jerome, *Epístola* XXII.29 (PL 22.416).
[5]. Jürgen Leonhardt, *Latin: Story of a World Language* (Cambridge: Harvard University Press, 2013), 2.
[6]. Keith Sidwell, *Reading Medieval Latin* (Cambridge: Cambridge University Press, 1995), 5.
[7]. Reginald Foster and Daniel McCarthy, *Ossa Latīnitátis Sōla ad Mentem Reginā́ldī Ratiōnémque: The Mere Bones of Latin according to the Thought and System of Reginald* (Washington, DC: Catholic University of America Press, 2016), 592.

the culture to which they belonged, the literary and historical allusions they made, and the type of audience they sought to reach.[8]

In short, the Latin from which we have drawn in this book is really only different in one respect: its subject matter. The Latin that we have featured encompasses any period, any place, and any person who is considered a Christian. And it also comprises Latin from all levels of society, all points of interest, and all modes of communication.[9] This form of Latin was the language that Christians used in treatises, hymns, poems, letters, classrooms, courtrooms, debates, cemeteries, graffiti, laws, and liturgies from the second century all the way until today. It is the language that pervaded all aspects of Western civilization.

IS THE LATIN LANGUAGE DEAD?

Before we make too much of the tired refrain that "Latin is dead," we need to remember that some people also believe in Bigfoot, and still others remain convinced that the first walking on the moon was staged. But more seriously, the argument that Latin is dead is somewhat analogous to the fact that Hebrew was "dead" at the beginning of the previous century. It was only at the creation of the nation of Israel in the middle of the twentieth century that Hebrew was revived for the purpose of speaking. This is not to say that a *Rōma Nova* will soon be created, but it most certainly is to say that technology has revivified the *Lĭngua Latĭna*, if there was even any need of revivification. Today, Latin is spoken as naturally as the rising of the Sun. Whether in podcasts, retreat centers, college classrooms, church services, magical formulas, private prayers, or Hollywood, the language is managing quite well, thank you very much. There is already an abundant industry of Latin materials that can be found in written publications, video productions, and audio recordings, but what's to say that there will not soon be full-length movies in Latin, TV channels, and even specific regions of the world where it is the official language (other than the Vatican)? Stranger things have happened.

Before you pull out the aluminum foil and label me a conspiracy theorist, I hasten to make my main point: *Lĭngua Latĭna vīva est*, "the Latin language is alive!" It has been read, spoken, prayed, murmured, and sung every single day for thousands of years. And that isn't changing any time soon. On the contrary, bright days lay ahead for this language, as well as you for learning how to read, understand, and translate it.

"MY DAYS ARE FEW"

But enough lauding of this prestigious language. As we approach the *fĭnis librī*, "the end of the book," I am reminded of the words of Alcuin of York. In a letter to a friend, he wrote: *Paucī sunt diēs meī*, "my days are few."[10] Our study of the Latin language may be coming to a finale, but it will not be forgotten. It is my hope and desire that you have benefited greatly from the study of this magnificent language, including the kind of learning extending beyond the basics of grammar and vocabulary.

---

8. See Frank Mantello and A. G. Rigg, *Medieval Latin: An Introduction and Bibliographic Guide* (Washington, DC: Catholic University of America Press, 1996), particularly 3–5, 71–76.

9. There are Christians writing today who continue to do so in Latin. Aside from the Vatican, there are individuals who write in Latin as well as speak in seminars, workshops, worship services, and school rooms. See, for example, Bernard Lonergan, *Early Latin Theology*, vol. 19 of *Collected Works of Bernard Lonergan*, trans. Michael Shields (Toronto: University of Toronto Press, 2011).

10. Alcuin of York, *Epistola* VIII (PL 100.149).

"BEFORE STUDY"

Rather than give my own concluding remarks, I bid you farewell in the words of our friend Thomas Aquinas. His writings have come to posterity in the form of systematic theologies, biblical commentaries, philosophical discourses, ethical treatises, intimate letters, and personal prayers. Of the latter, Thomas composed many for both public and private occasions. One of my favorite personal prayers of his is one that he often recited before studying, preaching, and writing. It goes by the name *Ante Stúdium*, "Before Study." I am including only an excerpt. May you take this *ōrā́tiō* to heart as you continue your study of the Latin language. Until next time, *valḗte, sodā́lēs*, "farewell, comrades."

Dā mihi intelligéndī acū́men,	Grant to me keenness to understand,
retinéndī capācitā́tem,	capacity to remember,
addiscéndī modum et facilitā́tem,	manner and facility to learn,
interpretā́ndī subtīlitā́tem,	subtlety to interpret,
loquéndī grā́tiam cōpiósam.	abundant grace to speak.
Ingréssum ī́nstruās,	May you guide my beginning,
Progréssum dī́rigās,	direct its progress,
ēgréssum cómpleās.	and bring to completion its conclusion.
Tū quī es vērus Deus et homō,	You who are true God and true man,
quī vīvis et rēgnās in saécula saeculṓrum.	who live and reign forever. Amen.
Āmēn.[11]	

---

11. The full prayer appears in *The Thomas Aquinas Prayer Book: The Prayers and Hymns of St. Thomas Aquinas* (Manchester, NH: Sophia Institute, 2000), 41–43.

APPENDIX I

Exercitia

Welcome to the practice portion of this book! The exercises below correspond to each of the chapters already discussed. For instance, Capitulum I corresponds to Exercitium I. I recommend completing the exercise that corresponds to each chapter before turning to the next chapter. When completing the exercises, simply follow the instructions and do your best. I often provide examples as well as footnotes to help you, but it is good practice to have a Latin dictionary always available (there are many free online Latin dictionaries).[1]

Because I always provide you with the exact source of a sentence, you are encouraged to locate these sentences online if you would like more context or want to translate larger sections. This is especially the case since, as I have said frequently in the book, context is key to understanding Latin properly. This means that you may not automatically understand the intent of every author or the exact point being discussed. What is more, not every sentence provided is a complete sentence. No matter—the encouraging news is that you should have the necessary component parts to make a suitable translation even if it does not translate into a complete and grammatically correct English sentence. If you get stuck, however, you can turn to the answer key or look up the passage online to better ascertain the context of the writing. One more note: it goes without saying that there are multiple acceptable ways to translate most any sentence, so do not be concerned if your translations do not perfectly mirror mine. This will particularly be evident when translating the *Convertendum in Anglicum*, or "English Translation" section at the end of each exercise.

Whereas all of the Latin in the book chapters are coded with diacritics like acute accents and macra to encourage consistent and accurate pronunciation, none of the Latin in the exercises below contain diacritics since primary works do not contain them. This will be excellent practice for you as you prepare to read primary Latin texts on your own. As you read more Latin without diacritics, I still recommend that you pronounce the Latin out loud or in your head before completing your translation.

EXERCITIUM I: *Nouns and Prepositions*

I. Prepositions. Translate the underlined preposition. As you do so, keep in mind three important things. First, the goal of these exercises is to reinforce concepts discussed in the chapter. Focus on what you can answer, not the words and concepts that you have not yet learned. (We all have to start somewhere.) Second, as mentioned in the instructions, not every sentence below is a complete sentence. Finally,

---

1. Here are two free online dictionaries that could be consulted among many others: William Whitaker's Words at the University of Notre Dame (http://archives.nd.edu/words.html) and Wiktionary, which is operated by Wikipedia.

because Latin does not have English words like "a," "an," or "the," and because there are sometimes multiple acceptable ways to translate a single word into English, it is unrealistic to expect identical translations for every question. So, do not be concerned if your translation does not perfectly match the number or size of the spaces allocated. Your focus should be providing an accurate translation, not worrying about whether your translation fits the number and size of the spaces.

Exemplum.[2] *Deinde ad exitus viarum servi diriguntur.* (Werner of St. Blaise)[3]

From that place the servants are directed to the exits of the ways.

1. Qui post hoc annum non supervixit. (Rudolph of St. Trudo)[4]

   And he did not survive _____ this year.

2. Quomodo enim, si non Dominus adsit, contra archangelum caro pugnet? (Bede)[5]

   For how, if the Lord is not present, can flesh battle _____ the archangel?

3. Dedit autem Deus gratiam populo coram Aegyptiis. (Alonso Tostado)[6]

   But God gave grace to the people _____ the Egyptians.

4. Et hoc facies ex potestate et ex misericordia. (St. Remigius)[7]

   And you will do this _____ power and _____ mercy.

5. Nomen per gratiam Spiritus Sancti in baptismate funditur in cunctos fideles. (Glossa Ordinária)[8]

   The name is poured out _____ (*in*) baptism _____ (*per*) the grace of the Holy Spirit to all the faithful.

II. Cases. Write in the blank line the case that best corresponds to the word(s) underlined, focusing on the prepositions (and not necessarily the accompanying words, which you may not recognize at this point). It may be helpful to review which prepositions pattern with which cases. Also, as noted above, not all examples are complete sentences.

Exemplum. *Hic est ex tribu Judae.*   *Ablative*
(Tychonius)[9] *He is from the tribe of Judah.*

---

2. "Example."
3. Werner of St. Blaise, *Deflorationes SS. Patrum* II (PL 153.1193).
4. Rudolph of St. Trudo, *Gesta Abbatum Trudonensium* III.2 (PL 173.320).
5. Bede, *Expositiones Allegoricae in Samuelem Prophetam* III.2 (PL 91.613).
6. Alonso Tostado, *Commentaria in Exodum* III (Venice: Giovanni Battista & Giovanni Bernardo Sessa, 1596), 20.
7. St. Remigius, *Enarrationes in Psalmos* LXI (PL 131.453).
8. Glossa Ordinária, *Canticum Canticorum* I (PL 113.1129). The noun following the underlined form of *in* is in the ablative case, which helps us understand how to translate it. Also, as you will detect, Latin sentences cannot always be translated into English in the same word order.
9. Tychonius, *Liber de Septem Regulis* VII (PL 18.62).

EXERCITIA

1. Qui panem <u>vitae</u> Christum non esurierunt. (Peter of Blois)[10] The one who had not hungered for Christ, the bread <u>of life</u>.

2. Nemo potest esse in Christo, quin prius datus sit <u>a Patre</u>. (Francis Turretin)[11] No one is able to be in Christ unless first offered <u>from the Father</u>.

3. <u>Ad arcem</u> perfectionis. (Gregory I)[12] <u>To the ark</u> of completion.

4. <u>O mitissime Pater et domine</u>, qui in vice Jesu Christi super oves Ecclesiae pastor constitutus es. (Hildegard of Bingen)[13] <u>Most mild father and master</u>, who has been established in the place of Jesus Christ as shepherd over the sheep of the Church.

5. Sicut unus panis <u>ex multis granis</u> conficitur . . . sic corpus Christi <u>ex multis membris</u> componitur. (Innocent III)[14] Just as one loaf of bread is prepared <u>from many grains</u> . . . so the body of Christ is composed <u>from many members</u>.

III. Genesis. Translate each sentence from Genesis into English, consulting a dictionary for any unfamiliar words. Some clues will be provided in the footnotes. At this early stage in translating, do not be discouraged if you need to compare your translation to an English one. (It is the first *capitulum*, after all.) You are already off to a great start.

Exemplum. *Pulvis es.* (III.19)   *You are dust.*

1. Sub caelo sunt. (I.9)[15]

2. Erit signum foederis inter me et inter terram. (IX.13)[16]

3. Vivat anima mea ob gratiam tui. (XII.13)[17]

4. Misit me Deus ante vos in Aegyptum. (XLV.5)[18]

---

10. Peter of Blois, *Poemata* V (PL 200.1141).
11. Francis Turretin, *Institutio Theologiae Elencticae* I.10.10 (New York: Robert Carter, 1847), 316.
12. Gregory I, *Commentariorum in Librum I Regum* III.21 (PL 79.211).
13. Hildegard of Bingen, *Epistola* VIII (PL 197.159). The use of *o* here indicates that these two nouns are not nominative; they are the cases used for direct address.
14. Innocent III, *De Sacro Altaris Mysterio Libri Sex* IV.36 (PL 217.879).
15. Translate *sunt* as "are," the subject of which is implied: "they."
16. Translate *erit* as "will," the subject of which is *signum foederis*, "the sign of the covenant."
17. Translate *vivat* as "may live," the subject of which is *anima mea*, "my soul." *Tui* translates as "your."
18. Translate *misit* as "sent," the subject of which is *Deus*, "God." The last word is a nation. It still exists today.

5. Do tibi partem unam extra fratres tuos. (XLVIII.22)[19]

EXERCITIUM II: *First-Declension Nouns; Sum, Esse, Fui, Futurus; and Et, -Que, and Ac*

I. First-Declension Nouns. Translate the underlined first-declension nouns in the blank lines. If there is a corresponding preposition, I will usually underline it to indicate that it is patterning with the noun. Note that more than one blank line per sentence indicates that more than one word may be needed to complete the translation (even if that blank line is not immediately next to the noun). Do not be concerned if your translation does not perfectly match the number of blank lines allocated.

Exemplum. *Neque enim aut anima corpus aut corpus anima est.* (John Calvin)[20]

For neither is the soul body nor is the body soul.

1. Vos resurrectionis gloriam in isto saeculo jam tenetis. (Cyprian of Carthage)[21]

    You all already possess in this age _____ _____ of the resurrection.

2. Apostolorum vices in hac ecclesia agere debemus. (Riculfus of Soissons)[22]

    We must exercise the succession of the apostles _____ this _____.

3. Agricola vel vinitor primos fructus laboris sui degustat. (Peter Lombard)[23]

    _____ _____ or a vinedresser tastes the firstfruits of his labor.

4. Dixit quoque Deus: Fiat firmamentum in medio aquarum: et dividat aquas ab aquis. (Gen. I.6)

    God also said: Let there be a firmament in the middle _____ _____ _____; and let it divide _____ _____ _____.

5. Talis coacervatio sententiarum[24] est hic liber Salomonis. (Philip Melanchthon)[25]

    Such a collection _____ _____ is this book of Solomon.

---

19. Translate *do* as "I give." The words *tibi* and *tuos* both refer to "you," but the first is a dative pronoun and the second is an accusative adjective.

20. John of Calvin, *Institutio Religione Christianae* II.14.1 (CR 30.353). If this were an example for you to complete on your own, I would inform you that *anima* is the subject of the verb *est* and that it cannot be in the ablative case in these examples. By process of elimination, this would help you isolate the only possibility for *anima*: nominative case singular, hence the translation as "a soul," "the soul," or simply "soul."

21. Cyprian of Carthage, *De Habitu Virgunum* XXII (PL 4.462).

22. Riculfus of Soissons, *Statuta Riculfi* I (PL 131.15).

23. Peter Lombard, *Collectanea in Epistolae D. Pauli, In Epistola II ad Tim.* II (PL 192.368). The word *agricola* is in the same case as *vinitor*.

24. Even though you may not have seen this word, you should instantly recognize it as a first-declension word due to its ending. The word *sententia, sententiae* (f) can be translated in many different ways. In this sentence, you can assume it is a noun that means "saying," but of course you will need to render it into English in accordance with its case and number.

25. Philip Melanchthon, *Expositio Proverbiorum Salomonis*, Praefatio (CR 14.2).

EXERCITIA

II. Cases. In the space provided, specify the case and number of the underlined noun. Because of either prepositions embedded in the Latin sentence (which you will have to find) or context clues that I will offer, there is only one possible answer for each question. Do not worry that you cannot understand everything about the Latin sentences. Simply concentrate on the task at hand of identifying the case of the noun by assessing its ending and/or determining whether there is a preposition that patterns with it.

Exemplum. *Linum enim de terra oritur.*   *Ablative singular*
(Isidore of Seville)[26]

1. Tunc super miserum et miserabilem hominem ira Dei descendit. (Adam of Dryburgh)[27]

2. In illa Dominica carne Divinitas pro anima fuit. (Leo I)[28]

3. Multi patres matresque familias Christo ministrantes. (Augustine of Hippo)[29]

4. Terra arida et fructuosa, per peccatum hominis maledicta, produxit tribulos et spinas. (Eucherius of Lyon)[30]

5. Sic et de vita aeterna habeas necesse est testimonium Spiritus. (Bernard of Clairvaux)[31]

III. The "To Be" Verb. Translate the underlined form of the verb "to be," "to exist" into Latin.

Exemplum. *I am not alone.*   *Non sum solus.* (Hugo of Flavigny)[32]

1. You have, therefore, four: those that exist[33] truly, those that exist, those that do not exist, truly, those that do not exist.

   Habes igitur quatuor: quae vere _____, quae _____, quae non vere, non _____, quae non _____ (Gaius Marius Victorinus).[34]

2. You all are of Christ.

   Christi _____. (Isidore Mercator)[35]

---

26. Isidore of Seville, *Prolegomena* I.11.3 (PL 81.60).
27. Adam of Dryburgh, *Sermo* XXVI.3 (PL 198.246). I will give you a hint: *ira* is the subject of the sentence here.
28. Leo I, *Epistula* VII (PL 54.1246).
29. Augustine of Hippo, *In Ioannis Evangelium, Tractatus* LI.13 (PL 35.1769).
30. Eucherius of Lyon, *Commentarii in Genesim* I.10 (PL 50.893). *Terra* is the subject of the sentence.
31. Bernard of Clairvaux, *Sermo* I (PL 183.383).
32. Hugh of Flavigny, *Chronicon* II (PL 154.371).
33. Another way to translate this would be "are."
34. Gaius Marius Victorinus, *Liber de Generatione Verbi Divini* XI (PL 8.1026).
35. Isidore Mercator, *Epistola Clementis Papae ad Jacobum Fratrem Domini* (PL 130.43). Isidore Mercator was a pseudonym.

3. God is Spirit.

   Deus Spiritus _____. (Jerome)[36]

4. We are not servants, but free children, if we should believe in Christ.

   Non _____ servi, sed liberi, si credamus in Christum. (Ambrose of Milan)[37]

5. You are a priest forever.

   Tu _____ sacerdos in aeternum. (Bede)[38]

IV. Exodus. Translate each sentence into English, consulting a dictionary for any unfamiliar words. Some clues will be provided in the footnotes. At this early stage in translating, do not be discouraged if you need to compare your translation to an English one. You are doing a great job!

Exemplum. *Deus est aemulator.* (XXXIV.14)   *God is jealous.*

1. Ego sum qui ego sum (III.14).[39]

2. Aaron frater tuus erit propheta tuus. (VII.1)[40]

3. Et reduxit super eos Dominus aquas maris. (XV.19)[41]

4. Nec contra nos est murmur vestrum, sed contra Dominum. (XVI.8)[42]

5. Gloria Domini apparuit in nube. (XVI.10)[43]

EXERCITIUM III: *Second-Declension Nouns*

I. Second-Declension Nouns. Translate the underlined second-declension nouns in the blank lines. If there is a corresponding preposition, I will usually underline it to indicate that it is patterning with

---

36. Jerome, *Epistola* LVIII (PL 22.581).
37. Ambrose of Milan, *Epistola* LVIII (PL 16.1258).
38. Venerable Bede, "Exodus XXVIII–XXXI," *In Pentateuchum Commentarii* (PL 91.328).
39. The pronoun *Ego* emphasizes the subject of the verb, which is already implied by the verb. Translate *qui* as "who."
40. *Tuus* means "your" in both instances, and *erit* is the future tense of *est*, "will be." You should be able to identify the name of the person specified, who is the subject of the sentence.
41. Translate *reduxit* as "has brought back," the subject of which is *Dominus*. The word *maris* could be translated as "of the sea."
42. Use your ear, context, and word derivation to translate *murmur* into English, being sure to translate the word *vestrum* as "your" before it (so your translation could start as "Your . . .") You can go ahead and translate *nec* as "not" and *nos* as "us."
43. Translate *apparuit* as "has appeared," the subject of which is the first word in the sentence.

the noun. Note that more than one blank line per sentence indicates that more than one word may be needed to complete the translation (even if that blank line is not immediately next to the noun). Do not be concerned if your translation does not perfectly match the number of blank lines allocated.

Exemplum. *Benedictus episcopus, servus servorum Dei.* (Benedict VIII)[44]

Bishop Benedict, *the servant of the servants of God*.

1. Est enim per Iesum Christum et [per] Deum patrem. (Martin Luther)[45]

   For it is _____ _____ _____ and _____ _____ the Father.

2. Filius Dei non est Filius Spiritus Sancti, sed est Filius Dei Patris. (Robert Bellarmine)[46]

   _____ _____ of God is not _____ _____ of the Holy Spirit, but is _____ _____ of God the Father.

3. Aquas viles praecipuum convertit in vinum. (Grimaldus of St. Gallen)[47]

   He changed ordinary waters _____ precious _____.

4. Deinde baptizari voluit a Joanne, rex a milite, Dominus a servo. (Eleutherius of Tournai)[48]

   Then he wished to be baptized by John, the king by his soldier, the Lord _____ his _____.

5. In sacramento panis et calicis ipsum Christi corpus et sanguis offertur. (Fulgentius of Ruspe)[49]

   In the sacrament of the bread and of the chalice, the very body and blood _____ _____ is offered.

6. Liber iste continet Novum et Vetus Testamentum. (Rabanus Maurus)[50]

   This _____ contains the New and Old Testament.

7. Apostoli sunt doctores in novo Testamento immediate vocati a Christo. (Philip Melanchthon)[51]

   _____ _____ are teachers in the New Testament who are directly called _____ _____.

---

44. Benedict VIII, *Epistolae et Decreta* IV (PL 139.1585). The title used here was a common one for the pope.
45. Martin Luther, *In Epistolam S. Pauli at Galatas* I (WA 40 Part 1.58). I have faith that you will be able to translate *Iesum*. Here's a hint: Although it is actually a fourth-declension noun, here it looks just like a second-declension masculine noun.
46. Robert Bellarmine, *Christianae Doctrinae Copiosa Explicatio* (Cologne: Ioannes Crithium, 1609), 21.
47. Grimaldus of St. Gallen, *Liber Sacramentorum* (PL 121.862).
48. Eleutherius of Tournai, *Sermo de Natali Domini* (PL 65.95).
49. Fulgentius of Ruspe, *Ad Monimum* II.11 (PL 65.190).
50. Rabanus Maurus, *Commentariorum in Ecclesiasticum* VI (PL 109.941).
51. Philip Melanchthon, *Scripta Dogmatica* (CR 21.1100).

8. Non enim audeo respicere contra Deum. (Renier of St. Laurent)[52]

   For I do not dare to look back _____ _____.

9. Vir mulierem diligit. (Hugo)[53]

   _____ _____ loves his wife.

10. Omne peccatum impatientiae adscribendum. (Tertullian)[54]

    Every _____ must be ascribed to impatience.

II. Cases. In the space provided, specify the case, gender, and number as well as the nominative and genitive singular form of the underlined noun. If there seems to be more than one possibility, context clues will narrow it down to only one correct answer.

Exemplum. *Sonus igitur de ore Domini procedit, cum consubstantialis ei Spiritus ad nos per Filium veniens.* (Gregory I)[55]   *Accusative masculine singular from* filius, filii

1. Beatus quoque apostolus Paulus, a Domino electus. (Cyprian of Carthage)[56]

2. Simon Petrus dixit tu es Christus Filius Dei vivi. (Matt. XVI.16)

3. Orabitque pro eo sacerdos et pro peccato eius. (Lev. V.6)

4. Tibi recte ascribitur, cunctis dare oculos. (Felix Ennodius)[57]

5. Nonne a Deo data est? (Minicius Felix)[58]

III. Augustine of Hippo. Augustine lived from 354 to 430, mostly in North Africa. He is one of the most influential theologians of all time. Of his myriad works, his *Confessiones*, "Confessions," ranks as one of the most beloved. Translate each sentence from Augustine's *Confessiones* into English, consulting a dictionary for any unfamiliar words.[59] Some clues will be provided in the footnotes. Keep up the good work.

---

52. Renier of St. Laurent, *De Claris Scriptoribus Monasterii Sui* (PL 204.38).
53. Hugh of St. Victor, *De B. Mariae Virginitate* IV (PL 176.875).
54. Tertullian, *De Patientia* V (PL 1.1258).
55. Gregory I, *Moralia in Iob* XXVII.16 (PL 76.419).
56. Cyprian of Carthage, *Epistula* LVIII.10 (PL 4.381).
57. Felix Ennodius, *Epistula* XIX (PL 63.31).
58. Minicius Felix, *Octavius* XVIII (PL 3.287).
59. All of the excerpts come from Augustine of Hippo, *Confessiones* I.1–5 (PL 32.659–63).

Exemplum. *Laudare te vult homo.*   *Humankind wants to praise you.*

1. Magnus es, Domine.[60]

2. Sapientiae tuae non est numerus.[61]

3. Non enim ego iam inferi.[62]

4. Non ergo essem, deus meus.[63]

5. Angusta est domus animae meae.[64]

EXERCITIUM IV: *Third-Declension Nouns*

I. Third-Declension Nouns. Translate the underlined third-declension nouns in the blank lines. If there is a corresponding preposition, I will usually underline it to indicate that it is patterning with the noun. Note that more than one blank line per sentence indicates that more than one word may be needed to complete the translation (even if that blank line is not immediately next to the noun). Do not be concerned if your translation does not perfectly match the number of blank lines allocated.

Exemplum. *Benedictus Domini es et Christi sacerdos.* (John of Salisbury)[65]   *You are blessed of the Lord and a priest of Christ.*

1. <u>Nomen</u> enim Deorum et angelis et sanctis omnibus a Deo est impositum. (Leo I)[66]

    For _____ _____ of deities, angels, and all holy creatures was established by God.

2. Damus igitur unum <u>corpus</u> Christi ex virgine sumptum in multis locis oferri. (Peter Martyr Vermigli)[67]

    Therefore, we concede that the one _____ of Christ from the virgin was taken up to be consecrated in many places.

---

60. Translate *magnus* as "great." It is referring to the person addressed in the vocative case.
61. Translate *tuae* as "to your . . ."
62. Translate *iam* as "now" and *inferi* as "in Hell."
63. Translate *essem* as "I would exist," and *ergo* as "therefore." Also, recognize that *deus meus* is in the vocative case. You can probably tell that *meus* means "my" here.
64. Translate *angusta* as "narrow" and *domus* as "house." Based on the sentence before, you should be able to guess what *meae* means. I suggest starting your translation with the subject—*domus*.
65. John of Salisbury, *Epistola* CCLVII (PL 199.300).
66. Leo I, *Appendix ad S. Leonis Magni Opera* (PL 56.690).
67. Peter Martyr Vermigli, *Defensio Doctrinae Veteris et Apostlicae* I (Zurich: Christoph Froschauer, 1559), 13.

3. Sed quid de Trinitate dicam? (Ambrose of Milan)[68]

   But what shall I say _____ _____ _____?

4. Aemulator erat mansuetudinis et pacis. (Gaufrid)[69]

   He was an imitator _____ _____ and _____ _____.

5. Filius Dei judicaturus est, nec tamen in ea forma apparens, in qua Deus est aequalis Patri, sed in ea qua filius hominis est. (Augustine of Hippo)[70]

   The Son of God will come to judge, but not, however, appearing in that form in which he is God equal _____ _____ _____, but in which he is the son _____ _____.

II. Cases. In the space provided, specify the case(s), gender, and number as well as the nominative and genitive singular of the underlined third-declension noun(s). If there seems to be more than one possibility, context clues will narrow it down to only one correct answer, or I will provide a clue in a footnote. In the sentences, focus on the words that you are familiar with. It is important to gain exposure to Latin and identify what you do understand.

Exemplum. *Vidit autem aliud somnium, et narravit illud patri suo et fratribus suis?* (Ambrose of Milan)[71]

Dative masculine singular from pater, patris
Dative masculine plural from frater, fratris

1. Semen est verbum Dei. (Francisco de Toledo)[72]

2. Deo igitur auctore homo hominem fallit. (Melchior Cano)[73]

3. Hic fecit ordinationes duas in urbe Roma per mensem Februarium et Martium. (*Liber Pontificalis*)[74]

4. Sensus corporis corporalia nuntiant cordi. (Prosper of Aquitane)[75]

---

68. Ambrose of Milan, *Expositio Evangelii secundum Lucam* I.26 (PL 15.1544).
69. Gaufrid, *S. Bernardi Vita Prima* VII.27 (PL 185.319). The word *mansuetudo, mansuetudinis* (f), is a third-declension noun that means "gentleness."
70. Augustine of Hippo, *De Trinitate* I.13.28 (PL 42.841).
71. Ambrose of Milan, *De Joseph Patriarcha* I.2.8 (PL 14.164). Here's a hint with this sentence: *patri* and *fratribus* are in the same case.
72. Francisco de Toledo, "Annotatio XXIII," in *Commentaria in Prima 12 Capita . . . Evangelii secundum Lucam* (Venice: Giovanni Battista Ciotti, 1600), 685. Once you recognize the verb *est*, you should realize which case *semen* has to be in. Hint—it is in the same case as *verbum*.
73. Melchior Cano, *De Locis Theologicis* II (Louvain: Servatius Sassenus and John Stelsius, 1564), 11.
74. "Felix Papa IV," in *Liber Pontificalis* (PL 65.10).
75. Prosper of Aquitaine, *Liber Sententiarum ex Operibus S. Augustini Delibatarum* CCCXXXVII (PL 51.480).

EXERCITIA

5. Episcopus ad <u>regem</u> deductus. (Gregory of Tours)[76]

III. Alonso Tostado. Known as "El Tostado," the Spanish theologian Alonso Tostado was born in 1410 and died within a year of assuming the office of Bishop of Avila in 1454. A prolific author, Tostado wrote on many subjects, especially biblical and theological ones. The excerpts below contain Tostado's exegesis of Exodus III from his commentary on that biblical book. Translate each sentence from Tostado's *Commentaria in Exodum* into English, consulting a dictionary for any unfamiliar words.[77] Some clues will be provided in the footnotes.

Exemplum. *Deus facit per modum, quem ipse facit.*

God acts by the means that he himself establishes.

1. Ego autem valde parvus [sum].

2. Christus gratias agit Patri.[78]

3. Deus autem ubique est.

4. Deus expulit septem populos.[79]

5. Domine, istud negotium valde magnum est.[80]

EXERCITIUM V: *First-, Second-, and Third-Declension Adjectives*

I. Adjectives. Translate the underlined adjectives in the blank lines. Note that more than one blank line per sentence indicates that more than one word may be needed to complete the translation (even if that blank line is not immediately next to the noun). Do not be concerned if your translation does not perfectly match the number of blank lines allocated.

Exemplum. <u>Benedictus</u> Domini es et Christi sacerdos. (John of Salisbury)[81]

You are <u>blessed</u> of the Lord and a priest of Christ.

---

76. Gregory of Tours, *Historia Francorum* VI.11 (PL 71.385).
77. All the excerpts come from Alonso Tostado, *Commentaria in Exodum* III (Venice: Giovanni Battista & Giovanni Bernardo Sessa, 1596), 17–18.
78. The word *agit* is a verb that constitutes a common expression in Latin: *gratias agere*, "to give thanks." The first word in the sentence is the subject of the verb *agit*.
79. Translate *expulit* as "has driven out," the subject of which is the first word. Do not worry that *septem* and *populos* <u>seem</u> to have mismatched endings; this is because *septem* is indeclinable and has no case or number.
80. Translate *istud* as "this." The first word in the sentence is in the case of direct address.
81. John of Salisbury, *Epistola* CCLVII (PL 199.300).

1. Mysterii totius <u>brevis</u> explicatio. (Gaius Marius Victorinus)[82]

   This is a _____ explanation of this complete mystery.

2. Suavissimus et dulcissimus est fructus ejus, et in ore, et corde <u>sapientis</u> dulcescit. (Anselm of Canterbury)[83]

   Her fruit is the most pleasant and most sweet, and she is sweet on the mouth and on the heart __ _____ _____.

3. Cum enim homo in poenitentia peccatorum orat . . . <u>sanctus</u> nominatur. (Hildegard of Bingen)[84]

   For when a person prays in the repentance of his sins, he is called _____.

4. <u>Omnipotentem</u> genuisse <u>omnipotens</u> intelligitur. (Peter Lombard)[85]

   _____ _____ is understood to have produced _____ _____.

5. Nostra enim corpora . . . sunt templa Spiritus <u>Sancti</u>. (Theodore Beza)[86]

   For our bodies are temples _____ _____ _____ Spirit.

II. Cases. In the space provided, specify the case, gender, and number as well as the complete "dictionary form" of the underlined adjective (if there is more than one option, list all of them). Because of prepositions or nouns, which may be close to the adjective underlined, there is only one possible answer for case and number (but not necessarily gender). Once again, it is good to encounter Latin with which you are not familiar. For this section, only focus on the words that you do know.

Exemplum. *Perstent tamen in <u>vera</u> pietate.* (John Calvin)[87]   <u>*Ablative feminine singular from* verus, vera, verum</u>

1. Cyprianus ejusque collegae episcopi Africanae ecclesiae . . . <u>bonos</u> mores <u>fidelium</u> informarent. (Carthaginian Council)[88]

2. David certe regnabat, et cum abundaret thesauris, ac manu forti <u>infinitis</u> populis imperaret, humilem se canit. (Leander of Seville)[89]

---

82. Gaius Marius Victorinus, *Eujusdem Libri Duo in Epistolam ad Ephesios* (PL 8.1238).
83. Anselm of Canterbury, *Meditatio de Salutatione B. V. Mariae* (PL 149.579).
84. Hildegard of Bingen, *Epistola* LIII (PL 197.273).
85. Peter Lombard, *Sententiarum Libri Quatuor* I.20.4 (PL 192.579). You will want to translate this sentence first with *omnipotens*. Remember to focus primarily on word endings, not word order.
86. Theodore Beza, *Adversus Sacramentariorum Errorem pro Vera Christi Praesentia in Coena Domini* (1574), 14.
87. John Calvin, *Praelectionum in Duodecimo Prophetas Minores*, in *Micheam* IV.4 (CR 71.349). Because *vera* by itself could be in several cases, here are two clues: The preposition *in* only patterns with two cases, and the case ending of the noun that *vera* modifies (*pietas, pietatis*) further limits the adjective.
88. Carthaginian Council, *De Infantibus Baptizandis* (PL 3.1011).
89. Leander of Seville, *Regula* XIV (PL 72.887). You have two options here since this adjective is modifying *populis*, meaning that it

3. Quia cum <u>iratus</u> fueris: misericordiam facis. (Mixed Missal)[90]

4. <u>Multos</u> enim videre licet, qui ab initio recta feliciter incedunt, post pauca vero a vana gloria omnium <u>bonorum</u> consiliorum peste in transversum aguntur. (Huldrych Zwingli)[91]

5. Almitatem vestram pro nobis orantem summus arbiter orbis ab <u>alta</u> coelorum arce tueri dignetur. (Trecea)[92]

III. Philip Melanchthon. Born in 1497, Philip Melanchthon was a colleague of Martin Luther's at the University of Wittenberg. He was a highly regarded thinker and a constant writer. Among the many biblical commentaries that he wrote, he penned several versions of a commentary on Proverbs called *Explicatio Proverbiorum Salomonis*, which was finalized in 1559.[93]

Exemplum. *Praecepta moralia scripserunt Phocylides, Theognis, et alii.*	*Phocylides, Theognis, and others have written moral precepts.*

1. Breves sententiae traduntur.[94]

2. Sententia . . . est breve dictum.[95]

3. Proverbium est valde celebratum dictum.[96]

4. Haec dicta monent primum de doctrina.[97]

5. Hic dolor iniustus est.[98]

---

cannot be in the genitive case. A hint: The verb *impero, imperare, imperavi, imperatus* can take a different case for its direct object other than the accusative case. And here *infinitis* is not in the ablative case, so that should make it clearer.

90. Mixed Missal, *Missalis Mixti Pars Posterior* (PL 85.988).
91. Huldrych Zwingli, *Quo Pacti Ingenui Adolescentes Formandi Sint* (CR 89.547).
92. Trecea, *Epistola XVI* (PL 96.836).
93. All excerpts come from the preface of Philip Melanchthon, *Explicatio Proverbiorum Salomonis* (CR 14.2–3).
94. Translate *traduntur* as "are transmitted," the subject of which is *sententiae*. There are many ways to translate *sententia, sententiae*. In these examples, the best translation is probably "saying."
95. The two nouns here share a semantic range but do not translate them with the same word in English.
96. Translate *celebratum* as "celebrated," which is an adjective modifying *dictum*.
97. Here you can translate *haec* as modifying the plural noun *dicta*, which is the subject of the sentence. You can translate it as "these." The verb *monent* here means "warn" or "admonish."
98. The word *hic*, "this," is modifying the noun *dolor*, which is the subject of the sentence.

EXERCITIUM VI: *Fourth-Declension Nouns, Positive, Comparative and Superlative Adjectives, and Ablatives*

I. Fourth-Declension Nouns and Comparative and Superlative Adjectives. Translate the underlined fourth-declension nouns or adjectives in the blank lines. If there is a corresponding preposition, I will usually underline it to indicate that it is patterning with the noun. Note that more than one blank line per sentence indicates that more than one word may be needed to complete the translation (even if that blank line is not immediately next to the noun). Do not be concerned if your translation does not perfectly match the number of blank lines allocated.

Exemplum. *Potest ergo sensus iste esse huius versus: Memor ero tui de terra Iordanis.* (Martin Luther)[99]

Therefore, that sense of this verse can be: "I will be mindful of you from the land of Jordan."

1. Acceptoque in manus novo testamento gallico. (Theodore Beza)[100]

   And receiving _____ my _____ a French New Testament.[101]

2. De tribu enim Juda nasci voluit Dominus Jesus Christus. (Primasius of Hadrumetum)[102]

   For the Lord Jesus Christ had wished to be born _____ _____ _____ of Judah.

3. Angelus virgini amplius exponit quod in origine, adventu, conceptu ac nativitate huius pueri omnia . . . essent eventura. (Caspar Schwenkfeld)[103]

   Moreover, the angel explained to the virgin that all these things would come to pass in the beginning, _____ _____ _____, _____ _____ _____, and in the birth of this boy.

4. Hic est cultus filiorum Caath. (Num. IV.4)[104]

   This is the _____ of the sons of the Kohathites.[105]

5. Dilectissimo fratri Caesario Bonifacius. (Boniface II)[106]

   Boniface to his _____ _____ brother Caesarius.

---

99. Martin Luther, *Psalmus XLI* (WA 1 3.237).
100. Theodore Beza, *Vita Calvini* (CR 49.161).
101. Here the preposition *in* makes it clear that *manus* can only be one case. However, it could be singular or plural so list both options.
102. Primasius of Hadrumetum, *Commentaria in Apocalypsim* (PL 68.842).
103. Caspar Schwenkfeld, *Clara Testimonia ex Libris Novo Testamenti* (1558). In your English translation, I recommend using both an article and a preposition for each corresponding noun.
104. Willem Apollonius, *Tractatus Theologicus de Jure Magistratus circa Res Ecclesiasticas* (Middelburg, Netherlands: Jacob Fierensius, 1642), 4.
105. This usage is singular and also the subject of the sentence.
106. Boniface II, *Epistola I* (PL 65.38). Caesarius was the archbishop of Arles who died in 542. The adjective *dilectus, dilecta, dilectum* means "beloved."

II. Cases. For each of the fourth-declension nouns or adjectives used in the Latin Bible below, identify the specific case, gender, and number as well as the "dictionary form." If there is more than one option, a preceding preposition or context should clarify. All examples come from the Latin Vulgate.

Exemplum. *Dixit ad illum in visu Dominus.*   *Ablative masculine singular from visus, visus*
(Acts IX.10)

1. Deinde ii qui sunt Christi, qui in adventu ejus crediderunt. (I Cor. XV.23)

2. Et dices ad eos: Haec dicit Dominus exercituum: Convertimini ad me, ait Dominus exercituum. (Zech. I.3)

3. Cum subito raptus in spiritu, ad tribunal judicis pertrahor. (Jerome)[107]

4. Pontifex, id est, sacerdos maximus inter fratres suos ... caput suum non discooperiet, vestimenta non scindet. (Lev. XXI.10)[108]

5. Ipse enim Spiritus testimonium reddit spiritui nostro quod sumus filii Dei. (Rom. VIII.16)

III. Francis Turretin. Born in 1623, Francis Turretin was an Italian-Swiss pastor and professor within the Reformed tradition. His most famous work was *Institutio Theologiae Elencticae*, "Institutes of Elenctic Theology," written over the course of several years. It wonderfully illustrates what is sometimes called Reformed scholasticism. The excerpt below comes from a subsection of that book.[109] Other than the *exemplum*, which hails from the section immediately prior, all five parts for you to translate comprise one long sentence, meaning that your translation will not be a complete sentence until the end. Translate each sentence into English, consulting a dictionary for any unfamiliar words. Some clues will be provided in the footnotes.

Exemplum. *Theologia supernaturalis consideratur, vel systematice prout notat compagem doctrinae salutaris ... vel habitualiter et per modum habitus in intellectu residentis.*

Supernatural theology is considered either systematically, as denoting the structure of saving doctrine ... or dispositionally, which is through the manner of a quality residing in the intellect.

1. Ut triplex datur Schola Dei—Naturae, Gratiae et Gloriae—et triplex Liber—Creaturae, Scripturae et Vitae.[110]

---

107. Jerome, *Epistula* XX.30 (PL 22.416).
108. As explained in one of the boxes for this *capitulum*, this form comes from the irregular adjective *magnus, major, maximus*.
109. The excerpt comes from Francis Turretin, *Institutio Theologiae Elencticae* I.2.9 (New York: Robert Carter, 1847), 6.
110. The word *ut* is paired here with *ita*, which appears in the portion below. You could translate this pair as "Just as" for *ut* and "in the same way" for *ita*. The word *datur* is a verb, which you can translate here as "is given," You will notice the hyphens here. Keep them in

2. Ita trifariam solet distingui Theologia.[111]

3. Ut prima sit naturalis, secunda supernaturalis, tertia beatifica.[112]

4. Prima ex lumine rationis, secunda ex lumine fidei, tertia ex lumine gloriae.[113]

5. Illa est hominum in mundo, ista fidelium in Ecclesia, haec beatorum in coelo.[114]

EXERCITIUM VII: *Fifth-Declension Nouns, Indeclinable Nouns, and Numbers*

I. Fifth-Declension Nouns and Numerals. Translate the underlined fifth-declension nouns or numerals in the blank lines. If there is a corresponding preposition, I will usually underline it to indicate that it is patterning with the noun. Note that more than one blank line per sentence indicates that more than one word may be needed to complete the translation (even if that blank line is not immediately next to the noun). Do not be concerned if your translation does not perfectly match the number of blank lines allocated. Note that some words may come from the boxes in the *capitulum*, not just the *Vocabulorum Index*.

Exemplum. *Lausannae pridie idus Ianuarii.*
(Theodore Beza)[115]

From Lausanne on the day before the ides of January.

1. Nam Paulus haec tria sic conectit, Deum, fidem, et baptismum. (John Calvin)[116]

   For Paul thus connects these _____: God, _____, and baptism.

2. Genesis, iuxta fidem historiae, describit fabricam mundi. (Isidore of Seville)[117]

   Genesis, _____ _____ _____ _____ of history, describes the creation of the world.

---

your translation. Please note that all six nouns within the hyphens—*naturae, gratiae, gloriae, creaturae, scripturae, vitae*—are all in the same case, number, and gender. And I will give you a clue: they are in the genitive case. Finally, *triplex* is an adjective; in the first instance, it is modifying *schola*, and in the second instance it is modifying *liber*.

111. In this clause, *theologia* is the subject, *trifariam* is an adverb that will appear in a dictionary, and you can translate the verbs *solet distingui* as "is customarily divided."

112. Translate *Ut* as "So that" and *sit* as "would be." You can supply the verb *sit* for each of the next two parts, with the result that your translation would have three identical components: "The first would be ___, the ___ would be ___, the ___ would be ___." Remember that this is not a complete sentence.

113. Go ahead and supply the verb *est* after *prima, secunda,* and *tertia*. There is an implied noun from the examples above that *prima, secunda,* and *tertia* are modifying, but you can translate them as "The first," "the second," and "the third" (similar to the example above).

114. For the sake of ease, translate *illa* as "The first," *ista* as "the second," and *haec* as "the third." We will learn these demonstratives soon enough. You can translate *est* as "belongs to," and supply it for the next two components, so that your translation would be something like this: "The first belongs to people . . . , the second belongs to . . . , and the third belongs to . . ." Note that both *fidelium* and *beatorum* are substantive adjectives, so they can be translated as nouns.

115. Theodore Beza, *Epistula* MMLXXXI (CR 43.378). The "ides" of a month is the thirteenth or fifteenth depending on the exact month. In January, it would be the thirteenth day, so the day before would be January 12. By the way, *idus, iduum* (f) is a fourth-declension noun that only occurs in the plural (which is why I listed it as such just now).

116. John Calvin, *Institutio Religionis Christianae* I.8.16 (CR 1.103).

117. Isidore of Seville, *In Libros Veteris ac Novi Testamenti Proemia* XIX (PL 83.159).

3. Creatura hominis <u>sexta die</u> perfecta est. (John Cassian)[118]

   The creation of humankind was completed _____ _____ _____ _____.

4. <u>Prima</u> poena de jejunii prevaricatione intraverat. (Ambrose of Milan)[119]

   The _____ punishment had entered from the transgression of fasting.

5. Id est quod unus idemque verus sit Deus visibilium et invisibilium conditor <u>rerum</u>. (Vigilius of Thapsus)[120]

   That is so that the one and the same true God may be the preserver _____ visible and invisible _____.

II. Cases. For each of the fifth-declension nouns or numerals below, identify the case and number as well as "dictionary form." If there is more than one option, I will provide a clue to narrow your choices.

Exemplum. *Fide Abel plurimam hostiam obtuli quam Cain. Ecce fides distinguit inter Abel et Cain.* (Martin Luther)[121]

Ablative singular from fides, fidei
Nominative singular from fides, fidei

1. <u>Unus</u> est mediator Dei. (Leo I)[122]

2. Haec <u>tria</u> remediorum genera spiritualiter commendavit nobis coelestis Medicus, eleemosynam videlicet et jejunium et orationem. (Augustine of Hippo)[123]

3. Cunctae <u>res</u> difficiles. (Eccl. I.8)[124]

4. Deus vero est objectum <u>fidei</u>. (William Ames)[125]

5. Totum <u>secundum</u> caput est adhortatio ad audiendam et discendam hanc doctrinam. (Philip Melanchthon)[126]

---

118. John Cassian, *Commentarii in Genesim* II.1 (PL 50.902).
119. Ambrose of Milan, *De Elia et Jejunio* III.7 (PL 14.700).
120. Vigilius of Thapsus, *Dialogus contra Arianos* I.1 (PL 62.181).
121. Martin Luther, *Sermo de Indulgentiis Pridie Dedicationis* (WA 1.96).
122. Leo I, *Sermo* LXIV.3 (PL54.360).
123. Augustine of Hippo, *Sermo* LXIV.12 (PL 39.1869). In order to determine most accurately the case and number of this adjective, you will need to determine the case and number of the noun it is modifying: *genera*, which comes from the word *genus, generis* (n). And I will give you one clue: the word is not the subject of the sentence (nom) or direct address (voc), so that only leaves one option. (*Medicus* is the subject.)
124. If you are in the market for a life verse, look no further. There is an implicit *sunt* here, which should help you more easily identify the case of *res*. You should also be able to translate this sentence with no help. When combined, the implied *sunt* tells you the case of *res*, *cunctae* tells you its gender, and *difficiles* tells you its number.
125. William Ames, *Medulla Theologica* I.6 (Amsterdam: Ioannes Ianbonius, 1556), 1.
126. Philip Melanchthon, *Explicatio Proverbiorum Salomonis* II (CR 14.9). Here you have three possible options. I will give you a clue: The case and number of *secundum* is the same as the predicative nominative *adhortatio*.

BASICS OF LATIN

III. Bonaventure. Bonaventure was a Franciscan theologian and bishop who lived from 1221 to 1274. He was a schoolmate and friend of Aquinas. The following excerpt is taken from *De Reductione Artium ad Theologiam*, "On the Reduction of the Arts to Theology." Here Bonaventure argues that all knowledge emanates from the light of God. Translate each sentence into English, consulting a dictionary for any unfamiliar words. Some clues will be provided in the footnotes.

1. Iacobus [scribit] in Epistulae suae primo capitulo.[127]

2. Primum lumen illuminat respectu figurae artificialis.[128]

3. Secundum [lumen illuminat] respectu forma naturalis.[129]

4. Tertium [lumen illuminat] respectu veritatis intellectualis.

5. Quartum et ultimum [lumen illuminat] respectu veritatis salutaris.

EXERCITIUM VIII: *Verbs and Four Principal Parts*

I. Principal Parts. Identify the principal part of each underlined verb. Although you have not yet encountered all these verbs, and I do not provide translations, focus on the word underlined and use what you know about principal parts to recognize whether it is (1) a first-person present tense, (2) present active infinitive, (3) perfect active indicative, or (4) a perfect passive participle.

Exemplum. Ab avo venire monstratur. *Second (principal part)*
(Isidore of Seville)[130]

1. Cur non dicunt: scandalosum est panem et vinum ante consecrationem vocare? (Huldrych Zwingli)[131]

2. Nunc sanctos angelos in aere contra adversarias potestates belligerare vidi. (Venantius Fortunatus)[132]

---

127. Bonaventure, "De Reductione Artium ad Theologiam I," in *Doctoris Seraphici S. Bonaventurae Opera Omnia Tomus V* (Florence, Italy: College of St. Bonaventure, 1891), 319. Translate *scribit* as "writes," the subject of which is *Iacobus*. We have seen this biblical name before. And here is a hint: despite its appearance as "Jacob" (which is correct based on the Old Testament name), we usually translate it as a different name in English. Both *Epistulae* and *suae* are in the genitive case, the latter of which means here "his." Both *primo* and *capitulo*, meanwhile, are in the ablative case.

128. Translate *illuminat* as "enlightens." The word *respectu* can be translated as "with respect to," and it is followed by the genitive case, which in these examples can be translated as if they are the direct object. This construction is repeated in each of the remaining sentences.

129. The words in parentheses are implied for the rest of the sentences, so go ahead and translate them.

130. Isidore of Seville, *Librum Etymologiarum* VI.17 (PL 82.558).

131. Huldrych Zwingli, *De Canone Missae Epicheris* (CR 89.588).

132. Venantius Fortunatus, *De Vita S. Columbae* III.6 (PL 88.762).

3. Sed quidquid alii quondam censuerint, iam inter Catholicos <u>dubitare</u> non licet. (Luis Alcazar)[133]

4. Nunquam <u>visus</u> est in lectulo soporatus. (Adalgerus)[134]

5. <u>Venio</u> nunc. (Paulinus of Nola)[135]

6. Si sancti Dei regnum Dei sunt, quomodo super terram, id est, sanctam Ecclesiam <u>regnare</u> dicuntur? (Ambrose of Milan)[136]

7. Lazarus constiterat ad vocem, et e sepulcro <u>vocatus</u>. (Hilary of Poitiers)[137]

8. Cum corpore suo denique pacem <u>habere</u> cupiebat. (Augustine of Hippo)[138]

9. Nam fides amicitiae corde <u>constare</u> debet. (Alcuin of York)[139]

10. Neque ego tantum haec juxta intimum animi mei sensam asserere <u>debeo</u>. (Ana Maria van Schurman)[140]

II. The Quicumque. The *Quicumque*, a word that comes from the opening line meaning "whosoever," is a creed traditionally ascribed to Athanasius, the bishop of Alexandria who lived in the fourth century. However, the actual author may never be known. The document has been passed down generation after generation in forty lines of concise Latin. The parentheses after each sentence provide the verse number.[141] Translate each sentence into English, consulting a dictionary for any unfamiliar words. Some clues will be provided in the footnotes.

1. Fides autem catholica haec est. (III)[142]

---

133. Luis Alcazar, *Vestigatio Arcani in Apocalypsi* (Antwerp: Martinus Nutius, 1619), 3.
134. Adalgerus, *Admonitio ad Nonsuindam Reclusam* IV (PL 134.920).
135. Paulinus of Nola, *Epistola* XXIII.10 (PL 61.263).
136. Ambrose of Milan, *In Apocalypsim Expositio* (PL 17.810).
137. Hilary of Poitiers, *De Trinitate* VI.3 (PL 10.184).
138. Augustine of Hippo, *De Civitate Dei* IX.12.1 (PL 41.638).
139. Alcuin of York, *Epistola* VIII (PL 100.149).
140. Ana Maria van Schurman, *Eukleria, seu Melioris Partis Electio* (Altona: Cornelius van der Meulen, 1673), 5.
141. For the complete text in Latin, see Daniel Waterland, *A Critical History of the Athanasian Creed Representing the Opinions of Ancients and Moderns concerning It* (Cambridge: Cambridge University Press, 1728), 229–43.
142. You may want to reverse the word order when translating. Begin your translation with *haec est*, "This is . . ." The adjective *catholica* comes from a Greek word meaning "universal" or "according to the whole." It is debatable whether the term here should simply be translated as "universal" or "Catholic." (The two meanings at this time naturally overlapped and were often thought of as one and the same—the "universal" church was also the "Catholic" church. However, the further adjective "Roman" came centuries later to refer to the Roman Catholic Church.)

2. Alia est enim persona Patris, alia Filii, alia Spiritus Sancti. (V)[143]

3. Et tamen non tres [sunt] aeterni, sed unus [est] aeternus. (XI)

4. Ita [est] Deus Pater, Deus Filius, [et] Deus Spiritus Sanctus. (XV)

5. Ascendit ad caelos [et] sedet ad dexteram Dei Patris. (XXXVII)[144]

EXERCITIUM IX: *Present Actives and Present Passives*

I. Verbs. Translate the verbs underlined. I recommend using the simple or undefined aspect when translating. Note that most verbs will need to be translated with more than one word in English. Do not be concerned if your translation does not perfectly match the number of blank lines allocated.

Exemplum. *Usque hoc tempus historiagraphus in Chronicīs* <u>scribit</u> *Eusebius.* (Gregory of Tours)[145]

The historian Eusebius <u>writes</u> in Chronicles up to this time.

1. Libera autem electione agere <u>videmur</u>. (John Calvin)[146]

   But _____ _____ _____ to act from free choice.

2. Cor enim contritum et humilitatum Deus non <u>despicit</u>. (Gabriel Biel)[147]

   For God _____ not _____ a contrite and humble heart.

3. Tales libri <u>amantur</u>, <u>habentur</u> in manibus, <u>leguntur</u>, <u>praedicantur</u> a stultis. (Philip Melanchthon)[148]

   Such books _____ _____, _____ _____ in the hands,
   _____ _____, and _____ _____ by the foolish.

4. Solus sine peccato est et ingreditur sine macula, apud quem <u>manet</u> ipsum sanctitatis unguentum. (Paulus Orosius)[149]

   He [that is, Christ] alone is without sin and he [alone] proceeds without a stain, before whom himself _____ an aroma of holiness.

---

143. Translate the first *alia* as "one" and the other ones as "another."
144. Translate *ascendit* as "he has ascended" and *sedet* as "he sits."
145. Gregory of Tours, *Historia Francorum* I.34 (PL 71.179).
146. John Calvin, *Institutio Christianae Religione* II.2.3 (CR 30.187). The passive voice of this verb is usually better translated as "seems" or "appears," but we will stick with a more wooden translation for now.
147. Gabriel Biel, *Expositio Sacri Canonis Missae* (Antwerp: John Beller, 1565), 15.
148. Philip Melanchthon, *Explicatio Proverbiorum* (CR 1.1023).
149. Paulus Orosius, *Liber de Arbitrii Libertate* (PL 31.1186).

EXERCITIA

5. Personae divinae <u>sunt</u> tres: Pater, Filius, et Spiritus Sanctus. (Henricus Alting)[150]

    The divine persons _____ three: Father, Son, and Holy Spirit.

6. <u>Dicit</u> Sanctus ad illam. (Gregory of Tours)[151]

    The Holy man _____ to her.

7. Villicus enim iste pro dissipatione bonorum domini villicus iniquitatis <u>nominatur</u>. (Odo of Tournai)[152]

    For this steward _____ _____ a "steward of wickedness" on account of the destruction of the good masters.

8. Gratias <u>ago</u> et ipse Deo. (Bernard of Clairvaux)[153]

    And I myself _____ thanks to God.

9. Quisquis autem Spiritum Christi non <u>habet</u>, ad hunc orbem terrarum non pertinet. (Richard of St. Victor)[154]

    But whoever does not _____ the Spirit of Christ does not belong to this world.

10. Tunc fratres omnes <u>veniunt</u>, orationi insistere non desistunt, laudantes nomen Domini quod est benedictum in saeculis. (Stephen of Muret)[155]

    Then all the brothers _____. They did not cease to persevere in prayer, praising the name of the Lord because it has been blessed forever.

II. Verb Conjugation. Identify the person, number, and voice and give the present infinitive active form of each of the underlined verbs. All examples come from the Latin Bible.

Exemplum. *Haec tibi <u>scribo</u>, sperans me ad te venire cito.* (I Tim. III.14)   *First person singular active from* <u>scribere</u>

1. Superbus et arrogans <u>vocatur</u> indoctus, qui in ira <u>operatur</u> superbiam. (Prov. XXI.24)[156]

2. Nos autem <u>praedicamus</u> Christum crucifixum. (I Cor. I.23)

---

150. Henricus Alting, *Methodus Theologiae Didacticae* III (Amsterdam: Aegidius Jansonnius, 1656), 17.
151. Gregory of Tours, *De Miraculis S. Martini* I.19 (PL 71.927).
152. Odo of Tournai, *Homilia de Villico Iniquitatis* XXX (PL 160.1147).
153. Bernard of Clairvaux, *Epistola* LXXIX.1 (PL 182.200). Remember that the phrase *gratias agere* is an expression in Latin.
154. Richard of St. Victor, *De Missione Spiritus Sancti* (PL 196.1022).
155. Stephen of Muret, *Vita S. Stephani Grandimontensis* III (PL 204.1050). Perhaps you noted correctly that *desistunt* is also a present active verb. It comes from the verb *desisto, desistere, destiti, destitus*, "to cease" or "to desist."
156. The infinitive form for *operatur* will look slightly different; it is *operor*.

3. Beati omnes qui <u>diligunt</u> te, et qui gaudent super pace tua. (Tob. XIII.18)

4. Cur ita <u>agis</u> contra servos tuos? (Exod. V.15)

5. Capitulum autem super ea quae <u>dicuntur</u>. (Heb. VIII.1)

III. Wolfgang Musculus. Born in 1497, Wolfgang Musculus was a Reformed pastor, professor, and theologian most active in the cities of Augsburg and Bern. He wrote many biblical and theological works, including a highly regarded commentary on the Gospel of John, excerpts of which are included below.[157] This commentary was first published in 1545. In the section below, Musculus is commenting on the opening lines of the Gospel of John.

1. Divinitatis Christi duplex est consideratio.[158]

2. Sic Paulus vocat Christum imaginem Dei invisibilis.

3. Non autem dicit, in principio fecit Deus verbum.[159]

4. Sicut Moses dicit, in principio fecit Deus coelum et terram.

5. Hoc est secundum praedicatum Evangelistae de Christo verbo Dei.[160]

EXERCITIUM X: *Imperfect Actives, Imperfect Passives, and Adverbs*

I. Imperfect Tense. Translate the imperfect verbs underlined. I recommend using the past continous aspect when translating. Note that most imperfect verbs in Latin will need to be translated with more than one word in English. Do not be concerned if your translation does not perfectly match the number of blank lines allocated.

Exemplum. *Abraham non ex causa sua, sed solo mandato Dei <u>volebat</u> occidere Isaac.* (Alonso Tostado)[161]	*Abraham <u>was desiring</u> to kill Isaac not for his own sake, but only on account of the command of God.*

---

157. All excerpts come from Wolfgang Musculus, *Commentarii in Evangelium Ioannis in Tres Hepladas Digesti* (Basil: Hervagius 1564), 1–2.
158. I suggest starting your translation with "There is . . ."
159. The implied subject of *dicit* is Moses. You can put "Moses" or "he" in your translation. You can translate *fecit* as "made."
160. You can translate *hoc* as "This" and *praedicatum* as "declaration."
161. Alonso Tostado, *Commentaria in Exodum* III (Venice: Giovanni Battista & Giovanni Bernardo Sessa, 1596), 20.

EXERCITIA

1. Illud semper ante Dei oculos perfectae miserationis sacrificium <u>approbatur</u>. (Isidore of Seville)[162]

   That sacrifice of complete compassion _____ always _____ _____ before the eyes of God.

2. Illi enim genu <u>flectebant</u>, opus bonum male <u>operabantur</u>. (Amalarius of Metz)[163]

   For they _____ _____ at the knee; they _____ _____ a good work badly.

3. Domum taliter <u>regebat</u> Ecclesiae. (Felix Ennodius)[164]

   In such a way he _____ _____ the house of the Church.

4. Et tunc stat quod Abraham non ageret contra legem, quia non <u>occidebat</u> innocentem. (Alonso Tostado)[165]

   And it then stands that Abraham did not act against the law because he _____ not _____ the innocent.

5. Ergo, dices, illis erit promissa res, a quibus Christus <u>videbatur</u>. (Tertullian)[166]

   Therefore, you will say, what was promised will be given to those by whom Christ _____ _____ _____.

II. Adverbs. Translate the adverbs underlined.

Exemplum. *Si <u>subito</u> finis humani corporis esset, hoc mandarentur membra sepulta loco.* (Ermoldus Nigellus)[167]

If the end of the human body were <u>suddenly</u> unexpected, the buried members were assigned to this place.

1. Nos omnes mortem <u>iam</u> comedimus, quicunque in Adamo sumus. (Sebastian Franck)[168]

   We all _____ eat death, whosoever of us is in Adam.

---

162. Isidore of Seville, *Concilia Hispaniae* (PL 84.503). The verb *approbare* means "to approve."
163. Amalarius of Metz, *De Ecclesiasticis Officiis* I.13 (PL 105.1027). We encountered the verb *flectere* in conjunction with fourth-declension verbs; it means "to bend"; the form *operabantur* comes from a verb meaning "to work," "to labor," or "to perform." Although it has a passive form, translate it in the active voice because it is deponent.
164. Felix Ennodius, *Vita B. Epiphanii Episcopi Ticinensis* (PL 63.212). This verb, from *rego*, means "to govern" or "to rule."
165. Alonso Tostado, *Commentaria in Exodum* III (Venice: Giovanni Battista & Giovanni Bernardo Sessa, 1596), 20. The verb *occido* means "to kill."
166. Tertullian, *De Resurrectione Carnis* XXXIV (PL 2.844).
167. Ermoldus Nigellus, *De Rebus Gestis Ludovici Pii* II (PL 105.602). This is formatted slightly differently to represent its genre as poetry.
168. Sebastian Franck, *De Arbore Scientiae Boni et Mali* (Mülhausen: Peter Schmidt, 1561), 4.

2. Nam gloria, ut inquit D. Augustinus, parens est omnis haeresis. Et tamen nihil minus volunt videri, dum <u>semper</u> vel hoc unum in ore habeant, omnia facere se pro gloria Dei. (Martin Luther)[169]

   For boasting, as St. Augustine says, is the parent of all heresy. And, nonetheless, people want nothing less than to seem so inclined while they _____ have even this one thing on their lips—that they do all things for the glory of God.

3. Sed quia <u>adhuc</u> populus Hebraicus erat imperfectus, et Deus volebat eos movere ad magna. (Alonso Tostado)[170]

   But the Hebrew people _____ were incomplete, and God was wanting to move them to great things.

4. Haec <u>etiam</u> triplex confessio notatur in illo breviloquio. (Peter Cantor)[171]

   This threefold confession is notated _____ in this brief speech.

5. Haec historia secundae hebdomadae <u>partim</u> ex propheticis, <u>partim</u> ex evangelicis libris assumitur. (Sicard of Cremona)[172]

   This story of the second week is taken up _____ from the prophetic books and _____ from the evangelical ones.

III. Cajetan. Tommaso de Vio, otherwise known as Thomas de Vio or simply Cajetan, was born in 1469 and died in 1534. He became a Cardinal in the Roman Catholic Church in 1517. A year later, he was sent by the pope to interrogate a young Augustinian monk named Martin Luther at the Diet of Augsburg in Germany. Cajetan was also an able biblical commentator, eventually composing commentaries on most books of the Bible. These commentaries, written in concise Latin, illustrate the emergence of the so-called critical era of biblical interpretation. The following comes from his biblical commentary on James, *Iacobus* in Latin.[173]

1. Non est usquequaque certum an Epistula haec sit Iacobi fratris Domini.[174]

2. Nec ipse seipsum nominat Apostolum, sed tantum servum Iesu Christi.[175]

---

169. Martin Luther, *Praelectiones in Prophetas Minores, Sacharja* XII.7 (WA 13.657). Despite the strange spelling, *Sacharja* is how the book of Zechariah is written in German. Also, although *facere* is an infinitive, I have translated it so you can focus on the deponent infinitive *videri*.

170. Alonso Tostado, *Commentaria in Exodum* III (Venice: Giovanni Battista & Giovanni Bernardo Sessa, 1596), 18.

171. Peter Cantor, *Verbum Abbreviatum* (PL 205.343).

172. Sicard of Cremona, *Mitrale* V.2 (PL 213.206).

173. Thomas de Vio, *In Omnes D. Pauli et Aliorum Apostolorum Epistolas Commentarii: Tomus Quintus* (Lyon: Iacobus & Petrus Prost, 1639), 362–63.

174. Translate *est* with an implied subject of "It." You can also translate *an* as "whether," *haec* as "this" (which is modifying *Epistola*), and *sit* as "is." The last three words are all in the same case.

175. You can translate *ipse* as "he" and *seipsum* as "himself."

3. Et mittitur ad duodecim tribus dispersas.[176]

4. Unde magis libri quam Epistolae titulum merebatur.[177]

5. Et est sermo de opere animi quod intus est.

EXERCITIUM XI: *Future Actives and Future Passives*

I. Future Tense. Translate all the verbs underlined, each of which is in the future tense. Note that future verbs will need to be translated into English with more than one word. Do not be concerned if your translation does not perfectly match the number of blank lines allocated.

Exemplum. *De tactu loquar, quinto sensu corporis nostri.* (Sidonius Apollinaris)[178]

I will speak about touch, the fifth sense of our body.

1. Tibi dabitur corona in aeterna gaudia. (Bernard of Clairvaux)[179]

    A crown _____ _____ _____ to you for everlasting joys.

2. Hic est Dominus Deus noster, qui regnat cum Patre et Spiritu Sancto, Filius Dei, ipse reget nos in saecula. Amen. (Arnobius the Younger)[180]

    This is our Lord God, who reigns with the Father and with the Holy Spirit, the Son of God; he _____ _____ over us in eternity. Amen.

3. Si vos ad sinum sanctae matris vestrae non deducimus, ita vos in Deum peccabitis, si nostram vocem audire omittatis. (John VIII)[181]

    If we are not leading you all to the bosom of your holy mother, then _____ _____ _____ _____ against God, if you all fail to obey our voice.

4. Ambulabunt gentes in lumine domus sanctae. (Victor III)[182]

    The nations _____ _____ in the light of your holy house.[183]

---

176. You can supply the subject of *mittitur* as "The letter." The word *dispersas* could simply be translated as an adjective meaning "scattered." It is modifying the noun next to it, unveiling the noun's case and number.
177. You can translate *Unde* as "Hence," followed by "more was obtained . . ." Here you can assume that both *libri* and *Epistolae* are in the genitive case.
178. Sidonius Apollinaris, *Epistola* XIV (PL 58.584). Although the form of this verb is passive, it is translated as active because it is deponent.
179. Bernard of Clairvaux, *Liber de Modo Bene Vivendi* 169.LXXIII (PL 184.1305).
180. Arnobius the Younger, *Commentarii in Psalmos* XLVII (PL 53.392).
181. John VIII, *Epistolae et Decreta* CCXVIII (PL 126.833).
182. Victor III, *Liber de Messiae Adventu Praeterito* XVI (PL 149.353).
183. Did you notice that *sanctae* is modifying *domus*, even though they look nothing alike? Hopefully, you know why they are in the same case, number, and gender but still look worlds apart. If you do not remember, return to the *capitulum* discussing adjectives.

5. Ideo hanc doctrinam contra Sathanam et mundum semper defendit et conservavit, estque defensurus[184] et conservaturus eam usque ad diem gloriosi sui adventus, in quo sanctis suis <u>exhibebit</u> omnia. (Johann Aepinus)[185]

Therefore [God] has guarded and preserved this teaching against Satan and the world, and he will always guard and preserve it until the day of his glorious return, in which he _____ _____ all things to his saints.

II. Conjugating the Future Tense. Returning to the sentences above, list the person, number, and voice as well as the infinitive form of each of the verbs underlined.

Exemplum. *First person singular passive from* loqui[186]

1. _____
2. _____
3. _____
4. _____
5. _____

III. Beatitudes. The English word "Beatitudes" derives from the Latin word *beatitudo, beatitudinis* (f), "blessedness" or "happiness." The Beatitudes contain some of Jesus's most memorable turns of phrases. They are part of a larger section called "the Sermon on the Mount," *Sermo Montis* in Latin, which is found in Matthew V—VII. The Beatitudes provide a good place to practice translating future verbs. In this exercise, translate the following sentences as best you can. Each one features at least one future verb. Consult a dictionary for unfamiliar words. Here are the first tips I will give you: Translate *ipsi* as "they," *qui* as "those who," and recognize that some sentences have an implied *sunt*, "are." Finally, do not fail to miss the connection between Jesus's *Beatitudines* and the *Decem Verba* that Moses reported. When you have time, compare the *Beatitudines* below with the *Decem Verba* listed in the *Opusculum Theologicum*.

1. Beati qui lugent quoniam ipsi consolabuntur. (V.4)

2. Beati mites quoniam ipsi possidebunt terram. (V.5)

3. Beati qui esurient et sitiunt iustitiam quoniam ipsi saturabuntur. (V.6)

4. Beati misericordes quia ipsi misericordiam consequentur. (V.7)[187]

---

184. The use of *defensurus* and *conservaturus* with *est* is another way to describe a future action, but this is part of a larger discussion under the purview of participles. Also, remember that *estque* is just the combination of *est* with one of the words for "and," *-que*.
185. Johannes Aepinus, *De Iustificatione Hominis* (Frankfurt: Petrus Brubachius, 1557), 1.
186. Remember that the verb is technically in the passive voice, even though it is translated in the active voice.
187. The verb in this sentence is in the passive form; however, translate it like it is active because it is deponent.

5. Beati mundo corde quoniam ipsi Deum videbunt. (V.8)[188]

6. Beati pacifici quoniam filii Dei vocabuntur. (V.9)

7. Beati qui perseutionem patiuntur propter iustitiam quoniam ipsorum est regnum caelorum. (V.10)[189]

EXERCITIUM XII: *Irregular Verbs*

I. Irregular Verbs. Translate the verbs underlined, each of which is considered an irregular verb. Note that most verbs will need to be translated into English with more than one word. Do not be concerned if your translation does not perfectly match the number of blank lines allocated.

Exemplum. *Moyses erat distans ab Angelo, qui loquebatur in rubo de medio ignis.* (Alonso Tostado)[190]

Moses was away from the Angel, who was speaking from the middle of the bush of fire.

1. Sed non sic erit. (Hildegard of Bingen)[191]

   But it _____ not _____ thus.

2. Potest enim intelligi duas esse civitates unius nominis. (Remigius)[192]

   For _____ _____ be understood to be two towns with the same name.

3. Nos ergo qui regem volumus habere perfectum, Dominum nolumus habere perfectum? (Ambrose of Milan)[193]

   We, therefore, who _____ to have a perfect king, _____ _____ _____ also _____ to have a perfect Lord?

4. Ergo post passionem Christi poterant observari sine peccato mortali. (Adriaan van Utrecht)[194]

   Therefore, after the passion of Christ, they _____ be observed without mortal sin.

---

188. Note that the use of *mundo* here is as an adjective; it is not the noun form, which means something different.
189. The verb here in the future tense can be found in the dictionary under *patior, pati*. Like in Matt. V.7, this verb contains a passive form but active meaning. (We will learn all about these wily verbs soon enough.) Also, while we are at it, go ahead and translate *ipsorum* as "theirs."
190. Alonso Tostado, *Commentaria in Exodum* III (Venice: Giovanni Battista & Giovanni Bernardo Sessa, 1596), 18.
191. Hildegard of Bingen, *Liber Divinorum Operum Simplicis Hominis* IV (PL 197.899).
192. Remigius, *Commentarius in Genesim* XXXIII (PL 131.110). You can supply the subject as "it."
193. Ambrose of Milan, *Apologia Altera Prophetae David* (PL 14.910). Keep in mind that the negative nature of the word *nolo* will necessitate the word "no" in our translation, and also we will reverse the word order since it is a question.
194. Adriaan van Utrecht, *Quaestiones in Quartum Sententiarum Praesertim circa Sacramenta* (Paris: Jodoci Badij, 1516), n.p.

5. Ego enim verba exhortationis edere <u>possum</u>, sed ille mentes vestras in melius promovere <u>potest</u>, qui ego quidem plantare et rigare <u>possum</u>, ille autem dare sufficit incrementum. (Herve de Bourg-Dieu)[195]

For _____ _____ _____ to set forth the words of exhortation, but he _____ _____ to better promote in your minds, indeed, _____ _____ _____ to plant and to irrigate, but he is adequate to give the growth.

II. Irregular Verb Conjugation. For each of the verbs underlined, list the person, number, tense, and voice as well as the infinitive form of the verb. All examples come from the Latin Bible.

Exemplum. *Domus autem Israhel <u>nolent</u> audire te quia <u>nolunt</u> audire me.* (Ezek. III.7) *But the house of Israel <u>will not want</u> to listen to you since it <u>does not want</u> to listen to me.*

Third person plural future active from nolle
Third person plural present active from nolle

1. Omnia <u>possum</u> in eo qui me confortat. (Phil. IV.13) <u>I can</u> do all things in the one who strengthens me.

2. Et non <u>poterant</u> resistere sapientiae et Spiritui quo loquebatur. (Acts VI.10) And <u>they could</u> not resist the wisdom and the Spirit by which he spoke.

3. Ego sum vitis vos palmites qui manet in me et ego in eo hic <u>fert</u> fructum multum. (John XV.5) I am the vine; you are the branches. The one who remains in me, and I in him, <u>bears</u> much fruit.

4. Domine si <u>vis</u> potest me mundare. (Matt. VIII.2) If <u>you want</u>, Lord, you can make me clean.

5. Et misit servos suos vocare invitatos ad nuptias et <u>nolebant</u> venire. (Matt. XXII.3) And he sent his servants to call all those invited to the wedding but <u>they were not willing</u> to come.

III. Peter Damian. Peter Damian, or *Petrus Damianus*, was a Benedictine monk who lived in the eleventh century. He was a passionate reformer of the church and left behind a large collection of letters, sermons, prayers, and treatises. Translate the following sentences as best as you can. Each one contains at least one irregular verb. Consult a dictionary for unfamiliar words.

1. Vis audire qualiter obedias Deo? . . . Vis etiam audire qualiter obedias proximo?[196]

---

195. Herve de Bourg-Dieu, *Commentarii In Epistolas Pauli* (PL 181.1085).
196. Peter Damian, *Sermo* XXXII (144.680). Here you could translate *obedias* as "you may be subject to," and the word after it in both instances as if it is the direct object.

2. Deus vult probare constantiam suorum.[197]

3. Christum . . . ferebat in corde, Christum proferebat in voce.[198]

4. Domine Jesu Christe, qui es et qui eras Deus cum Patre ante saecula . . . Deus ex Deo vero.[199]

5. Usque in finem saeculi corpora sanctorum in sepulcris erunt.[200]

EXERCITIUM XIII: *Deponents and Semideponents*

I. Deponents and Semideponents. Translate all the verbs underlined, which are all deponents or semideponents. Note that some verbs may need to be translated into English with more than one word. Do not be concerned if your translation does not perfectly match the number of blank lines allocated.

Exemplum. *Non omnis qui underline{patitur} probra justus est; sed qui pro veritate innox patitur.* (Isidore of Seville)[201]

Not everyone who suffers shame is just; but the one who suffers innocently for the truth.

1. Non loquitur de principio vel Dei vel filii. (Wolfgang Musculus)[202]

   He does not _____ about the beginning either of God or of the Son.

2. Consolatur Deus Moysen dando ei societatem. (Alonso Tostado)[203]

   God _____ Moses by giving him fellowship.

3. Plantavit Dominus paradisum ad gratiam beatorum, posuit ibi hominem operari, et custodire eum. (Ambrose of Milan)[204]

   The Lord planted paradise for the well-being of the blessed. He placed humankind there _____ _____ and to protect it.

---

197. Peter Damian, *Epistola* XV (PL 144.369). Translate *suorum* as "their."
198. Peter Damian, *Sermo* XXXIII (Pl 144.681). Here you can supply the subject (or nominative) as "He," and insert an implied "his" before *corde* and *voce*.
199. Peter Damian, *Orátio* XXXIII (PL 145.929). In this sentence, because of the case used in the beginning of the sentence, the verbs will be translated more like third-personal singulars rather than second-personal singulars.
200. Peter Damian, *Additio Ad Tomum* III (PL 144.892).
201. Isidore of Seville, *Sententia* XXIX.24 (PL 83.631).
202. Wolfgang Musculus, *Commentarii in Evangelium Ioannis in Tres Heptadas Digesti* (Basil: Hervagius 1564), 2.
203. Alonso Tostado, *Commentaria in Exodum* III (Venice: Giovanni Battista & Giovanni Bernardo Sessa, 1596), 20.
204. Ambrose of Milan, *De Elia et Jejunio* III.7 (PL 14.700).

4. Ecce nunc et Pelagius, qui <u>ausus est</u>[205] <u>profiteri</u> se esse sine macula atque peccato. (Paulus Orosius)[206]

   Look, now also Pelagius, who _____ _____ _____ that he himself was without blemish and without sin.

5. Ita diversis modis possum <u>gloriari</u> in carne, sed non jam in talibus. (Herve de Bourg-Dieu)[207]

   Thus in many ways I can _____ in the flesh, but not yet in such things.

6. Et ad hoc <u>hortatur</u> omnes, qui legunt hunc psalmum. (Martin Luther)[208]

   And he _____ to this end all who read this psalm.

7. In hac lege Dei pius <u>meditatur</u>. (Martin Geier)[209]

   The holy person _____ on this law of God.

8. Figuram hujus praestantissimi ornamenti sacras Litteras non clare depingere <u>fateor</u>. (Salomon Van Til)[210]

   _____ _____ that the Holy Scriptures do not clearly depict the shape of this most excellent adornment.

9. Deus per suam magnam potentiam <u>operatur</u>. (Alonso Tostado)[211]

   God _____ through his own great power.

10. Ego ex animo <u>testor</u>. (Boethius)[212]

    _____ _____ from my soul.

II. Arnobius the Younger. Arnobius the Younger was a clergyman, originally from modern France, who lived in the fifth century. The following comes from his commentary on Psalms.[213] Each one contains at least one deponent or semideponent verb. Translate each sentence into English, consulting a dictionary for any unfamiliar words. Some clues will be provided in the footnotes.

---

205. This construction—*ausus est*—is part of the perfect system that we have not yet learned it. For now, translate all of *ausus est* as a past tense for that verb.
206. Paulus Orosius, *Liber de Arbitrii Libertate* (PL 31.1185).
207. Herve de Bourg-Dieu, *Commentarii In Epistolas Pauli* (PL 181.1300).
208. Martin Luther, *Dictata super Psalterium* XLIII (WA 1 3.246).
209. Martin Geier, *In Psalmos Davidis Praelectiones Publicae et Collectanea*, vol. 1 (Dresden, 1668), 7.
210. Salomon Van Til, *Commentarius de Tabernaculo Mosis* (Amsterdam, 1714), 51.
211. Alonso Tostado, *Commentaria in Exodum* III (Venice: Giovanni Battista & Giovanni Bernardo Sessa, 1596), 20.
212. Boethius, *De Consolatione Philosophiae*, Praefatio I (PL 63.579).
213. The excerpts come from Arnobius the Younger, *Commentarii in Psalmos* XLVIII (PL 53.393), 411–12.

1. Post haec confitebitur Deo invitus.[214]

2. Exaudi,[215] Deus, orationem meam cum tribulor, sive cum deprecor. Quam orationem?[216]

3. In matutinis[217] meditabor in [Deo], quia ipse est adjutor meus.

4. Non audebunt daemones loqui.

5. Rex tuus Christus Filius Dei laetabitur in Patre et Spiritu Sancto.

EXERCITIUM XIV: *Personal Pronouns and Demonstratives*

I. Pronouns. Translate all the pronouns underlined. Some may need to be translated with more than one word. Do not be concerned if your translation does not perfectly match the number of blank lines allocated.

Exemplum. *O quam admirabilis est esta conclusion!* (Philip of Harveng)[218]

How wonderful is this conclusion!

1. Hic est vetus ille et terrenus Adam. (Erasmus of Rotterdam)[219]

    _____ is _____ old and earthly Adam.

2. Breviter, quod omnia illius nostra sunt, et nos in illo omnia habemus, in nobis nihil. Super hoc inquam fundamentum aedificari nos convenit. (John Calvin)[220]

    In short, because all things _____ _____ are ours, and also we have all things in _____, but we have nothing in ourselves. Above _____ foundation, I say, we need to be built.

3. Itaque proclamet tibi tota substantia nostri in voce exultationis et confessionis. (Hugh of Flavigny)[221]

    Therefore, let every part of us cry out _____ _____ in a voice of exultation and of confession.

---

214. Note that *invitus, invita, invitum* should be translated here as a substantive adjective. Also, note that this verb will take its object in the dative case.
215. Translate as a command: "Hear."
216. The first part of this comes from Psalm LXIII.2 (in the Vulgate). You can translate *Quam* as "What."
217. *Matutinus, matutina, matutinum* is an adjective that is often used as a substantive.
218. Philip of Harveng, *Moralitates in Cantica* (PL 203.513).
219. Erasmus of Rotterdam, *Enchiridion Militis Christiani* (Cologne, 1519), 13.
220. John Calvin, *Institutio Christianae Religionis* III.15.5 (CR 30.583).
221. Hugh of Flavigny, *Chronica* II (PL 154.367).

4. Crudelitas vestra gloria est nostra. (Tertullian)[222]

   _____ cruelty is _____ fame.

5. Quid sit Theologia, et quondam sit ejus objectum. (Louis Abelly)[223]

   What theology is and what _____ object sometimes is.

6. In altera narrationis parte, de Dei erga suam Ecclesiam providentia disserit. (Jean de L'Espine)[224]

   In another part of the story, he speaks against _____ Church concerning the providence of God.

7. Aliquot ex epistolis illis, ab Urbano statim post suam electionem scriptis, supersunt. (Anonymous)[225]

   Several of _____ letters survive, which were immediately written by Urban after his election.

8. Venio nunc ad Iustinum Martyrem, quem Bellarminus deinde nobis objicit. (William Whitaker)[226]

   I come now to Justin Martyr, whom [Robert] Bellarmine then sets in opposition _____ _____.

9. Psalmus hic, qui a plurimis habetur prooemium ac brevis summa totius libri sequentis, tria complectitur membra: I. Statum piorum, II. Impiorum, III. Utriusque causas et originem. (Martin Geier)[227]

   _____ psalm, which is held by many to be the beginning and the short summary of the whole next book, contains three parts: (i) the status of the godly, (ii) of the ungodly, and (iii) the causes and origin of both.

10. Unde Proverbium illud, cuius primo libro memini, Aut Erasmus Lutherizat, aut Lutherus Erasmizat. (Florimund de Raemond)[228]

    Hence _____ proverb, which I recalled in the first book: either Erasmus Lutherizes or Luther Erasmusizes.[229]

---

222. Tertullian, *Liber ad Scapulam* V (PL 1.704).
223. Louis Abelly, *Tractatus de Fide, De Deo, ac de Trinitate*, vol. 1 of *Institutiones Theologicae* (Joseph Bay, 1825), xxi.
224. Jean de L'Espine, *Tractatus de Providentia Dei* (Geneva: Jean Le Preux, 1591), n.p.
225. Anonymous, *Vita Beati Urbani II* XXIII (PL 151.32).
226. William Whitaker, *Disputatio de Sacra Scriptura contra Huius Temporis Papistas* (Cambridge, 1588), 437.
227. Martin Geier, *In Psalmos Davidis Praelectiones Publicae et Collectanea*, vol. 1 (Dresden, 1668), 1.
228. Florimund de Raemond, *Historia de Ortu* (Gerhardus Greuenbruch, 1644), 7.
229. Here the author turns both Martin Luther and Erasmus into verbs.

II. Martin Luther. Born in 1483 in Germany, Martin Luther is one of the most famous (and infamous) theologians of all time. He is considered the father of Protestantism. Although he was a former monk and a lifelong preacher, his "day job" was as a professor at the University of Wittenberg. In Wittenberg, he taught and wrote constantly. Among his many writings are sermons. The following was preached in 1518. It is titled *Sermo de Poenitentia*, "Sermon on Repentance."[230] Translate each sentence into English, consulting a dictionary for any unfamiliar words. Some clues will be provided in the footnotes.

1. Sic enim B. Anselmus docet ascendere ad amorem Dei ex amore hominis boni.[231]

2. Signum est enim verae contritionis.[232]

3. Haec est poenitentia iucunda, vera, stabilis, et ex spiritu nata.[233]

4. Poenitentia enim debet esse dulcis.

5. Amor enim est vinculum perpetuum.

EXERCITIUM XV: *Reflexives, Possessives, and Intensives*

I. Pronouns. Translate all the pronouns underlined. One or more may need to be translated with more than one word. Do not be concerned if your translation does not perfectly match the number of blank lines allocated.

Exemplum. *Si Filius Dei es, mitte te deorsum.* (Matt. IV.4)

If you are the Son of God, throw yourself downward.

1. Christus ipse visam civitatem deplorat. (Wolfgang Capito)[234]

   Christ _____ laments the city he sees.

2. Per filium ergo suum facta est mater Filii Dei. (Arnobius the Younger)[235]

   Therefore, the mother of the Son of God was created by her _____ son.

---

230. All excerpts come from Luther, *Sermo de Poenitentia* (WA I.320).
231. Translate *B. Anselmus* as "Blessed Anselm." He is referring to the medieval theologian Anselm of Canterbury.
232. You can assume the subject of *signum* is "it."
233. You can assume that *Haec* is patterning with *poenitentia*. Translate *nata* as "born."
234. Wolfgang Capito, *In Hoseam Prophetam* (Basel: John Herwagen, 1528), 71.
235. Arnobius the Younger, *Conflictus de Deo Trino et Uno* II.11 (PL 53.286).

3. Ipsi quippe regales sunt sedes quas Deus inhabitat, ipsi reges et Patres Ecclesiae. (Peter Damian)[236]

   Indeed, _____ are the royal seats that God inhabits; _____ are the kings and patriarchs of the Church.

4. Sed qui viam suam corrigit, non confundetur. (Ambrose of Milan)[237]

   But the one who corrects _____ way will not be confounded.

5. Adam ipse factus ex materia non coinquinata. (Lorenzo Valla)[238]

   Adam _____ was made from matter, not from something defiled.

6. Castellio in versione sua reddit invadere . . . non videtur satis esse aptum. (Petrus Abresch)[239]

   In _____ version, [Sebastian] Castellio renders it as "to enter" . . . [but] that does not seem to be quite appropriate.

7. Filius vero primo loco ponitur, quod per ipsum omnia facta sunt. (Christianus Avianus)[240]

   But the Son is put in the first position because all things were made through _____.

8. Loquar charitati vestrae, fratres, quod pertineat ad contemptum praesentis saeculi, ad spem futuri saeculi. (Augustine of Hippo)[241]

   I will speak of _____ love, brothers, because it pertains to the contempt of the present world and to the hope of the one to come.

9. Ipsi homines caeteris animalibus praestant. (Diego Valades)[242]

   Humans _____ excel the other animals.

10. Hoc opus nunc suscepimus, et haec praesentis operis nostri est intentio, demonstrare qualiter vel quo thesaurus iste sit absconditus in agro. (Rupert of Deutz)[243]

    We have now undertaken this work and this aim _____ _____ in this present work is to show how or in what way this treasure was hidden in the field.

---

236. Peter Damian, *Testimonia Libri Sapientiae* II (PL 145.1156).
237. Ambrose of Milan, "Sermo Secundus," in *In Psalmus CXVIII Expositio* (PL 15.1208).
238. Lorenzo Valla, *De Libero Arbtrio* (Munich: Cratander, 1518), 11 recto.
239. Petrus Abresch, *Dissertatio Philologico-Theologica ad Dictum Gabrielis Luc. 1:35* (Groningen, 1784), 5.
240. Christianus Avianus, *Tractatus de Hebraea Lingua* (Leipzig, 1620), 12.
241. Augustine of Hippo, *Sermo* CCCXLV (PL 39.1517).
242. Diego Valades, *Rhetorica Christiana* (Perugia: Petrutius, 1579), 3.
243. Rupert of Deutz, *De Glorificatione Trinitatis* I (PL 169.15).

II. Ephesians. The following examples come from the Latin version of Ephesians. Keep in mind that not all of these are complete sentences. Nevertheless, translate each into English, consulting a dictionary for any unfamiliar words. Some clues will be provided in the footnotes.

1. Memoriam vestri faciens in orationibus meis. (I.16)[244]

2. Quae est corpus ipsius et plenitudo eius qui omnia in omnibus adimpletur. (I.23)[245]

3. Et vos cum essetis mortui delictis et peccatis vestris. (II.1)[246]

4. In quibus et nos omnes aliquando conversati sumus in desideriis carnis nostrae. (II.3)[247]

5. Deus autem qui dives est in misericordia propter nimiam caritatem suam. (II.4)

EXERCITIUM XVI: *Relatives, Interrogatives, and Indefinites*

I. Pronouns, Nouns, and Verbs. Translate the pronouns, nouns, and verbs underlined. Some may need to be translated with more than one word. Do not be concerned if your translation does not perfectly match the number of blank lines allocated.

Exemplum. *Post dies aliquot spiritum exhalavit.* (Innocent III)[248]

After *a few* days, he breathed out his spirit.

1. Quidam enim sunt pastores, quidam mercenarii, quidam lupi. Pastores sunt qui oves diligunt; mercenarii, qui lanam et lac accipiunt; lupi, qui carnes comedunt (Hugh of St. Victor).[249]

   For _____ [pastors] are shepherds, _____ mercenaries, _____ wolves. The shepherds are those _____ love the sheep; mercenaries, those _____ take wool and milk; wolves, those _____ devour the flesh.

2. Iam quaeritur, quo sensu hic veniat? (Petrus Abresch)[250]

   The question is now raised: _____ _____ sense does it come here?

---

244. You can translate *faciens* as "making."
245. As mentioned above, keep in mind that *ipse, ipsa, ipsum* does not always have to have the concept of "self" implied. Here, for instance, it does not. You can start your translation with "Which."
246. You can translate *essetis* as "you were."
247. You could translate *conversati sumus* as: "we lived . . ."
248. Innocent III, *Appendix at Regesta* XXXIV (PL 216.1253).
249. Hugh of St. Victor, *Miscellanea* CL (PL 177.533).
250. Petrus Abresch, *Dissertatio Philologico-Theologica ad Dictum Gabrielis Luc. 1:35* (Groningen, 1784), 5.

3. De qua lege aut de quo consilio dicit Salomon, cum ait: Custodi legem atque consilium? (Salonius the Viennese)[251]

   About _____ law or about _____ plan did Solomon speak when he said: "Keep the law and counsel" [Prov. III.21]?

4. Neque etiam addo argumentum gratitudinis et glorificationis. (Peter van Mastricht)[252]

   Nor also _____ _____ _____ an argument of gratitude or glorification.

5. Nam quilibet munificus donat illa quae possidet; Deus autem, qui est ineffabile bonum, se largitur in praemio. (Cassiodorus)[253]

   For _____ generous gives what he _____. But God, who is indescribably good, is more abundant in his reward.

6. Christus parabolas suas hominibus proposuit propter spiritualia vitia, quibus saepe falluntur, et etiam propter virtutes, quibus contra illa victoriose pugnant. (Hildegard of Bingen)[254]

   Christ taught his parables to people on account of spiritual vices, _____ _____ they are often deceived; and also on account of [spiritual] virtues, _____ _____ _____ _____ victoriously against them.

7. Ita Deus quoque immutat in varias et miserabiles species faciem hominis. (Johannes Cocceius)[255]

   In this way, God _____ alters into different appearances, even sad ones, the face of humankind.

8. Te oro, ut saepe mihi scribas. Scripsit ad me quispiam cui nomen est Morelio. (Philip Melanchthon)[256]

   Please write me often. _____ by the name of Morelio wrote me.

9. Habet ergo caro cibum suum, quo reficitur; habet et anima cibum suum, quo saginatur. (Hugh of St. Victor)[257]

   Therefore, the flesh has its own food _____ _____ it is refreshed; and the soul has its own food _____ _____ it is nourished.

---

251. Salonius the Viennese, *Expositio Mystica* (PL 53.971).
252. Peter van Mastricht, *Theoretico-Practica Theologia, De Sancta Trinitate* 1.2.24 (Societas, 1724), 244.
253. Cassiodorus, *Expositio in Psalterium* V (PL 70.58).
254. Hildegard of Bingen, *Solutiones Quaestionum* XXX (PL 197.1052).
255. Johannes Cocceius, *Opera Anecdota, Theologica, et Philologica* I.14 (Amsterdam, 1706), 166.
256. Philip Melanchthon, *Epistola* MMMCCCLXXII (CR 7.157).
257. Hugh of St. Victor, *Miscellanea* CXXII (PL 177.547).

EXERCITIA

10. Solem videmus in <u>quadam</u> coeli parte. (Hilary of Poitiers)[258]

    We see the sun in _____ part of the sky.

II. Salonius the Viennese. Salonius was a churchman and bishop raised in the monastery at Lerins in France during the fifth century. The following is an *Expositio Mystica*, "mystical commentary," that Salonius wrote on the book of Proverbs.[259] The commentary features a question-and-answer format between himself and his brother Veranus. In the following excerpts, Veranus asks all the questions. Salonius answers them. Translate each sentence into English, consulting a dictionary for any unfamiliar words. Some clues will be provided in the footnotes.

1. Parabolae qua lingua dicuntur?

2. Quare Salomon huic libro nomen istud imposuit?

3. Quomodo ergo interpretatur Salomon?[260]

4. Quid distat inter sapientiam et disciplinam?

5. Quid est ergo discere sapientiam?

6. Quot sunt timores Domini? Duo, hoc est, servilis et sanctus.

7. Quid est quod ait: *Inclina cor tuum ad intelligendam prudentiam*?[261]

8. Quomodo potest homo inclinare cor?

9. De qua lege aut de quo consilio dicit Salomon, cum ait: *Custodi legem atque consilium*?[262]

10. Quae est lex sapientiae?

---

258. Hilary of Poitiers, *Tractatus in CXVIII Psalmum* (PL 9.630).
259. The excerpts come from Salonius the Viennese, *Expositio Mystica* (PL 53.967–71).
260. Keep in mind that the verb used here is a deponent.
261. The italics here, and in the passage in the other example, are biblical quotes (both, of course, coming from Proverbs). You can translate *intelligendam* as "to understanding."
262. You can translate the word *custodi* as a command: "Keep."

BASICS OF LATIN

EXERCITIUM XVII: *Perfect Actives*

I. Perfect Active. Translate all the perfects underlined. You may do so using either the present completed aspect or simple past. Do not be concerned if your translation does not perfectly match the number of blank lines allocated.

Exemplum. *Claruit* in anno 453.   He *flourished* in the year 453.
(Salonius the Viennese)[263]

1. Postquam vero Dominus hominem ex abysso perditionis reductum sibi per gratiam adoptionis segregavit, quia illum regeneravit ac reformavit novam vitam. (John Calvin)[264]

    But after the Lord has withdrawn the person from the abyss of destruction and _____ _____ him for himself through the sake of adoption, [God] _____ _____ him and _____ _____ him to new life.

2. Hodie nobis Dominus patrem cum filiis duobus vocavit et produxit in medium. (Peter Chrysologus)[265]

    Today, the Lord _____ _____ and _____ _____ the father with two sons in our midst.

3. Iuxta priorem quidem statum, voluit Deus in Christo super terram, in carne seu homine apparere ac in humilitate inveniri. (Caspar Schwenkfeld)[266]

    Indeed, according to the earlier ordinance, God _____ _____ Christ upon the earth, to appear in flesh and to be found in lowliness.

4. Exposuimus hactenus varia adversariorum schemata. (Franz Albert Aepinus)[267]

    Up to this point, _____ _____ _____ the different concepts of our adversaries.

5. Et nos ergo ad imitandam verecundiam seduli, ad conferendam gratiam non usurpatores, quae illi Spiritus infudit[268] sapientiae, ea per illum nobis manifestata, et visu comperta atque exemplo, vobis quasi liberis tradimus. (Ambrose of Milan)[269]

    And we, therefore, diligent to imitate his reverence and to dispense grace without usurpation, hand over to you as children those things that the Spirit of Wisdom _____ _____ _____ him, which have been made clear to us through him and learned both by sight and by example.

---

263. Salonius the Viennese, *Expositio Mystica, Prolegomenon* (PL 53.967).
264. John Calvin, *Institutio Christianae Religionis* III.17.5 (CR 30.593).
265. Peter Chrysologus, *Sermo* I (PL 52.183).
266. Caspar Schwenkfeld, *De Duplici Statu, Officio, et Cognitione Christi* (Basel, 1546), n.p.
267. Franz Albert Aepinus, *Moralitas Graduum Academicorum ex Iuris Naturae Principiis contra Fanaticos* (Rostock: Wepplinguis, 1702), n.p.
268. If you consider the meaning of the prefix -in ("into"), you can easily figure out the meaning of this verb. One more hint: It is related to the vocabulary word we are learning for this *capitulum*: *fundo, fundere, fudi, fusus*.
269. Ambrose of Milan, *De Officiis Ministrorum* I.2 (PL 16.23).

EXERCITIA

II. Perfect Active in the Latin Vulgate. Fill in the blank with the correct Latin form of the perfect active of *sum, esse, fui, futurus*. All examples come from the Vulgate.

Exemplum. *Cum enim servi essetis peccati, liberi fuistis iustitia.* (Rom. VI.20)

For when you all were slaves of sin, <u>you all were</u> free from righteousness.

1. Dei enim Filius Jesus Christus, qui in vobis per nos praedicatus est, per me, et Silvanum, et Timotheum, non _____ Est et Non, sed Est in illo _____. (II Cor. I.19)

   For the Son of God, Jesus Christ, who was preached among you through me, Silvanus, and Timothy, <u>has</u> been not Yes and No, but he <u>has been</u> Yes in everything.

2. Sed habitavimus in tabernaculis, et obedientes _____ iuxta omnia quae praecepit nobis Jonadam pater noster. (Jer. XXXV.10)

   But we have dwelt in tents, and <u>we have been</u> obedient to everything that our father Jehonadab has commanded us.

3. _____ autem dies vitae Abrahae, centum septuaginta quinque anni. (Gen. XXV.7)

   Now the days of the life of Abraham <u>were</u> 175 years.

4. Et ego in infirmitate, et timore, et tremore multo _____ apud vos. (I Cor. II.3)

   And <u>I was</u> among you in weakness and in much fear and trembling.

5. Et ait illi: Euge bone serve, quia in modico _____ fidelis, eris potestatem habens super decem civitates. (Luke XIX.17)

   And he said to him, "Well done, good servant. Because <u>you have been</u> faithful in a small thing, you will have authority over ten cities."

III. Benedictus. We bring our discussion of Latin prayers from Luke I to a full circle here. Whereas the corresponding *capitulum* started with Mary's prayer in Luke I.46–55, called the *Magnificat* due to the first Latin word, we now conclude with Zechariah's prayer in Luke I.68–79, called the *Benedictus* due to its first word. The excerpt contains every part of the prayer other than the last verse. Translation notes are kept to a minimum, and not all sentences are complete sentences.

1. Benedictus Dominus Deus Israel, qui visitavit, et fecit redemptionem plebis suae.

2. Et erexit cornu salutis nobis, in domo David pueri sui.

3. Sicut locutus est per os sanctorum, qui a saeculo sunt, prophetarum eius.[270]

4. Salutem ex inimicis nostris, et de manu omnium qui oderunt nos.

5. Ad faciendam misericordiam cum patribus nostris, et memorari testamenti sui sancti.[271]

6. Ius iurandum, quod juravit ad Abraham patrem nostrum daturum se nobis.[272]

7. Ut sine timore, de manu inimicorum nostrorum liberati, serviamus illi, in sanctitate et iustitia coram ipso, omnibus diebus nostris.[273]

8. Et tu puer, propheta Altissimi vocaberis: praeibis enim ante faciem Domini parare vias eius.[274]

9. Ad dandam scientiam salutis plebi eius, in remissionem peccatorum eorum.[275]

10. Per viscera misericordiae Dei nostri: in quibus visitavit nos, oriens ex alto.[276]

EXERCITIUM XVIII: *Pluperfect Actives and Future Perfect Actives*

I. Pluperfect and Future Perfect Active. Translate all the pluperfects and future perfects underlined. Do not be concerned if your translation does not perfectly match the number of blank lines allocated.

---

270. For the meaning of *locutus est*, see 17.6. This verb is deponent and thus, though passive in form, should be translated actively. Also, you will notice that the adjective *sanctorum* and the noun it modifies, *prophetarum*, are separated by several words.
271. Translate *Ad faciendam* as "To show . . ."
272. You will sometimes see *ius iurandum*, "vowing an oath," as a complete verb: *jusjurandum*. The meaning is the same. Translate *daturum* as "that he would grant . . ." Your translation will not be a complete sentence.
273. Translate *serviamus* as "that we may serve . . ."
274. The first two verbs in this sentence are in the future tense; *parare* is an infinitive that you can translate as "to prepare."
275. Translate *Ad dandam* as "To give . . ."
276. The word *oriens* can refer to "[the] east," "[the] dawn," or "[the] rising [sun]," just as the original Greek word (ἀνατολή) does. In fact, modern English Bibles translate this word in any number of ways. Compare some different biblical translations for Luke I.78 before deciding how you would like to translate this word. There are several acceptable ways to render this word.

Exemplum. Tunc pater suus respondit illi, et dixit: Chirographum quidem illius penes me habeo: quod dum illi <u>ostenderis</u>, statim restituet. (Tob. V.3)

Then his father responded to him and said: "I have a note of his hand with me. For <u>when you will have shown</u> him, he will repay it immediately."

1. Si poenitentiam non <u>egeris</u>, incides in manus Domini secundum magnitudinem ejus. (Jerome)[277]

   If you _____ not _____ _____ penitence, you will fall in the Lord's hands according to his greatness.

2. Deus <u>dixerat</u> quod daret eis gratiam in conspectu Aegyptiorum, ut darent eis, quaecumque postularent. (Alonso Tostado)[278]

   God _____ _____ that he would give to them favor in the sight of the Egyptians so that they would give to them whatever they asked.

3. Sciebat enim Dominus quid faceret pro amicis, qui patienter utebatur inimicis: ac sic omnia <u>dederat</u> Pater in manus ejus, et in usum mala, et in effectum bona. (Augustine of Hippo)[279]

   For the Lord knew what he was doing for his friends and was patiently making use of his enemies; and, in this way, the Father _____ _____ all things into his hands, both evil things for their use, and good things for the result.

4. Nunc ex Gothescalci schola, quidquid antea <u>dixerit</u>, Fulgentii audite consilium, et credite dictis Augustini ac Prosperi, quae isdem Fulgentius paulo ante proposuit. (Hincmar of Rheims)[280]

   Now, from the school of Gottschalk, whatever he _____ _____ _____ earlier, listen to the advice of Fulgentius and trust the words of Augustine and Prosper [of Aquitaine], which Fulgentius proposed a little beforehand in the same words.

5. Si autem <u>ostenderitis</u> quoniam Bel comedat haec, morietur Daniel quia blasphemavit in Bel. Et dixit Daniel regi: Fiat iuxta verbum tuum. (Dan. XIV.8)

   But if _____ _____ _____ _____ _____ that Bel would eat these things, Daniel will die because he has blasphemed against Bel. And Daniel said to the king, "Let it be done according to your word."

II. Perpetua. Perpetua was a noblewoman from the Roman city of Carthage. She was martyred along with her slave Felicitas around the year 203. Apparently, she kept a diary while in prison, which was used to narrate her story of faith. Some of these sentences come directly from the mouth of Perpetua. The excerpt below describes Perpetua's death in the Roman stadium by wild animals.[281] Each sentence contains either a pluperfect or future perfect active. Some translation clues will be provided.

---

277. Jerome, *Epistola* XXXIV.3 (PL 30.243).
278. Alonso Tostado, *Commentaria in Exodum* III (Venice: Giovanni Battista & Giovanni Bernardo Sessa, 1596), 21.
279. Augustine, *In Joannis Evangelium* LV.5 (PL 35.1786).
280. Hincmar of Rheims, *De Praedestinatione Dissertatio Posterior* VIV (PL125.125).
281. This excerpt is found in *The Acts of the Christian Martyrs*, ed. Herbert Musurillo (Oxford: Oxford University Press, 1972), 106–30. Specific sections will appear in parentheses.

1. Ascendit autem Saturus prior, qui postea se propter nos ultro tradiderat (quia ipse nos aedificaverat), et tunc cum adducti sumus. (IV.5)[282]

2. Et confortavi eum dicens: Hoc fiet in illa catasta quod Deus voluerit. (V.6)[283]

3. Pro hoc ergo orationem feceram: et inter me et illum grande erat diastema ita ut uterque ad invicem accedere non possemus. (VII.6)[284]

4. Video locum illum quem retro videram et Dinocraten mundo corpore bene vestitum refrigerantem. (VIII.1)[285]

5. Et petiit silentium et dixit: Hic Aegyptius, si hanc vicerit, occidet illam gladio; haec, si hunc vicerit, accipiet ramum istum. (X.9)[286]

EXERCITIUM XIX: *Present Active and Present Passive Subjunctives*

I. Present Subjunctives. Translate each of the underlined words below. Each sentence contains at least one active or passive subjunctive. Do not be concerned if your translation does not perfectly match the number of blank lines allocated.

Exemplum. *Neque enim quaero intelligere ut credam; sed credo ut intelligam.* (Anselm of Canterbury)[287]

For nor do I seek to understand so that I may believe; rather, I believe so that I may understand.

1. Quid est ergo discere sapientiam? Scire et intelligere quomodo recte credere debeas. (Salonius the Viennese)[288]

---

[282]. *Saturus* is a person's name. The adverb *ultro* can be rendered many ways, but here you can go with "freely." You can translate *adducti sumus* as "we were arrested."
[283]. Note that the verb at the end of the sentence, *voluerit*, is actually a perfect subjunctive, not a future perfect indicative active.
[284]. The noun *diastema* comes directly from the Greek word translated as "space" or "interval."
[285]. This sentence contains the name of Perpetua's deceased brother, Dinocrates. She is explaining a dream she had had of her deceased brother while in prison. You can translate the word *retro* as "formerly," *vestitum* as "dressed," and *refrigerantem* as "refreshed." Finally, be sure to translate *mundo* as an adjective and not as a noun. The two words mean very different things.
[286]. You can supply the subject of these two initial verbs as "he." Here Perpetua is referring to "This Egyptian," one of the gladiators attempting to kill her and the other Christian martyrs. In this sentence, you can assume that *hanc* can be translated as "her" or "this one" (that is, Perpetua); *haec* as "she" or "this one" (that is, Perpetua); and *hunc* as "he" or "this one" (that is, the gladiator).
[287]. Anselm of Canterbury, *Proslogion* I (PL 158.227).
[288]. Salonius the Viennese, *Expositio Mystica* (PL 53.969).

What, therefore, is it to learn wisdom? To know and to understand how _____ _____ believe correctly.

2. Solet etiam quaeri utrum post hanc vitam aliqua peccata <u>remittantur</u>. (Peter Lombard)[289]

   It is customary to inquire whether any sins _____ _____ _____ after this life.

3. Ne venire imperiti ad magisterium <u>audeant</u>. (Gregory I)[290]

   The inexperienced _____ not _____ to obtain an office of authority.

4. Utrumque ergo <u>scias</u> necesse est, et quid sis et quod a te ipso non sis. (Bernard of Clairvaux)[291]

   Therefore, there are two things that _____ _____ _____: what you are and that you are not what you are by your own (power).

5. Sic et ecclesia orat, ut Deus nos per exempla sanctorum suorum <u>restauret</u>. (Martin Luther)[292]

   In this way also, the church prays that God _____ _____ us through the examples of his saints.

II. Present Subjunctives of the "To Be" Verb in Tertullian. Translate each of the examples of *sum, esse, fui, futurus* in the present subjunctive. All examples come from the fiery writer from North Africa, Tertullian. Do not be concerned if your translation does not perfectly match the number of blank lines allocated.

Exemplum. *Veritas autem sic unum Deum exigit defendendo, ut solius <u>sit</u> quidquid ipsius est.*[293]

But truth thus demands that God is one by defending that whatever <u>belongs</u> to God is his alone.

1. Habere enim filium debeo, ut pater <u>sim</u>.[294]

   For I have to have a son if _____ _____ _____ a father.

2. Si circumcidaris, jam non <u>sis</u> filius.[295]

   If you become circumcised, _____ _____ no longer _____ [God's] Son.

---

289. Peter Lombard, *Sententiarum Libri Quattuor* IV.22.1 (PL 192.895).
290. Gregory I, *Regulae Pastoralis Liber* I.1 (PL 77.14).
291. Bernard of Clairvaux, *De Diligendo Deo* II.4 (PL 182.976). Hopefully you noticed two subjunctives that I did not underline: two instances of *sit*. We will have exercises for subjunctives for the "to be" verb in the section below.
292. Martin Luther, *Sermo de Poenitentia* (WA 1.320).
293. Tertullian, *Adversus Hermogenem* V (PL 2.202).
294. Tertullian, *Adversus Praxeam* X (PL 2.165).
295. Tertullian, *De Monogamia* V (PL 2.936).

3. Deum autem unum esse oportet, quia quod summum sit, Deus est: summum autem non erit, nisi quod unicum fuerit.²⁹⁶

   But God must be one because that which _____ _____ supreme is God. And nothing will be supreme other than that which is unique.

4. Quin potius memores simus tam dominicarum pronuntiationum, quam apostolicarum litterarum, quae nobis et futuras haereses praenuntiarunt.²⁹⁷

   But _____ _____ rather _____ mindful of the dominical sayings as much as of the apostolic letters, which also predict to us future heresies.

5. Et hic enim illam Joannes commendavit, quod sint quaedam delicta quotidianae incursionis, quibus omnes simus objecti.²⁹⁸

   For also John himself has commended here that there_____ certain sins of daily infraction, to which _____ _____ _____ all subject.

III. Thomas à Kempis. Thomas à Kempis was a spiritual giant. Born in Germany in the year 1380, he spent most of his life in the Netherlands as a brother in the religious movement known as *Devotio Moderna*, "Modern Devotion." According to scholar John van Engen, à Kempis' book *De Imitatione Christi*, "On the Imitation of Christ," is "the most influential devotional book in Western Christian History."²⁹⁹ Written between 1418 and 1427, *De Imitatione Christi* explores core areas of Christian formation that are just as relevant today as they were when written six centuries ago. The excerpt below (containing several biblical verses in italics) is the introduction to the entire book.³⁰⁰

1. *Qui sequitur me non ambulat in tenebris* dicit Dominus.

2. Haec sunt verba Christi, quibus admonemur quatenus vitam eius et mores imitemur, si volumus veraciter illuminari, et ab omni caecitate cordis liberari.³⁰¹

3. Summum igitur studium nostrum, sit in vita Jesu meditari.³⁰²

---

296. Tertullian, *Adversus Hermogenem* V (PL 2.201).
297. Tertullian, *De Praescriptionibus* IV (PL 2.16).
298. Tertullian, *De Pudicitia* XIX (PL 2.1020).
299. John van Engen, *Devotio Moderna: Basic Writings* (New York: Paulist, 1988), 8.
300. The text comes from Thomas à Kempis, *De Imitatione Christi* I.1–3 (Egmondt, 1629), 11–12.
301. Both *illuminari* and *liberari* are present passive infinitives, which are the "to be -ed" verbal forms.
302. The verb *meditari* is also a present passive infinitive, but it is a deponent.

4. Qui autem vult plene et sapide verba Christi intelligere, oportet ut totam vitam suam illi studeat conformare.[303]

5. Quid prodest tibi alta de Trinitate disputare, si careas humilitate unde displiceas Trinitati? Vere alta verba non faciunt sanctum et justum, sed virtuosa vita efficit Deo carum.

EXERCITIUM XX: *Imperfect Active and Imperfect Passive Subjunctives*

I. Imperfect Subjunctives. Translate each of the underlined words below. Please keep in mind that the imperfect subjunctive may be rendered accurately in any number of ways. Each sentence contains at least one imperfect subjunctive. Do not be concerned if your translation does not perfectly match the number of blank lines allocated.

Exemplum. *Cum adhuc Romae demoraremur, voluimus disputando quarere unde sit malum.* (Augustine of Hippo)[304]

While we were still lingering in Rome, we wanted to inquire through discussion where evil comes from.

1. Certe omnium patrum consensu laudatum et probatum est, quia summam Christianae fidei historiam revera complecteretur. (Peter Ramus)[305]

   Certainly, by the consensus of all the fathers, [the Nicene Creed] has been praised and approved since it, in fact, _____ _____ the complete story of the Christian faith.

2. Sic autem est conditus, ut si peccaret mori posset. (Haimo of Halberstadt)

   But in this way he was created so that if he _____ _____, he _____ _____ _____ to die [or "of dying"].

3. Praeterea etiam si vera sententia esset, nec ibi congrue poneretur, nec aliquid ibi doctrinae pondus haberet. (Odo of Tournai)[306]

   Furthermore, indeed, if the judgment _____ true, neither _____ _____ _____ suitably there, nor _____ anyone _____ the weight of instruction there.

---

303. Both *intelligere* and *conformare* are present active infinitives, which can be translated as "to . . .". The verb *oportet* may be translated as "should."

304. Augustine of Hippo, *Retractionum* I.9.1 (PL 32.595).

305. Peter Ramus, *Commentariorum de Religione Christiana Libri Quattuor* I.2 (Frankfurt: Andreas Wechel, 1576), 11.

306. Odo of Tournai, *Homilia de Villico Iniquitatis* XXXIII (PL 160.1147).

4. Et ideo absentibus illis qui priores facti erant apostoli, Paulus a Domino perfectus est: ut quando cum eis contulit, nihil esset quod perfectioni ejus <u>adderent</u>: sed potius <u>viderent</u> eumdem Dominum Jesum Christum. (Augustine of Hippo)[307]

   Therefore, being absent from those who had formerly been made apostles, Paul was made complete by the Lord so that when he conferred with them, they _____ _____ nothing to his completion but, on the contrary, they _____ _____ the same Lord Jesus Christ.

5. Igitur mandatum est nobis, ut nos <u>praepararemur</u> ad pugnam. (Godfrey of Bouillon)[308]

   Therefore, we were commanded so that _____ _____ _____ _____ for combat.

II. Imperfect Subjunctives of the "To Be" Verb in Alcuin of York.

Translate the following imperfect subjunctives in the writings of Alcuin of York, an influential churchman in the eighth century who also served as an advisor to Charlemagne. Do not be concerned if your translation does not perfectly match the number of blank lines allocated.

Exemplum. *Dixit eis Jesus: Si caeci <u>essetis</u>, non haberetis peccatum. Cum sit caecitas ipsa peccatum. Si caeci <u>essetis</u>, id est, si vos caecos adverteretis, et ad medicum curreretis; si ergo ita caeci <u>essetis</u>, non haberetis peccatum.*[309]

Jesus said to them, "If <u>you were</u> blind, you would not have sin." (Because blindness itself is sin.) "If <u>you were</u> blind," that is, if you turned toward the blind and hastened to a doctor. If, therefore, <u>you were</u> thus blind, you would not have sin.

1. Utinam dignus <u>essem</u> pacem praedicare, non discordiam seminare, et signum portare Christi, non arma diaboli.[310]

   Would that _____ _____ _____ worthy to preach peace and not sow discord, to carry the sign of Christ and not the weapons of the devil.

2. Quid de piscibus vel alitibus, quae in aquis vel super aquas vivere possunt, intelligi debet; si in arca <u>essent</u>, an non.[311]

   What ought to be understood about the fish and birds, which are able to survive in water or above the water, if _____ _____ in [Noah's] ark or not?

3. Cur Deus quasi nesciens interrogavit, ubi <u>esset</u> Adam.[312]

   Why did God ask, as if he did not know, where Adam _____?

---

307. Augustine of Hippo, *Epistola ad Galatas* II (PL 35.2112).
308. Godfrey of Bouillon, *De Bello Sacro* XXVI (PL 155.633).
309. Alcuin of York, *Commentaria in Sancti Ioannis Evangelium* XXIV.39 (PL 100.882). This sentence is quoting and commenting on a verse from the Gospel of John. How many more imperfect subjunctives can you spot besides the three underlined?
310. Alcuin of York, *Epistola* VIII (PL 100.149).
311. Alcuin of York, *Interrogationes et Responsiones in Genesim* CXV (PL 100.529).
312. Alcuin of York, *Interrogationes et Responsiones in Genesim* LXXII (PL 100.524).

4. Christus pro nobis, cum inimici <u>essemus</u>, mori non dubitavit.[313]

   Christ did not hesitate to die for us although _____ _____ [his] enemies.

5. Erant itaque de mundo, sed per gratiam electi sunt de mundo, ut non <u>essent</u> in mundo, in quo nati sunt de peccati radice.[314]

   Therefore, they were from the world, but through grace they were chosen from the world so that they _____ not _____ in the world in which they were born from the root of sin.

III. Lorenzo Valla. An accomplished philosopher, philologist, and textual critic, Lorenzo Valla was an Italian humanist who lived from 1407 to 1457. Among his many writings, he published a philosophical treatise on free will in 1439. Christians had debated the topic of free will for centuries in the Christian tradition. The following excerpt comes from the preface of Valla's work.[315] In the opening line, Valla addressed the book to Bishop Garcia of Lerida, a region in Catalonia, Spain, using the vocative case. Be sure to notice all the imperfect subjunctives he used. The following is an uninterrupted and continuous group of sentences, so expect every part to connect to that which comes before. Be sure to consult a dictionary for unfamiliar words or grammatical concepts.

1. Maxime vellem Garsa Episcoporum doctissime et optime.[316]

2. Ac summopere optarem, ut cum caeteri Christiani homines, tum vero hi qui Theologi vocantur, non ita multum tribuerent philosophiae.[317]

3. Nec tantum in ea operae consumerent, et prope parem ac sororem, ne dicam patronam, Theologiae facerent.

4. Male enim sentire mihi videntur de nostra religione, quam putant philosophiae praesidio indigere.

5. Quod minime illi fecerunt, quorum iam multis seculis opera extant, apostolorum imitatores, et vere in templo dei columnae.[318]

---

313. Alcuin of York, *Epistola* XXIV (PL 100.179).
314. Alcuin of York, *Commentaria in Sancti Ioannis Evangelium* XXXVII.17 (PL 100.947).
315. Lorenzo Valla, *De Libero Arbitrio* (Basel: Andreas Cratander, 1526), 3.
316. Here, let us translate *vellem* as the main verb. If so, you can start your sentence with: "I could wish . . . ," followed by several vocatives referring to the bishop.
317. You can translate *summopere optarem* with: "I could very much choose . . ."
318. You can begin this sentence with the subject of the verb *fecerunt*, which is *illi*.

EXERCITIUM XXI: *Perfect and Pluperfect Subjunctives and Cum Clauses*

I. Perfect and Pluperfect Subjunctives. Translate each of the underlined words below. Each sentence contains at least one perfect or pluperfect subjunctive. Do not be concerned if your translation does not perfectly match the number of blank lines allocated.

Exemplum. *Cur in paradiso lignum vitae et lignum scientiae boni et mali creatum est? Ut per illud <u>potuisset</u> homo immortalis esse.* (Alcuin of York)[319]

Why was the tree of life and the tree of the knowledge of good and evil created in the garden? So that through it humankind <u>would have been able</u> to become immortal.

1. Si cum <u>evangelizasset</u> Paulus in Arabia, postea vidit Petrum, non ideo ut per ipsum Petrum disceret Evangelium; name ante eum utique vidisset. (Augustine of Hippo)[320]

   If Paul saw Peter after he _____ _____ _____ in Arabia, it was not, therefore, to learn the Gospel from Peter; otherwise he would have surely seen him beforehand.

2. Poenitentem hominem dico, qui diligit quod ante <u>neglexerit</u>, et quod fecerat obliviscitur. (Jerome)[321]

   I say that a repentant person who loves what he previously _____ _____ _____ also forgets what he had done.

3. Considera quid <u>fueris</u>, antequam <u>esses</u>. (Tertullian)[322]

   Consider what _____ _____ before _____ _____.

4. Et ego cum omni humilitate coram S[acra] majestate tua universoque Imperiiordine <u>comparuissem</u>. (Martin Luther)[323]

   And _____ _____ _____ _____ before Your Holy Majesty and the whole rank of the Empire in all humility.

5. Judaeos quidem, quod per praevaricationem legis Deum <u>inhonoraverint</u>: Gentes vero, quod, cum cognitum de creatura creatorem ut Deum debuerant venerari, gloriam eius in manufacta <u>mutaverint</u> simulacra. (Lanfranc of Milan)[324]

   Indeed, the Jews _____ _____ _____ God through the violation of the law, while the gentiles should have worshiped the God they knew as Creator from the creation. Instead, _____ _____ _____ _____ his glory into hand-made idols.

---

319. Alcuin of York, *Interrogationes et Responsiones in Genesim* VI (PL 100.517).
320. Augustine of Hippo, *Epistola ad Galatas* II.8 (PL 35.2110).
321. Jerome, *Epistola* XXIV.3 (PL 30.243).
322. Tertullian, *Apologeticus* XLVIII (PL 1.523).
323. Martin Luther, *Luther an Kaiser Karl V* (WA BR 2.307).
324. Lanfranc of Milan, *Prologus Specialis in Epistolam ad Romanos* (PL 150.105).

EXERCITIA

6. An Theologiae vox <u>usurpanda sit</u> in Scholis Christianis; et quot modis sumatur? (Francis Turretin)[325]

   Should the voice of theology _____ _____ in Christian schools? And in how many ways should it be assumed?

7. Nunquam tibi <u>scripsissem</u>, si <u>noluissem</u> pacem tecum habere, et pacem in Christo. (Alcuin of York)[326]

   _____ _____ never _____ _____ to you if _____ _____ _____ _____ to have peace with you and peace in Christ.

8. Sic in hac mundi Republica nisi unus <u>fuisset</u> moderator, qui et conditor, aut soluta <u>fuisset</u> omnis haec moles, aut nec condi quidem omnino <u>potuisset</u>. (Lactantius)

   In this way, in this Republic of the world, unless there _____ one who was the ruler, who also [was] the creator, either this entire mass _____ _____ _____ destroyed, or it _____ not even _____ _____ _____ to be created at all.

9. Si enim ab omnibus <u>essent liberati</u> peccatis, nequaquam per singulos dies offerret quis sacrificia. (Alcuin of York)[327]

   For if _____ _____ _____ _____ _____ from all sins, by no means would anyone offer sacrifices every day.

10. Jusserunt ergo militibus suis, ut pergerent videre si bellum vere esset, et reverterentur quantocius, quia ipsi mox <u>essent parati</u> venire. (Godfrey of Bouillon)[328]

    Therefore, they ordered their troops to advance to see whether there really was a battle, and they turned back as soon as possible because they themselves _____ _____ _____ _____ to come soon.

II. Perfect and Pluperfect Subjunctives of the "To Be" Verb in Thomas Aquinas. Translate each of the underlined words below. Each sentence contains at least one perfect or pluperfect subjunctive. Do not be concerned if your translation does not perfectly match the number of blank lines allocated. All examples come from Thomas's *Summa Theologiae*.[329]

Exemplum. *Ergo videtur quod dolor animae patientis in purgatorio, vel in inferno, vel etiam dolor Adae, si passus fuisset, major <u>fuisset</u> quam dolor passionis Christi. (III.46.6)*

Therefore, it seems that the pain of a soul suffering in Purgatory or in Hell, or even the pain of Adam, if he had suffered at all, <u>would have been</u> greater than the pain of Christ's suffering.

---

325. Francis Turretin, *Institutio Theologiae Elentica* I.1 (Geneva: Samuel de Tournes, 1679), 1.
326. Alcuin of York, *Epistola* VIII (PL 100.149).
327. Alcuin of York, *Expositio in Epistolas ad Hebraeos* X.1 (PL 100.1077).
328. Godfrey of Bouillon, *De Bello Sacro* XLIII (PL 155.665).
329. All excerpts are taken from Thomas Aquinas, *Summa Theologiae* Liber III.

1. Ergo superfluum <u>fuisset</u> assumere maximum dolorum. (III.46.6)

   Therefore, _____ _____ _____ unnecessary to assume the greatest of pains.

2. Ergo videtur quod dolor Christi non <u>fuerit</u> maximus dolorum. (III.46.6)

   Therefore, it seems that the pain of Christ _____ not the greatest of pains.

3. Videtur quod alius modus convenientior <u>fuisset</u> liberationis humanae quam per passionem Christi. (III.46.3)

   It seems that _____ _____ _____ a more convenient way of setting free the human race other than through Christ's suffering.

4. Ad primum ergo dicendum quod Christus, cum non <u>esset subjectus</u> peccato, neque morti erat obnoxius, neque incinerationi. (III.51.3)

   Therefore, one must say first off that because Christ _____ not _____ to sin, neither was he liable to die nor liable to the ashes.

5. Et ideo non oportet quod per descensum Christi ad inferos omnes <u>fuerint</u> a purgatorio <u>liberati</u>. (III.52.8)

   And, therefore, it was not necessary through Christ's descent into Hell that not all _____ _____ _____ _____ from Purgatory.

III. Bede. Born in England in 673, *Beda Venerabilis*, or "Venerable Bede," was a significant churchman and figure in medieval Britain. Probably his most well-known writing is *Historia Ecclesiastica Gentis Anglorum*, or "Church History of the English People," which narrates the Christianization of his nation. The following excerpt is famous in the history of Christian missions.[330] It describes the occasion when Pope Gregory I first encountered representatives of the "English" race. He was at the market in Rome when slave traders brought in young boys to sell. Gregory was taken by the beauty of this race and inquired whether they were Christians. When he heard that they were not, he was saddened because he thought these *Angli*, "English" or "Angles," looked just like *angeli*, "angels." This incident prompted him to approach the pope—for Gregory himself had not yet received that office—to send Christian missionaries to convert the English people. Denied, he had to wait until he became pope before he could send a mission to the island. He remained true to his promise, and the rest is history. When translating this passage, watch out for indirect speech. Bede represents an Anglo-Latin that differed from the writing on the European continent. The passage below is continuous and uninterrupted, even though divided into specific numbers.

1. Nec silentio praetereunda opinio, quae de beato Gregorio traditione maiorum ad nos usque perlata est; qua videlicet ex causa admonitus tam sedulam erga salutem nostrae gentis curam gesserit.[331]

---

330. Bede, *Historia Ecclesiastica Gentis Anglorum* II.1 (PL 95.80).
331. You can start your translation of this sentence as follows: "Nor is the report . . ."

2. Dicunt, quia die quadam cum, advenientibus nuper mercatoribus, multa venalia in forum fuissent conlata, multi ad emendum confluxissent.

3. Et ipsum Gregorium inter alios advenisse, ac vidisse inter alia pueros venales positos candidi corporis, ac venusti vultus, capillorum quoque forma egregia.[332]

4. Quos cum aspiceret, interrogavit, ut aiunt, de qua regione vel terra essent adlati. Dictumque est, quia de Brittania insula, cuius incolae talis essent aspectus. Rursus interrogavit, utrum idem insulani Christiani an paganis adhuc erroribus essent inplicati. Dictum est, quod essent pagani.[333]

5. At ille, intimo ex corde longa trahens suspiria: 'Heu, pro dolor!' inquit, 'quod tam lucidi vultus homines tenebrarum auctor possidet, tantaque gratia frontispicii mentem ab interna gratia vacuam gestat!' Rursus ergo interrogavit, quod esset vocabulum gentis illius. Responsum est, quod Angli vocarentur. At ille: 'Bene,' inquit; 'nam et angelicam habent faciem, et tales angelorum in caelis decet esse coheredes.[334]

EXERCITIUM XXII: *Present Active Participles, Future Passive Participles (Gerundives), and Gerunds*

I. Present Active Participles, Future Passive Participles, and Gerunds. In each of the following sentences, there is at least one present active participle, future passive participle, or gerund. Do not be concerned if your translation does not perfectly match the number of blank lines allocated.

Exemplum. *Pater est prima persona Deitatis, a nullo existens, quae Filium, essentialem sui imaginem, genuit ab aeterno.* (Henricus Alting)[335]

The Father is the first person of the Deity, existing from no one, who beget from everlasting a Son, the essential image of himself.

---

332. Because we are in indirect speech, the initial accusative cases here represent the subject. So, start your translation with: "Gregory himself had gone . . ."
333. You can start this sentence with: "After he [Gregory] looked at them, he asked . . ."
334. You can start this sentence with: "But he [Gregory], drawing long sighs from the bottom of his heart, said . . ."
335. Henricus Alting, *Methodus Theologiae Didacticae* III (Amsterdam: Aegidius Jansonnius, 1656), 18.

1. Causa, cur doctrina Christi, admirationi illis erat, explicatur, nimirum quia docebat, non quasi minister, aut doctor communis, aut quasi unus ex Prophetis, sed quasi auctoritatem <u>habens</u>, et quasi ex se <u>loquens</u>. (Francisco de Toledo)[336]

   The reason why Christ's teaching was admired by them, it is explained, without doubt was that he was teaching not as a pastor, not as a common professor, not as one of the prophets, but as one _____ authority and as one _____ on his own.

2. Sed sine mea doctrina audi angelum ad ipsum <u>dicentem</u>: *Accipe puerum et matrem ejus* (Matt. II.13). (Arnobius the Younger)[337]

   But without my teaching, hear the angel _____ to him: "Take the boy and his mother" (Matt. II.13).

3. Quicunque ad fidem <u>veniens</u> ante verba baptismi adhuc in vinculo est veteris debiti. (Caesarius of Arles)[338]

   Whoever _____ to the faith before the words of baptism is still in bond of an old debt.

4. Illud tamen <u>fatendum</u> est. (Florimund de Raemond)[339]

   Nevertheless, this _____ _____ _____ _____.

5. Credamus Domini Dei Patris testimonio, ubi super baptizatum Filium magnifica voce testatur <u>dicens</u>. (Alcuin of York)[340]

   Let us believe in the testimony of the Lord, God the Father, when, concerning the Son's baptism, he testified in a great voice, _____.

6. Sed quid es, nisi id quod summum omnium solum <u>existens</u> per seipsum, omnia alia fecit de nihilo? (Anselm of Canterbury)[341]

   But what are you, except that alone which, as the highest of all beings, _____ through yourself, created all other things from nothing?

7. De colore Pilei Sacerdotum quaedam breviter <u>subnectenda</u> sunt. (Salomon Van Til)[342]

   Regarding the color of the priest's hat, some things _____ _____ _____ _____ briefly.

---

336. Francisco de Toledo, *Commentaria in Prima XII Capita Evangelii secundum Lucam* IV (Venice: Giovanni Battista Sessa, 1600), 417.
337. Arnobius the Younger, *Conflictus de Deo Trino de Uno* II.11 (PL 53.285).
338. Caesarius of Arles, *Homilia* V (PL 67.1056).
339. Florimund de Raemond, *Historia de Ortu* (Gerhardus Greuenbruch, 1644), 8.
340. Alcuin of York, *Adversus Felicis Haeresin* III (PL 101.38).
341. Anselm of Canterbury, *Proslogion* V (PL 158.229).
342. Salomon Van Til, *Commentarius de Tabernaculo Mosis* (Amsterdam, 1714), 37. This participle comes from the verb *subnecto, subnectere, subnexui, subnexus*, "to tie" or "to bind."

8. Corpus Scripturae est doctrina ad bene <u>vivendum</u> sufficiens. (William Perkins)[343]

   The body of Scripture is a doctrine sufficient _____ _____ well.

9. Si fuerit Dominus mecum . . . dederit mihi panem ad <u>vescendum</u> et vestimentum ad <u>induendum</u>. (Johannes Brenz)[344]

   If the Lord were with me, he would have given me bread for _____ and clothing for _____.

10. Hic si quis interroget: Quid igitur, nihilne <u>credendum</u> est? (Philip Melanchthon)[345]

    Here if someone asks: "What, then, is nothing _____ _____ _____?"

II. Peter Ramus. Peter Ramus was incredibly influential on many Protestant theologians, especially during the late sixteenth, seventeenth, and eighteenth centuries. Born in France in 1515 and killed during the Saint Bartholomew's Day Massacre in 1572 that targeted Huguenots (or French Protestants in the Reformed tradition during the sixteenth century), Ramus was a polymath interested in many different subjects, including rhetoric, logic, dialectic, pedagogy, mathematics, philosophy, and theology. Each sentence below contains at least one of the following: present active participle, future passive participle (gerundive), or gerund.[346]

1. Sic Ioan. 14, "Ego sum via, veritas, et vita," ait de se Christus, indicans sua doctrina demonstrare viam qua sit ad optatam beatitudinis metam. (I.1)[347]

2. Capita symboli duo sunt, primum de Deo, secundum de ecclesia Dei: Haec enim duo capita summam quandam doctrinae Christianae continent, et tamen etiam per universam doctrinam praecipue extant atque apparent, ideo praecipue spectanda nobis et consideranda. (I.2)[348]

---

343. William Perkins, *Armilla Aurea* I.1 (Basel: Conrad Waldkirch, 1596), 5. Note the use of the preposition *ad*, showing that this gerund indicates purpose.

344. Johannes Brenz, *Commentaria in Esaia* IV.38 (Tübingen: George Gruppenbachius, 1560), 472. Note the use of the preposition *ad* before both of these forms, showing that they indicate purpose.

345. Philip Melanchthon, *Explicatio Proverbiorum* VI (CR 14.15).

346. Peter Ramus, *Commentariorum de Religione Christiana Libri Quattuor* (Frankfurt: Andreas Wechel, 1576), 6–35. The parenthesis following each excerpt indicates the books and chapters, respectively.

347. You can translate *optatam* as "pleasant" or "desired," which is modifying the noun *metam*. The quotation comes from John XIV.6.

348. I recognize that this is a long sentence, but there are many such sentences in Latin. Besides, we will not know the content of the participles *spectanda* and *consideranda* without the whole sentence. Be sure to translate *symboli* as "of the creed" [that, is the Nicene Creed], and *Haec . . . duo capita* are all working together despite the fact that all three words end differently. They are the subject of the entire sentence.

3. Transiens Deus ante Mosem clamavit. (I.3)[349]

4. Et modo quod dicimus, "Credo in Iesum," hoc ipso credendi testimonio Iesum esse Deum confitemur. (I.9)[350]

5. Sic Stephanus moriens servatorem Christum confitetur: "Domine Iesus Christe suscipe spiritum meum." (I.9)[351]

EXERCITIUM XXIII: *Perfect Passive Participles, Future Active Participles, and Periphrastic Constructions*

I. Participles. Translate all the participles and periphrastics underlined. Do not be concerned if your translation does not perfectly match the number of blank lines allocated.

Exemplum. *Evangelista hodie Judaeorum circa Christum proditurus invidiam.* (Peter Chrysologus)[352]

The Gospel writer today <u>is about to bring forth</u> the Jews' jealousy concerning Christ.

1. De septem tubis, una superest tuba novissima, postquam tuba ejusmodi nulla <u>cantura est</u>. (Rupert of Deutz)[353]

   Concerning the seven trumpets, one final trumpet remains. Afterward, no trumpet of this kind _____ _____ _____.

2. Quid enim sint hodie, videmus; quid cras <u>futuri sint</u>, ignoramus. (Augustine of Hippo)[354]

   For what they are today, we see; what tomorrow _____ _____, we do not know.

3. Erat Deus omnia <u>formaturus</u>. (John Cassian)[355]

   God _____ _____ _____ _____ all things.

---

349. I thought you would appreciate a short sentence after a long one. To hear what God said next, you will need to consult Exodus 34:6–7—in the Vulgate, of course.
350. As you probably know by now, you can translate *esse* as "to be."
351. This quote comes from Acts VII.58.
352. Peter Chrysologus, *Sermo* XLVIII (PL 52.333).
353. Rupert of Deutz, *Commentária in Apocalýpsim* VI.10 (PL 169.1003).
354. Augustine of Hippo, *De Baptismo Contra Donatistas S. Augustini* IV.3.4 (PL 43.156).
355. John Cassian, *Commentarii in Genesim* I.7 (PL 50.893).

4. Moyses in deserto positus [est] gregem pascit. (Salvian)³⁵⁶

   Moses _____ _____ in the desert, where he pastures the flock.

5. In eadem forma carnis atque substantia veniet judicaturus. (Alcuin of York)³⁵⁷

   He will come and _____ _____ _____ in the same form and substance of flesh.

6. Et levavit pallium Eliae, quod ceciderat ei: reversusque steti super ripam Iordanis. (II Kgs. II.13)

   And he picked up Elijah's cloak that had fallen from him; and _____ _____, he stood on the bank of the Jordan [River].

7. Christus in caelum profecturus. (Nicholas Sander)³⁵⁸

   Christ _____ _____ _____ _____ to Heaven.

8. Quinto loco profert Polycarpum, virum egregium et constantem, nobilissima Martyrii corona decoratum. (William Whitaker)³⁵⁹

   In the fifth place, he cites Polycarp, an excellent and firm man, who _____ _____ with the most noble crown of a martyr.

9. Tibi (quod est super omnia) natus est Christus. (Peter Chrysologus)³⁶⁰

   To you (because he is above all things) Christ _____ _____.

10. Quia enim pati Graece πάσχειν dicitur; ideo Pascha passio putata est, velut hoc nomen a passione sit appellatum. (Augustine of Hippo)³⁶¹

    For because in Greek it is called πάσχειν; therefore, Passover _____ _____ to mean "to suffer," as if this word was named on account of his passion.

II. Smaragdus. The following comes from a New Testament commentary by Smaragdus, a churchman who lived during the sixth and early seventh centuries.³⁶² Commentaries during this time were mostly compilations of previous interpreters, such as Augustine, Bede, and others. The opening quotation below in italics comes from Matthew XI.2–3, and the sentences afterward offer commentary on it. Each sentence below is continuous and uninterrupted, so the full meaning will become clearer as you keep translating. In fact, some of the sentences below are fragments, not complete sentences.

---

356. Salvian, *De Gubernatione* I.9 (PL 53.41).
357. Alcuin of York, *Adversus Felicis Haeresin* V.3.9 (PL 101.197).
358. Nicholas Sander, *De Clave David* I.1 (Rome, 1588), 14.
359. William Whitaker, *Disputatio de Sacra Scriptura contra Huius Temporis Papistas* (Cambridge, 1588), 436.
360. Peter Chrysologus, *Sermo* V (PL 52.201).
361. Augustine of Hippo, *In Joannis Evangelium* LV.1 (PL 35.1784).
362. Smaragdus, *Collectiones in Epistolas et Evangelia, Evangelium Matthaei* XI (PL 102.521).

1. *Cum audisset Joannes in vinculis opera Christi, mittens duos de discipulis suis, ait illi: Tu es qui venturus est, an alium exspectamus?*

2. Qui venturus est, id est, quem prophetae venturum praedicarunt.

3. Non ait: Tu es qui venisti, sed tu es qui venturus est, et est sensus, manda mihi, qui interficiendus ab Herode.[363]

4. Et ad inferna descensurus sum, utrum te et in inferis debeam nuntiare, qui nuntiavi superis?[364]

5. An non conveniat Filio Dei, ut gustet mortem, et alium ad haec sacramenta missurus es.[365]

EXERCITIUM XXIV: *Perfect, Pluperfect, and Future Perfect Passives; Fierī; Ablative Absolutes*

I. Perfects. In each of the following sentences, there is at least one passive from the perfect system. Do not be concerned if your translation does not perfectly match the number of blank lines allocated.

Exemplum. *In ipso adoptati sumus in filios et haeredes a patre coelesti.* (John Calvin)[366]

We *were adopted* in him as children and heirs from the heavenly Father.

1. Servator igitur humani generis Christus verus Deus ita promissus erat et quidem servator solus. (Peter Ramus)[367]

    Therefore, Christ, who is true God, is the Savior of the human race, who _____ _____ _____ in this way and, indeed, he is the only Savior.

2. Iuxta priorem quidem statum, Dominus Iesus Christus, verus homo de virgine Maria natus est, cum anima, corpore, sanguine, carne, ossibus ac quibuscumque aliis ad verum hominem spectantibus. (Caspar Schwenkfeld)[368]

---

363. Translate the first part of this sentence with an implied "he" [that is, John the Baptist] as the subject of the verb *ait*. John is the implied speaker throughout this sentence.

364. As in the sentence above, John the Baptist is the one speaking, and he is speaking to Jesus.

365. Do not be concerned that your final translation in this sentence will not make complete sense without the rest of context. Just do your best to translate the grammar as presented.

366. John Calvin, *Institutio Christianae Religionis* III.15.5 (CR 30.583).

367. Peter Ramus, *Commentariorum de Religione Christiana Libri Quattuor* I.9 (Frankfurt: Andreas Wechel, 1576), 35.

368. Caspar Schwenkfeld, *De Duplici Statu, Officio, et Cognitione Christi* (Basel, 1546), n.p.

Indeed, according to the first condition, the Lord Jesus Christ, the true man who _____ _____ from the Virgin Mary, with a spirit, with a body, with blood, with flesh, with bones, and with all other things that pertain to a true person.

3. <u>Timendus est</u> Deus propter poenam aeternam: multum quoque <u>timendus est</u> propter poenam post mortem purgatoriam. (Helinand of Froidmont)[369]

   God _____ _____ _____ _____ on account of eternal punishment. God _____ _____ _____ _____ also very much on account of punishment after the purgative death.

4. Si primo omnium <u>factum est</u> coelum et terra, angeli postmodum <u>facti sunt</u>: si angeli ante <u>facti sunt</u>, non primo omnium fecit Deus coelum et terram. (John Cassian)[370]

   If, in the beginning of all things, heaven and earth _____ _____, and the angels _____ _____ afterward; if the angels _____ _____ beforehand, then God did not create heaven and earth first of all things.

5. Haec ergo sequenda solemnitas, quam praescribit lectio. Sed etiam in Deuteronomio <u>scriptum est</u>: quia planxerunt filii Israel Moysen diebus triginta, et <u>consummati sunt</u> dies luctus (Deut. xxxiv, 8). (Ambrose of Milan)[371]

   Therefore, this solemnity is to be followed, which the reading prescribes. But also _____ _____ _____ in Deuteronomy: "The sons of Israel mourned for Moses for thirty days, and then the days of their mourning _____ _____."

6. Qui etiam domus David <u>dictus est</u>; quia ex semine David secundum carnem <u>natus est</u>. (Gregory I)[372]

   He also _____ _____ to be of the house of David because _____ _____ _____ from the seed of David according to the flesh.

7. In Hierosolymis autem post Hermonem Macarius <u>ordinatus est</u>, vir nomine suo dignus, et omnibus bonis <u>ornatus</u>. (Cassiodorus)[373]

   But in Jerusalem, Macarius _____ _____ after Hermon, a man worthy of his name, who also _____ _____ by all good things.

8. <u>Repleta est</u> terra iniquitate: non est veritas, non est misericordia, non est scientia Dei in terra. (Helinand of Froidmont)[374]

   The earth _____ _____ with iniquity. There is no truth, there is no mercy, and there is no knowledge of God in the land.

---

369. Helinand of Froidmont, *Sermo XVI* (PL 212.617).
370. John Cassian, *Commentarii in Genesim* I.1 (PL 50.893).
371. Ambrose of Milan, *De Obitu Theodosii Oratio* III (PL 16.1386).
372. Gregory I, "Psalmi Sexti Poenitentialis," in *Expositio in Septem Psalmos Poenitentiales* (PL.640–41).
373. Cassiodorus, *Historia Tripartita* I.13 (PL 69.903).
374. Helinand of Froidmont, *Sermo XXVIII, De Potestate et Probitate Ecclesiae* (PL 212.717).

9. Per ipsius sanguinem huic <u>sumus reconciliati</u>. (John Calvin)[375]

   _____ _____ _____ to him through his very blood.

10. Hoc symbolum est ab apostolis aut apostolorum discipulis <u>collectum</u> <u>proditumque</u>. (Peter Ramus)[376]

    This creed _____ _____ and _____ _____ either by the apostles or by the disciples of the apostles.

II. John Cassian. The monk and theologian John Cassian was born around 360 in the Balkans. After his travels in the Middle East, where he visited many monks and monasteries, he settled in modern-day France. There he introduced many Western Christians to the ascetic practices of Eastern Christians. Cassian wrote many influential books on Christian spirituality. The following excerpts come from his *De Incarnatione Christi*, "On the Incarnation of Christ."[377] Here, Cassian is teaching on the creed, and you can supply Christ as the subject of the first word: *hic* ("he" or "this one"). From now until the end of the book, all translations will appear in their original forms—as one continuous passage.

Hic est enim unus ex Deo in Deum natus: cujus jussione universitatis opus secutum est; cujus voluntas rerum ortus est; cujus imperium mundi fabrica est; qui cuncta dixit, et facta sunt: cuncta mandavit, et creata sunt. Hic ergo unus est ad patriarchas loquens, in prophetis manens, ex Spiritu conceptus, natus ex Virgine Maria, in mundo visus, inter homines conversatus, affligens ligno crucis chirographum peccatorum, triumphans in semetipso, adversarias nobis inimicasque virtutes morte occidens, resurgendi fidem omnibus tribuens, gloria sui corporis corruptionem humanae carnis interimens.

EXERCITIUM XXV: *Present Active and Passive Infinitives; Indirect Speech; Impersonal Verbs*

I. Present Infinitives. Translate each of the underlined words below. Each sentence contains at least one present active or passive infinitive. Do not be concerned if your translation does not perfectly match the number of blank lines allocated.

Exemplum. *Aliud est enim <u>videre</u>, aliud est totum videndo <u>comprehendere</u>.* (Bede)[378]

For it is one thing <u>to see</u>, but it is another <u>to understand</u> everything by seeing.

---

375. John Calvin, *Institutio Christianae Religionis* III.15.5 (CR 30.583).
376. Peter Ramus, *Commentariorum de Religione Christiana Libri Quattuor* I.2 (Frankfurt: Andreas Wechel, 1576), 11.
377. John Cassian, *De Incarnatione Christi* IV.9 (PL 50.87).
378. Bede, *In Epistolam S. Joannis* III (PL 93.99).

EXERCITIA

1. Quid est <u>discere</u> disciplinam? <u>Cognoscere</u> qualiter unumquemque oporteat <u>vivere</u>, et quid operando conveniat <u>agere</u>. (Salonius the Viennese)[379]

   What is it _____ _____ wisdom? It is _____ _____ how each person ought _____ _____ and what is proper _____ _____ by working.

2. <u>Amare</u> delectat et <u>amari</u>. (Richard of St. Victor)[380]

   He enjoys _____ _____ and _____ _____ _____.

3. Non ergo inventi sunt in aliquo <u>dissentire</u> ab illo, ut cum ille se perfectum evangelium accepisse diceret, illi negarent, et aliquid vellent tanquam imperfecto <u>addere</u>. (Augustine of Hippo)[381]

   Therefore, they were not found _____ _____ with him in anything, so that when he said that he had received the complete gospel, they [the Judaizers] denied him and wanted _____ _____ something as though it were incomplete.

4. Duobus modis potest divina revelatio <u>esse</u> obscura, seu inevidens. (Louis Abelly)[382]

   Divine revelation is able _____ _____ unknown or unclear in two ways.

5. Sic humanae vitae artes docent suis praeceptis bene <u>loqui</u>, bene <u>dicere</u>, bene <u>ratiocinari</u>, bene <u>numerare</u>, [et] bene <u>metiri</u>. (Peter Ramus)[383]

   In this way, the refined skills of life teach by their principles [how] _____ _____ well, [how] _____ _____ well, [how] _____ _____ well, [how] _____ _____ well, and [how] _____ _____ well.

6. Ergo nocenter magis <u>habere</u>, quam illud ipsum <u>habere</u> fit crimen. (Hilary of Poitiers)[384]

   Therefore, it is a greater crime _____ _____ something guiltily than _____ _____ something for its own sake.

7. Sed non sine causa <u>agi</u> debes <u>credere</u>, quando vinum aqua mistum <u>oferri</u> vides. (Alcuin of York)[385]

   But it is not without reason that you ought _____ _____ (*credere*) it _____ _____ _____ (*agi*) when you see the wine _____ _____ _____ (*oferri*) mixed with the water.

---

379. Salonius the Viennese, *Expositio Mystica* (PL 53.969).
380. Richard of St. Victor, *Adnotatio in Psalmum* CXVIII (PL 196.315).
381. Augustine of Hippo, *Epistola ad Galatas* II (PL 35.2112).
382. Louis Abelly, *Tractatus de Fide, De Deo, ac de Trinitate*, vol. 1 of *Institutiones Theologicae* (Joseph Bay, 1825), 54.
383. Peter Ramus, *Commentariorum de Religione Christiana Libri Quattuor* (Frankfurt: Andreas Wechel, 1576), 6.
384. Hilary of Poitiers, *Commentarius in Matthaeum* XIX.9 (PL 9.1026).
385. Alcuin of York, *Confessio Fidei* IV.6 (PL 101.1091).

8. <u>Videre</u> cupiunt et <u>videri</u>. (Richard of St. Victor)[386]

   They desire _____ _____ and _____ _____ _____.

9. Periculosum <u>esse</u> dixit Isocrates sine legibus <u>vivere</u>. (Basilius Faber)[387]

   Isocrates said that _____ _____ dangerous _____ _____ without laws.

10. Hanc nostram imbecillitatem vult nos Deus <u>agnoscere,</u> et similiter vult <u>regi</u> nos suo verbo in vocatione, et <u>timere</u> ipsum, ac fide <u>petere</u> auxilium divinum. (Philip Melanchthon)[388]

    God wants for us _____ _____ this our weakness and, similarly, he wants us _____ _____ _____ by his word in our calling, and _____ _____ him, and _____ _____ for his divine help in faith.

II. Impersonal Verbs in the Latin Vulgate. Translate the following impersonal verbs. Do not be concerned if your translation does not perfectly match the number of blank lines allocated. All examples come from the Latin Bible.

Exemplum. *Accidit autem ut moreretur Naas rex filiorum Ammon, et regnaret filius ejus pro eo.* (I Chron. XIX.1)

And *it happened* that Nahash, the king of the children of Ammon, died, and his son reigned in his place.[389]

1. Respondens autem Iesus, dixit ei: Sine modo, sic enim <u>decet</u> nos implere omnem iustitiam. (Matt. III.15)

   But Jesus, responding, said to him: "Let it be,' for thus _____ _____ _____ for us to fulfill all righteousness."

2. Dic ergo nobis quid tibi videtur, <u>licet</u> censum dare Caesari, an non? (Matt. XXII.17)

   Tell us, therefore, how does it seem to you? _____ _____ _____ give tribute to Caesar or not?

3. Et in omnes gentes primum <u>oportet</u> praedicare evangelium. (Mark XIII.10)

   And among all the gentiles, _____ _____ _____ for the gospel to be preached first.

---

386. Richard of St. Victor, *Adnotatio in Psalmum* CXVIII (PL 196.315).
387. Basilius Faber, *Disciplina Scholastica* (Leipzig, 1565), 6. Remember that *esse* is in indirect speech. The verb *dixit*, "said," has triggered it, so we will NOT use the customary "to-" form.
388. Philip Melanchthon, *Explicatio Proverbiorum Salominis* XVI (CR 14.35–36).
389. The third-person singular of *accidit* is identical in the present active and perfect active here.

EXERCITIA

4. Nunc scimus quia scis omnia, et non <u>opus est</u> tibi ut quis te interroget: in hoc credimus quia a Deo existi. (John XVI.30)

   Now we know that you know all things and that _____ _____ no _____ among you that anyone should ask you [anything]. By this, we know that you originated from God.

5. <u>Facere</u> misericordiam et judicium magis <u>placet</u> Domino quam victimae. (Prov. XXI.3)

   _____ _____ _____ (*placet*) more _____ to the Lord _____ _____ (*facere*) mercy and justice than to offer sacrifices.

III. Damasus I. Damasus was the pope of Rome from 366 to 384. His papacy was fraught with controversy, and he had many opponents. In Rome, he sought diligently to defend the papacy against interlopers, and he was actively engaged in significant building projects around Rome that attracted many pagan aristocrats. He is the pope who commissioned Jerome to revise the *Vetus Latina*, or "Old Latin Bible." Among his hobbies was the writing of poems, many of which were engraved on the tombs of martyrs (and, as such, were epitaphs). Below is the epitaph that he composed for himself.[390] It is composed in hexameter. As the focus of this *capitulum* is the infinitive, every line but the first and fourth features a present active infinitive.

   Qui gradiens pelagi fluctus compressit amaros
   Vivere qui prestat morientia semina terrae
   Solvere qui potuit letalia vincula mortis
   Post tenebras fratrem post tertia lumina solis[391]
   Ad superos iterum Martae donare sorori
   Post cineres Damasum faciet qui surgere credo.

EXERCITIUM XXVI: *Perfect and Future Infinitives and More about Indirect Speech*

I. Perfect and Future Infinitives. Translate each of the underlined words below. Do not be concerned if your translation does not perfectly match the number of blank lines allocated.

Exemplum. *Deinde dicit Jesum non <u>esse passum</u>.* (Isidore of Seville)[392]

Then he said that Jesus <u>was</u> not <u>to suffer</u>.

---

390. This poem comes from PL 13.408–9.
391. The noun *fratrem* is probably best translated in the line below.
392. Isidore of Seville, *Prolegomena* III.86.7 (PL 81.637).

1. Hodie Dominus <u>exasperasse</u> nonnullorum videtur auditum. (Peter Chrysologus)[393]

   Today the Lord seems _____ _____ _____ the hearing of some.

2. Respondeo, primum mihi Cypriani litteras <u>suggessisse</u> quod teneam, donec perspiciam quale sit quod coepit postea disputari. (Augustine of Hippo)[394]

   I respond in the first place that the letters of Cyprian _____ _____ to me what I should watch until I should understand what next began to be discussed.

3. His taliter altercantibus, Apostolus se medium interponens, ita partium dirimit quaestiones, ut neutrum eorum sua iustitia salutem <u>meruisse</u> confirmet, ambos vero populos et scienter et graviter <u>deliquisse</u>. (Lanfranc of Milan)[395]

   For these arguing in such a manner, the apostle, intervening between both parties, separates questions into parts in such a way that neither of them would prove _____ _____ _____ salvation on account of their righteousness, but both peoples _____ _____ _____ knowingly and manifestly.

4. Nemo igitur qui sane sapit, credit Jesum alium carnem aut sanguinem <u>habuisse</u>, quam quae nata est de Maria Virgine, et passa est in cruce. (Paschasius Radbertus)[396]

   Nobody, therefore, who is wise believes Jesus _____ _____ another body or [another] flesh other than that which was born from the Virgin Mary and which suffered on the cross.

5. Ad annum Domini 396, dicit auctor Paulinum Nolanum <u>fuisse</u> presbyterum ordinatum. (Flavius Lucius Dexter)[397]

   In the year of our Lord 396, the author says that Paulinus of Nola _____ ordained a priest.

II. John Wesley and Count Zinzendorf. John Wesley and Count Zinzendorf were two influential Protestant thinkers in the eighteenth century. Wesley was an indefatigable evangelist, writer, administrator, and theologian. Less known was Ludwig von Zinzendorf, the establisher of the Moravian Church, which profoundly shaped Wesley's own Anglican theology. Wesley and Zinzendorf became friends in the 1730s. Naturally enough, when the two spoke together, they turned to the only language that they both spoke fluently: Latin. The excerpt below contains a conversation that took place between the two of them in London on September 3, 1741. The topic was justification—a concept that eventually caused them to part ways. As you will likely conclude, the "W" indicates Wesley and the "Z" represents Zinzendorf.[398]

---

393. Peter Chrysologus, *Sermo* CLXIV (PL 52.632).
394. Augustine of Hippo, *De Baptismo contra Donatistas* III.5.7 (PL 43.143).
395. Lanfranc of Milan, *Prologus Specialis in Epistolam ad Romanos* (PL 150.105).
396. Paschasius Radbertus, *Epistola de Corpore et Sanguine Domini* (PL 120.1351).
397. Flavius Lucius Dexter, *Apologeticus pro L. Dextro* (PL 31.597).
398. The source is John Wesley, *Journal from October 14, 1735 to November 29, 1745*, vol. 1 of *The Works of the Rev. John Wesley* (London: Wesleyan Conference Office, 1872), 323–24.

W. Nondum intelligo quid velis.³⁹⁹

Z. Ego, cum ex Georgia⁴⁰⁰ ad me scripsisti, te dilexi plurimum. Tum corde simplicem te agnovi. Iterum scripsisti. Agnovi corde simplicem, sed turbatis ideis.⁴⁰¹ Ad nos venisti. Ideae tuae tum magis turbatae erant et confusae. In Angliam rediisti. Aliquandiu post, audivi fratres nostros tecum pugnare. Spangenbergium⁴⁰² misi ad pacem inter vos conciliandam. Scripsit mihi, "Fratres tibi injuriam intulisse." Rescripsi, ne pergerent, sed et veniam a te peterent. Spangenberg scripsit iterum, "Eos petisse; sed te gloriari de iis, pacem nolle." Jam adveniens, idem audio.

W. Res in eo cardine minime vertitur. Fratres tui (verum hoc) me male tractarunt. Postea veniam petierunt. Respondi, "Id supervacaneum; me nunquam iis succensuisse: Sed vereri, 1. Ne falsa docerent. 2. Ne prave viverent." Ista unica est, et fuit, inter nos quaestio.

EXERCITIUM XXVII: *Imperatives, Prohibitions, and Vocatives*

I. Imperatives and Vocatives. In each of the following sentences, there is at least one example from the imperative mood and/or the vocative case. Do not be concerned if your translation does not perfectly match the number of blank lines allocated.

Exemplum. *Intelligite, quaeso, dilectissimi, et intuemini.* (Adam of Dryburgh)⁴⁰³   *Please understand, my beloved, and consider.*

1. Veni et cognosce vera esse quae dicimus. (Cyprian of Carthage)⁴⁰⁴

   _____ and _____ that what we say is true.

2. Fac sacrum pro salute imperatorum. (Perpetua)⁴⁰⁵

   _____ a sacrifice for the health of the emperors.

---

399. You can translate *velis* as "you mean."
400. Here Zinzendorf is referring to an American colony, which is now an American state.
401. The word *idea, ideae* (f), "idea" or "thought," is used a couple of times in this excerpt. It comes from Greek.
402. This is referring to Augustus Spangenberg, whom Wesley had met on board a ship from England to the American colonies in 1735. Spangenberg was a Moravian who introduced Wesley to a more evangelically oriented type of faith. In this sentence, Spangenberg's name is in the accusative, but in a sentence below his name is in the nominative case.
403. Adam of Dryburgh, *Sermones* XIII (PL 198.317).
404. Cyprian of Carthage, *Liber ad Demetrianum* XV (PL 4.555).
405. Perpetua, VI.3, in *The Acts of the Christian Martyrs*, ed. Herbert Musurillo (Oxford: Oxford University Press, 1972), 122.

3. Ecce qualem, <u>fratres</u>, paraclitum de Domini promissione accepimus, ecce qualem consolatorem habemus. (Richard of St. Victor)[406]

   Look, _____, what kind of counselor we have received from the promise of the Lord, look what kind of comforter we have.

4. Et <u>attendite</u>, quia incitaturus nos B. Augustinus ad hanc unanimitatem, ad hanc animae et cordis in Deo unitatem. (Adam of Dryburgh)[407]

   And _____ _____ because the B[lessed] Augustine will be inciting us to this unanimity, to this unity of mind and soul in God.

5. De quaestione famosa peccati originalis, quae apud orthodoxos saepius ventilatur, locuturus, invoco te, <u>Sancte Spiritus</u>, ut adsis mihi, mentem linguamque custodiens in omnibus, ne quid fiat in hoc negotio sine beneplacito tuo. (Odo of Tournai)[408]

   I am about to speak about the famous question of original sin, which is more often tossed about among the faithful. I invoke you, _____ _____, that you be present with me, guarding my mind and mouth in all things, so that whatever comes to pass in this labor not be without your good pleasure.

II. Psalmus CXL. The book of Psalms provides a rich tapestry of imperatives, prohibitions, and vocatives. The following comes from selected *versiculi*, "verses," of Psalmus CXL (Psalm 141 in English versions). Being the scholar that you are, no help will be given. Pay especial attention to the use of imperatives, prohibitions, and vocatives.

Exemplum. *Corripiet me justus in misericordia, et increpabit me, oleum autem peccatoris non impinguet caput meum. Quoniam adhuc et oratio mea in beneplacitis eorum.*

The righteous will correct me in mercy, and he will reprove me, lest the oil of the wrongdoer fatten my head. For my prayer will still be in those things that are pleasing to them.

1. Domine, clamavi ad te: exaudi me; intende voci meae, cum clamavero ad te.

2. Pone, Domine, custodiam ori meo, et ostium circumstantiae labiis meis.

3. Non declines cor meum in verba malitiae, ad excusandas excusationes in peccatis; cum hominibus operantibus iniquitatem, et non communicabo cum electis eorum.

---

406. Richard of St. Victor, *De Missione Spiritus Sancti* (PL 196.1017).
407. Adam of Dryburgh, *De Ordine Habitu* VIII (PL 198.517).
408. Odo of Tournai, *De Peccato Originali* I (PL 160.1071).

4. Quia ad te, Domine, Domine, oculi mei; in te speravi, non auferas animam meam.

5. Custodi me a laqueo quem statuerunt mihi et a scandalis operantium iniquitatem.

III. Anselm of Canterbury. Born in 1033, Anselm was a writer, philosopher, and churchman. He became the archbishop of Canterbury in 1093 during the so-called Investiture Crisis, when bishops clashed with kings over the right to appoint clergy. Despite his regular clashes, exiles, and leadership setbacks, Anselm was a gifted writer, both before and while serving as archbishop. The following excerpt comes from the opening lines of one of Anselm's most famous works, *Proslogion seu Alloquium de Dei Existentia*, "A Discourse or Address on God's Existence."[409] This writing is both philosophical and devotional, reminiscent of Augustine's *Confessiones*, written seven centuries earlier (in Latin, of course). In this excerpt, you will encounter Anselm's frequent use of imperatives and vocatives.[410]

Eia, nunc homuncio, fuge paululum occupationes tuas, absconde te modicum a tumultuosis cogitationibus tuis. Abjice nunc onerosas curas, et postpone laboriosas distentiones tuas. Vaca aliquantulum Deo, et requiesce aliquantulum in eo. Intra in cubiculum mentis tuae, exclude omnia praeter Deum et quae te iuvent ad quaerendum eum, et clauso ostio quaere eum. Dic nunc, totum cor meum, dic nunc Deo: Quaero vultum tuum, vultum tuum, Domine, requiro. Eia nunc ergo tu, Domine Deus meus, doce cor meum ubi et quomodo quaerat ubi et quomodo te inveniat. Domine, si non es hic, ubi te quaeram absentem: Si autem ubique es, cur non video te praesentem? Sed certe habitas lucem inacessibilem. Et ubi est lux inacessibilis, aut quomodo accedam ad lucem inacessibilem? Aut quis me ducet, et inducet in illam; ut videam te in illa?

---

409. The excerpt comes from Anselm of Canterbury, *Proslogion seu Alloquium de Dei Existentia* I (PL 158.225). Anselm takes brief quotes from three biblical passages, two from Matthew and one from Psalms, each in italics. See if you can track down the exact quotes.

410. Do not be thrown off by the use of *Eia*, which is what the grammarians refer to as an "interjection," the equivalent of something like "Aha!" or "Come on!" in English.

APPENDIX II

Answer Key to Exercitia

The following are the answers to the Exercitia. When one question calls for more than one answer, the different answers are separated by a semicolon (;). A backslash (/) indicates that either translation listed is acceptable. In fact, most of my "answers" represent just one of many acceptable translations. As mentioned in the Exercitia, translating does not represent a one-to-one correspondence between the original language and the target language. There are sometimes multiple acceptable ways to translate a Latin phrase or sentence into English. As such, the following "answer key" comes with an important caveat. Your answers will not perfectly mirror mine. And this is certainly going to be the case when it comes to translations of full sentences. When comparing your answers, therefore, do so *cum grano salis*, "with a grain of salt." Try to focus on the general meaning of your translations rather than on having the same exact answers that I present.

EXERCITIUM I: *Nouns and Prepositions*

I. Prepositions
1. After
2. Against
3. Before/in the presence of
4. From/out of; from/out of
5. In; through

II. Cases
1. Genitive
2. Ablative
3. Accusative
4. Vocative
5. Ablative; ablative

III. Genesis
1. They are under the sky/heaven.
2. It will be the sign of the covenant between me and between the earth/land.
3. May my soul live on account of your grace.
4. God sent me before you in/into Egypt.
5. I give to you one portion beyond your brothers.

EXERCITIUM II: *First-Declension Nouns, Sum, Esse, Fui, Futurus, and Et, -Que, and Ac*

I. First-Declension Nouns
1. The glory
2. In church
3. A farmer
4. Of the waters; [the] waters from [the] waters
5. Of sayings

II. Cases
1. Nominative singular
2. Ablative singular
3. Accusative plural
4. Nominative singular
5. Ablative singular

III. "To Be" Verb
1. Sunt; sunt; sunt; sunt
2. Estis
3. Est
4. Sumus
5. Es

IV. Exodus
1. I am who I am.
2. Aaron, your brother, will be your prophet.
3. And the Lord has brought back upon them the waters of the sea.
4. Your murmur is not against us but against the Lord.
5. The glory of the Lord has appeared in the cloud.

EXERCITIUM III: *Second-Declension Nouns*

I. Second-Declension Nouns
1. Through Jesus Christ; through God
2. The Son; the Son; the Son
3. Into wine
4. By [his] slave/servant
5. Of Christ
6. Book
7. The apostles; by Christ
8. Against God
9. A man/husband
10. Sin

II. Cases
1. Ablative masculine singular from *dominus, domini*

2. Nominative masculine singular from *Petrus, Petri*; nominative masculine singular from *Christus, Christi*; nominative masculine singular from *filius, filii*; genitive masculine singular from *Deus, Dei*
   3. Ablative masculine singular from *peccatum, peccati*
   4. Accusative masculine plural from *oculus, oculi*
   5. Ablative masculine singular from *Deus, Dei*

III. Augustine of Hippo

Great are you, Lord.
There is no number to your wisdom. OR: Your wisdom cannot be counted.
For I am not now in Hell.
Therefore, I would not exist, my God.
The house of my soul/spirit is narrow.

EXERCITIUM IV: *Third-Declension Nouns*

I. Third-Declension Nouns
   1. The name
   2. Body
   3. About the Trinity
   4. Of gentleness; of peace
   5. To the Father; of man/humanity

II. Cases
   1. Nominative neuter singular from *semen, seminis*
   2. Nominative masculine singular from *homo, hominis*; accusative masculine singular from *homo, hominis*
   3. Accusative feminine singular from *mensis, mensis*
   4. Genitive neuter singular from *corpus, corporis*; dative neuter singular from *cor, cordis*
   5. Accusative masculine singular *rex, regis*

III. Alonso Tostado
   1. I, however, am exceedingly small/But I am very small.
   2. Christ gives thanks to the Father.
   3. God, however, is everywhere/But God is everywhere.
   4. God has driven out seven people(s).
   5. Lord, this business is very great.

EXERCITIUM V: *First-, Second-, and Third-Declension Adjectives*

I. Adjectives
   1. Short/brief
   2. Of the wise
   3. Holy/godly
   4. The almighty/the all-powerful; the almighty/the all-powerful
   5. Of the Holy

II. Cases
1. Accusative masculine plural from *bonus, bona, bonum*; genitive feminine/masculine/neuter plural from *fidelis, fidelis, fidele*
2. Dative masculine plural from *infinitus, infinita, infinitum*
3. Nominative masculine singular from *iratus, irata, iratum*
4. Accusative masculine plural from *multus, multa, multum*; genitive neuter plural from *bonus, bona, bonum*
5. Ablative feminine singular from *altus, alta, altum*

III. Philip Melanchthon
1. Brief/short sayings are transmitted.
2. A saying is a brief/short maxim/word/dictum.
3. A proverb is a very celebrated maxim/word/dictum.
4. These sayings warn/admonish, first of all, regarding teaching.
5. This pain is unrighteous.

EXERCITIUM VI: *Fourth-Declension Nouns, Comparative and Superlative Adjectives, and Ablatives*

I. Fourth-Declension Nouns and Adjectives
1. In/into hand/hands
2. From the tribe
3. In the coming/arrival/advent; in the conception
4. service/worship
5. Most beloved

II. Cases
1. Ablative masculine singular from *adventus, adventus*
2. Genitive masculine plural from *exercitus, exercitus*; genitive masculine plural from *exercitus, exercitus*
3. Ablative masculine singular from *spiritus, spiritus*
4. Nominative masculine singular from *maximus, maxima, maximum*
5. Nominative masculine singular from *spiritus, spiritus*; dative masculine singular from *spiritus, spiritus*

III. Francis Turretin
1. Just as there is given a threefold school of God—of nature, of grace, and of glory—and a threefold book—of creation, of Scripture, and of life.
2. In the same way, theology is customarily divided triply/in three ways.
3. So that the first would be natural, the second would be supernatural, the third would be blessed.
4. The first from the light of reason, the second from the light of faith, the third from the light of glory.
5. The first belongs to people on earth, the second belongs to the faithful in the Church, and the third belongs to the blessed in heaven.

ANSWER KEY TO EXERCITIA

EXERCITIUM VII: *Fifth-Declension Nouns, Indeclinable Nouns, and Numbers*

I. Fifth-Declension Nouns and Numerals
1. Three; faith
2. According to the faith
3. On the sixth day
4. First
5. Of things

II. Cases
1. Nominative singular from *unus, una, unum*
2. Nominative plural from *tres, tres, tria*
3. Nominative plural from *res, rei*
4. Genitive singular from *fides, fidei*
5. Nominative singular from *secundus, secunda, secundum*

III. Bonaventure
1. James writes in the first chapter of his letter.
2. The first light enlightens with respect to artificial shape.
3. The second light enlightens with respect to natural form.
4. The third light enlightens with respect to intellectual truth.
5. The fourth and last/final light enlightens with respect to saving truth.

EXERCITIUM VIII: *Verbs and Four Principal Parts*

I. Principal Parts
1. Second
2. Third
3. Second
4. Fourth
5. First
6. Second
7. Fourth
8. Second
9. Second
10. First

II. The Quicumque
1. However/But/Moreover, this is the universal/catholic faith.
2. For one is the person of the Father, another of the Son, another of the Holy Spirit.
3. And, nevertheless/nonetheless, three are not eternal, but one is eternal.
4. So, there is God the Father, God the Son, and God the Holy Spirit.
5. He has ascended into the heavens/skies and he sits at/to the right [hand] of God the Father.

EXERCITIUM IX: *Present Actives and Present Passives*

I. Verbs
1. We are (being) seen
2. Does (not) despise
3. Are (being) loved/cherished; are (being) held/possessed; are (being) read/selected/chosen; are (being) preached
4. Remains/stays/endures
5. Are
6. Says/speaks/is saying/is speaking
7. Is (being) called/is (being) named
8. Give/am giving
9. Have/possess/is having/is possessing
10. Come/go/are coming/going

II. Verb Conjugation
1. Third person singular passive from *vocare*; third person singular passive *operor*
2. First person plural active from *praedicare*
3. Third person plural active from *diligere*
4. Second person singular active from *agere*
5. Third person plural passive from *dicere*

III. Wolfgang Musculus
1. There is a twofold consideration of the divinity of Christ.
2. So/Thus Paul calls Christ the image of the invisible God.
3. But he/Moses does not say: God made the word in the beginning.
4. Just as Moses says: God made heaven and earth in the beginning.
5. This is the second declaration of the Evangelist about/concerning Christ the word of God.

EXERCITIUM X: *Imperfect Actives, Imperfect Passives, and Adverbs*

I. Imperfect Tense
1. Was being approved
2. Were bending; were performing/working
3. Was ruling/governing
4. Was (not) killing
5. Was being seen

II. Adverbs
1. Already/now
2. Always
3. Still
4. Also/even
5. Partly/in part; partly/in part

III. Cajetan
1. It is by no means certain whether this letter is from James, the brother of the Lord.

2. Nor does he call himself an apostle, but only a slave/servant of Jesus Christ.
3. And the letter/it is sent to the twelve scattered/dispersed tribes.
4. Hence more was obtained of the book than from the title of the letter.
5. And it is a word/message about the work of the soul/mind which is within/inside.

EXERCITIUM XI: *Future Actives and Future Passives*

I. Future Tense
1. Will be given
2. Will rule/reign
3. You all will sin
4. Will walk
5. Will reveal

II. Conjugating Future Tense
1. Third person singular passive from *dare*
2. Third person singular active from *regere*
3. Second person plural active from *peccare*
4. Third person plural active from *ambulare*
5. Third person singular active from *exhibere*

III. Beatitudes
1. Blessed are those who mourn because they will be comforted.
2. Blessed are the mild/meek/humble because they will possess the earth.
3. Blessed are those who hunger and thirst after/for/toward righteousness because they will be filled/satisfied/satiated.
4. Blessed are the merciful because they will receive mercy.
5. Blessed are the pure in heart because they will see God.
6. Blessed are the peacemakers because they will be called children/sons of God.
7. Blessed are those who suffer persecution on account of righteousness because theirs is the kingdom of the heavens/heaven.

EXERCITIUM XII: *Irregular Verbs*

I. Irregular Verbs
1. Will (not) be
2. It can/is able to
3. Want/wish/desire; do we not (also) want/wish/desire
4. Could/were able to
5. I am able; is able; I am able

II. Irregular Verbs Conjugation
1. First person singular active from *posse*
2. Third person plural imperfect active from *posse*
3. Third person singular present active from *ferre*
4. Second person singular present active from *velle*

5. Third person plural imperfect active from *nolle*

III. Peter Damian
1. Do you wish to hear how you may be subject to God? . . . Do you also wish to hear how you may be subject to your neighbor?
2. God wants/wishes to test/examine their steadfastness/firmness/perseverance.
3. He was bearing/carrying Christ in his heart, he was bringing forth Christ in his voice.
4. Lord Jesus Christ, who is and who was God with the Father before the ages/eternity . . . God from true God.
5. The bodies of the holy/saints will be in tombs until the end of the age.

EXERCITIUM XIII: *Deponents and Semideponents*

I. Deponents and Semideponents
1. Speak
2. Comforts
3. To work
4. Dared to confess/acknowledge/declare/profess
5. Boast/glory
6. Exhorts/encourages/urges
7. Meditates
8. I confess/acknowledge/admit
9. Works
10. I testify/bear witness

II. Arnobius the Younger
1. The unwilling/reluctant will confess God after these things.
2. Hear, God, my prayer when I am pressed/I complain or when I pray. What prayer?
3. In the [early] morning[s], I will meditate on God, because he [himself] is my helper.
4. The demons will not dare to speak.
5. Christ your King, the Son of God, will rejoice in the Father and in the Holy Spirit.

EXERCITIUM XIV: *Personal Pronouns and Demonstratives*

I. Pronouns
1. This; that
2. Of his; him; this
3. To you
4. Your; our
5. Its
6. His
7. Those
8. To us
9. This
10. That

ANSWER KEY TO EXERCITIA

II. Martin Luther
1. For in this way, Blessed Anselm teaches how to ascend to the love of God from the love of a good man/person.
2. For it is a/the sign of true contrition.
3. This repentance is pleasant, true, steadfast/firm, and born from the spirit.
4. For repentance ought to be sweet.
5. For love is an eternal/perpetual chain.

EXERCITIUM XV: *Reflexives, Possessives, and Intensives*

I. Pronouns
1. Himself
2. Own
3. They [themselves]; they [themselves]
4. His [own]
5. Himself
6. His [own]
7. Him
8. Your
9. Themselves
10. Of ours

II. Ephesians
1. Making memory of you in my prayers.
2. Which is his body and his fullness/the fullness of him who is filled all in all.
3. And when/because you were dead in/by means of your crimes and sins.
4. In which also we all once/formerly/at one time lived in the desires of our flesh.
5. Moreover/But God who is rich in mercy on account of his exceeding love.

XVI: *Relatives, Interrogatives, and Indefinites*

I. Pronouns, Nouns, and Verbs
1. Some/certain; some/certain; some/certain/others; who/that; who/that; who/that
2. In what/which
3. Which; which
4. Do I add
5. Anyone; possesses/has
6. By which; by which; they fight
7. Also
8. Somebody
9. By which; by which
10. Some/a certain

II. Salonius the Viennese
1. In which language/tongue are the parables spoken?

2. Why did Solomon put/place that name to this book?
3. Therefore, how/in what way does Solomon interpret/understand/explain?
4. What differs/differentiates between wisdom and teaching/instruction/training?
5. Therefore, what is it to learn wisdom?/Therefore, what is needed to learn wisdom?
6. How many fearers of the Lord exist? [There are] two, that is, the servile one and the holy one.
7. What is it that he says: "Incline your heart to understanding knowledge/prudence/discretion" (Prov. 2:2)?
8. How/in what way can a person incline his heart?
9. About which law or about which plan does Solomon speak when he says: "Keep the law and counsel" (Prov. 3:21)?
10. What is the law of wisdom?

EXERCITIUM XVII: *Perfect Actives*

I. Perfect Active
1. Has separated/removed; has regenerated; has transformed
2. Has called; has led forth
3. Has willed/wished/desired
4. We have expounded/explained
5. Has poured into

II. Perfect Active in the Latin Vulgate
1. Fuit; fuit
2. Fuimus
3. Fuerunt
4. Fui
5. Fuisti

III. Benedictus
1. Blessed [be or is] the Lord God of Israel, who has visited and has made/completed/done the redemption of/for his people.
2. And he has raised [up] a/the horn of salvation to/for us in the house of David, his servant/child.
3. Just as he has spoken through the mouth of his holy prophets, who are from ages past.
4. Salvation/safety from our enemies and from the hand of all who/that hate us.
5. To show mercy with/to our fathers and to remember his holy will/testament.
6. Vowing an oath that/since/because he has sworn/vowed to Abraham our father that he would grant it to us.
7. So that without fear, [having been] freed/liberated from the hand of our enemies, that we may serve him in holiness and righteousness/justice before him for/in all of our days.
8. And you, boy/child, will be called a/the prophet of the Highest: for you will go before the face of the Lord to prepare his ways.
9. To give knowledge of salvation to his people in/unto the remission of their sins.
10. Through the bowels of the mercy of our God: in whom he has visited us, rising from on high.

ANSWER KEY TO EXERCITIA

EXERCITIUM XVIII: *Pluperfect Actives and Future Perfect Actives*

I. Pluperfect and Future Active
1. Will have made/done/performed
2. Had said/spoken
3. Had given
4. Will have said/spoken
5. You all will have shown

II. Perpetua
1. But/However, Saturus ascended/went up first, who had afterward/subsequently handed himself over freely (because he himself had established us/built us up), and then we were arrested.
2. And I consoled/comforted him, saying: "In/on that scaffold what[ever] God had willed will happen."
3. Therefore, on his behalf I had made/said a prayer: and between me and him there was a large space so that neither of us could/was able to approach the other.
4. I see that place which formerly I had seen, and [I see] Dinocrates well dressed with/in a pure body [and] refreshed.
5. He requested/asked for silence and said/spoke: "This Egyptian, if he should conquer/overcome/will have conquered/will have overcome her/this one [Perpetua], he will kill her with the sword; if she conquers/overcomes/will have conquered/will have overcome him/this one [the gladiator], she will receive this branch."

EXERCITIUM XIX: *Present Active and Present Passive Subjunctives*

I. Present Subjunctives
1. You should/ought to
2. Should/may be remitted
3. Should/may [not] dare
4. You should know
5. Would/may restore

II. Present Subjunctives of the "To Be" Verb in Tertullian
1. I should/would be
2. You may be
3. Should/may be
4. We should be/let us be
5. Be/are/may be; we may be

III. Thomas à Kempis
1. "The one who follows me does not walk in darkness," says the Lord.
2. These are the words of Christ, by which we are admonished/warned to what extent/so that we should imitate his life and habits/customs/character, if we want/wish to truly be illumined/enlightened, and to be freed/liberated from all blindness of the heart.
3. Therefore, this should be/let this be our greatest/highest pursuit, to meditate on the life of Jesus.

4. But/however, the one who fully and wisely wants/wishes to understand the words of Christ should strive/seek/study to conform to his entire life.
5. What benefit/use is it to you to debate/argue high/deep things about the Trinity, if you lack humility that you displease the Trinity/if you lack the humility by which you displease the Trinity? Truly, high/deep words do not make one holy and righteous, but a virtuous/good life makes one dear to God.

EXERCITIUM XX: *Imperfect Active and Imperfect Passive Subjunctives*

I. Imperfect Subjunctives
1. Might embrace/was embracing
2. Should/might/would sin; would be able/could be capable
3. Was/may be; might be put; might/did have
4. Might add/would add; might see/would see
5. We might be prepared

II. Imperfect Subjunctives of the "To Be" Verb in Alcuin of York
1. I might/would be
2. They existed/were
3. Was
4. We were
5. Would [not] be

III. Lorenzo Valla
1. I could very much wish, Garza, the most learned and best of bishops.
2. And I could very much choose both that other Christian people and especially those who are called theologians would not concede so much to philosophy.
3. Nor that they would consume so much work on it and make it almost equal and a sister (I do not say a patron) to theology.
4. For they seem to me to feel/perceive poorly about/of our religion, which they think/reckon stands in need of the protection of philosophy.
5. They/These men have done this [very] little, those whose works now survive/remain/exist after many generations/ages, imitators of the apostles and the ones who were truly pillars in the temple/church of God.

EXERCITIUM XXI: *Perfect and Pluperfect Subjunctives and Cum Clauses*

I. Perfect and Pluperfect Subjunctives
1. Would have preached/had preached
2. Has disregarded/neglected
3. You were/have been; you existed/were
4. I would have been/I had appeared
5. Would have dishonored; they will have changed
6. Be exercised/performed/utilized
7. I would [never] have written; I would not wish/want
8. Is/be/had been; would have been; would [not even] have been able

9. They would have been freed/liberated/they had been freed/liberated
10. Would have been prepared

II. Perfect and Pluperfect Subjunctive of the "To Be" Verb in Thomas Aquinas

1. It might be
2. Was
3. It might be/there might have been
4. Was [not] subject[ed]
5. Would have been freed/liberated

III. Bede

1. Nor is the report to be disregarded/passed over in silence about the blessed Gregory, which has been conveyed/handed down to us by the tradition of our ancestors, namely, on account of taking such diligence toward the salvation of our people.
2. They say that on a certain day, when some merchants had recently arrived [in Rome], there were many things for sale in the marketplace, and many people had gone there to make purchases.
3. Gregory himself had gone with the others, and, among other things, he saw some boys were set to be sold, their bodies white, their countenances beautiful, and their hair very fine.
4. After he looked at them, he asked, as they say, "from what country or nation were they brought?" And it was told/reported, "from the island of Britain," whose inhabitants were of such personal appearance. He again asked the same, whether those islanders were Christians or still involved in the errors of the pagans. It was told/reported to him that they were pagans.
5. But he, drawing long sighs from the bottom of his heart, said, "Alas, what a pity that the author of darkness has possession of people of such fair countenances and that their minds should be void of inward grace." Therefore, he asked again what the name of that people was. It was answered that they were called "Angles." But he said, "this is well, for they have an 'angelic' face, and it is fitting for such to be coheirs with the angels in heaven."

EXERCITIUM XXII: *Present Active Participles, Future Passive Participles (Gerundives), and Gerunds*

I. Present Active Participles, Future Passive Participles, and Gerunds

1. Having; speaking
2. Speaking
3. Comes/coming
4. Is/ought to be admitted/acknowledged
5. Saying
6. Existing
7. Are/ought to be tied
8. Of/for living
9. Eating; putting on
10. To be believed

II. Peter Ramus

1. Thus John 14, "I am the way, the truth, and the life," Christ speaks about himself, indicating that his teaching shows the way by which it may be the pleasant aim of blessedness/happiness.

2. There are two chapters of the creed: the first concerning God, the second concerning the church. For these two chapters contain/comprise a certain sum/the greatest summary of Christian teaching/doctrine, and nevertheless they also exist and appear especially through the entire teaching/doctrine. Therefore, they are especially to be observed and considered.
3. God, passing before Moses, exclaimed . . .
4. And only when we say/presently because we say, "I believe in Jesus," we confess Jesus to be God in this very testimony of belief/to be believed.
5. Thus Stephen, while dying, confesses Christ as/the Savior, "Lord Jesus Christ, receive my spirit."

EXERCITIUM XXIII: *Perfect Passive Participles, Future Active Participles, and Periphrastic Constructions*

I. Participles
1. Will sing/sound/is about to sing/sound
2. Will be
3. Is about to shape/will shape
4. Was put/placed
5. He will judge
6. Having returned/upon returning/after he returned
7. Is about to depart/will depart
8. Was adorned/decorated
9. Was born
10. Was reckoned/thought/regarded

II. Smaragdus
1. When John had heard [while] in prison/chains [about] the works of Christ, he sent two of his disciples and said/spoke to him: 'Are you the one who is coming/is to come, or should we expect/anticipate another?'"
2. The one who is to come/is coming, that is, [the one] about whom the prophets preach[ed] is to come/will come.
3. He did not say, "You are the one who came, but [rather] you are the one who is to come/is coming, who has perceived, 'send/deliver/commission me,' the one who is about to be killed by Herod."
4. And I am about to descend/go down into hell/into the underworld. Should I also declare/report about you in hell/in the underworld what I declared/reported [about you] on earth/in the upper world?
5. Whether it may not be fitting for the Son of God to taste death, and you are about to send another to/in these sacraments/mysteries.

EXERCITIUM XXIV: *Perfect, Pluperfect, and Future Perfect Passives; Fierī; Ablative Absolutes*

I. Perfects
1. Had been promised
2. Was born
3. Is to be feared; is to be feared

4. Was made; were made; were made
5. It was written; were complete
6. Was said; he was born
7. Was ordained; was honored/commended
8. Was refilled/swollen
9. We were reconciled
10. Was collected/gathered; was produced/published

II. John Cassian

For he alone was born/begotten to be God from/of God, at whose command the work/creation of the universe followed, whose will originated/gave rise to/is the beginning of all things; whose empire/command is the fabric of the world; who has spoken all things and they came to pass/happened. He has ordered/commanded all things, and they were created. Therefore, he alone has spoken to the patriarchs/ancestors, remaining in the prophets, was born from the Spirit, was born from the Virgin Mary, was seen by/in the world, was pondered by/dwelt with people/humanity, striking the handwriting of [our] sins on the wood of the cross, triumphing in himself, killing the powers contrary and hostile to us by his death, giving/granting to all people faith in the resurrection, and abolishing the corruption of human flesh by his glory.

EXERCITIUM XXV: *Present Active and Passive Infinitives; Indirect Speech; Impersonal Verbs*

I. Present Infinitives
1. To learn; to know/be acquainted with; to live; to do
2. To love; to be loved
3. To dissent/differ; to add
4. To be
5. To talk/speak; to speak/talk; to think/reason; to count/enumerate
6. To have/hold/possess; to have/hold/possess
7. To believe; to be done; to be offered
8. To see; to be seen
9. It is; to live
10. To know/to be acquainted with; to be ruled/governed; to fear; to ask

II. Impersonal Verbs in the Latin Vulgate
1. It is fitting/proper
2. Is it lawful/allowable/permitted
3. It is necessary/it is proper
4. There is [no] need
5. It is more pleasing; to do/perform

III. Damasus I

The one, who walking, restrained the bitter waves of the sea
The one who would make the dying seeds of the earth to live
The one who is able to dissolve the bonds of death from Lazarus
After the darkness of three daylights
And to give anew a brother to his sister Mary upon the earth
I believe that he will make Damasus rise again after his death (literally: after the ashes).

EXERCITIUM XXVI: *Perfect and Future Infinitives and More about Indirect Speech*

I. Perfect and Future Infinitives
1. To have provoked
2. Have suggested
3. To have merited/deserved; to have transgressed/been in want
4. Had had/had possessed
5. Was/had been

II. John Wesley and Count Zinzendorf

Wesley: I do not yet understand what you mean.

Zinzendorf: When you wrote to me from Georgia, I loved you very much. At that time, I perceived/acknowledged that you were simple in heart. You wrote again. I perceived/acknowledged that you were simple in heart, but you were unsettled/disturbed in your ideas/thoughts. You came to us. At that time, your ideas/thoughts were more unsettled/disturbed and confused. You returned to England. Sometime afterward, I heard that our brothers were fighting with you. I sent Spangenberg to make peace among you. He wrote to me, "The brothers have occasioned/inflicted an injury on you." I wrote back that they should not persist but rather that they should ask your pardon. Spangenberg wrote again, "They have asked [for peace], but that you were boasting of these things and did not want peace." Coming now, I hear the same.

Wesley: The matter by no means turns on that point. Your brothers (it is true) treated me poorly/ill. Afterward, they asked pardon. I replied, "This is unnecessary; I had never been angry with them. But I was afraid/I did dread (1) that they taught falsities; and (2) that they lived improperly/wrongly." That is, and was, the only question between us.

EXERCITIUM XXVII: *Imperatives, Prohibitions, and Vocatives*

I. Imperatives and Vocatives
1. Come; learn
2. Make
3. Brothers
4. Pay attention
5. Holy Spirit

II. Psalmus CXL
1. Lord, I have cried to you: Hear me; hearken to/turn to/come to my voice when I will have cried/I cry to you.
2. Lord, put protection around/set watch on my mouth and a door surrounding my lips.
3. Do not incline my heart to words of evil/wickedness, to make excuses in sins; with people/men performing/working unrighteousness, and I will not communicate/share/partake with the choicest/elect/chosen of them.
4. Because to you, Lord, Lord, are my eyes; in you I have hoped; do not take away my life/soul.
5. Preserve/keep me from the snare, which they have laid/positioned for me and from the stumbling blocks of those who perform/work unrighteousness.

III. Anselm of Canterbury

Come now, little man! Flee your occupations for a little while. Hide yourself for a little bit from your restless thoughts. Cast aside now your burdensome cares and put away your toilsome employments.

Make a little time for God and rest a little in him. "Enter the chamber of your mind" (Matt. 6:6). Shut out all things other than God and those things that help you seek him and, "having shut the door" (Matt. 6:6), seek him. Speak now, all of "my heart," speak now to God: "I seek your face/countenance; Lord, I need/am asking for your face/countenance" (Ps. 27:8). Therefore, come now you, my Lord God, teach my heart where and how it may seek you, where and how it may find you. Lord, if you are not here, where may I seek you being absent/your absence? But if you are everywhere, why do I not see you being present/your presence? But certainly, you dwell in unapproachable light. And where is unapproachable light, or where may I approach unapproachable light? Or who will lead me and bring me to that light/it, that I may see you in it?

APPENDIX III

Latin-English Vocabulary

A

ā, ab (+ abl): by, from
ábeō, abī́re, ábiī (abī́vī), ábitus (2): to go away, to depart
abscónditus, abscóndita, abscónditum: hidden, concealed, secret
abscóndō, abscóndere, abscóndī, abscónditus (3): to conceal, to hide, to cover
accédō, accédere, accésī, accéssus (3): to go to(ward), to approach
accéndō, accéndere, accéndī, accénsus (3): to kindle, to light (a fire), to inflame
acceptábilis, acceptábilis, acceptábile: acceptable
accū́sō, accūsā́re, accūsā́vī, accūsā́tus (1): to accuse, to blame, to reproach
áciēs, aciḗī (f): sharpness, keeness, edge, line of sight, line of battle
accípiō, accípere, accḗpī, accéptus (3): to take, to receive
áccidit, accídere, accī́dit (impers): it happens
accómodō, accomodā́re, accomodā́vī, accomodā́tus (1): to suit, to arrange, to accommodate
acquisī́tiō, acquisītiónis (f): acquisition
ad (+ acc): to, toward, near to
addō, áddere, áddidī, ádditus (3): to add
addū́cō, addū́cere, addū́xī, addúctus (3): to bring in, to lead in, to draw in
adhaéreō, adhaerḗre, adhaésī, adhaésus (2): to cleave to, to cling to, to adhere to
adhū́c: still, yet, now, as, thus far
ádiuvō, adiuvā́re, adiū́vī, adiū́tus (1): to help, to assist
adnū́ntiō, adnūntiā́re, adnūntiā́vī, adnūntiā́tus (1): to announce, to proclaim, to report
adóleō, adolḗre, -, - (2): to smell
adṓrō, adōrā́re, adōrā́vī, adōrā́tus (1): to worship, to adore, to revere
adsum, adésse, ádfuī, adfutū́rus (+ dat): to be present, to arrive
advéntus, advéntūs (m): coming, arrival, approach
advérsus (+ acc): against
aedī́ficō, aedificā́re, aedificā́vī, aedificā́tus (1): to build, to erect
aéstimō, aestimā́re, aestimā́vī, aestimā́tus (1): to think, to judge, to reckon, to value
aetā́s, aetā́tis (f): age, era, period of time
ager, agrī (m): field
agō, ágere, ḗgī, ā́ctus (3): to do, to act, to make
agrícola, agrícolae (m): farmer
afféctus, afféctūs (m): devotion, love, affection

āit, āiunt: he/she/it says, they say
albus, alba, album: white
aliénus, aliéna, aliénum: strange, foreign, belong to another
alō, álere, áluī, altus (3): to nourish, to foster, to feed
altắre, altắris (n): altar, place for burnt offerings
alter, áltera, álterum: the other (of two), the second
aliquándō: sometimes, formerly, at one time
altus, alta, altum: high, deep, tall
ámbulō, ambulắre, ambulắvī, ambulắtus (1): to walk, to travel
amícus, amícī (m): friend
ambō, ambṓnis (m): lectern, pulpit
amor, amṓris (m): love
ampléctor, amplécti, ampléxus sum (3): to embrace, to esteem, to cherish
amplus, ampla, amplum: large, abundant, ample, splendid
ancílla, ancíllae (f): female servant, maid
ángelus, ángelī (m): angel, messenger
ángulus, ángulī (m): corner, angle
ánima, ánimae (f): soul, life, spirit
ánimus, ánimī (m): mind, heart, spirit
annus, annī (m): year
ante (+ acc): before, in front of
ántequam: before
antíquus, antíqua, antíquum: old, ancient; (plural) forefathers
antístes, antístis (m): bishop, overseer
appéllō, appellắre, appellắvī, appellắtus (1): to call by name
apóstolus, apóstolī (m): apostle
appắreō, appārḗre, appắruī, appắritus (2): to appear, to be visible
apprehéndō, apprehéndere, apprehéndī, apprehḗnsus (3): to lay hold of, to understand, to seize
appropínquō, appropinquắre, appropinquắvī, appropinquắtus (1) (+ dat): to come near, to approach
apériō, aperíre, apéruī, apértus (4): to open, to uncover
aqua, aquae (f): water
árdeō, ardḗre, arsī, arsus (2): to burn, to be in love
árbitror, arbitrắrī, arbitrắtus sum (1): to judge, to witness, to observe, to consider
arbor, árboris (f): tree
árguō, argúere, árguī, argútus (3): to assert, to declare, to accuse
arma, armṓrum (n): weapons, arms
ars, artis, ártium (f): skill, art, craft, knowledge
ascéndō, ascéndere, ascéndī, ascḗnsus (3): to go up, to climb (up), to ascend
aspéctus, aspéctūs (m): appearance, sight
aspíciō, aspícere, aspéxī, aspéctus (3): to look at, to observe, to regard
assúmō, assúmere, assúmpsī, assúmptus (3): to take up, to accept, to assume
atténdō, atténdere, atténdī, atténtus (3): to pay attention, to attend (to)
aúdeō, audḗre, ausus sum (2): to dare, to risk, to venture
aúdiō, audíre, audívī, audítus (4): to hear, to listen (to)
aúferō, auférre, ábstulī, ablắtus (3): to take away, to remove
aula, aulae (f): class, hall, church, court, palace
aúreus, aúrea, aúreum: golden, of gold
auris, auris, aúrium (f): ear

aurum, aurī (n): gold
aut: or
āvértō, āvértere, āvértī, āvérsus (3): to turn away, to avoid, to avert

B

baptísma, baptísmatis (n): baptism
baptízō, baptizáre, baptizávī, baptizátus (1): to baptize
bene: well
benedícō, benedícere, benedíxī, benedíctus (3): to bless, to praise, to speak well of
benedíctiō, benedictiónis (f): blessing, benediction
benedíctus, benedícta, benedíctum: blessed
bibō, bíbere, bibī, bíbitus (3): to drink
bis: twice, two times
blasphémō, blasphemáre, blasphemávī, blasphemátus (1): to blaspheme
bonus, bona, bonum: good
bráchium, bráchiī (n): arm
brevis, brevis, breve: short, brief, small, little

C

cadō, cádere, cécidī, cāsus (3): to fall (down)
caelum, caelī (n): heaven, sky
caécitās, caecitátis (f): blindness, darkness
caecus, caeca, caecum: blind (blind person)
caeléstis, caeléstis, caeléste: heavenly, celestial, divine
cālígō, cālíginis (f): mist, fog, gloom, darkness
calix, cálicis (m): cup, chalice
canō, cánere, cécinī, cantus (3): to predict, to prophesy, to foretell, to sing
cánticus, cánticī (n): song, chant
cantō, cantáre, cantávī, cantátus (1): to sing, to chant
cápiō, cápere, cēpī, captus (3): to take, to capture, to seize
caput, cápitis (n): head
carō, carnis (f): flesh, meat
castus, casta, castum: chaste
cathólicus, cathólica, cathólicum: catholic, universal
causa, causae (f): purpose, reason, motive, cause
cáveō, cavére, cāvī, cautus (2): to beware, to take care
cēdō, cédere, cessī, cessus (3): to go, to proceed, to happen, to surrender
célebrō, celebráre, celebrávī, celebrátus (1): to celebrate
celer, céleris, célere: fast, swift
cēna, cēnae (f): dinner, supper
cēnáculum, cēnáculī (n): dining room, upper room
cēnō, cēnáre, cēnávī, cēnátus (1): to dine, to eat supper
centum: one hundred
cēra, cērae (f): wax
céreus, céreī (m): candle
cernō, cérnere, crēvī, crētus (3): to discern, to distinguish, to separate, to see

cessō, cessāre, cessāvī, cessātus (1): to stop, to cease, to delay
Christus, Christī (m): Christ, Messiah, Anointed One
clārus, clāra, clārum: clear, famous, bright, renowned
claudō, claúdere, clausī, clausus (3): to close, to shut
clērus, clērī (m): clergy
cibus, cibī (m): food
circum (+ acc): around, about, nearby
citō: quickly
cīvitās, cīvitātis (f): city, citizenship, state
clam: secretly
clāmō, clāmāre, clāmāvī, clāmātus (1): to proclaim, to cry out, to shout
clārēscō, clārēscere, clāruī, - (3): to flourish, to brighten, to become clear
clāvis, clāvis, clāvium (f): key
clēmēns, clēmēns, clēmēns: merciful, mild, peaceful, clement
coépiō, coépere, coepī, coeptus (3): to begin
cōgitō, cōgitāre, cōgitāvī, cōgitātus (1): to think, to consider
cognóscō, cognóscere, cognóvī, cógnitus (3): to learn, to recognize, to be acquainted with
cōgō, cōgere, coēgī, coāctus (3): to collect, to compel, to assemble, to force
cólligō, collígere, collēgī, colléctus (3): to gather, to assemble, to infer
combūrō, combūrere, combūssī, combūstus (3): to burn up, to consume (with fire)
comédō, comédere, comēdī, comēsus (3): to eat, to eat up, to chew up, to consume
comes, cómitis (m, f): companion, partner; count, earl
compléctor, compléctī, compléxus sum (3): to embrace, to surround, to hug
concéptus, concéptūs (m): conception, embryo
concípiō, concípere, concēpī, concéptus (3): to conceive, to comprehend, to contain
conclūdō, conclūdere, conclūsī, conclūsus (3): to enclose, to shut in, to conclude
concupīscō, concupīscere, concupīvī, concupītus (3): to covet, to desire, to be desirous of
cōnfīdō, confīdere, cōnfīsus sum (3) (+ dat): to trust (in), to confide (in), to confess
cōnfíteor, cōnfitērī, cōnféssus sum (2): to confess, to acknowledge, to praise
cōnfúndō, cōnfúndere, cōnfūdī, cōnfūsus (3): to confound, to confuse, to shame, to unite
cóngregō, congregāre, congregāvī, congregātus (1): to gather, to assemble, to congregate
cōnspéctus, cōnspéctūs (m): sight, presence, view
cōnsūmō, cōnsūmere, cōnsūmpsī, cōnsūmptus (3): to consume, to devour, to eat
cōnor, cōnārī, cōnātus sum (3) (+ inf): to strive, to try, to attempt
cónsequor, cónsequī, cōnsecūtus sum (3): to follow, to pursue, to obtain
cōnsōlor, cōnsōlārī, cōnsōlātus sum (1): to console, to soothe, to alleviate
cōnstítuō, cōnstítuere, cōnstítuī, cōnstitūtus (3): to establish, to confirm, to set up
copiósus, copiósa, copiósum: abundant, full, copious
cōnstat (impers): it is evident, it is agreed, it costs
conténdō, conténdere, conténdī, conténtus (3): to strive, to assert, to contend
contíneō, continēre, contínuī, conténtus (2): to hold together, to contain
contrā (+ acc): against
convéniō, convenīre, convénī, convéntus (4): to come together, to agree, to be suited
convértō, convértere, convértī, convérsus (3): to turn (back), to convert, to change
convīva, convīvae (m): guest
cōram (+ abl): before, in the presence of
cor, cordis, córdium (n): heart
coróna, corónae (f): crown, wreath, tonsure

corṓnō, corōnā́re, corōnā́vī, corōnā́tus (1): to crown
cornū, cornūs (n): horn
corpus, córporis (n): body
creō, creā́re, creā́vī, creā́tus (1): to create, to produce, to make, to cause
crēscō, crḗscere, crēvī, crētus (3): to grow, to increase
cum (+ abl): with, when, because
cultus, cultūs (m): worship, church service
cūnctus, cūncta, cūnctum: all, whole
currō, cúrrere, cucúrrī, cursus (3): to run, to hasten
custṓdia, custṓdiae (f): guard, custody; prison, cell
custṓdiō, custōdī́re, custōdī́vī, custōdī́tus (4): to guard, to protect, to watch

D

dē (+ abl): about, concerning, on
dḗbeō, dēbḗre, dḗbuī, dḗbitus (2): to owe, ought, to keep from
decet, decḗre, dḗcuit (impers): it is becoming, it is proper
dēclī́nō, dēclinā́re, dēclinā́vī, dēclinā́tus (1): to bend, to deflect
décorō, decorā́re, decorā́vī, decorā́tus (1): to adorn, to decorate, to beautify, to honor
dēféndō, dēféndere, dēféndī, dēfénsus (3): to defend, to guard, to protect
dēfī́ciō, dēfī́cere, dēfḗcī, dēféctus (3): to waste, to forsake, to abandon, to fail
dḗleō, dēlḗre, dēlḗvī, dēlḗtus (2): to destroy, to terminate, to abolish, to end
dēlī́ctum, dēlī́ctī (n): crime, fault, offense, sin
dēmī́ttō, dēmī́ttere, dēmī́sī, dēmī́ssus (3): to send down, to bring down, to forgive
dēmóror, dēmorā́rī, dēmorā́tus sum (1): to delay, to abide, to linger, to dwell
dēprecā́tiō, dēprecātiṓnis (f): prayer, deprecation
déprecor, dēprecā́rī, dēprecā́tus sum (1): to beseech, to pray for, to deprecate
dērelī́nquō, dērelī́nquere, dērelī́quī, dērelī́ctus (3): to abandon, to forsake, to desert, to leave
dēsī́derō, dēsīderā́re, dēsīderā́vī, dēsīderā́tus (1): to want, to wish, to desire
dēsī́stō, dēsī́stere, déstitī, déstitus (3): to cease, to desist
dēspī́ciō, dēspī́cere, dēspéxī, dēspéctus (3): to look down upon, to despise, to disdain
deus, deī (m): God, god
diábolus, diábolī (m): devil, Satan
dīcō, dī́cere, dī́xī, dictus (3): to say, to speak, to talk
diēs, diéī (m, f): day
diffī́dō, diffī́dere, diffī́sus sum (3) (+ dat): to distrust (in), to despair (of)
dignus, digna, dignum: worthy, fitting, appropriate
dī́ligō, dīlī́gere, dīléxī, dīléctus (3): to love, to esteem, to cherish
discípulus, discípulī (m): learner, disciple, student
dísputō, disputā́re, disputā́vī, disputā́tus (1): to dispute, to argue, to debate, to discuss
disséntiō, dissentī́re, dissḗnsī, dissḗnsus (4): to dissent, to differ
dī́ves, dī́ves, dī́vitis: rich, wealthy
dī́vidō, dīvídere, dīvī́sī, dīvī́sus (3): to divide, to separate
dō, dare, dedī, datus (1): to give, to offer, to yield
doctrī́na, doctrī́nae (f): teaching, learning, doctrine
dóceō, docḗre, dócuī, dóctus (2): to teach, to instruct, to show, to inform
dóminus, dóminī (m): Lord, lord, master, sir
domus, domūs (f): home, house, household

donec: while, until, as long as
dōnō, dōnāre, dōnāvī, dōnātus (1): to give, to grant; to forgive, to pardon
dórmiō, dormíre, dormívī, dormítus (4): to sleep, to lie down
dúbitō, dubitāre, dubitāvī, dubitātus (1): to doubt, to waver, to hesitate
dūcō, dúcere, dūxī, ductus (3): to lead, to guide
duo, duae, duo: two

E

ē, ex (+ abl): from, out of
ecclésia, ecclésiae (f): church, assembly, gathering
effígiēs, effigéī (f): image, figure, likeness
effúndō, effúndere, effúdī, effúsus (3): to pour (forth), to shed, to cast out
ēgrédior, ēgrédī, ēgréssus sum (3): to go out, to go forth, to land, to disembark
éligō, ēlígere, ēlégī, ēléctus (3): to choose, to elect
ēnárrō, ēnārrāre, ēnārrāvī, ēnārrātus (1): to explain, to expound, to show, to relate
eō, īre, iī (īvī), ītus (4): to go, to proceed, to advance
errō, errāre, errāvī, errātus (1): to go astray, to wander, to err, to be wrong
ēvangelízō, ēvangelīzāre, ēvangelīzāvī, ēvangelīzātus (1): to evangelize, to preach the gospel
évenit, ēveníre, ēvénit (impers): it results
exáltō, exaltāre, exaltāvī, exaltātus (1): to exalt, to praise, to elevate
exaúdiō, exaudíre, exaudívī, exaudítus (4): to hear (favorably), to hearken
exclāmō, exclāmāre, exclāmāvī, exclāmātus (1): to cry out, to exclaim
éxeō, exíre, éxiī (exívī), éxitus (4): to go out (from), to exit, to depart
exércitus, exércitūs (m): army, host
exhíbeō, exhibére, exhíbuī, exhíbitus (2): to reveal, to show, to exhibit
expéctō, expectāre, expectāvī, expectātus (1): to wait for, to expect
éxplicō, explicāre, explicāvī, explicātus (1): to unfold, to explain, to set forth
expónō, expónere, expósuī, expósitus (3): to set forth, to explain, to expound
exténdō, exténdere, exténdī, exténtus (3): to extend, to stretch, to prolong, to enlarge
extínguō, extínguere, extínxī, extínctus (3): to extinguish, to quench
extrā (+ acc): outside (of), beyond

F

fáciō, fácere, fēcī, factus (3): to do, to make, to construct
família, famíliae (f): family
fáteor, fatérī, fassus sum (2) (+ acc; dat): to confess, to admit, to praise
ferō, ferre, tulī, lātus (3): to bring, to bear, to carry
ferrum, ferrī (n): iron
festínō, festīnāre, festīnāvī, festīnātus (1): to hurry, to hasten
fidélis, fidélis, fidéle: faithful, loyal, trustworthy
fidēs, fídeī (f): faith, faithfulness
fīdō, fídere, fīsus sum (3): to trust, to rely (on), to put confidence (in)
fília, fíliae (f): daughter
fílius, fíliī (m): son
fleō, flēre, flēvī, flētus (2): to cry, to weep, to lament, to grieve (for)
fortis, fortis, forte: strong, brave

frāter, frātris (m): brother
frūctus, frūctūs (m): fruit, crop, outcome, produce
fugō, fugāre, fugāvī, fugātus (1): to put to flight, to chase, to drive into exile
fundō, fúndere, fūdī, fūsus (3): to pour (out), to shed

G

gaúdeō, gaudḗre, gāvīsus sum (2): to rejoice, to be glad
gládius, gládiī (m): sword
glṓrior, glōriā́rī, glōriā́tus sum (1): to boast, to brag, to glory
gēns, gentis, géntium (f): nation, tribe, people
genū, genūs (n): knee
gignō, gígnere, génuī, génitus (3): to give birth to, to produce, to beget
glṓria, glṓriae (f): glory, fame
gradus, gradūs (m): step, degree, rank, position
grā́tia, grā́tiae (f): favor, grace
grex, gregis (m): flock, herd, crowd
gustō, gustā́re, gustā́vī, gustā́tus (1): to taste, to sample

H

hábeō, habḗre, hábuī, hábitus (2): to have, to hold, to consider
hábitō, habitā́re, habitā́vī, habitā́tus (1): to dwell, to live, to inhabit, to abide
habitā́tor, habitātṓris (m): inhabitant, resident, dweller
hábitus, hábitūs (m): habit, appearance, garment, disposition
hódiē: today
haéresis, haéresis (f): heresy
homō, hóminis (m): person, humankind, man
hortor, hortā́rī, hortā́tus sum (1): to urge, to exhort, to encourage
hospes, hóspitis (m): host, guest

I/J

iáciō, iácere, iēcī, iáctus (3): to throw, to cast, to hurl
iam (jam): already, now, anymore
īgnis, īgnis, īgnium (m): fire
ignṓrō, ignōrā́re, ignōrā́vī, ignōrā́tus (1): not to know, to ignore
ígitur: therefore, consequently, thus
imperī́tus, imperī́ta, imperī́tum: inexperienced, unskilled
ímperō, imperā́re, imperā́vī, imperā́tus (1) (+ dat): to command, to give orders to, to rule
ímpleō, implḗre, implḗvī, implḗtus (2): to fill (up), to satisfy, to cover, to complete
impṓnō, impṓnere, impṓsuī, impṓsitus (3): to place upon, to set upon, to lay upon
in (+ acc; abl): into, onto, against (acc); in, on (abl)
íncitō, incitā́re, incitā́vī, incitā́tus (1): to incite, to quicken, to provoke, to hasten
íncrepō, increpā́re, increpā́vī, increpā́tus (1): to rebuke, to reprove, to blame
indígeō, indigḗre, indíguī, - (2): to need, to want, to lack
ínferus, ínfera, ínferum: of hell, below
inī́quitās, inīquitā́tis (f): iniquity, unfairness, injustice

inde: from there, thence, thereafter, since
índicō, indicáre, indicávī, indicátus (1): to indicate, to point out, to show, to declare
índigēns, indegéntis (m, f, n): needy (person), in want
índuo, indúere, índuī, indútus (3): to clothe, to put clothes on, to cover
ingrédior, ingrédī, ingréssus sum (3): to go into, to enter, to walk
inquiétus, inquiéta, inquiétum: restless
ínsequor, ínsequī, īnsecútus sum (3): to follow, to pursue
intelléctus, intelléctūs (m): reason, understanding, intellect
inter (+ acc): between
ínterest (impers): it concerns
interfício, interfícere, interfécī, interféctus (3): to kill, to destroy, to murder
intrā (+ acc): within, inside
intrō, intráre, intrávī, intrátus (1): to enter, to go in
intróeō, introíre, intróiī, intróitus (4): to enter, to go in
intúeor, intuérī, intúitus sum (2): to look at, to consider, to observe, to regard
invénio, veníre, invénī, invéntus (4): to find, to discover, to come upon, to obtain
ínvocō, invocáre, invocávī, invocátus (1): to invoke, to call by name, to call upon
īra, īrae (f): anger, wrath
īrátus, īráta, īrátum: angry
iúbeo, iubére, iussī, iussus (2): to command, to order
iúdicō, iūdicáre, iūdicávī, iūdicátus (1): to judge, to determine, to decide
iūstíficō, iūstificáre, iūstificávī, iūstificátus (1): to make righteous, to justify
iūstítia, iūstítiae (f): righteousness, justice
iūstus, iūsta, iūstum: righteous, just

L

lac, lactis (n): milk
laetor, laetárī, laetátus sum (1): to rejoice, to be glad
legō, légere, lēgī, lēctus (3): to read, to select, to choose
levō, leváre, levávī, levátus (1): to raise, to lift up, to elevate, to lighten
lēx, lēgis (f): law
liber, librī (m): book
līber, líbera, líberum: free
libet, libére, líbuit (impers): it pleases
licet, licére, lícuit (impers): it is allowed, it is permitted
lignum, lignī (n): tree, wood
língua, línguae (f): tongue, language
litúrgia, litúrgiae (f): liturgy, service
lóquor, loquī, locútus sum (3): to speak, to say, to tell, to talk

M

magistérium, magistériī (n): office of authority, teaching office
magnus, magna, magnum: great, large, big
malus, mala, malum: bad, evil
mandō, mandáre, mandávī, mandátus (1): to order, to command, to give charge to
mandúcō, manducáre, manducávī, manducátus (1): to eat, to chew, to devour, to gobble up

máneō, manére, mānsī, mānsus (2): to stay, to remain
mānō, mānáre, mānávī, mānátus (1): to flow, to run, to drop
manus, manūs (f): hand, group of people
mare, maris, márium (n): sea
māter, mātris (f): mother
méditor, meditárī, meditátus sum (1): to meditate (on), to contemplate
méminī, meminísse, -, - (3): to remember, to be mindful of
mēnsis, mēnsis, ménsium (m): month
mercēs, mercédis (f): pay, wages, reward, salary, ransom
métior, mētírī, mēnsus sum (4): to measure, to distribute
metus, metūs (m): fear, dread
mīlle: one thousand
mīror, mīrárī, mīrátus sum (1): to be amazed (at), to wonder (at)
misericórdia, misericórdiae (f): mercy
missa, missae (f): Mass
míseror, miserárī, miserátus sum (1): to have pity on, to lament, to feel sorry for
mittō, míttere, mīsī, missus (3): to send, to let go, to discharge
mórior, morī, mórtuus sum (3): to die
múlier, mulíeris (f): woman
multíplicō, multiplicáre, multiplicávī, multiplicátus (1): to multiply, to increase
multus, multa, multum: many, much
mūtō, mūtáre, mūtávī, mūtátus (1): to change, to move, to modify, to transform
mūtus, mūta, mūtum: silent, mute, quiet
mystérium, mystériī (n): mystery, sacrament

N

nam: for, because, thus
nārrō, nārráre, nārrávī, nārrátus (1): to narrate, to report, to tell, to recount
nātus, nātī (m): child, son, offspring
necésse est (impers): it is necessary
negótium, negótiī (n): business, employment, labor, matter, trouble
nímius, nímia, nímium: too much, too great, excessive
nisi: unless, if not, except
nōlō, nōlle, nóluī: not to wish, not to want, not to will
nōmen, nóminis (n): name
nōn: no, not
nōscō, nóscere, nōvī, nōtus (3): to know, to recognize
nox, noctis, nóctium (f): night
númerō, numeráre, numerávī, numerátus (1): to count, to number, to reckon
númerus, númerī (m): number
num(quid): if, whether, surely not?
nūntiō, nūntiáre, nūntiávī, nūntiátus (1): to announce, to declare, to proclaim, to tell

O

ob (+ acc): on account of, according to, towards
óbeō, obíre, óbiī (obívī), óbitus (4): to go towards, to die

obsum, obésse, óbfuī, obfutū́rus (+ dat): to be against, to do harm to
óccidō, occídere, óccidī, occā́sus (3): to go down, to pass away, to fall down
occī́dō, occī́dere, occī́dī, occī́sus (3): to kill, to murder, to slay, to beat
ocúrrō, occúrrere, ocúrrī, occúrsus (3): to (go to) meet, to come to, to occur
óculus, óculī (m): eye
occúrrō, ocúrrere, occúrrī, occúrsus (3): to meet, to go to meet, to come to, to charge
ódium, ódiī (n): hatred, ill will, bitterness
ófferō, offérre, óbtulī, oblā́tus (3): to present, to offer, to sacrifice
omnípotēns, omnípotēns, omnípotēns: all-powerful, omnipotent, almighty
óperor, operā́rī, operā́tus sum (1): to work, to labor
opī́nor, opinā́rī, opinā́tus sum (1): to suppose, to deem, to think
opórtet (impers) (2): it is fitting
optō, optā́re, optā́vī, optā́tus (1): to wish, to desire, to hope for
opus est (impers): there is need
ōrā́tiō, ōrātiṓnis (f): prayer, speech, sentence
ṓrdior, ōrdī́rī, ōrsus sum (4): to begin, to commence
órior, orī́rī, ortus sum (4): to arise, appear, to rise, to get up
ōrnō, ōrnā́re, ōrnā́vī, ōrnā́tus (1): to equip, to prepare, to adorn
ōrō, ōrā́re, ōrā́vī, ōrā́tus (1): to pray, to plead, to deliver a speech
ōs, ōris (n): mouth, face, appearance
os, ossis (n): bone, soul
ósculor, ōsculā́rī, ōsculā́tus sum (1): to kiss, to embrace
ósculum, ósculī (n): kiss
óstium, óstiī (n): door, entrance
ovis, ovis (f): sheep

P

pācíficō, pācificā́re, pācificā́vī, pācificā́tus (1): to make peace, to negotiate peace, to pacify
pānis, pānis, pā́nium (m): bread, loaf
páriō, párere, péperī, partus (3): to bear, to produce, to beget
partim: in part, partly
parvus, parva, parvum: small, little, cheap
Pascha, Paschae (f): Passover, Easter, Pesach
passim: here and there, at random
pāstor, pāstṓris (m): shepherd
pater, patris (m): father
pátior, patī, passus sum (3): to suffer, to endure, to allow
paúper, paúper, paúper: poor
peccā́tum, peccā́tī (n): sin
peccō, peccā́re, peccā́vī, peccā́tus (1): to sin, to transgress
per (+ acc): through, by means of
percútiō, percútere, percússī, percússus (3): to beat, to strike, to pierce
perdō, pérdere, pérdidī, pérditus (3): to destroy, to ruin
péreō, perī́re, périī [perī́vī], péritus (4): to perish, to pass away, to die, to disappear
permáneō, permanḗre, permā́nsī, permā́nsus (2): to persist, to ensure, to endure, to persevere
persólvō, persólvere, persólvī, persolū́tus (3): to explain, to recite, to perform (a duty)
pertíneō, pertinḗre, pertínuī, - (2): to stretch out, to reach, to belong to

pervéniō, pervenīre, pervénī, pervéntus (4): to come, to arrive, to attain, to reach
placet (impers) (2): it pleases
plangō, plángere, plānxī, plānctus (3): to mourn, to bewail, to lament
pópulus, pópulī (m): people
porrō: furthermore, further, onwards
porténdō, porténdere, porténdī, porténtus (3): to foretell, to predict, to portend
portō, portáre, portávī, portátus (1): to carry, to bear, to sustain
possídeō, possidére, possédī, posséssus (2): to possess, to inherit, to own
possum, posse, pótuī, - : to be able, can
post (+ acc): after, behind
pósteā: afterward, then, next
poténtia, poténtiae (f): power, might
potéstās, potestátis (f): power, ability, authority
pótior, potírī, potítus sum (4): to be more able, to be more capable
pōtus, pōtūs (m): drink
praecéptum, praecéptī (n): lesson, command, precept
praecípiō, praecípere, praecépī, praecéptus (3): to command, to order, to enjoin
precor, precárī, precátus sum (1): to pray, to ask, to beseech
praédicō, praedicáre, praedicávī, praedicátus (1): to preach, to announce, to declare
praefigŭrō, praefigŭráre, praefigŭrávī, praefigŭrátus (1): to prefigure
praesúmō, praesúmere, praesúmpsī, praesúmptus: to presume, to take for granted
praeter (+ acc): beyond, except, besides
praeváricor, praevāricárī, praevāricátus sum (1): to sin against, to transgress
prex, precis (f): prayer, request, entreaty
prōcédō, prōcédere, prōcéssī, prōcéssus (3): to advance, to proceed
prōdō, pródere, pródidī, próditus (3): to bring forth, to produce, to bear
prōdúcō, prōdúcere, prōdúxī, prōdúctus (3): to produce, to bring forth, to beget
proélior, proeliárī, proeliátus sum (1): to fight, to battle, to contest
prōfíciō, prōfícere, prōfécī, prōféctus (3): to avail, to prevail
profíteor, profitérī, proféssus sum (2): to profess, to declare, to acknowledge
prōíciō, prōícere, prōiécī, prōiéctus (3): to throw, to thrust, to cast away
prōmíttō, prōmíttere, prōmísī, prōmíssus (3): to promise, to send forth
porta, portae (f): gate, entrance, door
prídiē: day before
prīmum: first, at first
prīmus, prīma, prīmum: first
prínceps, príncipis (m): chief, leader, ruler, prince
prō (+ abl): for, on behalf of, before, instead of
probō, probáre, probávī, probátus (1): to test, to prove, to try, to examine
prōgéniēs, prōgeniéī (f): race, progeny, offspring
prohíbeō, prohibére, prohíbuī, prohíbitus (2): to forbid, to prohibit, to hinder, to restrain
prophéta, prophétae (m): prophet
propter (+ acc): on account of, because of
puélla, puéllae (f): girl
puer, púerī (m): boy, child, servant
pugnō, pugnáre, pugnávī, pugnátus (1): to fight, to battle, to combat, to struggle
pulvis, púlveris (m): dust, powder, ashes
púniō, pūnīre, pūnívī, pūnítus (4): to punish, to avenge

putō, putā́re, putā́vī, putā́tus (1): to think, to consider, to reckon

Q

quaérō, quaérere, quaesī́vī, quasī́tus (3): to seek, to inquire, to ask, to require
quam: than, as
quaesō, quaésere, quaesī́vī, - (3): to beseech, to ask; please
quasi: as it were, nearly, almost
quátenus: so, so that, insofar as
quéror, querī, questus sum (3): to complain, to lament, to be indignant
quia, quod, quóniam: that, because, since
quidem: indeed, in fact
quiéscō, quiéscere, quiévī, quiétus (3): to cease, to rest, to be still, to be at peace
quidquid: whatever
quoque: also, even, indeed, likewise

R

ratiócinor, ratiōcinā́rī, ratiōcinā́tus sum (1): to reckon, to consider, to compute, to argue
recédō, recédere, recéssī, recéssus (3): to fall back, to retreat, to withdraw
récitō, recitā́re, recitā́vī, recitā́tus (3): to recite
recórdor, recordā́rī, recordā́tus sum (1): to remember, to call to mind, to recollect
redémptiō, redēmptiónis (f): redemption, ransoming
redímō, redímere, redémī, redémptus (3): to redeem, to ransom
rédeō, redī́re, rédiī (redī́vī), réditus (4): to turn back, to return, to go/come back
reddō, réddere, réddidī, rédditus (3): to give back, to return, to restore, to render
refōrmō, refōrmā́re, refōrmā́vī, refōrmā́tus (1): to renew, to reform, to transform, to remake
regénerō, regenerā́re, regenerā́vī, regenerā́tus (1): to regenerate, to reproduce, to bring back
rēgī́na, rēgī́nae (f): queen
rēgnō, rēgnā́re, rēgnā́vī, rēgnā́tus (1): to rule, to govern, to reign, to lord it over
regō, régere, rēxī, rēctus (3): to rule, to govern
régulō, rēgulā́re, rēgulā́vī, rēgulā́tus (1): to rule, to govern, to regulate
relínquitur (impers) (3): it remains
relígiō, religiónis (f): religion, devotion, reverence
réliquus, réliqua, réliquum: remaining, surviving
remáneō, remanḗre, remā́nsī, remā́nsus (2): to remain, to be left, to abide
répleō, replḗre, replḗvī, replḗtus (2): to fill again, to replenish, to refill
rēs, reī (f): thing
respíciō, respícere, respéxī, respéctus (3): to look at, to respect, to have regard for
respóndeō, respondḗre, respóndī, respónsus (2): to reply, to respond, to answer
restat (impers) (1): it remains
restaúrō, restaurā́re, restaurā́vī, restaurā́tus (1): to restore, to renew
restítuō, restitúere, restítuī, restitū́tus (3): to restore, to replace, to revive
rēgnum, rēgnī (n): kingdom
resístō, resístere, réstitī, - (3): to resist, to withstand, to oppose
rēvḗrā: actually, in fact, in truth, truthfully
révertor, revértī, revérsus sum (3): to return, to turn back
rēx, rēgis (m): king

rītus, rītūs (m): ceremony, rite
rogō, rogāre, rogāvī, rogātus (1): to pray, to beseech, to ask for

S

sacérdōs, sacerdōtis (m): priest
sacrāméntum, sacrāméntī (n): sacrament, mystery, oath
saepe: often
sagínō, sagināre, sagināvī, saginātus (1): to fatten, to feed, to nourish
salūtō, salūtāre, salūtāvī, salūtātus (1): to preserve, to keep safe, to salute, to greet
sálveō, salvēre, -, - (2): to be well, to be healthy
sānctus, sāncta, sānctum: holy, godly
salvātor, salvātōris (m): Savior
salvō, salvāre, salvāvī, salvātus (1): to save
sápiēns, sápiēns, sápiēns: wise
sapiéntia, sapiéntiae (f): wisdom
scelus, scéleris (n): crime, sin
sciéntia, sciéntiae (f): knowledge
scílicet: naturally, certainly, namely
sciō, scīre, scīvī (sciī), scītus (4): to know, to understand
scrībō, scrībere, scrīpsī, scrīptus (3): to write
scrīptūra, scrīptūrae (f): writing, scripture
secúndus, secúnda, secúndum: second
sed: but
sédeō, sedēre, sēdī, séssus (2): to sit, to be seated, to be established
ségregō, sēgregāre, sēgregāvī, sēgregātus (1): to separate, to segregate, to remove
sēmen, sēminis (n): seed
sēminō, sēmināre, sēmināvī, sēminātus (1): to sow, to plant
semper: always
sēnsus, sēnsūs (m): feeling, sentiment, sense
senténtia, senténtiae (f): thought, sentiment, sentence
séquor, sequī, secūtus sum (3): to follow, to pursue
sermō, sermónis (m): speech, word, conversation
servō, servāre, servāvī, servātus (1): to keep, to preserve
servus, servī (m): slave, servant
sī: if
sīgnum, sīgnī (n): sign, mark, miracle
símilis, símilis, símile: similar
simul: at the same time, simultaneously
sine (+ abl): without
sistō, sístere, stitī, status (3): to stand, to cause to stand, to set, to place
sīve: or
sōl, sōlis (m): sun
sōlémnitās, sōlemnitātis (f): solemnity, feast day, festival
sōlémne, sōlémnis (n): feast (day), ceremony, festival
sóleō, solēre, sólitus sum (2): to be accustomed to, to be used to
soror, sorōris (f): sister
spargō, spárgere, sparsī, sparsus (3): to sprinkle, to sow, to scatter

spéciēs, speciéī (f): species, form, appearance
spectō, spectáre, spectávī, spectátus (1): to observe, to watch, to look at, to consider
spērō, spēráre, spērávī, spērátus (1): to hope, to expect, to await
spēs, speī (f): hope
spīrō, spīráre, spīrávī, spīrátus (1): to breathe
spíritus, spíritūs (m): spirit, breath, wind
spōnsus, spōnsī (m): groom
statim: immediately, at once, then
stēlla, stēllae (f): star
stō, stāre, stetī, status (1): to stand, to stay
sub (+ acc): under, before (acc); under, beneath (abl)
súbitō: quickly, at once, immediately
subnéctō, subnéctere, subnéxuī, subnéxus (3): to bind (under), to tie (under), to subjoin
succéndō, succéndere, succéndī, succénsus (3): to kindle, to inflame, to set on fire
suffíciō, suffícere, sufféci, sufféctus (3): to be sufficient, to be enough
sumō, súmere, sumpsī, sumptus (3): to take (up), to seize, to obtain, to acquire
summópere: exceedingly, very much
super (+ acc; abl): above, beyond (acc); concerning (abl)
supérnus, supérna, supérnum: heavenly, celestial
suprā (+ acc): above, over, beyond
surgō, súrgere, surréxī, surréctus (3): to rise, to arise, to get up
sūrsum: above, upwards
suscípiō, suspícere, suspéxī, suspéctus (3): to look up to, to regard, to suspect
súscitō, suscitáre, suscitávī, suscitátus (1): to encourage, to stir up, to awaken
sustíneō, sustinére, sustínuī, susténtus (2): to uphold, to support, to sustain, to restrain

T

tabernáculum, tabernáculī (n): tent, tabernacle
táceō, tacére, tácuī, tácitus (2): to be silent, to say nothing, to be quiet
tam: so, so much, to such a degree
tamen: nonetheless, nevertheless
tangō, tángere, tétigī, tāctus (3): to touch
templum, templī (n): temple, church
tempus, témporis (n): time, period, age
tendō, téndere, teténdī, tentus (3): to stretch, to extend, to bend
ténebrae, tenebrárum (f): darkness
téneō, tenére, ténuī, tentus (2): to have, to hold, to grasp
tentátio, tentatiónis (f): temptation
testis, testis, téstium (m): witness
téstor, testárī, testátus sum (1): to witness, to testify, to attest
tímeō, timére, tímuī, - (2): to fear, to be afraid
tollō, tóllere, sústulī, sublátus (3): to take away, to take up, to lift up
tōtus, tōta, tōtum: whole, complete, entire, total
terra, terrae (f): land, ground, earth
tractátus, tractátūs (m): treatment, treatise, tract
trādítiō, trāditiónis (f): tradition, teaching, instruction
trādō, trádere, trádidī, tráditus (3): to hand over, to deliver, to betray

trahō, tráhere, trāxī, tractus (3): to draw, to drag
tránseō, trānsíre, tránsiī, tránsitus (4): to go across, to traverse, to pass away
trēs, trēs, tria: three
tribus, tribūs (f): tribe
trínitās, trīnitátis (f): trinity
túeor, tuérī, túitus sum (3): to protect, to look at, to guard, to preserve
tunc: then, at that time
turba, turbae (f): crowd, multitude

U

ubi: where
ubíque: everywhere
umbra, umbrae (f): shadow
unde: from where, therefore
únitās, ūnitátis (f): unity, oneness
ūnivérsus, ūnivérsa, ūnivérsum: whole, entire
ūnus, ūna, ūnum: one
urbs, urbis (f): city
ūsus, ūsūs (m): practice, skill, use
ut: as, when; that, so that
utérque, utráque, utrúmque: each of two
ūtor, ūtī, ūsus sum (3) (+ abl): to use, to employ, to enjoy, to experience
útinam: would that
uxor, uxóris (f): wife

V

vādō, vádere, vāsī, - (3): to go, to hasten
valdē: greatly, exceedingly, very
váleō, valére, váluī, válitus (2): to be well, to be able, to be strong, to say goodbye
vel: or
velut: like, as
vēndō, véndere, véndidī, vénditus (3): to sell
vénia, véniae (f): indulgence, kindness, forgiveness
véniō, veníre, vēnī, ventus (4): to come, to approach
venter, ventris (m): womb, stomach, belly, bowels
ventus, ventī (m): wind
verbum, verbī (n): word
vēráciter: in truth, truthfully, really
véreor, verérī, véritus sum (2): to revere, to worship, to fear
vērō: but, indeed, in truth
vērus, vēra, vērum: true, real
vēscor, vēscī, -, - (3): to eat, to feed upon, to use
vestígium, vestígiī (n): footstep
vestis, vestis, véstium (f): garment, clothing
vetus, vetus, vetus: old, ancient, aged, former
via, viae (f): way, path, road

vīcī́nus, vīcī́na, vīcī́num: neighboring
vidḗlicet: namely, that is, that is to say
vídeō, vidḗre, vīdī, vīsus (2): to see, to look at, to understand
vídeor, vidḗrī, vīsus sum (2): to seem
vidḗtur (impers): it seems
vínciō, vincī́re, vinxī, vinctus (4): to bind, to tie up, to fasten, to fetter
vincō, víncere, vīcī, victus (3): to conquer, to win, to defeat
vínculum, vínculī (n): bond, chain
vīnum, vīnī (n): wine
vir, virī (m): man, husband
virgō, vírginis (f): virgin
virtūs, virtū́tis (f): power, virtue, character, strength
vīsus, vīsūs (m): sight, vision
vīta, vītae (f): life
vītis, vītis, vítium (f): vine
vítium, vítiī (n): crime, fault, sin, vice
vítulus, vítulī (m): bull, calf
vīvíficō, vīvificā́re, vīvificā́vī, vīvificā́tus (1): to bring (back) to life, to vivify
vīvō, vī́vere, vīxī, vīctus (3): to live, to be alive
vīvus, vīva, vīvum: alive, living
vocō, vocā́re, vocā́vī, vocā́tus (1): to call, to name, to designate
volō, velle, vóluī, - : to wish, to want, to will
volúntās, voluntā́tis (f): will
vōtum, vōtī (n): vow, prayer
vōx, vōcis (f): voice
vúlnerō, vulnerā́re, vulnerā́vī, vulnerā́tus (1): to wound, to hurt, to injure
vultus, vultūs (m): countenance, face, expression

APPENDIX IV

Bibliography

Allen and Greenough's New Latin Grammar. Edited by J. B. Greenough et al. Boston: Ginn & Company, 1903.

Allen, William. *Vox Latina: A Guide to the Pronunciation of Classical Latin.* 2nd ed. Cambridge: Cambridge University Press, 1989.

Baldi, Philip. *The Foundations of Latin.* Berlin: de Gruyter, 2002.

Clackson, James, and Geoffrey Horrocks. *The Blackwell History of the Latin Language.* Malden, MA: Wiley-Blackwell, 2007.

Collins, John. *A Primer on Ecclesiastical Latin.* Washington, DC: Catholic University of America Press, 1985.

Corrigan, Peter. *College Latin: An Intermediate Course.* New Haven: Yale University Press, 2015.

Foster, R. T., and D. P. McCarthy. *Ossa Latinitatis Sola ad Mentem Reginaldi Rationemque: The Mere Bones of Latin according to the Thought and System of Reginald.* Washington, DC: Catholic University of America Press, 2015.

Glare, P. G. W., ed. *Oxford Latin Dictionary.* 2 vols. Oxford: Oxford University Press, 2012.

Hall, William. *Latin Pronunciation according to Roman Usage.* Anaheim, CA: National Music Publishers, 1971.

Hardon, J. M. *Dictionary of the Vulgate New Testament.* New York: Macmillan, 1921.

Harrington, K. P. *Medieval Latin.* 2nd ed. Revised by Joseph Pucci. Chicago: University of Chicago Press, 1997.

Jones, Peter, and Keith Sidwell. *Reading Latin: Grammar and Exercises.* 2nd ed. Cambridge: Cambridge University Press, 2016.

Leonhart, Jürgen. *Latin: Story of a World Language.* Cambridge, MA: Harvard University Press, 2013.

Lewis, Charlton T., and Charles Short. *Harper's Latin Dictionary.* New York: American Book Company, 1907.

Lindsay, W. M. *The Latin Language: An Historical Account of Latin Sounds, Stems, and Flexions.* Cambridge: Cambridge University Press, 2010.

Medieval Latin: An Introduction and Bibliographical Guide. Edited by F. A. C. Mantello and A. G. Rigg. Washington, DC: Catholic University of America Press, 1996.

McInerny, Ralph. *Let's Read Latin: Introduction to the Language of the Church.* South Bend, IN: Dumb Ox Books, 1995.

Meissen, Randall. *Scholastic Latin: An Intermediate Course.* Rome: Pontifical Athenaeum Regina Apostolorum, 2012.

Nunn, H. P. V. *An Introduction to Ecclesiastical Latin.* Cambridge: Cambridge University Press, 1922.

Oniga, Renato. *Latin: A Linguistic Introduction*. Oxford: Oxford University Press, 2014.

Panhuis, Dirk. *Latin Grammar*. Ann Arbor: University of Michigan Press, 2006.

Probert, Philomen. *Latin Grammarians on the Latin Accent: The Transformation of Greek Grammatical Thought*. Oxford: Oxford University Press, 2019.

Scanlon, C. C., and C. L. Scanlon. *Latin Grammar: Grammar, Vocabularies, and Exercises in Preparation for the Reading of the Missal and Breviary*. Rockford, IL: TAN Books, 1976.

———. *Second Latin: For the Reading of Philosophy, Theology, and Canon Law*. Rockford, IL: TAN Books, 1976.

Schoenstene, Robert. *Reading Church Latin: Techniques and Commentary for Comprehension*. Chicago/Mundelein, IL: Hillenbrand Books, 2016.

Seigel, Mike. *Latin: A Clear Guide to Syntax*. London: Anthem Press, 2009.

Sidwell, Keith. *Reading Medieval Latin*. Cambridge: Cambridge University Press, 1995.

Smith, R. U., Jr. *Ecclesiastical, Medieval, and New-Latin Sentences*. Mundelein, IL: Bolchazy-Carducci Publishing, 2013.

Solodow, Joseph. *Latin Alive: The Survival of Latin in English and Romance Languages*. Cambridge: Cambridge University Press, 2010.

Stelten, L. F. *Dictionary of Ecclesiastical Latin*. Peabody, MA: Hendrickson, 2003.

Wheelock, F. M. *Wheelock's Latin: The Classic Introductory Latin Course based on the Writings of Cicero, Vergil, and Other Major Roman Authors*. Revised by Richard LaFleur. 7th ed. New York: HarperCollins, 2011.

INDEX

ablative case, 7–8
   ablative of comparison, 57–58
   ablative absolute, 251, 257–58
   other uses of ablative, 257–59
abbreviations, xvi
accent, xxii, xxiii, xxiv, xxv, xxvi–xxvii
   acute, xvi, xxiii, xxiv, xxvii
accusative case, 6–7, 8
Acts of Peter, 238–39
adjective, 39–46
   attributive, 41
   comparative, 54–55, 57
   degrees, 53–57
   first declension, 42–44
   positive, 53
   predicate, 41–42
   second declension, 42–44
   substantive, 42
   superlative, 55–56
   third declension, 44–46
adverb, 90–93
alphabet, xxii–xxiii
Ames, William, 224
and, 18–19
Antioch, Ignatius of, 90
Aquinas, Thomas, xxi, 38–39, 209–10, 212, 267–68, 347–48, 298
article, 6
aspect, 80, 85, 93, 95, 97, 170, 172, 173, 178, 204, 240, 263, 273, 275

Beatitudes, 42
Bingen, Hildegard of, 283–84

Caesar, Julius, xvii, xviii, xix, 13, 257, 296
Calvin, John, 30, 148

Canterbury, Anselm of, 223
Carthage, Cyprian of, 30–31
case system, 5–8
Cicero, xvii–xviii, 148, 158, 176, 201, 295–96
command. *See* imperative; prohibition
conditional sentence, 191n3, 203n5, 204n6
conjugation, 74, 79
consonant, xxv–xxvi
Constantine (I), 60
creeds (Latin), 71–72
   Catechismus Maior ("Larger Catechism"), 279
   Symbolum Apostolorum ("Apostles' Creed"), 77, 88, 101, 111–12
cum clause, 217–18

Damasus (I), 271–72
dative case, 6, 8
   dative of agent, 247
days of week (Latin), 60–61
declension, 13–14
   fifth, 61–63
   first, 15–18
   fourth, 49–52
   second, 23–26
   third, 30–34
      i-stems, 34–36
deponent, 126–30
diacritics, xvi
diaresis, xxv
diphthong, xxiv–xxv
direct object, 4, 6, 8, 128, 138

Felici, Pericle, 78–79
five solas, 38–39
future tense, 103–10, 181–83, 255

active indicative, 104–6, 107–9
passive indicative, 106–7, 109–10
perfect active indicative, 181–83
perfect passive indicative, 255

gender, 10–11
genitive case, 6, 10, 16, 29, 33, 235
   objective, 140
   partitive, 140
gerund. *See under* participle
Greek, 79, 90, 91, 102, 176, 230, 244, 256, 257, 271

Hebrew, 17, 22, 51, 63, 64, 102, 230, 297
Hippo, Augustine of, xviii, xix, xxiii, xxviii, 72, 115–16

imperative, 285–90
   future active, 289–90
   future passive, 289–90
   present active, 286–88
   present passive, 288–89
imperfect tense, 93–99, 201–6
   active indicative, 95–97
   active subjunctive, 202–4
   aspect, 93–94
   passive indicative, 97–99
   passive subjunctive, 204–5
impersonal verbs, 267–68
indicative mood, 69, 167, 185, 188, 189, 190, 192, 193, 212, 218, 290, 291
indirect object, 5, 8, 24, 138
infinitive, 262–65, 273–78
   future active, 276–77
   future passive, 277–78
   perfect active, 273–74
   perfect passive, 275–76
   present active, 263–64

present passive, 264–65
inflection, 4–5

Jerome, 295–96
Jesus, 3, 12, 13, 22, 23, 37, 38, 39, 42, 51, 71, 72, 79, 88, 90, 137, 138, 152, 155, 177, 187, 238, 239, 250, 254, 271

Latin, xvii–xix, 296–97
   classical, xxii
   ecclesiastical, xxii
   national, xxii–xxiii
Leonhardt, Jürgen, xvii, 296
Lérins, Vincent of, 89–90
locative case, 7, 8
Loyola, Ignatius of, 187–88, 191–92
Luther, Martin, xviii, 38, 48–49, 187, 200–201, 235

Maccovius, Johannes, 224
Mastricht, Peter Van, 224
mood, 73

Newton, Isaac, 261–62
Nicene Creed, 71, 72
noun, 4–5, 8, 10–11, 13
   indeclinable, 63–64, 343
   neuter, 26
   parsing, 23, 27–28
nominative case, 6, 8
   predicative nominative, 27
number, 10, 73
numerals, 65
   cardinal, 65
   ordinal, 65
   Roman, 65–66

Owen, John, 176–77

parsing. *See under* noun
participle, 223–28
   gerund, 233–35
   future active, 242–43
   future passive (gerundive), 231–33
   present active, 228–31
   perfect passive, 240–42
Patrick (Saint), 156–57
perfect system, 177–78
perfect tense, 169–73, 211–12, 214–16, 252–53
   active indicative, 169–73
   active subjunctive, 211–12
   passive indicative, 173, 252–53
   passive subjunctive, 214–16
periphrastic, 243–47, 252
   active, 244–45
   passive, 245–46
Perkins, William, 224
person, 73
pluperfect tense, 176–81, 212–14, 216–17, 253–54
   active indicative, 176, 178–81
   active subjunctive, 212–14
   passive indicative, 254–55
   passive subjunctive, 216–17
prayers (Latin)
   Actus Caritatis ("Act of Love"), 269–70
   Actus Contritionis ("Act of Contrition"), 248–49
   Agnus Dei ("Lamb of God"), 59
   Angelus ("Angel"), 250–51, 260
   Anima Christi ("Spirit of Christ"), 147, 155, 166
   Ante Studium ("Before Study"), 298
   De Profundis ("From the Depths"), 198–99, 207–8
   Deus Intende ("God . . . Come"), 220
   Fatimae ("Fatima"), 68
   Gloria Patri ("Glory to the Father"), 20–21
   Magnificat ("Magnifies"), 175, 184
   Nunc Dimittis ("Now Dismiss"), 293–94
   Pater Noster ("Our Father"), 37, 47
   Psalmus CL ("Psalm 150"), 237
   Sanctus ("Holy"), 29
   Signum Crucis ("Sign of the Cross"), 3–4
   Te Deum ("We . . . God"), 125, 133
preposition, 8–10
present tense, 80–87
   active indicative, 80–84
   active subjunctive, 192–94, 195–96
   passive indicative, 84–87
   passive subjunctive, 194–95, 196–97
prohibition, 290–91
pronoun, 137–39
   demonstrative, 142–46
   indefinite, 162–64
   interrogative, 161–62
   intensive, 152–54
   reflexive, 149–50
   relative, 157–61
   personal, 139–42
   possessive, 150–51
pronunciation (Latin), xxii–xxvii
proper noun/name, 25–26, 53, 63, 64, 81
principal parts, 75
punctuation, xxviii

Ramus, Peter, 223

semideponent, 130–31
speech, 265–66
   direct, 265–66
   indirect, 266–67, 274–75
subjunctive mood, 188–91, 200–201, 203–4, 205, 210, 211, 212, 215–16, 217–18, 285–86, 289, 290, 291
syllable, xxvi

Ten Commandments, 102–3
tense, 73
   compound, 251–52
Tertullian, xviii, 3–4, 22–23, 30, 126–27, 180, 254, 264, 295–96
translation, 5–6

verb, 72–75
   irregular, 115–23
   regular, 74–75
vocative case, 285, 291–92
voice, 73
vowel, xxiii–xxiv
Virgil, xvii, xviii, 176, 295, 296
Vulgate, xxiii, xxix, 4, 12, 64, 79, 102, 116, 137, 145, 152, 153, 169, 198, 235, 256, 257

word ending, 14–15
word order, 5, 275

www.ingramcontent.com/pod-product-compliance
Lightning Source LLC
Chambersburg PA
CBHW060417300426
44111CB00018B/2881